−2

EDIBLE HISTORIES, CULTURAL POLITICS

Towards a Canadian Food History

D0144979

Just as the Canada's rich past resists any singular narrative, there is no such thing as a singular Canadian food tradition. This new book explores Canada's diverse food cultures and the varied relationships that Canadians have had historically with food practices in the context of community, region, nation and beyond.

Based on findings from menus, cookbooks, government documents, advertisements, media sources, oral histories, memoirs, and archival collections, *Edible Histories, Cultural Politics* offers a veritable feast of original research on Canada's food history and its relationship to culture and politics. This exciting collection explores a wide variety of topics, including urban restaurant culture, ethnic cuisines, and the controversial history of margarine in Canada. It also covers a broad time-span, from early contact between European settlers and First Nations through the end of the twentieth century.

Edible Histories, Cultural Politics intertwines information about Canada's 'foodways' – the practices and traditions associated with food and food preparation – and stories of immigration, politics, gender, economics, science, medicine and religion. Sophisticated, culturally sensitive, and accessible, *Edible Histories, Cultural Politics* will appeal to students, historians, and foodies alike.

FRANCA IACOVETTA is a professor of history at the University of Toronto.

VALERIE J. KORINEK is a professor in the Department of History at the University of Saskatchewan.

MARLENE EPP is an associate professor of history at Conrad Grebel University College at the University of Waterloo.

Edible Histories, Cultural Politics

Towards a Canadian Food History

EDITED BY
FRANCA IACOVETTA, VALERIE J. KORINEK,
MARLENE EPP

UNIVERSITY OF TORONTO PRESS
Toronto Buffalo London

ISBN 978-1-4426-4476-2 (cloth)
ISBN 978-1-4426-1283-9 (paper)

Printed on acid-free, 100% post-consumer recycled paper with
vegetable-based inks.

Library and Archives Canada Cataloguing in Publication

Edible histories, cultural politics : towards a Canadian food history / edited by
Franca Iacovetta, Valerie J. Korinek, Marlene Epp.

Includes bibliographical references.
ISBN 978-1-4426-4476-2 (bound)   ISBN 978-1-4426-1283-9 (pbk.)

1. Food habits – Canada – History.   2. Food – Canada – History.   3. Food –
Social aspects – Canada – History.   4. Food – Political aspects – Canada –
History.   5. Canada – Social life and customs.   I. Iacovetta, Franca, 1957–
II. Korinek, Valerie Joyce, 1965– III. Epp, Marlene, 1958–

GT2853.C3E35 2012   394.1'20971   C2012-904248-X

University of Toronto Press acknowledges the financial assistance to its publishing
program of the Canada Council for the Arts and the Ontario Arts Council.

  Canada Council   Conseil des Arts   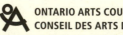 ONTARIO ARTS COUNCIL
for the Arts   du Canada   CONSEIL DES ARTS DE L'ONTARIO

University of Toronto Press acknowledges the financial support of the Government
of Canada through the Canada Book Fund for its publishing activities.

Contents

Illustrations

Preface

Why are so many people, Canadians included, talking so fervently about food these days? What explains the surge, or rather resurgence, of such massive interest in the politics of food and in its local and global connections? Why have a slew of recent books about how and what to eat become North American bestsellers? Why are Canadian historians participating in this 'culinary turn'? Why are our students excited about food history? How do we write a Canadian food history that is not strictly nation-bound but instead brings together local, regional, national, multicultural, and transnational histories?

Such questions and challenges were the 'tipping point' for this volume, which originated as a workshop funded by the Social Sciences and Humanities Research Council (SSHRC) and held at Conrad Grebel University College, University of Waterloo, in August 2008.[1] The workshop assembled a number of Canadian scholars, and a few invited international guests, to share their research, debate issues, and produce a volume in Canadian food history. The formal sessions offered valuable opportunities for in-depth discussion about a field of study that is relatively new in Canada. During mealtimes, as we sampled Mennonite-style perogies, borscht, and shoofly pie at Conrad Grebel (a Mennonite college affiliated with the University of Waterloo), we inevitably shared personal food memories. In the process, we realized both the diversity we represented – although those with a Christian background and a tradition of Sunday family dinner clearly dominated! – and that everyone had a 'food story' in their history.

As food theorists Carol Counihan and Penny Van Esterik have observed, 'food touches everything': it is the basis of every economy, 'a central pawn in political strategies of states and households,' a marker of social differences, borders, bonds, and contradictions, and the act of 'eating is an endlessly evolving enactment of gender, family, and community relationships.'[2] Like certain other aspects of human existence, food is so omnipresent – and also so ordinary – that it can be overlooked as a topic of 'serious' analysis. In reaffirming that food is a topic worthy of serious historical inquiry, we do not wish to depersonalize the subject – either our own or that of our historical subjects – but also caution against letting intriguing anecdotes or personal narratives of food substitute for careful analysis. As the large body of interdisciplinary work in the field demonstrates, food, both its presence and absence, plays a critical role in the shaping of identity and thus offers an excellent site for studies of identity formation and gendered subjectivities and for personal and family memory.

There are many compelling reasons for encouraging the further development of food history in Canada as elsewhere, including the need to historicize contemporary thinking about food systems, cultures, politics, and safety. An interest in food history is especially evident in the multicultural classroom and in other multicultural settings across the country. The ever-increasing volume of writing devoted to the economic, medical, ethical, and commercial importance of food also speaks to the tremendous interest in the subject. To cite just one example, in 2009, North American *E. coli* and listeriosis outbreaks heightened people's fears about food safety as they exposed the potentially dire gaps in industry and governmental monitoring of commercial food safety. Such events, and no doubt there will be more in the future, amplify both the importance of what we eat, and the academic significance of historicizing the social, cultural, and political histories of food production and consumption in Canada.

Even while we recognize that food is part of the personal, political, and everyday of Canadian society, we need also avoid the danger of giving so much explanatory power to food that it becomes everything and therefore nothing – or, 'all consuming.' Just as women and gender historians cannot assume that gender is always the answer, and labour and critical race historians cannot assume that, in every instance, it is class or race that most explains a given phenomenon, food historians must avoid reductionist or predictable arguments. As the academics flood into food history, there is also another challenge we might identify, namely, how to engage the debates, theorize the research, and capture the complexities, without losing the initial excitement, compassion, and curiosity that brought us to it in the first place. We hope that this volume of diverse chapters engages a wide assortment of readers and that the study of food in our collective past makes all of us more curious about Canadian history.

The book contributes towards mapping a terrain for a scholarly Canadian food history by providing a series of historical chapters that show how viewing the past through the lens of food and its attendant practices sheds important new light on the Canadian past and its diverse peoples. Taken together, the chapters demonstrate that while many view their food tastes as a matter of personal preference, food customs and practices are informed, prescribed, or mediated by many forces, including material conditions, class and cultural politics, state policies, experts, educational regimes, corporations, and the media. They show, too, that personal and collective choices also matter, and that the practices surrounding the purchase, preparation, and consumption of food have long provided both a cultural means of reaffirming family or community solidarity and a source of class, racial, gender and cultural conflict and negotiation. They explore how the contact zones created between newly arrived and more settled peoples have given rise to countless hybrid diets, and how the abundance or scarcity of food, or introduction of new foodstuffs, has shaped historical experience, both collective and individual. In short, the chapters show that the history of food is also about the history of power, or cultural politics that are classed, raced, sexed, and crossed with lines of authority, struggle, subservience, survival, and daily life.

We thank our invited international guests and their graduate students for participating in both the workshop discussions of the invited papers (these were solicited through a public call for papers) and in the public segment of our program, which drew a wider audience of faculty, students, and people from the community. Our keynote speaker Jeffrey Pilcher (University of Minnesota) – a noted Latin American and global food historian whose *Food in World History* has become an important course text[3] – offered a provocative overview of the relevance and future of food history. A leading scholar of migration history and author of the much-cited *We Are What We Eat: Ethnic Food and the Making of Americans*,[4] Donna Gabaccia (University of Minnesota) illustrated the value of cookbooks as historical sources through a fascinating tale about women and food myths of Charleston, South Carolina, and encouraged us to become pro-active about getting repositories to preserve food records. Finally, Daniel Bender (University of Toronto), a United States labour and cultural historian, gave an engaging demonstration of how he teaches global food history to the diverse student body at Toronto's Scarborough campus – and why he thinks students in the multicultural classroom are so captivated by food both as part of a global trajectory in which they see themselves and as part of everyday life and negotiation in a pluralist society – while cooking a colonial-era Anglo-Indian chicken curry dish.

We also thank all of the other people who helped make our workshop a success. Valerie and Franca thank Marlene for being an organized and gracious host and the administrative and food services staff at Conrad Grebel University College. We thank Paul Born, Helen Epp, and Michael Born for the fabulous dinner at the Epp/Born household, and Lucas Born for technical assistance at the workshop. We gratefully acknowledge the financial support of the Social

Sciences and Humanities Research Council, whose funds enabled us to bring together our contributors in energizing dialogue. Our focused conversations contributed enormously towards the completion of this volume and to its overall thematic coherence. At University of Toronto Press, we thank Len Husband for his enthusiastic support of our project. Finally, we thank our partners and families for their support. Food is for sharing and we share this food history book with them.

NOTES

1 See Malcolm Gladwell, *The Tipping Point: How Little Things Can Make a Big Difference* (Boston: Little Brown, 2000).
2 Carole Counihan and Penny Van Esterik, Introduction to their edited *Food and Culture: A Reader* (New York: Routledge, 1997), 3.
3 New York: Routledge, 2006.
4 Cambridge, MA: Harvard University Press, 1998.

EDIBLE HISTORIES, CULTURAL POLITICS

Towards a Canadian Food History

Introduction

FRANCA IACOVETTA, VALERIE J. KORINEK, AND MARLENE EPP

So often, new histories reflect contemporary interests and anxieties as well as social, political, and cultural developments – and food is no exception. Food issues have become very topical in the early twenty-first century because of widespread concern over the quality, availability, and cost of food. Food has become the site of major political mobilization as well as cultural transformations in everyday behaviour. Recent news coverage has focused on spiking food prices which, combined with depleting food resources (or the inequitable division of those resources), has fuelled our anxieties about a 'hungry planet.' We have been alarmed by exposés about the impact of 'fast food' diets, a spreading epidemic in obesity, especially among children, and the increase in obesity-linked diseases like diabetes.[1] Simultaneously, our fears are increasing about issues like produce, meat, and water tainted by *E. coli*, listeria, mad cow disease, and other preventable outbreaks. In Canada, as elsewhere, anti-globalization activists have taken to the streets to decry genetically modified foods, as well as pesticide-drenched and other unsafe foods; to denounce both human-made famines and the use of food for biofuels; and to protest a capitalist order that fattens the rich of the global North while starving the already poor of the global South.

In response to this doom-and-gloom picture, individuals, households, and communities have become food activists. 'Ethical eating' has become a commonplace topic for discussion and initiative, leading to a growing popularity in vegetarianism (and all its variants) and to the adoption of such other food practices as localism (which includes the '100 mile diet'), organic eating, and the 'slow foods movement.' Topics like 'food security' and 'food sustainability' have become urgent agendas for experts and populists alike. North American bestsellers such as Barbara Kingsolver's *Animal, Vegetable, Miracle*, an account of her family's year of growing, harvesting, and eating their own food, illustrate both the popularity of such recent trends and the zeal with which devotees embrace such culinary conversions.[2] In like vein, having alerted us to the societal, medical, and environmental costs of the typical North American diet in *The Omnivore's Dilemma*, Michael Pollan returned with the bestselling *In Defense of Food*, whose thesis (enumerated in the subtitle) is 'eat food, not too much, mostly plants.'[3] Canada's Wayne Roberts similarly offers both distressing and hopeful news in *The No-Nonsense Guide to World Food*.[4] These works, and countless others, attest to a fairly widespread anxiety over food and an expanding food activism that has turned many Canadians (and others worldwide) into 'foodies' – people with a passion for eating, talking, and thinking about what we eat.

Food is fundamental – and personal – to each one of us. Since we all must eat, and most of us cook at least some of our meals, we all have a personal stake in food. Moreover, many of us are fascinated by food because it is such a fundamental part of our lived reality, past and present, and of memory, good and bad. We share our food memories with others, noting our nostalgic longings for certain foods and hatred of others. No doubt, this helps explain the popularity of books that use food – its preparation, consumption, and its presence in memory – as an organizing theme. These include memoirs like *Lilla's Feast*, the chronicle of a woman who compiled a cookery book while in a state of semi-starvation in a Japanese concentration camp during the Second World War. U.S. food memoir literature includes *Crazy in the Kitchen*, a narrative of growing up in an Italian-American family in which memories of migration and generational conflict focus on recipes and eating, and *Miriam's Kitchen*, which tells how a fiercely left-wing Jewish American woman comes to respect the religious worldview of her mother-in-law, a survivor, by sharing time, recipes, and stories in her kitchen.[5] Canadian food memoirs, which also highlight ethnic and family themes, include Janice Wong's *Chow: From China to Canada – Memories of Food and Family*, and Maria Cioni's *Spaghetti Western: How My Father Brought Italian Food to the West*.[6]

Novels featuring food have enjoyed both critical and popular success. Canadian examples include Rudy Wiebe's *A Discovery of Strangers* and Timothy Taylor's *Stanley Park*, both of which explore the themes of aboriginality and colonialism through food. Judy Fong Bates' *Midnight at the Dragon Café* utilizes a Chinese immigrant café as the setting for a novel about one extended Asian family's experiences in small-town Ontario, while Austin Clarke's *Love and Sweet Food* mixes food, rum, and cultural memory to portray the Caribbean immigrant experience and challenge Anglo-Canadian cultural hegemony. *Comfort Food for Breakups* depicts the overlapping themes of sexual and ethnic identity, as a Ukrainian-Canadian woman cooks her way through relationship endings.[7] Homeland foods act as critical signposts of memory and identity in the novels of South Asian Canadian writers like Anita Rau Badami (*Can You Hear the Nightbird Call?*) and Anar Ali (*Baby Khaki's Wings*).[8]

Food movies are a genre unto themselves. Those popular with art film goers and featuring sumptuous meal scenes include *The Big Night*, where two Italian-American brothers create an Italian feast for an entertainer who never arrives, and the German-made restaurant love story *Mostly Martha*. In the critically acclaimed Danish film, *Babette's Feast*, spinster sisters living a pious but drab village life agree to their housekeeper's wish to use her lottery winnings to create a lavish banquet. *Julie and Julia* features writer-director (and self-declared foodie) Nora Ephron directing Meryl Streep as Julia Child in a popular Hollywood fantasy about the transformative power of French cuisine. Against the backdrop of the Canadian High Commission in New Delhi, a wily housekeeper and an ambassador's 'house husband' make mouth-watering curries and dosas in *Cooking with Stella*, a 2009 film by Canadian Dilip Mehta.

The mass popularity of food TV in North America has made elite chefs household names and created many popular food gurus. Many university and college students enjoy the Food Network and growing numbers of them have taken up chef and cooking programs. In Canada during the late 1980s and the 1990s, Margaret Visser, the cultural anthropologist who penned the delightful *Much Depends on Dinner* (1986) and *The Rituals of Dinner* (1992) gained a large radio audience with her engaging style. An internationally successful writer, her instalments on the popular Canadian Broadcasting Corporation (CBC) radio program, *Morningside*, expanded Canadian knowledge about the history and symbolism of food, at least among a CBC-listening public.[9] These are just a few examples of how 'foodie' interests have permeated aspects of 'popular' and 'high' culture.

Canadians' interest in food has been bolstered since the mid-twentieth century by the ever greater diversity in food cultures that we can sample. Note the variety of cookbooks – practical-minded classics, 1970s vegetarian stalwarts, bestsellers with artful photographs, and 'ethnic' or regional collections – that today grace both the kitchen shelves and living-room coffee tables of more and more households.[10] We have plenty of positive examples of the shift towards 'multicultural eating' and 'world fusion diets' on both national and international fronts. Many Canadians now expect a greater degree of variety in their food shops, meals, and restaurants and have welcomed the increased opportunities available in a pluralist society to have new sensual pleasures, expand cultural horizons, and participate in a spreading 'culinary pluralism.' Despite recurring efforts to marginalize or homogenize the 'foreign' foods of successive waves of newcomers,[11] immigrant foodways (a term that encompasses the eating habits and other food-related cultural and social practices of a particular group, region, or historical period[12]) have transformed the culinary landscape in Canada as elsewhere. It is popular to cook and 'eat ethnic,' a phrase that now refers to non-Western foods, although the phrase itself is problematic since we all carry some form of ethnicity. Corporations have both responded to and encouraged the global food trend; when, for example, Loblaws' newly installed CEO Galen Weston Jr set out to reinvigorate the company's flagging sales, he did so with a television and print campaign touting a new line of prepared ethnic foods, beginning with that Indian staple Naan bread. Today, many Canadian 'foodies' (ourselves included) participate in a culinary pluralism enriched by the growing global migration from the South (which has brought us Indian, Thai, and other cuisines) while mindful that this migration is itself partly a product of the same global forces producing so many troubling inequities and that we open ourselves to critiques of culinary imperialism.

Situating Food History

Given the amount of information and discussion about food issues, a growing number of historians, ourselves included, have been drawn to study these subjects in earlier eras. Witness the recent proliferation of scholarly food histories on the international scene and the signs of an emerging food history in Canada. As so often happens, when we search for historical roots to contemporary phenomena – or seek to historicize claims about 'new' trends or crises – we discover both the familiar and unfamiliar. We find earlier food exchanges among peoples and global food systems as well as earlier critiques of food entrepreneurs and capitalists. We encounter earlier generations of people, both Aboriginal and white settlers, who effectively lived the mythical 100 mile diet, even if largely by circumstance. We discover earlier famines and alarming levels of global food inequity as well as efforts to respond to the problems through various means of social and political activism. We find that encounters between peoples of different races and religions resulted in eating evolutions and revolutions that altered the cultures of all sides. Our research also uncovers marked differences between earlier and current developments, whether between the Columbian food exchange of the sixteenth century and today's transnational agricultural industry, between the health food movement of earlier and current eras, or between the reception of immigrant foods in a more xenophobic past versus the multicultural present. By more fully exploring food topics in all of their dimensions, we can deepen our understanding of the Canadian past and also provide critical contexts for assessing contemporary understandings and debates.

We see many signs of the growing scholarly legitimacy of and interest in food history and food studies. Certainly, the academic study of food, from a wide range of disciplinary vantage points, has been growing exponentially over the past few decades, many researchers embarking from earlier theoretical works by Claude Lévi-Strauss, Roland Barthes, or Mary Douglas, for example.[13] Wide-ranging histories of food habits, customs, and patterns, such as *Curry: A Tale of Cooks and Conquerors*, and *Fish on Friday: Feasting, Fasting and the Discovery of the New World*, offer fascinating and illuminating perspectives on world history.[14] Caroline Walker Bynum's ground-breaking *Holy Feast and Holy Fast: The Religious Significance of Food to Medieval Women* effectively brought together the histories of women, religion, and food.[15] A number of book-length studies of single food commodities demonstrate how access to and distribution of foods like sugar, coffee, salt, tea, cod, and the potato have been transformative in world history.[16] U.S.-based social histories of popcorn and 1950s icons like Spam and meatloaf provide intriguing observations of mass culture while left and labour histories of U.S. food companies offer hard-hitting critiques of corporate and global capitalism.[17] Broad-ranging studies of food across space and time submit new ways of thinking about the past not organized around wars, rulers, or exploration – or at least interpret such developments in significantly different ways. Jeffrey M. Pilcher's *Food in World History*, for instance, traces the 'influence of food in the global transition to modernity' by focusing on such themes as the diffusion of foodstuffs, agricultural versus pastoral conflicts, class distinctions, social identities, and the role of the state.[18]

Another sure sign of the growing academic legitimacy of food as a topic is the appearance of scholarly journals, organizations, and conferences on food. The new, multidisciplinary journals in food studies include *Food & Foodways* (1985), *Gastronomica* (2001), and the e-journal, *CuiZine: The Canadian Journal of Food Cultures* (2008). Professional Canadian networks include the Culinary Historians of Ontario (1994) and the Canadian Association for Food Studies (CAFS, 2006). In 2008, the CAFS and contributors to this volume held the first cross-disciplinary panel in food history at the Canadian Historical Association meetings. Besides our own workshop (see preface), food conferences recently held in Canada include one on Transnational Foodways (2012) hosted by the University of Toronto's Centre for Diaspora and Transnational Studies and one on Canadian Domestic Foodscapes (2008) held at Concordia University.

The Canadian historical canon in food history though small is growing. Until very recently, food-related topics have not attracted much serious academic attention of Canadian historians, although some might consider the approach

of Canada's staples-focused historians, from Harold Innis' fish to the special-
ists of wheat, to represent a form of commodity-based food history.[19] In addition, the large and multidisciplinary body of scholarship on Aboriginal peoples
contains valuable food-history material related to such critical issues as human
interactions with the environment, agricultural and other food systems, and
gender, nutrition, and health.[20] Various feminist histories of farm, working-
class, and immigrant women and ethnic communities and labour histories of
men in work camps also include useful discussions about food.[21] By contrast,
however, the United States has a much more established scholarly historiography in U.S. food history. It includes Harvey Levenstein's pioneering social
histories of changing American diets and eating regimes, *Revolution at the
Table* and *Paradox of Plenty*. It also includes full-length women's, cultural, and
ethnic histories written by scholars such as Laura Shapiro, Sherrie A. Inness,
Warren Belasco, Janet Theophano, Donna Gabaccia, Hasia Diner, and Psyche
A. Williams-Forson.[22] A number of these U.S. scholars have also produced
or participated in recent collections in food studies that already have become
influential in the field.[23]

   In Canada, it is really the community-based writers and public historians
with museums and heritage organizations who have laid the groundwork for
a Canadian food history through their efforts to collect cookbooks and otherwise document historical foodways in Canada. Since its appearance in 2006,
culinary historian Dorothy Duncan's national study, *Canadians at Table: Food,
Fellowship, and Folklore, a Culinary History of Canada*, has been an important
starting point for anyone wanting to consider some aspect of food and foodways in the Canadian past.[24] More recent compendiums of twentieth-century
Canadian foodways – including *A Century of Canadian Home Cooking* (1992)
by home economists Carole Ferguson and Margaret Fraser, and Elizabeth Driver's 2008 *Culinary Landmarks*, a comprehensive and annotated bibliography
of Canadian cookbooks published before 1950 – are both important research
projects and indispensable tools for historians in search of sources in food
history.[25] So, too, is Thelma Barer-Stein's 1979 encyclopedic compendium of
ethnic food traditions in Canada, entitled *You Eat What You Are*.[26] A few studies
on specific ethnic cuisines have been produced, including two collections, on
Chinese and Italian foodways respectively, published by the Ontario Historical Society and edited by food writer Jo Marie Powers.[27] Scholarly contributions to an emerging Canadian food history have appeared as part of feminist
and gendered studies of women's magazines, farm settlements, refugee and
immigrant narratives, and nutrition and food campaigns.[28] A ground-breaking
monograph in the field is Steven Penfold's *The Donut: A Canadian History*;
published in 2008, it reveals how the evolution of a particular food commod-

ity – or snack item – reflects and influences the cultural, social, and economic history of the nation.[29] Also leading the way in Canadian food scholarship is Nathalie Cooke's 2009 collection of essays, *What's to Eat? Entrées in Canadian Food History*.[30] Cooke's volume is more specifically focused on defining evolving 'Canadian' culinary tastes and traditions and more explicitly cast within a national framework than is our book, but both volumes explore such key themes as gender codes, ethnic foodways, and corporate advertising.

Our book contributes to the growing scholarship in Canadian food history, broadly defined, by bringing together in one volume a large sample of current research in the field. We highlight the different ways in which Canadian historians and historically minded scholars in other fields are engaging with and contributing to the rapidly expanding international scholarship in food history. This volume provides empirically based research on food topics that generate new understandings of or shed new light on the Canadian past. Cognizant of the valuable work in political science, sociology, nutrition, and other disciplines, many of our authors draw, to differing degrees, on theoretical insights or research from outside of history. But this is primarily a volume written by and for historians, although we hope others will also find it useful. We stress, too, that while Canada's diverse peoples and their foods and food-related issues are the subjects of analysis, the book is not a nationalist project per se. It does not aim to define a 'Canadian' culinary tradition or history, although, of course, we scrutinize food as a potential site for identity formation and the making of local, regional, national, imperial, and other, such as class, racial-ethnic and gender-based, subjectivities. Nor does the focus of analysis stop at the nation's borders; rather, our approach is expansive and seeks to bring together the many local, regional, national, multicultural, diasporic, and transnational histories that necessarily inform Canada's history. We hope that, like this volume, food history in Canada will attract a diversity of historians and remain a site of informed and critical debate over meaningful matters.

At a time when food history courses in Canada are becoming more numerous, and the demand for them is growing at both the graduate and undergraduate level, this volume will help fill a current and expanding need for Canadian-specific research on a wide range of food history topics. At twenty-three chapters, this is a big but readily manageable and accessible book that contains a mix of fourteen longer essays (main entrées, if you will) dealing with new and major themes in food history and eight shorter case studies and a photo essay (tasty appetizers) that are more specifically focused on a particular item, event, source, or question. We adopted this mixed structure for several reasons. For one, it enabled us to include a larger sample of current work in the field for a more versatile book that can be used productively in a wide range of full-year or semester-length food history courses whether in the post-secondary undergraduate classroom or graduate seminar. We also know that students and veteran readers alike enjoy variety in their reading (in length as well as in topic and focus) and that short chapters that whet their appetite will encourage them to read more. Furthermore, the shorter case studies and photo essay, by concretely demonstrating how adopting an informed food lens even on a specific document or question, or a selection of documents, interviews, or images, can yield meaningful statements about the past, will help equip students to develop their own 'do-able' research projects. The longer essays provide more in-depth or wide-ranging investigations of a broadly defined theme or research question. These objectives, and not any desire to rank the topics covered, explain the inclusion of chapters that conform to the conventional scholarly article or essay length as well as the shorter case studies and photo essay.

We eliminated the repetitive citation of Canadian food historiography in the individual essays because a full citation of that literature is found in this introduction. In all cases, the contributions are condensed versions of longer papers presented at the 2008 workshop.

Themes in Canadian Food History

Food history is much more than what people ate or cooked and at what point in time; it is even more, perhaps, about what food and its attendant customs meant and mean. Historians, and researchers in other disciplines such as anthropology, sociology, and literature, are showing us that the study of food – its production and consumption, its exchange and evolution, its abundance or scarcity – can illuminate social relations between individuals and groups, the exertion of power (political and otherwise), how cultural norms and aberrations are created, and how personal and group identity is constructed. Our volume demonstrates that adopting a food lens will enhance our historical understandings of a whole range of processes and activities in the Canadian past.

Although no single volume in food history can be fully comprehensive, taken together, the contributions here represent a wide range of subjects from across the chronological spectrum, from the contact and colonial eras to the end of the twentieth century and into the present. Our contributors include women and men who are gender, social, cultural, environmental, and migration historians as well as historically minded scholars in health, religious, ethnic and cultural studies, art history, and literary criticism. Readers will encounter a variety of perspectives including feminist, racial, anthropological, Marxist, transnational, environmental, Foucauldian, post-colonial, sexuality, and global food systems approaches. A few of the essays are explicitly interdisciplinary. Along with a significant chronological and geographical coverage is the diversity of sources mined. The sources include personal writings and memoirs, interviews, government documents, corporate promotional materials, newspaper and magazine articles and advertisements, and radio and television commercials, as well as (to the historian) less conventional ones, like sculptures and cookbooks.

By using the subject of food as a focal point of inquiry, the chapters in this book offer insight into a number of major issues. The volume is structured along eight dominant themes, although, of course, many of the chapters address more than one theme, and certain categories, such as women and gender, and race and ethnicity, link many of the contributions, either topically or analytically. The first theme, cultural exchanges and cuisines in the contact zone, speaks to the multiplicity of ethnic, racial, class, and other group identities that have mingled within 'Canada's' borders, and still do. Food is a pivotal site for the interactions of peoples and for the creation and reinforcement of intergroup perceptions. We must understand that eclectic eating habits and hybrid diets are not solely postmodern phenomena born of recent globalization. As Donna Gabaccia has demonstrated for the United States, blending, borrowing, and juxtaposing foodways is a long-standing pattern.[31] In Canada, the tendency towards 'ethnic fusion eating' also has a long history, and themes of culinary borrowing, mingling, erasing, and hybridity (defined here as the presence of mixed cuisines that emerge as the product of the encounters, whether forced or consensual, between peoples with different culinary practices and traditions) were evident both in colonial and modern settings. The exchange of food between European colonizers and Aboriginals, between employer and 'foreign' domestic, between Anglo- and Franco-Canadians and immigrants, was more than just a material encounter. The exchange of food signified an absorption and thus evolution of culture, a breaking down of boundaries – although often the creation of new ones – and a determination of power, influence, and hegemony.

Much of the fascinating work in the Canadian setting comes from researchers exploring the role of food and foodways in the 'contact zones' between 'Natives and newcomers.' These studies treat neither group as static communities but, instead, seek to illuminate how the foodways of different groups of Aboriginals and white settlers underwent modification in given times and places. For example, the potato, a European crop, became a staple of the Aboriginal diet of west coast Native Canadians. Here, Alison Norman's essay returns us to a familiar Canadian source, the writings of British gentlewoman pioneer settlers in Ontario, such as the sisters Susanna Moodie and Catharine Parr Traill. But she focuses on a neglected theme, settler women's food exchanges and culinary relations with the Native women of their area, highlighting the new hybrid diets that resulted from this mingling. These changes in diets, she argues, reflected greater changes taking place in both cultures. For the First Nations, changing food customs were part of the wider shift towards becoming a Christian, agrarian, and patriarchal people, a process that also represented a dilution of 'traditional' culture, heritage, and identity, and also in some ways, the creation of a new Anglo-Native identity. For British settlers, the consumption of Native Canadian foods was part of the process through which they came to self-identify as 'Canadians.'

Yet, by the nineteenth century, Euro-Canadian settlers were part of a culture that derided Native culture and part of an economic and political system that spanned the Atlantic. In Ontario, as imported tea and coffee eventually became available, indigenous ingredients were forgotten. Or, as Julia Roberts' discussion of the colonial meals of 'native' duck illustrates, indigenous ingredients might be transformed, in this case, through the application of wheat flour, imported spices, European cooking methods, and the dining rituals of elite Anglo-Canadian males, into 'imperial food.' In an essay that brings together food and drink history, Roberts' exploration of 1840s Ontario tavern suppers is explicitly critical of the colonizers' adaptations and appropriations of indigenous foodstuffs and dishes. Drawing on the wider literature in colonial food history, and the questions it raises about the hybridity, or 'creolization,' of cuisine (the latter term usually denoting that the process of intermingling of food traditions occurred under conditions of colonialism) within imperial-colonial contexts, Roberts suggests that the public consumptive rituals that helped elite men enact their identity were partly predicated on a process of cultural appropriation of indigenous cuisine served in the form of hybrid colonial dishes like the fancy snipe supper she deconstructs for us. Drawing on the cultural history of performance, pageantry, and spectacle,[32] Roberts probes the 'performance' of these gentlemanly tavern suppers – such as snipe and wine, followed by musical entertainment, billiards, and more drink – as sites of elite male identity formation.

A positive example of food hybridity and mingling in a modern, 'multicultural' contact zone is offered by Michel Desjardins and Ellen Desjardins in their chapter on food and Christianity in Canada. They note the significant changes brought about in Christianity by major developments such as Vatican II (1962), the Quebec Quiet Revolution of the 1960s, and especially the greater cultural and religious diversity of the post-1967 immigrants who hail from around the globe but particularly from South and East Asia, parts of Africa, Latin America, and the Caribbean. Acknowledging that tensions do exist, they highlight the progressive efforts of long-standing Christian groups who continue to do charitable work, like run soup kitchens and out-of-the-cold programs, and who also now participate in both multi-Christian and multi-faith philanthropic efforts. Their case study notes the positive impact of increased religious pluralism and racial diversification of the Canadian Christian population, which has resulted in multi-faith encounters between, for instance, Catholic and Muslim students in Montreal, and shows how racially mixed Christian congregations have created opportunities for teaching and learning mutual lessons on worship and tolerance. Thus, looking at foodways within contact zones from colonial eras to the present reveals much about how cultural groups create and exchange aspects of identity.

Given the geographical scale of Canada, and the regional diversity, it is not surprising that regional food identities and traditions, our second theme, are stronger for many people, and are often regarded as more authentic than attempts to codify and create a generic 'national' cuisine. Several chapters examine regional food identities and the way that region, ethnicity, and race coalesce in the creation of such foodways. Maura Hanrahan's case study of the enduring foodways of rural Newfoundlanders takes a long historical view from colonial times to the present and highlights the critical and persistent interconnections between local environment, foodways, and group and regional identity. Unlike for much of the rest of North America, Newfoundland food practices are not rooted in agriculture but, instead, represent adaptations of indigenous hunting, gathering, and fishing patterns. These links between the diet and the land and sea, so necessary to establishing settler society in the 1600s, have remained central to Newfoundlanders' cultural identity, she argues, even through urbanization, late twentieth-century industrialization, the loss of the cod fishery, and the animal rights campaigns that have both sanctioned and condemned (particularly internationally) the annual seal hunt in the province of Newfoundland and Labrador.

On the other side of the country, Megan Davies' case study of early twentieth-century foodscapes – meaning the culinary cultures of a place – that developed among the Euro-Canadian settlers who established pioneer communities in the Peace River area of northern British Columbia and Alberta between 1900 and 1940 reveals a similar melding of settler food traditions with indigenous knowledge and practices. The early settlers were able to eke out a subsistence existence by combining agriculture, hunting, and berry picking, while they sought to tame and transform the Peace, ultimately hoping to replicate the Anglo-Canadian pastoral landscape they idealized. Davies' case study of the narratives of individuals and families who settled in this region (also a contact zone) reveals important themes, among them that the indigenous residents ensured 'food security' (meaning the availability and accessibility of food) for the settlers and that the latter adopted an ecological approach to the use of space and place for food production that mirrored that of Aboriginal peoples, who saw land as both a vital source of resources necessary for survival and a site of individual and social identities.

Turning to the period 1900 to 1960, Caroline Durand's chapter considers the role of francophone and Catholic educators in shaping a provincial or, rather, a specifically francophone Quebec culinary identity through domestic science manuals and education. She explores the francophone home economics curriculum in twentieth-century Quebec schools before the Quiet Revolution through an analysis of prescriptive texts on cooking, nutrition, diet, and home economics. Lauded as scientific texts imparting the latest rational knowledge on diet, these manuals, she shows, were deeply ideological or value-laden texts written by well-placed and influential advocates of a traditional French Canadian nationalism influenced by the Roman Catholic Church. Durand's essay demonstrates how nutrition can be adapted to an ideological and cultural project, in this case, to buttress the traditionalist goals of Catholic educators.

A number of the chapters address a third theme, the centrality of foodways and memories to the formation of group identity within specific ethnic and racial communities, and often in specific regions or urban locales and class or social location. Women usually figure in real and symbolic ways in the formation of such collective identities. Stacey Zembrzycki's case study of the childhood food memories of a group of Ukrainian men and women who grew up in prairie farm households and in northern Ontario working-class boarding houses demonstrates some of the ways in which food shaped people's narratives of the past. Like other oral historians, she acknowledges the romanticized and nostalgic nature of these childhood recollections – most of her participants told tales not of struggle or hunger but of enough food, resourceful mothers, and family and community togetherness. She also carefully mines these valuable sources to discern similarities and differences of experience across regional, political, and gender lines. As a contribution to memory history, Zembrzycki's chapter demonstrates how her narrators' food memories, both good and bad, profoundly informed their understanding of being Ukrainian in Depression-era Canada.

The notion of collective memory is also explored in S. Holyck Hunchuck's cultural interpretations of the giant folk-art food sculptures erected in Ukrainian towns in rural Alberta and Saskatchewan. Some contemporary writers view these colossi simply as super-sized tourist kitsch, but this essay alerts us to the need to understand them as important representations of Ukrainian cultural identity and collective memory as expressed through folkloric food customs and cultural rituals. Informed by the tragic events of twentieth-century Ukraine, where invasion, revolution, famine, war, and displacement caused much hunger, suffering, and loss, Ukrainian memories of food trauma (the enduring physical and psychological shock and injury resulting from food deprivation), Holyck Hunchuck argues, continue to inform the active memory and cultural practices of Ukrainians in Canada today, where, for example, holiday foods and food rituals commemorate the ancestors. At the same time, these folk art colossi are public and political statements of Ukrainian cultural survival in Canada.

Recent transnational studies of diasporic communities have enriched our understanding of the movement and transformation in foods as they travel the same transnational circuits as the migrants of a given diaspora and of the emergence of new identities within these contexts.[33] One of today's largest diasporas in Canada comprises South Asians in Toronto, now one of the most racially diverse cities on the globe. Like Montreal and Vancouver, the multicultural metropolis of Toronto represents its own culinary micro-region where a plethora of food experiences, culinary fusion, hybridity, and experimentation are daily in evidence. Julie Mehta, herself a transnational scholar, explores the daily negotiations and emerging subjectivities of young South Asian university students interacting with their other Asian and Canadian classmates and others in Toronto. She does so in an interdisciplinary case study on contemporary South Asian foodways in Toronto that combines history, literary allusions, restaurant research, interviews, sociological observation, and personalized scholarship.[34] As noted earlier, it is ahistorical to declare, as do many media and food writers, that such culinary diversity is the product of postmodernity; nevertheless, Mehta's contribution does highlight the particularities of a large and still rapidly expanding South Asian diaspora in Canada and the multiplicity of both regional and standard South Asian cuisines in Toronto. The chapter captures a contemporary sensibility in addition to showing how transnational scholars can study 'the global' in 'the local' setting of diasporic sites like Toronto.

Food, of course, is gendered in so many ways, and particularly in a feminine way, as grocery shopping, food preparation, and clean-up are all coded as women's responsibility – regardless of how many men may perform these functions. The fourth theme, then, is gendering food in cookbooks and family spaces. There are many stereotyped notions of food and gender, whether it is beefsteak and maleness, or jello and femaleness, both of these foods also being markers of social class. As Inness, a leading American theorist of food and gender, bluntly puts it: 'if we are to study women's gender roles ... we need to study food.'[35] Her 2001 collection of essays, *Cooking Lessons*, demonstrates how particular food items – meatloaf, jello, fried chicken, for instance – offered women power and influence in their households and communities.[36] For Canada, Valerie Korinek and Franca Iacovetta's 2004 study of the gender politics of food shows how, after the Second World War, nutritionists, writers, and policy makers – gatekeepers of the Canadian way – in Canada focused on women's roles in purchasing food and preparing family meals. The capacity of immigrant women, in particular, to 'eat Canadian' at home, whether it meant embracing jello salads or rejecting spicy salami, affected the potential of the state to promote a homogeneous citizenry in an era when the makeup of the population was undergoing dramatic change.[37]

Immigrant women used the culinary table as a site of connection between the old and new worlds. Especially in ethnically distinct communities, women are often viewed as cultural carriers with responsibility for maintaining traditions, customs, language, and other group distinctiveness across generations. Marlene Epp, in her chapter on mid-twentieth-century Mennonite cookbooks, focuses on an ethno-religious community for whom foodstuffs and foodways – like language, dress, and architecture – have often been cultural trademarks of community identity. She shows how cookbooks were an important medium through which Mennonite women of the 1950s and onwards offered public declarations of their (normally private) food labours and which solidified certain cultural aspects of community, both internally and externally, and, in the case of bestsellers, to wider sectors of society as well. Her essay highlights the women's interactions and sense of community, as well as value of the cookbooks as philanthropic tools whose sales contributed to the running of churches, larger denominational institutions, and mission boards. Beginning in the mid-1970s, Mennonite women were also responding to a series of food crises through the publication of 'social justice' or 'world community' cookbooks that advocated cooking methods that used less of the world's resources so that 'others could eat enough,' and by 2005, featured 'recipes that celebrate fresh, local foods.'

Andrea Eidinger's essay provides a valuable analysis of how cookbooks, far from simply being 'just recipes,' offer a critical entry point into how group efforts to create tools for shaping a community ethnic identity target women, in this case, Jewish women. She combines textual and social historical analysis of a popular Jewish cookbook, *A Treasure for My Daughter: A Reference Book of Jewish Festivals with Menus and Recipes*. Originally published in the 1950s, by the Ethel Epstein Ein Chapter of Hadassah-WIZO in Montreal, it holds a place of honour in the home of many Canadian Jewish women. On the surface, *A Treasure for My Daughter* appears to be a simple cookbook and guide to the major religious celebrations in the Jewish calendar, but it actually contains within it a particular discourse on 'Jewishness,' one that represented a new Jewish orthodoxy taking shape among established, middle-class Jews in the 1950s against a backdrop of increasing acculturation, competing cultures, and changing roles for women.

Gender roles are central to Sonia Cancian's chapter, in which she explores how two generations of Italian women living in post-1945 Montreal accepted, negotiated, or resisted their role as family food provider. Among the second-generation women – those who came to adulthood during the women's movement of the 1970s – she finds a much greater degree of ambivalence about performing this role, leading some of them to adopt strategies that lessened the burden of daily and festive cooking. Based on a small but rich sample of interviews, this case study demonstrates well how a limited research base can reveal intriguing, indeed, meaningful, patterns of behaviour worthy of investigation. Cancian's research also underscores a related theme, the importance of food to ethnic identity creation.

The gendered nature of foodways and foodscapes is a relatively new area of academic inquiry; however, the commerce of foodstuffs and, in particular, food staples has a lengthy history. Seeking ways to more creatively explore and explain global trade, the history of exploration and discovery, and the commensurate spread of colonies and empires, historians in recent years have turned to food commodities as the organizational principle for such transnational work. Many food scholars have illuminated the social, economic, and political developments occurring during a particular era by exploring the history of a singular food commodity. Among the most important and influential of these global histories has been Sidney Mintz's study of sugar, entitled *Sweetness and Power.* Some chapters in this book focus on a particular food item, but James Murton's essay on marketing apples and Nathalie Cooke's on cultural debates over margarine most explicitly adopt a single-food-commodity approach, which constitutes our fifth theme.

Murton combines a commodities-oriented with an environmental and global systems approach to explore an experiment in imperial marketing in which Canada was expected to fulfil a role as both agricultural producer and imperial consumer. He examines the promotional efforts of the British government's Empire Marketing Board (EMB) during the1920s and early 1930s to create markets in Britain for goods produced in the British dominions and colonies overseas. By focusing on Canadian apples, he explores the EMB's challenges of trying to create a global market in food, which included practical considerations, such as the complexities of preserving perishable products as they travelled great distances, and cultural ones, such as normalizing the idea of consuming fruit, meat, and other goods from the other side of the world. Socioeconomic concerns existed, as well, such as creating a web of information that would connect colonial farmers and packing houses with British wholesalers, merchants, and customers. Above all, Murton's chapter reminds us that there is nothing natural or inevitable about global food markets. They have to be built, a process that, as contemporary critics of the world food system note, often involves the complicit role of supportive governments that enact laws that protect multinationals over local farmers and ranchers and provide financial inducements to facilitate global trade.[38] This historical essay explores issues of local versus imported foods that are central to contemporary critiques of global food systems.

In her essay, Nathalie Cooke focuses on that familiar edible oil product, margarine, and explores the broader social, cultural, and political ramifications emanating from its production, marketing, and distribution. She examines the debates prompted by margarine's appearance especially as they unfolded in postwar Quebec (and Ontario), highlighting the narrative scenarios that cast the main characters – farmer, consumer, policy maker, marketer, and even butter and margarine as rival characters in their own right[39] – in the story in dramatically different ways. Dairy farmers and cheese makers, for example, tried to scare consumers into sticking with butter with alarmist claims about the threats that falling butter consumption would have on the agricultural industry and related industries, and even on the quality of soil. For their part, the margarine advocates stressed its lower cost while also trying to improve its image as 'a poor man's substitute for butter,' and its bland appearance, by including a packet of yellow colouring with every product.

Protests over the price of and access to food, as well as issues of mindful eating and social justice, have been important components of the politics of food – our sixth theme. There is a long history of working-class and poor mothers who publicly protested rising food prices, and historians have documented for both the pre-industrial and industrial eras women's active roles and leadership in urban bread riots, sugar boycotts, and Jewish women's 'kosher' protests.[40] Julie Guard's chapter fits into this history of women's consumer mobilizations, asking a specific question: how did radical women fighting rising prices in Canada during the Depression mobilize a large, broad-based grassroots movement? They did so largely, her case study reveals, by tapping into the extraordinary material and symbolic meanings of milk and the hyperbole that exaggerated milk's fundamental importance to health. In discussing how the milk price campaign transformed a marginal group of women into a highly respectable consumer organization, the Toronto Housewives Association, Guard notes that the group's biggest achievement was not simply lower prices but stimulating a popular education campaign about the political economy of milk.

Catherine Gidney, in her essay on student food politics at a Canadian university, examines food protests of a very different kind. She explores students' relationship to dining-room food and a wider university culture by looking at two residence food protests held at Victoria University, University of

Toronto. The first one, in 1913, occurred in the women's residence, and the students' complaints about declining food quality and service quietly resulted in the removal of a recently hired dietician. The second, in 1948, took place in the men's residence, where the students' protest over reduced amounts of milk (and jam) and mismanagement of the now cafeteria-style dining room, included a publicity-earning gimmick of bringing two calves into the dining room. By revealing the disruptions in the normal functioning of the university residence dining room and its traditional elite culture of bourgeois gentility, both events provide rare insights into largely middle-class students' social and cultural life in an era before the dramatic democratization of universities, and the class and gender relations embedded in highly ritualized performances of bourgeois civility.

Taking a different approach to food politics, Catherine Carstairs explores the topic of 'mindful eating' by considering the Canadian (and North American) health movement of the 1960s and 1970s. She significantly revises the dominant and baby-boomer–fuelled images of that movement – baby boomers growing sprouts, baking whole grain breads, and making yogurt and granola – by pointing out its much earlier roots and its broad constituency of peoples and ages. She notes the ironies, and problematic politics, of some of Canada's early health food activists. What these male and female activists had in common, Carstairs shows, was a desire to find a sense of control in their lives through carefully monitoring what and how they ate or, in other words, mindful eating. Other themes that link past to present in her essay are holistic health, concerns about pesticides and food additives, the promotion of vitamins and herbal remedies, and vegetarianism, a topic also explored by Valerie Korinek.

In an essay that brings together food and sexuality history, Korinek explores how a 1990 commercial for PETA (People for the Ethical Treatment of Animals) entitled 'Meat Stinks' and featuring singer k.d. lang, triggered an angry and homophobic backlash in her cattle-dependent home province of Alberta. Drawing on a variety of newspapers in prairie small towns and cities, Korinek covers local, provincial, and national reactions to lang's decision to 'come out' as a vegetarian. Angry protest towards lang came from a variety of corners, but the best-publicized reaction was from cattle industry activists who defaced the welcome sign of lang's hometown of Consort, Alberta (which read 'home of kd lang') to read 'Eat beef dyke.' The lang episode sheds light on the role that gender, sexuality, and food symbolism have played in the shaping of contemporary prairie viewpoints on matters of social cohesion and regional diversity.

Food and its related practices have been intimately linked to the construction of group and national as well as imperial identities, through, for example, cookbooks and cultural spectacles. This seventh theme, shaping national identity, is of acute interest to historians of Canada, a country that is both a white settler society with a troubled past (and present) of Aboriginal-settler relations and a significant immigrant-receiving nation where liberal pluralist ideologies continually bump up against persistent Anglo-French conflicts and a still racialized vertical mosaic.[41] Food can function as an important signifier of difference and identity among people of disparate ethnic and racial backgrounds. In an officially designated multicultural nation like Canada, in which celebrations of diversity coexist with pressures to assimilate, the evolution of food practices reveals the tensions, negotiations, and power struggles that existed (and continue to exist) between ethnic groups, between white and non-white, and also within the sphere of national identity making that occurs at many levels. Chapters in this collection illuminate both the possibilities and tensions between a nation-building agenda that emphasizes commonality and the celebration of multiculturalism that assumes differences.

The efforts at putting forth a collective identity through food-as-public-spectacle are addressed by Molly Pulver Ungar, in her case study of the elaborate banquets served during the British Royal Tour of 1939, when reigning monarch King George VI and Queen Elizabeth visited Canada. Ungar explores how the chefs, organizers, and participants happily served up 'Canadian nationalism on the menu' while also displaying much imperial enthusiasm. Through a close textual reading of two hotel restaurant menus preserved from this highly public spectacle, she effectively draws out the symbolic and cultural role played by these themed and extravagant menus, and shows how the artfully presented meals were meant both to act as representations of Canadian national pride and imperial enthusiasm and to create a sumptuous feast and fantasy fit for a king. Indeed, in Ungar's chapter, the menus and meals themselves take on a performative quality in their own right and in so doing helped create certain exceptional moments in grand culinary theatre.

Turning to the 1950s and 1960s, Franca Iacovetta explores the efforts of a mixed group of middle- and working-class Anglo, ethnic, and immigrant women at the International Institute of Toronto to help bring about a 'multicultural reimagining' of the postwar city and nation, in part by mounting ethnic banquets and a multi-ethnic Christmas cookbook and other pluralist projects aimed at shifting, however modestly, a hegemonic politics of Anglo-conformity to one more respectful of cultural difference. Like other multi-ethnic Canadian (and U.S.) cookbooks that helped to create a safe cultural terrain on which, particularly, the dominant 'hosts' could be encouraged to accept 'difference,' the institute's 1963 cookbook was a hybrid culinary text, the product of a process of mainstreaming the foreign foods until they were no longer considered dangerously foreign yet still retained enough of the exotic to make experimenting with them worthwhile. The essay also portrays the institute banquets as spectacles: the staff promised colourful displays and festive food, and the events featured costumed women performing their ethnicity and serving up their culture for Canadian consumption.

A final important theme concerns the role of nutritional standards, whether marketed or imposed on targeted populations. In her photo essay, Cheryl Krasnick Warsh considers the advertising campaigns of food companies that exploited parents' concerns about children's nutrition by selling children's foods aimed at enhancing 'vim and vigour.' Focusing on the period 1914 to 1954, she explores the major trends in power foods, such as yeast, oatmeal, Ovaltine, and breakfast cereals, and contextualizes them within both the medical and maternal concerns of a given time frame (whether it be weakly children, high infant morbidity and mortality rates, or the flu epidemic) and socio-cultural preoccupations (whether it be school performance for boys, single parenthood during wartime, or ensuring optimal health in the post-1945 era). The ads themselves invite a discussion of the power of images and both their intended, or coded meanings and the meanings that readers may have attributed to them.

Taking a different approach, the essays by Ian Mosby and Krista Walters address the matter of constructing national identities by means of establishing or imposing nutritional standards. Mosby explores the social construction of healthy eating recommendations during the Second World War by examining the Canada's Official Food Rules campaign, launched by the government in 1942. It was the first truly national public health effort aimed exclusively at improving Canadians' dietary habits and remains to this day the basis of modern Canadian nutritional advice. Mosby shows that the rationale behind the Food Rules went beyond reinforcing cultural norms to also define good citizenship in terms that fit the priorities of a wartime state keen to ensure industrial productivity, agricultural sustainability, and military fitness. An exaggeration of the problem of widespread malnutrition, he adds, enabled policy makers to frame inadequate nutrition as a problem of poor education rather than class or income inequalities.

Through an analysis of a decade-long, state-funded nutritional survey of Aboriginal Canadians, conducted by professional nutritionists between 1965 and 1975, Walters shows how nutrition can be adapted to ideological and cultural projects. Far from simply a benign effort to raise national health standards, the project, she argues, instituted hegemonic dietary regulations based on Western norms and, once again, used dietary health as a colonial tool for assimilating Aboriginal peoples. Government experts defined the behaviours and habits of poor and marginalized Aboriginal women and their families as pathological or culturally deviant and then used their findings to justify arguments about placing such 'deviant' bodies under the increasing control of federal authorities. Nutritional ideals and the marketing of those ideals, then, are shaped by the political and social norms existing at a given time and so must be viewed in historical context.

In conclusion, our knowledge of Canada's peoples, institutions, cultures, and identities is enhanced by probing the past using food as a lens of examination. Historical research on food can converge with global food studies addressing issues related to environmentalism, justice, and development in a contemporary context. Food history has much to offer those interested in Canadian history, and enables us to more critically approach contemporary political, cultural, medical, and environmental aspects of how Canadians grow, market, trade, and consume food. It reminds us that so much of our present-day concerns about food accessibility and safety, about the costs of the global food marketplace, and about commercially and medically constructed notions of how and what to eat have lengthy histories – as does our notion of ourselves as 'cosmopolitan' eaters.

Food history offers a new vantage point on long-standing history questions about cultural politics and power, gender relations, ethnic and racialized histories of inclusion and exclusion, imperial designs and nation building, sexual and gendered performances, class struggles and cultural identities, regional diversity, and the role of the state or corporation in shaping daily practice. Those looking for a 'Canadian food culture' should look elsewhere, but for those interested in thinking critically about the history of what Canadians eat, and what that signifies about our society, country, and people, we welcome you to this smorgasbord. Bon appetit!

NOTES

1 Nor has our worry over anorexia nervosa and other disorders abated as we observe girls, and boys, affected by the fashion and celebrity world's obsession with thinness. Joan Jacobs Bumberg, *Fasting Girls: The History of Anorexia Nervosa* (Cambridge, MA: Harvard University Press, 1988).
2 Barbara Kingsolver, *Animal, Vegetable, Miracle: A Year of Food Life* (New York: HarperCollins, 2007).
3 Michael Pollan, *The Omnivore's Dilemma: A Natural History of Four Meals* (Waterville, ME: Thorndike, 2006); Michael Pollan, *In Defense of Food: An Eater's Manifesto* (New York: Penguin, 2008), 1.
4 Toronto: Between the Lines, 2008.
5 Frances Osborne, *Lilla's Feast: A True Story of Food, Love and War in the Orient*

(New York: Random House, 2004); Louise DeSalvo, *Crazy in the Kitchen: Food, Feuds, and Forgiveness in an Italian American Family* (New York: Bloomsbury, 2004); Elizabeth Ehrlich, *Miriam's Kitchen: A Memoir* (New York: Penguin, 1997).

6 Janice Wong, *Chow: From China to Canada – Memories of Food and Family* (Vancouver: Whitecap Books, 2005); Maria L. Cioni, *Spaghetti Western: How My Father Brought Italian Food to the West* (Calgary: Fifth House, 2006).

7 Rudy Wiebe, *A Discovery of Strangers* (Toronto: Knopf, 1994); Timothy Taylor, *Stanley Park* (Toronto: Knopf, 2001); Judy Fong Bates, *Midnight at the Dragon Café* (Toronto: McClelland and Stewart, 2004); Austin Clarke, *Love and Sweet Food: A Culinary Memoir* (Toronto: Thomas Allen, 2004); Marusya Bociurkiw, *Comfort Food for Breakups: The Memoir of a Hungry Girl* (Vancouver: Arsenal Pulp Press, 2007).

8 Anita Rau Badami, *Can You Hear the Nightbird Call?* (Toronto: Knopf, 2006); Anar Ali, *Baby Khaki's Wings* (Toronto: Penguin, 2009). On these and other cited novels, see also the chapters by Julie Mehta and Julia Roberts in this volume.

9 Margaret Visser, *Much Depends on Dinner: The Extraordinary History and Mythology, Allure and Obsessions, Perils and Taboos, of An Ordinary Meal* (New York: Harper Collins, 1986); *The Rituals of Dinner: The Origins, Evolution, and Meaning of Table Manners* (New York: Harper Collins, 1992).

10 For just one example of each type, Irma S. Rombauer and Marion Rombauer Becker, *Joy of Cooking* (Indianapolis, IN: Bobs Merrill, 1931, reprinted in 1940s, 1950s; reprinted in 1962, 1963, 1964, 1975, 1995, 1997, 1998, and the 75th anniversary edition in 2006); Anna Thomas, *The Vegetarian Epicure* (New York: Vintage Books, 1972); Julie Rosso and Sheila Lukins, *The Silver Palette Good Times Cookbook* (New York: Workman, 1984); Lucy Waverman and James Chatto, *A Matter of Taste: Inspired Seasonal Menus with Wines and Spirits to Match* (Toronto: Harper Collins, 2004); Nigella Lawson and James Merrell, *Feast: Food to Celebrate Life* (London: Hyperion, 2004).

11 For example, earlier racial stereotypes of Italians as smelly garlic eaters, like more recent stereotypes of South Asians as smelly curry eaters and Asian Canadians as dog eaters, show how popular portrayals of eating habits serve to racialize and 'other' particular racial and ethnic groups. The 1999 legal dispute between neighbouring Toronto households over the smoke and fumes produced by a Chinese Canadian family's wok cooking quickly became, in the media anyway, also a clash of ethnicities.

12 Here, we offer general definitions for this and other concepts in food history literature that may be unfamiliar to non-specialists, but we encourage readers to consult the individual chapters to see how the authors have borrowed and applied the more scholarly or complex theoretical definitions in their work.

13 Roland Barthes, *Mythologies* (Paris: Seuil, 1957; transl. 1970); Claude Lévi-Strauss, *The Raw and the Cooked* (Paris: Plon, 1964; transl. 1966); Mary Douglas (Collected Works), *Food in the Social Order: Studies of Food and Festivals in Three American Communities* (New York: Basic Books, 1984).

14 Brian Fagan, *Fish on Friday: Feasting, Fasting, and the Discovery of the New World* (New York: Basic Books, 2006); Lizzie Collingham, *Curry: A Tale of Cooks and Conquerors* (New York: Oxford University Press, 2006). These are just two examples of a huge multidisciplinary literature covering regions around the world. One place to consult for new as well as reprinted and revised editions of older studies is California Studies in Food and Culture, a multidisciplinary book series at the University of California Press.

15 It showed how practices of fasting and eating of the Eucharist were empowering to Christian women. Berkeley: University of California Press, 1987.

16 Sidney W. Mintz, *Sweetness and Power: The Place of Sugar in Modern History* (New York: Penguin, 1985); Mark Pendergrast, *Uncommon Grounds: The History of Coffee and How It Transformed Our World* (New York: Basic Books, 1999); Mark Kurlansky, *Cod: A Biography of the Fish that Changed the World* (New York: Walker, 1997); Redcliffe N. Salaman, *The History and Social Influence of the Potato* (Cambridge, MA: Cambridge University Press, 1985); Mark Kurlansky, *Salt: A World History* (New York: Penguin, 2003); Elizabeth Abbott, *Sugar: A Bittersweet History* (Toronto: Penguin, 2008); John Reader, *Potato: A History of the Propitious Esculent* (New Haven, CT: Yale University Press, 2009). This a small sample of a burgeoning literature.

17 Andrew F. Smith, *Popped Culture: A Social History of Popcorn in America* (Columbia, SC: University of South Carolina Press, 1999); Carolyn Wyman, *Spam: A Biography* (San Diego, CA: Harcourt Brace, 1999); John Soluri, *Banana Cultures: Agriculture, Consumption, and Environmental Change in Honduras and the United States* (Austin, TX: University of Texas Press, 2005); Daniel Sidorick, *Condensed Capitalism: Campbell's Soup Company and the Pursuit of Cheap Production in the Twentieth Century* (Ithaca, NY: Cornell University Press, 2009). Levenstein's *Paradox of Plenty* offers a useful discussion of new left critiques of American imperialism and the so-called banana republics of Latin America.

18 Jeffrey M. Pilcher, *Food in World History* (New York: Routledge, 2006).

19 Harold Innis, *The Cod Fisheries: The History of an International Economy* (New Haven, CT: Yale University Press, 1940); Douglas McCalla, 'The Wheat Staple and Upper Canadian Development,' *Canadian Historical Association Historical Papers* (1978): 34–46; John McCallum, *Unequal Beginnings: Agricultural and Economic Development in Ontario and Quebec* (Toronto: University of Toronto Press, 1980). More pertinent, perhaps, are environmental histories such as John F. Varty, 'On Protein, Prairie Wheat and Good Bread: Rationalizing Technologies

and the Canadian State, 1912–1935,' *Canadian Historical Review* 85/4 (2004): 721–53.

20 A tiny sample includes Bruce Trigger, *The Children of Aataentsic: A History of the Huron People to 1660* (Montreal and Kingston: McGill-Queen's University Press, 1976); Mary Ellen Kelm, *Colonizing Bodies: Aboriginal Health and Healing in British Columbia, 1900–1950* (Vancouver: UBC Press, 1998); Cole Harris, *Making Native Space: Colonialism, Resistance and Reserves in British Columbia* (Vancouver: UBC Press, 2002); Allan Greer, *Mohawk Saint: Catherine Tekakwitha and the Jesuits* (New York: Oxford University Press, 2005).

21 A small sample includes Marjorie Cohen, *Women's Work, Markets, and Economic Development in Nineteenth-Century Ontario* (Toronto: University of Toronto Press, 1988); Varpu Lindström, *Defiant Sisters: A Social History of Finnish Immigrant Women in Canada* (originally Lindström-Best; Toronto: Multicultural History Society of Ontario, 1988; repr. University of Toronto Press, 1992); Marlene Epp, 'The Mennonite Girls' Homes of Winnipeg: A Home away from Home,' *Journal of Mennonite Studies* 6 (1988): 100–14; Frances Swyripa, *Wedded to the Cause: Ukrainian Canadian Women and Ethnic Identity* (Toronto: University of Toronto Press, 1993); Ian Radforth, *Bushworkers and Bosses: Logging in Northern Ontario, 1900–1980* (Toronto: University of Toronto Press, 1987); and Depression-era studies such as Lara Campbell, *Respectable Citizens: Gender, Family, and Unemployment in Ontario's Great Depression* (Toronto: University of Toronto Press, 2009).

22 Harvey Levenstein, *Revolution at the Table: The Transformation of the American Diet* (New York: Oxford University Press, 1988); Levenstein, *Paradox of Plenty: A Social History of Eating in Modern America* (New York: Oxford University Press, 1993); Laura Shapiro, *Perfection Salad: Women and Cooking at the Turn of the Century* (New York: Farrar, Straus and Giroux, 1986); Laura Shapiro, *Something from the Oven: Reinventing Dinners in 1950s America* (New York: Viking, 2004); Sherrie A. Inness, *Dinner Roles: American Women and Culinary Culture* (Iowa City, IA: University of Iowa Press, 2001); *Secret Ingredients: Race, Gender and Class at the Dinner Table* (London: Palgrave Macmillan, 2006); Janet Theophano, *Eat My Words: Reading Women's Lives through the Cookbooks They Wrote* (New York: Palgrave, 2002); Warren Belasco, *Appetite for Change: How the Countercultures Took in the Food Industry* (New York: Pantheon,1989, 1990, rev. ed., 1993); Warren Belasco, *Meals to Come: A History of the Future of Food* (Berkeley, CA: University of California Press, 2006); Donna R. Gabaccia, *We Are What We Eat: Ethnic Food and the Making of Americans* (Cambridge, MA: Harvard University Press, 1998); Hasia R. Diner, *Hungering for America: Italian, Irish, and Jewish Foodways in the Age of Migration* (Cambridge, MA: Harvard University Press, 2001); Psyche A. Williams-Forson, *Building Houses Out of Chicken Legs: Black*

Women, Food, and Power (Chapel Hill, NC: University of North Carolina Press, 2006).

23 For just a few examples, Sherrie A. Inness, ed., *Cooking Lessons: The Politics of Gender and Food* (Lanham, MD: Rowman and Littlefield, 2001); Warren Belasco and Philip Scranton, *Food Nations: Selling Tastes in Consumer Societies* (New York: Routledge, 2002). We could also include multidisciplinary volumes in food studies such as Arlene Voski Avakian and Barbara Haber, eds., *From Betty Crocker to Feminist Food Studies: Critical Perspectives on Women and Food* (Amherst, MA: University of Massachusetts Press, 2005), and Carole Counihan and Penny Van Esterik, eds., *Food and Culture: A Reader* (New York: Routledge, 1997).

24 Toronto: Dundurn Press, 2006.

25 Carole Ferguson and Margaret Fraser, *A Century of Canadian Home Cooking* (Scarborough, ON: Prentice-Hall, 1992); Elizabeth Driver, *Culinary Landmarks: A Bibliography of Canadian Cookbooks, 1825–1949* (Toronto: University of Toronto Press, 2008).

26 Thelma Barer-Stein, *You Eat What You Are: People, Culture and Food Traditions* (Willowdale, ON: Firefly Books, 1999).

27 Jo Marie Powers, ed., *From Cathay to Canada: Chinese Cuisine in Transition* (Toronto: Ontario Historical Society, 1998); Jo Marie Powers, ed., *Buon Appetito! Italian Foodways in Ontario* (Toronto: Ontario Historical Society, 2000). In keeping with the multidisciplinarity of food studies, both volumes resulted from conferences involving professional and community historians, industry people, and the public.

28 Valerie J. Korinek, *Roughing It in the Suburbs: Reading Chatelaine Magazine in the Fifties and Sixties* (Toronto: University of Toronto Press, 2000); Franca Iacovetta and Valerie J. Korinek, 'Jell-O Salads, One-Stop Shopping, and Maria the Homemaker: The Gender Politics of Food,' 190–230, and Marlene Epp, 'The Semiotics of Zwieback: Feast and Famine in the Narratives of Mennonite Refugee Women,' 314–40, both in Marlene Epp, Franca Iacovetta, and Frances Swyripa, eds., *Sisters or Strangers? Immigrant, Ethnic, and Racialized Women in Canadian History* (Toronto: University of Toronto Press, 2004); Franca Iacovetta, *Gatekeepers: Reshaping Immigrant Lives in Cold War Canada* (Toronto: Between the Lines, 2006); Marlene Epp, *Mennonite Women in Canada: A History* (Winnipeg: University of Manitoba Press, 2008); Royden Loewen, *Family, Church, and Market: A Mennonite Community in the Old and the New Worlds, 1850–1930* (Urbana, IL: University of Illinois Press, 1993); R.W. Sandwell, *Contesting Rural Space: Land Policy and Practices of Resettlement on Saltspring Island, 1859–1891* (Montreal and Kingston: McGill-Queen's University Press, 2005); Stacey Zembrzycki, '"There Were always Men in Our House": Gender and the Childhood Memories of Working-Class Ukrainians in Depression-Era Canada,' *Labour/Le Travail* 60

(Autumn 2007): 77–105; Elizabeth Beaton, ed., *Connecting the Dots: Social and Scientific Perspectives on Agricultural Rural Life in Atlantic Canada* (Sydney: Cape Breton University Press, 2009).

29 Toronto: University of Toronto Press, 2008.

30 Montreal and Kingston: McGill-Queen's University Press.

31 Gabaccia, *We Are What We Eat.*

32 Such historical inquiry is interested in the systematic scrutiny of cultural spectacles, such as pageants and parades, for what they can tell us about the process of identity formation and the production of social meaning at the level of participant or spectator, civic, labour, or ethnic group, and at the national and international level. A small sample includes Eric Hobsbawm and Terence Ranger, eds., *The Invention of Tradition* (Cambridge: Cambridge University Press, 1983); John Bodnar, *Remaking America: Public Memory, Commemoration and Patriotism in the Twentieth Century* (Princeton, NJ: Princeton University Press, 1993); Robert Cupido, 'Appropriating the Past: Pageants, Politics and the Diamond Jubilee of Confederation,' *Journal of the Canadian Historical Association* 9/1 (1998): 155–86; H.V. Nelles, *The Art of Nation Building: Pageantry and Spectacle at Quebec's Tercentenary* (Toronto: University of Toronto Press, 1999); Ian Radforth, *Royal Spectacle: The 1860 Visit of the Prince of Wales to Canada and the United States* (Toronto: University of Toronto Press, 2004); Craig Heron and Steve Penfold, *The Workers' Festival: A History of Labour Day in Canada* (Toronto: University of Toronto Press, 2005); and, with a focus on public sites of consumption and performance, Beat Kümin and B. Ann Tlusty, eds., *World of the Tavern: Public Houses in Early Modern Europe* (Aldershot: Ashgate, 2002).

33 A few examples are E.M. Collingham, *Curry: A Tale of Cooks and Conquerors* (New York: Oxford University Press, 2006); Krishnendu Ray, *The Migrant's Table: Meals and Memories in Bengali-American Households* (Philadelphia, PA: Temple University Press, 2004); Dick Hebdige, *Cut 'n Mix: Culture, Identity and Caribbean Music* (London: Methuen, 1987).

34 On personalized scholarship, Franca Iacovetta, 'Post-modern Ethnography, Historical Materialism and Decentring the (Male) Authorial Voice: A Feminist Conversation,' *Histoire Sociale / Social History* 32/64 (1999): 275–93.

35 Sherrie A. Inness, 'Introduction: Thinking Food/Thinking Gender,' in *Kitchen Culture in America: Popular Representations of Food, Gender, and Race* (Philadelphia, PA: University of Pennsylvania Press, 2001), 4.

36 See her 'Introduction: Of Meatloaf and Jell-O,' in *Cooking Lessons*, xi.

37 Iacovetta and Korinek, 'Jell-O Salads, One-Stop Shopping, and Maria the Homemaker.' See also Korinek, *Roughing It in the Suburbs*, esp. chapter 5.

38 Such as the many scholarly articles by sociologist Harriet Friedmann, which include her earlier 'World Market, State, and Family Farm: Social Bases of

Household Production in the Era of Wage Labour,' *Comparative Studies in Society and History* 20/4 (1978): 545–86; and her 'Circles of Growing and Eating: The Political Ecology of Food and Agriculture,' in Raymond Grew, ed., *Food in Global History* (Boulder, CO: Westview Press, 1999).

39 On the notion that material objects can have a life of their own, see Arjun Appadurai's *The Social Life of Things: Commodities in Cultural Perspective* (Cambridge: Cambridge University Press, 1986).

40 For just two North American examples, see Ruth Frager, *Sweatshop Strife: Class, Ethnicity and Gender in the Jewish Labour Movement of Toronto, 1900–1939* (Toronto: University of Toronto Press, 1992); Ardis Cameron, *Radicals of the Worst Sort: Laboring Women in Lawrence, Massachusetts, 1860–1912* (Urbana, IL: University of Illinois Press, 1993).

41 Alan C. Cairns, *Citizens Plus: Aboriginal People and the Canadian State* (Vancouver: UBC Press, 2000); Charles Taylor, *Reconciling the Solitudes: Essays on Canadian Federalism and Nationalism* (Montreal and Kingston: McGill-Queen's University Press, 1993); Eve Haque, '"Multiculturalism within a Bilingual Framework": Language and the Racial Ordering of Difference and Belonging in Canada,' doctoral dissertation, University of Toronto, 2007; Sherene Razak, ed., *Space and the Law: Mapping a White Settler Society* (Toronto: Between the Lines, 2002).

PART ONE

Cultural Exchanges and Cuisines in the Contact Zone

1 'Fit for the Table of the Most Fastidious Epicure': Culinary Colonialism in the Upper Canadian Contact Zone

ALISON NORMAN

In a letter dated 9 May 1833, Catharine Parr Traill, the English immigrant settler woman who would gain a reputation as a colonial writer, reported that the local Aboriginal women (whom she called 'squaws') 'have been several times to see me; sometimes from curiosity, sometimes with the view of bartering their baskets, mats, ducks, or venison, for pork, flour, potatoes, or articles of wearing apparel. Sometimes their object is to borrow "kettle to cook," which they are very punctual in returning.'[1] Traill and her sister Susanna Moodie belonged to a small group of British pioneer women whose writings have received plenty of attention by Canadian historians and literary scholars. To date, however, histories of colonial Ontario have largely left unexplored the subject of Traill's 1833 letter, settler women's food exchanges and culinary relations with the Native people of their area. This chapter helps to fill that gap.

My essay explores the culinary and cultural exchanges that took place between Aboriginal and white British settler women in Upper Canada/Canada West (1791–1867), focusing in particular on the new hybrid diets that resulted from this mingling of peoples. It does so by undertaking a gendered reading of the diaries, letters, and books penned by British immigrant women (and some men) who settled in or travelled through the regions around Peterborough, Toronto, and Brantford. Their texts help to document significant patterns. Within the contact zones of the backwoods of Ontario, where women exchanged food, recipes, material culture, and culinary information, the diets of middle-class British immigrants changed with the incorporation of 'Native' foods such as corn, wild rice, herbal teas, pumpkins, venison, duck, fish, and, of course, the legendary maple syrup. Native diets also changed. Modifications of the diets of the First Nations of southern Ontario already had occurred before the War of 1812, and more changes took place with increased British immigration in the 1830s. I argue that these changes in diets reflected greater changes taking place in both cultures. For the First Nations, changing food customs were part of the wider shift towards becoming a Christian, agrarian, and patriarchal people. That process also represented a dilution of 'traditional' culture, heritage, and identity, and in some ways, the creation of a new Anglo-Native identity. For British settlers, the consumption of Native Canadian foods was part of the process through which they came to self-identify as Canadians. Changes made to the backwoods settler diet became 'Canadian fare,' a transformation that was evident in the cookbooks that appeared throughout the nineteenth and twentieth centuries. Although not all settlers or First Nations had direct contact with each other, there was a mingling of cultures in the backwoods of Upper Canada which resulted in changed diets, culinary customs, and lifestyles.

Diets are always changing, and the ecological imperialism wrought by what Alfred Crosby has termed the 'Columbian Exchange' had a great impact on diets on both sides of the Atlantic.[2] Plants, animals, and microbes travelled both ways on ships, along with the explorers and settlers. When British settlers arrived in Upper Canada at the end of the eighteenth century, some new species were already well established there. However, the exchange continued with settlers who cut down trees, brought in cows, sheep, and pigs, and planted foreign species. Catharine Parr Traill, for instance, asked relatives in England to mail her the seeds of fruits and flowers to plant in her backwoods garden.[3] This ecological imperialism, facilitated by British settlers, meant that some settlers could eat foods from home, and some First Nations could eat new foods. It also meant that the physical environment in Upper Canada was changing, as land was cleared by both settlers and First Nations people to plant crops.[4]

The Native Diet

The First Nations living in what was Upper Canada already had a long history of contact with Europeans before Loyalist settlers began arriving in the 1790s. Their diets had changed through contact with fur traders and missionaries, and continued to do so in the face of ongoing attempts by the colonial government to make them into settled agricultural and Christian people. Furthermore, there was a long history of pre-colonial trade involving foodstuffs among the First Nations groups who lived in the Great Lakes region prior to European settlement. Communities in the south traded their corn and tobacco to Georgian Bay communities in exchange for furs, dried fish, and meat.[5] When Europeans arrived and began trading, they were participating in a well-established trade economy, one that featured complex cultural exchanges between the participants.

This chapter covers the period 1790s–1860s, and I am particularly interested in the years immediately following the arrival of the Loyalists after the American Revolution, and the subsequent period of increased British immigration that occurred in the years after the end of the Napoleonic Wars in 1815. During this time, the people living on the land in southern Upper Canada were the Anishnaabeg (or Ojibwa) and the Haudenosaunee (or Iroquois). Prior to reserve life, Anishnaabeg people in Upper Canada ate wild rice, often seasoned with maple sugar or combined with duck or venison. Fish was a major part of their diet, as they tended to live along waterways. They gathered wild berries and fruit, which they also used as trade items to get squash and pumpkins from the Haudenosaunee, who farmed those vegetables. Food preparation – including harvesting, drying, and pounding rice – was women's work, while hunting and fishing were considered men's work.[6]

After the move to reserves, many Anishnaabeg adopted a farming lifestyle.[7] They were provided, at least initially, with housing, farming equipment, seed, and stock. They planted crops (such as potatoes, corn, wheat, oats, and peas), kept cows, and used oxen to work the fields. Field work was done by the men.[8] Surplus food and crafts were sold to non-Native neighbours and, at times, men found work on neighbouring farms.[9] Not all Anishnaabeg settled onto reserves or missions, however, and many continued to hunt. But as white settlement further encroached onto their hunting lands, they found it increasingly difficult to survive and, at times, the reserves and missions became a refuge.[10] Peter Jones, the Mississauga chief and Methodist missionary, noted in his *History of the Ojebway People* that while some people continued to hunt game using traditional methods for sustenance, 'the Indians who live within the bounds of the English settlements depend, in a great measure, for their livelihood on making baskets, brooms, wooden bowls, ladles and scoop shovels, which they sell to the white people in exchange for provisions.'[11] Evidently, communities could not always grow enough food to sustain themselves and had to supplement their diets by trade with settlers. Contact with white settlers and the colonial government produced changes in gender relations and culture, and also in the Anishnaabeg diet.

The Haudenosaunee were the other major Native group who came into contact with white settlers in what is now southern Ontario. Prior to their migration to Upper Canada, and before contact and assimilation with Anglo-Americans, the Haudenosaunee of upstate New York were farmers, fishers, hunters, and gatherers. The central crop of the Haudenosaunee was maize, or Indian corn, and it 'played an important part in Iroquois culture and history.'[12] Corn was cultivated on a large scale, which necessitated permanent settlement, resulting in heavily fortified villages and the construction of longhouses. In Haudenosaunee society, the gendered division of labour made men responsible for hunting and warring, while women took care of the crops and gardens.[13] As the need for warring ended after the War of 1812, men had more time to participate in field labour, although it was still primarily the women's domain, with the clan matrons being responsible for ordering the planting, cultivation, and harvesting.[14] Corn was grown with beans and squash, or pumpkin, together known as the three sisters, in a traditional method that saved land and labour and allowed the plants to benefit from each other. The corn provided a structure for the beans to climb, the beans provided nitrogen that enriched the soil in which the squash and corn were planted, and the squash spread out over the ground, preventing weeds and creating a microclimate to retain moisture in the soil.[15] The system also reflected the Haudenosaunee belief that these vegetables were guarded by three inseparable sister spirits and that the plants would not thrive if planted separately.[16] Corn was eaten in many different ways, but one common usage was to pound the corn into meal or flour and then bake it in breads or cakes.[17] Haudenosaunee women (and children) gathered wild roots, berries, nuts, and herbs, and developed methods of making maple sugar out of sap.[18] Men fished using nets in the summer and went ice fishing in the winter; they hunted deer, wild turkey, muskrat, and beaver.

A number of these traditions underwent change while the Haudenosaunee were undergoing conversion to Christianity and also learning Anglo-Canadian farming methods. Several thousand Haudenosaunee migrated to Upper Canada after the end of the American Revolution when, in 1784, they were granted tracts of land in the British colony in return for their loyalty to the Crown. These Six Nations people travelled from New York and settled along the shores of the Grand River, as well as at Tyendinaga, near Deseronto.[19] They brought with them their culinary customs, including the three sisters. Many of the Six Nations were already Christian converts having had centuries of contact with Anglo-American missionaries in the United States. They were successful farmers whose methods resembled those of their non-Native neighbours.[20] They grew corn, oats, wheat, and barley, and kept cattle. Subsistence gardening was more common among the traditional Longhouse families than among the Christian farmers.[21] The men continued to hunt. Scottish traveller John Howison visited the Mohawk village at Grand River in the late 1810s and noted that 'when the hunting season approaches, many of the inhabitants forsake their homes and agricultural occupations and assume, for a time, the savage mode of life from which they have been but partially reclaimed.'[22] Howison's Eurocentric comments do provide evidence that Six Nations people had not wholly converted to a Euro-Canadian way of life, despite their relatively productive farms. Like the Anishnaabeg, the Haudenosaunee in Upper Canada retained some of their culinary customs, but they also adopted new farming practices which led to changes in their diets.

The First Nations in Upper Canada, then, already had contact with Europeans or Anglo-Americans, and by the late eighteenth century, when Upper Canada was formed, their diets had already undergone change. Generally speaking, hybrid diets were common, to varying degrees, as many Native people adopted Euro-American farming methods, but still retained certain aspects of their own agriculture, gardening, gathering, hunting, or fishing. When they came into contact with British or Anglo-American settlers in Upper Canada, they did not have 'traditional' Native diets but had preserved enough of their culinary customs to teach some of them to the new British arrivals struggling to survive in the bush.

The British Diet

The diets of British settlers, who came from different social backgrounds and included rural and city dwellers both, would change upon their settlement in Upper Canada. Our focus here is on the middle-class immigrants – the wives of half-pay officers (disbanded soldiers with a pension), merchants, tradesmen, and sons of wealthy families – precisely because they produced written records, from private letters to publications, about their travels and daily life. (We know far less about the diets of the labouring poor.) By the time of their arrival, British food customs themselves had undergone significant changes at both the regional and national level, and the culinary fare once recognized throughout Europe had fallen into decline during the Victorian era.[23] Also, the historically close association between women and food growing, gathering, and preparation had undergone serious change between 1750 and 1850,[24] as upper class women and wealthy middle-class women, distancing themselves from actual kitchen work, assumed new duties as managers of the household and of its cook and servants.[25] The industrial boom created a new middle class that by the second half of the nineteenth century was hiring more and more cooks, housemaids, and other domestic help.[26] Accustomed to hired help, many of the middle-class British women who settled in Upper Canada lacked the skills to cook for their own families. As for diets in Britain at this time, wealthier families ate multicourse meals, prepared and served by servants, that might include elaborate soups, vegetables, fish, poultry, meat with sauces and gravies, as well as pastries, breads, and desserts.[27] The 'lesser gentry,' like the families of writers Jane Austen and the Bronte sisters, were more self-sufficient in food production, growing fruits and vegetables, raising poultry and cattle, making cheese, brewing beer, baking bread, and preserving hams and pickles.

They had only to buy tea and sugar.[28] The home life of the Austens is similar to the Strickland family, whose members Samuel Strickland, Susanna Strickland Moodie, and Catharine Parr Strickland Traill all emigrated to Canada and wrote about their experiences.

The British who emigrated to Upper Canada between 1820 and Confederation (1867) were considered desirable immigrants who could help the colonial government create 'a really British colony.'[29] In the 1820s and 1830s, when the colony actively encouraged immigration, the travel literature exaggerated the wealth of the colony and understated the amount of labour required to achieve success.[30] In his 1821 travel book, John Howison typically declared that Upper Canadians 'live much better than persons of a similar class in Britain,' and many a backwoods hut displayed 'many substantial comforts, such as immense loaves of beautiful bread, entire pigs hanging round the fireplace, dried venison, trenchers of milk, and bags of Indian corn.'[31] But as continuing changes in agriculture and industry threatened people's customary way of life in Britain, one million people responded to the call to come to British North America between 1815 and 1855.[32] The 'Canada mania' that 'pervaded the middle ranks of British society,' wrote Susanna Moodie, produced many settlers 'perfectly unfitted by their previous habits and education for contending with the stern realities of emigrant life.'[33] They also brought with them preconceived notions of Aboriginals and wrote about their disappointment at meeting 'Indians' in Western clothing who did not match their romantic image of the noble savage.

The Settler Diet in the New World

From the moment they embarked on the outgoing ships, where deficient supplies were a common complaint, the emigrants' diet underwent change. The emigrants were told what to bring aboard ship – 'very basic foods' like potatoes, salted beef or pork, cheese, eggs, dried fish, flour, root vegetables, bottled beer or cider, and 'if possible some apples, oranges, or lemons'[34] – and were desperate to eat fresh food after landing in Quebec. As they travelled west, stopping at taverns or inns along the way, they expressed some disapproval over their more informal arrangements. (Unlike English inns, many Upper Canadian taverns, as Julia Roberts' chapter in this volume explains, were 'American-style' places, where people of different classes, races, and genders might mingle.) Calling the tavern fare barely tolerable, they complained about the cornmeal bread, poor butter, weak tea, and salted or greasy meat – an inauspicious beginning.[35]

Many British immigrants arrived in a completely unfamiliar landscape, where the population was largely rural and the towns that did exist were small. The majority of homes were log houses or shanties, and although roads had been built between the larger towns, travel was time consuming and difficult.[36] Since many settlers bought large tracts of land, settlement in the backwoods was sparse, and neighbours were rarely close by. This probably helps explain why they sometimes sought out First Nations people as acquaintances. Settlers' lives were dominated by seasonal work such as clearing land and planting, tending, and harvesting their crops.[37] It was a life of subsistence – running a farm in order to provide food for the family. 'Next to childcare,' observes Jane Errington, 'preparing and cooking meals was one of the most important and time-consuming responsibilities of colonial wives.'[38]

Work was gendered. Men hunted, fished, ploughed the garden and the fields, and did other heavy labour, although there are some examples of bachelor men who cooked for themselves. Pioneer settler John Langton wrote frequently about his culinary adventures in his backwoods kitchen but was relieved when his sister Anne, who would also write about her experiences, arrived to take over the domestic duties.[39] 'It was the women,' he wrote, 'who planted, tended, and harvested the garden' on the farm, 'oversaw the poultry and worked the dairy,' and 'supervised or undertook the butchering of meat and the preservation of meat, fruit, and vegetables'[40] – most of them newly learned skills. As Traill noted in her 1855 book, *The Canadian Settler's Guide*, one of the more popular domestic manuals aimed at helping newly arrived women in the backwoods kitchen, since 'the materials' and 'method' of food preparation 'varies greatly between the colony and the Mother-country,' she had included 'the most approved recipes for cooking certain dishes, the usual mode of manufacturing maple-sugar, soap, candles, bread, and other articles of household expenditure.'[41]

In contrast to England, middle-class British folk in Upper Canada might commonly have only one domestic servant, if they could keep her at all, and thus did more of the cooking themselves. Many settler journals and letters discuss the difficulty in procuring 'help' and retaining it, as the demand exceeded the supply.[42] Traill also explained the custom of hiring servants in Upper Canada (they tended to be hired on a monthly basis) as well as the appropriate wages and noted how they should be treated as one of the household.[43] Many domestics were Irish immigrants, although some American women occasionally did this work. Rarely were they Native women.[44] An English emigrant, Mrs Edward Copleston stressed the difficulty of running her family home near Orillia with the 'bush girl' help who knew very little herself:

It was quite one thing to order your dinner, as in days of yore, and quite another business to set to work and cook it yourself. I was on the horns of a dilemma never contemplated. To dismiss the bush girl at first set off was impracticable, as she had come from a long distance. To have plenty of provisions, and not know how to use and cook them was too absurd. I could not help being both amused and ashamed of my own incapability, so I turned to my different cookery guides for information and counsel.[45]

This lack of domestic servants, as English traveller Alfred Domett observed, also meant that Upper Canadian daughters found themselves doing the housework once performed by domestics.[46]

The staples of the typical diet in Upper Canada were potatoes, bread, and salt pork or beef, augmented by the products of hunting, fishing, and gardening.[47] This diet began with the Loyalists, who were given flour, pork, a small amount of beef, and a little butter and salt as provisions upon their arrival in 1784.[48] After the rations ran out, however, many settlers were forced to subsist on soups, 'the herbs, roots, bark and berries to be found in the woods,' as well as game and fish. Apart from the lack of corn, this diet was quite typical of a First Nations diet in Upper Canada.[49] Whether by choice or necessity, life in the backwoods forced settlers to adopt Native culinary traditions. As the Loyalist diet improved, it included beef, mutton, salt pork, fish, and game. Wheat flour was ground for bread; before the mills for grinding were built, settlers ate coarse bread, or more often, breads made from cornmeal.[50] Porridge made from cornmeal was sweetened with maple sugar. An item much prized by Aboriginals, wild rice was another grain that became popular with Loyalists.[51] As tea was expensive, Loyalists used hemlock, sassafras, and New Jersey tea as substitutes. When settlers who came after the War of 1812 arrived, their diet did not differ greatly from this Loyalist one. For backwoods settlers, access to goods and the ability to afford them largely determined what people ate. For instance, flour and salt pork, which were packed in barrels and easily transported, became and remained staples.[52] Problems with acquiring foodstuffs often led settlers to turn to Native foods, if they could get them. Many British settlers tried to retain their British culinary habits but this was not always possible.

Yet, settler women's central role in food production in Upper Canadian kitchens (as well as in the fields and gardens) could be an empowering, if gruelling, experience for women who had not cooked for their families before. For example, Errington argues that women's ability to produce the family's 'multicourse' dinners on 'an open fire or cook-stove,' a task that required skill and hard work, was highly valued because feeding families was so integral to ensuring the farm's development. In short, 'the success of the dinner attested to [the Upper Canadian housekeeper's] abilities.'[53] In *The Guide*, Traill stressed the demands of New World households, saying that many women would need to become acquainted with 'the duties of the house,' as it was their responsibility to care for the family's well-being, especially if and when they had no female servant.[54] Similarly, Anne Langton explained that in times of scarcity, it was the woman's task to 'spread a decent table before the family.'[55] Acquiring and using Native foods was one way that women could improve the settler diet and take better care of their family.

Domestic Contact in the Backwoods

In the first few decades of the nineteenth century, British settlers moved onto lands previously occupied by the First Nations, and often still inhabited by them. The backwoods of Canada became a contact zone for domestic exchange between Natives and settlers, with some settlers establishing friendly relations with Native families. Contact with Native people often happened through trading and informal meetings (for example, when settlers went looking for 'Indians' and visited camps). In many of these instances, food was exchanged or shared, as was customary in both Haudenosaunee and Anishnaabeg cultures. Where friendly relations prevailed, settlers engaged in direct trade with Natives, whereas those with less direct contact learned Native methods indirectly, from other settlers or cookbooks. In either case, Native culinary practices seeped into Upper Canadian culture. Some of the settler writers who described their meetings with Natives, such as Anne Langton and Mary O'Brien, made only brief mentions, suggesting only superficial contact. But other writers, including the Strickland sisters, seem to have had more frequent and friendly domestic contact. Of course, it is likely that other contact occurred, and went unrecorded by either these writers or other backwoods settlers.

Certainly, Susanna Moodie and Catharine Parr Traill in their writings refer to frequent and friendly relations with the Native peoples who lived or camped near their new backwoods settlements. They had both arrived in 1832, and for most of the 1830s, they lived on bush farms along the south side of Lake Katchewanooka (northeast of Peterborough), as did their brother, Samuel Strickland. Susanna later moved to Belleville, and Catharine to several different homes on Rice Lake. This land had been the traditional homeland of the Anishnaabeg people, but much of it had been surrendered throughout the nineteenth century, and many of their people began to live on reserves including at Rice Lake, Sugar Island, Alnick, and Mud Lake.[56] But since the Native peoples of the area still used Lake Katchewanooka and Rice Lake as hunting and fishing grounds, the Strickland siblings had plenty of contact with them.

Susanna Moodie and her husband seemed to have had particularly friendly relations with the Mississauga who lived on the shores of Lake Katchewanooka.

She notes that a dry cedar-swamp near her home 'had been their usual place of encampment of many years' and that 'the whole block of land was almost entirely covered with maple trees, and had originally been an Indian sugar-bush.'[57] In a chapter of *Roughing It in the Bush* entitled 'The Wilderness, and Our Indian Friends,' Moodie explains that almost every week they visited her, adding that 'as my husband never allowed them to eat with the servants ... but brought them to his table, they soon grew friendly and communicative, and would point to every object that attracted their attention, asking a thousand questions ... and if we were inclined to exchange it for their commodities.'[58] Moodie wrote about trading with her Mississauga neighbours, who gave her family birch baskets and canoes and foodstuffs like venison, duck, fish, and grapes in exchange for salt pork, flour, garden vegetables, and clothing. Traill also writes of trading food with local Aboriginals:

> The squaws [sic] came frequently to get pork and flour from me, and garden vege-tables, in exchange for fish, venison, or baskets. For a few pounds of salt pork they will freely give you a haunch of venison, or dried salmon trouts. They are fond of peas, Indian corn, melons, pumpkins, or indeed any vegetables; sometimes they will follow me into the garden, and beg 'onion,' or 'herb,' to put in soup: potatoes they never refuse. They often beg the shells of green peas to boil in their soups and pottage, and will eat them by the handfuls.[59]

For both Moodie and Traill, these female encounters involved domestic matters and commonly occurred in the kitchen or garden. Moodie's relationship with her Native neighbours seems to have been so friendly that during particularly difficult times, they gave her ducks, fish, venison, and other food items. 'For many a good meal I have been indebted to them,' she writes in moving prose, 'when I had nothing to give in return, when the pantry was empty, and "the hearth-stone growing cold," as they term the want of provisions to cook at it.'[60] When writing of friends who left food on her doorstep, she singled out John Nogan (an Anishnaabeg from the Curve Lake Reserve) who 'would slip away without saying a word, thinking that receiving a present from a poor Indian might hurt our feelings, and he would spare us the mortification of returning thanks.'[61]

Exchange of Food and Recipes

British settlers as well as Native people created new hybrid diets in Upper Canada. Along with new foods came new methods of cooking, and new reci-pes. Some skills that settlers brought from home were useful in cooking and acquiring foodstuffs, but others, such as ice fishing, rice harvesting, and maple sugaring, had to be learned. As in other colonies, many meals were combinations of Old and New World foods and recipes. For settlers, the most important new foods were maize, maple sugar, wild rice, teas, fish, and venison. Maize, or Indian corn as it was called by settlers, was adopted by British immigrants who had settled in the Americas before settlers arrived in Upper Canada during the nineteenth century. Johnny cakes or cornmeal porridge, called *supporne*, were common foods in colonial America. 'With the exception of wheat,' wrote Traill, 'there is not a more valuable grain, or one more various and valuable in its uses to man, than Indian-corn.'[62] Most settlers planted corn as soon as possible after arriving in the backwoods. Traill tells readers of *The Guide* that pumpkins should be grown with corn, but later also writes that beans should be planted with climbing poles.[63] It is unclear whether she knew about the method of planting all three sisters together, or decided against it,[64] but in advising settlers to plant pumpkin with corn, she encouraged at least part of the Haudenosaunee method.

Maple syrup is perhaps the most famous of the First Nations foods that settlers adopted. The settlers, however, rarely credited the First Nations for having invented maple syrup (and maple sugar), and through the process of cultural appropriation, maple syrup is now considered a traditional 'Canadian' food. Both the Anishnaabeg and the Haudenosaunee tapped maple trees for their sap during the late winter months and collected it in birch bark containers.[65] Prior to contact with Europeans, sap could not be boiled down enough to make syrup because they did not have adequate containers, although it was reduced by a process involving the placing of hot stones into large vessels made of wood.[66] Once brass kettles were more commonly owned, Native people used them to boil the sap into syrup, or vinegar. In Brant County, as in much of southern Upper Canada, 'to satisfy the sweet tooth, the pioneer had maple sugar made from maple sap.'[67] Maple sugar became the most commonly used sweetener as Muscavado sugar was expensive and difficult to acquire.

For settlers, finding a sugar bush and learning how to make maple syrup and maple sugar became very important. Samuel Strickland devotes an entire chapter in his book, *Twenty-Seven Years in Canada West*, to describing the process, which took a significant amount of effort.[68] As a letter penned by Tom Stewart, another settler, suggests, without instruction or advice, maple sugar making was a difficult business: 'In April, we tried to make some sugar; but as we had nobody to tell us how to set about it, we did not succeed at all.'[69] Thus, books like Traill's *Canadian Settler's Guide* went to great lengths to describe the process.[70] It seems that most settlers learned how to make maple products from other settlers, rather than directly from Native people, but the methodology was a First Nations invention, adopted and altered by settlers. They could also buy maple sugar from Native people. This 'Indian sugar,' explained Traill, 'looks dry and yellow, and is not sold in cakes, but in birch boxes, or mowkowks, as they call them,' and 'owes its peculiar taste to the birch bark vessels that the sap is gathered in, and its grain to being constantly stirred while cooling.'[71]

By the end of the eighteenth century, tea (sweetened by sugar) had become a common and important drink in the British diet, and the difficulty of acquiring it in Upper Canada resulted in substitutes being used.[72] The making and sharing of tea and coffee substitute recipes between Native and settler people offers an excellent example of how both groups came to 'drink the other' in the backwoods. Several plants were used to make hot drinks, including Labrador tea, New Jersey tea, and Sassafras tea, all commonly used by the First Nations.[73] Traill gives recipes for several types of tea in her *Guide*, including several Native recipes. She notes, for instance, that 'the Indians boil the chips and bark of the sassafras, or spice-wood tree, as a luxury, as well as a medicine, and bring it from distant parts of the country. I once tasted the decoction, and found it very pleasant, besides tasting the bark, which had a fine aromatic flavour, like the nutmeg.'[74] Coffee was another drink missing in the backwoods, and settlers came up with various brews to replace it. Most were made from toasted or burned plants. Moodie apparently invented a recipe of roasted dandelion roots which she shared with backwoods neighbours. She writes: 'For years we used no other article; and my [Anishnaabeg] Indian friends who frequented the house gladly adopted the root, and made me show them the whole process of manufacturing it into coffee.'[75] The Haudenosaunee traditionally made a similar coffeelike brew out of burned corn, so it is possible that Moodie and other settlers adopted their method.[76]

Wild rice was another important food to both settlers and Natives, and settlers learned Native methods of harvesting and cooking the rice.[77] In her *Guide*, Traill explains how Native women in the Rice Lake area harvested rice using canoes, and preserved it through drying.[78] Traditional Native methods of cooking the rice in a pot over fire before adding it to soups and stews are explained in detail. Traill provides several Native recipes, as well as one for wild rice pudding – the Westernization of a New World food.[79] She also comments on the availability of wild rice and its production by Native women: 'Indian-rice is sold in the stores at 10s. a bushel: it affords a great quantity of food. The Indians sow it up in mats or coarse birch-bark baskets: it is dearer now than it used to be, as the Indians are indolent, or possibly, employed in agricultural pursuits or household work.'[80] Traill's guidebook was published in 1855, over thirty years after she arrived in Upper Canada, and clearly she had witnessed change. Evidently, as the Anishnaabeg moved to reserves and became more dependent on farming for their livelihood, wild rice harvesting decreased, which made it more difficult for settlers to acquire.[81]

Finally, much fish and game were procured through hunting and fishing or through trade with First Nations people. Settlers farther removed from villages tended to rely more heavily on fish and game.[82] British settlers might have learned to fish at home, but new methods were learned in Upper Canada, with the most common appearing to be two traditional fishing methods of the Anishnaabeg: night fishing, using lanterns or torches and spears, and ice fishing.[83] Elizabeth Simcoe, wife of the first lieutenant governor of Upper Canada, John Simcoe, described going night fishing for salmon on the Don River in York in November in 1793: 'At 8 this dark Evening we went in a Boat to see Salmon speared. Large torches of white birch bark being carried in the Boat the blaze of light attracts the fish which the Men are dextrous in spearing.' 'The manner of destroying the fish is very disagreeable,' she added, 'but seeing them swimming in Shoals around the boat is a very pretty sight.'[84] Several decades later, Traill noted that 'we often see the lighted canoes of the fishermen pass and repass of a dark night before our door.' She adds that her brother Samuel Strickland 'is considered very skilled as a spearsman, and enjoys the sport so much that he seldom misses a night favourable for it.'[85] Anne Langton complained about the 'four fishing lights in the lake to-night, which look very pretty moving up and down, but this holds no prospect of fish tomorrow. The Indians find it more convenient to take their produce at once to the [Fenelon] Falls where they have certain sale of it.'[86]

Settler writers also wrote about ice fishing. In *The Backwoods of Canada*, Traill describes the Native method of ice fishing, in which a hole is made with a tomahawk, and the fisherman waits above it, covered in a blanket, using a wooden fish decoy, until he is able to spear a fish. She notes that a fish called 'masquinongé' was often caught this way and 'may be bought very reasonably from the Indians. I gave a small loaf of bread for a fish weighing from eighteen to twenty pounds.'[87] John Langton learned to ice fish and described his efforts in letters written to his family in England.[88] Many settlers commented on this tasty fish, now more commonly known as 'muskie,' part of the pike family. Another settler, Thomas Need, learned to fish for masquinongé using a net he purchased from a Native.[89] Several recipes for cooking this fish and others appear in settler letters and publications, and most are derived from Native methods of cooking over an open fire or buried in coals. Susanna Moodie's description is perhaps the most eloquent. After detailing the method of cleaning and then burying the fish in hot coals, she adds: 'when the flesh will part from the bone, they draw it out of the ashes, strip off the skin, and it is fit for the table of the most fastidious epicure.'[90]

Many settlers apparently grew sick of their salt pork and happily traded it for venison hunted by neighbouring First Nations. Traill writes that 'they who live in the backwoods, often have venison brought in, either by their own people or by the Indian hunters, who gladly exchange it for salt-pork, flour or vegetables.'[91] Venison and meat from other hunted animals often broke up the monotony of the backwoods diet. In her *Guide*, Traill provides several recipes for cooking venison, including roasting and frying it, as well as making venison pies, soup, and venison ham. She also provides recipes 'to supply the female settler with information to meet her daily want' and offers advice for preparing food 'as practised in this country.'[92] Consequently, she includes sections on preparing partridges, pigeons, black squirrels, hare, wild ducks, and wild geese, but no recipes for cooking beef. She likely assumed that British women knew how to do that already, and beef was eaten less often in the backwoods.

Despite their willingness to trade for Native foodstuffs and to try some of their recipes, some settlers were still apprehensive when it came to eating foods that Native women prepared themselves. 'I have heard much of the excellence of Indian cookery,' wrote Susanna Moodie, 'but I never could bring myself to taste anything prepared in their dirty wigwams.'[93] She also commented on the preparation of a Native meal which she terms 'Indian hotch-potch':

> It consisted of a strange mixture of fish, flesh and fowl, all boiled together in the same vessel. Ducks, partridges, muskinonge, venison, and muskrats, formed a part of this delectable compound. These were literally smothered in onions, potatoes, and turnips, which they had procured from me. They very hospitably offered me a dish of this odious mixture. Which the odour of the muskrats rendered everything but savoury; but I declined. My little boy tasted it, but quickly left the camp to conceal the effect that it had upon him.[94]

Moodie seems to have a problem with the mixed nature of the meal, but 'hodge-podge' was a favoured recipe in *Mrs Beeton's Book of Household Management*, and it was a common dish in Victorian Britain. But it was generally a meal meant to economize leftovers, and was likely more popular with the lower classes.[95] This might explain Moodie's distaste of the 'Indian hotch-potch.' Settler comments on Native foods also tell us about the settlers, of course. Despite her willingness to experiment with some Native cooking methods, Moodie's sense of superiority regarding British cooking methods comes through strongly.

Moodie observed in the 1830s that the Anishnaabeg women who camped near her home were cooking with an 'iron spider.'[96] This was a Euro-Canadian long-handled frying pan with legs, which allowed it to stand over a fire, and its use suggests a change in cooking techniques for Native women.[97] Cecilia

Morgan submits that ownership and use of such domestic items were important indicators of proper Christian womanhood for missionaries in the area.[98] Settler commentators like these help us see how Native eating patterns were changing with increased contact in the backwoods areas of Upper Canada. Some Aboriginal writers also commented on such changes. For instance, Peter Jones explained that 'the Indians are well pleased to discard these [traditional items of cookware] for English pots and kettles, which they find much more convenient.'[99] So while some Aboriginal traditions persisted, others were probably lost or used less frequently. But the same, of course, is true of the settlers. Although they brought with them a culinary tradition, by necessity or choice, their food customs transformed as they adapted to life in the backwoods. A culinary exchange model allows us to better consider the complex interactions that occurred between these two peoples than do approaches that stress one-way exchange in which the First Nations benefit from 'civilized' and progressive European settlers. As we have seen, mutually beneficial relations were established through exchanges of food and culinary traditions.

Conclusion

In the backwoods of Upper Canada, both Native and settler communities underwent changes in the contact zone. What did this mean for their identity? I argue that for British settlers, their adoption of wild rice, masquinongé, and maple syrup does not make them 'White Indians.'[100] Instead, it indicates an acceptance of Native foods and culture as part of their new life in Canada, and also that eating Native foods was part of their transformation from Britons to Canadians. For the First Nations of the region, the changes that took place over this period are part of a longer trajectory of colonialism in which state officials and missionaries attempted to 'civilize' the 'Indians,' in part by changing their eating habits. Food reflects a community's culture, and the adoption of Euro-American culinary customs among the First Nations suggests that they had assimilated to some extent.

   Specific and repeated attempts were made to encourage the First Nations all over Canada to become settled Christian farming households, in which men worked the fields and women cooked and looked after the house. For the most part, these efforts were successful at erasing culture (and foodways), although, as I have suggested, some traditions persevered. Many were revived in the late twentieth century. It is also important to note that although the colonizing efforts of missionaries and the colonial government included changes to diet, Native people, and women in particular, seemed eager to trade for British foods. Both the settlers and First Nations were willing to experiment with food in Upper Canada. By the middle of the nineteenth century, contact between these groups began to change. As the number of British settlers grew, Native people were increasingly forced to leave their traditional lands and move to reserves. Settlers also moved to towns, or built new communities, and as a result, contact between settlers and Natives decreased in the 1840s and beyond. The influence on each other's diet and identity remains.

ACKNOWLEDGMENT

I offer thanks to Cecilia Morgan, Heidi Bohaker, Jennifer Bonnell, Cara Spittal, Robin Grazley, and Kristine Alexander for their comments on earlier versions and presentations of this essay, which is based on my Master's research paper, supervised by Jane Errington.

NOTES

1 From a letter dated 9 May 1833. Catharine Parr Traill, *The Backwoods of Canada: Being Letters from the Wife of an Emigrant Officer, Illustrative of the Domestic Economy of British America* (Toronto: McClelland and Stewart, 1989 [1836]), 135.

2 Alfred W. Crosby, *The Columbian Exchange: Biological and Cultural Consequences of 1492.* Foreword by Otto Von Mering (Westport, CT: Greenwood, 1972); Alfred W. Crosby, *Ecological Imperialism: The Biological Expansion of Europe, 900–1900* (New York: Cambridge University Press, 1993).

3 Traill, *Backwoods of Canada*, 124–5.

4 See also William Cronon, *Changes in the Land: Indians, Colonists, and the Ecology of New England* (New York: Hill and Wang, 1983).

5 Bruce Trigger, 'The Original Iroquoians: Huron, Petun, and Neutral,' in Edward S. Rogers and Donald Smith, eds., *Aboriginal Ontario: Historical Perspectives on the First Nations* (Toronto: Dundurn Press, 1994), 44.

6 Frances Densmore, *Uses of Plants by the Chippewa Indians* (Washington, DC: Bureau of American Ethnology, 1928), 306, 313–17. See also Albert Ernest Jenks, *The Wild Rice Gatherers of the Upper Lakes: A Study in American Primitive Economics* [Annual report of the Bureau of American Ethnology to the Secretary of the Smithsonian Institution] (Washington, DC: Government Printing Office, 1901), vol. 19, part 2, 1013–1137; Gardner P. Stickney, 'Indian Use of Wild Rice,' *American Anthropologist* 9/4 (1896): 115–22; Thomas Vennum, *Wild Rice and the Ojibway People* (St Paul, MN: Minnesota Historical Society Press, 1988).

7 Cecilia Morgan, 'Turning Strangers into Sisters? Missionaries and Colonization in Upper Canada,' in Marlene Epp, Franca Iacovetta, and Frances Swyripa, eds., *Sisters or Strangers? Immigrant, Ethnic, and Racialized Women in Canadian History* (Toronto: University of Toronto Press, 2004), 23–48.

8 Peter S. Schmalz, *The Ojibwa of Southern Ontario* (Toronto: University of Toronto Press, 1991), 176–7.

9 Ibid., 179.

10 Ibid., 178–9. It appears that Christian Anishnaabeg continued to increase in numbers on their southern Ontario farmlands, while the 'pagans' were decreasing on their hunting grounds. Schmalz, *The Ojibwa*, 135.

11 Peter Jones, *History of the Ojebway Indians with Especial Reference to Their Conversion to Christianity* (London: A.W. Bennet, 1861), 73. Jones' history was published posthumously, and material for the book was likely gathered in the 1830s and 1840s.

12 Arthur Caswell Parker, *Iroquois Uses of Maize and Other Food Plants* (Albany, NY: University of the State of New York, 1910), 5. See also F.W. Waugh, *Iroquois Foods and Food Preparation* (Ottawa: Canada Department of Mines, Geological Survey, 1916).

13 Parker, *Iroquois Uses of Maize*, 22–3. Much has been written on the gendered division of labour in Haudenosaunee communities. See also W.M. Beauchamp, 'Iroquois Women,' *Journal of American Folklore* 13/49 (1900): 81–91; Judith K. Brown, 'Economic Organization and the Position of Women among the Iroquois,' *Ethnohistory* 17/3 (1970): 151–67; Gretchen Green, 'Gender and the Longhouse: Iroquois Women in a Changing Culture,' in Larry D. Eldridge, eds., *Women and Freedom in Early America* (New York: New York University Press, 1997), 7–25; Nancy Shoemaker, 'The Rise or Fall of Iroquois Women,' *Journal of Women's History* 2/3 (1991): 39–57; William Guy Spittal, ed., *Iroquois Women: An Anthology* (Ohsweken, ON: Iroqrafts, 1990); Elizabeth Tooker, 'Women in Iroquois Society,' in Jack Campisi, ed., *Extending the Rafters: Interdisciplinary Approaches to Iroquoian Studies* (Albany, NY: State University of New York Press, 1984), 100–23.

14 Parker, *Iroquois Uses of Maize*, 24.

15 Harriet V. Kuhnlein and Nancy J. Turner, *Traditional Plant Foods of Canadian Indigenous Peoples: Nutrition, Botany, and Use* (Philadelphia, PA: Gordon and Breach, 1991), 99–100.

16 Parker, *Iroquois Uses of Maize*, 91–2.

17 Ibid., 69–78.

18 Ibid.

19 Charles M. Johnston, 'The Six Nations in the Grand River Valley, 1784–1847,' in Rogers and Smith, *Aboriginal Ontario*, 167–81.

20 Sally M. Weaver, 'The Iroquois: The Consolidation of the Grand River Reserve in the Mid-Nineteenth Century, 1847–1875,' in Rogers and Smith, *Aboriginal Ontario*, 186.

21 Ibid.

22 John Howison, *Sketches of Upper Canada, Domestic, Local, and Characteristic to which Are Added, Practical Details for the Information of Emigrants of Every*

Class: And Some Recollections of the United States of America (London: G. & W.B. Whittaker, 1821), 147.

23 Gilly Lehmann, *The British Housewife: Cookery-Books, Cooking and Society in Eighteenth-Century Britain* (Totnes: Prospect, 2003); Colin Spencer, *British Food: An Extraordinary Thousand Years of History* (London: Grub Street with Fortnum & Mason, 2002); C. Anne Wilson, *Food and Drink in Britain: From the Stone Age to Recent Times* (Harmondsworth: Penguin, 1984); C. Anne Wilson, *Eating with the Victorians* (Stroud: Sutton Publications, 2004).

24 Spencer, *British Food*, 21–2, 25, 104, 194, 269.

25 Julie Elb, 'Beauty and the Feast: Food and Feminine Identity in England, 1750–1850,' doctoral dissertation, University of Memphis, 2003, iii.

26 Spencer, *British Food*, 251.

27 Ibid., 253.

28 Ibid., 255. See also Maggie Lane, *Jane Austen and Food* (London: Hambledon Press, 1995).

29 Sir John Colborne, lieutenant governor of Upper Canada. Gerald M. Craig, *Upper Canada: The Formative Years, 1784–1841* (Toronto: McClelland and Stewart, 1999), 227. See also E. Jane Errington, 'British Migration and British America, 1783–1867,' in Phillip A Buckner, ed., *Canada and the British Empire* (New York: Oxford University Press, 2008), 140–59.

30 Daniel Keon, 'The "New World" Idea in British North America: An Analysis of Some British Promotional, Travel, and Settler Writings, 1784–1860,' doctoral dissertation, Queen's University, 1984.

31 John Howison, *Sketches of Upper Canada* (London: Geo. B. Whittaker, 1825), 3rd ed., 270.

32 Helen I. Cowan, *British Immigration before Confederation* (Ottawa: Canadian Historical Association, 1978), 3.

33 Susanna Moodie, *Roughing It in the Bush, or, Life in Canada* (Toronto: McClelland and Stewart, 1989 [1852]), 14.

34 Elizabeth Jane Errington, *Emigrant Worlds and Transatlantic Communities: Migration to Upper Canada in the First Half of the Nineteenth Century* (Montreal and Kingston: McGill-Queen's University Press, 2007), 66.

35 Edwin Clarence Guillet, *Pioneer Days in Upper Canada* (Toronto: University of Toronto Press, 1964), 33–5. See also Julia H. Roberts, 'Taverns and Tavern-Goers in Upper Canada, the 1790s to the 1850s,' doctoral dissertation, University of Toronto, 1999; Julia H. Roberts, '"A Mixed Assemblage of Persons": Race and Tavern Space in Upper Canada,' *Canadian Historical Review* 83/1 (2002): 1–28.

36 Estimates from 1831 suggest that three-quarters of the housing in Upper Canada was log construction. Randall White, *Ontario, 1610–1985: A Political and Economic History* (Toronto: Dundurn Press, 1985), 83.

37 Elizabeth Jane Errington, *Wives and Mothers, School Mistresses and Scullery Maids: Working Women in Upper Canada, 1790–1840* (Montreal and Kingston: McGill-Queen's University Press, 1995), 7.

38 Ibid., 91.

39 John Langton and W.A. Langton, *Early Days in Upper Canada: Letters of John Langton from the Backwoods of Upper Canada* (Toronto: Macmillan, 1926). See esp. 35, 38, 57–60, and 83.

40 Errington, *Wives and Mothers*, 92. See also Marjorie Griffin Cohen, *Women's Work, Markets, and Economic Development in Nineteenth-Century Ontario* (Toronto: University of Toronto Press, 1988); L.A. Johnson, 'The Political Economy of Ontario Women in the Nineteenth Century,' in Janice Acton, Penny Goldsmith, and Bonnie Shepard, eds., *Women at Work: Ontario, 1850–1930* (Toronto: Canadian Women's Educational Press, 1974), 13–31.

41 Catharine Parr Traill, *The Canadian Settler's Guide* (Toronto: McClelland and Stewart, 1969 [1860]), xviii.

42 Errington, *Wives and Mothers*, 107–8.

43 Traill, *Canadian Settler's Guide*, 6–7.

44 Susanna Moodie mentions that she had hired a Native woman: 'A woman, that occasionally worked for me, had a disagreeable squint; she was known in Indian by the name of *Sachábó*, "cross-eye."' Moodie, *Roughing It in the Bush*, 297. However, it seems that hiring Native women was uncommon in the early to mid-nineteenth century.

45 Mrs Edward Copleston, *Canada: Why We Live in It, and Why We Like It* (London: Parker, Son, and Bourn, 1861), 69–70.

46 Alfred Domett, E.A. Horsman, and Lillian Rea Benson, *The Canadian Journal of Alfred Domett, Being an Extract from a Journal of a Tour in Canada, the United States and Jamaica, 1833–1835* (London, ON: University of Western Ontario, 1955), 61.

47 Errington, *Wives and Mothers*, 92.

48 Guillet, *Pioneer Days in Upper Canada*, 26.

49 Ibid. See also William Canniff et al., *History of the Settlement of Upper Canada (Ontario): With Special Reference to the Bay Quinté* (Toronto: Dudley & Burns, 1869).

50 Guillet, *Pioneer Days in Upper Canada*, 26–8.

51 Ibid., 28.

52 Ibid., 38.

53 Errington, *Wives and Mothers*, 96.

54 Traill, *Canadian Settler's Guide*, 2–3.

55 Anne Langton and H.H. Langton, *A Gentlewoman in Upper Canada: The Journals of Anne Langton* (Toronto: Clarke, 1967), 189.

56 Map of Peterborough Region Locales. Carl Ballstadt, Elizabeth Hopkins, and Michael A. Peterman, eds., *I Bless You in My Heart: Selected Correspondence of Catharine Parr Traill* (Toronto: University of Toronto Press, 1996), xvii; Map. Schmalz, *The Ojibwa of Southern Ontario*, xvi.
57 Moodie, *Roughing It in the Bush*, 280.
58 Ibid.
59 'A Visit to the Camp of the Chippewa Indians,' in Carl Ballstadt and Michael A. Peterman, eds., *Forest and Other Gleanings: The Fugitive Writings of Catharine Parr Traill* (Ottawa: University of Ottawa Press, 1994), 150.
60 Moodie, *Roughing It in the Bush*, 299.
61 Ibid., 149.
62 Traill, *Canadian Settler's Guide*, 110.
63 Ibid., 110–22, 135; Traill, *Backwoods of Canada*, 153–4.
64 See Parker, *Iroquois Uses of Maize*, 91.
65 Densmore, *Uses of Plants by the Chippewa Indians*, 308–13; Parker, *Iroquois Uses of Maize*, 102–3.
66 Parker, *Iroquois Uses of Maize*, 308.
67 Jean H Waldie, 'White Settlers Learned Homely Cures from Indians in the Early Settlement,' in *Brant County: The Story of Its People* (Brantford, ON: J.R. Hasting Printing & Lithographing, 1984), 60.
68 Samuel Strickland, *Twenty-Seven Years in Canada West; or, the Experience of an Early Settler* (London: Bentley, 1853).
69 Basil Hall, *Travels in North America: In the Years 1827 and 1828* (Edinburgh: R. Cadell, 1830), 3rd ed., 315. As quoted in Jodi Aoki, 'Culinary Themes in the Writings of Frances Stewart, Genteel Pioneer of Duoro Township,' *Culinary Chronicles*, no. 46 (2005): 3–7.
70 Traill, *Canadian Settler's Guide*, 142–50. See also Langton and Langton, *Gentlewoman in Upper Canada*, 113; Audrey Saunders Miller, ed., *The Journals of Mary O'Brien, 1828–1838* (Toronto: Macmillan, 1968), 93; Traill, *Backwoods of Canada*, 129–31.
71 Traill, *Canadian Settler's Guide*, 146. See also Frances Densmore, *Uses of Plants by the Chippewa Indians*, 388.
72 Spencer, *British Food*, 216–18.
73 Densmore, *Uses of Plants*, 317. See also Guillet, *Pioneer Days in Upper Canada*, 44; Nancy J. Turner, Adam F. Szczawinski, and National Museum of Natural Sciences (Canada), *Wild Coffee and Tea Substitutes of Canada* (Ottawa: National Museum of Natural Sciences, National Museums of Canada, 1978).
74 Traill, *Canadian Settler's Guide*, 137.
75 Moodie, *Roughing It in the Bush*, 355. For a recipe, see Turner et al., *Wild Coffee and Tea Substitutes of Canada*, 43–4.

76 Parker, *Iroquois Uses of Maize*, 77.

77 This, despite the fact that the British looked down on rice because it was associated with Chinese labourers in London at the end of the eighteenth century. Spencer, *British Food*, 225; Densmore, *How Indians Use Wild Plants*, 313–17.

78 Traill, *Canadian Settler's Guide*, 105–6.

79 Ibid., 106–7.

80 Ibid., 106.

81 See also Vennum, *Wild Rice and the Ojibway People*.

82 Guillet, *Pioneer Days in Upper Canada*, 48.

83 Mary F. Williamson, *'To Fare Sumptuously Every Day': Rambles among Upper Canadian Dishes and Repasts Together with Authentic Menus and Culinary Receipts* (Peterborough, ON: Peterborough Historical Society, 2004), 14–15.

84 Elizabeth Simcoe and Mary Quayle Innis, *Mrs Simcoe's Diary* (Toronto: Macmillan, 1978), 111. Night fishing often occurred in the fall when darkness falls earlier, and when salmon spawn.

85 Traill, *Backwoods of Canada*, 132. See also Susanna Moodie's poem, 'The Indian Fisherman's Light,' in *Roughing It in the Bush*, 303–4.

86 Langton and Langton, *Gentlewoman in Upper Canada*, 94.

87 Traill, *Backwoods of Canada*, 134.

88 Langton and Langton, *Early Days in Upper Canada*, 59.

89 Thomas Need, *Six Years in the Bush; or, Extracts from the Journal of a Settler in Upper Canada, 1832–1838* (London: Simpkin, Marshall, 1838), 68.

90 Moodie, *Roughing It in the Bush*, 302.

91 Traill, *Canadian Settler's Guide*, 155–6.

92 Ibid., 157–60.

93 Moodie, *Roughing It in the Bush*, 301.

94 Ibid., 301–2.

95 Mrs Isabella Beeton, *The Book of Household Management* (London: Cox and Wyman, Printers 1861); Spencer, *British Food*, 276.

96 Moodie, *Roughing It in the Bush*, 294. In this instance, Tom Nogan's wife was boiling bark, which might have been used or eaten in many different ways.

97 Fiona Lucas, *Hearth and Home: Women and the Art of Open Hearth Cooking* (Toronto: Lorimer, 2006), 10–11.

98 Morgan, 'Turning Strangers into Sisters? Missionaries and Colonization in Upper Canada,' 33–5.

99 Jones, *History of the Ojebway Indians*, 74.

100 James Axtell, 'The White Indians of Colonial America,' *William and Mary Quarterly* 32/1 (1975): 55–88.

2 'The Snipe Were Good and the Wine Not Bad': Enabling Public Life for Privileged Men

JULIA ROBERTS

When we look at Harriet Clench's *Country Tavern*, we see the artist's appreciative rendering of fine furniture in the lovely windsor chairs and tavern table. We see, too, the tavern blended harmoniously into a 'progressive' colonial society represented by the settled town across the bay, with its steamers and steeples. And in the foreground we see a woman at work, serving a tray of drinks to gentlemen consumers. Clench's canvas thus addresses the relationship between the leisure of consumption and the labour of production. In so doing, it offers us valuable evidence about the material comfort of a minor public house in the countryside and the place of drink in public sociability. It also tells us about the willingness of men, specifically gentlemen, to patronize these taverns and how the work of women enabled a public enactment of gentlemanliness.

These themes are also addressed in the diary of a thirty-three year-old government clerk named Harry Jones, who also brought the relationship between the culture of drink and of food into sharp relief in an entry, dated 12 May 1842, that describes a late night of male camaraderie in Kingston, Ontario. He wrote of arriving in the afternoon to be told that 'the game supper for which I was to stand treat [at a saloon] had been ordered to be ready at the billiard rooms at 10 o'clk,' adding 'our party [of] Dr Stewart, Hitchings, Brough, McKenzie, Galt and myself [thought] the snipe were good and the wine not bad – after which the singers sung and the whole party drank hot stuff of all sorts until 2 [a.m.].' The affair had cost him 8 dollars.[1] The saloon was Alexander Smith's British North American, frequented for its 'fruits and rarities,' 'fresh oysters,' 'superior spiced oysters,' 'choicest wines and liquors,' 'excellent pastry cook,' 'assiduous' service, and its snipe.[2] Unlike the country house of Clench's canvas, Smith's North American was a principal tavern, or hotel, located in the centre of town.

1.1 Harriet Clench, *A Country Tavern near Cobourg*, Canada West, 1849, oil on canvas. Art Gallery of Ontario, used with permission.

Hybridity and Colonial Cuisines

The food and drink served and consumed in colonial taverns and hotels make social relationships visible to historians. As in much food history, there is a consumption story told here, about gentlemen dining on snipe, wine, and hot stuff, and how their mutual sociability enabled them to craft, sustain, and display a distinctive public identity.[3] There is also a production story, often left untold, about kitchen workers and public house servants who transformed indigenous, local, and imperial ingredients into a colonial cuisine fit for gentlemen.

The scenario allows us to address questions central to colonial food history regarding the hybridity or creolization of cuisine, such as to what extent did colonial cuisine, through its adoption, reinterpretation, or possession of indigenous ingredients, represent an act of cultural mutuality or appropriation? Other contributors in this volume explore 'hybridization,' most particularly Alison Norman (in a colonial context) and Julie Mehta (in the contemporary context), but my emphasis on appropriation and exploitation comes closest to Krista Walters' chapter on Canadian nutritionists and Aboriginal women. Moreover, in contrast to all of the other contributions, this chapter brings together two historiographies – food and drink – that are usually treated separately.

The essay highlights the links between *public* consumption and production for public consumption. In nineteenth-century public houses, consuming patrons defined, transgressed, and subverted the multiple boundaries among them – of class, 'race,' and gender. Gentlemen, and sometimes ladies, used food and drink to separate themselves from the rest of the mixed company in the public houses. They purposefully interpreted food and drink in terms of cultures of class and national identity. In 1832, for example, Thomas Need, an Oxford-educated gentleman, justice of the peace, militia officer, and prominent settler on 3,000 acres near Peterborough, described how privileged Englishmen viewed routine tavern consumption, noting that a great rush of people 'instantly responded' to the bell announcing a tavern's opening and how 'the work of destruction' immediately began, as 'plates rattled – cups and saucers flew about, and knives and forks found their way indifferently into their owners' mouths or the various dishes on the table.' After describing his own meal of 'sweet-meats crowned with a "pièce de resistance" … a huge greasy dish of beef steaks and onions,' he turned to the rest of the customers, saying they were 'a motley' crew of 'Yankees and emigrants, washed and unwashed, storekeepers, travellers and farmers' and 'a large unshaven backwoods' settler' who sat opposite 'a little prim, puritanical store-keeper' wearing a hat. 'Ten minutes sufficed,' he concluded, 'for the dispatch of the meal.'[4] The snipe dinner could not stand in sharper contrast in everything from its timing, select company, wine and haute cuisine, duration, and convivial sociability, making it a distinctly different experience and one in which food and drink carried different meanings.

Consumption and the Labour of Production

Historians know much more about consumption, especially of alcohol, in public houses than about production,[5] yet the history of production is a crucial corollary, making the public houses visible as sites of the domestic labour that supported public life, particularly that of a consciously privileged male public life. A tiny, delicately flavoured wetland game-bird like snipe, for example, had to be shot, prepared, and cooked. Although an indigenous bird, in the colonial worlds of the 1840s, snipe was also strongly associated with an old world genteel, even aristocratic, European sporting tradition. Early Americans considered snipe a great delicacy, for example,[6] and, as late as 1874, snipe appeared on the menu for the Earl and Countess of Dufferin at the Arlington Hotel in Cobourg, Ontario.[7] Wine carried similar connotations of gentility, politeness, and refined taste, so much so that the well-heeled men appointed to the Legislative Council in the first government of Upper Canada once tried to tax more 'democratic' drinks like whiskey and rum.[8] Hot stuff was a mixed drink based on rum, brandy, or whiskey and made expensive by the old imperial products in it – spices such as mace or nutmeg, citrus peels and juices, cane sugar, and by the showmanship of its production and presentation at the bar or at the table.

Each element of the supper at Smith's – the snipe, wine, and hot stuff – illustrates the relationships between the consumers (Jones and his cronies) and the producers, which included Smith, a black tavernkeeper. Presumably, Smith would have welcomed paying customers of all types, but the stocks of his larder and bar, his house, and the skills of his household and staff clearly enabled elite consumption. Jones and friends had all been professional gentlemen,[9] and the 8 dollar tab was enough to keep a family in modest respectability for a week and double the monthly wage of a female domestic.[10] In this regard, our diarist penned a consumption story about privileged men mutually enacting rituals of sociability in a tavern.[11] Although he did not write explicitly about the people who supplied and served them, Jones' description reveals a production story involving the labours of non-elite women and men, including, to introduce a third group of producers, Aboriginals who supplied game to colonial taverns.

Certainly, the men at the snipe supper engaged in a colonialist enterprise that naturalized Anglo-American hegemony but it did not necessarily represent a straightforward assertion of cultural precedence. In her study of chocolate in New Spain, historian Marcy Norton documents coloniz*ers* acculturating *to* and adopting the foodways *of* the coloniz*ed* in ways that exposed the contradictions and uncertainties of cultural hierarchy in the colonial enterprise.[12] Similarly, both literary scholar Helen Pike Bauer (for colonial India) and historian Donna Gabaccia (for America) have shown kitchen space and cooking practices to be sites where 'an uneasy mix of Empire building and respect for indigenous [or African-American] knowledge' combined.[13] In rare instances, the colonizer, not the colonized, (the slaving, not the enslaved) acculturated the food of the 'other.' In Canada, it has been novelists more so than historians who have more fully explored how food 'locates us in particular cultural spaces with important cultural boundary markers'[14] and addressed the theme of indigeneity.[15] In a novel like Timothy Taylor's *Stanley Park*, the indigenous ingredients (dandelion greens, grey squirrels, Canada geese) used to make an alternative cuisine to that of the Anglo-Canadian one carry the potential to subvert or undermine the seeming certainties of colonizers and 'host' societies.[16] Similarly, very recent immigrant histories suggest how women, disempowered in many ways, nevertheless forged foodways that could stand apart from mainstream norms,[17] thereby historicizing anthropologist Mary Douglas' classic statement that food 'encodes' messages about 'different degrees of hierarchy, inclusion and exclusion, boundaries and transactions across the boundaries.'[18] Such insights help us complicate the supper at Smith's saloon, although little disruption occurred there. It allows us to see that a simple narrative of privileged consumption was contingent, or dependent, on the unacknowledged appropriation of indigenous items and on the labour of others.

Consuming and Producing in Public

Consumed in public places, food and drink encoded equally powerful messages. Whether in the early modern inns frequented by the European elite, or the restaurants of late eighteenth-century Paris popular among the bourgeoisie, or the saloons of industrial North America where working-class men, and some women, gathered, the glasses, tankards, brown bottles, and cups brimming with drink always crowded tabletops and bars alongside the trenchers, bowls, plates, and serving dishes bearing food.[19] This mix of food and drink was intrinsic to the legal definition of a tavern in early Canada. These were sites licensed to sell liquor by small measure (the pint, half-pint, gill, and glass) and legally obligated to provide refreshment (food) at all hours. In the industrializing centres of North America, publicans routinely supplied a free lunch to barroom patrons for the price of a beer. At Joe Beef's tavern in Montreal, for example, buying a drink meant sailors, deckhands, and other workers could help themselves from 'great piles of bread, cheese, and beef' laid out on the bar.[20] Despite such linkages, food and drink are rarely linked in the work of historians, especially in Canada, where drink studies tend to highlight temperance activism and pathologies like alcoholism and violence.[21] By contrast, however, the scholarship that treats drink as symbol tends to explore the rituals associated with it (such as treating and toasting) in ways familiar to food historians. In these analyses, drink is most revealing of the sets of social interactions and cultural definitions it enabled, whether these served to draw drinking companions into a warm sense of mutual belonging or to exclude others from the group.[22] The tavern offers a promising way to integrate food history with the 'drink as symbol' school of alcohol studies because they share a mutual interest in consumption rituals and how these encoded social and cultural meaning in discrete historical moments.[23]

Taverns, Tavernkeepers, and Making Colonial Cuisine

Tavernkeeping was a female trade and tavern work was women's work in the many hundreds of small taverns that dotted Ontario towns and rural roadways by mid-century.[24] Thus, we know that when Peter, a Mississauga man, stopped at Jacob Finkle's tavern with a companion in 1805 to exchange his ducks for whiskey, it was his wife, Susanna, who transformed the indigenous wild fowl into colonial cuisine.[25] That the labour involved was mainly female places women and their domestic labour firmly within the processes of colonization. Indeed, the history of colonial Canada can be viewed as a history of women's work and how it supported men's work and the work of Empire, family survival, and cultural formation. There were no Canadian cookbooks published in Susanna Finkle's day. American books like Amelia Simmons' *American Cookery*, popular in the colony by 1801, did not contain any recipes ('receipts') for game or wild fowl.[26] But Catherine Parr Traill's 1854 *Hints on Canadian Housekeeping* suggests what a domestic labourer had to do with a 'native' duck. As a repository of common colonial knowledge about creating colonial cuisine rather than a cookery book, Traill's book contained what a female settler like Susanna would have known about dealing with such local materials as partridges, pigeons, black squirrels ('a very delicate food'), hare, wild ducks, geese, and blackbirds. *Canadian Housekeeping* attested to the place of the indigenous in more than ingredients. Moreover, Traill treated the labour of First Nations women at the wild rice harvest with respect and recommended some 'Indian' recipes. There is even a hint here of the colonizer's embrace of indigeneity and its power to shape colonial knowledge of cuisine. As to the ducks, 'the *usual* mode of cooking' Traill wrote, 'and the best, is to roast them.' Roasting involved many stages: the duck, like all wild fowl had to be plucked and then drawn (cutting off the head and removing crop, gullet, windpipe, heart, liver, and gizzards), cleaned, perhaps stuffed 'with bread-crumbs, sage, onion, and a good deal of pepper and salt,' and perhaps a gravy made of the innards boiled in water 'with a few rings of onion and a crust of browned bread' or 'a little cream, flour, and a little nutmeg grated.'[27] Another popular cookbook, written by eighteenth-century 'celebrity chef' John Farley of the London Tavern, and published with the ordinary housekeeper in mind, offered similar instructions, and described making duck gravy out of 'the gizzard and pinions,' onion, lemon pickle, peppercorns, mace, catsup, and browning.[28]

These instructions, one from the colonial backwoods, the other from the imperial centre, highlight two related points. First, domestic labour *was* labour – hard, physical, time-consuming, and skill-based. Uniquely, in tavern households, it also became tangibly productive: it produced income on the account books. In the record of patrons' debits and payments for meals, drinks, and other domestic services is a record of their indebtedness to the products of pre-dominantly female labour.[29] Second, the processes of cookery described and the ingredients involved make evident the transformation and appropriation of the duck, an indigenous ingredient, into colonial understandings of taste and cuisine.

Onion and sage grew in every kitchen garden in the colony. Susanna Finkle had four cows for butter, and salt and pepper were larder staples. Parr Traill's nutmeg and the mace, lemon pickle, and catsup of Farley's recipe were far more 'exotic' in their connotation of far away places and long-distance trade. Although the economic historian Douglas McCalla has noted that the varied 'palate of seasonings' available to country cooks was not borne out by purchasing patterns in country general stores, nevertheless, each was available in the towns of York and Kingston well before 1805.[30] And even very early tavern-keepers, to whom storekeepers often addressed their advertisements, certainly stocked the exotics. James Donaldson, who kept a tavern in Amherstburg in 1801, Matthew Dolsen at the Thames from the 1790s, Abner Miles and Ely Playter in early York, all kept on hand the several citruses, sweet spices, and the loaf sugar needed by their elite or free-spending barroom patrons.[31] By cooking a wild duck, then, female colonists like Finkle integrated indigenous foods into a colonial and Anglo-American cuisine flavoured by the products of empire. Certainly, when William Cooper advertised the opening of his prominent Cof-fee House in York, he promised to keep it as 'nearly on the footing of an English inn as local circumstances will permit,' referencing an English understanding of an up-market establishment. He also employed a 'clean, sober Woman who understands Cooking well' and made clear the connections between her food work and empire as he pledged to keep at hand the 'shrub, fresh lime juice … Devonshire, Navy, and Cavis sauces' culled from the produce of 'foreign' pos-sessions.[32] His is a straightforward statement about the cultural and culinary benefits wrought by empire.

The Language of Colonial Cuisine

Colonizers measured the success of the colonial enterprise, in part, through the dinners they consumed. When John Elmsley, the son of a former chief justice of Upper Canada who had been raised mostly in England, and himself a retired naval officer, office-holder, and businessman, returned to the colony in 1825 as a member of the local elite, he wrote to his mother, saying, 'What think you of a Dinner' for twenty-two people 'consisting of Fish soup, veni-son, Turkey, three entire courses, served on a complete service of China, side dishes, silver, champagne, claret, and cider' and mahogany tables, where once 'the head of a pork barrel' might be used for a table, a meal meant 'a single dish' of 'Chowder or Lobskouse,' 'R[a]tion Rum' was the only drink, 'and fingers and thumbs the principal utensils.'[33] Elmsley's letter represents what literary scholar Karin Becker has termed an 'imaginative text' located within a discourse about cuisine that involved both writer and reader in a 'culinary cult' of elites claiming positions as judges of taste and presentation. As Becker shows, fiction writers who used food as metaphor, such as Balzac, Flaubert, Zola, and Maupassant, helped create a language of cuisine (one very different from that of modern Canadian novelists). So, too, did cookbook authors, as the settlers recognized. In Montreal, for instance, Levi Adams wrote his poem, 'The Charivari,' with a stanza about a woman named Annette: 'But oh, her pastry 'twas said to surpass / that of the queen of the pie crusts, Mrs Glasse,' or, Hannah Glasse, the author of the immensely popular *Art of Cookery*, in multiple editions from 1747.[34]

The much-published British travellers to the British colonies and the United States similarly joined in this making of a language of cuisine. Like Elmsley's letter, their writings about food invariably highlighted its role as cultural marker that, for example, denoted English or Western European civility as against a troubling otherness, or a hierarchy of access to elite tastes or services as opposed to a democratic levelling too redolent of republican values, or a culturally specific ideal of 'cuisine' or 'dining' as opposed to, as one traveller put it, 'simply a feeding.'[35] In defining English foodways as the basis of 'proper cuisine,' these travellers also came to distinguish between 'Canadian' and 'American' ways. For example, William Berczy, the Swiss-born artist, author, and colonizer of Upper Canada wrote to his wife in 1798 that he had 'supped very well and very cleanly ... with fish and a very good goose' at a place near Cornwall where they knew 'how to serve folk properly.' It was, he added, 'no Yankee tavern.' Another traveller, Thomas Fowler, in 1832, assuming a readership knowledgeable of French cuisine, reported that a dinner 'de quatre services' on board a steamboat actually had been an 'excellent dinner ... elegantly displayed.' At a 'splendid new establishment, the Mansion House,' in tiny Grafton in 1833, a traveller reported that the food had been as 'civilized' as its tavern sign, which displayed the British Arms in bold relief and 'the national emblems of the constituent parts of the united empire.' And Anna Jameson, unaware, it seems, of the centrality of whitefish to local Algonquian cuisine, wrote scathingly of the 'epicures of our degenerate times [who] have nothing of that gastronomical enthusiasm which inspired their ancient models, else we should have them all coming here to eat whitefish at the Sault.' In displaying their collective ability to pass judgment on what connoted fine cooking and service, the proper ordering of courses, elegance, and luxury (as opposed to mere substance), in the acknowledgment of epicurean standards, and in the assumption appropriating indigenous ingredients was right and just, these travellers, in company with their audiences, gave witness to a shared discourse about consumption that operated as a powerful expression of social and cultural status.[36]

Hotels, Principal Houses, and Conspicuous Consumption

Public sites of consumption proliferated in Upper Canada. With a population of almost half a million in 1842, exploding to nearly one million by 1851, urban centres grew apace, in what was, nevertheless, an overwhelmingly agrarian colony. In that decade, Toronto doubled from 15,000 to 30,000 persons; Hamilton grew from 4,000 to 14,000; Kingston from 6,000 to 11,000; and both Ottawa and London reached 7,000.[37] Large town and city streetscapes began to look urban, with their late Georgian masonry, planked sidewalks, street lighting, and, by 1856, railway stations. Manufactories began to employ a just emerging industrial workforce alongside traditional mercantile and artisanal shops. Increasingly, varied forms of commercialized leisure, such as amusement parks, theatres, circuses, and bowling lanes in purpose-built structures, coexisted with the older forms of wandering menageries and travelling panoramas, often linked to taverns. In Toronto, as earlier in Montreal, and even earlier in New York City and Philadelphia, new opportunities for epicurean consumption appeared. What contemporaries called 'monster' hotels claimed whole blocks of street frontage and offered luxuriously appointed public dining rooms, well staffed by a retinue of waiters, many of them black, serving meals prepared by professional cooks. They complemented, and added a new dimension to, the range of dining experiences available in the principal taverns.

A small number of principal taverns had always existed to meet the demands of an up-market clientele. The principal houses, often called hotels, differed from the rest in their scale, location, and especially in their provision of fashionable living. Located in towns and cities, at Niagara Falls, and occasionally along important routes, they gave the public who could afford them a quality of service not available elsewhere. Principal houses claimed 'central' and 'marketplace' locations and promised a 'table d'hotel … kept in the very best style,' with the 'finest fish and fowl,' 'mutton chops and lobster,' 'salmons, sardines,' 'choice' wines and liquors, and apartments of 'excellence and comfort.' Their dining rooms offered 'handsomely and substantially' finished furnishings, such as walnut dining tables and chairs. Personal crockery and serving dishes met standards of elegant respectability as did the tablecloths, cruet sets (for season-ings, sugar, vinegar, and oil), knives and forks, teacups with saucers, teapots and coffeepots, as well as expensive glass plates, wine glasses, 'cut' glass tum-blers, and decanters. All of these were expensive investments made to support polite sociability.[38]

Gendering Elite Public Sociability

Novelist John Richardson recognized the place of such public consumption in elite sociability in his 1840 *Canadian Brothers*, where he writes about offic-ers who, 'glittered in the gay trappings of military uniforms,' drank and rev-elled behind the windows of the principal hotel while the townsfolk 'collected round' to watch.[39] The sense in which consumption acted as a literal stage for the performance of masculine elite identity is enhanced in this depiction by the presence of an audience. The passage also points to the powerfully gen-dered freedoms elite men had to define classed masculine identities in public, through such pageants of consumption. Richardson told a male story of pub-lic consumption, but others wrote about mixed-gender places,[40] including Sir James Alexander, a military officer who served in Canada for seven years in the 1840s. He wrote about 'country parties' of officers and ladies at Fink's Inn, near Kingston, with a 'well-ordered repast' and dancing 'to the music of two or three violins.' Gentleman and settler Samuel Strickland recalled a celebra-tion in honour of the accession of King William IV in 1830 where 'workmen' enjoyed an outdoor fête and the elite 'a ball and supper at Reid's Hotel.' And historians have long noted the crucial presence of women in the creation and enactment of polite society.[41]

Still, women's presence in public house sociability was and had always been managed by male gatekeepers. By the 1840s, it was being defined in new and rigorous ways; the redefinition of the gendered nature of the public itself, and new ideas about alcohol, both challenged women's historic access to such places. Certainly, economically privileged women lacked the comparable freedom to sit at night in a public house table dressed in the 'glittering' and 'gay' garb that distinguished them as ladies. And they lacked the freedom of Richardson's officers to perform before the eyes of the townspeople.

Patterns of elite male consumption, such as the snipe supper at Smith's saloon, then, affirmed 'gentlemanly' privilege in its multidimensional sense of a classed, gendered, and racialized identity. The elite supper party depended, for its realization, on the domestic labour of the very men and women against whom gentlemen defined themselves.

Racializing Elite Public Sociability

Although the provenance of the 1842 snipe is unknown, the history of colonial game supply to tavernkeeping households invokes racialized hierarchies. Just as tavernkeeper Finkle traded with Mississauga for ducks, the merchant and tavernkeeper Matthew Dolsen traded extensively with Lenape (Delaware) and other Native suppliers on the Thames River. Printer Charles Fothergill's tavern landlord 'bought a brace of partridges' from an unnamed Native supplier, and another Kingston tavernkeeper acquired a 'very fine' maskquinonge (a large whitefish) from a Native fisher in 1833.[42] Alternatively, the gentlemen diners celebrated a successful hunting expedition.[43] Hunting snipe, however, was not an everyday event; it required a hunting party, as the marsh bird was among the most difficult to shoot. Well camouflaged, it could spot 'the sportsman or his dog at great distance' and went off in a rapid zigzag flight.[44] A recent food history argues that early republican Americans identified wild game with 'frontier food,' and prized domestically 'produced' food, instead, as they moved towards a national sense of identity; our snipe supper suggests no similar move in Canada.[45] Instead, at the saloon, the choice of snipe reflected a continued investment in indigeneity's dual meanings, as a prime ingredient for appropriation and as a link, via hunting tradition, to a privileged social status.

In consuming hot stuff at the end of their snipe supper, Jones and his companions participated in a pageant of racialized identity in another sense. Although it was happenstance that tavernkeeper Smith was black, the production of such drinks involved his performing before a group of elite white men.[46] That Smith was well paid for his labour in support of gentlemanly sociability does not detract from its racialized content. The power and privilege of 'whiteness' was rendered visible in other ways as well. At the Rossin House Hotel in Toronto, for example, English author and traveller Isabella Bishop complained about the waiters who were 'runaway slaves' and 'very inattentive and uncivil.'[47] With a less scathing tone, Mrs Copleston, an American diner eating at Sword's, also in Toronto, in 1856, wrote that 'the attendants (all negroes)' outnumbered the guests. As 'they marched in single file, each bearing a dish,' their 'principle assumed all the airs of a generalissimo'; when he signalled, 'down went the dishes on the table all at once – a pause – another signal – and off flew the covers with similar precision and alacrity ... repeated at each course until the meal was over.' In making the racialized content of her hotel dining experience explicit, she declared that 'black countenances and gloveless black hands made the effect all the more ridiculous, although to some not altogether pleasing.'[48]

Similarly, at the Clifton at Niagara Falls, English gentlewoman and settler Susanna Moodie wrote in more positive tones about the 'well-dressed negro waiters,' who, with 'perfect ease and dexterity,' showed great 'politeness' when taking 'so many complicated orders' without making 'a single mistake.' Indeed, it all 'seemed natural to them.' She also commented that 'some, in spite of their dark colouring,' were 'handsome, intelligent looking men.'[49] While clearly impressed, Moodie's passage is a blueprint of colonialist responses dressed up in the guise of 'tolerance.' It is overlaid with racialized assumptions, including the naturalness of racial hierarchy. In assuming a racial prerogative to objectify and rate the black waiters, Moodie's comments about the food servers shed light on how this staged racialized encounter worked to bolster the whiteness of elite identities through the act of public consumption.

Gender and Production Stories

Women's domestic labour, both waged and unwaged, was crucial to enabling elite sociability, and the very presence of women as classed and gendered others reaffirmed the naturalness of male precedence and privilege. Many tavern and hotel patrons openly acknowledged women's production in kitchens, and, sometimes explicitly, more often implicitly, defined it as work. As one client put it, 'our hostess exerted herself and we soon sat down to a sumptuous feast consisting of a brace of fine fat wood ducks and fried black bass.' A 'comely young woman' cooked and served food to military men in a Grand River tavern in 1829. At the Palmer, in Sandwich, 'the girl that waited at table ... a very pretty girl ... when last I saw her was doing lady.' In another case, the tavern-keeper 'asked us into his parlour, while his wife prepared dinner.'[50]

Although women's work was crucial, the use of adjectives like 'comely' and 'pretty' suggests, too, that some gentlemen tavern-goers elided women's work and women's bodies into one sexualized whole. One traveller liked a house where 'the waiters are females, fat and plump' and hoped to catch a glimpse of petticoat and flesh.[51] Writing about domestic servants' clothing, Christine Rinne highlights the sexuality of the small, white maid's apron; it conceals her body but 'the shape and material are reminiscent of what is under her outer layer, hence more arousing.' Similarly, Peter Bailey notes that nineteenth-century English barmaids were expected to exude 'sex appeal' as part of their job, making them an 'item of allurement' alongside the increasingly fine furnishings and appointments.[52]

When elite colonial men assessed female keepers and staff in sexualized ways, they denied them dignity, and visibility, as workers. To counteract this masculine bias in the historical record, historians need to understand that colonial public houses were not exclusively male spaces,[53] and that women's *waged* domestic labour, as kitchen maids or domestic servants, set them apart both from gentlemen and from the idealized construction of early Victorian womanhood – the lady, whose domestic duties were equally idealized as un-work because performed as unpaid duty.[54]

But kitchen work really was not sexy; picking, trussing, and cooking snipe for several gentlemen was a fussy, many-stepped process. Parr Traill's *Hints on Canadian Housekeeping* advised that 'snipe and woodcock are cooked the same as in other countries,' and the recipe books admonished cooks to take 'great care' with the 'exceedingly tender' skin or your hands will destroy 'the beautiful appearance of the bird.' Skewering meant not only the careful alignment of thighs with pinions; one also had to 'skin the head, turn it, take out the eyes and put the head on the point of the skewer with the bill close to the breast.' Roasting meant building a hot 'brisk' fire and carefully managing it because the snipe 'spoiled' easily. For presentation, one layered two snipe per diner over toast just 'nicely brown,' held 'a quarter of a pint of gravy' in a 'chafing dish for three or four minutes,' and then sent it 'up hot to table' accompanied with herbed and cloved onions, mushrooms, caper-seasoned sauce, fried bread crumbs, and wild or domestic greens.[55] Waiting at table meant, for female tavern workers, also enduring the sexualized gazing suggested in the writings of gentlemen travellers.

Conclusion

In arguing that, through their public consumption in principal taverns and hotels, elite men in colonial Ontario enacted a particular colonial identity that depended on the labour of classed, gendered, and racialized others for its support, my chapter makes a case for food history as a revealing history – an entrée into social relationships both at the symbolic level and as it played out in daily life and labour. By focusing on the darker side of culinary hybridity, it does not suggest that early Canadian history contains no examples of the anti-colonialist view Marcy Norton found in chocolate. To give one example, as a young explorer in the employ of the Hudson's Bay Company in 1770, Samuel Hearne expressed his appreciation for an indigenous meal produced in the Chipewyan style, noting that 'to heighten the luxury … the partridges are boiled in a kettle of deer fat, which it must be allowed renders them beyond all description finer flavoured than when boiled in water or common broth.'[56] A focus on food sheds light on the complex racial, gender, and class dynamics of the colonial world and, in the Canadian case, helps us trace the rise of that hegemonic 'Canadian' cuisine that twentieth-century immigrants confronted in all its bland certainty.

NOTES

1 Lambton County Archives (LCA), Henry John Jones Journal, 1831–1883, 12 May 1842. (Hereafter HJ).

2 *Kingston Chronicle and Gazette*, 27 Feb. and 21 Sept., 1841, 26 Jan 1842, 28 June 1843 (Smith's advertisements).

3 The phrase 'consumption story' is from Douglas McCalla, 'A World without Chocolate: Grocery Purchases at Some Upper Canadian Country Stores, 1808–1861,' *Agricultural History* 79/2 (2005): 147–72.

4 Thomas Need, *Six Years in the Bush: Or, Extracts from the Journal of a Settler in Upper Canada, 1832–1838* (London: Simpkin, Marshall, 1838), 34–5. See also Jeanne Hughes, 'Inns and Taverns,' in *Consuming Passions: Papers Presented at the 101st Annual Conference of the Ontario Historical Society* (Willowdale, ON: Ontario Historical Society, 1990), 93–112.

5 An excellent synthesis is Craig Heron, *Booze: A Distilled History* (Toronto: Between the Lines, 2003).

6 James E. McWilliams, *A Revolution in Eating: How the Quest for Food Shaped America* (New York: Columbia University Press, 2005), 149, quoting John Lawson, *A New Voyage to Carolina* (London, 1709), 12–13.

7 Menu reprinted in Edwin C. Guillet, *Pioneer Inns and Taverns Combined Edition* (Toronto: Ontario Publishing Co., 1964), vol. 2, book 1, 125.

8 Richard D. Merritt, 'Early Inns and Taverns: Accommodation, Fellowship, and Good Cheer,' in Richard Merritt, Nancy Butler, and Michael Power, eds., *Capital Years: Niagara-on-the-Lake, 1792–1796* (Toronto: Published for the Niagara Historical Society by Dundurn Press, 1992), 201 and 208n43.

9 The allusion is to R.D. Gidney and W.P.J. Millar, *Professional Gentlemen: The Professions in Nineteenth-Century Ontario* (Toronto: University of Toronto Press, 1994). See also Julia Roberts, 'Harry Jones and His Cronies in the Taverns of Kingston, Canada West,' *Ontario History* 95/1 (2003): 1–21.

10 Elizabeth Jane Errington, *Wives and Mothers, Schoolmistresses and Scullery Maids: Working Women in Upper Canada 1790–1840* (Montreal and Kingston: McGill-Queen's University Press, 1995), 113.

11 Roberts, 'Harry Jones and His Cronies'; Thomas Brennan, *Public Drinking and Popular Culture in Eighteenth-Century Paris* (Princeton, NJ: Princeton University Press, 1988); David S. Shields, *Civil Tongues and Polite Letters in British America* (Chapel Hill, NC: University of North Carolina Press, 1997); Jean-Robert Pitte, 'The Rise of the Restaurant,' in Jean-Louis Flandrin and Massimo Montanari, eds., trans. Clarissa Botsford et al., *Food: A Culinary History from Antiquity to the Present* (New York: Columbia University Press, 1999), 473. Many scholars have

explored modes of consumption as forms of social representation and indices of, especially, privileged class formation. For example, Stuart M. Blumin, *The Emergence of the Middle Class: Social Experience in the American City, 1760–1900* (Cambridge: Cambridge University Press, 1989); Leonore Davidoff and Catherine Hall, *Family Fortunes: Men and Women of the English Middle Class, 1780–1850* (Chicago, IL: University of Chicago Press, 1987).

12 Marcy Norton, 'Tasting Empire: Chocolate and the European Internalization of Mesoamerican Aesthetics,' *American Historical Review* 111/3 (2006): 660–91.

13 Helen Pike Bauer, 'Eating in the Contact Zone: Food and Identity in Anglo-India,' in Tamara S. Wagner and Narin Hassan, eds., *Consuming Culture in the Long Nineteenth Century: Narratives of Consumption, 1700–1900* (Lanham, MD: Lexington Books, 2007), 98; Donna R. Gabaccia, *We Are What We Eat: Ethnic Food and the Making of Americans* (Cambridge, MA: Harvard University Press, 1998), 31.

14 Enoch Padolsky, 'You Are Where You Eat: Ethnicity, Food, and Cross-Cultural Spaces,' *Canadian Ethnic Studies,* Special Issue on 'Ethnicity: Space and Place,' 37/2 (2005): 30.

15 On Rudy Wiebe, Austin Clarke, and others, see the introduction to this volume.

16 Timothy Taylor, *Stanley Park* (Toronto: Knopf, 2001), 389.

17 Marlene Epp, 'The Semiotics of Zwieback: Feast and Famine in the Narratives of Mennonite Refugee Women,' 314–340, and Franca Iacovetta and Valerie J. Korinek, 'Jello-O Salads, One-Stop Shopping, and Maria the Homemaker: The Gender Politics of Food,' 190–232, in Marlene Epp, Franca Iacovetta, and Frances Swyripa, eds., *Sisters or Strangers? Immigrant, Ethnic and Racialized Women in Canadian History* (Toronto: University of Toronto Press, 2004).

18 Mary Douglas, 'Deciphering a Meal,' in Carole Counihan and Penny Van Esterik, eds., *Food and Culture: A Reader* (New York: Routledge, 1997), 36, 41; Helen Day, 'Möbial Consumption: Stability, Flux, and Interpermeability in "Mrs Beeton,"' in Wagner and Hassan, *Consuming Culture*, 50. See also, Margaret Visser, *The Rituals of Dinner: The Origins, Evolution, Eccentricities, and Meaning of Table Manners* (Toronto: Harper Collins, 2000 [1991]), 106.

19 Beat Kümin, 'Eating Out before the Restaurant: Dining Cultures in Early-Modern Inns,' in Marc Jacobs and Peter Scholliers, eds., *Eating Out in Europe: Picnics, Gourmet Dining and Snacks since the Late Eighteenth Century* (Oxford: Berg, 2003), 76; Rebecca L. Spang, *The Invention of the Restaurant: Paris and Modern Gastronomic Culture* (Cambridge, MA: Harvard University Press, 2000), 87; Craig Heron, 'The Boys and Their Booze: Masculinities and Public Drinking in Working-Class Hamilton, 1890–1946,' *Canadian Historical Review* 86/3 (2005): 411–52. See also Bonnie Huskins, 'From Haute Cuisine to Ox Roasts: Public

Feasting and the Negotiation of Class in Mid-19th-Century Saint John and Halifax,' *Labour/Le Travail*, no. 37 (1996): 9–36.

20 Peter de Lottinville, 'Joe Beef of Montreal: Working-Class Culture and the Tavern, 1869–1889,' *Labour/Le Travail*, nos. 8/9 (1981/2): 9–40; Heron, *Booze*, 99, 175; Perry Duis, *The Saloon: Public Drinking in Chicago and Boston, 1880–1920* (Urbana, IL: University of Illinois Press, 1983), 15–45. See also Madelon Powers, *Faces along the Bar: Lore and the Workingman's Saloon, 1870–1920* (Chicago, IL: University of Chicago Press, 1998), 209–12; Warren Cron Miller, 'Inns, Taverns and Places of Refreshment,' in Warren Cron Miller, ed., *Vignettes of Early St Thomas* (St Thomas, ON: Sutherland Press, 1967), 255.

21 For example, Janet Noel, *Canada Dry: Temperance Crusades before Confederation* (Toronto: University of Toronto Press, 1995); Cheryl Krasnick Warsh, ed., *Drink in Canada: Historical Essays* (Montreal and Kingston: McGill-Queen's University Press, 1993).

22 Examples include Brennan, *Public Drinking and Popular Culture*; David Conroy, *In Public Houses: Drink and the Revolution of Authority in Colonial Massachusetts* (Chapel Hill, NC: University of North Carolina Press, 1995); Peter Thompson, *Rum, Punch and Revolution: Tavern-Going and Public Life in Eighteenth-Century Philadelphia* (Philadelphia, PA: University of Pennsylvania Press, 1999); Beat Kümin and B. Ann Tlusty, eds., *World of the Tavern: Public Houses in Early Modern Europe* (Aldershot: Ashgate, 2002); and Julia Roberts, *In Mixed Company: Taverns and Public Life* (Vancouver: UBC Press, 2009).

23 These issues also have contemporary relevance in a multicultural Canada (and United States), where 'eating ethnic' has been viewed both as a positive act (pluralist, global) and a negative one (cultural colonialism). See Lisa Heldke, *Exotic Appetites: Ruminations of a Food Adventurer* (New York: Routledge, 2003).

24 Roberts, *In Mixed Company*, 153–60.

25 Ibid., 105.

26 See Elizabeth Driver, *Culinary Landmarks: A Bibliography of Canadian Cookbooks, 1825–1949* (Toronto: University of Toronto Press, 2008).

27 Catharine Parr Traill, *The Female Emigrant's Guide, and Hints on Canadian Housekeeping*, 153, x, 107–9, 153–5, 156 (emphasis added) (Toronto: Maclear, 1854).

28 John Farley, *The London Art of Cookery and Domestic Housekeeper's Complete Assistant,* 12th ed. (London: Scatcherd and Letterman, 1811) 43.

29 Men's cookery work tended to be more prestigious. Sarah Freeman, *Mutton and Oysters: The Victorians and Their Food* (London: Gollancz, 1989), 151–5.

30 Bev Hykel, 'Surviving on the Homestead,' in *Consuming Passions*, 73–92; Assessment Roll of Fredricksburgh Tp., Lennox and Addington Co., 1808, online at

www.sfredheritage.on.ca (cows); McCalla, 'A World without Chocolate,' 155, 157, 160–1; on storekeepers' stocks, 'Quetton St George & Co. Advertises,' [1803] in Edith G. Firth, ed., *The Town of York, 1793–1815: A Collection of Documents of Early Toronto Publications of the Champlain Society* (Toronto: Champlain Society, 1962), 125.

31 Archives of Ontario (AO), Surrogate Court Records, Essex Co., Wills 1801 (#20) James Donaldson; Chatham-Kent Museum Archives, Chatham, Ontario, Matthew Dolsen Journal, 1797–1799; AO, Playter [EIy], Diary; Baldwin Room, Metropolitan Toronto Reference Library. Abner Miles Account Book, 1 Sept. 1795 – 15 Dec. 1796. Accounts of a General Store and Tavern.

32 *Upper Canada Gazette*, 27 Nov. and 4 Dec. 1802.

33 Edith G. Firth, ed., *The Town of York, 1815–1834: A Further Collection of Documents of Early Toronto* (Toronto: Champlain Society, 1966), 318–19.

34 Karin Becker, 'The French Novel and Luxury Eating in the Nineteenth Century,' in Jacobs and Scholliers, *Eating Out in Europe*, 199–214; Levi Adams, 'The Charivari, or, Canadian Poetics: A Tale after the Manner of Beppo' (Montreal, 1824).

35 Patrick Shirreff, *A Tour through North America* (Edinburgh: Oliver & Boyd, 1835), 161–2.

36 William Berczy, quoted in Guillet, *Pioneer Inns and Taverns*, vol. 2, book 1, 86; Thomas Fowler, *Journal of a Tour through British America* (Aberdeen: L. Smith, 1832); *Cobourg Star*, 27 Nov., 1833, quoted in Guillet, *Pioneer Inns and Taverns*, vol. 2, book 1, 100; Anna Jameson, *Winter Studies and Summer Rambles* (London: Saunders), vol. 3; Shirreff, *A Tour through North America*, 161–2.

37 Population statistics are from Frederick H. Armstrong, *Handbook of Upper Canadian Chronology*, rev. ed. (Toronto: Dundurn Press, 1985), 275.

38 The quotations are from tavernkeepers' newspaper advertisements; see (Toronto) *Colonial Advocate*, 6 Jan. 1831; (Toronto) *Globe*, 9 July 1844, 14 Oct. 1845, 31 Mar. 1849; (Toronto) *Correspondent and Advocate*, 11 Jan. and 14 June 1837; *Kingston Chronicle*, 23 Jan. 1830, 1 Jan. 1831; *Stratford and Perth County Intelligencer*, 2 Nov. 1855; (Toronto) *Canadian Freeman*, 2 Dec. 1830; Jeanne Minhinnick, *At Home in Upper Canada* (Toronto: Clarke, Irwin, 1970), 200–1.

39 John Richardson, *The Canadian Brothers, or the Prophecy Fulfilled: A Tale of the Late American War* (Montreal: Armour, 1840), 196–7.

40 Of course, historians have critiqued the 'separate spheres' argument. For just two examples, Errington, *Wives and Mothers*; Mary Kelley, 'Beyond the Boundaries,' *Journal of the Early Republic* 21/1 (2001), 95–113.

41 Samuel Strickland, *Twenty-Seven Years in Canada West, or the Experiences of an Early Settler* (London: R. Bentley, 1853), vol. 1, 292; James Edward Alexander, *L'Acadie, or Seven Years' Explorations in British America* (London: H. Colburn, 1849), vol. 1, 123. On women's role in polite sociability, Amanda Vickery, *The

Gentleman's Daughter: Women's Lives in Georgian England (New Haven, CT: Yale University Press, 1988).

42 Dolsen Journal, 1797–1799; Adam Fergusson, *Practical Notes Made during a Tour in Canada and a Portion of the United States in 1831. Second Edition to Which Are Now Added Notes Made During a Second Visit to Canada in 1833* (Edinburgh: William Blackwood, 1834), 120; Thomas Fisher Rare Book Room, University of Toronto, Charles Fothergill Collection, Charles Fothergill, 'A Few Notes Made on a Journey from Montreal through the Province of Upper Canada in 1817,' 56.

43 HJ, 1 May 1842.

44 Thomas Bewick, *A History of British Birds* (Newcastle Upon Tyne: Frank Graham, 1972 [1826]), vol. 2, 6th ed., 51–2.

45 McWilliams, *Revolution in Eating.*

46 William Clarke, *Clarke's Complete Cellarman: The Publican and Innkeeper's Practical Guide* (London: Sherwood, Gilbert and Piper, 1830), 180–1.

47 Bishop, *Englishwoman in America*, quoted in Guillet, *Pioneer Inns and Taverns*, vol. 2, book 3, 154.

48 Mrs Edward Copleston, *Canada: Why We Live in It and Why We Like It* (1861), quoted in Guillet, *Pioneer Inns and Taverns*, vol. 1, book 1, 194.

49 Susanna Moodie, *Life in the Clearings versus the Bush,* (London: R. Bentley, 1853), 348–9.

50 Strickland, *Twenty-Seven Years*, vol. 1, 73 (ducks & bass); Basil Hall, *Travels in North America in the Years 1827 and 1828*, vol. 1, 127 (Grand River) (Philadelphia, PA: Carey, Lea and Carey 1829); HJ, 21 Sept. 1837 (waitress); Morleigh, *Life in the West* (London: Saunders and Otley, 1842), 211.

51 John MacTaggart, *Three Years in Canada* (London: H. Colburn, 1829), 309–10.

52 Christine Rinne, 'Consuming the Maidservant,' in Wagner and Hassan, eds., *Consuming Culture*, 71; Peter Bailey, 'Parasexuality and Glamour: The Victorian Barmaid as Cultural Prototype,' *Gender and History* 2 (Summer 1990): 148–72.

53 Diane Kirkby, *Barmaids: A History of Women's Work in Pubs* (Cambridge: Cambridge University Press, 1997).

54 Anne McClintock, *Imperial Leather: Race, Gender, and Sexuality in the Colonial Contest* (New York: Routledge, 1995), 80.

55 Parr Traill, *The Female Emigrant's Guide*, 156; Francis Collingwood and John Woolams, *The Universal Cook, and City and Country Housekeeper...* (London: Printed by R. Noble, for J. Scatcherd, 1797), 2nd ed., 84, 131.

56 Samuel Hearne, *Journey from Prince of Wales Fort in Hudson's Bay to the Northern Ocean ... in the Years 1769, 1770, 1771 and 1772* (London: Strachan and Cadell, 1795), 213–14.

3 The Role of Food in Canadian Expressions of Christianity

MICHEL DESJARDINS AND ELLEN DESJARDINS

Food has always been a vital part of religious life. Based on their religious beliefs, people, in Canada and elsewhere, have restricted the food they eat, fed the spirit world, ingested the divine, offered food to others as charity, and celebrated important religious occasions with special food. Focusing historically, and in the present, on food and religious experience is one way to examine the lives of Canadian Christians. Despite the increasingly secular and multicultural nature of Canada, over three-quarters of the population still currently self-identify as Christian, and over half of these are Roman Catholic.[1] In this chapter, we examine changes to Canadian Christian food practices that have occurred since the late 1960s, when altered immigration policies and the emergence of multiculturalism as a core Canadian value led to an increasingly multi-ethnic and multi-religious population, especially in the larger cities.

Historical Links between Food and Canadian Christianity

Canadian Christians have expressed their religiosity through food in ways quite similar to other Christians throughout the world, but their experiences have also been coloured by the European colonization of this land and its peoples, the multi-ethnic European immigrant presence throughout the country, tensions between 'the French' and 'the English' founding peoples, and deep-seated antagonisms between Catholics and Protestants. This section reviews the main Christian food-related categories, highlighting some of their Canadian characteristics.[2]

Christianity in its early decades distinguished itself from its parent, Judaism, by declaring members free from dietary restrictions.[3] But temporary food restrictions, sometimes called fasts, have a long history within Christianity.[4] Christian fasts focus on the avoidance of animal products, including butter, eggs, and meat itself. They often but not only precede special religious days, such as Christmas, Easter, and Sundays, with their length and severity varying between Christian groups and over time.

Canadian Roman Catholics on the whole have taken fasting far more seriously than Protestants. As a result, Catholic Friday and Lenten practices, especially in the early centuries of colonization, contributed significantly to the sense that Catholicism and Protestantism were not only different branches of the same religion, but entirely different religions. Until recently most Catholics abstained from meat on Fridays, often replacing it with fish, as a type of self-denial in memory of the day on which Jesus was said to have suffered and died. Fish was not the only substitute: as Stacey Zembrzycki notes in her chapter in this volume, Ukrainian Canadians often replaced meat with their signature ethnic food – perogies – for their Friday fast. During the forty-day Lenten period that precedes Easter, Catholics also removed from their diet various sensory delights, including sweets (for the children) and animal dietary products. The weekly Friday food restriction was determinative: if there is one thing that Protestants knew about Catholics, it was that Catholics did not eat meat on Fridays.

Christian Sunday worship gatherings since the earliest days of Christianity have focused on a food ritual. Called by various names – Eucharist, the Lord's Supper, Communion – this ritual symbolizes a wide range of possibilities, including thanksgiving, the invocation of the Spirit, the memory of Jesus' sacrifice, the memory of the Last Supper, and hope of the upcoming Kingdom that Christians believe awaits them when Jesus returns.[5] For the majority of Christians over the centuries, the Eucharist has not only been symbolic, but substantive: the bread and wine (or their substitutes) were thought to be changed, or 'transubstantiated,' into the actual body and blood of Jesus, giving believers direct corporal access to God through food.

In the Canadian context, sharply divided as it was until recent decades between Catholics and Protestants, the Eucharist, like Friday fasting, played a major part in delimiting boundaries. While Christians as a whole honoured this ritual, Protestants typically saw transubstantiation as akin to magic, and Catholics considered it a fundamental act of faith. In both cases, however, as well as for the Eastern Christian communities that also helped shape Canada for over a century,[6] the Eucharistic food ritual was a primary conduit to the divine.

Canadian Christians have long celebrated religious occasions with special foods linked to their ethnic backgrounds. Canadian Ukrainian cookbooks are full of old country recipes prepared for Christmas and Easter, as are Mennonite cookbooks, as illustrated by Marlene Epp in this volume.[7] Colourful rituals have often complemented these special foods. For instance, some Christian immigrants from Eastern Europe continued the tradition of bringing elaborate food baskets to church on the Saturday before Easter, to be blessed by the priest and returned home. That blessed food, including bread, sausage, butter, cheese, and decorated eggs, became a vital part of the Easter meal. In her chapter in this volume, Franca Iacovetta describes a Latvian ethnic celebration that introduced Torontonians to the particular foods and recipes that were part of Latvian immigrant Easter rituals. Across the country, each Christian community has similar stories – of French-Canadian *réveillons* following Christmas midnight mass, Slovenian women working together to produce their Easter *potica*, or walnut role cakes, and Dene feasting on smoked moose and dried fish. Religion, ethnicity, and location have merged in distinct ways with food. Women, in particular, have played an important role in transmitting this knowledge from generation to generation.

Food has often accompanied religious services and gatherings in this country, for good reasons: shared snacks and meals bring people together and foster community, banquets can raise money for various needs, and commensality – the act of eating together – helps people get through long, cold winters. Canadian church cookbooks attest to this reality of Christians gathering after a service or to commemorate a special event. Moreover, church potlucks, post-service coffee and cookies, and bake sales have been around since the time that Europeans arrived on the shores of Canada.

The community building that each group did, however, also separated them from others. Food, after all, brings some people together and keeps them apart from others. But there have always been exceptions to this segregation, particularly in smaller communities where Christians of different denominations toiled and sometimes ate together, despite having religious food traditions that worked to keep them apart. An elderly informant we interviewed in 2006 in the Waterloo Region of southwestern Ontario recounted a local childhood memory that speaks to this reality:

> Growing up on a farm, we needed to work with our family's neighbours to get the crops in – including our Protestant neighbours. This meant that the Catholic wives had to prepare meat on Fridays, because the Protestant men expected it, and it meant that the Protestant women had to prepare fish on Fridays, because the Catholic men needed it. These original experiences of cooperation between Catholic and Protestant farmers gave me a grounding in interfaith dialogue from a very early age.[8]

The most explicit link between religion and food for many Christians has been food charity, supported by biblical injunctions that encourage followers of Jesus to feed the poor. Canadian Christians of all denominations since the founding of New France have given food and meals to the poor, raised money for Christmas food baskets, and as soon as they were able sent money abroad for hungry populations. Until recently, Christian denominations have tended to perform this religious service independently of one other.

One expression of this food charity is work done by the Salvation Army, an evangelical Protestant group that arrived in Canada from London in 1882, establishing itself as a 'soup and salvation' mission that fed the hungry with a view to converting them to Christianity.[9] The 'Sally Ann' focused on food charity, be it in the context of emergency and disaster food supply, homeless and addiction services, safe houses, or services for the mentally and physically needy.

Another group well known for its Christian food charity is the Society of St Vincent de Paul, which began in Paris in 1833 with the intention of encouraging more Roman Catholics to help the poor. First established in Canada in 1847, the Society developed support groups in most Canadian Catholic parishes to ensure that less fortunate families received at least some material support. A good deal of that support came in the form of food, with major fundraising and distribution of that food taking place before and during the Christmas season.

Changing Patterns to the Role of Food in Canadian Christian Life

Much of what we have just reviewed continues to be practised by Canadian Christians. In some respects, food shapes Christian lives today in ways that have not changed much over time: The Salvation Army representatives still greet immigrants to this country, churches hold bake sales to raise money and foster community building, cities have their soup kitchens and out-of-the-cold programs run by local Christian churches, Sunday services usually include Eucharistic celebrations, Lent for many still evokes the thought of food restrictions, Easter baskets still get blessed in churches, and the major religious feasts have the smells and tastes of past places and times that sometimes extend beyond the Canadian shores.

In what follows, we focus less on continuity than on change. Canadian expressions of Christianity have undergone a transformation over the past forty years. We explore ways in which food has been implicated in these changes. Before turning to the federal government catalysts for these changes, we touch on two other events that significantly challenged Canada's Catholics in the 1960s and helped to pave the way for new religious realities in this country. These were Vatican II and Quebec's Quiet Revolution.

The rulings that emerged from Vatican II, a series of meetings of Catholic

Church leaders held from 1962 to 1965 in Rome, affected everyday Canadian Catholics like nothing they had personally known before. What these Catholics experienced were church services now being held in the vernacular language instead of Latin, the altar table being turned around with the priest facing them rather than away, and a removal of the requirement to abstain from meat on Fridays. In addition, they were encouraged to work more closely with Christians of other denominations, and to some extent also with religious people outside Christianity.

The implications for religious food culture were profound. The Eucharist now more closely resembled a meal, with priests openly conducting the transformative food ritual and parishioners being allowed to receive the food (and drink) in their hands. More significantly for many Catholics, the centuries-long rhythm of different Friday food was broken, a legal relaxation that surprisingly prompted a good number of Catholics to reconsider their participation in the church.

Yet, for Church leaders all was not doom and gloom. The ecumenical thrust of Vatican II led to an increasing number of new initiatives, with Catholics working more closely with other Christians on a variety of projects. A recent example is Catholic participation in the Canadian Foodgrains Bank (CFB), a Christian charitable project meant to alleviate world hunger. CFB started in 1983 out of the Mennonite Central Committee, and now it is owned by fifteen Canadian church agencies. One of these agencies is the Canadian Catholic Organization for Development and Peace, which seeks to 'pool resources, both human and financial, and work collaboratively together in a Christian Response to Hunger.'[10] For the younger members of the churches, this inter-Christian involvement with food aid is now all they have ever known; for at least some older Catholics, who in their early years would have considered Mennonites as far removed from their faith as Buddhists (the reverse is equally true of Mennonites), the change has been enormous.

Quebec's Quiet Revolution added another significant factor, particularly to the religious practices of francophone Catholics. Coined to represent the major cultural and religious changes that took place in Quebec during the early 1960s, this movement shifted control of education and health from the Catholic Church to secular governmental agencies, as part of a larger drive to strip the Church of the power it had wielded over Quebec Catholics for centuries.[11] It 'marked an acceleration of the process of secularization of the Québec State,'[12] a process mirrored by Christians in other parts of Canada as well.[13]

The changes wrought by Vatican II and Quebec's Quiet Revolution meant that fewer and fewer Canadians, particularly those with long family roots in this country, concern themselves with religious food restrictions and with the

Eucharist. But these practices have not disappeared. One need only look at Friday menus to see that 'fish on Fridays' is alive and well throughout Canada, if not in Catholic homes, then at least in restaurants. And one need only look at the Christian churches filled with new immigrants, whose food practices often resemble what used to exist in Canada a generation or two ago. It is to that reality that we now turn.

The Vatican and Quebec changes were complemented by Canadian federal government legislation introduced in 1967 and 1971. The Immigration Act of 1967 significantly increased Canada's ethnic diversity by introducing the 'points system,' replacing the old system of accepting immigrants to Canada that had discriminated against non-Caucasians. As a result of this Act, any applicant with enough points became equally competitive, regardless of race, colour, and religious affiliation. Along with this change, in 1971, the federal Liberal government introduced the official policy of Canadian 'multiculturalism.'[14] The result was a flood of new immigrants into Canada from all over the world – particularly South and East Asia, parts of Africa, Latin America, and the Caribbean – accompanied by changes to the self-identity of this country and a growing appreciation for the Aboriginal communities.[15]

A major consequence of these changes has been the increased presence of immigrants involved in other religious traditions, particularly Islam, Hinduism, and Sikhism.[16] Over the past forty years, Vancouver and Montreal, and especially Toronto, have been transformed into cities containing extraordinarily mixed populations. What is less well known, however, is that most immigrants to Canada continued to be Christian, especially Roman Catholics, from the Philippines, Asia, Latin America, and other parts of the global South.

Increased religious pluralism and ethnic diversification of the Canadian Christian population certainly has had an effect on the intersection of food and Christianity. We begin by looking at ethnic diversification through the looking glass provided by Paul Bramadat and David Seljak's *Christianity and Ethnicity in Canada*.[17] This book, with chapters addressing different Christian denominations, reveals that not all Christian communities have been affected to the same extent by Canada's changing ethnic mix. The Eastern Christian communities that are more ethnically and regionally specific (e.g., Serb, Greek, Coptic, Ukrainian, Russian) have been influenced far more by the arrival of other Christians from their home countries than by ethnic diversification.[18] The same applies to the Christian Reformed Church, where over 98 per cent of members still claim European ancestry.[19] By contrast, to be a member of the United Church has long ceased to mean being an anglophone Protestant with family roots in the British Isles. Similarly, Presbyterians, Catholics, and even Anglicans at church gatherings in Canada are now sometimes encouraged by their new parishioners to serve tortillas alongside the cabbage, and beans instead of pork. In other words, the vital sensory links made between food and religious place are currently being reconfigured in Canadian Christian communities – in some communities more than in others.

Quebec religious life has been affected by the influx of immigrants from new parts of the world. Solange Lefebvre observes that because of a 1977 ruling that required immigrant children in Quebec to attend French schools, a large number of francophone Roman Catholic parishes have become multi-ethnic.[20] Changes in food practices followed suit. Montreal Catholics, in particular, Lefebvre notes, when they invite their Muslim friends to share meals with them, are learning that respect includes an understanding of Muslim dietary restrictions. Moreover, since most immigrants tend to be socially more conservative, the new ethnic mixes have meant that the preparation of food for religious events often reverts back to the kitchens, to the control of women.

These types of examples are repeated across Canada, across many Christian traditions. Presbyterians are seeing their Scottish roots, and food fare, mix with those of Koreans.[21] The United Church of Canada, the country's largest Protestant denomination, has been a leader in dealing with the implications of ethnic diversity. As Greer Anne Wenh-in Ng notes, the Amazing Grace Taiwanese Mission in Fraser, B.C., celebrates the Chinese Lunar New Year and the Mid-Autumn Festival with their food-rich traditions (moon cakes, pomelos, etc.).[22] For their part, most Lutherans in Canada, although still grounded in their German roots and accompanying German food, are also embracing ethnic diversity. In Surrey, B.C., for example, 'there are English, Chinese, Korean, and Spanish services at Faith Evangelical Lutheran Church, comprising four "worshipping fellowships" ... [One of the leaders] is also training lay people of Hispanic, Hindi and Mandarin backgrounds [and has hired] a Hindu convert to Christianity as an evangelist ... On festival days Faith Lutheran brings all four worshipping fellowships together for joint worship services, followed by a pot-luck lunch where ethnic foods are shared.'[23] One imagines ethnic fusion in potlucks, with the pork sausages complemented by noodles, pickled vegetables, dhal, and tacos. All of this matters because Christians tend to associate particular food with special religious occasions, and as that food culture changes so, too, does a person's religious culture. Sermons and biblical texts might be fodder for theologians, but food is universally significant.

Ethnic diversification in Canadian congregations has helped to create greater global awareness, including more calls by Christians for global justice.[24] Moreover, it has increased sensitivity to the problems inherent in the traditional model of Christian charity which, as Janet Poppendieck for one has noted, both at home and abroad has at times offered token rather than structural solutions.[25]

Moving from ethnic diversification within the Christian tradition to religious pluralism more broadly, one sees tensions throughout Canada, to be sure,[26] but also an abundance of positive discoveries and sharing. One example among many is a Quebec group, Astrolabe, which since 2004 has been introducing Muslims to the *cabanes à sucre* that was traditionally a French-Canadian Catholic rite of spring, blessed by priests and, in francophone Catholic communities outside Quebec, often held adjacent to the church.[27] Still, we should not paint too rosy a picture. Interreligious understanding has a long way to go before all Christians in this country appreciate, for instance, the visceral negative response that Muslims, many Jews, and some Indians feel about pork, but we are far from the mid-twentieth century mindset that simply assumed Christianity and Christian food practices as the norm.

Christian encounters with people of other religious traditions have sometimes had unexpected results. On the Wilfrid Laurier University campus in Waterloo, Ontario, some Catholic students who are trying to revitalize their own faith by returning to their tradition's fasting roots are modelling themselves on their Muslim classmates.[28] Inspired by their classmates' piety during Ramadan, fasting for these young Catholics now entails total abstinence from food and drink from sunrise to sunset during the forty days of Lent, a practice not otherwise followed in the Catholic tradition.[29] Another example of hybridization can be seen with the House of Friendship food bank in the Waterloo Region, which now receives food donations from a local Hindu temple, a local Sikh gurdwara, and the Muslim Shi'a community. In addition, a sectarian Sikh farming community fifty kilometres away regularly sends truckloads of produce to this food bank during the summer. This self-professed 'Christian' food bank has willingly been adopted and altered by members of other faith traditions. In sum, not only are Christians being nourished by the presence of other religious traditions, and not only are Christian expressions of food charity likely to be interdenominational, as noted above, but traditional forms of Christian charity are also being transformed into multi-faith expressions.[30]

Conclusion

Food remains intertwined with Canadian Christian life in ways that reflect the old practices and beliefs as well as the changes brought about as a result of the increased diversification of Canadian culture. With fewer Christians attending church services, fewer restrictions imposed on adherents, and fewer women spending long hours in the kitchen (their place not often replaced by men), the traditional religious connections to food are changing for many Christians who grew up in this country – including Aboriginal Christians, many of whom are now nurturing their pre-Christian religious traditions, at the same time as their traditional food sources are increasingly threatened by environmental changes.

The central Eucharistic feast is not usually celebrated by the whole community, the days of long fasts for many are a thing of the past, and the huge Sunday and religious feast-day dinners have become potlucks and take-outs that rarely include the whole extended family. Moreover, lingering after service to share food and drink is an opportunity taken up by a minority, and the donations at work or at the door to the United Way and the Cancer Society often replace Christian calls for food charity. Indeed, the Canadian components of the categories with which we began this case study have all become more complex.

One result of this complexity is that food is no longer as divisive a force as it once was between Christian groups. Many churchgoing Canadian Christians share in 'worldwide communion day,' a Sunday when Christian churches across the world are conscious of having a shared Eucharist, and Christians also work together to address social inequities.[31] On the whole, the Catholic-Protestant feuding that so marked the first centuries of Canada no longer resonates with the intensity it did before.

Canada's increasing degree of secularization has also meant a shift of food from the category 'religion' to 'ethnicity,' to the extent that one can make this distinction. With that shift has come increased celebration of difference. The turkey and meat pies for Thanksgiving and Christmas, and the ham for Easter, are becoming more cultural than religious artefacts – as are the religious holidays themselves. Canadians tend to be more interested, for example, in tasting 'local Mennonite food' or supporting the Mennonite sale of Fair Trade coffee, than they are in attending Mennonite religious services.

So how is the religious role of food affected by the rise of secularism, the growing ethnic diversity among Christians, and the increasing presence, visibility, and interactions of Canadians belonging to multiple religious groups? First, we are witnessing movement in two opposite directions: while many Canadian-born Christians are moving away from some of the previouslyheld links between food and religious life, immigrants on the whole are reinscribing those links, in diverse ways. Second, food traditions or 'ethnic markers' associated with a wide array of immigrants, including ones attached to religious traditions, are becoming accepted into the food culture of the larger secular society. Third, there is considerable interreligious exchange in this country, leading to greater awareness of religious food restrictions and fasting as practised by Muslims, Jews, and Hindus – resulting at times in unexpected partnerships, such as the attraction of young Christians to vegetarianism, fed not only by the environmental movement but also by immigrant Hindu, Sikh, and Jain religious food practices that are gaining more public exposure. In short,

Canadians are experiencing intercultural exchanges and movement in several directions – with food so often at the centre, serving as a mirror to the past and the present.

NOTES

1 Reginald Bibby, *Restless Gods: The Renaissance of Religion in Canada* (Toronto: Stoddart, 2002), 85. For an overview of the demographics of Christianity in Canada, see Peter Beyer's Appendix, in Paul Bramadat and David Seljak, eds., *Christianity and Ethnicity in Canada* (Toronto: University of Toronto Press, 2008), 437–40. The 2001 Census identified 12,793,125 Roman Catholics, spread across every province and territory (5,939,715 in Quebec, 3,911,760 in Ontario).

2 There is some overlap between these categories and those in Daniel Sack's *Whitebread Protestants: Food and Religion in American Culture* (New York: St Martin's Press, 2000), which organizes the data under Liturgical Food, Social Food, Emergency Food, Global Food, and Moral Food. Sack's categories effectively represent the American Protestant model; ours are more representative of the global connections between food and religion that we have found in our research, and we think they better represent the Canadian Christian experiences.

3 Paul, for example, taught: 'Food will not commend us to God' (1 Cor 8:8). A few Christian groups over the centuries have had dietary restrictions (e.g., Seventh Day Adventists), but they have been rare.

4 The important role of fasting throughout Christian history is well represented in David Grumett and Rachel Muers, *Theology on the Menu: Asceticism, Meat and Christian Diet* (London/New York: Routledge, 2010), 1–71.

5 See Hal Taussig, *In the Beginning Was the Meal: Social Experimentation and Early Christian Identity* (Minneapolis, MN: Fortress, 2009), for a study that highlights the significant role of this early Christian food ritual, while encouraging modern Christians to revitalize this ritual.

6 The term 'Eastern Christianity' is used here, as it is by Myroslaw Tataryn in *Christianity and Ethnicity in Canada* (Toronto: University of Toronto Press, 2008), to bring together 'those branches of the Christian world that historically developed quite independent of both the ancient Church of Rome (Roman Catholicism) and the churches of the Reformation [Protestantism]' (289). Eastern Christianity includes Orthodox communities, many of which come from Eastern Europe, the Middle East, and India.

7 E.g., *Ukrainian Daughters' Cookbook*, by the Ukrainian Women's Association of Canada, Daughter of Ukraine Branch (Regina, SK, 1984). Research by Marlene Epp and others also shows that Canadian Mennonite women, in particular, since

the early 1800s have integrated belief and religious identity through food. See 'The Semiotics of Zwieback: Feast and Famine in the Narratives of Mennonite Refugee Women,' in Marlene Epp, Franca Iacovetta, and Frances Swyripa, eds., *Sisters or Strangers? Immigrant, Ethnic, and Racialized Women in Canadian History* (Toronto: University of Toronto Press, 2004), 314–40; Pamela Klassen, 'What's Bre[a]d in the Bone: The Bodily Heritage of Mennonite Women,' *Mennonite Quarterly Review* 68 (1994): 229–47.

8 This interview was conducted in the House of Friendship building in Kitchener, Ontario, 10 Aug. 2006, as part of our ongoing research project on the religious role that food plays in people's lives, across religious traditions and across the world. We have conducted well over 150 interviews over the last four years, across South and East Asia, North Africa, Europe, the Middle East, part of the Caribbean, and North America, and we are currently preparing a book that will address thematic differences and similarities within and between traditions.

9 For a broad history of the Salvation Army in Canada, see R.G. Moyles, *The Blood and Fire in Canada: A History of the Salvation Army in the Dominion, 1882–1976* (Toronto: Peter Martin, 1977).

10 Available at http://www.foodgrainsbank.ca/member_churches.aspx.

11 For background information see Michael Gauvreau, *The Catholic Origins of Quebec's Quiet Revolution, 1931–1970* (Montreal and Kingston: McGill-Queen's University Press, 2005).

12 These words come from what has come to be known as the Bouchard-Taylor Report, 139. Another relevant quote from that report is: 'In our view, secularism comprises four key principles. Two of the principles define the final purposes that we are seeking, i.e. the moral equality of persons or the recognition of the equivalent moral value of each individual, and freedom of conscience and religion. The other two principles express themselves in the institutional structures that are essential to achieve these purposes, i.e. State neutrality towards religions and the separation of Church and State' (135). This report, published in 2008, was commissioned by the Quebec government. See Gérard Bouchard and Charles Taylor, *Building the Future: A Time for Reconciliation*, available at http://www.accommo- dements.qc.ca/documentation/rapports/rapport-final-integral-en.pdf.

13 Tracking the 'no religion' category in the 1981, 1991, and 2001 census figures, we see an increase from 7.4% to 12.3% to 16.2%. The results are difficult to assess since, e.g., many members of the large Chinese population in Canada typically choose 'no religion' because they have trouble isolating a single religious tradition to which they adhere. Nevertheless, the rise in this figure is significant.

14 The multiculturalism policy became a statute in 1988. The term is much more prevalent outside Quebec, which has had an ambivalent relationship to the notion of multiculturalism. The Bouchard-Taylor Report prefers the notion of intercul-

turalism, which, in their view, 'seeks to reconcile ethnocultural diversity with the continuity of the French-speaking core and the preservation of the social link' (19).

15 For a challenge to the reality of multiculturalism, see Neil Bissoondath, *Selling Illusions: The Cult of Multiculturalism in Canada* (Toronto: Penguin, 1994).

16 Muslims in Canada, e.g., made up 0.4% of the population in 1981 (98,000), 0.9% in 1991 (253,265), 2% in 2001 (579,640), and they are now estimated to make up 2.5% (785,700). Hindus and Sikhs in 2001 also had a combined figure of 557,615. A good number of Muslims are also Indian, some having come to Canada indirectly from East Africa.

17 This book is a sequel to their *Religion and Ethnicity in Canada* (Toronto: Pearson, 2005).

18 See the chapter by Myroslaw Tataryn, 'Canada's Eastern Christians,' in Bramadat and Seljak, *Christianity and Ethnicity in Canada*, 287–329. There are currently about 650,000 'Eastern' Christians in Canada, many having come in recent years from Eastern Europe and the Middle East.

19 Stuart Macdonald, 'Presbyterian and Reformed Christians and Ethnicity,' in Bramadat and Seljak, *Christianity and Ethnicity in Canada*, 174.

20 Solange Lefebvre, 'The Francophone Roman Catholic Church,' in Bramadat and Seljak, *Christianity and Ethnicity in Canada*, 105–6.

21 Macdonald, 'Presbyterian and Reformed Christians,' 184.

22 'The United Church of Canada: A Church Fittingly National,' in Bramadat and Seljak, *Christianity and Ethnicity in Canada*, 211.

23 Bryan Hillis, 'Outsiders Becoming Mainstream: The Theology, History, and Ethnicity of Being Lutheran in Canada,' in Bramadat and Seljak, *Christianity and Ethnicity in Canada*, 271.

24 See Cathy C. Campbell, *Stations of the Banquet: Faith Foundations for Food Justice* (Collegeville, MN: Liturgical Press, 2003), for an example of a Winnipeg Anglican Church minister taking creative actions to raise awareness of global justice among her congregants.

25 Janet Poppendieck, 'Want Amid Plenty: From Hunger to Inequality,' in Carole Counihan and Penny Van Esterik, eds., *Food and Culture: A Reader*, 2nd ed. (New York: Routledge, 2008), 572–81. For more critical engagement with practices of charity, see also the two accompanying articles in that collection: Jennifer Clapp, 'The Political Economy of Food Aid in an Era of Agricultural Biotechnology' (539–53), and Karen Coen Flynn, 'Street Credit: The Cultural Politics of African Street Children's Hunger' (554–71).

26 Tensions have run the highest in Quebec. The Bouchard-Taylor Report was commissioned to understand the sources and nature of these tensions, which intensified from May 2002 to February 2006 and led to a time of turmoil from March

2006 to June 2007, and to make recommendations on resolving them. Some of the incidents that generated these tensions emerged from differences in food culture, particularly over kosher laws with orthodox Jews; see 48–60 for a description of the main incidents.

27 See www.astrolabequebec.org.

28 For a related study of how Catholics in America are revisiting their fasting traditions, see Kathleen M. Dugan, 'Fasting for Life: The Place of Fasting in the Christian Tradition,' *Journal of the American Academy of Religion* 63/3 (1995): 539–48. For the significance of fasting in the broader U.S. Christian framework, see R. Marie Griffith, '"Don't Eat That": The Erotics of Abstinence in American Christianity,' *Gastronomica* 1/4 (2001): 36–47.

29 Ironically, Muslim fasting during the month of Ramadan itself may have emerged in the seventh century from early Christian fasting practices. See Grumett and Muers, *Theology on the Menu*, 103–5, and Kees Wagtendonk, *Fasting in the Koran* (Leiden: Brill, 1978).

30 We see similar influences in the reverse, with Canadian Muslims, e.g., setting up food banks and shelters based on Canadian Christian models.

31 An example of this inter-Christian activity is *See You Next Week: An Ecumenical Community Ministry in an Ontario Downtown* (Kitchener: Community Ministry, 2007), that describes a decade of work by local Lutheran and United churches in providing Lenten Wednesday dinners at which both street people and church members sit to eat together.

PART TWO

Regional Food Identities and Traditions

4 Pine-Clad Hills and Spindrift Swirl: The Character, Persistence, and Significance of Rural Newfoundland Foodways

MAURA HANRAHAN

Diet has always tied Newfoundlanders to the land and sea, as we will see in this survey of historical foodways in rural Newfoundland since early European settlement some four hundred years ago. This is true of the indigenous Mi'kmaq and Beothuck of the island as well as the centuries-old settler society, which is the focus of this chapter. The links between diet and the land and sea have been central to life in rural Newfoundland and, to a lesser extent, in the island's cities. Land- and sea-based food traditions have been remarkably persistent, although some of these traditions are threatened by the ground fish moratoria imposed by the federal government in 1992 as a response to mechanized overfishing.

Unlike much of the rest of North America, most Newfoundland food practices are not rooted in agriculture. In Western Europe, as well as most of North America, commensality traditions (eating together) have the fall harvest as their focus, as seen in Thanksgiving celebrations. But Newfoundland's settler society was never an agrarian one, mainly but not entirely because arable land is scarce on the island. This case study will identify and explain some of the strategies of survival for people in regions where large-scale farming is not central or even possible. In rural Newfoundland, food acquisition and consumption practices were heavily influenced by indigenous hunting, gathering, and fishing patterns. Indeed, adapting to these practices allowed the first Europeans to overwinter instead of merely spending the summer fishing in Newfoundland waters, as had been their initial practice. These adaptations first planted the seeds of the settler society in the 1600s. For rural Newfoundlanders, in particular, they retain cultural significance to this day.

Newfoundland Settler Society

The early Europeans came from the west country of England, specifically

Devon and Dorset, the south of Ireland, especially Waterford and Wexford, coastal France, and the Iberian Peninsula. From the 1550s, Europeans from many nations took part in a lucrative seasonal fishery in Newfoundland waters. In 1583, Sir Humphrey Gilbert claimed the island for Queen Elizabeth I. Britain and France fought over it through the centuries, and the French retained rights along the island's French Shore until 1904. The British imposed a settlement ban in an attempt to prevent other Europeans from gaining a toehold on the island itself. Thus, year-round settlement was slow. But hundreds and then thousands of Britons, Irish, and French sneaked into coves and bays along the island's and Labrador's 11,000 kilometre coastline. The population grew substantially in the mid- to late-1700s as restrictions on settlement were modified. The first wave of migration to Newfoundland was over by the early 1800s, and most present-day Newfoundlanders count their ancestors among these early settlers.[1] The foodways of these people, learned not from recipes but through word of mouth and performance,[2] are at the heart of Newfoundlanders' cultural identity, even through urbanization, late twentieth-century industrialization, and the loss of the cod fishery. The Thai, Greek, and vegetarian restaurants in St John's may be popular, but it is salt fish and blueberries that are laden with meaning – if not romanticism – for most Newfoundlanders.

Newfoundland Foodways

Why didn't agrarian society take root in Newfoundland? The main and obvious determinative factor for Newfoundland's stunted agricultural development is the geophysical environment. The island of Newfoundland consists of boreal forest and subarctic tundra. There is limited arable land, the notable exceptions being areas of the Northeast Avalon Peninsula, including St John's West, and parts of the west coast, especially the Codroy Valley. The eastern parts of the island are located near the intersection of the warm Gulf Stream and the frigid Labrador Current, resulting in unpredictable weather marked by long, damp winters, a short summer, and hurricanes through the late summer and early fall ('August gales' are dreaded by every fisherman). Long ago glacial action left thin layers of soil, and although agriculture is not impossible (root crops grow well here), it is difficult and limited. In the words of one historian, agriculture in Newfoundland was 'meager and limited.'[3] For the very earliest settlers, relying on fatty meat, ale, biscuits, and peas, food shortages were a seasonal occurrence.[4] The image of the resilient Newfoundlander is at least partly rooted in this fact. A 1933 Royal Commission noted, 'usually of good physique, the Newfoundlander is hardy and long-lived.'[5]

Early plantations or colonies failed because of their reliance on agriculture.

It might have been possible to live off agriculture in southern England but not in Newfoundland – the John Guy plantation at Cupers Cove, Conception Bay, being a prime example of this. Sponsored by merchants in Bristol, England, in 1610, the colony, as it was called, was one of the first in the New World. The colonists found that soil and climate were not as good as they had hoped. They were successful in raising vegetables like potatoes and turnips but not grain, and they did not harvest enough hay to keep their animals through the winter of 1613.[6] After Guy left, interim leader Henry Crout concluded that the fishery was not as exploited as it should have been; too many colonists, he said, 'scorned to torne a Fish.' This history of the Cupers Cove colony shows that vegetable gardening was possible on the island but livestock raising was probably too demanding for the geophysical environment.[7] In addition, occupational pluralism was necessary to survive in Newfoundland, especially if a profit was expected, as with this experiment.

As the most abundant, reliable food resource, fish had to remain central. Indeed, while the geophysical environment made agriculture a challenge, the sea offered an unimaginable bounty: the fishing grounds off Newfoundland's shores and on its Grand Banks were the richest in the world. Cod is extremely protein-dense; because it has virtually no fat, it salts and dries well. As if there were no other species in the sea, the early settlers called it simply 'fish,' as their descendants still do.[8] Cod – *gadhus morhua* – was also dubbed 'King Cod,' appeared on Newfoundland stamps, and remains a recurring motif in the island's art.

But 'making fish,' as gutting and drying it is called, is a labour-intensive and time-consuming process. It involved entire families working from dawn until late at night during the summer fishing season. Accordingly, there were few available hours to devote to agriculture. On the northeast coast, with its relative concentration of communities, the demands of preparing for the fishery in the winter and spring and then prosecuting the fishery through the summer and early fall were so great as to preclude large-scale agriculture with its own substantial requirements of time and effort. In addition, the settlement ban in itself would have limited agricultural development.[9] With each passing generation, any agricultural knowledge that might have originated in Europe was lost, and much of it might not have applied in the Newfoundland environment anyway. There is ample evidence of fisheries- and woods-based ecological knowledge among rural Newfoundlanders – as seen in the range of traditional medicines, for example[10] – but the absence of agricultural expertise has proven an obstacle to agricultural development.[11]

This is not to say that agriculture did not occur in Newfoundland, and the endurance of rural 'kitchen gardens' should be noted. In spite of the simultaneous demands of the fishery, families grew turnips, potatoes, carrots, cabbage, and the like for household consumption. Such gardens were located right on household doorsteps, in communal gardens, as on Bell Island, and, in the case of the Great Northern Peninsula, on the side of the road.[12] But food was rarely grown for commercial purposes, with the Codroy Valley on the island's west coast and one or two other regions being notable exceptions. In the main, agriculture was always supplemental, if not tangential, to the general economy. Kitchen gardens were the result of manual, not mechanized labour; they featured little sexual division of labour, and were family activities.[13] Food produced was for household consumption, part of the subsistence-based household economy.

As indigenous people knew, the land provided nutritious food. There was game, caribou and Arctic hare, several kinds of vitamin-rich berries, including blueberries, blackberries, partridgeberries, and bakeapples (called cloud berries elsewhere), and, in addition to ocean fish like cod and herring, the rivers were full of salmon and trout. Settlers who failed to adopt the indigenous economic adaptations faced even more food scarcity than was natural, as well as compromised diets.[14] This danger was understood by indigenous people in Newfoundland and across North America.

The Mi'kmaq and Beothuck moved from one place to another in order to maximize the benefits of available resources. They spent summers at the mouths of good salmon and eel rivers; they went to the coast in the spring to hunt seals; they went to the best berry grounds in the fall; they followed the migrating caribou and trapped small game in the winter. They used their extensive knowledge of the land and water to purposely hunt, gather, and fish. Meanwhile, the settlers developed a less elaborate pattern of seasonal transhumance.[15] The settlers had summer houses near the ocean so they could easily access fish; in late fall, when the fishery ended, they moved into the woods to their winter houses to be near fur-bearing animals. Thus, their round of food acquisition activities resembled indigenous adaptations more than it did those of ancestors in Europe. Later generations would speak often and deeply about land rights: their 'right to fish' and their 'right to hunt' – post-moratoria public discourse is filled with such language, without any recognition that it appropriates indigeneity.

The practice of living off the land without altering it – harvesting rather than farming – shaped Newfoundlanders' relationship to the land, thus showing that, as Julia Roberts demonstrates in her chapter, appropriation of indigeneity is not the complete story but certainly part of it. In other words, Newfoundlanders adapted to and adopted indigenous land-use patterns as well as cultural outlooks and approaches. This is illustrated by the lyrics of the still popular anthem, written when Newfoundland was a self-governing Dominion within the British Empire, like Canada and the other 'white' dominions. The country's anthem is a celebration of the natural environment: 'When sunrays crown thy pine-clad hills and summer spreads her hand / When silvern voices tune thy rills / We love thee smiling land ... / When blinding storm gusts fret thy shore / And wild waves lash thy strand / Thro' sprindrift swirl and tempest roar / We love thee, wind-swept land.'

Newfoundland Food as Symbolic and Political

Farming could not save early settlers in what is known as 'the hungry month of March.' But wild food could. It was, in fact, a marine resource in the form of seal that allowed the early settlers on the island's northeast coast to survive winters that were much longer than those they knew back in Europe. (It is disconcerting to imagine the early settlers' quite valid fears when spring failed to appear when they expected it.) But arriving on the ice floes in late March and April, seal, so central to indigenous diets, provided life-giving vitamins and protein. We will never know how many people would have died if it were not for the availability of nutrient-dense seal meat.[16]

Today, in the face of international condemnation and sometimes virulent opposition from well-organized activists, such as Greenpeace and Paul McCartney, many Newfoundlanders, along with their government, remain steadfastly loyal to the seal hunt, just as Albertans cling to their pride in ranching culture. A small but increasing number of Newfoundlanders are publicly against the seal hunt but none of them has the stature or symbolism of k.d. lang, an Albertan who squared off against the ranching community, as is discussed by Valerie Korinek in her chapter in this volume. If such a person emerged, it is quite possible that he or she would be personally vilified, at least by some. The loyalty to the seal hunt is not necessarily logical; like ranching, the seal hunt involves dangerous work, and it is long associated with fatalities.[17] Moreover, the industry is now an economically marginal one, with only several hundred (ageing) men taking part. The highly symbolic western Canadian family farm of which Korinek writes is also endangered. In spite of its probable disappearance, for many – but not all – Newfoundlanders, the seal hunt is culturally important and worth preserving. This loyalty is one manifestation of Newfoundlanders' relationship with the sea and its food resources, rooted in the ethno-genesis of settler society.[18] Thus, in a play on the activists' placards, popular buttons read 'Save a Newfoundlander; eat a seal,' and a t-shirt proclaims 'I ♥ seals.' Simply put, there might not be a Newfoundland society without seals and the hunt, as many Newfoundlanders recognize and assert.

One of the most beloved of Newfoundland food traditions is the 'boil-up'; it, too, is a clear expression of Newfoundlanders' relationship to the land. The boil-up is a break from work in the woods or at sea, involving freshly brewed tea, sometimes stirred with a pine branch, and Newfoundland food such as salt fish or capelin (small fish, the arrival of which heralds the summer season). As most Newfoundlanders will assert, a boil-up is not a picnic with checkered cloth, wicker baskets, and specialty foods or wine. A boil-up is not a leisurely pastime of the affluent classes. During a boil-up, people sit on the ground or on boughs gathered from the woods as they rest from berry picking or setting rabbit snares; they eat food carried in their bread box or grub bag.[19] A boil-up is a reassertion of Newfoundlanders' relationship to the land, a way of claiming a sort of ownership of the land and an intimacy with it. There is an element of class loyalty in the continuing attachment to the boil-up; as O'Brien explains, the boil-up is an assertion and validation of rural culture.[20] This is particularly true at present when rural culture is under threat because of the ongoing ground-fish moratoria; the political aspect of boil-ups is emphasized in a popular poster that defiantly proclaims 'There's nothing like a cup of tea in the woods.' With its communal nature – boil-ups occur in family or community groups – the practice affirms and reinforces Newfoundland's cultural identity. The parallels to Western culture as depicted by Valerie Korinek in her chapter are clear; the affirmation of beef consumption, and the valorization of family values and the virile cowboy, reinforce Albertan identity. These practices and values are held so dear that to publicly criticize them, as singer k.d. lang did, results in personal vilification rather than debate and discussion of the health and environmental problems inherent in eating meat. As with rodeos and ranches in western Canada, Newfoundland's boil-up ritual may be romanticized – particularly for Newfoundlanders who have moved off the island[21] – but, like other foodways, it is certainly enduring.[22]

In some ways, then, the boil-up is akin to indigenous commensality practices such as the Labrador Metis tradition of gathering on the beach and sharing the first salmon of the season among all community members.[23] Group identity is reinforced here, as wild food becomes a symbol. Neither the boil-up nor the sharing of the salmon are a celebration of human alteration of the land, as happens with agriculture and Thanksgiving. Rather, both are celebrations of the land itself and the life-sustaining food it offers.

The emphasis on the land- and sea-based economy changed rapidly with the Second World War and the introduction of large-scale wage labour, replacing the barter or 'truck' economy. And it had always been different in St John's, Harbour Grace, and other urban centres where conventional commerce thrived and from where Newfoundland seafood products were exported to southern

Europe, the Caribbean, and South America. In these cities and towns there would have been elaborate rituals – colonialist enterprises – similar to the 'snipe dinner' that Julia Roberts describes in her chapter. Like the snipe dinner, these would have had encoded in them unmistakable messages about hierarchy, exclusion, and inclusion. But the sumptuous eight-course meals enjoyed by the hated merchants of Newfoundland history do not loom large in the collective psyche. It is as if they are deliberately pushed to the side and the table spread with roast caribou, salt fish, and fresh berries.

Through the capitalist era, then, and in a rapidly urbanizing context, vestiges of subsistence food acquisition have survived. This includes roadside gardening on the Great Northern Peninsula and widely practised autumnal moose hunting. Commensality practices in Newfoundland reflected hunting, fishing, and gathering traditions, many rooted in age-old indigenous practices. Highly symbolic and even politicized in some cases, Newfoundland foodways have proven remarkably tenacious.[24]

ACKNOWLEDGMENT

Thanks to Marg Ewtushik for research assistance and to Paul Butler for his copyediting services.

NOTES

1 Later waves of migration, beginning in the 1800s, included but were not limited to Russian and Eastern European Jews, Chinese men (as in Canada, Chinese women were not permitted to immigrate), German artisans, and Norwegian whalers. More recent (twentieth and twenty-first centuries) immigrants include African, Middle Eastern, and South American refugees, especially Sudanese, Palestinian, and Colombian people. Newfoundland gained representative government in 1833, responsible government in 1855, and confederated with Canada in 1949.

2 P.J. Gray, 'Traditional Newfoundland Foodways: Origins, Adaptation and Change,' MA thesis, Memorial University of Newfoundland, 1977.

3 Sean Cadigan, *Hope and Deception in Conception Bay: Merchant-Settler Relations in Newfoundland, 1785–1855* (Toronto: University of Toronto Press, 1995).

4 P.A.N. Gard, 'Health: Nutrition,' in Joseph R. Smallwood, ed., *Encyclopedia of Newfoundland and Labrador* (St John's: Newfoundland Book Publishers, 1984), vol. 2, 880–5; P.J. Gray, 'Foodways,' in *Newfoundland Traditions* (St John's: Department of Folklore, Memorial University of Newfoundland, ca. 1976), 27. See also various entries in Maura Hanrahan and Marg Ewtushik, *A Veritable Scoff:*

Sources on Foodways and Nutrition in Newfoundland and Labrador (St John's: Flanker Press, 2001).

5 *Newfoundland Royal Commission Report*. Newfoundland Royal Commission, 1933.

6 The colonists also had to surrender livestock to the pirate Peter Easton for protection.

7 This would change to a degree with the technological and transportation innovations that came much later.

8 Gray, 'Foodways,' 27.

9 A.P. Dyke, 'Subsistence Production in the Household Economy of Rural Newfoundland,' in M.L. Skolnik, ed., *Viewpoints on Communities in Crisis,* 26–60 (St John's: Institute of Social and Economic Research, Memorial University of Newfoundland, 1968).

10 R.R. Andersen, J.K. Crellin, and B. O'Dwyer, *Healthways: Newfoundland Elders: Their Lifestyles and Values* (St John's: Creative Publishers, 1998); J.K. Crellin, *Home Medicine: The Newfoundland Experience* (Montreal and Kingston: McGill-Queen's University Press, 1994); L.F. Felt and P.R. Sinclair, eds., *Living on the Edge: The Great Northern Peninsula of Newfoundland* (St John's: Institute of Social and Economic Research, Memorial University of Newfoundland, 1995).

11 John T. Omohundro, 'Living off the Land,' in L.F. Felt and P.R. Sinclair, eds., *Living on the Edge: The Great Northern Peninsula of Newfoundland* (St John's: Institute of Social and Economic Research, Memorial University of Newfoundland, 1995), 103–27.

12 M. Fleming, 'Roadside Gardening on the Great Northern Peninsula,' *Newfoundland Farm Forum* 3/8 (1981): 1.

13 Omohundro, 'Living off the Land.'

14 F. Fraser, M. Frecker, and P. W. Alderdice, 'Seasonal Variation of Neural Tube Defects in Newfoundland and Elsewhere,' *Teratology* (1986): 31; G. Johnson, 'Nutritional Deficiency Diseases in Newfoundland and Labrador: Their Recognition and Elimination,' unpublished paper, n.d. (ca. 1980); D. Steven and G. Wald, 'Vitamin A Deficiency; A Field Study in Newfoundland and Labrador,' *Journal of Nutrition* 21 (1941): 461; W.R. Aykroyd, 'Beriberi and Other Food-Deficiency Diseases in Newfoundland and Labrador,' *Journal of Hygiene* 30 (1930): 357–86; W.R. Aykroyd, 'Vitamin A Deficiency in Newfoundland,' *Irish Journal of Medical Sciences* 28 (1928): 161–5; V.B. Appleton, 'Observations of Deficiency Diseases in Labrador,' *American Journal of Public Health* 11 (1921): 617–21; J.M. Little, 'Beriberi Caused by White Flour,' *Journal of the American Medical Association* 58 (1912): 2029–30.

15 In the case of the small Beothuck group, the incursion was such that they lost access to the natural marine resources on which they depended; this, coupled

with disease and several violent incidents, would result in their tragic demise as a people. (There is, however, Beothuck 'blood' in some Mi'kmaq and European Newfoundlanders.)

16 Ryan Shannon, *The Ice Hunters: A History of Newfoundland Sealing to 1914* (St John's: Breakwater Books, 1994).

17 The worst of these occurred in 1914 when 77 men were trapped on the ice for two days and nights and perished; that same year the S.S. *Southern Cross* sank with the loss of over 200 sealers.

18 Shannon, *Ice Hunters.*

19 A.M. Tizzard, *On Sloping Ground: Reminiscences of Outport Life in Notre Dame Bay, Newfoundland* (St John's: Breakwater Books, 1984).

20 Andrea O'Brien, '"There's Nothing like a Cup of Tea in the Woods": Continuity, Community and Cultural Validations in Rural Newfoundland Boil-ups,' *Ethnologies* 21/1 (1999): 65–83.

21 James Overton, 'Coming Home: Nostalgia and Tourism in Newfoundland,' *Acadiensis* 14/1 (1984): 84–97.

22 O.H. Anderson, 'Boiled Dinner still Preferred,' *Canadian Hospital* 39/2 (1962): 61.

23 Maura Hanrahan, 'Industrialization and the Politicization of Health in Labrador Metis Society,' *Canadian Journal of Native Studies* 20/2 (2002): 231–50; Maura Hanrahan, 'Salmon at the Centre: Ritual, Identity and the Negotiation of Life Space in Labrador Metis Society,' in Darrin McGrath, ed., *From Red Ochre to Black Gold* (St John's: Flanker Press, 2001), 146–65.

24 Omnifacts Research, 'Report on the Consumption of Fish Products in Newfoundland' (St John's: Fishing Industry Advisory Board, 1978); Anderson, 'Boiled Dinner still Preferred,' 61. See also various entries in Hanrahan and Ewtushik, *A Veritable Scoff.*

5 Stocking the Root Cellar: Foodscapes in the Peace River Region

MEGAN J. DAVIES

A pioneer settler from Lakeview, British Columbia, Frances Nicolson has memories of the cool family cellar as a vast seasonal larder. Bins of potatoes and carrots were layered with sand for freshness, 'carefully placed eggs' set in crocks, and pans of milk placed in a dairy cupboard and rotated for maximum cream and butter production.[1] Frank Palsson, in Progress, an early Peace River settler locale, remembers sealers filled with wild strawberries, saskatoons, currents, and raspberries, and canned moose meat, fresh butter in big tubs, and mutton and pork hanging in the smokehouse.[2] Alice Summers recalls that her mother Emily Tompkins, living in the tiny community of Halfway, canned berries, rhubarb, and vegetables in the summer so the family could have fruit and vegetables year-round.[3] The settler strategy of gathering indigenous food items and cultivating culturally familiar plants and livestock was typical of food in the Peace River during the period of Euro-Canadian family settlement, from the 1910s through the 1940s.

These industrious narratives speak to the theme of plenty, with virtually all food either foraged or grown locally in the limited cash economy of British Columbia's Peace River region during the early twentieth century. 'I can never remember being hungry, or very cold. Wild meat and fruit was plentiful and Mom always canned, dried or cured an abundance of it for winter, with garden fruit and vegetables,' recalled Blanche Dopp Hipkiss about homesteading in Taylor Flats (then Bear Flats) in 1917.[4] The McRanns kept beehives as well as a general vegetable garden, chickens, and milk cows at their Landry homestead, and they made their own cheese and pork sausage.[5] Soldier-settler S.H. Tuck of Pouce Coupe reported growing a forty-four-pound Copenhagen market cabbage in 1923.[6] Fred and Marian Thompson moved up to Sunset Prairie from the Fraser Valley in 1930, 'believing they could handle the Depression better on a "pioneer" basis.' Although rabbits decimated their gardening efforts for the first three years, they were eventually able to cultivate 'winter-keeping' vegetables and such exotic fare as tomatoes, citron, marrow, and asparagus.[7]

The communities of Lakeview, Progress, Halfway, Taylor Flats, and Sunset Prairie are located in the Peace River lowlands, an area that transverses the northern boundaries of the provinces of Alberta and British Columbia and includes some twelve million hectares on the B.C. side. Wide plateaus of parkland and boreal shrub forest are bisected by the river known locally as 'The Peace.'[8] Treaty Number 8, signed in 1899 between representatives of the Canadian government and the Dene Tha' First Nation peoples, was a first step towards Euro-Canadian settlement.[9] The transfer of some 500,000 acres to British Columbia from the federal government of Canada, the introduction of new strains of hardy, early maturing wheat, and the promotion of the area as 'one of the world's great wheat and mixed farming reserves' and a place where agricultural development was 'making a prosperous country out of the wilderness' helped attract a sizeable influx of Euro-Canadian settlers into the region in the interwar period.[10] Between 1921 and 1931, the area's population increased from 2,144 to 7,013, and by the time the railway reached Dawson Creek in 1930, aspiring Peace River farmers included those leaving behind Depression drought and abandoned prairie homesteads.[11] Despite efforts by the provincial state, the Red Cross, the philanthropic Rockefeller Foundation, and the British Fellowship of the Maple Leaf to bolster Euro-Canadian agricultural settlement in the region, the area remained economically marginal and isolated until construction of the Alaska Highway began in 1941.[12]

This chapter explores the foodways of Euro-Canadians in British Columbia's Peace River area during the 1910–1940 settlement era as a slice of a larger history of regional health and healing in the Peace.[13] Here, I focus on the production rather than the consumption of food and, drawing on a combination of local histories, memoirs, and oral history interviews, I organize my discussion around the topics of gardening and gathering.[14] Since my sources were generally crafted from the memory boxes of successful settlers and their descendants, the theme of hunger, although not absent, is a minor note. Other scholars have observed how memories of food tend to emphasize the social relations around food and foodways,[15] but in my research I also located consistent themes of abundance, food work, and fostering food security.

In this case study, I apply critical insights regarding food security, food and identity, and food as a means of creating body-place-memory in a new location to my research on Peace River settlers.[16] Dr James Cull, director of the Peace River Health Unit in the 1930s, saw the use of the 'food of the area' as part of what distinguished the rural people of the Peace from their urban cousins.[17] Indeed, settlers lived almost exclusively on the mythical 100 mile diet, the focus of much interest today; they simply had no money to purchase goods beyond basic necessities.[18] Far from the prosperous and productive wheat farms envisioned by staff at the Beaverlodge Dominion Experimental Station, over the border in Alberta, Peace River homesteaders ran subsistence enterprises that look a lot like the homesteads of Ruth Sandwell's late nineteenth-century Saltspring Island pioneers.[19] A study of settler food and foodways in the Peace underscores the importance of local variables, self-sufficiency, and the productive labour of women and children, encouraging us to use the lens of food security to revision historical understandings of the family farm as a dynamic, male-dominated unit of economic production.[20] As in the analyses presented by Julia Roberts, Alison Norman, and Maura Hanrahan in this volume, food also functioned as a series of intersections between the individual, the family, and the community. Assistance from First Nations peoples of the region, and a strong ethos of helping those in need of food, particularly new arrivals, were in essence an ongoing reworking of entitlement relations. And as food scholars note, the exchange of food represents an important social connection in many cultures, so it is reasonable to assume this process was meaningful for both Aboriginal and Euro-Canadian participants.[21] As my data make clear, there were generational and collective patterns to food production.

This was a borderlands phase of food production and gathering, characterized by indigenous-settler exchanges of goods and knowledge and the cultivation of imported species alongside the harvesting of local plants and animals. Although frontier circumstances gave a measure of fluidity to male and female roles, settler tasks around the production of food were, nevertheless, highly gendered. Frontier women of the Peace were intimately connected with the work of creating and maintaining healthy settler bodies: food production was thus part of 'motherwork' which included everything from community midwifery to jam making.[22] Men hunted wild game, caught fish, and raised livestock – key sources of protein – and their periodic and seasonal waged labour allowed for the purchase·of staples like flour and rarer commodities like apples, oranges, and coffee. In both cases, gendered food work served practical purposes, but also it fostered social relations and frontier identities. 'Feeding her children was always Mother's first concern,' is the description of North Rolla settler Amelia Dahlen's life priorities.[23] Food production was part of the identity of women like Dahlen as hardworking and capable frontier women and served as a basis of female authority and power.[24] For men, hunting and farming were food-related tasks that operated alongside land ownership, an ability to support dependants, and house building to create a 'male' meaning of the relentless hard work of homesteading on the frontier.[25] In broader terms, this process likely paralleled what Alison Norman found in her chapter in this volume about food consumption in nineteenth-century Ontario, where the adoption of a 'Canadian' diet that incorporated both Aboriginal and non-Aboriginal foods informed the formation of a 'Canadian' identity.

Food fostered links between actual places, settler and Aboriginal bodies, and social relations. Food sites like berry patches, gardens, and fishing holes met the nutritional needs of settler bodies and were part of the process of creating a mental map of the complex possibilities of a new place. District nurses like Nancy Dunn of Sunset Prairie taught 'nutrition' through the Women's Institutes (rural women's organizations), but oral and local histories demonstrate that many settlers already had a good empirical understanding of diet that incorporated both local produce and culturally familiar foods to produce a balanced diet throughout the year. Rain, sun, snow, planting, and harvest served to demarcate seasonality and construct settler time and settler food tasks.[26] Food production and procurement were framed in the context of the 'everyday' and 'the local' and shaped by availability. 'It is rather amusing,' missionary Monica Storrs wrote in a May 1930 diary entry, just at the moment of the year when fresh fruits and vegetables were virtually unattainable, 'how the staple diet runs strictly according to natural home-grown supply.'[27]

Growing

Primary food production, along with the construction of house and barn, required the imposition of Euro-Canadian agrarian forms on the Peace River landscape. This daily food work of settlers, tending gardens, poultry, and livestock, needs to be appreciated as part of a collective project of crafting 'home' through the recreation of familiar foodways and informal community patterns of sharing food with those who did without. As others have noted, understandings of cultural power relations and gendered identities, such as I found in the creation of Euro-Canadian foodways in the Peace, require an appreciation for material conditions, everyday 'life-world' experiences, and the ways in which the body serves as a canvas for the creation of civic society.[28]

Creating a vegetable garden was one of the important tasks facing the newly arrived settlers. People who arrived after planting time faced a hard winter and early spring, often relying on the kindness of new neighbours to see them through. Ella Paradowski, who settled in Sweetwater in 1932, recalled, 'One of the major projects was to prepare the land for a garden. We grew a grand garden.'[29] When Agnes Rosenau (née Kerr) planted the rhubarb roots she had brought from Scotland to the family homestead at Progress, she was investing in an insurance policy against scurvy and recreating Old World foodways in a new home space.[30] These were large endeavours, and some families created plots in several different locations. The Hendricks family of Pouce Coupe had two garden plots – one by the house, another one quarter of a mile away by the river.[31] A half-mile up the Clearwater River, the elderly Tom Starnes had a garden of about five acres that produced food for his son and family of four and enough to give away as well.[32]

Although entire families laboured to establish gardens, and likely worked together each year adding horse manure or using bush fires to delay winter frosts, tending the plot over the growing season was clearly designated women's work in the settler family.[33] Women did the planting, hoeing, pulling of weeds, and harvesting of vegetables, work that could be done with young children in tow or folded into other chores due to the relative proximity to the family house.[34] It is likely that children also worked pulling garden weeds. Although some gardens were physically located a distance from the family home, this duality of female and child activity served to link the two spaces together.

Plants and produce from the Edinger family garden demonstrate that food-ways through the Peace involved the establishment of Euro-Canadian food systems through a complex series of community diffusions. Sent 'tame fruit' plants from friends in their previous home of Trail, BC, the Edingers shared Old World agricultural produce like rhubarb, raspberries, strawberries, and horseradish among Peace River neighbours in need; they also dispensed horti-cultural knowledge and actual plants of these species by clippings and division throughout the region.[35] Food worked as a form of social exchange within the settler community: one neighbour might supply another with beef and receive help building a structure or fencing in return.[36]

Settlers worked to establish a herd of livestock and a stock of poultry stand-ard to the Euro-Canadian farm – not an easy task when cows failed to survive the winter and crafty weasels depleted the precious supply of hens and chicks.[37] The cows, chickens, and pigs that Henry and Mary Studley brought with them when they came to Sweetwater, in 1930, formed the basis of their farm stock and meant that the family had a supply of meat, eggs, and diary products.[38] In the Barrington household, a steer was butchered each November and a pig in the spring, ensuring a steady supply of meat.[39] Here, again, we see cooperative community patterns that reworked entitlement relations to ensure access to food. The Dahlen family history, for example, reported that neighbours in the North Rolla area shared milk and eggs during the scarce winter months when livestock production was limited.[40] Other families traded or bartered eggs and butter, reflecting research done on women and dairying in other parts of rural Canada.[41] The Church of England Harvest Thanksgiving services described by missionary Monica Storrs – although inaccessible to many because of physical or denominational distance – were nevertheless public, ritualized expressions of the season's Old World bounty, with sheaves or wheat nailed to the lectern, enormous cabbages and loaves of bread on the alter, and an impressive rendering of the harvest hymn, 'We Plough the Fields and Scatter.' Following the festivities, the produce was shared with Providence Hospital in Fort St John and the Red Cross, for distribution to families in need.[42]

Although comparatively minor markings on the larger landscape of the Peace, settlers' homes, barns and outbuildings, livestock, gardens, and fields also served to recreate the landscape as Euro-Canadian. The visual and cultural order imposed on the Peace River landscape by the Hutton-Potts family farm is evident through the descriptions of a red barn, white fences, a root cellar, and an English garden complete with flowers, a rockery, a sundial, and a badminton court.[43] Other Canadian historians have addressed the way in which the New World landscape was revisioned to offer Old World vistas, but the example of Peace River gardens demonstrates a very practical, pragmatic application of this process.[44]

Gathering

Deeply connected to place in spatial and material terms, foraging and hunting put settlers beyond the realm of the farm and into the wider forum of natural regional foodways, locating, remembering, and sharing information about specific sites where hunting, fishing, or berry picking brought reliable returns year after year. I see Euro-Canadians adopting perspectives and using space and place for food production in a fashion that mirrors that of Aboriginal peoples: land was both a vital source of resources necessary for survival and a site of individual and social identities.[45] Early settlers saw landscape as 'foodscape' – as full of food potential as a well-stocked autumnal root cellar. Hunting and berry picking, both often undertaken as collective tasks, served valued social functions and helped construct settler identities.

Like many others in the Peace during the 1930s, hunting and foraging for food gave the Stevenson family food security in an era when 'money was scarce, and jobs non-existent.'[46] Similar data collected by Meg Luxton in Flin Flon, Manitoba, demonstrate that fishing and hunting and gathering edible wild plants were food security strategies practised during lean times by a generation of Depression-era Canadians.[47] Moreover, the linkage between settlers and First Nations was more than just a common ecology: there are many indications in local histories that early settlers learned about gathering food from indigenous residents.[48] Exploration of settler foraging and hunting in the Peace thus sets into relief an aspect of Aboriginal–Euro-Canadian contact which was a critical element of food security for early settlers – a theme that also emerges in Maura Hanrahan's chapter on the foodways of early Newfoundland settlers, who relied on the skills and practices of the Mi'kmaq and Beothuk.

Foraging began with the space right outside the back door. At Cecil Lake, scurvy was avoided by the first spring greens – lamb's quarters or 'pigweed' as it was known locally – which grew copiously on the farmyard manure pile.[49] Alice McArthur, an English immigrant, found that dandelions, another exotic plant introduced to the Canadian West by settlers, made good greens and used them to help construct an adequate family diet after a lean first spring.[50]

But the larger sphere of foraging was in the vast thickets of saskatoon berries, cranberry bushes, and strawberry plants that could be found across the Peace. Wild berries thrive in open spaces, shrub lands, and disturbed habitats, and it is likely that prime locations, picking times, drying methods, and use were identified for the first settlers by First Nations peoples.[51] Ethno-botanists emphasize the widespread importance of berries, especially saskatoons, as sweeteners and trading items among Native peoples, noting as well the socio-cultural aspects of intertribal berry gathering at key picking sites.[52] Like Aboriginals, some Euro-Canadian settlers made significant seasonal journeys to obtain berries for eating and keeping. Saskatoon Island, a First Nations berry-picking site just over the Alberta border, was recalled as the site of a two-day campout and berry-picking excursion.[53] Taylor Flats, on the north side of the Peace River, had been swept by fire – perhaps intentionally set – several times before the arrival of Europeans, and offered a profusion of wild strawberries, raspberries, saskatoons, and cranberries.[54]

These were tasks delegated by gender and age. Following established Aboriginal foraging patterns and those found elsewhere in Canada among Euro-Canadians, berry picking was a job done by women and children, who gathered wild strawberries, raspberries, saskatoons, blueberries, and cranberries.[55] Indeed, the Peace River family biographies, generally written by the children of settlers, convey a similar delight in the novelty and sociability in these excursions, as Neil Sutherland found in his historical study of childhood in Canada.[56] Settler offspring have strong memories of summers spent in search of wild fruit: the activity is presented as a yearly adventure and chance to visit with other women and children. 'We picked berries,' recalled Pearl Fellers (née Kezer), whose family came to Progress in 1930, 'often camping out for days, miles from home, to pick, and my mother canning the large boxes of them when we returned.'[57] Frances Nicolson (née Golata) remembered day-long expeditions, 'Because we usually went with friends, they were social outings, and I never fully realized that they were necessities of life rather than pleasures.'[58]

Hunting was primarily male work, although there are many stories of women and children shooting prairie chickens and snaring rabbits. Fathers and sons or male neighbours and friends would regularly go out together to hunt moose and deer. The front page of the 13 October 1938 *Peace River Block News* reported the death of Rolla resident Ole Moland on a hunting trip down the Pine River to the Peace. Moland, reaching over to swat a fly, accidently discharged a rifle. The bullet passed through his abdomen and then hit hunting companion Walter Lee in the chest.[59] Bear, valued by some for grease that could be rendered and used in cookies and piecrust, were rarer than deer or moose.[60] The Tompkins family of Halfway ate fish from the river as well.[61]

Bagging game was not a sport, but a necessity, particularly in the early years of Euro-Canadian settlement. An inability to hunt was a liability in places where game was a critical part of the settlers' diet.[62] A lack of hunting skill severely limited the diets of some newcomers. When the Haddows arrived in Sunrise Valley in 1929, they reported, 'There were lots of evidence lying around of moose and deer but none of us know much about hunting, therefore we were confined to a diet of beans, rice and raisons.'[63] The first Euro-Canadian settlers on the Pouce Coupe Prairie learned where to locate wild game and when to kill it from First Nations peoples who had used the area as a summer camping ground.[64] At Cecil Lake, Aboriginal hunters brought fresh moose meat to trade for flour or tobacco.[65] Hunting was hard work, especially in the winter when it involved traversing miles of snow-filled landscapes on snowshoes, on skis, or on foot.[66] The cost of ammunition was another factor to be calculated. Shells cost about 15 cents each in the Peace during the 1930s.[67]

Technically, provincial regulations restricted Euro-Canadian settlers to a limited period of hunting in the fall, but Peace River settlers found ways to circumnavigate this obstacle. Moose meat shot out of season could be quickly canned before the local game inspector was aware of a breech in hunting codes.[68] Seth Gunter of Tupper Lake got a trap line to ensure year-long access to wild game. Clarence Tibbetts and his neighbours at Carpio took a more straightforward approach, explaining to the police that there were real short-ages of food in the locality, and reaching a suitable agreement: they could hunt as long as there was no waste.[69] Game, especially a large killing like a moose, was routinely shared by local hunters, along with seeds, clothing, and baking.[70] The Gunters of Peavine Lake always shared wild meat with neighbours who either did not have a gun or did not know how to use one.[71]

Conclusion

Lidia Marte describes foodways as 'choreographies of the daily survival of fam-ilies and individuals,' processes that link home, family, and region, and reach back to memories of food gathered, prepared, and consumed in places far distant in time and space from the present.[72] Peace River settlers performed a similar sequence of everyday steps, temporal and imagined, combining the new with the familiar, nurturing settler bodies, and crafting memories that linked body, people, and place. Food was intensely local, grown in gardens, raised in the barnyard or pasture, foraged from the thickets, or hunted in the boreal forest. Embedded in the social relations of the region, and strongly linked to the formation of individual and collective identity, food was shared through knowledge, through the activities of procuring food, and through actual seeds, clippings, game, and produce. The hybridity of creating settler food security in this early period suggests a model of conceptualizing settler foodways – systems that persisted in remote regions with limited cash economies well into the twentieth century.

The Peace served as a hybrid 'foodscape' in multiple ways – as a site of food security through a complex mediation of place, task, season, and civic responsibility, as a meaningful aspect of Aboriginal and non-Native contact, and as a canvas for the (re)creation of Euro-Canadian frontier identities and the Euro-Canadian home spaces. In the post–Second World War era access to a cash economy, non-local food, grocery stores, and freezers reshaped foodways in the Peace River region and across rural Canada. Historians can make evocative contributions to current discussions of foodways and food security by emphasizing foraging and hunting – aspects ignored by many food theorists – and by exploring the subsequent processes that disconnected rural people from the 'foodscapes' that once bound together place, community, and body.

ACKNOWLEDGMENT

I would like to thank the Wellcome Trust for funding this research, and also Gerry Clare of the Dawson Creek Archives, Donna Redpath of the Fort St John Museum and Archives, and staff at the B.C. Archives and the Rockefeller Archives Center for their assistance.

NOTES

1 L. York, ed., *Lure of the South Peace: Tales of the Early Pioneers to 1945* (Fort St John and Dawson Creek, B.C.: South Peace Historical Book Committee, 1981), 923–4. Nicolson settler biography. Root vegetables including potatoes, carrots, turnips, beets, cabbage, and onions were placed in dug cellars where a lack of cribbing created a cool, damp place ideal for storage.
2 York, *Lure of the South Peace*, 595–8. Palsson settler biography.
3 Field notes; interview with Alice Summer, 26 July 2005, Hudson's Hope, B.C.

Like other interviewees, Alice noted that her mother was the person in the household who was in charge of the family diet.

4 C. Ventress, M. Davies, and E. Kyllo, compilers, *The Peacemakers of North Peace* (n.p., 1973), 52–5. Dopp settler biography.

5 York, *Lure of the South Peace*, 412–14. McRann settler biography.

6 Report of Dominion Government Experimental Sub-Station, Beaverlodge, Alberta, 1928.

7 York, *Lure of the South Peace*, 768–70. Thompson settler biography. Muriel Claxton made this point as well, noting that settlers realized that they were better off in the Peace than in cities. Muriel Claxton, 'Pioneering in the Peace,' *Public Health Nursing Bulletin* 2/1 (1933): 7–9.

8 B. McGillivray, *Geography of British Columbia: People and Landscapes in Transition* (Vancouver: UBC Press, 2000), 7.

9 The original Aboriginal population of the area was Dene Tha', but by the twentieth century, Cree, Saulteaux, and Metis peoples had migrated into the Moberly Lake region. McGillivray, *Geography of British Columbia*, 66–79. It is important to note that non-Native settlement in Canada inevitably involves the displacement of Aboriginal peoples from lands that had served as cultural foodways.

10 F.H. Kitto, *The Peace River Country Canada: Its Resources and Opportunities* (Ottawa: National Development Bureau, 1930), 7, 26. There is no sustained scholarly history of the region, but for works contemporary to the period, see Kitto, *Peace River Country*; C.A. Dawson and R.W. Murchie, *The Settlement of the Peace River Country: A Study of a Pioneer Region* (Toronto: Macmillan, 1934); and 'The Peace River Country, Canada,' in W.A. Mackintosh, *Prairie Settlement: The Geographical Setting* (Toronto: Macmillan, 1934), 151–71. Jonathan Swainger's important work on crime and community in the Peace includes his 'Police Culture in British Columbia and "Ordinary Duty" in the Peace River Country, 1910–1950,' in J. Swainger and C. Backhouse, eds., *People and Place: Historical Influences on Legal Culture* (Vancouver: UBC Press, 2003), 198–223, and 'Creating the Peace: Crime and Community Identity in North-eastern British Columbia, 1930–1950,' in L.A. Knafla, ed., *Violent Crime in North America* (Westport, CT: Praeger, 2003), 131–54.

11 McGillivray, *Geography of British Columbia*, 7.

12 Ken Coates and W.R. Morrison, *The Alaska Highway in World War II: The U.S. Army of Occupation in Canada's Northwest* (Toronto: University of Toronto Press, 1992). The work of the Fellowship of the Maple Leaf in the Peace River is detailed in two volumes of missionary Monica Starr's diaries: W.L. Morton and Vera K. Fast, eds., *God's Galloping Girl: The Peace River Diaries of Monica Storrs, 1929–1931* (Vancouver: UBC Press, 1979), and Vera K. Fast, ed., *Companions of the Peace: Diaries and Letters of Monica Storrs, 1931–1939* (Toronto: Univer-

sity of Toronto Press, 1999). I consider the Peace in the context of other interwar public health initiatives in British Columbia in Megan J. Davies, 'Competent Professionals and Modern Methods: State Medicine in British Columbia during the 1930s,' *Bulletin of the History of Medicine* 76/1 (2002): 56–83. On the controversial educational reforms in the region, see Alan H. Child, 'A Little Tempest: Public Reaction to the Formation of a Large Educational Unit in the Peace River District of British Columbia,' *BC Studies* 16 (Winter 1972): 57–70.

13 On women and informal settler health care, see my 'Mother's Medicine: Women, Home and Health in the Peace River Region of British Columbia, Canada, 1920–1940,' in J.T.H. Connor and Stephan Curtis, eds., *Medicine in the Remote and Rural North, 1800–2000* (London: Pickering and Chatto, 2011), 199–214.

14 A series of published primary settler accounts gathered in the 1970s and 1980s are my main source for this chapter, although food also came up in oral histories about health and healing, undertaken in 2002 and 2005.

15 D. Lupton, 'Food, Memory and Meaning: The Symbolic and Social Nature of Food Events,' *Sociological Review* 42/4 (1994): 664–85.

16 Historical studies of food benefit from an interdisciplinary approach; for example, the food-mapping notion of body-place-memory serves to convey the manner in which food of the Peace fostered links between actual places, settler bodies, and social relations. I adapt this conceptualization from Lidia Marte, 'Foodmaps: Tracing Boundaries of "Home" through Food Relations,' *Food and Foodways* 15 (2007): 261–89.

17 Sleepy Hollow, New York State, Rockefeller Archives Center, RG 5 IHB/D, Series 3, Sub-Series 427J, Box 175, Folder 2171, J.S. Cull, 19 Jan. 1937, 'Second Annual Report of the Peace River Health Unit.'

18 Alisa Smith and J.B. MacKinnon, *The 100-Mile Diet: A Year of Local Eating* (Toronto: Random House, 2007); Barbara Kingsolver, *Animal, Vegetable, Miracle: A Year of Food Life* (New York: Harper Collins, 2007); and Colin Beavan, No Impact Man blog at http://noimpactman.typepad.com/.

19 R.W. Sandwell, *Contesting Rural Space: Land Policy and Practices of Resettlement on Saltspring Island, 1859–1891* (Montreal and Kingston: McGill-Queen's University Press, 2005). David Wood's important study of farm settlement in the boreal forest makes a similar point. J. David Wood, *Places of Last Resort: The Expansion of the Farm Frontier into the Boreal Forest in Canada, c.1910–1940* (Montreal and Kingston: McGill-Queen's University Press, 2006).

20 This suggests ways in which the historical study of food could allow Canadian historians to expand upon Marjorie Cohen's important work on women and dairying in her *Women's Work, Markets, and Economic Development in Nineteenth-Century Ontario* (Toronto: University of Toronto Press, 1988).

21 Carole M. Counihan and Steven L. Kaplan, eds., *Food and Gender: Identity and Power* (Amsterdam: Harwood Academic, 1998), 3.

22 The phrase 'motherwork' is from Harriet Rosenberg's, 'The Home Is the Workplace: Hazards, Stress and Pollutions in the Household,' in S. Arat-Koc, M. Luxton, and H. Rosenberg, eds., *Through the Kitchen Window: The Politics of Home and Family* (Toronto: Garamond, 1990), 57–80. It refers to the caregiving activities of women in the home and in the community, and includes a culturally organized set of tasks relating to children and other dependent family members. See also M. Luxton, *More Than a Labour of Love: Three Generations of Women's Work in the Home* (Toronto: Women's Press, 1980).

23 York, *Lure of the South Peace*, 457.

24 Historians of women in rural western Canada spotlight the connection between work and female identity. See Veronica Strong-Boag, 'Pulling in Double Harness or Hauling a Double Load: Women, Work and Feminism on the Canadian Prairie,' in R. Douglas Francis and Howard Palmer, eds., *The Prairie West: Historical Readings* (Edmonton: Pica Pica Press, 1992), 401–23; Christine Georgina Bye, '"I Like to Hoe My Own Row": A Saskatchewan Farm Woman's Notions about Work and Womanhood,' *Frontiers* 26/3 (2005):135–67; Catherine A. Cavanaugh, '"No Place for a Woman": Engendering Western Canadian Settlement,' in *The Prairie West as Promised Land* (Calgary: University of Calgary, 2007), 261–90.

25 Cecilia Danysk, 'A Bachelor's Paradise,' in Catherine Cavanaugh and Jeremy Mouat, eds., *Making Western Canada: Essays on European Colonization and Settlement* (Toronto: Garamond, 1996), 154–85; George Colpitts, *Game in the Garden: A Human History of Wildlife in Western Canada to 1940* (Vancouver: UBC Press, 2002), chapter 3; Wood, *Places of Last Resort*, 27–9.

26 I am working here with ideas about historical time and seasonality. E.P. Thompson, in *Customs in Common: Studies in Traditional Popular Culture* (New York: New Press, 1993), 357–8; L. Gofton, 'Food Fears and Time Famines: Social Aspects of Choosing and Using Food,' *British Nutrition Foundation Bulletin* 15: 79–95, cited in David Bell and Gill Valentine, *Consuming Geographies: We Are Where We Eat* (New York: Routledge, 1997), 3–5; Judith Fingard, 'The Winter's Tale: The Seasonal Contours of Pre-Industrial Poverty in British North America, 1815–1860,' *Historical Papers* 9/1 (1974): 65–94.

27 Morton and Fast, *God's Galloping Girl*, 105.

28 It is worth contextualizing this in a broader picture, however, for 'home space' food production and entitlement relations also served to redefine rural British Columbia as Euro-Canadian. The important work on gender, race, and 'white' British Columbia is Adele Perry, *On the Edge of Empire: Gender, Race and the Making of British Columbia, 1849–1871* (Toronto: University of Toronto Press,

2001). See the editors' introduction to K. Pickles and M. Rutherdale, eds., *Contact Zones: Aboriginal and Settler Women in Canada's Colonial Past* (Vancouver: UBC Press, 2005), 1–14; K. Elswood-Holland, '"We Used to Scrump the Apples, We Used to Have Our Knickers Full of 'Em," Growing up in the Countryside: Forging Feminities in Rural Somerset c. 1950–1970,' in J. Little and C. Morris, eds., *Critical Studies in Rural Gender Issues* (Aldershot: Ashgate, 2005), 123–40. For specific analysis of colonialism and the body, see M. Jolly, 'Colonizing Women: The Maternal Body and the Empire,' in S. Gunew and A. Yeatman, eds., *Feminism and the Politics of Difference* (St Leonard's, Australia: Allen and Unwin, 1993), 103–27.

29 York, *Lure of the South Peace*, 865–6. Paradsowki settler biography.

30 Ibid., 193–4. Rosenau settler biography.

31 Ibid., 712–15. Hendricks settler biography.

32 Ventress et al., *Peacemakers of North Peace*, 22–7. Starnes settler biography.

33 York, *Lure of the South Peace*, 736–8. Magusin settler biography. Ibid., 905–6. Morin settler biography.

34 This list of garden chores comes from Edwina Morin's settler biography. Ibid., 905–6.

35 Ibid., 684–6. Edinger settler biography.

36 Ibid., 412–14. McRann settler biography.

37 Ventress et al., *Peacemakers of North Peace*, 19. Herald settler biography.

38 York, *Lure of the South Peace*, 765–6. Studley settler biography.

39 Field notes: interview with Winnie Williams, 27 July 2005, Sunset Prairie, B.C. Winnie recalled that the pig was butchered and then salted and buried in an oat bin for storage.

40 York, *Lure of the South Peace*, 457. Dahlen settler biography.

41 Cohen, *Women's Work*. Sandwell also notes the role of women raising hens and chickens on Saltspring Island, in *Contesting Rural Space*, 132.

42 Morton and Fast, *God's Galloping Girl*, 270–1.

43 Rolla History Book Committee, compilers, *'Rolla Remembers,' 1912–1952* (Edmonton: Art Design Printing, 1991), 143–4. Hutton-Potts settler biography.

44 For example, Colin M. Coates, 'Like "The Thames towards Putney": The Appropriation of Landscape in Lower Canada,' *Canadian Historical Review* 74/3 (1993): 317–43.

45 For an exploration of this understanding of land from an Aboriginal perspective, see Kathleen Wilson, 'Therapeutic Landscapes and First Nations Peoples: An Exploration of Culture, Health and Place,' *Health and Place* 9 (2003): 83–93.

46 York, *Lure of the South Peace*, 831–3. Stevenson settler biography.

47 Luxton, *More than a Labour of Love*, 122–4.

48 For example, a section in *Lure of the South Peace* contains settler memories of
watching Beaver (Dene) catch fish and eels, 115–16.

49 Field notes: collective interview with Jean Mensink and Dorthea Smith, 30 July
2002, Cecil Lake, B.C. The consumption of pigweed was recalled with some
humour. Pigweed, or lamb's quarters, although not native to northern British
Columbia, grows in cultivated land. Its leaves can be eaten raw or boiled. Andy
MacKinnon, Jim Pojar, Ray Coupé, eds., *Plants of Northern British Columbia*
(Vancouver: Lone Pine, 1999), 199. Turner notes that pigweed was boiled and
eaten as greens by other southern Aboriginal peoples of the province. Nancy J.
Turner, *Food Plants of Interior First Peoples* (Victoria: Royal B.C. Museum Hand-
book, 1997), 173.

50 York, *Lure of the South Peace*, 897–8. McArthur settler biography.

51 Descriptions of these berries and their growing areas can be found in MacKinnon et al., *Plants of Northern British Columbia*. Late nineteenth-century mission
records and the 1879–80 Dominion Geological Survey note Beaver, Cree, and
Metis berry picking in the Alberta and B.C. Peace River regions.

52 Turner, *Food Plants of Interior First Peoples*, 20–4, 124, 139–41, 143–4.

53 York, *Lure of the South Peace*, 665–7. Browncombe settler biography.

54 The environmental history of Taylor Flats is sketched out in Ventress et al., *Peacemakers of North Peace*, 34. Although it is not noted, First Nations peoples have
traditionally managed fire to create cultivation spaces and may have done so at
Taylor Flats.

55 Turner emphasizes the role of First Nations women in berry picking in *Food
Plants of Interior First Peoples*, 22–6. Luxton found an historical pattern of berry
picking by women and children in Flin Flon, a practice dating back to the Depres-
sion years when the town was founded. *More Than a Labour of Love*, 122–4. Neil
Sutherland, *Growing Up: Childhood in English Canada from the Great War to the
Age of Television* (Toronto: University of Toronto Press, 1997), 153–5.

56 Sutherland, ibid.

57 York, *Lure of the South Peace*, 721–3. Kezer settler biography.

58 Ibid., 923–4. Golata settler biography.

59 *Peace River Block News*, 13 Oct. 1938, 1.

60 Field notes: Toulie Hamilton, 26 July 2005, Hudson's Hope, B.C. Phyllis Higens
described her husband Ike as an 'ardent hunter' who 'nearly always got his moose
and deer.' But he apparently only got one bear over his hunting career. York, *Lure
of the South Peace*, 347–50. Higens settler biography.

61 Field notes: interview with Alice Summer, 26 July 2005, Hudson's Hope, B.C.

62 York, *Lure of the South Peace*, 702–4. Haight settler biography. The beans, rice,
and raisins were likely provisions brought by the family for survival purposes

when they migrated into the region. Colpitts stresses the importance of wild meat in the Western diet into the late nineteenth century. The case of the Peace River suggests that this pattern persisted in more marginal regions well into the twentieth century. Colpitts, *Game in the Garden*, 75–8.

63 York, *Lure of the South Peace*, 528–32. 'Sunrise Valley History.'

64 This is noted in the Starnes settler biography. Ventress et al., *Peacemakers of North Peace*, 22–7.

65 Ibid., 368.

66 York, *Lure of the South Peace*, 698–700. Gunter settler biography.

67 Ibid., 831–3. Stevenson settler biography.

68 This specific illustration comes from the Dahlen settler biography, but this was a relatively common occurrence. Ibid., 456–62. Dahlen settler biography.

69 Ibid., 699–700. Gunter settler biography. Ibid., 771–3. Tibbetts settler biography.

70 Ibid., 503–5. McGilivary settler biography. Ibid., 572–5. Wendt settler biography.

71 Ibid., 698–700. Gunter settler biography.

72 Marte, 'Foodmaps,' 263.

6 Rational Meals for the Traditional Family: Nutrition in Quebec School Manuals, 1900–1960

CAROLINE DURAND

'A healthy diet,' wrote the authors of *Vitalité*, a French-language Quebec educational guide published during the Second World War to advise teachers in their classroom lessons on nutrition and diet, 'makes for harmoniously developed bodies that are vigorous, strong, straight and fairly tall, faces that are welcoming, alert and lively, and eyes that are clear, bright and interested in life; lips are florid and break into easy smiles revealing teeth that are in good condition and perfectly regular; hair is soft, supple and shiny.' In addition to these highly desirable physical benefits, the writers also asserted, flowed yet more beneficial consequences, among them that 'concentration is easily maintained' and 'helpfulness and camaraderie promote good relations between youth and their parents or teachers,' leading ultimately to the production of children who not only 'perform better in school' but become 'masters of the world, the future is theirs!' Penned by Father Albert Tessier, a cleric and educator, and Thérèse Marion, the first dietician hired by the City of Montreal's Board of Health in 1942, this excerpt alone from their school text clearly shows what religious and government authorities in Quebec hoped to achieve by teaching cooking and nutrition in the schools: the creation of superior individuals who would be productive, competitive, and highly accomplished.[1]

This chapter examines a range of school texts on cooking, nutrition, diet, and home economics published by the Quebec government's education department and used in francophone Catholic schools between 1900 and 1960, with the aim of unearthing the values imbedded in their arguments and explanations. It explores how such values related to the ideals and campaigns espoused by the advocates of traditional French Canadian nationalism, which was heavily shaped by the Roman Catholic clergy, as well as by the proponents of economic liberalism. The essay demonstrates how the scientific and rational knowledge available on diet was used to support a conservative and nationalistic conception of the family and French Canadian womanhood while simultaneously promoting a representation of the individual that was rational and tailored to the requirements of a liberal capitalist system.

The focus is on the prescriptions, arguments, and advice contained in the aforementioned writings. Research conducted thus far reveals little about how people negotiated this discourse; nevertheless, it is clear that these prescriptions were legitimized through the authority of the well-placed people and institutions that produced and disseminated them. In short, science, religion, and the state lent them considerable credibility, as did claims to francophone cultural survival within a primarily anglophone Canada. This did not mean that everyone gave up their tastes and habits to follow these recommendations, or that they ignored competing messages, such as those conveyed in advertisements that stressed the sheer pleasure of eating rich foods like ice cream or told women to save time and trouble by using convenience foods, such as tinned pie fillings and jams, to feed their family.[2] Still, these educational texts, with their promotion of both French Canadian nationalism and economic liberalism, constituted a reference point against which individuals, especially women, could judge and legitimize their own or other people's practices, or, alternatively, develop a sense of guilt and inadequacy in relation to the normalized ideal, that is, the ideal portrait that was presented to them as normal and within everyone's reach.[3]

In considering the links between nutritional education, nationalism, and the promotion of a liberal capitalist ideology, my study of the Quebec school system both parallels what earlier Anglo-Canadian historians have revealed about the ideological content of the domestic science curriculum in English-speaking Canada and brings to light some key differences. As for similarities, the home economics programs that arose in English Canada during the period 1890s–1930s, and studied by historians such as Barbara Riley and Terry Crowley, similarly constituted a conservative reaction against the supposedly dangerous influences of industrialization and urbanization. These courses, too, were designed to keep young women at home (and away from the modern factory) and as tools for modernizing (and elevating) domestic work.[4] In addition, the historical scholarship on educating women for motherhood in the early twentieth century, produced by scholars such as Katherine Arnup and Cynthia Comacchio, shows that in English Canada, too, scientific or medical discourses on motherhood contributed to a social regulatory agenda aimed at reforming mothers in ways that both reflected and benefited nationalist and pro-capitalist goals. The ideological application of nutritional instruction in English Canada continued into the post-1945 era highlighted here, including, as Franca Iacovetta documents, in the food campaigns meant to transform immigrant women into ideal gendered citizens.[5] But there are also significant differences in the history of nutritional and home economics education in Franco-Catholic Quebec and Anglo-Protestant Canada that must be remembered. One is that the very long and close collaboration that existed in Quebec between the Catholic Church and the provincial government over educational matters is unique in Canada's history. A second is that the minority situation faced by francophones in Quebec, who felt disadvantaged and marginalized even in their own province, fuelled French Canadian nationalism. That is, it was matters of cultural survival and not, as some English-speaking Canadians have dismissively or incorrectly assumed, a state of 'cultural backwardness,' that helps explain the appeal of this nationalist ideology. In turn, the twin forces of cultural nationalism and Catholicism made francophone school texts appear far more traditional in content than their English Canadian counterparts. This conservatism is evident, for instance, in the many references to the superiority of a rural way of life and in the assumption that every Quebec girl will become a mother and homemaker rather than a professional or wage-earning cook, dietician, or cafeteria manager.[6] More detailed or refined comparisons with anglophone Canada will require further research on Quebec's nutritional history, although Quebec-based research should not be valued solely in these terms. Indeed, my chapter makes a valuable contribution to Quebec historiography by shedding new light on the cultural, social, and ideological aspects of women's educational history in the province, a scarcely explored topic since the 1980s.[7] The first section provides some necessary historical context for the primary sources under review, the texts selected for analysis being typical of the manuals produced and used in twentieth-century Quebec schools before the 1960s. The second section highlights how the discourses on cooking, diet, and nutrition were infused by French Canadian nationalism, while the final section probes the scientific and rational aspects of these prescriptions and how they also supported an ideology of economic liberalism.

Sources and Context

Originating with the Quebec government and with Roman Catholic religious orders such as the Sisters of Charity of Montreal (also known as the Grey Nuns) and the Congregation of Notre-Dame,[8] these educational texts were intended for young girls attending public primary school or older girls attending domestic science schools. Equally noteworthy is that these mainly twentieth-century manuals were published in an era before the 1960s, when the Quebec government funded education in its province (education being a provincial responsibility in Canada) but delegated almost all of its powers in this arena to one

Catholic and one Protestant confessional committee. The Roman Catholic Church, whose high-ranking fathers, including the archbishop, sat on the confessional committees, shaped and approved all of the manuals used in the Catholic schools in Quebec. The Catholic clergy also made up most of the writers of the teaching materials for Catholic schools as well as the teachers and administrators. The omnipresence of the Catholic Church in the Quebec school system helps to explain some of the distinguishing features of the nutritional and domestic science texts, including, perhaps, why several authors invoke divine motives when promoting their vision of the ideal French Catholic woman and of the machinelike French Canadian body. During the period of their existence, from 1882 to the end of the 1960s, the main objective of Quebec's domestic science schools was to reproduce, mainly through the training of successive generations of girls and young women, the Catholic, rural, and patriarchal family considered to be the fundamental core of the French Canadian nation.[9] The tremendous growth that these organizations experienced reflected the fervour of their promoters. In 1938, there were sixteen schools training 230 students; by 1959, more than 7,000 female students were enrolled in 204 schools.[10] In addition, beginning in 1923, home economics was also officially included in the Catholic primary school curriculum. Falling under the responsibility of the Department of Agriculture, the course was welcomed by educational authorities as a means of encouraging more young people, particularly those from rural backgrounds, to remain at home through depictions of domestic life in highly attractive, even romantic, terms. By creating the conditions that made it conducive for more youth to freely choose to stay in their rural town or village rather than venturing into the big cities of Quebec, English-speaking Canada, or the United States, where 'Anglo' and 'modern' cultures of secularism and consumerism prevailed, these courses, it was hoped, could help protect successive generations of francophone families from exposure to what Catholic leaders considered modern influences dangerous to French Canadian survival.[11]

Nor were the domestic science schools the only institutions outside of the regular public school system that taught young francophone women about cooking and feeding families in ways that bolstered the French Canadian nation. The Department of Agriculture sought to reach women through public talks on nutrition, cooking, and the benefits of respecting French Canadian traditions, and through the *Cercles des fermières* (rural women's circles that operated much like the Women's Institutes in rural anglophone Canada) that upheld traditional ways. In addition, the *Fédération nationale Saint-Jean-Baptiste*, the leading women's nationalist and philanthropic organization in Quebec that also lobbied on behalf of women's rights, gave cooking demonstrations and evening nutrition courses in various Montreal parishes.[12] Since the women speakers and teachers who participated in these various activities themselves may well have studied at one of the province's domestic science schools, they were communicating a state-sanctioned body of knowledge to broader audiences. The manuals on home economics and cooking undoubtedly exerted some influence outside of these venues as well, as copies made their way into certain social agencies and even private home, although it remains difficult to determine how widely they were distributed and used. And, of course, the extent to which girls and women were exposed to this literature varied considerably depending on their origins (including rural or urban) and the length and type of studies they pursued.

We should note, too, that boys and young men could also come under the purview of experts, or at least dispensers, of diet and nutritional advice. In school, boys might receive nutritional advice from physical education teachers, for example, who discussed the relationship between a good diet and physical health and sports performance.[13] School medical examinations and milk distribution offered opportunities for speaking to all children about nutrition. In addition, Canada's Food Rules were intended for the entire population. By contrast, however, the target audience of the francophone school publications under scrutiny was primarily female. Like the Canadian nutritional experts who surveyed Aboriginal populations (the subject of Walters' chapter in this volume) and the social work staff who hoped to modernize immigrant women's food customs even as they celebrated ethnic foods (a theme in Iacovetta's chapter), Quebec educational authorities targeted women precisely because they saw mothers as the key to producing healthy children and proper families.

Indeed, it bears repeating that while the focus here is on Quebec, many of the observations made regarding domestic science training and ideals of health and motherhood were not specific to francophone Catholic Quebec. Rather, the discourse observed was part of a vast body of literature whose content crossed ethnic, linguistic, and religious lines. The English Canadian studies already cited and other chapters in this volume make this abundantly clear. For example, the stereotype of the mother as guardian of religious and cultural traditions who sacrifices herself for her family was familiar not only to Catholics but, as Andrea Eidinger and Marlene Epp respectively show, to Jewish and Mennonite women as well. And Anglo-Celtic and Protestant women, too, were subject to the same exhortation. Moreover, the education of mothers into proper citizens aware of their duties to family and nation sometimes transcended provincial jurisdiction, as when the federal government initiated or supported campaigns meant to improve or 'uplift' national health and mothering standards.[14]

It is equally important to recognize that nutritional science did not simply operate in a vacuum. As Ian Mosby's chapter in this volume shows, a seemingly neutral tool like Canada's Food Rules serves national political and economic objectives. Similarly, in her analysis of nutritionists and Aboriginals, Walters demonstrates how the federal government's definition of the behaviours of certain poor and marginalized groups as pathological helped to justify its arguments about placing them under the increasing control of federal authorities. In the Quebec case, the distinguishing feature of all of its educational programs was the considerable degree to which they were informed by the tenets of traditional French Canadian nationalism, with its emphasis on respect for patriarchal families, Catholicism, and other conservative values. This nationalist ideology permeated the education of girls and boys until the Quiet Revolution of the 1960s, which witnessed the end of clerical control over provincially funded education.[15]

French Canadian Nationalism and Traditionalism

It is not surprising that cooking and home economics courses were in tune with the values and aims of French Canadian nationalism. After all, the Quebec Department of Agriculture, which assumed some responsibility for teaching home economics, made clear that its central objective in implementing such a program was to counter the undesirable impact of industrialization and urbanization by keeping French girls in the countryside. In short, it sought to 'ruralize' home economics. Beginning in the early twentieth century, it tried to stem the exodus to Quebec and American cities by convincing girls that the occupation of rural homemaker was a noble and sacred calling and by instructing them in their duty as 'Christian mothers, worthy of bearing the glorious title of farmer's wife [*cultivatrice*].' This is the argument contained in *La Bonne Ménagère*, for example, which told girls not to 'run after the unknown' and 'abandon the fields of their childhood for the foul air of cities.'[16]

The same objectives underlay the home economics curriculum that was established and revised, sometimes significantly, in numerous schools across the province between the 1910s and the 1940s. Indeed, the conservative and nationalist agenda informing the program was explicitly invoked by several of its prominent promoters, including Reverend Adélard Dugré who, in 1916, wrote that such an education would keep rural Quebec populated by patriarchal families.[17] Similarly, at the second provincial conference on home economics, held in 1934, Superintendent of Public Instruction Cyrille Delâge and Alphonse Désilets, an agronomist with the Department of Agriculture, both claimed that home economics courses would safeguard French Canadian domestic virtues, values, and traditions against modernism and Americanism.[18] These educational leaders, along with the nuns and others who taught the curriculum on the front lines of the classroom, all expected that properly educated girls would become the prolific and devoted Catholic French Canadian mothers that the nation needed in order to flourish.

Thus, the laid-out lesson plans for the teaching of cooking classes were designed to promote the farm and countryside and its rural traditions. In their manuals, some authors provided a comparison of the budgets of rural and urban households and claimed that food produced and consumed in the countryside was fresher and less expensive.[19] Others invoked romantic or nostalgic images of farm life in earlier generations and harkened back to the nation's glorious past in an effort to inspire women readers to remain in their rural homeland: 'All the energy of our race, our ancestral traditions, all the glorious past of our forebears resonate within these walls!' declared a home economics text published in 1929 by the Congregation of Notre-Dame.[20] In similar vein, the woman author of the 1926 *Manuel de la cuisinière économe et pratique* evoked the 'virtues of frugality that made for the gaiety and robust health of our ancestors.'[21] In manuals produced during and after the Second World War, nationalist goals also affected the discourse on domestic appliances and cooking utensils. Whereas elsewhere in Canada, the latest stoves were being touted as instruments of modernity,[22] in Quebec domestic science manuals written by female religious, old wood stoves and even 'antique hearths' were presented as superior to 'banal' modern stoves at least until the middle of the twentieth century.[23] In the 1950s, a series of manuals that featured a young woman named Louise and her elders, with titles like *Louise et sa maman* and *Louise et ses éducatrices*, adopted a similar position in favour of a superior and curative countryside. Louise's grandparents are farmers who have lived for years in a house that was more than a century old and they possess a bread oven. Her grandmother prefers her old cast iron stove to a modern one because the foods simmer longer and thus taste better, and because it is equipped with a practical food warmer.[24] When Louise gets sick, she visits her aunt and grandmother at the family farmhouse to recover her health and learn new culinary skills.[25] When the young Louise engages in domestic duties, she is complimented by the men in her family. Having observed Louise cleaning, her grandfather pronounces that she 'had what it took to keep house' while her uncle Pierre revels in her homemade molasses cupcakes.[26] Throughout the series, the Quebec farmer is depicted as a man to conquer and please, and his praise constitutes an official stamp of approval.

The province's teaching nuns used the cooking classes as an opportunity to inculcate into the girls qualities considered essentially feminine and necessary to the making of a successful wife and mother, such as devotion, sacrifice, flexibility, decisiveness, and simplicity.[27] Ideal Christian wives, they taught, neglected themselves in order to better serve others and, moreover, did so effortlessly because their actions were motivated by genuine love. Such devotion to loved ones, they added, was not only necessary to familial happiness, but also an essential part of feminine nature. As one text declared, 'women must sacrifice – this is one element of their happiness.'[28] It was equally important, the nuns instructed their students, for the model homemaker to be even-tempered, eager to please, charitable, prudent, gentle, compassionate, lenient, and patient. Indeed, she was elevated to saint or martyr status in manuals that explained how she had to demonstrate 'quasi-divine Christian strength' and 'heroic abnegation' in the face of troubles and disappointments. To this long list of virtues was added modesty.[29]

Domestic science classes taught that cooking was essential to the strength and vigour of the French Canadian nation. Like campaigns elsewhere that drew a link between food customs and nation building, much moral and ideological weight was attached to a seemingly instrumentalist function like cooking and feeding a family. Authors hammered home the message to young women that their husbands' and children's work productivity, educational success, good humour, and genuine happiness all depended on their cooking. Health guaranteed national vigour. As one author put it, 'wives and mothers, the responsibility for building robust health, the foundation of a robust nation, is yours. Your husbands and children need abundant nourishment.'[30] During the Second World War, preserving health became even more important to the achievement of patriotic and nationalistic objectives, with the authors of *Vitalité* calling it 'a strict obligation binding every individual to God and Nation!'[31] Despite its feminine aura, cooking was also intended to serve more masculine ambitions. Women had to feed their men so as to develop their muscles, minds, and endurance and thereby enable them to become the 'robust citizens that Church and Nation are demanding for the difficult work ahead.'[32]

A woman's ability to serve good meals was considered essential to ensuring marital happiness, or at least peaceful coexistence, both concepts being defined along patriarchal lines, namely, the principle of satisfying the husband. 'By suggesting ways of avoiding common errors and of binding their future husband to the home,' affirmed the teacher Amélie DesRoches in 1912, 'I am giving [women], if not the recipe for perfect happiness, at least the solution to many difficulties.'[33] In the manuals written by DesRoches and her male and female colleagues, good cooking was, indeed, held up as an antidote to many dangers and social ills. By keeping men at home, a woman's strong culinary skills kept husbands away from the bar and thus prevented alcoholism among workers, and had the added benefit of improving their productivity. It also protected couples and families from entering into public social places considered unwholesome, such as restaurants, where, according to Reverend Charles A. Lamarche, the wife would 'simper, sometimes smoke, and make eyes at the customers.'[34] Good cooking was even attributed with the power to counter the rural exodus to the city. Reverend Lamarche made this and other arguments at a 1926 congress on the teaching of domestic science, saying that through their influence over their husbands' and children's bodies, health, and mood, women had influence over society. 'Holding the frying pan is holding the sceptre of the world,' he declared.[35]

Such pleas grew more passionate by the end of the 1950s as the Quiet Revolution dawned and social change began calling traditional ideologies into question. In response, the clerical and other advocates of traditional French Canadian nationalism made a final push to keep women in the kitchen by depicting their role as natural and providential. A sense of urgency already is evident in the texts published in the late 1950s, such as the 1957 edition of *La cuisine raisonnée*. All possible arguments were raised to convince women to remain in the kitchen and thus the moral centre of her traditional family and culture. Writers appealed to women readers to follow their heart, or alternatively, their mind. They cautioned against any concession to dangerous influences and emphasized the need for determined efforts to act as the family's moral centre. Through such devotion to loved ones, these manuals stressed, women would also be exerting a positive and moral influence on their society, economy, and country. In support of a nationalist agenda informed by culturally conservative values, these authors heralded the value of the latest developments in modern domestic science. Hence, they glorified the 'intellectual joys' that resulted from being able to apply the principles of anatomy, physics, chemistry, and hygiene to meal preparation. They stressed the aesthetic pleasures that came from cooking fine meals as well as the pragmatic benefits accrued from educated mothers who feed families well while also saving money. Above all, writers stressed the sacred aspect of women's domestic and moral mission.[36]

Reason, the Science of Nutrition, and Economic Liberalism

Significantly, however, the motherhood discourse that appealed to religious and nationalistic sentiments with increasing frequency by the end of the 1950s was not the only discourse evident in these francophone school texts. The domestic science manuals invoked reason as a basis for educated motherhood and promoted the value of scientific and 'balanced' cooking. These scientific concepts were introduced gradually into these publications, their incorporation being made in fairly close succession to the advancements made in nutrition.

A comparison of domestic science manuals published in the early and later part of the twentieth century well illustrates the growing application of scientific approaches. In the early 1900s, the advice given reflected the government's ideas about the eating habits of farm families and relied on an almost folksy approach. For example, *La bonne ménagère*, a manual produced by the Department of Agriculture advised that women serve so-called ordinary dishes such as pea soup, lard; ham, vegetables, and eggs that would 'sustain farmers in their gruelling labour' and allow them to recover their strength. Meals also had to be of good quality and served promptly, so that workers did not wait.[37] To be sure, certain standards were applied; for example, the food had to be appetizing, nourishing, varied, well prepared, and economical. But that was largely the extent of the book's rational and scientific arguments. The recipes it contained differed in form and level of detail from those appearing in later publications. Rather than giving instructions in a 'scientific' manner that spelled out the two main parts or stages (a list of the ingredients to assemble and then a detailed description of the procedure to be followed), *La bonne ménagère* offered its instructions using a customary language and commonsensical style. Hence, the directions for roux (a thickener for sauces that combines flour and butter) read: 'To make a roux any housewife must know she must start out by browning some butter, then adding a little flour cut with enough water to obtain the desired amount of sauce. Everything is allowed to boil quite awhile with or without meat.'[38] Similarly, further on in the book, it is explained that the cabbage soup was to be cooked 'slowly' and salt added 'appropriately.'[39] In issuing such directions, Department of Agriculture staff was clearly relying on personal experience, some trial and error, and a strong dollop of common sense.

By contrast, in manuals produced only a few years later, the promotion of specific foods, such as milk, meat, eggs, fruit, and vegetables, necessitated explanations as to their nutritional value. For example, in 1922, *La cuisine à l'école primaire* mentioned the importance of 'active principles,'[40] likely a reference to the recently discovered vitamins contained in various foods.[41] This new knowledge was quickly incorporated into the manuals. Beginning in 1927, the *Manuel de diététique à l'usage des écoles ménagères des Soeurs grises de Montréal* included a table that displayed the vitamin A, B, and C content of foods.[42] As knowledge about nutrients grew, calories, vitamins, minerals, fats, sugars, and proteins become a familiar feature of the content of school manuals. By the end of the period under review, some cooking manuals devoted long sections to these components. In the 1957 edition of *La cuisine raisonnée*, the nutrition section ran to almost sixty pages and included numerous tables on vitamins and other nutrients, menus applying nutritional principles, and examples of servings containing 100 calories. That same year, the Department of Public Instruction developed a nutrition-based dietary program for the family institutes.[43]

The 'rational' approach increasingly adopted in domestic science teaching materials also appeared in graphic and iconographic from. In addition to the illustrations of food items, dishes, and meals, food was frequently displayed in a form more conducive to laboratory analysis than culinary use. Cooking and domestic teaching books, for instance, often featured images of test tubes filled to varying degrees that were meant to represent the precisely measured nutrient quotient of specific foods such as milk, meat, or eggs.[44] Presumably, the use of test tubes added scientific authenticity to the manuals and their advice. Even the human body became subjected to such schematic and scientific representations. *La cuisine raisonnée*, for example, presented a 1957 rendition of the human body that, far from appearing lifelike, was divided into its various elements (ten gallons of water, twenty-four pounds of carbon, one-quarter of an ounce of iron), with each of the ingredients pictured being mixed in a giant test tube.[45] The second image clearly suggests that humans were neither biological nor organic but rather chemical.

Indeed, the authors who penned some of the later manuals often used a language informed by chemistry or medicine. The kitchen was transformed from being a room in the house into 'the laboratory of family health,'[46] while preparing healthy meals was elevated into practising the principles of 'preventive medicine.'[47] In a manual written in the late 1940s, Sister Marie de Sainte-Thérèse de Jésus affirmed that 'Good food is scientific – it does not consist of a series of rules and "old wives" recipes.'[48] Recipes became 'culinary techniques' referred to as 'standard formulas' or 'standard preparations' and were sometimes presented in table format.[49] In the family institutes' 1957 food program, the term 'recipe' was not used, the Department preferring the term 'culinary preparation.'[50]

In addition to being depicted as a complex chemical compound, the body in these school texts was viewed as an economy, with foods meeting physiological needs in the same way that markets met consumer needs, and with the calories ingested having to 'balance' like money in a budget. In this fiscal conception of the body,[51] calories were income, physiological needs were expenses, and fat was a necessary saving (although potentially dangerous when too abundant). As early as 1917, Dr Charles-Narcisse Valin described food as 'any substance able to repair the losses suffered by our tissues and provide, through combustion, the energy needed to maintain normal warmth.'[52] He placed great importance on balancing the body's energy expenditure and food intake, with the latter having to be tailored to a person's work, age, and gender and to the local climatic conditions. Reaching and maintaining an ideal weight signalled that equilibrium had been reached, which was represented by the image of a scale.[53]

The converse was also presented. References to calories were generally accompanied by warnings and threats that poor consumption habits would produce illnesses such as weight loss, obesity, and weakness as well as diabetes and kidney problems. In these texts, health involved the scientific process of achieving a perfect balance between calories ingested and energy expended.[54] In the later publications, and in the literature that was more specifically geared to older students, the evaluations based on calories and the calculation of needs became more complex. The 1957 edition of *La cuisine raisonnée* devoted an entire chapter to evaluating individual food requirements; it featured combustion scales by level of expenditure and practical applications based on the work performed by an individual of average size.[55]

At the heart of this scientific argumentation was the premise that man was like a machine, a comparison that appeared frequently in the literature examined. Although not the only image employed,[56] it almost always accompanied any discussion of concepts related to rationality and equilibrium. Already in 1917, the machine-as-body imagery was reflected in the lexicon being used by experts like Dr Valin as he urged readers to eat rationally, with words such as 'usure' (wear and tear), 'combustible' (fuel), 'charbon' (coal), 'machine,' 'rénovation' (renewal), 'entretien' (maintenance), 'rendement' (performance), 'production,' 'épargne' (savings), and 'travail' (work).[57] In the 1920s, Mrs Alphonse Désilets[58] and the Grey Nuns[59] also started comparing the body to a machine. And in the 1940s, Reverend Tessier and co-writer Marion accompanied their version of this metaphor with an illustration of the heart rendered as part of the gears in a factory: this machinery is also carefully fuelled and lubricated with proper foods, represented as an oil container.[60] They, too, referred to order, rigour, precision, production, the expertise of the staff maintaining this machine, and the expenses involved in repairing breakdowns. During the same period, Sister Marie de Sainte-Thérèse de Jésus similarly noted that keeping the 'human machine' healthy enabled people to reach 'the highest levels in their professions, in business, or in school.'[61] These commentators saw success and upward mobility as being directly related to nutrition.

The pervasiveness of this metaphor of human body as machine, which went hand in hand with the rational vision of cooking inspired by nutritional knowledge, served cultural and ideological goals. It helped promote the concept of the body as an instrument of production that every individual had the power to improve or even perfect to obtain maximum performance. It was through rational and reasonable choices that everyone could achieve this ideal. Furthermore, an individual's relationship to his or her body was not only rationalized by science, but was compared to, and integrated into, the liberal industrial and capitalist economic model. This conception of the body assumed that individuals took responsibility for their health, which was a daily priority, and that their food choices were always rational. It neglected the importance of factors such as social and economic status, working conditions, and environment, just as it overestimated the role of health arguments in food choices.[62]

In all of the sources cited, which together offer a representative sample of the francophone nutritional and home economics texts used in Quebec schools in the era before the Quiet Revolution, options were proposed as if every housewife could choose freely between them. Aside from a few references to budgetary concerns or seasonal constraints, people's ability or willingness to follow the advice provided was never questioned in the school manuals. Even when people's incomes were low, it sufficed, the authors suggest, to know how to purchase, preserve, and cook food and to educate one's tastes to appreciate appropriate food items and resist unhealthy gluttony. Certainly, some authors did recognize that malnutrition could be associated with poverty and that more underprivileged people might well be less receptive to their advice. But it did not change the central message communicated in the schools, namely, that through rational and scientific cooking, prepared by a self-sacrificing but well-informed Christian homemaker deeply devoted to her family, everyone could have a healthy and productive body that allowed participation in the real or promised economic prosperity of the era.

Conclusion

In a 1960 text, Sister Sainte-Thérèse-de-la-Foi accurately summarized the spirit of the school manuals on cooking and diet, with its mix of homemaker ideology, religious vocation, and nutritional science, when she wrote:

> It is up to every individual to form or reform his or her eating habits [...] The woman of the house, who is responsible for preparing menus and for the family's health, must strive to acquire solid knowledge of nutrition and culinary arts. This means that guests will find the menu contains the elements needed for a balanced diet as well as a sufficient variety of foods to satisfy their appetite. Did not God in his wisdom create appetite and taste to facilitate the duty of eating reasonably?[63]

As this excerpt suggests, Quebec's educators regarded nutrition as a scientific and rational science but valued it ultimately for its capacity to serve what they invoked as divine purposes to thus allow individuals to draw the maximum benefit from the body God had given them. In 1929, the nuns of the Congregation of Notre-Dame affirmed this position, writing: 'This human machine is admirably well constructed since it is directed by an intelligent motor [...]

acting on a marvellous instinct and following a personal, independent government that only God the Creator could achieve.'[64] Reverend Tessier joined this chorus of voices, declaring that 'the body' was 'the dwelling of the spirit' that 'is freely provided by the Creator,' and instructing his readers: 'We must take great care of it, treat it with respect, maintain it well, and use common sense in nourishing it.'[65] As these quotations illustrate, nutrition was to be placed in the service of Creation, but also of the nation and its prosperity. The ultimate goal of nutritional advice offered in these Quebec domestic science manuals was to develop 'human capital' in the service of God, the nation, and the economy. A good Christian was a rational individual who made moral choices that corresponded to the good decisions made in a market economy. Gluttony, originally a capital sin, became an infraction to food rules denoting a lack of self-control that was as damaging to a person's spirit as it was to health.

In Quebec, the Catholic Church required science to be subordinate to religion; scientific disciplines were not to question religious doctrines and the established social order. Nutrition was taught not to help women cook less or to convince men that they, too, could contribute to family meals, thereby allowing married women to spend more time outside the home. On the contrary, in pre-1960s Quebec, nutrition was used as an argument to convince girls and young women that their role as mother, wife, and homemaker was not only gratifying, but also providential and necessary to the survival of the Catholic and patriarchal family considered the backbone of the French Canadian nation. It was against a backdrop of social conservatism that these traditional and clerical-nationalist objectives were able to benefit from more modern and liberal scientific concepts without contradicting them.

At the same time, however, these prescriptions on diet and nutrition and the portrait of the ideal woman they promoted suited not only the traditional French Canadian nationalists but the liberals and capitalists as well and in equal measure. Despite the differences existing between these ideological groupings, they could all agree with the hierarchy of values expressed, as well as the dominance of traditional representations of the family and gender roles. Thus, a consensus was possible. Modern aspects of nutrition such as rationality, science, and economy were promoted but they served a higher objective, namely, reproduction of the traditional French Canadian Catholic family. This family's existence was based on having a mother in the home who was a good Christian woman devoted to her husband and children. For it was the men and children who represented the future of the nation; they were essential to its productivity and prosperity, and thus were required to have healthy, well-nourished bodies. Certainly, daily life did not correspond to this ideal everywhere in Quebec. It was not until the 1960s and 1970s, however, that changes in educational materials began to appear.[66] Even since the Quiet Revolution, however, men and women have not always had the same role in the kitchen, and individuals have been encouraged by health experts to use their reason to control the machine that is their body. This is the lesson that children to this day are taught in Quebec schools.

NOTES

1 Albert Tessier and Thérèse Marion, *Vitalité* (Province of Quebec: Department of Public Instruction, Department of Social Welfare and of Youth, n.d. [between 1941 and 1944]), 16. All translations are my own.

2 The examples are from the magazine *La Revue moderne*, ad for Joubert ice cream, Dec. 1931, 39, and for Meadow Sweet pie filling, Dec. 1928, 44.

3 Other postwar Canadian studies that use this concept include Mary Louise Adams, *The Trouble with Normal: Postwar Youth and the Making of Canadian Heterosexuality* (Toronto: University of Toronto Press, 1997); Mona Gleason, *Normalizing the Ideal: Psychology, Schooling, and the Family in Postwar Canada* (Toronto: University of Toronto Press, 1999); Krista Walters' chapter in this volume.

4 Barbara Riley, 'Six Saucepans to One: Domestic Science vs. The Home in British Columbia,' in Barbara K. Latham and Roberta J. Pazdro, eds., *Not Just Pin Money: Selected Essays on the History of Women's Work in British Columbia* (Vancouver: Camosun College, 1984), 159–81; and Terry Crowley, 'Madonnas before Magdalenes: Adelaide Hoodless and the Making of the Canadian Gibson Girl,' *Canadian Historical Review* 67/4 (1986): 520–47.

5 Katherine Arnup, *Education for Motherhood: Advice for Mothers in Twentieth-Century Canada* (Toronto: University of Toronto Press, 1994); Cynthia Comacchio, *Nations Are Built of Babies: Saving Ontario's Mothers and Children, 1900–1940* (Montreal and Kingston: McGill-Queen's University Press, 1993); Franca Iacovetta, *Gatekeepers: Reshaping Immigrant Lives in Cold War Canada* (Toronto: Between the Lines, 2006).

6 A difference underlined by Marta Danylewycz, Nadia Fahmy-Eid, and Nicole Thivierge, 'L'enseignement ménager et les "Home Economics" au Québec et en Ontario au début du xxe siècle: Une analyse comparée,' in J. Donald Wilson, ed., *An Imperfect Past: Education and Society in Canadian History* (Vancouver: UBC Press 1984), 67–119.

7 Several historians made important contributions to the study of women's education in Franco-Catholic Quebec in the 1980s, but the literature on domestic science is not as well developed as it is for English Canada, and it has not attracted serious scholarly attention in recent years. See Nicole Thivierge, *Écoles ménagères et*

instituts familiaux: Un modèle féminin traditionnel. Histoire de l'enseignement ménager-familial au Québec, 1882–1970 (Quebec City: Institut québécois de recherche sur la culture, 1982); Nadia Fahmy-Eid and Micheline Dumont, eds., *Maîtresses de maison, maîtresses d'école: Femmes, famille et éducation dans l'histoire du Québec* (Montreal: Boréal, 1983); Micheline Dumont and Nadia Fahmy-Eid, *Les couventines: L'éducation des filles au Québec dans les congrégations religieuses enseignantes, 1840–1960* (Montreal: Boréal, 1986); Marta Danylewycz, *Profession: Religieuse. Un choix pour les Québécoises, 1840–1920* (Montreal: Boréal, 1988); and Danylewycz et al., 'L'enseignement ménager.'

8 The Congregation of Notre-Dame published its celebrated *Manuel de Cuisine Raisonnée* for the first time in 1919. Since then, the work has been revised, corrected, enlarged, and reissued at least once a decade. The most recent edition dates from 2003. The same congregation published many general works on home economics for students in the primary and upper grades. All were not consulted, because they repeat themselves to a large degree, but a sample was analysed.

9 Thivierge, *Écoles ménagères.*

10 Ibid., 241.

11 Armand Beauregard, 'L'Art ménager,' in *École sociale populaire*, no. 129 (Montreal: École sociale populaire, Action paroissiale, 1924), 10.

12 See, e.g., the annual reports for the years 1919–20 and 1931–32 documenting the high attendance at these courses and demonstrations. Service des archives, Université de Montréal, Fonds E81, Écoles ménagères provinciales, E81/3B, 4, 'Rapports budgétaires.'

13 See, e.g., Roméo Gauthier, *Cours pratique, éducation physique rationnelle et chrétienne* (Saint-Hyacinthe: France-Québec Publicité, 1954).

14 See, e.g., Franca Iacovetta and Valerie Korinek, 'Jell-O Salads, One-Stop Shopping, and Maria the Homemaker: The Gender Politics of Food,' in Marlene Epp, Franca Iacovetta, and Frances Swyripa, eds., *Sisters or Strangers? Immigrant, Ethnic, and Racialized Women in Canadian History* (Toronto: University of Toronto Press, 2004), 190–230.

15 On the Quiet Revolution, see, e.g., Kenneth McRoberts, *Quebec: Social Change and Political Crisis* (Toronto: Oxford University Press, 1993).

16 *La bonne ménagère: Notions d'économie domestique et d'agriculture à l'usage des jeunes filles des écoles rurales de la province de Québec* (Province of Quebec: Department of Agriculture, [1900?]), 5–7. On these migrations and urban work experiences, see, e.g., Yukari Takai, *Gendered Passages: French Canadian Migration to Lowell, Massachusetts, 1900–1920* (New York: Peter Lang, 2008); Bettina Bradbury, *Working Families: Age, Gender and Daily Survival in Industrializing Montreal* (Toronto: McClelland and Stewart, 1993); Le Collectif Clio, *L'histoire des femmes au Québec depuis quatre siècles*, 2nd ed. (Montreal: Editions Le Jour, 1992).

17 Adélard Dugré, *La désertion des campagnes: Ses causes, ses remèdes* (Quebec: Department of Agriculture, 1916), 23.

18 *Deuxième congrès provincial de sciences ménagères et d'éducation familiale tenu à l'École ménagère provinciale de Montréal du 29 mai au 1er juin 1934* (Quebec: Department of Public Instruction, 1934), 27, 28, and 52–6.

19 Soeurs grises de Montréal, *Cours d'enseignement ménager: 3ième année* (Montreal: École ménagère régionale des Soeurs de la charité (Soeurs grises), 1929), 24–5.

20 Congrégation de Notre-Dame, *L'économie domestique à l'École primaire supérieure, 9 ième et 10 ième années* (Montreal: Les presses de l'Action sociale, 1929), xi.

21 Mrs Alphonse Desilets, *Manuel de la cuisinière économe et pratique* (Province of Quebec: Department of Agriculture, Home Economics Service, 1926), 3.

22 See, e.g., *La revue moderne*, ad for McClary stove, May 1956, 34; Joy Parr, 'Shopping for a Good Stove: A Parable about Gender, Design, and the Market,' in Joy Parr, ed., *A Diversity of Women: Ontario, 1945–1980* (Toronto: University of Toronto Press, 1995), 75–97 .

23 Congrégation de Notre-Dame, *L'économie domestique à l'école élémentaire: 4e, 5e, 6e et 7e années* (Montreal: Congrégation de Notre-Dame, 1942), 26. Sister Sainte-Madeleine-de-la-Passion, *Louise et ses éducatrices, Deuxième livre d'économie domestique à l'école primaire: Sixième année, septième année* (Montreal: Congrégation de Notre-Dame, 1951), 147.

24 Sister Sainte-Madeleine-de-la-Passion, *Louise et sa maman* (Montreal: Congrégation de Notre-Dame, 1953), 37; *Louise et ses éducatrices*, 147.

25 Sister Sainte-Madeleine-de-la-Passion, *Louise et ses éducatrices*.

26 Ibid., 24 and 50.

27 Sister Sainte-Marie-Vitaline, *La cuisine à l'école primaire, théorie et pratique* (Quebec City: Les presses de l'Action sociale / École normale classico-ménagère de Saint-Pascal, 1922), v; Soeurs grises de Montréal, *Cours d'enseignement ménager: 1ère année* (Montreal: École ménagère régionale des Soeurs de la charité (Soeurs grises), 1929), preface.

28 Congrégation de Notre-Dame, *L'économie domestique à l'École primaire supérieure, 9ième et 10ième années* (Quebec City: Les presses de l'Action sociale, 1929), 7.

29 Congrégation de Notre-Dame, *L'économie domestique à l'École primaire supérieure*, 8 and 9.

30 Sister M. de Ste-Thérèse de Jésus, S.C.I.M., nun at L'Institut du Bon Pasteur de Québec, *La cuisinière économe et avisée: Menus et recettes pratiques conformes aux nécessités des temps* (Quebec City: Ateliers de l'Institut St-Jean-Bosco, 1947), 296.

31 Tessier and Marion, *Vitalité*, 3.

32 Ibid., 12.

33 Amélie DesRoches, *Hygiène de l'alimentation et propriétés chimiques des aliments, suivi d'un cours théorique sur l'art culinaire* (Neuville (Comté de Port-neuf), QC, 1912),viii.

34 Charles A. Lamarche, 'Le foyer domestique affermi par l'éducation ménagère,' in *Premier congrès pédagogique provincial d'enseignement ménager: Les 6, 7, 8, 9 septembre 1926 à l'École Normale Classico-Ménagère de Saint-Pascal* (Quebec City: Les presses de l'Action sociale, 1927), 213.

35 Lamarche, 'Le foyer domestique,' 215.

36 Sister Sainte-Marie-Vitaline, ed., Congrégation Notre-Dame, *La cuisine raisonnée*, 8th ed. (Quebec City: Les presses de l'Action sociale, 1957),vii and viii.

37 *La bonne ménagère*, 14 and 15.

38 Ibid., 21.

39 Ibid., 25.

40 Sister Marie-Vitaline, *La cuisine à l'école primaire* (Quebec City: Les presses de l'Action sociale, 1922).

41 The first vitamins were identified in 1911, and a significant number of vitamins were discovered between 1915 and 1930. Practical methods for measuring the quantities in foods did not emerge before the 1930s, which made transforming this discovery into advice on food amounts to eat quite uncertain. Harvey Levenstein, *Revolution at the Table: The Transformation of the American Diet* (Berkeley, CA: University of California Press, 2003), 148–9.

42 Soeurs Grises de Montréal, *Manuel de diététique à l'usage des Écoles ménagères des Soeurs grises de Montréal* (Montreal: Imprimerie des Sourds-Muets, 1927), 26–8.

43 Département de l'Instruction publique, Service de l'éducation familiale, *Alimentation 1ière, 2ième, 3ième et 4ième années des Instituts familiaux* (Government of Quebec, 1957).

44 See, e.g., Sister Sainte-Marie-Vitaline, *La cuisine à l'école primaire*, 44.

45 Sister Sainte-Marie-Vitaline, *La cuisine raisonnée*, 12.

46 Sister Sainte-Marie-Vitaline, *L'économie domestique à l'école complémentaire et au cours de Lettres-Sciences* (Quebec City: printed at the Ateliers de l'Action catholique, 1943), 43.

47 Congrégation de Notre-Dame, *L'économie domestique à l'école élémentaire: 4e, 5, 6e et 7e années*, 149.

48 Sister Marie de Sainte-Thérèse de Jésus, S.C.I.M., *Aliments et nutrition* (Quebec City: Soeurs du Bon Pasteur, 1946–48), 13.

49 Congrégation de Notre-Dame, *L'économie domestique à l'école élémentaire: 4e, 5, 6e et 7e années*, 177, or Sister Sainte-Marie-Vitaline, *L'économie domestique*, 185.

50 Department of Public Instruction Service de l'éducation familiale, *Alimentation 1ière, 2ième, 3ième et 4ième années des Instituts familiaux*, 26.

51 The expression is used by the American sociologist Barry Glassner in *The Gospel of Food: Everything You Think You Know about Food Is Wrong* (New York: Harper Collins, 2007).

52 Dr Charles-Narcisse Valin, *Hygiène alimentaire à l'usage des écoles ménagères et des familles* (Province of Quebec: Department of Agriculture, 1917), 5.

53 Ibid., 10–12.

54 Sister Marie de Sainte-Thérèse de Jésus, S.C.I.M., *Aliments et nutrition*, 17.

55 Sister Sainte-Marie-Vitaline, *La cuisine raisonnée*, 25–38.

56 The human body was also sometimes compared to plants or animals, especially by saying that if a farmer understands the importance of feeding these well, he should understand that he must do the same with his own body. See the foreword by Father Martin, domestic science school inspector, in Valin, *Hygiène alimentaire*, 3.

57 Ibid., 4–7.

58 Desilets, *Manuel de la cuisinière économe et pratique*, 4: soups are [my translation] 'oils that help the human machine in its various physical functions.' The author was a graduate of the École ménagère de Roberval, founded in 1882 by the Ursulines.

59 Soeurs grises de Montréal, *Cours d'enseignement ménager: 1ère année*, 76.

60 Tessier and Marion, *Vitalité*, 22–3.

61 Sister Marie de Sainte-Thérèse de Jésus, S.C.I.M., *Aliments et nutrition*, 12.

62 On this last point, see Avner Offer, *The Challenge of Affluence: Self-Control and Well-Being in the United States and Britain since 1950* (Oxford: Oxford University Press, 2006), esp. chapter 7.

63 Sister Sainte-Thérèse-de-la-Foi, *L'enseignement ménager au cours secondaire: Dixième et onzième années* (Montreal: Fides, 1960), 197.

64 Congrégation de Notre-Dame, *L'économie domestique à l'École primaire supérieure, 9ième et 10ième années*, 145.

65 Tessier and Marion, *Vitalité*, 23.

66 See, e.g., Marielle Préfontaine, Mariette Blais, and Suzanne Simard-Mavrikakis, *L'alimentation: Ses multiples aspects* (Montreal: Guérin, 1972).

PART THREE

Foodways and Memories in Ethnic and Racial Communities

7 'We Didn't Have a Lot of Money, but We Had Food': Ukrainians and Their Depression-Era Food Memories

STACEY ZEMBRZYCKI

Ukrainian men and women who grew up on farms in small rural communities in Manitoba and Saskatchewan and in Sudbury boarding houses in northern Ontario during the 1930s shared a variety of memories with me when they recounted their Depression-era experiences.[1] In particular, some declared that it had been a difficult decade for their working-class families, and others simply stated that they had not been affected by the economic circumstances of the times. Region played a significant role in shaping the experiences of those who lived in these places. Terrible weather, insects, drought, and a poor market for crops and livestock wreaked havoc on those who lived on some farms in western Canada, while those who resided in Sudbury faced a shorter economic crisis because of the region's nickel and the global demand for it; the local nickel market nearly collapsed in 1931 and 1932, but it quickly recovered between 1933 and 1937, stumbled in 1938, and then exploded with the outbreak of the Second World War.[2]

As Ukrainian men and women recalled their Depression-era experiences in regionalized terms, they drew on memories of food to tell their stories. Interestingly, this pattern cut across the regional, ideological, political, and religious differences that often separated them. These recollections not only helped my interviewees understand the prosperity and/or poverty that they experienced as children, but also acted as powerful cultural markers that enabled them to affirm their distinct ethnic identities.[3] They may not have had either the luxury of choice or the opportunity to ask for seconds, but they 'never knew what it was like to be hungry.'[4]

Analysing these narratives remind us that memories are composed of many layers which tend to be 'situated in place and time from the perspective of the present.'[5] In other words, these adult memories about childhood in the 1930s cannot simplistically be read as revealing the entire story. Nostalgic recollections of youth – their layers and the meanings inherent in them – have shifted with the passage of time. As adults share their memories, they have a tendency to view the past 'through a golden haze,' and consequently, '[unhappy], embarrassing, shameful, or unpleasant events [may] … be transformed or omitted as [they move towards their] … "happy ending."'[6] While there is no doubt that the Depression years presented my interviewees and their families with many challenges – Julie Guard's chapter in this collection emphasizes this kind of narrative – they chose, instead, to frame this period in positive terms, highlighting memories that spoke of immigrant and working-class pride as well as tales about coping strategies and, ultimately, survival. There may be glaring omissions, silences, and even secrets in their stories, but these were the personal truths that they shared with me.[7]

Mothers played a vital role in ensuring their families' survival.[8] As Andrea Eidinger and S. Holyck Hunchuck also note in this collection, mothers assumed the responsibility of providing their families with physical sustenance while they engaged in culinary exchanges that reinforced distinct ethnic traditions and ethnic boundaries.[9] These traditions and boundaries, as we shall see, continue to be practised and enforced by the children of these women. Food has left indelible marks on their memories, helping them maintain a sensual and tangible link with their pasts and, particularly, their Ukrainianness.

The Gendered Production, Purchasing, and Preparation of Food

All of the interviewees in this case study, regardless of where they grew up, stressed that the production, purchasing, and preparation of food was left up to their mothers, not their fathers. Additionally, region had little impact on Ukrainian food pathways and the dishes that resulted. All mothers planted crops, raised small animals, and relied on local stores for the ingredients that they needed to produce traditional meals for their families.

To a large degree, these women depended on the foods they could obtain from their families' labours. They maintained large gardens and tended to the animals that were raised on their farms and in their backyards.[10] In undertaking these endeavours, mothers ensured that they would have fresh vegetables, eggs, milk, and meat to feed their families. These resources alleviated the effects of the Depression, making it easier for families to cope with the natural catastrophes and economic crashes of the 1930s.

Gardening in Sudbury did, however, present mothers with notable challenges. In addition to a short growing season, those who lived in this mining community had to deal with the dangerous sulphur fumes that came from the open roasting yards where nickel was smelted. This pollutant not only burned and eventually killed most of the trees and crops in the area, but also created a yellow haze over the town which made the air difficult and uncomfortable to breathe. Due to this pollution, women often struggled to keep their gardens alive. As Mary Brydges (née Ladyk) noted, it burned the tops off of her progressive mother's lettuce crops every summer.[11] The sensory memories of Sudbury's Ukrainians are quite different from the ones that were recounted by those who grew up on rural western Canadian farms; the low-lying yellow haze was nothing like the smell of fresh bread baking in outdoor clay ovens.[12] A fond memory, many were quick to point out all of the time and effort that went into making bread from scratch. They were appreciative of their mothers' labour, but few wanted to return to this period in their lives, even if the bread tasted much better than it does today. ·

In addition to relying on the food grown on their properties, mothers in both parts of the country depended on the regional fruit-producing plants that grew in the wild around their homes. Consequently, summer and autumn were busy seasons for mothers. They spent much of their time preparing for the winter by preserving fresh fruits and vegetables, and especially cabbage. I make special reference to cabbage because many Ukrainian men and women vividly recalled the large barrels of sauerkraut that their mothers made every fall. Specifically, they would fill the barrels with layers of sauerkraut and heads of cabbage. When the barrels froze they would then use a small axe to chop off what they needed, ensuring that they would have sauerkraut to eat and cabbage leaves to make cabbage rolls throughout the winter.

Meat was an important part of most meals. Because it was an expensive commodity to purchase, women on the prairies and in Sudbury kept pigs, chickens, rabbits, and cows to ensure some degree of survival for their families (cows being a more common possession for prairie families). To make certain that there would be enough meat throughout the winter, many of these animals were 'fattened up' and slaughtered each year before the first snowfall, and then they were strung up in barns and front porches where they could be kept frozen. Like the barrels of sauerkraut, mothers used what they needed and kept the rest of the meat for future meals, never leaving any waste.

Although much of the food that mothers used to feed their families came from their farms and backyards, they also relied on local merchants for some supplies. In addition to providing basics, like sugar and flour, these stores functioned as important community centres, where local, and in places like Sudbury, multicultural networks took root. When Ernie Lekun's Ukrainian Catholic mother Mary went to the neighbourhood store, she gossiped and shared recipes with the other women who were shopping there. In explaining how this social network affected him, Ernie recalled a number of the Finnish dishes that he enjoyed as a child, noting that his mother learned how to make these meals from the Finnish women she routinely met at the store. Ernie was still in awe when speaking about his mother's activities, declaring 'somehow, despite the fact that no one spoke the same language, they still communicated.'[13] Local general and neighbourhood stores also acted as important resources for women who were struggling to feed their families during difficult times. Even when they had no money to pay for goods, women could still go into some stores and get what they needed through either credit or bartering or exchanges. In this case, totals were added to an ongoing bill and women paid the merchants back in instalments when they had the money. None of my interviewees admitted that their families had trouble paying their bills; however, we know that the extension of too much credit forced some merchants to close their stores and perhaps even declare bankruptcy.[14] Children had little to do with their families' finances but most would have been aware of any tensions that may have been caused by the Depression. In highlighting positive memories, my interviewees held onto a narrative that emphasized respectability rather than shame.

Although Sudbury mothers tended to rely on merchants more than the women who lived on farms in western Canada, it is interesting to note that the dishes that appeared on tables in both of these regions were similar: mothers prepared ethnic food to meet the dietary needs of their families. According to Robert Harney, Italian boarding house operators and their boarders used food and language to insulate themselves from cultural change.[15] For Ukrainian mothers, ethnic food and language appear to have had more to do with economics and less to do with an explicitly conscious effort to preserve ethnic culture and traditions. Ukrainian women stuck to what they did best and did not spend the few spare moments of their days pondering how food and language defined ethnic boundaries. These women, like most immigrant women feeding families on tight budgets, took their roles as food providers seriously and drew on customary ways of stretching meals and using familiar ingredients and recipes to feed their households.[16]

Perogies and cabbage rolls were, for instance, labour-intensive ethnic staples, usually made once a week by mothers; since Friday was a day of fasting for Ukrainian Catholics, they frequently ate perogies because it enabled them to abstain from eating meat. These foods fed many hungry mouths and could be made in large quantities for a relatively low price. Perogies required flour, lard, and potatoes, and cabbage rolls were made with cabbage, lard, shredded meat (usually salt pork), and/or rice. Mothers tended to adapt these specialties to fit the seasons, filling perogies and cabbage rolls with whatever they had on hand. Some of these adaptations resulted from ethnic intermarriage. For instance, Lorraine Jurgilas' (née Burke) Croatian mother would make 'Ukrainian-style' cabbage rolls and then serve them cold, like Croatian *sarma*.[17] These ethnic dishes were easily altered to fit the needs of working-class families because, as Jacob Bzdel noted, 'they could be made with whatever was around.'[18] Necessity more than choice dictated ingredients and methods of preparation during the 1930s.

Since meat was the most expensive food to purchase, Ukrainians rarely ate it as a main dish. Roasted and fried meats were reserved for special meals, like holidays. If Ukrainian mothers prepared meat, then it was usually boiled and added to either a water-based soup or stew; these were foods that required little preparation and could also be made quite inexpensively. Moreover, wild meat was infrequently eaten by Ukrainian men and women. Again, these were special dishes that were prepared a couple of times a year, usually in the fall during hunting season. In addition to cooking wild game, like partridge, prairie chickens, rabbits, and deer, mothers, especially in Sudbury, served pigeon meat with cream. Many of my interviewees admitted that they still enjoyed the taste of wild game, but they were quick to state that they would not eat pigeon meat today. Although those I interviewed longed to return to the 'good old days' of their youth, this food memory speaks to some of the challenges that families faced at this time. Hunger made pigeons a cheap and necessary dietary option, not a preferred one.

Mothers who lived on farms and in boarding houses assumed the responsibility of providing physical sustenance for those who lived in their homes, depending on their labours for the ingredients that they needed to make three meals a day. While Sudbury mothers tended to shop at local stores more often than prairie mothers, all mothers produced similar ethnic dishes that fed their families throughout the Depression.

Identity and the Consumption of Food

Like the production, purchasing, and preparation of food, memories about consuming ethnic dishes pointed to similar patterns that cut across the regional, ideological, political, and religious lines that set Ukrainians apart. Mothers may not have thought about the cultural implications of preparing and serving ethnic food, but the children who consumed these dishes certainly did. When my interviewees recounted their childhood experiences, they used memories about ethnic food to assert, maintain, and reinforce their Ukrainian identities. For them, the consumption of Ukrainian food was part of an important exchange that both symbolized and marked the boundaries of their culture.

Food has played a central role in popular Ukrainian Canadian identity. 'So closely identified with the family while uniting its members in a larger communion,' Frances Swyripa states, 'food formed a particularly significant bond and aspect of Ukrainianness.'[19] While there is no doubt that memories about food symbolized the ethnic heritage of Ukrainian men and women who grew up in western Canada and northern Ontario, they were also signifiers of difference. The smells and tastes experienced in their homes set them apart from their peers, serving as important reminders of the immigrant world of their parents. To this end, Charlie Rapsky declared that he always knew which houses were Ukrainian because the smell of cabbage emanated from them, and Katherine Timchuk (née Harach) noted that her mother used garlic to ward off sickness and so her house often smelled like this 'Ukrainian penicillin.'[20]

Although discussions about preparing and consuming ethnic foods had a clear economic dynamic, they also served as important and powerful cultural markers, providing Ukrainian men and women with a sensual link to their ethnic pasts. While many of my interviewees maintained a connection to their heritage through memberships at ethnic churches and/or ethnic halls, few continued to eat Ukrainian food on a regular basis; the labour-intensive nature of this food and its high fat content led many to place limits on traditional dishes. Memories about consuming food were, therefore, quite important, allowing them to make important cultural connections to an ethnic past which has, in many respects, been lost.

Conclusion

Depression-era memories about purchasing, preparing, and consuming food organized the narratives of Ukrainian men and women who grew up on rural farms in Manitoba and Saskatchewan and in Sudbury boarding houses during this decade. Although region impacted the stories they told, it ultimately had little effect on food pathways in these parts of the country. The community of consumption, which shared memories helped to forge, also cut across the religious, political, and ideological differences that set Ukrainians apart. Mothers assumed much of the responsibility of providing their families with physical sustenance, drawing on customary ethnic dishes to meet their families' dietary needs because they made economic sense. My interviewees not only stressed the economic necessity of these dishes, but also declared that Ukrainian specialties were important cultural markers. Food memories gave Ukrainian Catholic, Orthodox, nationalist, and progressive men and women a tangible, and often easily accessible means through which they could understand their identities and Depression-era experiences and make important cultural distinctions.

NOTES

1 This case study is based on 82 life story oral history interviews that Olga Zembrzycki, my grandmother, and I conducted with Ukrainians who were either born
   in, raised in, or came to the region of Sudbury, Ontario, prior to 1945: 50 of our
   interviewees were women and 32 were men; 23 of them grew up in Manitoba and
   Saskatchewan, 49 grew up in northern Ontario, and the 10 remaining grew up
   elsewhere, mostly in Eastern Europe.
2 On how the Depression affected the Sudbury region, see C.M. Wallace and Ashley
   Thomson, eds., *Sudbury: Rail Town to Regional Capital* (Toronto: Dundurn,
   1993); Stacey Zembrzycki, 'Memory, Identity, and the Challenge of Community
   among Ukrainians in the Sudbury Region, 1901–1939,' doctoral dissertation, Car-
   leton University, 2007, 200–332; Stacey Zembrzycki, '"There Were always Men in
   Our House": Gender and the Childhood Memories of Working-Class Ukrainians in
   Depression-Era Canada,' *Labour / Le travail* 60 (Fall 2007): 77–105. For a more
   general discussion about the decade and its impact on Canadians, see, e.g., Lara
   Campbell, *Respectable Citizens: Gender, Family, and Unemployment in Ontario's
   Great Depression* (Toronto: University of Toronto Press, 2009); Katrina Srigley,
   Breadwinning Daughters: Single Women in a Depression-Era City (Toronto: Uni-
   versity of Toronto Press, 2010); Denyse Baillargeon, *Making Do: Women, Family,
   and Home in Montreal during the Great Depression*, translated by Yvonne Klein
   (Waterloo, ON: Wilfrid Laurier University Press, 1999).
3 For a related discussion that historicizes the relationship between food, identity,
   and power, see the introduction to this collection. Also see Donna Gabaccia, *We
   Are What We Eat: Ethnic Food and the Making of Americans* (Cambridge, MA:
   Harvard University Press, 1998); Nathalie Cooke, ed., *What's to Eat? Entrées
   in Canadian Food History* (Montreal and Kingston: McGill-Queen's University
   Press, 2009).
4 Lorraine Jurgilas (née Burke), interview, Sudbury, 8 Nov. 2004.
5 Natalie Zemon Davis and Randolph Starn, 'Introduction: Special Issue on Memory and Counter-Memory,' *Representations* 26 (Spring 1989): 2. Also see Kathleen
   Stewart, 'Nostalgia: A Polemic,' *Cultural Anthropology* 3/3 (1988): 227–41.
6 Neil Sutherland, 'When You Listen to the Winds of Childhood, How Much Can
   You Believe?' in Nancy Janovicek and Joy Parr, eds., *Histories of Canadian Children and Youth* (Oxford: Oxford University Press, 2003), 23. Personal biographical memories often give individuals a way to understand their lives as well as
   the societies in which they live. See Michael Frisch, *A Shared Authority: Essays
   on the Craft and Meaning of Oral and Public History* (Albany: State University
   of New York Press, 1990); Luisa Passerini, *Fascism in Popular Memory: The*

Cultural Experience of the Turin Working Class, translated by Robert Lumley and Jude Bloomfield (Cambridge: Cambridge University Press, 1987); Joan Sangster, 'Telling Our Stories: Feminist Debates and the Use of Oral History,' *Women's History Review* 3/1 (1994): 5–28; Marlene Epp, 'The Memory of Violence: Soviet and East European Mennonite Refugees and Rape in the Second World War,' *Journal of Women's History* 9/1 (1997): 58–87; Pamela Sugiman, 'Passing Time, Moving Memories: Interpreting Wartime Narratives of Japanese Canadian Women,' *Histoire sociale / Social History* 37/73 (2004): 51–79.

7 See Annette Kuhn, *Family Secrets: Acts of Memory and Imagination*, 2nd ed. (London: Verso, 2002).

8 This is a thread that winds through the chapters by Caroline Durand, S. Holyck Hunchuck, Julie Guard, Andrea Eidinger, Marlene Epp, and Sonia Cancian. For a related examination of the significant roles played by mothers who lived in rural settings, see, e.g., Royden Loewen, *Ethnic Farm Culture in Western Canada* (Ottawa: Canadian Historical Association, 2002), 23; Royden Loewen, *Family, Church, and Market: A Mennonite Community in the Old and the New Worlds, 1850–1930* (Urbana, IL: University of Illinois Press, 1993), 43–8, 101–5, 219–26; Stella Hryniuk, *Peasants with Promise: Ukrainians in Southeastern Galicia, 1880–1900* (Edmonton: Canadian Institute of Ukrainian Studies Press, 1991), 22–30.

9 For a related discussion about the impact that food has had on the identities of Mennonite women, see Marlene Epp, 'The Semiotics of Zwieback: Feast and Famine in the Narratives of Mennonite Refugee Women,' in Marlene Epp, Franca Iacovetta, and Frances Swyripa, eds., *Sisters or Strangers? Immigrant, Ethnic, and Racialized Women in Canadian History* (Toronto: University of Toronto Press, 2004), 314–40.

10 Although public health by-laws enacted in the late nineteenth and early twentieth centuries prohibited animals like chickens and pigs from being kept close to homes in most districts within the Sudbury region, many interviewees admitted that their mothers ignored these rules until the early 1930s, so that they could ensure some degree of survival for their families. That these by-laws could be ignored with little repercussion reflects the pace of development in this region. Whereas large urban centres, like Montreal and Toronto, outlawed animals from being kept in residential areas in the mid-nineteenth century, northern mining communities in the Sudbury region did not begin to seriously enforce similar by-laws until much later. See Wallace and Thomson, *Sudbury*; Mike Solski, ed., *The Coniston Story* (Sudbury: Journal Printing, 1983), 13–17; Bettina Bradbury, *Working Families: Age, Gender, and Daily Survival in Industrializing Montreal* (Toronto: McClelland and Stewart, 1993), 163–8; Bradbury, 'Pigs, Cows, and Boarders: Non-Wage Forms of Survival among Montreal Families, 1861–91,' *Labour / Le travail* 14 (Fall 1984): 9–46.

11 Mary Brydges (née Ladyk), interview, Sudbury, 28 Oct. 2004.
12 For a discussion about the important role that senses play in memory, see Joy
     Parr, *Sensing Change: Technologies, Environments, and the Everyday, 1953–2003*
     (Vancouver: UBC Press, 2010).
13 Ernie Lekun, interview, Sudbury, 9 May 2005.
14 Zembrzycki, 'Memory, Identity, and the Challenge of Community.'
15 Robert Harney, 'Boarding and Belonging: Thoughts on Sojourner Institutions,'
     Urban History Review 2 (1978): 27.
16 Food is central to understanding the narratives of immigrants, especially immi-
     grant women. See, e.g., Franca Iacovetta, *Gatekeepers: Reshaping Immigrant
     Lives in Cold War Canada* (Toronto: Between the Lines, 2006), 137–69; Marlene
     Epp, 'The Semiotics of Zwieback,' 314–40; Rhonda Hinther, '"Sincerest Revo-
     lutionary Greetings": Progressive Ukrainians in the Twentieth Century,' doctoral
     dissertation, McMaster University, 2005, 136–8.
17 Lorraine Jurgilas, interview. Franca Iacovetta also notes that culinary pluralism
     was common among ethnically mixed families. See Iacovetta, *Gatekeepers*, 162.
18 Jacob Bzdel, interview, Val Caron, 10 Jan. 2005.
19 Frances Swyripa, *Wedded to the Cause: Ukrainian-Canadian Women and Ethnic
     Identity, 1891–1991* (Toronto: University of Toronto Press, 1993), 245.
20 Charlie Rapsky, interview, Sudbury, 6 June 2005; Katherine Timchuk (née Har-
     ach), interview, Sudbury, 2 Nov. 2004.

8 Feeding the Dead: The Ukrainian Food Colossi of the Canadian Prairies

S. HOLYCK HUNCHUCK

This chapter examines an aspect of Canadian food history that can be gleaned from an ensemble of seven giant statues of Ukrainian foods built in rural Alberta and Saskatchewan between 1973 and 2001.[1] To the casual viewer, these colossal figures may seem to be little more than examples of the modern trend in North America of constructing tourist art in the form of huge, hyperrealistic, roadside attractions.[2] As a feminist art historian with an interest in Ukrainian Canadiana,[3] and in the deep history behind symbols, myths, and folkloric practices,[4] my position, however, is that these statues bear closer examination. They are more than easily dismissed ethnic kitsch aimed at the tourist market. These particular sculptures, sited where they are and representing what they do, are laden with profound meaning specific to the Ukrainian community's traditional relationship to food symbolism, cultural identity, and collective memory as informed by food trauma (the enduring physical and psychological injury resulting from food deprivation) and death, and as expressed through foodstuffs and food rituals.

It is little exaggeration to state that food trauma has scarred the Ukrainian community throughout its existence, from the prehistoric to the contemporary.[5] My reading of these statues is based on the premise that food trauma continues to inform both the active memory and the collective unconscious of the ethnoculture, even within today's Canada with its multicultural society, modern conveniences, prosperous lifestyle, and peaceful history.[6]

As a consequence, 'food is more than a meal on the table' for Ukrainians, according to Toronto poet Marusya Bociurkiw.[7] While Stacey Zembrzycki's chapter reveals that traditional foods were an important part of the day-to-day cultural lives of Depression-era Ukrainian workers and farmers in Canada, my essay is an aetiological one that analyses the same foods that have come to be rendered, decades later, as monumental public art. What do these food colossi mean? They were erected during an era of prosperity and modernity. Their builders – small town politicians, business people, and service club members of Ukrainian ancestry – are financially comfortable, socially arrived, and assimilated members of Canadian society. They no longer rely on peasant cuisine for sustenance or to provide their sense of place in Canada; nevertheless, their ties to traditional Ukrainian dishes remain strong on a symbolic level. To consider the semiotic aspects of food, and to know the Ukrainian tradition of artistic and ritualistic responses to a history of food trauma, is to better understand these sculptures on the tabletop of the prairie landscape and their place in Canadian food history.

Simply put, these sculptures are a continuation of Ukrainian folkways in which traditional cuisine and food rituals play a significant role as a collective memento mori.[8] They do so as public art, in permanent materials, on a spectacular, traffic-stopping scale. Their existence raises issues that concern not only Ukrainians or the aesthetics of monumental sculpture,[9] but the relationships of all of us to contemporary, multicultural Canada through food, through women's work, and ultimately, through our memorials to the dead. Those women and those deceased not incidentally include the *Babi* (peasant grandmothers).[10] Bociurkiw describes them as nothing less than the 'heart and centre' of Ukrainian culture,[11] and Zembrzycki notes that the Babi 'have played a central role in defining the Ukrainian identity of their descendants [in Canada].'[12] Yet, they are seldom given their due respect in written accounts either of Ukrainian history or the Ukrainian Canadian immigration story.[13] In regard to food alone, the Babi are the ones who help to clear the land for agriculture and to grow and harvest food, and it is they who prepare traditional Ukrainian peasant dishes, serve them, and pass down the recipes, cooking practices, and preservation techniques that keep the living alive. They are also the bearers of the ancient food rituals that keep the dead remembered. These rites, in turn, are intrinsic to the Ukrainian folkloric belief that the community consists of three parts: the living, the dead, and the generations to come. All must be 'fed' – and traditionally, it is Ukrainian peasant women who do the feeding, with Ukrainian peasant foods.

Two of the seven colossi are studied here as representative examples: the *Pysanka* of Vegreville, Alberta of 1973–75,[14] and the *Lesia* of Canora, Saskatchewan of 1980–81.[15] The former is a 9.4 m high statue of a traditional Ukrainian decorated egg (also known as an Easter Egg), rendered in steel, aluminium, and reinforced concrete; the latter is a 7.6 m female figure in traditional Ukrainian peasant costume, constructed of fibreglass and plywood. She bears a *rushnyk* (sacramental cloth) upon which rest salt and a circular, braided bread or *kolach*.[16]

8.1 *Pysanka* (Ukrainian Easter Egg), Vegreville, Alberta. Ron Resch, Paul Sembaliuk, John Sikoski and Two Hills Construction et al. (1973–5). Photo: S. Holyck Hunchuck, 2008.

The symbolism and ritual purpose fulfilled by these statues can be clarified by examining four intertwined aspects of Ukrainian culture: the use of food as sacrament, the special place accorded the dead, the ongoing significance of peasant dishes to modern Ukrainian Canadians, and the role of food trauma in Ukrainian history. Traditional foods can provide more than physical sustenance of workers or support the day-to-day assertion of their ethnic

8.2 *Lesia* (Ukrainian Maiden Bearing Bread and Salt), Canora, Saskatchewan. Nicholas Lewchuk and Orest Lewchuk (1981). Photo: S. Holyck Hunchuck, 2008.

identity. These modern statues demonstrate that, on a semiotic level, food can provide a link to ancient folkways in which sacrificial offerings, memorials to the ancestors, and tributes to women's labour can have an ongoing and highly visible place both in defining a landscape and in articulating the immigrant experience – including that of Ukrainian Canadians, and with it, their history of food trauma. In the process, these food sculptures have a further, historiographic role to play. They are public art projects that redress in part the gaps and absences to be found in most Western textual accounts of Ukrainian and Ukrainian Canadian history.

Sacramental Quality of Ukrainian Food

For Ukrainians, 'all food is soul food,' according to Saskatoon anthropologist Zenon Pohorecky.[17] He adds, 'it has sacramental qualities and political thrust.'[18] As explored by Zembrzycki, Marlene Epp, Andrea Eidinger, Franca Iacovetta, and Julie Mehta in their chapters in this volume, meal sharing is an important way for various minorities in a host society to assert their existence as ethnics, to renew their cultural practices, and to reinforce their social bonds. These practices can be seen as nourishing the community's 'soul.' Furthermore, for those displaced and marginalized, as are all groups in diaspora, by geography, ethnicity, language, and often by class, both banquets and public art are focal points of collective identity and thus serve as political statements of minority survival.

For modern Ukrainians in Canada, moreover, the peasant foods depicted in the statues also bear an indefinable imprimatur of cultural authenticity. Ukrainian cuisine varies with regional climates and historical influences; nevertheless, it is appreciated as a genuine traditional artform that survives relatively intact despite Ukraine's many colonizers in its past, despite the diaspora of the past century-and-a-half,[19] and despite the pretensions of the assimilated and the nouveaux riche today. In so doing, it invokes associative, reassuring memories of the Babi, the all-giving matriarchs and artisans of the peasant kitchen. Indeed, it pays tribute to them.

Finally, while all food is a source of spiritual comfort for the living, for Ukrainians it also performs this function for the dead. This last meaning of 'soul food' is perhaps the least-known to historians of food or to travellers on Canadian highways, but the use of foodstuffs as sacrificial ornament, as votive offering, and as a means of ancestor worship may be the most important symbolic role of these monuments in the prairie landscape.

That the sculptures take the form of Ukrainian cuisine requires an examination of the foods themselves. Eggs, bread, and salt are among the basic ingredients in any well-stocked Eastern European kitchen.[20] For Ukrainians, the rushnyky used to wrap, present, bless, and serve meals are an important part of folkways in which the dead are buried in the earth but 'live' in the sky,[21] social relations are marked by 'a fierce, almost bullying, hospitality' centred on meals,[22] and food is a physical, social, spiritual, emotional, and mnemonic connector between the living and the dead, between the present and the past and, ultimately, between memory and oblivion. In this cosmology, even the most seemingly ordinary foods and food-related items, prepared and served by the humblest Baba, are therefore the stuff of sacrament.

Eggs occupy a revered place in Ukrainian peasant culture, both in the cuisine proper and in the food rites that connect the living and the dead. Eggs are extremely nutritious and calorie-rich, but they are also universal symbols for potentiality, women's fertility, and life itself.[23] Perhaps the most famous of all Ukrainian folk arts is the *pysanka*, a powerful totem of life, divine protection, and the possibilities of regeneration, renewal, and rebirth.[24] While most pysanky makers in Canada today put their decorated eggs on display with the good china, for the Babi who originated them, pysanky are holy. They believe above all that the universe would last only as long as pysanky are made. Traditionally, the eggs are hung from trees, gates, and doorways as protective emblems, buried in the soil to mark boundaries and ensure the fertility of the protected zone, and left as ritual food for the ancestors out in the land on top of their graves.[25] Pysanky have been called nothing less than 'icons of the universe,'[26] but their source material is, as at Vegreville, a simple food item treasured by Ukrainians, the egg.

Bread, too, occupies a special place in the Ukrainian food pantheon of life and death. The ancient Ukrainian word for 'grain' (*zbizhzhia*) translates as the 'totality of divinity';[27] the rite of baking is considered an act of magic (even the fire is seen as sacred); and bread is considered 'the holiest of foods' and 'a gift from God.'[28] When a peasant drops a bread crumb on the floor, she will pause, pick it up, and kiss it in apology and veneration.[29] The reverence for grains and breads spans traditional Ukrainian culture in both the old and new worlds. Savella Stechishin, the Ukrainian Canadian home economist, points out that bread is 'a sacred item,'[30] and 'no significant event can take place without it, where it is used to bring blessings to any family activity.'[31] Canadian food historian Thelma Barer-Stein goes further, noting that 'there is no aspect of Ukrainian life or afterlife that is not celebrated with the holiness of grain.'[32] A loaf of bread is used to bless the bride and groom at their wedding; grains of wheat are placed in the coffin with the corpse; and in the *Panikhyda* (memorial service), the deceased is toasted not with alcohol but with a piece of bread.[33]

Ukrainian cookery has dozens of bread types, but the special holiday loaves are always egg-rich[34] and therefore doubly important as ritual objects. Appropriate artistic care is paid to their forms and decorations. These vary with the occasion but are usually kolachs (circular in shape)[35] and sculpted into a braid, as seen at Canora. The shapes of these artisanal breads serve a semiotic purpose: as braids formed in a round, they symbolize both eternity and the tripartite, intertwined nature of the Ukrainian collectivity. More elaborate breads may also be topped with a single white candle (as at *Sviat Vecher*, the Holy Supper held on Christmas Eve), with bread-sculpted birds (the *korovai*, or wedding loaf), or with crosses and spirals (the *paska*, or Easter bread).[36] The intersection of private family life with the broader world of outsiders and strangers is also marked with ritual bread: the most sincere form of greeting is that seen with the *Lesia*: a kolach with a mound of salt (*sil*).

The history of salt is similarly linked with the history of Ukrainian food sacrality.[37] Ancient salt mines dot the Carpathian Mountains shared by Hungary, Poland, Romania, Slovakia, and Ukraine, but giftgiving of bread and salt is a pan-Slavic tradition derived from the ancient Greeks who colonized the Black Sea coast of this region. To be presented with a round, sculpted bread and a mound of salt, mounted upon a rushnyk, as is the visitor to Canora, is therefore to be welcomed with the sacred gift of community inclusion and protection.[38]

The links between the living and the deceased in Ukrainian food rituals are further underlined by the use of the rushnyk, or long white cloth traditionally handwoven of hemp, linen, or cotton, and hand-embroidered in floral or geometric designs.[39] Rushnyky, like ritual breads and decorated eggs, come in different sizes and patterns, and are used to mark all important occasions, including the blessing and serving of food. More than a mere towel, dish cloth, or place mat,[40] a rushnyk is nothing less than a sacro-religious statement in physical form. The presence of a rushnyk says, in effect: 'Pay attention: this is important' – or to borrow a phrase pronounced during the Divine Liturgy of the Eastern Christian church, 'Wisdom! Let us be attentive.' Rushnyky are described as a material 'link between the living and the dead,'[41] and, arguably, the greatest difference between the two states of being is the sharing of food.[42] The Panikhyda uses a rushnyk to remind the living of this simple truth: the memorial service ends with a rushnyk-swaddled bread being lowered, broken into pieces, and eaten by the mourners in memory of the deceased.[43]

The Special Place Accorded the Dead in Ukrainian Life

No event in Ukrainian life is complete without a meal, but when the living sit down to eat they also welcome the ancestors to the table. Borciurkiw notes, 'Our rituals of cooking and eating are a kind of memory machine ... that evoke spectral presence.' She adds, 'The idea being [that] the ghosts of the dead are always with us; the border between this life and the next [is] permeable as a cloud.'[44] Ukrainian foodways that honour the dead occur in subtle form on a daily basis and are explicit during five major holidays, including Christmas and Easter.[45] Even everyday meals do not commence with the expression of social niceties, such as Ukrainian equivalents to 'Cheers!' or 'Bon appetit!' but with the invocation, 'Eat, eat; *tomorrow there may be no food.*' This statement is an invitation to bodily pleasure aimed at the living ('Eat, eat') as well as a spoken memorial to those who died from hunger in famines past and a notice to hoard food against a perpetually uncertain life to come.

The Christmas Eve Holy Supper is the single most important meal in the Ukrainian calendar. Held on 6 January, it was originally one of many wintertime pagan feasts but, in typical Ukrainian 'dual-faith'[46] fashion, became blended into Christian celebrations from the tenth century onward. No gifts are exchanged, for the point of the evening is the twelve-course feast that takes months of women's labour to prepare, hours to serve, and is a true 'community' event.[47] Guests are welcomed at the threshold, as they are at Canora, with a ritual offering of sil and a round, braided kolach, proffered on a rushnyk. The meal is served on another rushnyk/tablecloth, and the centrepiece is a three-layered, candle-topped kolach which triply alludes to the interwoven and endless cycles of life, death, and rebirth.[48]

The dead have an honoured place in Holy Supper rituals. A *didukh* (ceremonial sheaf of wheat representing the ancestors)[49] is wrapped in a rushnyk and placed in the 'holy corner,'[50] where it oversees the meal. The first course, a bowlful of *kutia* (hot cereal of wheat or barley, nuts, honey, and poppyseed)[51] is brought out by the head of the household. He begins the feast by offering a bowl of kutia to the didukh and tossing another to the ceiling. If it sticks (or is accepted by the souls in heaven above), a good year will follow. That is, before the living can eat, the ancestors must be appeased with food. In addition, a special place at the table is left empty – 'place setting for the dead' – with the expectation that this night, the ancestors may reappear and join in the Supper.

Propitiating the deceased with food also occurs in springtime. At Easter, pysanky, along with other food items including bread and salt,[52] are wrapped in rushnyky and taken to church to be blessed. These are then brought back home for the family's Easter meal, a celebration of resurrection that is preceded by a fast and begins with a simple boiled egg. In many families, the living literally dine with the dead during this time: picnics are eaten on top of the graves, with vodka poured into the soil, and pysanky left behind in the cemetery for the ancestors to partake.

These invocations, decorative elements, and ritual acts around Ukrainian meals, and particularly around holiday feasts, indicate a collective awareness of the ancestral presence: the dead may be absent in person, but not in spirit, and they are to be fed. The meals may be a grand community banquet or a modest family snack, while the dining 'table' may be found in a peasant kitchen, a Christian church, a community hall, or out in the open on top of a grave.

Traditional Ukrainian Cuisine and Modern Ukrainian Canadians

Folk arts such as Ukrainian cookery, egg decorating, and the making of sacramental cloths have been created for millennia, but the Babi who are willing to undertake the arduous, repetitive, and unpaid labour of producing them are now a scarce, ageing, and declining demographic. As a result, these traditional Ukrainian foodways, once taken for granted by the community, have acquired the status of the rare and the valued. As early as 1981, Pohorecky finds that for Ukrainians in Canada, 'food' is the single most important form of their ethnic expression, outranking language, religion, politics, music, visual art, and dance.[53] It is little accident that the sculptures began to be built around the same historical moment of the mid-1970s to the early 2000s when their builders – the assimilated and prosperous Ukrainians in small-town Alberta and Saskatchewan – were becoming gentrified but losing the 'low' peasant culture that sustained previous generations. The Ukrainian food colossi in Canada can, therefore, be read as social memorials to ancient foods and foodways. Ultimately, they stand as a semiotic substitute, in permanent materials, on a gigantic order, in public, to the private sense of memory, ethnic identity, and the consolations of 'soul food' that used to be commonplace with traditional Ukrainian meals provided by the Babi. As such, the statues commemorate those peasant women at the culture's 'heart and centre.' In the process, they allude to the culinary labour produced by peasant women as an artistic response to food trauma.

The Role of Food Trauma in Ukrainian History

Ukraine is mainly a grain-growing region, prone to the unpredictable cycles of feast and famine typical of all agrarian cultures. However, it is also bears the status of a 'classic shatter belt'[54] for its place in the history of human conflict, with food seizures, food shortages, and outright famine along with other hardships doubtless accompanying each of countless invasions, wars, and battles within this narrative.

The twentieth century was a period of almost unrelieved suffering and loss that likely left no family in diaspora untouched. Both world wars, as well as major revolutions, counter-revolutions, and civil wars occurred in the Ukrainian region in the past hundred years, and tens of millions of Eastern Europeans were killed by these conflicts.[55] Non-combatant peasants, such as the ones who formed 90 per cent of the Ukrainian population prior to 1939, were often caught on the front lines of battle. Peacetimes were also characterized by mass suffering and premature death, with food trauma at the centre. The Holodomor ('Death from Starvation') of mainly 1932–33 was a genocide engineered by Joseph Stalin aimed particularly at the Ukrainian peasantry. It claimed between two million and twelve million lives, mainly within the Ukrainian Soviet Socialist Republic (UkrSSR). During the Holodomor, emigration from the UkrSSR was banned by the Soviet government, the borders were sealed, and the food-seizure protocols of the 1932 Law of Protection of Socialist Property were so relentless that to store or hoard grain of any kind – presumably even in the form of a didukh – became a crime punishable by death.

The earliest wave of Ukrainian immigrants from the late nineteenth century carried with them to Canada a cultural knowledge of food trauma alongside a legacy of food worship and reverence for the ancestors. However, the chronicle of Ukrainian food trauma has scarcely been recorded or documented by Western historians, including those in Canada, let alone redressed or commemorated in a systematic fashion. The lives of Ukrainian women have been the subject of even less study by writers or heroic treatment by artists, especially the plight of the Babi. Nevertheless, the history of Ukrainian conflict, suffering, displacement, and premature death, particularly among its female members is, arguably, the single largest influence on the successive waves of immigration to Canada during the past 120 years. This narrative can be said to inform the cultural memory of every enlightened Ukrainian Canadian and her attitudes even today, to food, to history, to the Babi, and to feeding the dead.

Conclusion

The Ukrainian food colossi on the Canadian prairies are, above all, highly visible, deeply symbolic, but little-understood public art. If the power of visual art lies at least in part in its ability to convey messages that are otherwise unspoken, using the power of allusion, suggestion, and associative meaning, then the food statues can be seen as a means of breaking silences in the Ukrainian chronicle of food trauma. If the response of Ukrainians in Canada to a lack of understanding or common awareness of this history should turn out in at least some circumstances to be non-textual in medium, but take the form of non-discursive visual art as it does with the food colossi, it logically follows that the art refers back to the traditional sources that are seen as manifesting authentic

Ukrainian culture: peasant food. That is, for people who cannot always rely on the accuracy of written accounts of their experiences, the difference between memory and oblivion (particularly around food trauma) can be provided by such visual art as these sculptures, with their emphatic reassertion of folk art and folkways, and their celebration of the individuals who not only occupy the centre of the cultural legacy but whose life experiences have largely been written out of most, if not all, of the historical narratives: the Babi.

To put it simply, if art can speak the unspeakable, then the Ukrainian food colossi are art in the form of giant votive offerings: an updated version of peasant foods left out to feed the dead. Their place setting-cum-altar is the tabletop of the Canadian prairies – or by extension, the vast *mohyla* (gravemound) that is the earth itself. In so doing, they stand also as memorials to the now-disappearing Babi, those women whose labour, artistry, and sacred power created Ukrainian foodstuffs and foodways that keep the living alive – and the dead, fed, and thus remembered.

ACKNOWLEDGMENTS

This chapter is dedicated to the memory of Stephania Holyck Hunchuck (1921–2009) matriarch of Howland Avenue, Toronto. She was a generous soul, an indefatigable labourer, an extraordinary cook, a gifted craftswoman, and a Baba whose kitchen door was always open to generations of Torontonians. *Vichnaya Pamyat*/Eternal Memory. I also offer thanks to Marshall Nay and the Alberta Ukrainian Heritage Foundation, Edmonton, for underwriting the photo-documentation of the colossi.

NOTES

1 The Vegreville *Pysanka*, Glendon *Perogy* (1991), Vilna *Mushrooms* (1993), Mundare *Kielbassa* (2001), and by extension, the Andrew *Duck* (1997) and Smoky Lake *Pumpkins* (1998) (all Alberta), and the *Lesia* of Canora, Saskatchewan.

2 Studies of the pop architecture and roadside signage in North America arguably begin with *Learning from Las Vegas: The Forgotten Symbolism of Architectural Form*, by American architects Robert Venturi, Denise Scott Brown, and Steve Izenour (Cambridge, MA: MIT Press, rev. ed., 1972) and include 'Travels in Hyperrereality,' by Italian linguist-philosopher Umberto Eco, in his *Travels in Hyperreality: Essays* (San Francisco: Harcourt, Brace Jovanovich, 1975), 3–58, and art historian Karal Ann Marling, *The Colossus of Roads: Myth and Symbol*

along the American Highway (Minneapolis, MN: University of Minnesota Press, 1984). Canadian works include Henri Robideau, *From the Pacific to the Atlantic, Canada's Gigantic!* (Toronto: Summerhill, 1988), 7–14, and Holland Gidney, 'Canadian Gigantica: Genus Roadside,' *This Magazine* 40/1 (2006): 26–7.

3 English-language readers will find the fundamentals of Ukrainian history, politics, and culture in the five-volume *Encyclopaedia of Ukraine (E.U.)* (Toronto: University of Toronto Press, 1984–95). On Ukrainian Canadian history, see Orest Martynowych, *Ukrainians in Canada: The Formative Years, 1891–1924* (Toronto: University of Toronto Press, 1991), and Vadim Kukushkin, *From Peasants to Labourers: Ukrainian and Belarusan Immigration from the Russian Empire to Canada* (Montreal and Kingston: McGill-Queen's University Press, 2007). For studies of Ukrainian Canadian material culture, see folklorist Robert Klymasz, *Continuity and Change: The Ukrainian Folk Heritage in Canada* (Ottawa: Museum of Man, 1972), and his *Sviéto: Celebrating Ukrainian-Canadian Ritual in East-Central Alberta* (Edmonton: Alberta Ministry of Culture and Multiculturalism, 1992); Ukrainian Women's Association of Canada, *Ukrainian Canadiana* (Edmonton: Author, 1976); Mariya Lesiv, *Pysanka: The Ukrainian Easter Egg in Canada*, M.A. thesis, University of Alberta, 2005.

4 The history of archetypes and symbols are surveyed by Carl Jung in *Man and His Symbols* (New York: Dell, 1968), and the semiotician C.J. Cirlot, *A Dictionary of Symbols* (London: Routledge and Kegan Paul, 1961). For a feminist examination of the myths and symbols particular to the material culture of Baltic, Central, and Eastern Europe, see Marija Gimbutas, *Language of the Goddess* (San Francisco: Harper and Row, 1991).

5 V. Markus, 'Famine,' *E.U.*, vol. 1, 853–5.

6 Ukrainians first immigrated en masse to Canada in the late nineteenth century as economic and political refugees, followed by smaller post-revolution waves in the 1920s; postwar refugees and Displaced Persons in the late 1940s; and economic migrants since Ukraine's independence in 1991. Today, Ukrainians comprise a small minority of the overall Canadian population (approx. 3%). Most of the first arrivals settled in about equal proportions as industrial workers in large cities or in such frontier towns as Sudbury, Ontario, and especially as farm workers on the prairies. In certain small bloc settlements in rural east-central Saskatchewan and east-central Alberta (as well as southern Manitoba), Ukrainians have formed a sizeable minority for over a hundred years.

7 Marusya Bociurkiw, *Comfort Food for Break-Ups: Memoirs of A Hungry Girl* (Vancouver: Arsenal Pulp Press, 2007), 63. Writing generations earlier, Ukrainian Canadian essayist William Paluk describes the *horshok* (ceramic serving dish) as a 'kind of shrine around which the family gathers periodically, and which binds it

together until death.' 'Plight of the *Perih [Perogy]*,' in *Canadian Cossacks: Essays, Articles, and Stories on Ukrainian-Canadian Life* (Winnipeg: Canadian Ukrainian Review, 1942), 64.

8 Literally, 'Remember you must die.' The theme of memento mori as expressed through an abundance of foodstuffs is the basis of the *Vanitas* painterly tradition in Western art.

9 Critical views of the Ukrainian food sculptures are to be found in Myrna Kostash, *All of Baba's Children* (Edmonton: NeWest, 1977), 404–5, and Frances Swyripa, *Wedded to the Cause: Ukrainian-Canadian Women and Ethnic Identity, 1891–1991* (Toronto: University of Toronto Press, 1993), 181–2.

10 The term *Baba* is pan-Slavic and is used colloquially to describe any female elder, especially agricultural labourers and urbanites with lower-income status. While current usage of 'Baba' may connote female clumsiness, ignorance of social graces, and contrariness, my use is honorific.

11 Bociurkiw, *Comfort Food*, 39

12 Stacey Zembrzycki, 'Sharing Authority with Baba,' *Journal of Canadian Studies / Revue d'études canadiennes* 43/1 (2009): 5.

13 Exceptions include Martha Bohachewsky-Chomiak, *Feminists despite Themselves* (Edmonton: Canadian Institute of Ukrainian Studies and the University of Alberta Presses, 1984); Swyripa, *Wedded to the Cause*; Marusya Bociurkiw, *Halfway to the East* (Vancouver: Lazara, 1999).

14 Ron Resch, Paul Sembaliuk, Two Hills Construction, et al.

15 Nicholas Lewchuk and Orest Lewchuk.

16 Also known as *kalach*. Bread types include *baba*, *babka*, *challah*, *dyveh*, *iezhen*, *klib*, *knysh*, *korovai*, *kulich*, *paska*, and *shysky*, among others.

17 Zenon Pohorecky, 'Ukrainian Cultural and Political Symbols in Canada: An Anthropological Approach,' in Manoly Lupul, ed., *Visible Symbols: Cultural Expression among Canada's Ukrainians* (Edmonton: Canadian Institute of Ukrainian Studies Press, 1981), 143.

18 Ibid.

19 Mass Ukrainian emigration began in the nineteenth century, with the United States as the primary destination. Emigration to Canada only began in the 1890s.

20 As are potatoes and dough (Glendon *Perogy*), mushrooms (Vilna *Mushrooms*), and garlicky pork sausage (Mundare *Kielbassa*). Duck and pumpkin (Andrew and Smoky Lake) were local Alberta additions c. 1900 to the dietary staples of the Ukrainian pioneers, 1891–1939. See also, Marshal Nay, *Trailblazers of Ukrainian Emigration to Canada* (Edmonton: Brightest Pebble, 1997).

21 For explanations of rushnyky form and symbolism, see curators Oksana I. Grabowicz and Maria Shust, *Traditional Designs in Ukrainian Textiles:An Exhibition* (New York: Ukrainian Museum, 1977); Lidia Lykhach and Sophia Kachor, *Kolory*

i Melodiyi Ukrainskoho Sviata: Colours and Melodies of Ukrainian Holidays (Winnipeg: Oseredok Ukrainian Cultural and Educational Centre, 2008); D. Horniakevytch and L. Nenadkevych, 'Embroidery,' *E.U.*, vol. 1, 816–18, and M. Mushynka, 'Rushnyk,' *E.U.*, vol. 4, 441–3 .

22 Bociurkiw, *Comfort Food*, 39.

23 Egg ornamentation is a folk art practised by many traditional cultures including those of Balkan, Baltic, Central, and Eastern Europe.

24 Ukrainian egg decorating is today associated with Easter, the Christian rite of remembrance of the death and resurrection of Jesus Christ, but the making of pysanky is ancient and pagan. Traditionally, these delicate objets d'art are made from foodstuffs in springtime, using secret techniques that are passed on from mothers to daughters in celebration of the end of winter and the arrival of the fertile seasons of spring and summer.

25 Within pysanky iconography, standard motives allude to the supernatural forces that govern fertility, the interdependency of farming culture with nature, and especially, the cycles of life and death. The Vegreville *Pysanka* is decorated with circular rows of triangles in a classic protective motif described by Western semioticians as a *vagina dendata*, and by Ukrainians as 'wolves' teeth.' Its secondary motif is the star, symbolizing enlightenment, mystical presence, and divine protection.

26 Mary Tkachuk, Marie Kishchuk, and Alice Nikolaichuk, *Pysanka: Icon of the Universe* (Saskatoon: Ukrainian Women's Association of Canada and the Ukrainian Museum of Canada, 1997).

27 Savella Stechishin, 'Foods, Traditional,' *E.U.*, vol. 1, 915.

28 Ibid., 915.

29 Bociurkiw, *Comfort Food*, 39.

30 Stechishin, 'Foods, Traditional,' 915.

31 Ibid., 915.

32 Thelma Barer-Stein, *You Eat What You Are* (Toronto: McClelland and Stewart, 1979), 527.

33 Stechishin, 'Foods, Traditional,' 915.

34 In *Festive Ukrainian Cookery*, the American food historian Marta Pisetka Farley describes a recipe from 1891 for an 'esoteric' variety of Easter bread 1 m in height and containing 140 egg yolks (Toronto: University of Toronto Press, 1991), 38. For more practical bread recipes, see numerous entries in Savella Stechishin, *Traditional Ukrainian Cookery* (Winnipeg: Trident, 1957, 12; rev. ed., 1980).

35 Stechishin, 'Foods, Traditional,' 915.

36 Occasionally, wedding and funeral breads are also decorated with ribbons, skewers, flags, marshmallows, and other ornaments. For Ukrainian bread types and forms, see Olya S. Marko, *Pracja Zhinka (Women's Work): An Introduction to the Art of Ukrainian Ritual Breads* (exhibition catalogue) (Winnipeg: Oseredok

Ukrainian Cultural and Educational Centre, 1987), and numerous entries in Farley, *Festive Ukrainian Cooking*.

37 Salting is one of humankind's earliest ways of flavouring and preserving food, and salt's cleansing and scouring qualities make it an ideal medium to purify the work surfaces used in cooking, food preparation, and food storage. Thus, salt is an appropriate, universal metaphor for longevity, vitality, and purity.

38 Similar to the Classical Greek concept of *xena*, it is exemplified by the Ukrainian proverb, '*Hist' u Xatu, Boh u Xatu*' ('To Honour a Guest Is to Honour God'), cited by Robert Klymasz, *Folk Narrative among Ukrainian-Canadians in Western Canada* (Ottawa: Canadian Centre for Folk Culture Studies, National Museum of Man, 1973), 7.

39 Some rushnyky motives are woven rather than embroidered, and more recent examples are machine printed.

40 Rushnyk is often mistranslated as 'towel.'

41 Mushynka, 'Rushnyk.'

42 The use of ornamental ritual cloths for these purposes is common to the indigenous cultures of Balkan, Baltic, Central, and Eastern Europe. In peasant homes, rushnyky mark all points of sanctity. They are draped around icons, over doors and windows, above the marital and birthing beds, and, significantly, around the dish cupboard.

43 During a Panikhyda, the priest holds up to heaven a kolach on a rushnyk. This, in effect, makes the peasant bread equal in holy status to the Bible and icons of the Christian saints, which are also draped with rushnyky.

44 Bociurkiw, *Comfort Food*, 59.

45 The rite of the funeral feast was practised by the pre-Classical Greeks and is at least 5,000 years old in Ukrainian territory: see Yu. Ya. Rassamakin, 'The Steppe Neighbours of the Ancient Trypilians: Second Quarter of the Fifth to the Beginning of the Third Millennium BC,' in Krzysztof Ciuk, ed., *Mysteries of Ancient Ukraine: The Remarkable Trypilian Culture, 5400–2700 BC* (Toronto: Royal Ontario Museum, 2008), 49. Other holidays in which Ukrainians feed the dead include *Provody* ('Blessing of the Graves,' the first Sunday after Easter); *Zeleni Sviat* ('Green Holiday,' 40–50 days after Easter, also known as *Rosalia*, a pagan feast celebrating fertility as well as death); and *Dmytra* (Saturday before the feast of St Dmytro, 26 November).

46 The phrase 'dual-faith' describes the blending of Christian traditions with ones from pagan, pre-Christian, and often matriarchal traditions that even today seem to have a presence in virtually every Ukrainian Christian custom. For introductions to the subject of historical and current dual-faith practices see, '*Provody*,' *E.U.*, vol. 4, 253–4; I. Korovystky, 'Demonology,' *E.U.*, vol. 1, 656–7; P. Odarenko, 'Christmas,' *E.U.*, vol. 1, 461–2; B. Kratsiv, 'Folk Beliefs' and 'Folk Customs and

Rites,' *E.U.*, vol. 1, 904–5; B. Kratsiv and B. Medwisky, 'Mythology,' *E.U.*, vol. 3, 521; Z. Kuzelia and P. Odarenko, 'Easter,' *E.U.*, vol. 1, 780–1; and M. Mushynka, '*Rosalia*,' *E.U.*, vol. 4, 407–8.

47 Regional differences occur in the observances of the *Sviat Vecher*, but the meal never contains red meat or dairy products and generally includes versions of *kutia*, *borscht/borshch* (beet soup), beans, mushrooms, *holubtsi* (cabbage rolls filled with rice, buckwheat, and onions), *perogies/perihy* (dumplings usually filled with potato), *kapusta* (pickled cabbage with carrot and onion), fish (fresh, smoked, and pickled), bread with salt and garlic, cookies and cakes, and dried fruit compote.

48 For Ukrainian Christians, the three tiers and tripartite braids of the Christmas Eve kolach doubly represent the Holy Trinity of Father, Son, and Holy Spirit, while the twelve courses refer to the twelve Apostles.

49 From *Dido* ('Grandfather'). The stalks of the didukh are gathered from the very last remains in the fields after the fall harvest and are traditionally burned in spring as fertility offerings to the new crop.

50 The east or northeastern corner (also known as the 'sacred corner' and 'icon corner'). The archeological evidence of a special corner for votive images in Ukrainian domestic architecture has been traced back as far as Trypilian/Cuceteni domestic architecture (c. 5000 BCE). See Natalia B. Burdo, 'Magic and Symbolism among the Ancient Trypilians: Reconstructing Domestic Life' (178), and 'Spirituality and Artistic Expression' (213), in Ciuk, *Mysteries of Ancient Ukraine*.

51 According to Savella Stechishin, *kutia* is also 'inseparable' from traditional Ukrainian burial rituals. It is the first course of the funeral meal, because it 'represents the resurrection of the dead.' See Stechishin, 'Food, Traditional,' 916.

52 Other meal items in the sanctified Easter basket typically include kielbassa, butter, green onions, garlic, horseradish, and a beeswax candle.

53 Pohorecky, 'Ukrainian Cultural and Political Symbols in Canada,' 143. Almost seventy years ago, William Paluk envisioned the decline of traditional Ukrainian meals in Canada to such modern intrusions as canned vegetables and store-bought bread. See 'Plight of the Perih,' 64–6.

54 Peter Ennals and Deryck Holdsworth, *Homeplace: The Making of the Canadian Dwellling over Three Centuries* (Toronto: University of Toronto Press, 1998).

55 Norman Davies, *A History of Europe* (London: Pimlico, 1999), 1329.

9 Toronto's Multicultured Tongues: Stories of South Asian Cuisines

JULIE MEHTA

I begin this chapter on the culinary journey of South Asians negotiating their complex identities in multicultural Toronto and its environs with some stories about *roti* – the handmade bread used by almost all South Asian immigrants, particularly the Sikhs from the Indian state of Punjab – and its long roots in the vexed immigrant history of Canada. Since the Sikhs were the first and largest group of South Asian immigrants to Canada, I use this particular community to launch the exploration. In some form or another, the ubiquitous roti is the crucial cultural symbol that unites hyphenated Canadian-South Asians in their diverse histories of arrival and settlement in Canada. Fearing them as 'brown people' and as wage competitors, the predominantly Anglo-Canadian population responded to their growing numbers in Canada, which in 1908 stood at five thousand people, most of them in British Columbia, with much hostility.

A related concern was the polluting of a primarily 'clean' Canadian cultural landscape, through assertions of identity by supposedly 'un-assimilable' settlers with their 'smelly' cuisines, as well as strange modes of dress and habit. As a *Vancouver Sun* editorial declared, in opposition to the male migrants' desire to bring their families, these people (incorrectly called Hindu) 'are not a desirable people' in 'a white country with white standards of living and morality,' adding, we 'will never be able to absorb them' and 'must not permit their women to come in at all.'[1] In response, the Canadian government, then guardians of an essentially white Canada policy, responded by limiting immigration to people who arrived from South Asia by 'continuous voyage' from their land of origin. Since one could not get to Canada from India or Sri Lanka (Pakistan and Bangladesh were a part of British India and not created yet) non-stop without docking at some intermediate port of call, the law produced the intended effect, virtually stopping the entry of immigrants from South Asia. Between 1909 and 1943, only 878 South Asians entered Canada.[2]

After the Second World War, Sikhs gained some rights: in 1947, they won the right to vote and, in 1950, in Mission, B.C., Narajan Singh Grewal became the first Sikh elected to a city council. But it was not until the decades after 1967, when Canada dismantled its most explicit racist quotas and liberalized its admission rules, that Sikhs (and other South Asians) began arriving in significant numbers, settling in major centres across the country. The waves of Sikh immigrants who came after the first arrivals established strong networks of community in Canada by starting up grocery stores, restaurants, and meeting places aligned to their places of worship, the *gurudwaras*. Enterprising and heavily invested in preserving their cultural values, Sikh families began to use food 'to chart viable alternatives to "official" and "traditional" models of national definition,' as the Toronto-based Indo-Caribbean author Shani Mootoo showcases in her story *Out on Main Street*.[3] In the writings of contemporary Asian Canadian novelists such as Anita Rau Badami and South Asian poets, the word roti swaddles in its folds the agrarian economy of Punjab and the identity of an entire race. Here, wheat is the currency of life, and roti becomes a unifying symbol for all Punjabis in the Canadian diaspora and awakens familial, community, and cultural memory.[4] Roti is also the link that connects Canada's Sikh community to the vexed history of the arrival of the steamship *Komagata Maru* in Vancouver in 1914, and the subsequent maltreatment of the 'brown invaders' by the Canadian authorities who finally sent the shipload of immigrants back to India amid a South Asian Canadian uprising. Accounts speak of how the Indo-Canadians already in Canada made rotis in their homes and supplied these to the 'prisoners' aboard the steamer, to keep them alive.[5]

For second- and third-generation Sikh immigrants, roti has an immediacy as food they may share at home during meals *and* is woven into the fabric of Sikh cultural history in Canada, as established by the 2008 apologies by Canadian Member of Parliament Ruby Dhalla and Prime Minister Stephen Harper, for the suffering the Canadian government had imposed on the *Komagata Maru* passengers. Thus, roti, for Indo-Canadians across generational lines, is a signifier of struggle. A perceptive Punjabi student in my University of Toronto course in Asian Cultures and Literatures in Canada spoke eloquently on the subject in his essay with these final words: 'what has struck me most is the recurrent image of food as a marker of diasporic rapture and rupture. For me I have rediscovered my identity through these texts we have discussed and I now understand why my grandmother insists I eat her ghee-laden rotis and converse only in Punjabi.'

South Asian Culinary Landscapes in Toronto

Today, the landscape of Toronto and the Greater Toronto Area (GTA) is marked by a multiplicity of South Asian cuisines reflecting the many diverse regional groups from South Asia who have become a blended reality of Canadian immigrant life. In 2006, Canada's South Asian population, with groups from India, Pakistan, Sri Lanka, and Bangladesh, as well as second-generation South Asians from elsewhere, stood at 1.26 million (followed by the Chinese at 1.21 million). Contributing significantly to Toronto's transformation as one of the most multicultural cities on the globe, some 298,074 South Asians represented the largest perception of 'visible minority groups' in the city in 2006. Together, these racial groupings are poised to become the city's majority by 2012 (and also in Vancouver). As for the GTA, the Census Metropolitan Area of Toronto numbered 684,070 South Asians in 2006, or 13.5 per cent of the 'visible minority groups' (followed, again, by the Chinese at 486, 330 or 9.6%). Of the South Asian groups, the largest concentration of Sikhs are in Brampton, while Mississauga is home to the greatest numbers of Indians, Pakistanis, and Bangladeshis; and Scarborough has the densest Sri Lankan Tamil population.[6]

For the many diverse South Asians who are negotiating their place and identity in Canada's most multicultural city, this culinary landscape constitutes a crucial site of identity formation, one affected by the intersections of many South Asian and other groups and by contested notions of language, belonging, and identity. My case study, itself a hybrid of empirical research, participant observation, and personalized scholarship, explores the crucial but neglected subject of South Asian North American identities in multiracial Toronto by exploring two major sources that speak to the key importance of food in the formulation of identity: South Asian restaurants and cuisines and the narratives of students in the multicultural university classroom and wider Toronto landscape. Like other chapters in this volume, I explore the relationship between food and identity in situations of encounter, track the rise of ethnic foodways, and explore the phenomena of cultural hybridity and creolization. However, while these other chapters deal largely with Europeans encountering dominant majority Canadians in earlier periods,[7] or with Euro-Canadian-Aboriginal encounters,[8] my case study, while informed by history, focuses on racialized non-Western immigrants whose cultural presence on the contemporary culinary and literary landscape has helped define a certain Canadian diasporic cosmopolitanism.

This project was sparked by classroom discussions in a third-year Asian Cultures in Canada course I have been teaching at the University of Toronto since 2006.[9] Here, young Asian Canadian undergraduates have been vigorously engaged in finding their *own* hyphenated, diasporic Asian-North American identities through two crucial cultural markers: food and language. The students explore their 'cosmopolitan' pluralities through the food they share at home in a multigenerational gathering, or consume at restaurants either with their families or peers, or through the language they often lose in the overwhelming urgency to acculturate to 'Canadian ways.' Like the immigrant protagonists in South Asian literature, such as Leela Bhatt,[10] Su-Jen,[11] Miyo Mori,[12] Arjun Chelvaratnam,[13] or Nurdun Lalani,[14] the students must sort out who they are. They come to understand that a journey involves learning where one comes from. With their classmates to help them unveil their own pasts, my students are allowed a glimpse into their *present*. Each year in the course, these final-year students, approximately 85 per cent of them Asian, assert they are 'seeking our own identities as minorities in Canada,' as one of them put it.

My research into South Asian foodways has continued outside of the classroom and into the culinary urban environment. Significantly, Toronto provides an *unmatched* opportunity to test my culinary interest in cooking at least fifteen different regional cuisines of South Asia in my own kitchen, with the best and 'most authentic' ingredients available in more than one hundred ethnic grocers all over the GTA. Add to that the approximately two hundred South Asian restaurants that aggressively jostle for a toehold on the culinary landscape, and this becomes a paradise for a food enthusiast. My project also excavates the powerful connection that 'imaginary homelands' in immigrant communities have to food, and how revisionary menus and recipes that are recreated in a diaspora are bound to collective memory.[15] Drawing from history, anthropology, and cultural studies, I ask these questions: Can food operate as substitute for and thereby support disaggregated and/or hybrid identities in the world of diasporic formations? To what extent might such culinary productions, alone, be the bearers of displaced identities or must they be accompanied by the continuing use of the language of origin to achieve their full effects? Indeed, what is the role of language and food as vehicles of identity, and does creolization and/or bilingualism necessarily diffuse their significance?[16]

My informed observations and interviews confirm the value of Etienne Baliban's concept of 'eternal strangers' in a global world, namely, that food is a great connector for many diverse peoples who have all migrated, relocated, or been refugees.[17] So, too, does it reinforce Sarah Daynes' point that food 'is the easiest tool to transport memories,'[18] an insight that informs other contributions in this volume.[19] I argue that food is a marker of belonging and identity among 'imagined communities,' as Benedict Anderson configures them.[20] Having spent twenty-five years as an independent researcher and author of books on cultures of Asia, and having lived in Australia, Singapore, India,

Thailand, Vietnam, Cambodia, and now Canada, I also know that the presence of regional cuisines from different provinces within a single city affects the specific notions of a community's identity and its distinctive sense of 'self.' One finds in Toronto many examples of generic South Asian foods, including variants of the pan-Indian 'characterless' butter chicken and overspiced, listless samosas, that, in Simon During's words, reflect a 'global sameness.'[21] Nevertheless, one also finds a diversity of regional foods, and this multiplicity of South Asian cuisines has given rise to some distinctive notions of being South Asian in Canada.

Global Palates versus Regional Pockets

Being South Asian in Canada inevitably involves a sense of hybridity – simply defined as a blending of cultures – that is highly contested. Susan Stanford-Friedman asserts that for cosmopolitan postmodern diasporics like the burgeoning numbers of South Asian immigrants on the move in the world, hybridity is transgressive in that it is a creative force that disrupts, denaturalizes, and potentially dismantles hegemonic cultural formations. Acknowledging that 'the politics of hybridity is fiercely contested, with advocates, denouncers, and ambivalents lining up on all sides,' she maintains:

> The fundamental question is how hybridity relates to power relations in the borderlands between difference. Is hybridity imposed or embraced? Who benefits? Is it reciprocal or one-sided? Does it enhance one group's power at the expense of others? Is it the luxury of the privileged? The unchosen reality of the least empowered? Is it revolutionary or regressive? Does hybridity talk represent a much-needed alternative to the binaries of center-periphery, First and Third World, self-other? To the excesses of identity politics? Or, does hybridity talk fall back into romantic utopianism, obscuring the real relations of power that maintain inequitable structures of difference?[22]

An important aspect of South Asian food in diaspora includes the tension between the standardization of cuisine versus, and alongside, the continuity of regional specialization. With all these questions in mind, I have explored the South Asian cuisines found on the streets of Toronto and its environs and asked whether they represent global sameness or regional diversity. In Toronto, as noted earlier, one finds both. There are three restaurants serving generic but high quality South Asian fare in the GTA and Toronto that come under the category of the solid 'standard Indian' though ubiquitous eatery – Host, Dhaba, and Nirvana. All of them are conceptualized and run by Punjabis (some like the owner of Nirvana, is Sikh), who come from the northwest province of Punjab, in India, a primarily agricultural society that is also the homeland of the wheat-growing farmers, the Sikhs. This 'Punjabi style' cuisine dominates the culinary map of India even *within* India, which has forty-eight different kinds of cuisines and eighteen official languages. It is the kind of cooking that produces butter chicken, palak-paneer (cottage cheese and spinach), and tandoori chicken.

Host, which has three main branches – in Richmond Hill, Mississauga, and downtown Toronto (near upscale Yorkville) – is a well-known establishment run by Sanjeev Sethi, and a collection of hand-picked, skilled, and informed staff, each of whom is committed to 'establishing alternative networks of intimacy' in the community and beyond, to anchor the cultural values that come with preserving a way of life through traditional cuisine, as Anita Mannur posits in her compelling study of South Asian diaspora and its cuisines.[23] The fourth location of Host is at Wellington and Blue Jays Way, which opened in 2008, and already has won the palates of die-hard foodies with their tandoori lamb chops with vindaloo sauce, signposting a trend whereby some Indian restaurants are bravely going avant-garde. The Mississauga branch is perhaps the most active with the largest turnaround on Sunday buffets, where South Asians from all over the GTA queue up to 'get a taste of home' and 'celebrate as a community.' A hands-on chef in the kitchen, owner Sanjeev Sethi has made Host a reliable and standard brand that whips up north Indian fare that is ubiquitous: chicken butter masala, mutton curry, roti, naan, and a range of vegetable curries that include broccoli, capsicum, and carrots – not the traditional vegetables found in an Indian kitchen. The inspiration, Chef Sanjeev maintains, is his mother's cooking and her commitment to 'cook with love as the primary ingredient.'[24]

Located in the city's financial and business district of Toronto, Dhaba is another popular Indian restaurant that fits the high-quality brand of non-regional, ubiquitous curry restaurants serving mostly Punjabi fare that is pan-Indian today. It is run by P.K. Ahluwalia, the chef owner-operator, and competes with Host for a steady curry-loving clientele. The lunchtime buffet offers a varied fare of at least twenty salads and ubiquitous items like fish Amritsari (a version of fish and chips, with a large dollop of masala) and butter chicken. Dhaba takes on a new image for dinner, however, reinventing itself for the white Canadian palate and serving up exotic versions of the Orient: the 'fusion' cuisine on the evening à la carte menu features venison and lamb, but also vegetarian alternatives. For its attempt to straddle the world of butter chicken at lunch and Indian fusion at night, Dhaba has been called 'inventive' and 'innovative' by reviewers.[25]

Nirvana was launched in Mississauga in 2004 as 'a unique concept gallery restaurant with a definitive Indian theme.' As an experiment in Indian fine dining, owner Sukhi Ghumman wanted 'not only to initiate authentic Indian cuisine for the South Asian and the Canadian palate, but to club this with a culture statement. We want to focus on art, culture and fashion.'[26] Nirvana's pride lies in the fiery caverns of the twin tandoors, the clay ovens that spew out delicious mutton seekh kebabs and prawn kebabs. The Sikh population of the GTA generally agrees that Nirvana makes the best baigan bharta (smoked eggplant puree), saag gosht (spinach and mutton curry), and tandoori rotis, giving it their stamp of approval from a *desi*, or provincially Indian perspective.

All three of these Punjabi-style restaurants have established themselves as strong catering pods that host many wedding banquets and other celebrations. Offering a comparable price range, they cater primarily to a large, mixed clientele of white Canadians who want good quality standard Indian food coupled with fine dining and trained servers who can converse and entertain as required. Still, critics have disparaged this form of vernacular globalization, arguing that the marking of butter chicken as 'Indian' national cuisine leads to a kind of misguided global acceptance of what is 'Indian' cuisine, resulting in a sort of global uniformity that homogenizes all regional South Asian food into 'curry.' In other words, it is Toronto's version of the characterless British offering of a nouveau national dish, chicken tikka masala, which has *no* precedent or roots in Indian cuisine.

However, in Toronto and the GTA region, vernacular cuisine from South Asia flourishes not as an ever-present 'curry' common to all but rather as highly specialized restaurants with very specific menus, or catering units with highly focused offerings. In these specialized locales, people of a specific community from South Asia draw members of *their* community or *others* and establish a specific cultural and geographical culinary cuisine.

Interestingly, most of the culturally diverse styles of cooking are preserved by women chefs in these establishments. And the competition between similar styles of regional or provincial cooking is fierce. For example, in a corner of Ridgeway, located on the border between Mississauga and Oakville, is White Gold Sweets – a Gujarati restaurant tucked into a warehouse complex, where Neeta Patel offers up rare regional delicacies such as Undhiyu, a mixed vegetable tempered with asafetida and Indian oregano and topped with fried lentil pakoras (balls).

Similarly, in a nondescript strip mall on Bartley Bull Boulevard in Brampton is Anjappar Chettinad, another fine regional restaurant. The chefs, trained in Chennai, Tamilnadu, in India, are hand-picked for the Canadian outlets in Toronto (Brampton and Scarborough). Its fiery chili and pepper-based cuisine has roots in a thousand-year community history among the chettiars, from southern India, and is highly popular with the Tamil community. Anjappar also attracts others, including white Canadians who come from as far away as Guelph for the mutton sukka veruval, king fish curry, and chicken chettinad. For manager Ellalan Guname, 'the proof of multiculturalism in Toronto and the GTA lies in the 30 per cent clientele who make up our regulars.' As he explains, 'Anjappar practises a very, very specialized form of cooking, which is not available in even the larger metros of India like Calcutta and Mumbai. And the food, one would imagine, is extremely hot for the white Canadian palate.' They were, thus, happily surprised by the positive response, 'first from the Tamil community, who are *not all Brahmins* or vegetarians.' Brahmins, the highest caste among the four castes among Hindus, are often vegetarians, since eating meat is considered unclean for a high-born, priestly class person, whose caste purity depends sometimes on his or her diet. Tamils of the other castes – the Kshatriyas (warrior class), Vaishyas (business class), and Shudras (servers and lower class) – are non-vegetarians, and often eat flesh and fish. 'And then,' adds Guname, were 'the many other Indians and white Canadians' who also became regulars. As a result, the business grew 'to such an extent' that it can 'survive even in these tough economic times.'[27]

This is not to suggest we have seen the end of the stereotyping of South Asian cuisine as pungent and offensive, and as 'disturbing' the ethos of a pristine, unpolluted white Canadian neighbourhood. In Toronto and the GTA, real estate agents 'warn' prospective Canadian house owners and renters of the 'smells' that emanate from unfamiliar cooking spices and herbs. Conversely, the grilling of meats on a barbecue by Euro-Canadians might remind new South Asian immigrants, who may be vegetarian, of a crematorium where the smell of charred flesh symbolizes last rites. However, since they are a minority, this aspect of food as a highly complex and culturally nuanced marker is often neglected by the mainstream. Still, one of the best sites for exploring the meanings and power of food to shape identity and cultural exchange is the multicultural classroom.

Tongue as the Seat of Cultural Power

Each year in the Asian Cultures class, we have looked closely at Michael Ondaatje's bio-text, *Running in the Family*. A second-generation Filipino Canadian student, Maria Teresa Camu, was most taken by a short passage in the book where Ondaatje describes the joy of slurping up crab curry and rice with his fingers. In her class presentation, she effectively connected the communal experience of eating with fingers in a Filipino household or at a Filipino festival with Asian Canadian author Ondaatje's recollections of eating crab curry with his fingers when he had returned to Sri Lanka to collate the history of his family. Ondaatje insists that crab curry must be savoured with the fingers; anything else would be a travesty. Socially, it would not sit well if one person in a communal setting insisted on using cutlery in the midst of a meal. Inspired by these discussions, Maria chose for her course essay to study the specific utensils used to cook Filipino food in the traditional Filipino kitchen. Her oral interviews with older family members and friends made for some truly groundbreaking research and provided the class with rare glimpses into the food rituals of the Filipinos within the Canadian multicultural landscape.

As this example suggests, in my classroom, cultural quirks and rituals are *not* denied out of some kind of self-conscious ethnicity but rather brought to the fore, and in the comfort zone that is created, students no longer feel embarrassed about their family food customs. My students have shared with their classmates stories of family meals and rituals about which they have rarely spoken publicly. Indeed, they have spoken of feeling empowered by their cultural practices; instead of relying on cliché dismissals of their elders' old-fashioned or traditional ways, they have admitted to understanding why their grandparents so stringently clung to food habits and practices. Here, an important catalyst was reading Asian Canadian novels such as Badami's book *Can You Hear the Nightbird Call?* and Judy Fong Bates' book *Midnight at the Dragon Café*, which launched class discussions about *how* food becomes a transformative experience – either as an assertion of community values or a zone of familiarity and identity in the midst of interracial tensions *among minorities within* Canada. In this context, students were inspired to share their own stories about how their grandparents or parents had turned to 'homeland' food to create a secure 'cultural space' within a new Canada of multicultural elements. Student Anne Gnanatheepan, whose parents migrated from Sri Lanka, was clearly concerned about issues of hyphenation and acculturation; she wrestled all year with a whole range of issues about her 'once homeland' intellectually. As we ran the grid with South Asian writers, and engaged in many long class discussions, she slowly began to articulate her insightful formulations and synthesized the two crucial cultural markers – food and language – into a clever metaphor of 'the tongue.' As she put it, the *tongue* was the symbolic residence of the two most rich and complex markers of culture.

Smelling Hybridity

I have used food to provoke discussion in my other courses. During an Effective English Writing class I was teaching in the summer of 2009, I decided to introduce to my students the idea of compare and contrast by bringing to class two different types of samosas: sample A, the traditionally spicy potato and peas samosa, which came with the pungent tamarind and fennel seed chutney, and sample B, a tofu and onion samosa. The students were to write down three words that described each of the samples. In the front row sat a second-generation Canadian student of Eastern European origins, who picked up sample A first. As a classmate offered her the chutney, she turned away in disgust, exclaiming, 'It smells like urine.' A complete whoosh of silence rippled right through the lecture hall. 'Okay, what about the samosa itself?' I asked. 'That really burned my taste buds,' she explained, quite honestly.

Just as I was overcoming my initial shock over this student's urine comment and wondering how to handle it, another young white Canadian student from the back of the class raised his hand and exclaimed: 'Why, which planet have you been on? Haven't you ever tasted a samosa before?' A Jamaican-born Canadian student said, 'Sample A is the real thing. I love it.' And another young white Canadian added, 'This is Toronto. If you've gone to school here, and are now at university here, how come you have no idea of the most multicultural Indian snack?' Interestingly, it was not a South Asian or Chinese immigrant, but instead two young, white Torontonians and a Jamaican, who stood up for the samosa. In her defence, the original student later explained to me that for her the concept of hybridization had more to do with her European affiliations, and she could more readily relate to the idea of experimenting with and merging various European cultures. Along with the food, the concept of nineteenth-century European gentility and sophistication also appealed to her. The incident exposed me, a South Asian scholar recently transplanted to Canada, to a form of cultural hybridity that, as other chapters in this volume highlight, involves white Europeans negotiating a Euro-Canadian identity whether in hostile or familiar immigrant contexts. It alerted me to the fact that hybridity as applied to Asian visible minorities is not the only form that rears its head in a multicultural space like contemporary Toronto. Even today, when immigrant cultures are largely understood as non-Western, hybridity can still refer to a mix of European cultures.

Homi Bhabha's ideas about hybridity can help us understand the opinions of second- and third-generation hyphenated Canadians – students in the classroom who wrestle with multiple identities, cultures, and ideas of home, especially in the context of diasporic food and language that informs their everyday encounters in living with multigenerational members of their families. Bhabha traces the hyphenated subject as split and mobile, located in a somewhat ambivalent 'third' space that disrupts the more conventional binaries of 'self' and 'other.' 'The third space,' he writes, 'may open the way to conceptualizing an international culture, based not on the exoticism of multiculturalism, or the diversity of cultures, but on the inscription and articulation of culture's hybridity.'[28]

Over the years, my students in the Asian Cultures course have grappled with such complex issues. In our annual class excursion into the vast and varied cuisine hubs of the city, one clear favourite has been the Host, for its satisfying range of the familiar butter chicken, tandoori chicken, and paneer makhni. But, my students have also made some new suggestions about regional cuisine stops. One that is popular among the Pakistani students is Tandoori Time, where whole families gather to taste the nahari, a delicious slow-cooked beef curry; or haleem, a punchy lentils-and-beef dish. Many of these students' memories of family celebrations on special occasions, such as Eid, a Muslim holiday that marks the end of Ramadan (the Islamic holy month of fasting), involve one of two Tandoori Times in Toronto.[29] Typically, the Pakistani families in Mississauga flock to Desi Corner (a corner of homeland), a take-out place on Dundas and Hurontario, where a team of women cooks make an excellent range of biriyanis (chicken, mutton and beef) from morning to midnight, under the supervision of Mrs Siddiqui, who owns the restaurant with her husband. Her son is a University of Toronto student who often helps out in the shop, learning about his national cuisine as he works. Another favourite is Eastern Foods International, which also serves delicious kormas of mutton and chicken that evoke the 'real' thing back in the best restaurants of Lahore or Karachi or even at Charbaugh, in Lucknow, famous for its superb Muslim fare. These places become critical sites of identity formation.

Conclusion

To return to my opening narratives about roti, my Asian Canadian student's perceptive insight into why he ate his grandmother's 'ghee-laden rotis' and talked with her 'only in Punjabi' speaks equally well not only to the power of food as a marker of difference but to its productive creativity; food can be harnessed through language both to produce and maintain memories of the past and to acculturate to the new cultural realities of the present. Like earlier generations of white European immigrants who used food and language as resources for forging an ethnic or hyphenated Canadian identity, young South Asian students in today's multicultural Toronto and GTA are actively engaged in shaping their identities. If, in contrast to white European immigrants and Euro-Canadians, South Asians in contemporary Toronto and GTA have not been able to access a white subjecthood, the multiplicity of regional South Asian cuisines have given them a more particular sense of place – of the 'here' and 'there' – and thus of a hyphenated diasporic South Asian Canadian identity. Perhaps Keya Ganguly, a diasporic hyphenated woman academic, with a healthy appetite for culinary adventure, best sums up the South Asian diaspora's obsession with food to nurture and protect its cultural wealth, when she says, 'It is difficult, if not impossible to think of immigrant Indian existence ... without at the same time thinking of Indian food.[30]

NOTES

1 *Vancouver Sun*, 17 June 1913, Editorial, 6.
2 Gurcharan S. Basran and B. Singh Bolaria, *The Sikhs in Canada: Migration, Race, Class and Gender* (New Delhi: Oxford University Press, 2003).
3 Shani Mootoo, *Out on Main Street* (Vancouver: Press Gang, 1993).
4 Anita Rau Badami, *Can You Hear the Nightbird Call?* (Toronto: Knopf, 2006); Proma Tagore, 'Kichuri Afternoon,' in Rishma Dunlop and Priscilla Uppal, eds., *Red Silk: An Anthology of South Asian Canadian Women Poets* (Toronto: Mansfield Press, 2004), 137.
5 Norman Buchignani and Doreen M. Indra, with Ram Srivastava, eds., *Continuous Journey: A Social History of South Asians in Canada* (Toronto: McClelland and Stewart, 1985); Hugh Johnston, *The Voyage of the Komagata Maru: The Sikh Challenge to Canada's Colour Bar*, 2nd ed. (Vancouver: UBC Press, 1989); Milton Israel, ed., *The South Asian Diaspora in Canada: Six Essays* (Toronto: Multicultural History Society of Ontario, 1987). See also filmmaker Ali Kazimi's film *Continuous Journey*.
6 Toronto's Racial Diversity, City of Toronto, http://www.toronto.ca/toronto_facts/diversity.htm[1]; Statistics Canada, http://www40.statcan.gc/101/cst01/demo50a-eng.htm[2].
7 For example, the chapters by Andrea Eidinger, Marlene Epp, and Franca Iacovetta in this volume.
8 For example, the chapters by Alison Norman, Julia Roberts, Megan Davies, and, in a different manner, Krista Walters, in this volume.
9 Made possible by an endowment from Senator and Chancellor Emeritus Vivienne Poy, 'Asian Cultures and Literatures in Canada' is taught under the aegis of Canadian Studies at University College, University of Toronto, and is meant to encourage discourse on multiculturalism in the academy.
10 Badami, *Can You Hear the Nightbird Call?* Set in India and Canada, the novel narrates the story of three women, including Beby-ji and Leela Bhat, whose lives are linked tragically to the political turmoil unleashed in the Punjab, first by the partition of India and Pakistan, in 1947, and, later, in the 1980s, by the Khalistani

separatist movement and the Air India bombing in which hundreds of Canadians died mid-air over the coast of Cork, Ireland.

11 Judy Fong Bates, *Midnight at the Dragon Café* (Toronto: McClelland and Stewart, 2001). This is a tale about growing up in 1950s Canada of a young, immigrant Chinese girl who is renamed and struggles to find her hyphenated identity. Swinging between a Canadian identity during the day (while at school and learning to speak English), and a Chinese persona at home, Annie-Su Jen has to cope with her inflexible 'Chinese' mother's deep dark secret of an affair with her stepbrother, even as Su Jen witnesses her old, Chinese father's gargantuan efforts to give her a better life in Canada.

12 Kerri Sakamoto, *One Hundred Million Hearts* (Toronto: Knopf, 2003). The story is about a second-generation Japanese Canadian girl, Miyo Mori, who goes back to Japan looking for her roots and to find answers about her father Masao's mysterious life as a Japanese Kamikaze. Her loss of her language, Japanese, and her inability to feel at home in Canada or in Japan reflects the in-betweenness of what many immigrants encounter in their new home.

13 Shyam Selvadurai, *Funny Boy* (Toronto: McClelland and Stewart, 1994). A story about a young boy's coming out and his traumatic realization of his sexuality during his early teens that cleverly sutures the national narrative of Sri Lanka's beleaguered civil war between the Sinhalese and the Tamils with the personal story of Arjun Chelvaratnam's rude awakening to battle his way through prejudice because he is 'funny' and 'gay.' This award-winning novel is perhaps the most applauded by students trying to locate their identities in a new homeland.

14 M.G. Vassanji, *No New Land* (Toronto: McClelland and Stewart, 1991). Nurdun Lalani is the typical victim of racial prejudice and unfathomable hatred in one of the short stories in the collection, which reiterates the condition of the Asian immigrant male who faces a kind of preconceived bias because of his reputation as a chauvinist and potential molester or rapist among a largely white Canadian population.

15 Two other concepts are integral to this project: acculturation – where groups of individuals having different cultures come into continuous contact, with subsequent changes in the original culture patterns of either or many groups; and Fernando Ortiz' concept of transculturation where, by constant juxtaposition of different cultures, there is a natural tendency of peoples to resolve conflicts. See his *Cuban Counterpoint: Tobacco and Sugar* (Durham, NC: Duke University Press, 1995 [1947]).

16 This literature includes Akhil Gupta and James Ferguson, eds., *Culture, Power, Place: Explorations in Critical Anthropology* (Durham, NC: Duke University Press, 1997); Benedict Anderson, *Imagined Communities* (London: Verso, 1983); Susan Stanford-Friedman, *Mappings: Feminism and the Cultural Geographies*

of Encounter (Princeton, NJ: Princeton University Press, 1998 [e-book, 2001]); Dick Hebdige, *Cut 'n' Mix: Culture, Identity and Caribbean Music* (London: Methuen, 1987); Simon During, *Cultural Studies: A Critical Introduction* (Oxford: Routledge, 2005).

17 Etienne Baliban to the author in a question and answer session at McMaster University in June 2006.

18 Sarah Daynes, *Music, Place and Space* (London: Routledge, 2007), 25.

19 For example, see Stacey Zembrzycki's chapter on Depression-era memories among Ukrainians in Canada. See also, Marlene Epp, 'The Semiotics of Zwieback: Feast and Famine in the Narratives of Mennonite Refugee Women,' in Marlene Epp, Franca Iacovetta, and Frances Swyripa, eds., *Sisters or Strangers? Immigrant, Ethnic, and Racialized Women in Canadian History* (Toronto: University of Toronto Press, 2004), 314–40.

20 Anderson, *Imagined Communities*, 6.

21 During, *Cultural Studies*, 8.

22 Stanford-Friedman, *Mappings*.

23 Mannur, *Culinary Fictions*.

24 Interview with Sanjeev Sethi, Jan. 2009.

25 Interview with P.K. Ahluwalia, Jan. 2009.

26 Interview with Sukhi Ghumman, Feb. Jan 2009.

27 Interview with Ellalan Guname, Oct. 2008.

28 Homi K. Bhabha, *The Location of Culture* (London: Routledge, 1994).

29 One is at Winston Churchill and Eglinton West, the other on Burnhamthorpe, close to Mavis Street.

30 Keya Ganguly, *States of Exception: Everyday Life and Postcolonial Identity* (Minneapolis, MN: University of Minnesota Press, 2001).

PART FOUR

Gendering Food in Cookbooks and Family Spaces

10 More than 'Just' Recipes: Mennonite Cookbooks in Mid-Twentieth-Century North America

MARLENE EPP

Mennonite women have often been stereotyped by their associations with food, whether they are preparing it, eating it, or cleaning up after its preparation and consumption. The linkages are often seen in popular booklets about Mennonites written mainly for tourists, or in media reports about Mennonite relief sales, where quilts and baked goods abound, or in the cookbook-publishing industry, which has thrived on the public's interest in Mennonite and Amish foodways. One such example is within the *Food that Really Schmecks* series of cookbooks by Canadian cookbook icon, the late Edna Staebler (who was not Mennonite). Even while focusing on the foodways of the smaller culturally conservative Mennonite subgroups, Staebler offered a broad portrayal of Mennonite women with descriptors such as 'plump,' 'placid,' and 'well-rounded.'[1] Such adjectives, because located in a cookbook, had the effect of linking women's physicality and their personality with their foodways. The gendered nature of food and its practices is also prominent in Mennonite community histories and in auto/biography. For instance, in her memoir, writer Katie Funk Wiebe noted that in her understanding, growing up and becoming a Mennonite woman 'in essence meant learning to cook.'[2]

Mennonite women, of course, are not singular in bearing a food-related identity – most women throughout history share this characterization, as chapters by Iacovetta, Cancian, and others in this collection demonstrate – however, this chapter focuses on a distinctive ethno-religious community for whom foodstuffs and foodways have often been cultural trademarks of community identity. Mennonites are a small (about 1.5 million members worldwide) Protestant denomination with sectarian origins in the sixteenth-century Reformation. They were characterized by religious convictions on believers' (or adult) baptism, pacifism, and nonconformity to the world, all of which historically brought them into conflict with states and societies and which led to patterns of diasporic migration and settlement in close-knit communities that were also 'closed' in varying degrees. These religious beliefs and patterns of living led to the development of ethnic characteristics among some Mennonite groups; the nature of their ethnicity depended on the geographical and human environment in which they established settlements. Cultural markers – language, dress, architecture, or foodways, for instance – that evolved from the intersection of religious belief and ethnic experience, became significant features of community identity at various times and places.[3]

The site at which foodways – and thus identity – were simultaneously maintained and transformed was the kitchen table, where families sat together and ate, at the church potluck, and through the medium of cookbooks, which offer a literary window into the preservation of foodways within a community. By 'reading' the recipes for meaning beyond culinary instruction, and by analysing the intent and presentation of the cookbook itself, I argue that the cookbook is a significant source that shaped both Mennonite self-understanding and generated external perceptions and knowledge about Mennonite ethno-religious identity; indeed, cookbooks may rival writings on history and theology in terms of communicating ideas about who Mennonites are to a broad sector of society. Furthermore, cookbooks, as a literary exhibit of women's culinary labour, provide a glimpse into the relationships between gender, foodways, and community identity.[4] The cookbooks examined in this essay offer glimpses into a number of themes: the role of women in fundraising for Mennonite mission and service initiatives, the connections between foodways and ethno-religious identity, the evolution of identity in the midst of modernization and acculturation, and the possibility of food practices as political statement.

Women, especially in ethnically distinct communities, were often viewed as cultural carriers, with responsibility for maintaining traditions, customs, language, and other group distinctives across generations. For the first generation of immigrants in Canada, regardless of which historical era saw them arrive, foodways were often the site at which the old and new worlds met. The preparation of ethnic foods was one means for newcomer Mennonites to 'survive psychologically'[5] as they made other difficult transitions in climate, language, and host society environments. The notion of maintaining traditional meals as a statement of cultural survival is also put forward by Hunchuck in her chapter in this volume on Ukrainian food sculptures on the Canadian prairies. Their capacity for food production nurtured women's entrepreneurial initiatives that were sometimes spurred on by economic necessity, such as occurred during the Depression, or for refugee newcomers after the Second World War, or for those sectarian Mennonite groups that strove for self-sufficiency. For women with minimal institutional power, foodways were a way to contribute in essential ways to the life of faith communities. The church kitchen was 'the center of their power'[6] for women whose denominations barred them from the pulpit and from most leadership positions.

Cookbooks as Historical Source

One important way in which Mennonite women capitalized on their reputation for kitchen production – whether in church or home – was in the creation and publication of cookbooks. I argue that the oft-trivialized recipe book, ubiquitous in Mennonite homes in the latter half of the twentieth century, was an important medium through which women offered public declarations of their food labour and which solidified certain cultural aspects of community, both internally and externally. Cookbooks, associated with the mundane, with the material, and with women's work, have rarely been regarded 'as having any serious historical value.'[7] In recent years, however, the study of cookbooks as a genre of writing and their usage as historical source is becoming more prominent. Janet Theophano suggests, 'There is much to be learned from reading a cookbook besides how to prepare food ... The cookbook, like the diary and journal, evokes a universe inhabited by women both in harmony and in tension with their families, their communities, and the larger social world.'[8] Carol Gold, in her study of Danish cookbooks over three centuries, writes, 'Cookbooks tell stories, as do all books. Perhaps the stories are not linear; they do not have a beginning, a middle, and an end, but they are stories nonetheless. Reading ... cookbooks, one can learn about changes in the economy, in the social makeup of the society, in women's roles, and in what it means to be a nation state and to be a member of that nation state.'[9] Further, analysts of community-based cookbooks suggest that in such volumes, women tell of their 'lives and beliefs' and 'present their values.'[10] Stories and values can all be found through a careful and curious reading of Mennonite cookbooks.

Cookbooks, as possibly the best-selling genre of books, were (and are) produced in abundance by Mennonite women as a means to raise funds and to celebrate a long history of food production. The creation of community cookbooks, whether they raised funds or not, brought the food-related labour of women in the so-called private sphere to the public sphere of church, community, and in the case of some best sellers, to wider sectors of society. They placed food production into a written medium, thus increasing the value of women's kitchen labour to literary-minded Mennonites. As 'culinary writing,' published cookbooks were a means for women to 'define themselves and their cultural groups, to preserve the past, and to shape the future';[11] this was also the case for Canadian Jewish women, as demonstrated by Andrea Eidinger in her chapter in this volume.

Although many Mennonite women did keep journals and write letters, for those who were not comfortable with or were disinclined towards that form of reflective expression, writing down and making public their favourite or prized recipes was a way of 'making themselves visible.'[12] While cookbooks do not explicitly reveal the events and circumstances of a woman's life, as does the memoir or diary, they do capture and illuminate an aspect of her domestic life that is 'evanescent and often unnoticed,'[13] yet consumes so much of her labour activity. The 'compiled' cookbooks, often the product of church and community women's groups, and often created as fundraisers, are texts that present what is commonly eaten within the households and collective gatherings of a community and reflect food preferences, food aspirations, and what might be considered culinary trademarks of the group that compiles the cookbook.

Furthermore, the business and clerical aspects of cookbook production also allowed women to exhibit and hone their organizational and administrative abilities. And in the very writing down of instructions to create dishes for both everyday and extraordinary occasions, women were indicating that their food labour was an occupation that required knowledge and skills, and that wasn't intrinsic to their sex. Indeed, the cookbook served to 'professionalize' the everyday act of cooking.

Mennonite Community Cookbooks

Norma Jost Voth, in her survey of Mennonite foodways that migrated from south Russia to North and South America, notes that 'few, if any' printed cookbooks accompanied families across the ocean. A few handwritten collections of recipes were brought by immigrants, but mostly women carried cooking knowledge 'in their heads.'[14] The recording of a recipe, Voth suggests, was to retain memory of how to prepare a dish eaten at another's home, or for foods made only at certain times of the year, not for regularly eaten things such as zwieback (double-decker buns) or cabbage borscht. After migrating to Canada or the United States, some women began to record recipes of unfamiliar dishes they learned to prepare while working as domestic labour in non-Mennonite households.

I am not aware of any formally published Mennonite cookbooks in the first half of the twentieth century. By the 1950s, however, the creation of an assembled cookbook for recipes that were not simply passed along on recipe cards or orally or by example was symptomatic of a new generation of cooks that were thought to require the scientific and professionalized instructions offered by tried and tested cookbooks. After the Second World War, in Canada, as in the United States, female domesticity and vocational homemaking were called to standards of perfection even while homemakers themselves were searching for ways to make their jobs easier.

Most small compilations of church or community recipes have a life mainly on kitchen shelves; virtually no library or archives that specializes in Mennonite studies makes a concerted effort to collect cookbooks, in the same way that they might accumulate church histories or theological writings.[15] Mennonite cookbooks vary from typewriter-written and staple-bound manuscripts circulated within a small area as projects to raise funds, to glossy and professionally published collections that, in a few cases, have become national best sellers.[16] In this brief study, I focus on a small number of cookbooks that are popular and widely used books found in many North American Mennonite households and produced in the second half of the twentieth century.

The *Mennonite Community Cookbook: Favorite Family Recipes*, by Mary Emma Showalter, was first published in 1950. A professor in home economics at a Mennonite college in Virginia, she compiled the cookbook in an effort to preserve the recipes contained either in 'worn and soiled' handwritten booklets or in the memories of the Mennonite women of her mother's generation.[17] In 1947, Showalter wrote to the 'wives of Mennonite pastors' in Canada and the United States, asking them to solicit 'favorite family recipes' from within their communities. Of the over 5,000 recipes she received, about 1,150 went into the published book.[18] The purpose of the cookbook, Showalter said, 'is an attempt to preserve for posterity our own peculiar type of cookery that has been handed down for many generations.'[19] Two decades later, Showalter remarked, 'I had no idea it would be such a success.'[20] A report on Showalter's retirement from teaching in 1972, noted that the *Community Cookbook* had gone through sixteen printings and sold about 200,000 copies.[21] In 2008, close to 500,000 had been printed, with 4,000 copies continuing to sell annually, and the *Cookbook* was on the publisher's best-seller list.[22] When Showalter died, in 2003, it was said that the *Community Cookbook* was 'the parent of a whole family of Mennonite and Amish related cookbooks which came along in the half century since its first publication.'[23]

Ten years after the *Community Cookbook* appeared, a comparable cookbook project was launched in Manitoba. The simple, spiral-bound 1,000-recipe *Mennonite Treasury of Recipes*, compiled by a committee of women, would become a best seller among Mennonite books in Canada. First published in 1961, by the mid-1980s, the book had gone through thirteen printings and sold 42,000 copies. By 2008, 350,000 copies had been printed. The inspiration for the book came at the 1960 annual Conference of Mennonites in Canada sessions at Steinbach, Manitoba, when, after cooking meals that resulted in 5,000 plates for several hundred delegates over six days, a group of women agreed that it would be a good idea to write down recipes for mass cooking for future reference. The introduction to the cookbook points out that 'the delightful Mennonite custom of gathering in large numbers and dining together' was gaining in popularity as travel increased, and thus 'a sheet' to explain how to cook popular Mennonite recipes for large groups was necessary. Many of the recipes, the compilers noted, hailed from 'days of want and austerity' but they felt future generations might find them interesting.[24]

The project became a joint initiative of the women's societies at a number of southern Manitoba churches with the Ebenezer Verein (society) of Steinbach Mennonite Church taking the lead.[25] The Ebenezer women's organization had begun their work in 1948, holding auctions and bazaars to raise money for missions, church institutions, schools, and hospitals. One of the *Treasury*'s organizers, Anna (Derksen) Rosenfeld, recalled that despite a consensus among the women that 'yes it would be nice' to produce a cookbook, 'nobody thought we would go ahead as we had no money.' She summoned 'all [her] courage' and approached her brother who operated a local printing company. When the project committee learned that the printer wanted to produce 3,000 copies to start, one woman expressed deep scepticism that such a number would ever be sold, stating 'you will never get rid of them.'[26] The 'enormity' of the project became clear to Rosenfeld when she realized that the women's group was carrying a debt of $3,750.[27] At times, she recalled, she wanted to 'throw up my hands in despair' but encouragement from 'Mrs Warkentin [who] had so much faith in this venture' and also from her brothers at the printer's persuaded her to forge ahead.[28]

The creation of the cookbook involved many hours of 'considerable asking, writing, and begging' women across the country to contribute recipes.[29] The submissions then had to be sorted, translated, and organized into categories, and were typed 'days and evenings' by Rosenfeld's daughter. The time demands of the project prompted the committee of women to go to a cottage by the lake for two weeks in order to better concentrate on their work, and so their husbands were 'left to shift for themselves.'[30] When the first books came off the press in December 1961, Rosenfeld recalled, 'I was humbled and so thankful; it was a beautiful book. All the work had finally paid off! So often we had been discouraged, and now it was a reality!'[31] Her 1990 obituary noted that her greatest success lay in the publication of the *Mennonite Treasury of Recipes*.[32]

The announcement of the *Treasury*'s publication in the national English-language Mennonite newspaper, the *Canadian Mennonite* in February 1962, noted that the book sold for $2.25 and was compiled by 'a committee of ladies' from Steinbach, Manitoba. Hedy Durksen, who wrote a regular column enti-tled 'Just around the House' stated that she was 'very well pleased' with the new cookbook which was 'also very handsomely assembled' and 'attractive as well as useful.' She also reported that proceeds from the sales of the *Treasury* were to be used 'in the interest of missions.'[33] The 1962 edition that I possess begins with a poem entitled 'The Housewife' that exalts the 'small affairs,' 'tri-fling worries,' and 'little cares' that consume the life of a homemaker, among which was 'A hungry husband to be fed.' Reflective of its particular social era, the cookbook's individual recipe authors are named according to their hus-bands, as in 'Mrs John Rempel,' or 'Mrs F.E. Reimer,' while the single women contributors are labelled as 'Miss.' (The 1982 edition – the one being sold by the printer in 2008 – maintains the same naming system.)

Cookbooks as Fundraisers

One important purpose of producing local community or church compila-tions of recipes was fundraising. Janet Theophano notes that the 'ubiquitous community fund-raising cookbook' dates back to the 1600s.[34] And Barbara Kirshenblatt-Gimblett observed that 'fundraiser cookbooks are by far the more prolific genre of Jewish cookbooks.'[35] The *Mennonite Community Cookbook* did not have obvious fundraising goals and, while the *Mennonite Treasury of Recipes* was not initiated with fundraising goals in mind, the popularity of the cookbook meant that it soon was able to generate money for charitable projects. Sales of the *Treasury* quickly reached a level that the creators were able to recoup their costs, pay their debt, and start contributing funds towards various church and mission projects. Indeed, they repaid their debt less than three months after the books were printed and at the same time were able to deposit $108.09 in the bank. In 1964, the Ebenezer Verein at Steinbach Men-nonite Church decided that the $1,000 at their disposal from the sale of the *Treasury* would be donated to the church organ fund. In the following year, the $1,000 earned was designated to 'salaries for missionaries.'[36]

Money continued to come in over the years from sales of the *Treasury* and was used for a wide range of mission and service projects. In the period from July 1962 through January 1986, the royalties from the sale of the *Treasury* amounted to $38,000, most of which was donated to charitable causes.[37] It is clear that the project was a money maker that undergirded improvements made to the local church – facilities and equipment – and also the community and international work of service and mission organizations. This was also true for many other church and community cookbooks. It was women's organizational work and economic labour that undergirded the successful functioning of local churches, larger denominational institutions, and mission boards. For women's societies such as the Ebenezer Verein, domestic labour as exhibited in the community cookbook became, as for Jewish women, a 'philanthropic tool.'[38]

Cookbooks and Ethnic Identity

If Mennonite women's culinary labour and the formal expression of that labour through the production of cookbooks furthered the financial goals of their community, perhaps of greater import was that labour to the preservation of ethnic identity. As numerous analysts have observed, 'foodways serve as … powerful metaphors of group identity,'[39] and thus cookbooks have a pivotal role to play in explicitly shaping that identity, as is demonstrated in Iacovetta's discussion in this volume, of the ethnic cookbooks produced by the International Institute of Toronto. One of the main characteristics of many Mennonite cookbooks was their inclusion of a section on 'ethnic foods' – recipes for what were considered to be 'Mennonite' foods. As such, cookbooks functioned (and continue to do so) as powerful identity markers of Mennonite ancestry, migration, settlement, and cultural evolution. Especially by mid-twentieth century, when the routine preparation of Mennonite ethnic foods began to decline in the midst of modernization and acculturation (although not among all Mennonite groups), reproducing such recipes in published cookbooks served to reinvigorate collective cultural identity. In this way, cookbooks, as Theophano remarks, 'served as a place for readers to remember a way of life no longer in existence or to enter a nostalgic recreation of a past culture that persists mostly in memory.'[40] This may have been especially the case for Mennonites of Dutch-Russian-Ukrainian ethnic identity, many of whom left their homelands abruptly and involuntarily and with a sense of loss and displacement. For Mennonites wrenched from places in which rich cultural traditions and memories had been formed, the collection of recipes representative of those traditions may be described as 'nostalgia cookbooks' or 'collective memory cookbooks.'[41]

So-called Mennonite foods evolved in response to a historical context that saw different Mennonite groups migrate to and settle in disparate parts of the world over the past centuries. So-called Russian Mennonite foods emerged from Dutch, Prussian/Polish, and Ukrainian traditions, while Swiss-Pennsylvania German Mennonite foods drew from Swiss and south German influences. Thus, a meal in the Russian Mennonite tradition would often include borscht (meat-based cabbage soup), zwieback (white double buns), vereniki (filled dumplings akin to Ukrainian perogies), and portzelky (deep-fried fritters similar to the Dutch oliebollen). A Swiss Mennonite table was often ordered by the adage of 'seven sweets and seven sours' and might hold wiener schnitzel, sauerkraut (pickled cabbage), a variety of pickles, apple butter, fruit pie, and custard.

In these varying geographical and cultural contexts, Mennonites interacted with their neighbours and absorbed aspects of resident foodways and recipes that were hitherto unknown to them. It was through the kitchen labour of women that new ethnic flavours were incorporated into Mennonite cooking. As it was women who prepared the meals for their household, they were the ones who were introduced, in the case of Russia, for instance, to Ukrainian borscht and vereniki, by the Ukrainians who worked for them as domestic and farm help. They acquired Ukrainian methods for drinking tea and techniques for pickling cucumbers and watermelon. Similarly, Mennonites who were identified ethnically as Swiss had engaged in food exchange in the Alsace and Palatinate regions of Europe and later in Pennsylvania with a range of new settlers of Germanic origin in an ethnic fusion that would later become known as Pennsylvania German.

These fusions of ethnic foodways became most obvious, beyond the dinner table, in Mennonite cookbooks. While the *Mennonite Community Cookbook* did not isolate ethnic recipes in a separate section, the entire book is imbued with the sense that there exists a distinctive 'Mennonite cookery.' For their part, the women who compiled the *Mennonite Treasury of Recipes* included a 'Mennonite section' when the printer suggested that they do 'something different with a lot of sales appeal.'[42] Almost all Mennonite cookbooks that contained a section on 'ethnic' or 'traditional' foods included a recipe for zwieback, considered the 'hallmark of Mennonite baking,' with origins that possibly went back to the sixteenth-century Netherlands.[43]

That an interest in writing down and publishing 'Mennonite' recipes appeared at mid-century and in the decades that followed is not coincidental. While the preparation and consumption of such 'traditional' Mennonite foods as the laborious vereniki may have begun to decline by the 1950s and 1960s, the inclusion of recipes for such foods in Mennonite cookbooks was a means to prevent the disappearance of such foods from historical memory. Perhaps the epitome of the ethnic food celebration is found in the 1990 two-volume *Mennonite Foods and Folkways from South Russia*, by Norma Jost Voth. Published by the Mennonite-owned publisher Good Books in Pennsylvania, which in recent decades has achieved international sales success with its 'slow cooker' cookbooks, *Foods and Folkways* is part recipe collection and part anthropological-historical analysis of Mennonite foods with origins in the Netherlands, West Prussia, and south Russia from the seventeenth through the early twentieth centuries.[44] Alongside the recipes are essays and anecdotes illuminating the food customs and traditions that were central to Russian Mennonite identity.

The author indicates that, recognizing the passing of the 'old traditional foods familiar in [her] mother's kitchen,' she felt a sense of urgency to preserve the recipes and the stories connected to them.[45]

The two volumes are a veritable 'feast' of reflections and information that portray a community whose cultural and, indeed, religious identity is closely tied to its foodways. The particularity of eating goes so far as to encompass 'Mennonite Seasonings for Soup' or 'Eating Watermelon – Mennonite Style.' Following the intent of *Foods and Folkways*, is a 2006 publication, entitled simply *Mennonite Ethnic Cooking*, which states as its purpose 'to honour the ingenuity of Mennonite women of past decades, which we want to remember and preserve.'[46] In this case, the author-compiler is both reviving the foodways aspect of Mennonite identity and valorizing the historic culinary labour of women. While some would dispute the usefulness of ethnicity as a feature with which to identify Mennonites (most of whom would consider themselves to be primarily a religious group), to the extent that shared cultural markers enhance the cohesion of a community, the public acknowledgment of distinctive 'Mennonite' foodways in cookbooks has played a key role in creating community identity.

As Mennonite ethnicity has diversified especially in the latter decades of the twentieth century and into the twenty-first, foodways and cookbooks may well provide a venue through which that 'multiculturalim' can be publicly showcased. In 2001, an Ontario Mennonite church published a cookbook that included a section on its 'Swiss' cultures, its 'Russian' cultures, and also on the 'Other' cultures represented among its members.[47] Another example is a Spanish-language Mennonite cookbook published in Mexico in 2000. It was published in a series that celebrates Mexico's ethnic food traditions and in this case Mennonites whose ancestors had a migratory path that took them from south Russia to the Canadian prairies and then to north-central Mexico in the 1920s. Most of the recipes derive from the Russian Mennonite tradition, so that 'Paska' – a decorative Easter bread of Ukrainian origin – becomes 'Pan de Pascua.'[48] This compilation points to an 'ethnic fusion' of Dutch-Russian and Mexican in a unique form of cookery that has become a well-known aspect of Mennonite identity in Mexico today.

Cookbooks as Signposts of an Era

Even while Mennonite cookbooks possessed a character and included features such as 'ethnic' recipes that made their particularity recognizable, such cookbooks also reflected wider societal interests and emphases. They identified the historical moment and context in which women's culinary labour was situated. As Anne L. Bower noted in her study of community cookbooks, such projects tell the story of women's lives at a particular point in history; they indicate a 'collective value system' and are signposts of the changes underway in a community in a given era.[49]

Cookbooks published after 1960 reflect a formerly rural and separatist community that was acculturating and modernizing in a rapidly changing postwar Canada. Royden Loewen notes that the 1961 publication of the *Treasury of Recipes* was indicative of a mid-century 'new middle-class ethnicity' among some Manitoba Mennonites.[50] It portrayed the labour of urban (that is, resident in town as opposed to on the farm) women who were, perhaps subconsciously, professionalizing their work in the kitchens of both home and church. Befitting the professionalized homemaker, such skilled labour required instructions, whether for traditional Mennonite fare – prepared from memory by previous generations – or for modern 'English' recipes (English meaning cultures that were not Mennonite), or for many other aspects of middle-class homemaking.

That cooking and baking were part of the overall vocation of homemaking is indicated by the inclusion, in many Mennonite cookbooks like the *Treasury*, of a section devoted to a range of non-culinary 'household hints.' The *Treasury*, for instance, offers advice on how to hang pictures, how to clean bathroom fixtures and shower curtains, how to pick up slivers of broken glass from a rug, and how to recover an ironing board. Another cookbook's 'Hints' offered counsel on whitening yellowed piano keys, using ice cream containers for house plants, and how to prevent clothes from sticking to an outdoor laundry line on a cold winter day.[51] The hints were indicative of a mid-twentieth century ethos of domesticity that placed a great deal of emphasis on perfectionism in homemaking on the part of women, Mennonites not excepted. Cookbooks like the *Mennonite Treasury of Recipes* pointed to the fact that women's domestic labour was in transition in the last half of the twentieth century. This was true for their presentation of homemaking ideals and for the culinary recipes and food practices they contained. For example, the *Treasury* illuminated the changing foodways of a generation of women who were cooking traditional rural ethnic foods alongside modern urban and partly processed dishes. So in the *Treasury* one finds ancestral Germanic dishes like Plumi Moos (cold fruit soup) and Rollkuchen (deep-fried fritters) together with recipes for 'Cheerios Cocktail Snacks' and 'Checkerboard Casserole.' The incorporation of both old and new world recipes in Mennonite cookbooks of the late twentieth century offered 'a message of history, of modernity, of social change, and of culinary inventiveness.'[52]

Cookbooks as Culinary Politics

To the extent that Mennonite cookbooks exhibited culinary and homemaking practices that were evolving in response to a modernizing world, the very labour activity involved in their creation had a political message. As oft-overlooked texts of female expression, not unlike diaries, quilts, and samplers, cookbooks both reflect and construct the worlds in which women live. With limited access to 'recognized status-bearing discourse' – which in the church and conference might include sermons, reports, and meeting minutes – the printed and distributed cookbook was a form of 'public participation.'[53] It was an assertion of women's place and labour within the structure of church and community. The rationale for the *Treasury* in wanting to publicize recipes designed to feed large groups was an indirect way of asserting women's fundamental roles in the running of large Mennonite conference gatherings. While women did not have a voice in the discussion and decision making of Mennonite bureaucracies, their culinary labour was essential to the functioning of meetings that brought the men together. In the writing down, compiling, and publishing of recipes for quantity, women's institutional labour was no longer hidden from view. The creation of community cookbooks as fundraising endeavours was a means for women to influence, however obliquely, the economic impact of their denominational bodies in terms of monied contributions. Cookbooks can, thus, be read for their political meanings, safely situated within the non-threatening context of culinary instructions.

By the latter decades of the twentieth century, Mennonite women were politicizing their cookbook creations even more. A succession of what could be described as 'social justice' cookbooks, also referred to as 'world community cookbooks,' began appearing in the mid-1970s, the first of which was Doris Janzen Longacre's immensely successful *More-with-Less* cookbook, that advocated cooking methods and ingredients that used less of the world's resources. In short, the purpose of the project was to 'challenge North Americans to consume less so others could eat enough.'[54] First published in 1976, the *More-with-Less* cookbook had sold 840,000 copies in forty-seven printings twenty-five years later, and had far surpassed the expectations of its creators.

The book was politically ahead of its time – and thus not without critics – in responding to the 'food crisis' of the 1970s and, in particular, in suggesting that North Americans eat less meat and thus reduce the amount of grain grown for meat production. With recipes drawn from many global cultures that focused on the eating of grains and legumes, the cookbook was eagerly taken up by a generation of Mennonites and other North American social activists. In his analysis of the *More-with-Less* cookbook, Matthew Bailey-Dick argues that it moulded a Mennonite identity based on principles of discipleship (serving and helping others) and simple living and, thus, was extremely important as a shaper of ideology and values within the Mennonite community but also well beyond.[55]

Another analyst of the cookbook who was involved in its creation, commented, 'If you consider the theological teaching and witness of this cookbook, its impact far outweighs that of most Mennonite writings in theology and ethics.'[56]

The *More-with-Less* cookbook was followed in 1991 by *Extending the Table: A World Community Cookbook*, a compilation that declared itself to be 'in the spirit of *More-with-Less*' but focused on global education through food-ways by sharing stories and recipes from ordinary people and places around the world. An indication that the book was not just another collection of international cuisine, author Joetta Handrich Schlabach stated her belief that 'the experience of preparing new foods and meeting people through stories can broaden our understanding of other people and their problems.'[57] In this case, the labour of cookbook production reflected and also elicited a late twentieth-century interest in transnational relationships, international connections, and global understanding.

Continuing the tradition of cookbook as socio-political statement is a 2005 collection by two Mennonite women entitled *Simply in Season*, organized around the theme of cooking with foods that are in season in a given locale: 'recipes that celebrate fresh, local foods.'[58] Once again in tune with the times, *Simply in Season* offered practical and simple approaches to eating local, seasonal, and fairly traded foodstuffs; the authors organized the recipes around foods that were locally available (depending on the region) during the four seasons of the year. Here again, it is largely women's labour – from producing the dishes, to articulating the recipes, to compiling them in a collection, to utilizing them in daily meal preparation – that shaped an identity for the Mennonites that reflected a changing social and cultural environment.

Conclusion

If understood in terms of their wider goals and impact, cookbooks have served as a female voice in the otherwise male-dominated discourse on Mennonite beliefs and identity. This is true whether one refers to the *Mennonite Treasury of Recipes* – a simple compilation that celebrated traditional notions of Mennonite ethnicity while also reflecting a mid-twentieth century emphasis on domesticity – to the polished *More-with-Less* cookbook that situated North American Mennonites on the cutting edge of political calls for attention to inequities in global resources. Both were and continue to be immensely successful within their respective realms. Cookbooks, initiated and produced by women, shaped both Mennonite cultural self-understanding and generated external perceptions and knowledge about Mennonite historical development and ethnic identity. Indeed, one should not understate the importance of the lowly and mundane cookbook – a product of female labour – to the creation and evolution of Mennonite community identity.

NOTES

1 Edna Staebler, *More Food that Really Schmecks* (Toronto: McClelland and Stewart, 1979), 12, 15. This volume was preceded by Staebler's *Food that Really Schmecks* (Toronto: McGraw-Hill Ryerson, 1968).
2 Katie Funk Wiebe, *The Storekeeper's Daughter* (Scottdale, PA: Herald Press, 1997), 163.
3 For a reflection on the varieties of Mennonite ethnicity, see Royden Loewen, 'The Poetics of Peoplehood: Ethnicity and Religion among Canada's Mennonites,' in Paul Bramadat and David Seljak, eds., *Christianity and Ethnicity in Canada* (Toronto: University of Toronto Press, 2008), 339.
4 Norma Jost Voth, in writing about the 'distinctive way of living' for Mennonites with Russian ethnic identity, argues that cultural forms including housing styles, language, educational systems, and work routines were all imbued with both the necessity and pleasure of eating. See *Mennonite Foods and Folkways from South Russia* (Intercourse, PA: Good Books, 1991), vol. 2, 6.
5 Anne Harder, *The Vauxhall Mennonite Church* (Calgary: Mennonite Historical Society of Alberta, 2001), 13.
6 Daniel Sack, *Whitebread Protestants: Food and Religion in American Culture* (New York: St Martin's Press, 2000), 2–3.
7 Matthew Bailey-Dick, 'The Kitchenhood of All Believers: A Journey into the Discourse of Mennonite Cookbooks,' *Mennonite Quarterly Review* 79 (April 2005): 155.
8 Janet Theophano, *Eat My Words: Reading Women's Lives through the Cookbooks They Wrote* (New York: Palgrave, 2002), 6.
9 Carol Gold, *Danish Cookbooks: Domesticity and National Identity, 1616–1901* (Seattle, WA: University of Washington Press, 2006), 176.
10 Anne L. Bower, 'Bound Together: Recipes, Lives, Stories, and Readings,' in Anne L. Bower, ed., *Recipes for Reading: Community Cookbooks, Stories, Histories* (Amherst, MA: University of Massachusetts Press, 1997), 2.
11 Theophano, *Eat My Words*, 52.
12 Ibid., 9.
13 Ibid., 122.
14 Voth, *Mennonite Foods*, vol. 2, 273.
15 Since I began my research and analysis of Mennonite cookbooks, the assistant librarian at my own institution, Conrad Grebel University College, has begun a deliberate effort to enhance the cookbook collection in our library and archives.

16 For instance, Good Books, a Mennonite and Amish specialty publisher in Penn-
    sylvania, has produced a series of recipe collections for slow cookers that have
    appeared numerous times on the *New York Times* best-seller list and sold thousands
    of copies.
17 Mary Emma Showalter, *Mennonite Community Cookbook: Favorite Family Reci-
    pes* (Scottdale, PA: Mennonite Community Association, 1950), x.
18 Catherine R. Mumaw, 'A Tribute to Mary Emma Showalter Eby,' *Minding Men-
    nonite Memory* (July 2005): 10.
19 Showalter, *Mennonite Community Cookbook*, x.
20 Jewel Showalter, 'Community Cookbook Author Retires from Teaching,' *Mennon-
    ite Reporter* 2/26 (1972): 4.
21 Ibid., 4.
22 E-mail communication, 9 June 2008, from Levi Miller, director, Herald Press.
23 Ibid., quoting e-mail from Levi Miller to Philip C. Kanagy.
24 *The Mennonite Treasury of Recipes* (Steinbach, MB: Derksen Printers, 1962).
25 *25 Jaehriges Jubilaeum der Steinbach Mennoniten Gemeinde 1968* (Steinbach,
    MB: Steinbach Mennonite Church, 1968), 13.
26 Lydia Penner, 'The Mennonite Treasury of Recipes, a Canadian Bestseller,' in *Fifty
    Years Ebenezer Verein, 1936–1986* (Steinbach, MB: Ebenezer Verein, 1987), 53–4.
27 Ibid.
28 Ibid., 54.
29 'Bericht des "Eben-Ezer" Nähvereins,' in *25 Jaehriges Jubilaeum der Steinbach
    Mennoniten Gemeinde 1968*, 27. Translation by Helen L. Epp.
30 Penner, 'Mennonite Treasury of Recipes,' 54.
31 Ibid.
32 Obituary of Anna Derksen Rosenfeld, *Der Bote* 67/34 (1990): 7.
33 Hedy Durksen, 'Just around the House: Recipe Books,' *Canadian Mennonite* 10/6
    (1962): 8.
34 Theophano, *Eat My Words*, 12.
35 Barbara Kirshenblatt-Gimblett, 'Recipes for Creating Community: The Jewish Char-
    ity Cookbook in America,' *Jewish Folklore and Ethnology Review* 9/1 (1987): 8.
36 *Fifty Years Ebenezer Verein*, 41–2.
37 Penner, 'The Mennonite Treasury of Recipes,' 54.
38 Kirshenblatt-Gimblett, 'Recipes for Creating Community,' 10.
39 Linda Keller Brown and Kay Mussell, 'Introduction,' in Linda Keller Brown and
    Kay Mussell, eds., *Ethnic and Regional Foodways in the United States* (Knoxville,
    TN: University of Tennessee Press, 1984), 8. This linkage is also demonstrated in
    chapters by Eidinger, Iacovetta, Zembrzycki, Hunchuck, Cancian, and Mehta, in
    this volume.
40 Theophano, *Eat My Words*, 8.

41 Carol Bardenstein, 'Transmissions Interrupted: Reconfiguring Food, Memory, and Gender in the Cookbook-Memoirs of Middle Eastern Exiles,' *Signs: Journal of Women in Culture and Society* 28/1 (2002): 357.

42 Penner, 'Mennonite Treasury of Recipes,' 54.

43 Voth, *Mennonite Foods and Folkways*, vol. 2, 33.

44 Voth, *Mennonite Foods and Folkways*, vols. 1 and 2. A similar volume that focused on the Pennsylvania German cultural tradition is Phyllis Pellman Good, *Cooking and Memories: Favorite Recipes from 20 Mennonite and Amish Cooks* (Lancaster, PA: Good Books, 1983).

45 Voth, *Mennonite Foods and Folkways*, vol. 1, 32.

46 Anne Harder, *Mennonite Ethnic Cooking* (Alberta: Author, 2006), i.

47 *Be Present at Our Table: 150th Anniversary Cookbook, Erb Street Mennonite Church, 1851–2001* (Waterloo, ON: Erb Street Mennonite Church, 2001).

48 Katherine Esther Emilia and Renpenning Semadeni, *Recetario Menonita de Chihauhau* (Mexico, D.F.: CONCULTA, 2000).

49 Bower, 'Bound Together.'

50 Royden Loewen, *Diaspora in the Countryside: Two Mennonite Communities and Mid-Twentieth-Century Rural Disjuncture* (Toronto: University of Toronto Press, 2006), 65.

51 Showalter, *Mennonite Community Cookbook*, 450–9.

52 Theophano, *Eat My Words*, 78.

53 Bower, 'Bound Together,' 5–6.

54 'About More-with-Less,' World Community Cookbook, Mennonite Central Committee, www.worldcommunitycookbook.org. Doris Janzen Longacre, with her *More-with-Less Cookbook: Suggestions by Mennonites on How to Eat Better and Consume Less of the World's Limited Food Resources* (Scottdale, PA: Herald Press, 1976), introduced the world to 'eating simply'; it now has its own Internet homepage, and was celebrated in a twenty-fifth anniversary edition in 2000.

55 Bailey-Dick, 'Kitchenhood of All Believers,' 153–63. An analysis of some contemporary Mennonite cookbooks that focuses on the intersection of eating habits, social justice, and aesthetics is Rebekah Trollinger, 'Mennonite Cookbooks and the Pleasure of Habit,' *Mennonite Quarterly Review* 81 (Oct. 2007): 531–47.

56 Gayle Gerber Koontz, quoted in 'About More-with-Less,' World Community Cookbook, Mennonite Central Committee, www.worldcommunitycookbook.org.

57 Joetta Handrich Schlabach, *Extending the Table: A World Community Cookbook* (Scottdale, PA: Herald Press, 1991).

58 Mary Beth Lind and Cathleen Hockman-Wert, *Simply in Season* (Scottdale, PA: Herald Press, 2005).

11 Gefilte Fish and Roast Duck with Orange Slices: *A Treasure for My Daughter* and the Creation of a Jewish Cultural Orthodoxy in Postwar Montreal

ANDREA EIDINGER

In a 2007 article that traced the history of the traditional matzah-and-egg dish that was a family favourite of many Montreal Jews during Passover,[1] Montreal *Gazette* writer Susan Schwartz noted: 'nostalgia is a key ingredient, so cooks strive to get their family recipe just right.'[2] For Montreal Jews, the relationship between their sense of 'Jewishness,' holiday celebrations, and food remains as strong today as it was nearly sixty years ago when, in 1950, the Ethel Epstein Ein Chapter of Hadassah-WIZO in Montreal published *A Treasure for My Daughter: A Reference Book of Jewish Festivals with Menus and Recipes*. Edited by Bessie W. Batist, with recipe sections edited by Sarah Ein, Anne Warshaw, and Mary Davids, this cookbook highlights critical connections between Jewish women, food, and identity. Indeed, the book has achieved near legendary status in Montreal's Jewish community, where it holds a place of honour in the home of many a Canadian Jewish woman who received it as a wedding gift from her mother.

This essay addresses a complex question – how did Jewish-Canadian women *learn* to be both Jewish and Canadian? – through an exploration of the post–Second World War origins, recipes, and character of *A Treasure for My Daughter*. The cookbook was produced by and for Jewish Canadian women in Montreal who were of middle-class background and of Ashkenazic and Eastern European descent. Its female creators sought to educate young Jewish women at a time of increasing acculturation and assimilation into Canadian culture and opposition from dissenting groups in the Montreal Jewish community. In publishing the book, the women contributed towards a 1950s-era crystallization of Montreal Jewish cultural practice and the creation of a new orthodoxy among this particular group of Jews, one that rejected their own immigrant heritage in Eastern Europe in favour of the biblical past and modern Israel. The cookbook reflects these apparent contradictions. For example, the authors stress the

Middle Eastern origins of their customs, yet their values were distinctly North American and middle class in character. This, in turn, contradicted the Eastern European origin of the recipes in the cookbook. Finally, the dominant gender code clearly placed the burden of cultural reproduction on the shoulders of Jewish mothers who were to educate and inspire their children through 'joy,' 'peace,' 'beauty,' and 'wisdom.'

A Treasure for My Daughter also had a far wider reach. Worldcat lists over 130 libraries across Canada, the United States, and Israel that contain the book. It has been sold all over the world, including in England, Australia, Indonesia, South Africa, South America, and Israel. According to the daughter of the editor, 'every Jewish woman who came of age in the '50s and early '60s is the proud owner of a very spotted, tattered beloved copy' of it. The most recent edition notes that 'demand from all over North America' promoted 'the twelfth edition of this unique cookbook' and 'heirloom in many Jewish households.'[3] Thus, this study, though focused on Montreal, has implications for the broader Canadian and even international context. Although its publication was not a watershed moment in Canadian Jewish cultural history, the book reflects and illustrates changes that were taking place in the postwar period.

Despite the prominence of *A Treasure for My Daughter* (and many other cookbooks like it) in many Jewish households, the relationship between Jewish women, food, and culture is seldom discussed.[4] This chapter focuses on food as an important site for the negotiation and contestation of ethnic and gendered identity by examining the creation of a new food culture by Ashkenazi Jewish women in Montreal in the postwar period.[5] In this, it complements chapters by Sonia Cancian, Marlene Epp, and Julie Mehta in this volume, which also demonstrate the critical importance of food to ethnic identity creation.

The terms 'Jew' and 'Judaism' can encompass a whole range of people, beliefs, and value systems. In light of my desire to challenge the homogenization of the terms 'Jew' and 'Jewish,' I draw on the concept of 'Jewishness,' a cultural construct, which can include religious, ethnic, and social dimensions of identity. Deborah Dash Moore makes 'Jewishness' a central theme in her book *At Home in America: Second-Generation New York Jews*. She describes the shifting definition of what it means to be Jewish, which relies on the 'assumption of a common cultural heritage,' while simultaneously recognizing that Jewish ethnicity is pluralistic in nature.[6] In other words, each individual defines for himself or herself what it means to be Jewish, depending on language, nationality, ethnicity, class, gender, generation, and wave. There are as many different ways of being Jewish as there are individuals. This chapter considers the formation of ethnic identity among Jewish women in a particular place and time, Montreal after the Second World War, as a way of complicating the question: What is a Jew?

'I Am So Glad to Be Your Daughter!'

The Ethel Epstein Ein Chapter of Montreal Hadassah-WIZO was founded on 17 December 1947 in memory of Mrs Hyman Ein. Hadassah-WIZO was and continues to be a powerful organization of Jewish women volunteers that devotes itself primarily to providing education and health care for women and children in Canada and Israel. Bessie Wittenberg Batist had originally proposed the idea of a cookbook following the first meeting of this Hadassah chapter. *A Treasure for My Daughter* grew out of her work with organizations involving young Jewish women, who often asked her about Jewish practices. One of the founders and volunteers of the library of the Young Women's Hebrew Association, Batist (born 1905 or 1906) came to Canada as a child from Odessa. Having learned about Jewish customs from her mother and father, both Eastern European Jews, she felt strongly that information about Jewish cultural practices was vitally important for the community and that it was her duty to ensure its transmission.[7]

The creation of *A Treasure for My Daughter* was 'undertaken and followed through by a group of homemakers with no previous experience [in publishing or writing] but with a great sense of dedication and the will to succeed.'[8] Like many publications, this was a collaborative work, and a number of individuals in the Montreal Jewish community outside of Hadassah circles participated in its creation as well. The introduction thanks many prominent individuals, most notably several men, for their assistance. Several prominent rabbis read and reviewed the manuscript, including Rabbi Wilfred Shuchat of the Orthodox Shaar Hashomayim Congregation and Rabbi Maurice Cohen from the Conservative Shaare Zion Congregation. David Rome, noted scholar of the Montreal Jewish community, helped with the project. According to Bessie Batist's daughter, her father Joseph Batist played a significant role: 'Mom did the text with *much help from my Dad*,' she recalled, adding, 'we remember the arguments! And my sister had never even heard them raise a voice until then.'[9]

The names and institutions acknowledged in the book are significant in and of themselves. The members of Hadassah-WIZO were mostly middle-class women who had the time and financial resources to engage in philanthropic activities.[10] Most of the names on the book committee mentioned in the preface and acknowledgments are of Eastern European and Germanic origin (Singer, Raginsky, Weinstein, Schwartz), suggesting that the authors were of Ashkenazic descent. The rabbis who endorsed the book were affiliated with two of the wealthiest and most important synagogues in the city; the high membership price for each of them restricted access to Shaar Hashomayim and Shaare Zion to those with surplus income. More specifically, these named individuals belonged to a distinct subset of the Jewish community of Montreal – Eastern

European Jews who had fled pogroms and entered Canada between 1880 and 1914, or their descendants. By the end of the Second World War, these Jews were the dominant and largest component of Montreal's Jewish community. They had successfully integrated into the wider Canadian society and achieved financial success. Most labels are problematic but I will use the term 'established Jewish Canadians' to refer to this group. Given their prominence, and their role in creating the cookbook, we can reasonably assume that the form of Jewishness contained within *A Treasure for My Daughter* was that promoted by the elite of this established group. With this context in mind, I now turn to the cookbook itself.

A Treasure for My Daughter is unlike most cookbooks. Rather than simply a collection of recipes organized like a dinner menu, this cookbook is organized according to the Jewish calendar and its most important holidays. Following a description of the meaning and traditional observances of each holiday is a selection of dinner menus appropriate for the occasion. The explanatory text is written in the form a conversation between a mother (hereafter known as Mother) and her daughter, Hadassah, who is about to be married. It is written in a way that assumes that such interaction is how this type of information is normally passed down and disseminated. This assumption is reinforced in the conversation as well. For example, in the section on Chanukah,[11] Hadassah and her mother discuss the menorah. While admiring the beauty of it, Hadassah exclaims: 'It is your mother's and my own grandmother's! Was she a wonderful mother like you? Was she a mother to guide and advise, was she a comrade to discuss all the aspects of living? I am so glad to be your daughter.'[12] In this passage, Hadassah makes a clear association between holidays, ritual objects, her mother, and her grandmother. Further, she implies that a good (or wonderful) mother necessarily passes down the information that is considered crucial for every young Jewish woman wishing to set up a home. This type of transmission is also assumed to be natural. When Hadassah first asks her mother about how to prepare for Shabbat, Mother responds that it 'is something that will come *naturally* to you because you were brought up with it.'[13]

However, the message that young Jewish women need this kind of book implies a breakdown in communication, even that something has gone terribly wrong. It suggests that young Jewish women, despite being well meaning, are largely ignorant of the proper way to observe Jewish holidays and rituals in the home. In several places, Hadassah laments her own ignorance, at one point saying, 'I have some qualms about my ability to manage my own home in the traditional Jewish way.'[14] The neglect of Jewish traditions is an important theme in *A Treasure for My Daughter*. While at times deploring her own lack of knowledge, Hadassah actively criticizes Jewish women who neglect Jewish traditions. We see this happen in the section on Chanukah. As Mother recounts the story of the Jewish Maccabees, she notes that 'during the reign of [the Greek ruler] Antiochus Epiphanes (Illustrious) of Syria, Palestine was a part of his realm' and the 'Jews were greatly persecuted,' forced even 'to worship Greek idols' and 'become assimilated' or risk being 'put to death, martyrs for our faith.'[15] Here, Antiochus is portrayed as a villain who tried to assimilate the Jews by forcing them to give up their religion and traditions. Through this story, Mother asserts her view that assimilation entails the ultimate betrayal of the Jewish faith, such that even death is preferable. Hadassah responds by saying that she wants to learn how to prepare for the holidays partly because 'I have always taken the routine of this home for granted.'[16] Elsewhere in the text, Hadassah also notes that many of her friends have expressed a lack of enthusiasm for holiday celebrations, even feeling that Jewish holidays usually were sad and difficult events. She asks her mother, 'How did you manage to convey the spirit of the Jewish ceremonies and customs to us without making us think them burdensome?'[17]

By the 1950s, the over-assimilation of the latest generation of young Jewish women appears to have become a significant problem for community leaders. In the history of Jewish communities, public leaders have desired external acculturation but internal continuity with their traditions. The Jewish community met this goal through the creation of 'religious, educational, and philanthropic institutions that maintained Jewish particularism.'[18] In other words, while Jewish individuals were expected to adopt the English language and Canadian clothing, they were also expected to retain Jewish traditional values and customs. Jewish leaders were (and are) largely hostile to total assimilation, and they actively sought to retain Jewish cultural distinctiveness even as they adopted external markers of Canadianness. In post-1945 Canada, however, the distinctiveness of Jewish identity in Canada appeared to be under threat.

More than just elite alarmism, there were indications that young Jewish women growing up in postwar Montreal actively rejected their Jewish identities and strove to act as Canadian as possible. The 1950s was a time when many young adults chose to '[shift] their allegiances from the old ethnic ties to the new nuclear family ideal.'[19] Ethnic diversity was not a prized quality in this period, but cultural uniformity was.[20] A tendency towards conformity to the dominant anglophone culture likely helps explain some of the demographic changes occurring in the Montreal Jewish population, where, for example, family size was continually decreasing and marriages between Jews and non-Jews rose from 4.9 per cent in 1926 to 12 per cent in 1953. These changes provoked a great deal of concern from community leaders, who viewed assimilation and acculturation as a serious threat to the future of the Jewish people in Canada.[21]

Intergenerational relationships were a key factor in the over-assimilation of young Jewish women. In contrast to the Montreal Italian women whom contributor Cancian interviewed,[22] the conflicts between Jewish immigrant mothers and Jewish-American daughters were common and well-documented aspects of the history of Jews in North America. In *The World of Our Mothers*, Sydney Stahl Weinberg describes how American-born children often felt ashamed of their European parents, for their backward ways and inability to speak English. In one case, the 'sister wanted her family to be American too, and she resented the fact that they were not like the parents of her native-born friends and felt ashamed of their home on the Lower East side.'[23] Much of this resulted from the education of the children in American schools, which preached the superiority of American values.[24] Another point of contention was religion. Oftentimes a young woman's job would require her to work on Saturday, something forbidden under Jewish law. Other parents worried that a young woman's desire to be American would result in her abandoning Judaism, even going so far as to eat non-kosher hot dogs.[25] As time went on, second-wave feminism prompted yet more conflicts between Jewish immigrant parents and Canadian daughters. In *Her Works Praise Her*, Hasia Diner and Beryl Lieff Benderly argue that feminism made it increasingly difficult for Jewish women to be content with simply being a helpmate, and brought questions about the role of Jewish women in the modern world into sharp focus. In postwar Montreal, too, feminism led some young Jewish Canadian women to move away from Judaism as a way of rejecting the domestic outcome of their mothers' lives.[26]

Chicken Noodle Soup, with Biblical French Fries on the Side

The obvious solution to this problem was to educate young women in their duties as Jewish women. To this end, *A Treasure for My Daughter* devotes a great deal of space to describing religious rituals. Moreover, the book presents many of these rituals detailed as dating back to biblical times. Whenever explanations of the origins of certain ritual practices are offered, the same words are repeated: 'history,' 'tradition,' 'ancient,' and 'ancestors.' Indeed, the 'ancestors,' specifically those of biblical times, are cited frequently as a major authority on modern Jewish customs and practices. Further, all of these words in the text are connected to the words 'Palestine,' 'Israelites,' and 'the Exodus.' When Mother explains the origins of Succot to Hadassah,[27] she says that the holiday is significant because 'our ancestors in Palestine celebrated it as the festival of the ingathering of the harvest,' and because it commemorates the temporary shelters used by the Israelites while wandering in the desert.[28] Significantly, these explanations are not simply described as religious. Instead, throughout this text, there is a conflation of religion and history. Consider, for example, the explanation offered for Shabbat observance:[29]

> The Sabbath is one of the first institutions observed by our ancestors dating back to the days of the Exodus. There are two foundations for the Sabbath: one the religious, that God created the world in six days and rested on the seventh day; therefore the Sabbath is the anniversary of the Creation. The other approach is historical. When the Israelites were freed from slavery they received the Ten Commandments on Mount Sinai, the fourth of which is 'Remember the Sabbath to keep it Holy.'[30]

Although Mother says that the first explanation is religious and the second is historical, both originate in religious scripture. There are numerous references to the Exodus in the sections under consideration. With the exception of Chanukah, each holiday and its customs is linked back to the Exodus, Moses, Mount Sinai, and the Ten Commandments.

While the established Jewish Canadian community was orienting itself to the past, it was also looking to the modern state of Israel for many of its customs. This, too, is reflected in the cookbook. For example, Mother explains that 'Oneg Shabbat' means the 'Pleasure of the Sabbath' and that it assumed its present form in Tel Aviv in 1923,[31] when Chaim Nachman Bialik modernized the old custom of group study of religious texts to include social events like sing-a-longs.[32] Similarly, in the section on Chanukah, Hadassah devotes two pages to describing public celebrations of Chanukah in Tel Aviv, as inspiration for her own, noting that the celebrations were 'unique and picturesque.'[33] The implication is that it is not enough to emulate the past. It is the duty of modern Jews to look to the Israeli example to learn how to 'modernize' ancient customs and bring them into line with contemporary values.

This orientation to the biblical past served a very specific purpose: to lend weight to the new cultural orthodoxy that is present (and subtly championed) in *A Treasure for My Daughter*. By 'inventing' the myth that the customs of the established Jewish Canadian community were of ancient heritage, the cookbook's creators legitimized their own practices and beliefs with respect to Judaism. Mother frames the argument most effectively in the section on Chanukah when she describes 'the privilege of belonging to an ancient nation of great tradition, a nation so great that even today the way of life of righteous men throughout the world is based on the Ten Commandments.'[34] And these customs must be strictly followed. 'I know that in carrying on the Jewish beliefs in your home,' Mother says to Hadassah, 'you will find it no more burdensome than I did. You may make minor changes here and there, but basically you will do as has been done for centuries, and Jews will continue to do as long as this world exists.'[35]

In asserting the primacy of their cultural system, the established Jewish Canadian community was implicitly comparing itself with other Jews, particularly those who were either too Jewish or too Canadian. The cookbook includes certain groups of Jews just as it excluded 'others.' Those excluded were the groups and denominations that the established Jewish Canadian community considered deviations from authentic Judaism. At the same time, the book also seems targeted to young Jewish women in general, suggesting that established Jewish Canadians were also actively spreading the way of life and cultural practices reflected in *A Treasure for My Daughter* to other Jewish groups. Indeed, the book constructed and reinforced the cultural orthodoxy it was trying to promote by virtue of its publication.

Just as complete assimilation was an undesirable outcome, so too, was it equally problematic to be the 'wrong kind of Jewish.' Thus, the book highlights the traditions associated with the established Jewish Canadian community while ignoring or excluding the customs of other groups. The only Jewish traditions featured in *A Treasure for My Daughter* are Israeli and Canadian ones. There is no attempt to display Sephardic, North African, and Western European Jewish traditions or Hassidic, Ultra-Orthodox, and Reform cultural practices. In sum, the text excludes all Jewish cultural practices that do not conform to the cultural practices of the established Jewish Canadian community.

While actively looking to the biblical past as a source of authority, the established Jewish Canadian community embraced values that were distinctly North American and middle class. Accordingly, *A Treasure for My Daughter* depicts the Jewish people as the originators of the most important North American and Christian traditions, particularly the Sabbath and Thanksgiving. It describes the Sabbath as 'one of the greatest contributions Israel has made to the world.'[36] This is so for a number of reasons. First, the Jews were the first to observe the Sabbath. As noted earlier, the use of this term is deliberate. Rather than using the Hebrew or Yiddish terms, Shabbat and Shabbos, the English word is used in order to more closely connect Jewish traditions with Christian traditions. This is further reinforced through Hadassah's involvement in 'Sunday school.'[37] Second, the Sabbath, specifically the fourth commandment, has been redefined as 'the first labour law of mankind,'[38] with Israel receiving acclaim for being the first nation to dedicate one day in the week to rest, a very enlightened principle.[39]

The Jewish people are also given credit for being the originators of Thanksgiving celebrations. In the opening section on Succot, the following conversation takes place between Mother and Hadassah:

'Mother, I asked David [Hadassah's fiancé] to have dinner with us tomorrow night. What will you serve?'

'How does turkey with all the trimmings appeal to you?'

'Fine, Mother, though it seems like a Thanksgiving menu and to-morrow is the first day of Succot.'

'Why, Hadassah, Succot is the Jewish Thanksgiving. As a matter of fact the Pilgrim Fathers in America based their thanksgiving on our festival because they were steeped in the knowledge of the Bible.'[40]

Yet, Hadassah's confusion seems understandable given that the menu is every inch a traditional North American Thanksgiving meal. There is nothing here to suggest this is a Jewish harvest celebration. The menu is distinctly American, right down to turkey, cranberry sauce, and mashed potatoes. The second Succot Dinner Menu is even more puzzling: cantaloupe basket, yellow split pea soup, southern fried chicken, honey, french fried potatoes, cabbage salad, peace tarts, date and nut loaf, and tea.[41] Moreover, a survey of all of the recipes in the cookbook reveals that two-thirds of the recipes are North American or Western in origin.

What do fried chicken and french fries have to do with the wanderings of the Jewish people in the desert for forty years or bountiful crops? Nothing. This is precisely the point. These menus attest to the fact that the established Jewish Canadian community was rooted firmly in the present and in North American values of family and freedom. Indeed, throughout the text, the words 'Church' and 'Christianity' could easily be substituted for 'synagogue' and 'Judaism.' These concerns and values are eloquently described in Mother and Hadassah's conversation about the special significance of Chanukah:

'It testifies that the Jew can be a solider when the need arises. This festival, how-ever, commemorates the victory of a great moral cause rather than the victory of the battlefield.'

'Yes, Hadassah. Our rejoicing is not at the defeat of our enemies, but at the rededication of the Temple [...]'

'Chanukah exemplifies the rebellion in defence of the inalienable rights of man. It is a protest against the denial of the freedom of worship. The victory of the Maccabees is that of godliness over paganism, Judaism over Hellenism, right over might, democracy over dictatorship. From this point of view, this victory assumes world-wide significance even today. Now we hope that our rededication to the ideals of our people will maintain the Jews as a contributing factor in the advance-ment of civilization.'[42]

This passage is significant for other reasons as well; the key words in this exchange are strong examples of Cold War military rhetoric. As Doug Owram observes, the Cold War 'seems to have been a less dominant force' in Canada than in the United States, but it was nevertheless 'a brooding presence that reminded people that their current situation was tenuous.'[43] The Cold War was perceived as an international diplomatic dispute as well as 'a moral crusade: evil against virtue, Christ against anti-Christ or, more accurately, a re-creation of the struggle between democracy and tyranny that predated the Second World War.'[44] In the 1950s, the reality of the Cold War loomed large, reminding Canadians of the fragility of their political institutions. It remained the duty of all Canadians, regardless of their ethnicity, to support their country and to live the ideal of democracy even in their daily lives.[45] With the use of keywords like godliness and democracy, the editors of the cookbook are declaring that the values and traditions of the established Jewish Canadians coincide with those of the wider middle-class Canadian society. After all, Jewish Canadians are the originators of some of the ideals that Canadians hold most dear. More importantly, the established Jewish Canadian community of Montreal was willing to actually, or at least symbolically, pick up arms in defence of Canada and the values of freedom and equality.

Part of the cultural orthodoxy presented in *A Treasure for My Daughter* also involves the appropriate roles for women as they internalize Canadian middle-class gender roles from the period. The 1950s saw a domestic revival that emphasized the importance of the nuclear family and associated traditional gender roles: man as father and breadwinner, and woman as mother and homemaker. For both the United States and Canada, scholars have suggested that the crises engendered first by the Depression and the Second World War and then the Cold War led to a resurgence of a family ideal based on this breadwinner/homemaker divide. According to this ideology, the home would contain and isolate subversive and potentially dangerous forces like working women, homosexuals, and communists. While the pervasiveness of this ideology is a hotly debated subject, what is clear is that these stereotypical images of men and women had considerable cultural currency.[46]

Many features of this cookbook play into this 1950s domestic ideal. *A Treasure for My Daughter* assumes the presence of a housewife, as evidenced by the complexity and expense of the recipes. For instance, Dinner Menu II for Rosh Hashanah[47] contains eight separate dishes.[48] One can only imagine what the grocery bill would look like to purchase the ingredients for such a menu, without even taking into account the notoriously expensive kosher products.[49] Further, many of the dishes take considerable time and care to prepare; roast duck with orange slices is not a recipe for a beginner.[50] The assumption is that the woman of the household does not need to work outside the home and thus can devote many hours to cooking food, cleaning house, and preparing for the holidays. Mother says to Hadassah, 'I worked hard to develop our home, as you will too, I am sure.'[51]

There are other contradictions. Although *A Treasure for My Daughter* pays much attention to the modern as well as biblical past of Jewish traditions, the Eastern European origins of the individuals who authored this cookbook is ignored entirely. This was likely a conscious decision owing to the challenges posed by immigration. For the established Jewish community, the lapse served a very specific purpose; by concealing their European origins, they were able to disassociate themselves from the newly arrived Jewish immigrants. The established community feared that any association with the newly arriving Jewish refugees might make them appear guilty of being 'too-Jewish by association.'

A significant distance existed between the members of the established Jewish Canadian community and many newly arrived Jewish immigrants, a lot of whom had a more difficult time than most adjusting to Canadian life.[52] Some of these newcomers felt offended by what they perceived as a negative reaction to their presence on the part of the established Jewish Canadian community, and believed that the established community could never understand their experiences in Europe. Others resented the established Jewish Canadians for their relative safety in North America. Some of these difficulties did lie with established Jewish Canadians. Some of them resented the immigrants, saying that they had a 'more persecuted than thou' attitude. The established Jewish Canadians also disliked the constant reminder that the immigrants evoked of the horror of war. Also, many in the established Jewish Canadian community feared that association with the newcomers, many of whom could not speak English and arrived with little or no financial resources, would challenge their own well-earned middle-class identities.[53]

Unfortunately, the editors of this cookbook did not entirely succeed in their objectives. Like many other myths, the history of the established Jewish Canadian community as described in *A Treasure for My Daughter* is contradictory and inconsistent. The initial disconnect between the actual ethnic identities of the authors and the heritage presented in the book becomes even more complicated when one looks beyond the explanatory texts to the recipes themselves. Indeed, Eastern European recipes such as gefilte fish, eier kichel, kishke, kugel, and potato pancakes (latkes), are central to most of the dinner menus.[54] A full one-third of the recipes in this cookbook are drawn directly from Eastern European cooking traditions. These humble foods, featuring cheap ingredients, were the recipes brought from the Old Country and were staples in immigrant diets. For example, gefilte fish, to this day one of the foods most often associated with Judaism, is made from household staples. Take whatever fish is available, an onion, a carrot, oil, sugar, salt, eggs, and water, blend the ingredients all together, and then shape the mixture into balls. This recipe makes eighteen to twenty-four balls, enough to feed a fair number of people.[55] Not only are these dishes cheap, but they provide filling foods for large numbers of people that are high in protein and carbohydrates.

Aside from some of the obvious benefits of such cheap nutritious food, these dishes evoked warm notions of home for most established Jewish Canadians. They were comforting and familiar foods that evoked childhood memories of grandmother's kitchen. As Valerie Korinek and Franca Iacovetta suggest, the collective identity that immigrants invested in ethnic dishes from the old country guarded against their easy displacement. Such foods had helped to ease the transition to a new country by providing some sense of continuity in a strange place.[56]

A Treasure for My Daughter thus reflects and expresses the creation of a new cultural orthodoxy in the Jewish community of Montreal in the 1950s. Established Jewish Canadians probably saw no contradiction between the Eastern European recipes and their newfound identity as Jewish Canadians with links to Israel; all were important aspects of their identities. In this particular case, the established Jewish Canadians looked to the Bible and modern Israel for their cultural traditions. Their Eastern European heritage was passed over in favour of a more ancient heritage. In the context of the Cold War, it did not make sense to be 'too Jewish'; instead, *A Treasure for My Daughter* reflects the internalization of Canadian middle-class values by this particular subset of the Jewish community of Montreal. However, despite disavowing their cultural links to the Old World, this collection of recipes demonstrates that the Eastern European heritage of second-generation Jewish Canadians was a fundamental, if implicit, part of their collective memory. The inconsistencies and contradictions in this new cultural orthodoxy reflect the complexity of the processes of assimilation and acculturation.

Like Mother, Like Daughter

The final major issue revealed by a critical reading of *A Treasure for My Daughter* involves the continued transmission of this cultural orthodoxy. It was not enough for the authors to publish the book but they had to ensure that all of its contents were transmitted whole to the next generation. In their introduction, the editors make it clear that they are writing this book for Jewish homemakers.[57] Throughout the text, women, marriage, and home are constantly in association with each other. Not only is this book a traditional wedding gift for

Jewish brides, but the context of the conversation that frames the cookbook is that of a young Jewish woman asking her mother for instruction in light of her upcoming marriage. Mother's response to this request reinforces the point: 'Soon you will be a homemaker yourself, and you will be busy preparing for the Sabbath and other holidays.'[58]

The fact that all of the women in the book are homemakers, wives, and mothers, and that it is their duty alone to ensure the survival of Jewish customs and traditions reflects the concerns of its creators. For them, the assimilation and acculturation of the younger generation of Jewish women would render them unable to fulfil their highest duty, to educate the next generation. Herein lies the greatest threat to the future survival of the Jewish community. This explains why *A Treasure for My Daughter* attaches so much importance to the mother's role in cultural transmission. When men are mentioned, they are usually associated with synagogues and formal religious services. For example, as Mother explains the domestic observance of Shabbat, Hadassah notes that 'when father comes home from the synagogue, there is also a deep feeling when he blesses each of the children by placing his hands on our bowed heads,' adding that 'after this solemn moment we all join him in singing "Shalom Aleichem," our joyous Sabbath hymn.'[59] This passage is important for two reasons: the father is closely associated with synagogue and is seldom present in the home, and he is also associated with the word 'solemn.' These associations appear repeatedly throughout the cookbook. Conversely, mothers are always associated with the home, with domestic rituals such as singing 'Shalom Aleichem,' and with the words 'joy,' 'peace,' and 'beauty.' A case in point is the conversation prompted by Mother's description of how she lights the Sabbath candles and adds a personal prayer:

> You know, mother, after you have lit the candles and said the prayer, when we gather around you to say 'Good Sabbath' peace and joy seem to settle over our home; sometimes I think I can see that peacefulness and joy, not only feel it.

> I, too, feel very much as you do, Hadassah. In fact you will experience it even more in your own home, because you will be the one who ushers in the Sabbath by lighting the candles, and you will bring that joy and peace into your household.[60]

Take also the name of Hadassah for the daughter. Although probably a nod to the name of the publishing organization, the word Hadassah is also associated with the Book of Esther. In fact, Hadassah is Hebrew for Esther, the beautiful Jewish maiden who attracts the attention of the Persian King and saves the Jewish people from execution.[61] This is Esther's legacy to modern Jewish women:

Jewish women must use their wisdom to save the Jewish people by making their homes beautiful, peaceful, and conducive to the transmission of 'Jewishness.' Mother reinforces this point when she tells Hadassah, 'It is by the observance of these holidays and customs in our homes that we have been able to retain the religion and traditions of our heritage.'[62] The significance of this name also testifies to the cultural project at stake: the book's editors and contributors are saving Judaism by making the homes of all Jewish women beautiful.

Rickie Berman has argued that the roles of Jewish women in religious life were fundamentally altered during the immigration process. While previously men were seen as the bearers of the religion, they were now forced to work for a living. This economic change, which took men away from synagogue and their religious studies, resulted in there being greater importance attributed to women's domestic rituals as 'key components in the transmission of a sense of Jewish identification and attachment.'[63] Although Berman is dealing with the British context, the shift she describes is also evident in Montreal. The formal observance of the Jewish religion is an important part of the Montreal Jewish community. Synagogue membership levels continued to rise in the 1940s and 1950s, particularly in Conservative and Reform congregations. Orthodox synagogues also took off following a revival in traditional Judaism in the postwar years. However, as Louis Rosenberg notes, the rise in synagogue attendance was motivated by a desire to belong to a community, rather than by religious belief. Most Jews in Montreal only attended synagogue for major holidays and life-cycle occasions (like bar mitzvahs).[64]

The importance of including children in domestic rituals is made clear in every section of this book. For each holiday, either Mother or Hadassah points out the special duties reserved just for children.[65] Following a lengthy discussion about Hadassah's supervision of her 'Sunday school' pupils in their Chanukah play, Hadassah remarks how this event marked a high point in their celebrations: 'the children, who have looked forward eagerly to this annual Chanukah parade, form a line of spectators, their little flags and Menorot clutched firmly in their hands.'[66] 'A ritual such as that of [lighting] the candles,' Mother adds, 'inspires even little children, and when we explain their meaning, the education and religious goal is attained. We cannot all be scholars in the Talmud, but we can all enjoy the practice of our religion in our homes and synagogues. Our heritage is so rich that it is our obligation to the children to impart as much of the meaning of our observances as we possibly can.'[67] The symbolism inherent in the lighting of the candles and the illumination of the children's minds cannot be overlooked. Through such simple acts, Jewish women are called on to transmit the 'Jewishness' learned in *A Treasure for My Daughter* to the next generation and thus ensure the survival of the Jewish people.

Similarly, the Jewish home as sanctuary appears in various places in the text, which also explains that creating such a sanctuary depends not on a woman's skill at interior decorating but rather, like Esther, on her choice of words. Hadassah praises her mother's ability to educate her about Jewish customs: 'Mother, you have always explained all the festivals – not only the Sabbath, – and made an interesting Jewish home for all of us.'[68] Mother responded, 'I wanted our home to be a gay place where our friends could come and enjoy themselves in a Jewish way.'[69] By carefully explaining the importance of domestic ritual observances, Mother is able to demonstrate their beauty and thus their value.

In the New World, domestic rituals came to be seen as the most effective method of transmitting cultural knowledge. By using beauty and wisdom, Jewish women would create happy Jewish homes, preserving both family and the Jewish religion. It was essential that Jewish women ensured the survival of Jewish culture by passing this knowledge and wisdom on to their children, by inspiring them, and by making their home a Jewish sanctuary.

Conclusion

On the surface, *A Treasure for My Daughter* may appear to be a simple cookbook and guide to the most important religious celebrations in the Jewish calendar. Yet, it is much more than that. Indeed, the cookbook contains within it a discourse on 'Jewishness' as constructed by a certain subset of the Montreal Jewish community during the early postwar period. This new Jewish orthodoxy took form in the 1950s against a backdrop of increasing acculturation, competing cultures, and changing roles for women. In response, a group of highly motivated women and men designed a cookbook that dispensed advice regarding appropriate behaviour particularly for young Jewish women. These Ashkenazic Jewish Canadian community leaders produced this book in an effort to counteract an apparent disinterest in religion on the part of the younger generations. They attributed this disinterest to over-assimilation, intermarriage, strained intergenerational conflicts, feminism, and the increasing Canadianization of young Jewish women. At the same time, these community elites also sought to shore up their own middle-class identities against the threat posed by the newly arrived Jewish immigrants from Europe.

The 'Jewishness' described in *A Treasure for My Daughter* has a distinct character. For established Jewish Canadians, their culture was outwardly modern, middle class, and Canadian, building on links to ancient and modern Israel. They described their 'traditions' as originating in the biblical past and modern Israel. Their orientation towards the biblical past and modern Israel was in line with their political ambitions; nevertheless, their espousal of middle-class North American values points to their desire to affirm their Canadianness. In this respect, they created a tripartite identity: Jewish, Israeli, and Canadian. In producing this book, the editors were asserting the primacy of their own brand of Judaism and in the process claiming to save the Jewish people as a whole. What is never explicitly acknowledged, however, is that this cultural identity is at odds with the authors' Eastern European origins, even though many of the recipes implicitly reference this heritage in that they originate in the humble and filling foods of the Old World. This tension between the professed culture of the established Jewish Canadians and the Eastern European origins of the recipes speaks volumes about the tension emanating from the simultaneous desire to assimilate and to retain some cultural distinctiveness. It also speaks to the power of the familiar. Further, in writing and publishing this book, the cookbook's creators helped to establish and reinforce the supremacy of their culture, making it into a new orthodoxy.

Finally, *A Treasure for My Daughter* highlights the important role that Jewish women played as bearers of this new cultural orthodoxy. In some respects, the cookbook reflects the gender norms of the wider Canadian society in that it portrayed Jewish women as homemakers with children, men as breadwinners, and nuclear families as the norm. For the Montreal Jewish community, however, these domestic rituals took on an additional importance. Jewish women became the critical keepers of 'Jewishness,' with a duty to keep the faith and to inspire and educate their children by transforming their home into a Jewish sanctuary. Women were an integral part of a newly constructed postwar orthodoxy according to which the line of cultural transmission from mother to daughter could not be allowed to break down.

Far from being static social categories, identity, tradition, and 'authenticity' are constantly negotiated and renegotiated. The fact that I have recently received my own copy of the most recent edition of *A Treasure for My Daughter* from my mother points to its continued importance in the Montreal Jewish community and the success of the 1950s orthodoxy. This 2001 edition was the thirteenth printing of *A Treasure for My Daughter*. The tremendous success of the book has contributed to a wonderful and vibrant culture that remains strong to this day, a mix of myth and reality, with one foot in the past, and another planted firmly in the present.

NOTES

1 Passover is the annual celebration of the liberation of the Hebrews from slavery in

Egypt as told in the Book of Exodus. This celebration usually occurs in the spring, according to the Jewish lunar calendar, and lasts for eight days. During this period, Jews refrain from eating leavened bread, as the ancient Hebrews had no time to let their bread rise when they fled Egypt. Instead, unleavened bread, called matzah or matzoh, is eaten.

2 Susan Schwartz, '8 Days of Matzo Brei,' *Montreal Gazette*, 28 March 2007.

3 Bessie W. Batist et al., eds., *A Treasure for My Daughter: A Reference Book of Jewish Festivals with Menus and Recipes*, rev. ed. (Montreal: Ethel Epstein Ein Chapter of Hadassah, 2000), 7.

4 Research on the history of Canadian Jewish women includes the following: Paula J. Draper, 'Abraham's Daughters: Women, Charity and Power in the Canadian Jewish Community,' in Jean Burnet, ed., *Looking into My Sister's Eyes: An Exploration in Women's History* (Toronto: Multicultural History Society of Ontario, 1986), 75–90; Ruth Frager, *Sweatshop Strife: Class, Ethnicity, and Gender in the Jewish Movement of Toronto, 1900–1939* (Toronto: University of Toronto Press, 1992); Lynne Marks, 'Kale Meydelach or Shulamith Girls: Cultural Change and Continuity among Jewish Parents and Daughters – a Case Study of Toronto's Harbord Collegiate Institute in the 1920s,' in Ruby Heap and Alison Prentice, eds., *Gender and Education in Ontario: An Historical Reader* (Toronto: Canadian Scholars' Press, 1991), 395–405. The limited work on Jewish women and food includes: Carol Bardenstein, 'Transmissions Interrupted: Reconfiguring Food, Memory, and Gender in the Cookbook-Memoirs of Middle Eastern Exiles,' *Signs: Journal of Women in Culture and Society* 28/1 (2002): 353; Hasia R. Diner, *Hungering for America: Italian, Irish, and Jewish Foodways in the Age of Migration* (Cambridge, MA: Harvard University Press, 2001).

5 In North America, the term 'Ashkenazi' refers to an ethnic group of Jews, who are largely descended from Eastern European Jews. Their ancestors spoke Yiddish as a lingua franca and adopted many of the foods and customs of the native peoples of this region. They are to be distinguished from Sephardic Jews, who are the descendants of Spanish-Portuguese Jews, who fled during the Inquisition, settled in North Africa and around the Mediterranean, and adopted many of the customs of these lands.

6 Deborah Dash Moore, *At Home in America: Second-Generation New York Jews* (New York: Columbia University Press, 1981), 9.

7 Nancy Gutterman, e-mail message, 29 Aug. 2007.

8 Ibid.

9 Ibid.

10 Gerald Tulchinsky, *Branching Out: The Transformation of the Canadian Jewish Community* (Toronto: Stoddart, 1998), 151.

11 Chanukah is the Jewish festival of lights. This holiday lasts for eight days and

commemorates the victory of the Maccabees over Greek persecution and the subsequent rededication of the Temple. It usually falls in the month of December.

12 Batist et al., *A Treasure for My Daughter*, 59.

13 Ibid., 19, emphasis added.

14 Ibid.

15 Ibid., 59.

16 Ibid., 19.

17 Ibid., 23.

18 Paula E. Hyman, *Gender and Assimilation in Modern Jewish History: The Roles and Representation of Women* (Seattle, WA: University of Washington Press, 1995), 17.

19 Elaine Tyler May, *Homeward Bound: American Families in the Cold War Era* (New York: Basic Books, 1988), 19

20 Doug Owram, *Born at the Right Time: A History of the Baby Boom Generation* (Toronto: University of Toronto Press, 1996), 19.

21 Tulchinsky, *Branching Out*, 282–3.

22 See Cancian's chapter in this volume. For some discussion of mother-daughter conflicts among Italians see, e.g., Miriam Cohen, *From Workshop to Office: Italians in New York* (Ithaca, NY: Cornell University Press, 1993).

23 Sydney Stahl Weinberg, *The World of Our Mothers: The Lives of Jewish Immigrant Women* (Chapel Hill, NC: University of North Carolina Press, 1988), 111.

24 Ibid., 114.

25 Ibid., 116.

26 Hasia R. Diner and Beryl Lieff Benderly, *Her Works Praise Her: A History of Jewish Women in America from Colonial Times to the Present* (New York: Basic Books, 2002), 377–98.

27 Succot is the Jewish harvest festival. It generally occurs between September and October. It commemorates the time spent by the Israelites wandering in the desert following their escape from Egypt. This event is commemorated by eating meals in a small hut, called a Succa, based on the ones used by the Israelites.

28 Batist et al., *A Treasure for My Daughter*, 48.

29 Shabbat, also called Shabbos in Yiddish, is the Jewish day of rest. It is marked from Friday at sundown until Saturday at sundown. During this period, religiously observant Jews refrain from all work, attend synagogue, and eat meals with their family.

30 Batist et al., *A Treasure for My Daughter*, 22.

31 Oneg Shabbat refers to the celebration of the Jewish Sabbath as a happy occasion. It is an informal gathering of Jews, often in a private home, and often involving a hearty meal, discussions, and singing.

32 Batist et al., *A Treasure for My Daughter*, 21.

33 Ibid., 57.
34 Ibid., 59.
35 Ibid., 23–4.
36 Ibid., 23.
37 Ibid., 57.
38 Ibid., 22.
39 Ibid.
40 Ibid., 48.
41 Ibid., 54.
42 Ibid., 58.
43 Owram, *Born at the Right Time*, 52–3.
44 Ibid., 162.
45 Ibid., 45.
46 For more on this debate, see, e.g., Joanne Meyerowitz, ed., *Not June Cleaver: Women and Gender in Postwar America, 1945–1960* (Philadelphia, PA: Temple University Press, 1994).
47 Rosh Hashanah is the Jewish New Year. It is usually celebrated in September and marks the beginning of the High Holidays. The High Holidays are a period of ten days following Rosh Hashanah where Jews are encouraged to reflect on the past year. It culminates with Yom Kippur, the Day of Atonement, where Jews fast for the entire day to atone for sins they might have committed in the past year.
48 Batist et al., *A Treasure for My Daughter*, 36.
49 Kosher is the English term for Kashrut, Jewish dietary laws. Kosher foods are foods that have been prepared in accordance with these laws as certified by a number of different organizations.
50 Batist et al., *A Treasure for My Daughter*, 36–7.
51 Ibid., 23.
52 Tulchinsky, *Branching Out*, 284.
53 Ibid., 266.
54 Batist et al., *A Treasure for My Daughter*, 25.
55 Ibid., 26.
56 Franca Iacovetta and Valerie Korinek, 'Jello-O Salads, One-Stop Shopping, and Maria the Homemaker: The Gender Politics of Food,' in Marlene Epp, Franca Iacovetta, Frances Swyripa, eds., *Sisters or Strangers? Immigrant, Ethnic, and Racialized Women in Canadian History* (Toronto: University of Toronto Press, 2004), 216.
57 Batist et al., *A Treasure for My Daughter*, xi.
58 Ibid., 19.
59 Ibid., 20.
60 Ibid.

61 Esther 1:10–21.

62 Batist et al., *A Treasure for My Daughter*, 123.

63 Rickie Berman, 'Women in Jewish Religious Life: Manchester, 1880–1930,' in James Obelkevich, Lyndal Roper, and Raphael Samuel, eds., *Disciplines of Faith: Studies in Religion, Politics, and Patriarchy* (London: Routledge and Kegan Paul, 1987), 51.

64 Quoted in Tulchinsky, *Branching Out*, 284.

65 Batist et al., *A Treasure for My Daughter*, 19.

66 Ibid., 57–8.

67 Ibid., 61.

68 Ibid., 23.

69 Ibid.

12 'Tutti a Tavola!' Feeding the Family in Two Generations of Italian Immigrant Households in Montreal

SONIA CANCIAN

'*Tutti a tavola!*' (Everyone to the table!) my mother would call out when I was a young girl. It wouldn't be long before my siblings and I would gather in the kitchen near my mother as the water for the pasta boiled and the *ragù* simmered on the stovetop. In the meantime, my father waited at the table with a glass of wine nearby, and soon enough, we were all served our mother's weekly traditional Italian Sunday dinner.[1] In the memories of my childhood, the preparation, cooking, and serving of family meals involved almost exclusively the women of the family. I grew up within the ideological context of second-wave feminism during the latter decades of the twentieth century. I understood that women and men have equal rights, that they perform equally valid roles in both the domestic and public spheres, and that I had a right to pursue my own personal and professional goals. Yet, in my everyday universe, I watched, learned, and absorbed a different message: that women were responsible for preparing, cooking, and serving the meals for their families.

Despite my resistance to practices and discourses that limited women's equality and essentialized their roles, by watching and learning the kitchen activity of women in my household, I subconsciously internalized the importance of serving others in the domestic realm.[2] Thus, I came to understand that a woman's primary responsibilities – whether she was employed full-time or not – were anchored in the domestic sphere as she adopted the roles of nurturer, feeder, and caregiver of her family. My coming to terms with this dichotomy in my own life – a dichotomy that represented a generational shift – has been a primary motivation for this discussion about a cohort of two generations of Italian immigrant women feeding their families at the dinner table in Montreal.[3]

In her influential article, Micaela di Leonardo identifies 'kin work' as part of women's responsibility inside and across kin and non-kin households.[4] In addition, Carol Gilligan observes, 'Women's place in man's life cycle has been that of nurturer, caretaker, and helpmate, the weaver of those networks of relationships on which she in turn relies.'[5] As this chapter shows, the roles that Italian immigrant women adopt and negotiate are closely related to the performances of gender that unfold at dinner tables and family gatherings within households. Many studies have shown that in a large percentage of households in North America, Europe, and the United Kingdom, the organization, preparation and serving of meals to individual families is women's domain.[6] The rewards for women's hard work in feeding and serving their families are anchored in personal gratification and pride as well as in feeling appreciated and valorized by everyone gathered around the table.[7] Yet, as feminist scholarship suggests, women do not simply accept these roles without responding to them and questioning them as well. Rather, they actively negotiate, resist, and skilfully make do of their roles and responsibilities in preparing, cooking, and serving their families, thus demonstrating that their roles in the domestic realm are complex.

The questions I explore in this case study revolve around the gendered practices at meal times in Italian immigrant households in Montreal after the Second World War, and how these practices were passed on from one generation to the next. Who was preparing and serving meals to whom and under what conditions? Especially, in light of the women's movement of the 1970s, I question how the second generation of women born in these families negotiated, resisted, or accepted traditional roles in their own households, and why the gendered responsibility for feeding families was so persistent across generations despite societal changes. Although the women's recollections evoke sentiments of nostalgia, this was not my primary concern. Here, I focus on the gendered understandings and expectations that were and are played out in family gatherings, as told by the women interviewed. For this study, oral interviews were conducted with two generations of Italian women in Montreal: the 'first generation' refers to women who were born in Italy, and who migrated to Canada in the years after the Second World War; the 'second generation' refers to women born in Canada to those postwar immigrants.

Family Gatherings and Feeding Families: The First Generation

From the women's stories, we learn that getting together over the years with family members on a regular and frequent basis was viewed as culturally normal. This was especially the case for the first generation of Italian immigrant women but also resonated with women who were growing up or coming of age in Montreal up to the early 1970s. This collective memory is especially evident in the descriptions of family meals and gatherings with immediate and/ or extended family on Sundays, during festive holidays, at birthday celebrations, and religious markings in family members' lives, such as baptism, confirmation, and marriage. For instance, in the first years after Pierina V. and her mother arrived from Cattolica Eraclea, Sicily, with her siblings in 1957, she remembers the women of her family heavily involved in the kitchen preparing meals for everyone and that these 'numerous, loud' and sometimes smoke-filled, family gatherings included even the participation of boarders.[8] Conversely, Antonietta P. from Ampezzo Carnico, in the Friuli region, remembers family gatherings in smaller settings, in which for the most part, her mother prepared and cooked meals for the immediate family. Not all family gatherings involved large numbers or elaborate dinner preparations. For instance, Maria L. recalls, 'I don't remember anything like that … I imagine that we perhaps did get together … certainly, it was nothing special … the children of my step-father would eat in another room … even though we lived together, they ate on their own, and we would cook and eat on our own.'[9]

Family meals and meal rituals required careful preparation, effort, and time on behalf of women. A majority of the first-generation women recall that meal gatherings at family tables entailed enormous work for the women in multiple- and single-family households. Most first-generation women frequently prepared meals for family dinners and gatherings that numbered from four up to as many as thirty-nine guests, regardless of whether these women were employed outside the home or not (a double duty that will be addressed further on). In many cases, small- or large-scale meal preparation required making do within tight living quarters and with limited family budgets. The ritual of feeding one's family was also about creating a certain kind of family, whether expected or desired. Marjorie DeVault suggests that her interviewees, 'talk about their choices as pieces of a consciously crafted structure of family life. The times of coming together that result are thought of – though not entirely consciously – as making a family.'[10]

In some cases, women created meal rituals that spoke of solidarity and harmony with their immediate families, especially if that harmony was lacking in their family of origin. For instance, Maria L. fondly remembers preparing a complete American breakfast (composed of eggs fried in olive oil, bacon, toast, jam, espresso coffee, milk, and orange juice) for her husband and four young children on Saturday mornings. As she remembers, 'Saturday was a special day for me, when the children were still young. Saturday was sacred. Finally, we had a nice full breakfast together. I was happy to do everything.'[11] Maria's reflections on the importance of Saturday morning breakfasts with her family underscore that food and meals have symbolic and social meanings. A '"proper" meal,' for instance, is closely related to personal and social constructions of '"proper" family life.'[12] Understandings about the significance of meals reflect idealized versions of family life; as a result, women like Maria 'work hard at making their meals particular kinds of events,' like 'a calm time,' or 'an important getting together time.'[13]

Among first-generation Italian immigrant women in Montreal, it was assumed that feeding their families – and all the domestic tasks that this entailed – was women's role. This did not mean that men never helped. As other scholars of gender and food have pointed out, when men 'helped,' it was usually in the context of specialty cooking or elaborate meals for guests. For instance, during festive meals Antonietta's husband would also be involved in the kitchen, cooking a number of the family's favourite dishes like stuffed turkey with either a veal roast or French Canadian ham with vegetables, and a salad that included 'insalata rossa trevisana.'[14] In many cases, husbands of first-generation women became involved in domestic work, especially when the children left the family home, by 'helping' their wives in the kitchen, serving wine, and grocery shopping with their wives or alone. Men participated with women in the preparation of certain foods, especially with regard to home-prepared items that required preservation – dried meats like sausage, prosciutto, capicollo – and also ricotta and caciocavallo cheese, fresh pasta, tomato sauce, and Italian pickled vegetables, also known as *giardiniera*. They also worked with women at such seasonal tasks as growing a vegetable garden.

Yet, many recollections are about men who simply waited to be served and offered minimal to no assistance. For instance, when asked if her stepfather participated in the preparation of meals, Maria L. replied, 'Are you joking? He was a man of the old school with respect to today ... the man did nothing but work and at night, sit ... that's the way it was then ... and find dinner ready, and it was normal for my mother to cook, even though she too had been working outside the home. It was normal that the woman work [as waged worker] and then cook at home.'[15] The 'old school' of thought that Maria L. experienced was an ideology of gender-stratified domesticity that pervaded Western society in the 1950s and 1960s, when the Italian immigrants arrived in Montreal. An idealized notion – certainly not always manifest in real-life households – that male and female roles were clearly separate, and that women's place was in the domestic realm while men's was in the workplace and public realm, was pervasive in middle-class North America, generally, and not unique to Italians. In this context, as food and gender scholar Sherrie Inness observes, cooking was not only a serious matter for any girl or woman to attract and keep a mate, but also in expressing love and, in the case of Italians, 'respect' for every member of her family.[16] Included with this was the notion that cooking and serving meals for a husband and children and other family members was entirely a woman's domain.[17]

This strict division of labour in the household reinforced gender inequities in roles assumed by husbands and wives, an imbalance of equity in the household that is further captured in an interviewee's comment: 'There will never be two captains on a ship. Not that I'm inferior to my husband. I'm not. We talk, we discuss, but there will always be one captain to a ship.'[18] For first-generation Italian immigrant women, gender inequities were anchored in a strict division of labour in the household in which the responsibility of managing, organizing, preparing, and regularly serving as well as ensuring the meals' good taste to all members at the table was a task assigned almost exclusively to women.[19] The division of labour did not go unnoticed by the daughters of Italian immigrants. For instance, Pierina V., born in Italy in1951, whose mother was employed outside the home and also cooked for the family and cleaned the family home, watching her mother perform these tasks daily has meant 'it's not expected, it's accepted'[20] that women serve their husbands at the table. Not only is it accepted, in Pierina's eyes, but it's also a pleasure.

Acceptance or Resistance: The Second Generation

If feeding the family was an accepted pleasure for some first-generation Italian immigrant women in Montreal – even if also an exhausting and overwhelming task – how did these gendered familial roles transfer to their daughters, whether in practice or in ideology? And how did the realities of the daily and festive practice of cooking and serving translate into the practices of the next generation of Italian women within their own households? Like their mothers to a certain extent, the second-generation responses to expectations regarding 'feeding the family' were varied, representing a mix of acceptance and/or resistance. On the one hand, they were dealing with role models and teaching – of ideas and skills – that were passed from one generation to the next. On the other hand, for women who were born in Canada and who grew up and reached adulthood during the 1970s, feminist ideology and notions of gender equity and equality inevitably shaped their responses to domestic labour. In this, they were a generation in transition, as were all young Canadian women of this era.

Part of the reason that women accept (to varying degrees) their roles is attributed to how models and roles are learned by women in the home, and the cultural significance these daily actions engender. In response to a question about whether men are served first at her family table, Pierina responded, 'I feel that I have to do it ... because I saw my mother doing it all the time ... for me, she was the good teacher, the perfect teacher.'[21] Mothers serve as important role models for their daughters, and this is especially evident in Pierina's words. The sociologist Ann Oakley observes in her study on housewives,

'The mother is not only a female child's role-model for feminine behaviour, but for housework behaviour also. The daughter watches, imitates and later actively helps,'[22] leading to a more specific consequence in which standards and routines are learned and internalized by the daughter.[23] Marjorie DeVault's findings are similar: associations of specific gender activities in the household 'are learned early and enforced through everyday observation of prevailing patterns of gender relations.'[24] Mothers of the first generation became effective role models in terms of how their daughters came to idealize motherhood and its attendant tasks and responsibilities. Feminist scholarship has demonstrated that children, from an early age, observe their mothers at work in the household. In this way, girls were often recruited into 'womanly activities based on the principles of responsibility and attention.'[25] When these women become mothers themselves, the lessons they learned and internalized as children are reinforced through the urgency and immediacy of (their own) infants' needs.[26]

A further reason why these gender activities in the household are learned easily and 'naturally' is that they are 'rarely justified or even articulated explicitly,' leading these gendered cultural understandings to be part of a morally charged sense of how things should be.[27] This certainly appears to be the case for the younger women interviewed, who talked about responding to their mothers' expectations of their roles at different moments in their lives. In the case of first-generation women, interviews revealed that the image of women serving the plates and men sitting at the table waiting to be served mirrored the gendered understandings of how things *should be* in many Italian immigrant families of postwar Montreal. Their recollections speak of these gatherings, where women are visibly content to talk about the importance of pleasing others at the table. In doing so, as DeVault suggests, they subconsciously emphasize 'the self-imposed discipline they adopt as protection against "selfishness."'[28] Being 'selfless' was also a gendered quality and reinforced the service aspect of feeding one's family.

The opportunities that these activities entail for women are several and significant in nature; at the same time, the continued assumptions of these roles as part of women's domain underscore that 'gender relations of feeding and eating seem to convey the message that giving service is part of being a woman, and receiving it fundamentally part of being a man.'[29] Inevitably, these understandings of a woman's roles in feeding and serving her family provide resilient layers of assumptions on how a woman views herself in relation to others and how she feels she *should* behave once she has formed her own family. Such assumptions did not change easily for the second generation, even though the realities of their daily lives changed dramatically and their ideological environment was different. Yet, personal voices of resistance emerge (consciously or not), as we observe below from the comments of second-generation women.

In terms of cooking and serving practices in their immigrant households, as the second generation of women was growing up not all daughters as children were expected to participate equally in cooking and serving responsibilities. Older daughters were required to help much more than younger daughters. Some daughters of first-generation women were not expected to cooperate in the kitchen as they were growing up, that is, help their mothers and other women family members in the kitchen during gatherings; they, nonetheless, learned their primary roles as servers and cooks when they had their own households. Reflections like, 'I only learned to cook when I got married,' voiced by second-generation women like Melissa I., Angela S., Lisa F., and Judith B. help us to appreciate that while these women felt excluded from kitchen work as they were growing up, they still internalized the assumptions of what their roles would be when they were adult women with their own households. Once married and occupied with creating their own households with children, they quickly learned the work of feeding and serving their families.

For these women, what they learned as children and adolescents – despite coming of age in the aftermath of the women's movement of the late 1960s and early 1970s – was that it was viewed as normal for them to serve and cook for their husbands and children. They learned this through watching their mothers and other female kin operate as nurturers, feeders, and carers of their families. By participating in these gendered activities, they acquired a skill or capacity, 'that allowed them as adults to see the responsibilities that arise out of the needs of others and of a group.'[30] Thus, the influence of mothers and models of mothering have been extremely prominent in these young women's appropriation of their roles as feeders and caregivers in their own family structures, in conjunction with other factors such as how men in the family reinforced these roles to them as they were growing up. In part, this was the behaviour of their fathers, but it was also manifest in expectations of their brothers. When we consider the younger males in Italian immigrant families, there seems to be consensus among the older women interviewed that sons were not expected to participate in the kitchen or serve the plates. However, as adults, in some families the sons and sons-in-law are now being praised for helping and wanting to help in the kitchen. Pierina explains, 'Not that they don't want to. They're pretty good at that [helping out with tasks in the kitchen].' But, ultimately, the men are excluded from such preparations because, as she points out, 'when you're too many in the kitchen, you don't get anything done.'[31]

A determining factor in the degree to which the second-generation women fulfil their expected roles in the domestic sphere, including the kitchen, is whether or not they are full-time wage earners. Even though their mothers may also have worked outside the home for wages, the domestic roles for first-generation women took precedence over other employment, while for second-generation women, the 'working mother' was becoming the Canadian norm and thus the prioritization of their roles as women was conflicted. Some women felt they shouldn't have to carry the 'double load' in the same way as their mothers had. Melissa I. suggests, 'Of course, when I was home, it was more traditional roles, but when I went back to work, I said, "No."'[32] Once she returned to work, Melissa did not accept a double work day. She then made it clear to her husband that she needed him to participate equally in household work. Angela S., who is a stay-at-home mother, further explains, 'For me, it's like, he's a construction worker, he's tired, and I do it … it's not because my mother instilled it in me, this is the way I grew up. My husband doesn't have a problem [with] doing anything, but especially now that I'm a stay-at-home mom, I do 85 per cent. But it's only as expected, I mean, it's only normal. That's what I think.'[33]

On the other hand, while Lisa F. is also a stay-at-home mom and earning income through her home-based business, she admits to making 'supper usually, sometimes my husband will help. Usually I make the bulk of the meal. He'll help me. He's a good chopper. But yeah, I make the plates on the stove and I serve them, [or] sometimes the plates are in the middle and everyone serves themselves.'[34] Despite the participation of men in the domestic sphere in second-generation Italian immigrant households – whether through helping in the cooking process, serving, and/or cleaning up – these women's responses (all of whom have young children) underscore the connection noted earlier between mothering and preparing and serving meals.

For Italian married women of the second generation who are economically independent, the perspectives differ. Many responded with a viewpoint that privileges a more egalitarian work relationship in the domestic sphere with their partners. For instance, Melissa I., who now works full-time and has two young children in a daycare program, remarks, 'When I went back to work, there was more equality. My husband cooks almost every day when he gets home before me … He picks up the stuff in the home.'[35] Similarly, Nelia P. remarks, 'I cook. Roberto doesn't cook. It's the only thing he doesn't do. I don't think it's because he isn't capable, because the man does everything. So, I'm the one who cooks, I'm the one who prepares the meals, but when it's a question of serving, we both do it. When it's a question of cleaning afterwards, we both do it.'[36] For women like Melissa and Nelia, responsibility for the task of 'feeding the family' has become a question and negotiation, rather than an assumption. In this, their lives are indicative of the profound impact that second-wave feminism had on the division of labour in Canadian households, immigrant or otherwise.

While many Italian women grew up in Canada learning ideas and acquiring unspoken understandings from their mothers and the social and cultural environment that surrounded them about how wives and mothers *should* behave as feeders of their families, the additional dynamic of full-time wage work and women's personal ambitions to pursue careers complicates the picture further. Despite the resilience of 'the power of the socially organized practice and discourse of mothering,'[37] particularly in regards to feeding families in these households, full-time employment for these women serves as a mechanism for making egalitarian ideals of sharing the work of preparing and serving meals with their husbands more possible. Moreover, in my conversations with both cohorts of first-generation and second-generation women, a subtle distinction emerged in the ways that they articulated how they felt they negotiated these roles and expectations and whether they hoped for a more egalitarian approach in their households. The first-generation women seemed to speak more readily about 'making do' with the work involved, and about their skilled abilities and pride in accommodating and negotiating their roles as wives and mothers in feeding their families. In contrast, women of the second generation voiced more explicitly their resistance to their mothers' ideals and the desire for change by underscoring the ways in which they have modified or resisted some of the practices of feeding their families on a daily and occasional basis. For instance, many remarked that they now more frequently organize potluck dinners, in which 'everybody brings something,' rather than preparing meals for everyone themselves. Several women mentioned that the number of family gatherings is diminishing, and that they are hosting smaller family gatherings, usually privileging immediate family members. Others have confided that they have reacted to their mothers' views that 'it's always been done' and openly questioned them about why family gatherings have to continue with the same (as in their past experiences) understanding of food and care in the preparation and serving of meals.[38]

In describing their roles in the preparation of family meals, the younger women articulated more clearly a resistance to adopting fully the norms and roles that they've been socialized to accept by their mothers (and other women in their families, as well as men) and their social and cultural environments. In these interviews, they also emphasized the frustrations they felt when, even during present-day family meals and gatherings, the women continue to serve the meals, while the men remain seated and wait to be served.[39] However, as the above responses illustrate, these women are also actively changing the ways in which family meals are being organized in order to lessen their workload and encourage a more egalitarian approach to preparing and serving meals to their families.

Conclusion

Gender continues to be a significant player in the production, preparation, serving, and consumption of food in Canadian households, as other chapters in this volume by Marlene Epp and Stacey Zembrzycki also demonstrate. Gender roles and expectations around the kitchen table for Italian immigrant women of two generations were and continue to be an important part of these women's daily lives as well as their social and cultural universes. However, as this study has also demonstrated, many Italian Canadian women are actively engaged in accepting, making do, negotiating, and resisting their roles and responsibilities as nurturers of their families. In this, we see the significant impact that a changing social environment has had on Italian women's (and others) notions of who should 'feed the family.'

ACKNOWLEDGMENT

The research for this chapter was funded by a Social Sciences and Humanities Research Council of Canada postdoctoral fellowship. My thanks to Donna Gabaccia, Awa Abdi, and Elizabeth Zanoni for reading earlier versions. Thanks also to the women who were interviewed for this study, and particularly, my mother to whom I dedicate this work.

NOTES

1 'Sunday Dinner' means in this context, a three- to five-course meal served at lunchtime on Sundays with most or all members of the immediate family present. In my family, these dinners frequently followed mass service and included a first serving of antipasto (prosciutto and slices of cantaloupe, bread sticks, and pickled vegetables, known as *giardiniera*), a pasta dish, a meat dish with salad followed by fruit and cheese as dessert, and coffee for the adults. See also Carole M. Counihan, *Around the Tuscan Table: Food, Family, and Gender in Twentieth-Century Florence* (New York: Routledge, 2004), in particular, chapter 7 on the meanings of families eating together in Italian households. See also Murcott for an understanding of the composition and importance of cooked dinners in households in South Wales, especially on Sundays, in which a cooked dinner was identified as 'meat, potatoes, vegetables and gravy,' and viewed as a 'proper meal' as a result of 'not only its composition, but also, its preparation and taking.' Anne Murcott,

"'It's a Pleasure to Cook for Him": Food, Mealtimes and Gender in Some South Wales Households,' in Caroline B. Brettell and Carolyn F. Sargent, eds., *Gender in Cross-Cultural Perspective* (Englewood Cliffs, NJ: Prentice-Hall, 1993), 79.

2 Feminist scholarship has produced a plethora of studies on the relationship between women's subordination and the household. Consider, for instance, Marjorie L. DeVault, *Feeding the Family: The Social Organization of Caring as Gendered Work* (Chicago, IL: University of Chicago Press, 1991); Anne Murcott, ed., *The Sociology of Food and Eating: Essays on the Sociological Significance of Food* (Hants, England: Gower, 1983), and 'It's a Pleasure to Cook for Him,' 77–87; Heidi I. Hartmann, 'The Family as the Locus of Gender, Class and Political Struggle: The Example of Housework,' *Signs* 6 (1981): 366–94; Judith Lorber, *Paradoxes of Gender* (New Haven, CT: Yale University Press, 1994); Deborah Lupton, *Food, the Body and the Self* (London: Sage, 1996); Meg Luxton, *More than a Labour of Love: Three Generations of Women's Work in the Home* (Toronto: Women's Press, 1980); Ann Oakley, *The Sociology of Housework* (New York: Pantheon, 1974). See also, Wendy Edmond and Suzie Fleming, eds., *All Work and No Pay: Women, Housework, and the Wages Due* (Bristol, England: Power of Women Collective and Falling Wall Press, 1975).

3 Fifteen women from two generations of Italians living in Montreal were interviewed for this chapter in March and April 2008 in Montreal and in Fort Lauderdale, Florida, where three women spend their winters. Six of the women belong to the first generation of Italian immigrants who arrived in Canada in the immediate postwar period; all have been married for many years and have adult children who are either living with them or in their separate households. The other nine women interviewed are second-generation women born of Italian families in Canada; all have households of their own, they are either married or living in common law partnerships, and most have young children. All participants' responses originally given in Italian are my translations into English. Depending on participants' wishes, real names and pseudonyms have been used.

4 Di Leonardo identifies *kin work* as, 'the conception, maintenance, and ritual celebration of cross-household kin ties, including visits, letters, telephone calls, presents, and cards to kin; the organization of holiday gatherings; the creation and maintenance of quasi-kin relations; decisions to neglect or to intensify particular ties; the mental work of reflection about all these activities; and the creation and communication of altering images of family and kin vis-à-vis the images of others, both folk and mass media.' Micaela di Leonardo, 'The Female World of Cards and Holidays: Women, Families, and the Work of Kinship,' in Brettell and Sargent, *Gender in Cross-Cultural Perspective*, 323.

5 Carol Gilligan, *In a Different Voice: Psychological Theory and Women's Development* (Cambridge, MA: Harvard University Press, 1993 [1982]), 17.

6 See, e.g., Murcott, *Sociology of Food and Eating* and 'It's a Pleasure to Cook for Him'; Counihan, *Around the Tuscan Table*; and DeVault, *Feeding the Family*.

7 Murcott, 'It's a Pleasure to Cook for Him'; Counihan, *Around the Tuscan Table*; and Marlene Epp, 'The Semiotics of Zwieback: Feast and Famine in the Narratives of Mennonite Refugee Women,' in Marlene Epp, Franca Iacovetta, and Frances Swyripa, eds., *Sisters or Strangers? Immigrant, Ethnic, and Racialized Women in Canadian History* (Toronto: University of Toronto Press, 2004), 314–40.

8 Pierina V. recalls: 'We were seven people, my mom had boarders, plus we were always reunited with her cousins living in the same building ... so one night it was my mother [cooking], one night my cousin, but mostly it was my mother.' Interview, 11 April 2008, Fort Lauderdale.

9 Interview with Maria L., 14 April 2008, Fort Lauderdale.

10 DeVault, *Feeding the Family*, 78.

11 Interview with Maria L.

12 Murcott, *Sociology of Food and Eating*, 102. See also, DeVault, *Feeding the Family*; Lupton, *Food, the Body and the Self*; Counihan, *Around the Tuscan Table*; and Epp, 'The Semiotics of Zwieback.'

13 DeVault, *Feeding the Family*, 48–9.

14 A salad consisting of a red-leaf lettuce, typical of Treviso in the Veneto region of Italy. Interviews with Nelia P. and Antonietta P., 6 April 2008, and with Wanda P., 26 April 2008, all Montreal. Wanda P., e-mail message to author, 20 Feb. 2009.

15 Interview with Maria L.

16 Sherrie A. Inness, *Dinner Roles: American Women and Culinary Culture* (Iowa City, IA: University of Iowa Press, 2001), 146–7.

17 See Inness' argument about women and the association of kitchen work and women in the 1950s. Inness, *Dinner Roles*, 158.

18 Interview with Pierina V.

19 DeVault argues, 'The reasons for this emphasis on deferential service are complex. Certainly, such patterns are upheld by women's lack of power in the wider society, as well as family ideology that identifies "woman" as the subordinate partner in intimate relationships. But in addition, women often choose to provide service because they recognize that their work contributes to sociability in groups, and sometimes, to a group's very survival. The work is directed toward pleasing others as well as serving their more material needs for sustenance and comfort.' *Feeding the Family*, 233. Further, a similar argument can be made about domestic work in Italian immigrant households, in which interviews reveal that laundry work, ironing, cleaning house, in tandem with preparing home-cooked meals for families was viewed as 'normal' women's work and was at the same time, '"naturally" satisfying to women.' Inness, *Dinner Roles*, 163. See also, Murcott, 'It's a Pleasure to Cook for Him,' 78.

20 Interview with Pierina V.
21 Ibid.
22 Oakley, *Sociology of Housework*, 96.
23 Ibid.
24 DeVault, *Feeding the Family*, 148.
25 Ibid., 119.
26 Ibid.
27 Ibid., 148.
28 Ibid., 233.
29 Ibid., 234. Gilligan also observes, 'But while women have thus taken care of men, men have, in their theories of psychological development, as in their economic arrangements, tended to assume or devalue that care.' *In a Different Voice*, 17.
30 DeVault, *Feeding the Family*, 96.
31 Interview with Pierina V.
32 Interview with Melissa I., 19 March 2008, Montreal
33 Interview with Angela S., 4 April 2008, Montreal.
34 Interview with Lisa F., 4 April 2008, Montreal.
35 Interview with Melissa I.
36 Interview with Nelia P.
37 DeVault, *Feeding the Family*, 96.
38 Interview with Judith B., 4 April 2008, Montreal.
39 Interview with Lisa F. In her interview, Melissa I. made a similar comment: 'The women are still in the kitchen, even though they're a fourth generation removed.'

PART FIVE

Single Food Commodities, Markets, and Cultural Debates

13 John Bull and Sons: The Empire Marketing Board and the Creation of a British Imperial Food System

JAMES MURTON

The London Grocer John Bull and Sons Ltd was founded in 1928 as a successor to the venerable firm of John Bull, founded many years before in 450 AD. Historians are not clear as to what occupied the shelves of the older company, but John Bull and Sons was a specialist in the produce of the British Empire. Under signs bearing the slogan 'The Empire Is Your Garden,' JB&S's shelves groaned with South African pineapples, chickens and geese from the Irish Free State, and New Zealand lamb. 'Home' goods from Britain itself jostled with the products of 'British' farmers overseas. English rabbits, skinned and ready for cooking, might hang in the window for the consideration of stylish young women, or that space might be occupied by piles of Canadian apples. Gentlemen in top hats and spats left the store laden with bags bearing the firm's name, one that was redolent of the worldwide fraternity that the British Empire had become by the 1920s.[1]

Or so the promoters of the British government's Empire Marketing Board (EMB) would have hoped. In truth, Londoners of the 1920s could not have visited John Bull and Sons.[2] There was no actual storefront, no white-aproned shopkeepers helping housewives sort out Canadian Red Delicious from Winesap apples, and certainly no earlier firm going back to 450 AD. John Bull and Sons was a poster concept created by an artist in the employ of the EMB, which, from 1926 to 1933, had the job of creating markets in Britain for goods produced in British Dominions and colonies overseas.[3] And yet in a sense John Bull and Sons did exist. Its fictional windows and displays represented the problem of marketing foods produced a long way from home, of normalizing the idea of consuming fruit and lamb from the other side of the world. To get its piles of Empire apples JB&S would have faced, as did the EMB, the complexities of preserving perishable products as they travelled great distances. If there was no physical shopkeeper to dispense advice, there was a need to create

13.1 Poster: Shoppers at John Bull and Sons (1928) Ltd., by Harold Sanders Williamson. Courtesy of Library and Archives Canada, Acc. No. 1983-27-99.

a web of information connecting Canadian farmers and packing houses with British wholesalers, merchants, and customers. While the Empire Marketing Board built no physical shop, it did work towards creating a global market in food.

Such a global market transcended national and ecological boundaries. Before food could be traded globally, a whole set of connections between the local and global – cultural, infrastructural, and environmental – had to be worked out. The Empire Marketing Board did not initiate this process: food already was an important component of the world market that had developed from the mid-to-late nineteenth century. But the EMB did come along when the challenge of trading in perishable items like apples was being addressed. It was part of an attempt to reshape the British trading system around the Empire, following the crumbling of the world market during the First World War. The board reminds us that a global market in food was not – indeed, markets in general are not – natural or inevitable, but rather had to be built out of ecological conditions, farming practices, culture, and state policy. Focusing on a particular 'local' – Canada – and one food – apples – this chapter examines the ways in which the EMB worked to embed national agricultural economies and agro-ecosystems in a larger imperial, and ultimately global, market system.

Background

By the 1920s, Canadians were still in the process of (forcibly) transforming areas where First Nations procured food into the fields and fences of Euro-Canadian agriculture. In the future apple-growing region of British Columbia's southern Okanagan Valley, for instance, fields watered by a recently constructed government-sponsored irrigation project were crowding out the herds of the Osoyoos Band. Farther north in the Okanagan and in Canada's other primary apple-producing areas – Ontario's Niagara Peninsula and the Annapolis Valley of Nova Scotia – the process of dispossession and environmental transformation was further advanced. Orchards stood where others had shaped the land for hunting and mixed farming.

Such ecological imperialism was never entirely simple nor in only one direction. For example, the potato was a native of South America that became a staple crop of First Nations people in the Pacific Northwest after being introduced by European mariners. Alison Norman's chapter in this volume points out how early settlers in what is now Ontario adopted wild rice (cultivated by the Anishnaabeg) and pressed local plants such as Labrador tea and dandelions into service as replacements for tea and coffee. Yet, by the nineteenth century, Euro-Canadian settlers were part of a culture that derided Native ways. In Ontario, imported tea and coffee eventually became available. Indigenous ingredients were forgotten, or, as Julia Roberts' discussion in this volume of local duck illustrates, they might be transformed, in this case, through the application of wheat flour, imported spices, European cooking methods, and the dining rituals of elite male Anglo-Canadian sociability, into 'imperial food.' Ontario farmers turned quickly to the production of what English agricultural historian Joan Thirsk has called 'mainstream' European agricultural products – meat and cereals, and particularly in early Upper Canada, winter wheat.[4]

The extent to which the production of Upper Canadian wheat was aimed at British markets has been much debated by Canadian agricultural historians. The deeper question – how such markets were constructed – has been less studied. Yet, markets, as Canadian historical economists Harold Innis and Karl Polanyi argued some years ago, do not just exist but are built. Both Innis (through his study of the fur trade in Canada) and Polanyi showed that markets are built on a 'web of historical and cultural contingencies, and not simply from generalized, law-like movements of supply and demand.'[5] Key to the 'great transformation' (using Polanyi's phrase) to a market society in the early modern period was the making of elements of nature over into commodities. Yet, the elements of nature were never, as historian John Soluri notes in his history of the Honduran banana trade, 'passive or predictable.'[6] The production, extraction, shipping, and selling of furs, bananas, or, in the work of food historian Gabriella Petrick, lettuce, were inevitably shaped by the nature of those various items.[7] For example, since lettuce was extremely perishable and usually eaten raw, it required a delicate integration of growers and shippers with cooling and shipping technology, and the development of a new, hardier strain of the plant – iceberg lettuce. Culture, too, was crucial. When U.S. fruit companies faced a potential crisis as pathogens attacked banana plants in Honduras, they were compelled to develop a strain of banana that was both resistant to the disease and resembled the Gros Michel variety to which U.S. consumers were accustomed.[8] Finally, as Innis and Polanyi both insisted, and as Jeffry Frieden's history of global capitalism makes clear, making markets requires supportive governments to choose between competing interests – such as enacting land use laws that favour banana cultivation over ranching – and to enact tax, banking, and currency policies facilitating global trade.[9]

From the mid-nineteenth century on, successive governments supported an ever-widening global trade in food because it brought economic development to producing regions and supplied cheap food to city dwellers in Europe and eastern North America. Yet, global food came at a significant cost. Native peoples were displaced, and environments were transformed. In receiving areas, farmers were undermined. The extensive market gardens of Brooklyn, for example, were made redundant by the California fruit empire and were swallowed up by city.[10] As environmental historian William Cronon argues, people were increasingly separated from the place and process of agricultural production and so had little opportunity to appreciate that the packaged steak they bought came from a real cow participating in a real ecosystem somewhere. The effects of their food on the places that produced it became invisible to them.[11] As the leading historical critic of the world food system, historical sociologist Harriet Friedmann, argues, sustainable agriculture requires an agro-ecosystem that mimics the functioning of natural ecosystems. Constructing such an agro-ecosystem, in turn, requires a fine-tuned adaptation to place that is impossible in a system where production and consumption are heavily shaped by global multinationals.[12]

Understanding how these global food systems came about is important. Most analysts of our contemporary global food system see it as beginning after the Second World War. However, histories of pre-1939 food systems, and particularly those dealing with the role of European settler societies like Canada in them, are thin on the ground. One of the aims of this essay is to begin to fill this gap.[13] What scholarship does exist rarely considers the multiple interactions between the state, culture, and the environment, as I do here. American historians such as Cronon, Soluri, and Petrick have tended to concentrate on the power of big business while excluding or downplaying the role of the state.[14] Friedmann's earlier work on food systems before the Second World War makes clear the role of the state in fostering appropriate forms of trade and agriculture, but, like Cronon, she rarely systematically analyses the cultures of consumption that shaped what happened in the store or the home.[15] Yet, the state in the form of the EMB actively used cultures of imperialism to build a market in food. It trumpeted the very global connections that, according to critics like Friedmann and Cronon, food systems hide. Whereas historians of the EMB and of Canadian export agriculture have tended to assume that the existence of general laws of supply and demand predated cultural and political systems, this study questions those assumptions and, by implication, challenges explanations for the existence of the global food system itself.[16] This chapter shows how the food system under scrutiny was deliberately constructed. And an important part of that complex story is the Empire Marketing Board.

Origins of the Empire Marketing Board

By the 1880s, steamships, railways, telegraph lines, adherence to principles of free trade and what amounted to a global currency – the gold standard – had made possible the complicated 'international network of jobbers, shippers, shipping companies, millers, packers, and wholesalers' that made up the first global food system.[17] Countries in Europe, and long-industrialized Britain, in particular, were increasingly reliant on overseas agricultural producers, particularly the massive wheat farms of the Americas, Australia, and Russia, while producers were dependent on European markets. The First World War, however, delivered a massive shock to the system. Governments struggled to reintroduce the gold standard; tariffs and other protective measures became increasingly common. For a United Kingdom committed to free trade, the situation was particularly problematic: foreign countries could still sell in Britain while protecting their own markets.[18]

One solution that British businessmen and politicians across the ideological spectrum embraced was to turn to the Empire. Stephen Constantine has argued that imperialism, far from declining after the First World War, became newly popular.[19] Imperialists in Britain and the Dominions saw the Empire as a potential force for peace and civilization in the world. So uncontroversial was this idea that the Empire Marketing Board's posters were used in schools across Britain, Canada, and other parts of the Empire.[20] A cross-section of elite opinion favoured the idea of solving Britain's postwar economic problems by creating an Empire market. Imperial preference – that is, favourable duties on imports from the Empire coupled with higher duties on foreign imports – would take advantage of the variety of climates and economies within the expanded interwar Empire, and bolster the economies of Britain, the Dominions, and the colonies. At the Imperial Economic Conference of 1923, the Dominions got Britain to agree to the idea of preferential tariffs on certain Dominion food imports while the prime minister of Australia called for an Imperial Economic Committee to oversee Empire commerce. But, since it was politically impossible for the British government to raise the price of food through increased tariffs, the Conservative government of Stanley Baldwin instead established in 1925 the Imperial Economic Committee with a budget of £1 million ($5 million dollars), the estimated amount that the Dominions had lost in the foregone tariffs. The IEC, in turn, recommended the money be administered by an 'executive commission' that would replace tariffs with a program to increase the sale of Empire goods in Britain. This executive commission was constituted the next year as the Empire Marketing Board.[21] The IEC remained in existence, its relationship to the EMB murky.

Imperial enthusiasts saw these developments as a positive step towards Empire unity. The IEC, especially, saw itself as an 'imperial body' deriving from resolutions adopted at the Imperial conference and reporting to the various governments of the Empire. The EMB was more purely a creature of the British government, under the control of Secretary of State for Dominion Affairs Leo Amery.[22] Together they were, according to Sir Thomas Allen, one of the British representatives on the IEC, designed to create permanent bodies with the goal of turning the Empire into a 'single unit of commerce.'[23]

Such talk was not welcomed by the Canadian government. At the 1923 conference, Canadian Prime Minister William Lyon Mackenzie King delivered a speech of artful Kingsian vacuity, seemingly supporting imperial unity while stressing a laissez-faire model of global trade. His references to the 'great family' that was the Empire inevitably stressed its vastness and diversity. The need for component countries of the Empire to act in their own best interests was couched in the language of unity. 'Whatever is achieved which may be of advantage to one of the countries,' King noted, 'is certain to be of advantage sooner or later to the whole. Similarly, whatever is of advantage to the whole must be of advantage to each of the several parts.'[24]

We can assume that King was well aware that the interests of the local and the imperial would not necessarily coincide. Although committed to the

Empire, Canada under King would act in its own best interests. When giving instructions to one of the Canadian representatives on the IEC, King made it clear that Canada was anxious to increase consumption of Canadian products in Britain but wary of any permanent imperial institutions. The IEC was acceptable, King explained, because he had been assured that it would only meet on an ad hoc basis.[25] O.D. Skelton, the influential deputy minister of external affairs, agreed. When the Australian government suggested British subsidies of Dominion producers, restrictions on foreign imports into Britain, and the creation of an Empire Control Board to be run by Britain, Skelton demurred. All these measures, he argued, were either impractical or politically impossible. Instead, Skelton proposed that the £1 million grant be spent on advertising Empire products in Britain, a position supported as well by the Canadian minister of agriculture and Prime Minister King himself.[26] Canada's representative on the IEC, L.C. McOuatt, was thus understandably alarmed by people like Sir Hugh Allen, who called for permanent imperial institutions, especially as McOuatt believed Allen's position reflected the general opinion of the committee. In response, McOuatt noted that 'from the outset [Canada had] been alone in opposing this line of action.' He informed Skelton that the meetings seemed unlikely to produce a report that Canada could agree to.[27] Skelton's advice to McOuatt was to stand firm.[28]

In the end, matters broke the Canadian way. The final report recommended that the 'executive commission' (what would become the EMB) engage in marketing and in research into the production, storage, and shipping of foods. McOuatt was happy to note that there was 'nothing' in this activity that was 'harmful to Canadian interests.' In keeping with the wishes of all of the Dominion governments, produce would be labelled with the word 'Empire' and the name of the actual country that produced it. The EMB would be simply a 'small British commission.' Local interests would not be swallowed up by imperial ones.[29]

The victory was largely a mirage. The IEC remained in continuous existence. The EMB, although technically just an advisory board for the secretary of state for the Dominions, in practice was never just a small commission. It piggy-backed on the executive authority of the secretary, who was ex officio chairman. With a civil service staff of 120 (at its maximum), it was also not a small committee.[30] Within eight months, Canadian representatives were fighting to keep Dominion representatives off the EMB and to keep the EMB separate from the IEC on the ground that both actions would tend to make the EMB permanent.[31] Both fights were lost. The EMB would quickly turn to the encouragement of greater imperial unity. Most prominently, its marketing campaign worked hard to normalize the idea that the Empire was a single 'garden' and that Ceylon or New Zealand was as much a part of home as the East Riding or Surrey.

Normalizing the Empire Garden: The Propaganda Campaign

To carry out this message, the EMB employed all the techniques of 1920s mass media and advertising.[32] The EMB operated in an age in which advertising had been refined to a high art. Like other prominent commercial enterprises, such as the Metropolitan District Railway or the Canadian Pacific Railway, the EMB was best known for a series of striking poster images shown on commercial hoardings, in factories and grocers, and in public sites in towns and cities across the United Kingdom.[33] Yet, posters were only one form of media that the EMB employed. The board published full-page illustrated ads in a range of British newspapers, from the *Times of London* to *Women's Weekly* to *Punch*.[34] Pamphlets explained 'Why Every Woman Ought to Buy British,' and women were further targeted with a variety of recipe leaflets, each one focusing on a particular Empire food.[35] The board's exhibition pavilion, which mixed dioramas of Empire history with cooking demonstrations and an electrically lit marquee of the board's name, travelled around the United Kingdom and to Toronto for the Canadian National Exhibition (CNE) in 1928.[36] The board encouraged retailers to establish Empire Shopping Weeks, and sent lecturers to labour and women's organizations. It took to the radio waves on the BBC. Having been ordered to 'bring the Empire alive,' the EMB film unit also became a pioneer in documentary filmmaking.[37]

Many professional ad men were unimpressed, however, and criticized the board for its lack of catchy slogans and its failure to deliver a clear message. Its copy, they said, was wordy. Consumers were not being told precisely what they should do. The artwork was uninspired. In response, the EMB said their main job was educational. They were not selling any particular product or firm but, instead, seeking to inform British consumers about the true breadth and diversity of the Empire, and persuading them that it was in their interest to purchase Empire products.[38] Thus, they stressed that the Empire was a single economic unit; indeed, it was a single family. 'Every Time You Buy Empire Produce You Help the Empire to Buy the Goods You Make at Home,' declared one poster, erasing colonial relations of power via a vision of market-driven reciprocity. Vast distances and the social and ecological damages wrought by the conversion of smallholder to export agriculture disappeared into the image of the Empire garden, so that 'when it is winter with us, the sun somewhere else in the British Empire is reddening apples and putting the juice into oranges.' In this garden, 'you can eat Empire apples all year round.'[39]

The EMB, in other words, was engaged in a discursive campaign of geographical and ecological erasure and reimagining. As the following quotation suggests, this process involved highlighting, on the one hand, that there already had been 'A REVOLUTION IN YOUR FOOD': 'Your grandfathers ate little but the produce of the fields around them. The development of Empire lands overseas, the increasing speed of ships and railways, and the discoveries of cold storage have brought to the humblest households in our great towns the produce of distant territories and various climates.'[40] Consumers were encouraged to see themselves as part of a larger community constituted through global/imperial systems. 'The Sun Never Sets on the Orchards of Empire,' proclaimed one ad, graphically laying out almost the entire industrial-ecological matrix of the world/imperial food system. From top left, the sun feeds a row of fruit trees. A line of carts, ships, and trains brings the fruit to a group of inspectors, and finally to a dinner table pictured lower right.[41]

Yet, much of this revolutionary new food system did not involve the Empire. True, Britain was highly dependent on imported foods, but they came from all corners of the global economy. The Empire accounted for not quite half of the grain imported into Britain, despite the fact that Australia and Canada were major world producers. Empire dairy products accounted for a similar proportion, and Empire meat and fruit met only 25 per cent of British needs.[42] So, if one discursive move was to normalize the buying and consuming of food from the other side of the globe, the other was to make 'everything consciously imperial,' including 'products like milk and butter and everyday activities like shopping and cooking.'[43] Thus, the ads that ran in women's magazines and evening papers stressed the imperial implications of an everyday shopping trip. 'THE MEN TALK AND TALK, BUT ... Mrs John Bull,' went one such ad, 'carries in her purse a power that sets men working for her all over the world,' adding, 'because she must buy food for her family, farmers till the soil of a hundred countries, ships move in their thousands, wheels in their millions turn.'[44]

There was little effort to hide the workings of this food system; instead, the EMB trumpeted Britain's global food connections. In working to sell the idea and products of Empire, the EMB did something else as well. They sold the idea and practice of global food. Positive images attached to the Empire were employed to normalize the idea of obtaining one's dinner from the other side of the globe. Fruit from Australia or rice from India was not foreign, it was British. In buying it, in demanding it, the British consumer was consuming the products of her own garden.

Or so the EMB wanted British consumers to believe. However, the integration of the local and the global was not so easily done. First, although the EMB always argued that the overall effect of Empire buying would be economic benefits for all, British farmers were understandably not convinced. Hence, from the start, the EMB was forced into an at-times awkward compromise over the promotion of overseas versus British (or 'Home') produce. The board's solution was to emphasize that Britain, too, was part of the Empire, and to urge consumers to first ask for Home goods, and then the products of the Empire. Sometimes the promotion of Home goods came close to undermining the EMB's support for overseas products: 'what could be fresher or richer or cleaner,' one ad for British products asked, 'than the butter and eggs, the milk and cheese and bacon that come to us from the farmlands of these islands?'[45] Certainly, as the EMB argued, Empire buying allowed consumers to take advantage of varying climates and seasons, a position that justified products of tropical and southern hemisphere colonies. Such logic foundered for the case of Canada. Despite a plethora of advertising copy claiming a particular 'season' for Canadian apples, the board also issued a Calendar of Empire apples that made the environmental reality clear: at no time were Canadian apples available when Home apples were not.[46] Canadian producers could not hope to compete on environmental conditions alone.[47]

More fundamental than these problems of competition was the fact that distance and climatic heterogeneity posed as many challenges as they did opportunity. Imagine an idealized pre-industrial food system. Transportation is relatively short and straightforward. Retailers can buy based on personal knowledge of farmers and local ecological conditions. Organic wastes can be returned to the system.[48] None of this is true of a global system. The Empire was not really a garden, and even approximating such a reality would require the full application of industrial technology and state bureaucracy.

Thus, the discursive construction of an Empire garden was always intertwined with what the board called an 'even greater' work proceeding 'behind the scenes.'[49] Its main features were the encouragement of locally specialized production; the creation of the means of accessing information about markets and the agro-ecological conditions of distant places; support for scientific research into the problems of turning products of nature, like apples, into uniform, easily transportable commodities; and encouraging the infrastructure necessary to actually carry out the shipping and sale of overseas foods. The remainder of this chapter examines the way in which the board and the IEC tackled these problems in the case of the Canadian apple industry.

Uniting the Empire Garden: Apples

The export of Canadian apples to Great Britain began as early as the mid-nineteenth century with sporadic shipments of apples from Nova Scotia, although it was not until the 1880s that regular trade developed. From this point on, however, the Nova Scotian apple industry became almost entirely devoted to supplying the British market. Up until 1890, an average of almost one million bushels of applies were shipped each year from Nova Scotia to the United Kingdom. By contrast, apples grown in Ontario and British Columbia were far more likely to be sold on domestic markets. The total volume of Canadian exports to Britain grew steadily to an average of 4.5 million bushels annually over the five years after the First World War; it fell to 3.5 million bushels by 1925, and then resumed climbing.[50]

Yet, despite this forty-year history of the apple trade, the supply of apples to Britain, and their prices, could be erratic. One problem flowed from the workings of the U.S. market. U.S. apple producers aimed, first of all, at their domestic market of 120 million people, and only excess supply was exported to Britain. Such excess might be small or, because U.S. production was so large, it might reach a size that flooded Canadian exports to Britain, which arrived on the market at the same time.[51] These fluctuations in supply hurt Canadian producers, but they also destabilized the market in Britain since an unexpectedly large American harvest drove down prices. A further problem, and one with longer-lasting effects on the work of the EMB, was raised at the 1923 Imperial Conference by the Food Investigation Board of the British government's Department of Scientific and Industrial Research. Fresh fruit, they noted, was a living organism, and 'there is at present only very elementary knowledge as to how to control ... the conditions during the handling, storage and transport of large bulks of these commodities for considerable periods and over the long distances required.'[52] Shipments of damaged fruit destabilized prices and undermined the attempt to build a market for Empire apples. As the IEC would later point out while considering the EMB's ad campaign, 'publicity undertaken in respect of foodstuffs which are irregular in supply and insufficient in quantity will merely cause disappointment and dissatisfaction ... advertisement would be comparatively useless without continuity of supply.'[53]

All of these were problems that arose from the relationship between global markets, on the one hand, and on the other, the agro-ecology of apples and the geographies of their production in Canada and the Empire. When apples became global commodities, consistency and predictability of supply became important. Ecology and geography, however, introduced uncertainty. The Canadians proposed tariffs on U.S. fruit imports to Britain. This was essentially an attempt to reshape an unfavourable geography of production by making U.S. fruit more expensive than Canadian (as it would be if the United States was further away than Canada from the United Kingdom).[54]

The more fundamental problem was the agro-ecological. We can usefully think of this problem as one of quality, made acute by the perishability of apples. Supporters of global food systems spoke often of the problem of ensuring quality; this is not surprising given that, as historian John Soluri has said of the banana, quality and quantity are linked. As the market supplies more and more product, it becomes ever more important to distinguish individual products on the basis of their superior quality. Soluri largely considers quality as analogous to taste, in the same sense, in other words, that today we might believe Starbuck's coffee is superior in taste (or quality) to Tim Horton's. For apple growers and marketers, quality more often meant consistency. The object was to produce a properly shaped fruit free of blemish from insects or disease. Doing so required controlling nature.[55]

When the EMB came on the scene, there were several measures already in place for controlling nature and ensuring quality. Grading was a central one. Apples were sorted by uniformity of size and colour, the larger and more evenly coloured achieving a higher grade.[56] Grading sorted out the poor from the quality fruit, but the dividing line between what were in reality infinitely varied individual pieces of fruit was essentially arbitrary. A high quality harvest might sell for the same price as a fruit of lower quality that barely made the grade. The Fruit Marks Act of 1901, which legislated two grades, attempted to finesse this problem by allowing packers to add other descriptions of quality, so long as these could not be confused with the legislated marks.[57] The Fruit Act of 1931 legislated four grades for apples packed in barrels, and three for those packed in boxes. Within a particular grade, fruit was designated to be one of two to four standard sizes. Shippers were allowed to add a brand mark, known to the trade, to designate fruit of an especially high quality.[58]

Grading was thus a process of culturally constructing nature. As Ian Mosby's chapter in this volume shows, the seemingly neutral scientific rules of nutrition were imbedded in cultural notions of what constituted the bodies of the ideal Canadian. Similarly, grading developed an idea of a perfect apple. Although actual apples could only approximate this ideal, growers were nevertheless encouraged to try to produce it. However, they faced various obstacles. Growers had to determine what would grow under local conditions, keeping in mind what varieties were desirable to British consumers. The federal Department of Agriculture supplied information on favoured varieties – a 1903 pamphlet identified ten.[59] It was hoped that pruning, regular spraying, and careful picking would result in a large, ideally shaped fruit free of blemish from insects or diseases.

Grading and growing techniques, thus, were two different ways of controlling for the variation between apples. Another, perhaps larger problem was the perishability of the fruit. Just packing the apples was a delicate process requiring considerable skill and experience. Nova Scotia and Ontario growers shipped apples in a 96-quart wooden barrel with eight hoops. These barrels were first set face down and a layer of pulp or paper was inserted. Packers placed apples of uniform size and colour on the paper, the stem end facing down. Stems were clipped to avoid damaging other apples. A second layer was then placed on top of the first. Once the base layer was established, the next step was to gently pour in apples from baskets, 'the barrel being frequently jarred' to settle the apples and decrease space between them. When the barrel was almost full, a felt 'head' was placed on the load and the 'racking' (or rocking) process settled the fruit further. Racking also resulted in a level surface on which the final layers were arranged by hand, piled so that the fruit rose slightly above the top of the barrel. When the top was attached this protruding fruit was forced into the barrel, and the entire contents were thus placed under pressure. The amount by which the fruit should project above the barrel depended on the hardiness of the variety being packed and the packer's judgment. Too much pressure and the fruit would arrive bruised and wet. Too little, and it would not be adequately protected from jarring.[60] Though B.C. growers packed their apples in wired pinewood boxes that held a bushel (or about one-third the volume of a barrel), similar considerations applied to the packing process.[61] Apples were packed so that there was a slight bulge in the top and bottom of the box, which was made out of thinner wood. Thus, the fruit was held tight, although again, it was important to get the tension exactly right.

Shipping apples also required care and attention. Barrels and boxes had to be carried on their side in wagons equipped with springs, protected from rain and frost, and arranged carefully on ships. Early in the century, cold storage facilities, particularly for small shippers, were often not available or were inadequate. Butter compartments were sometimes used, although these were set at temperatures 10 degrees colder than was suitable for apples.[62] By the early 1930s, a network of refrigerator cars supplied by ice stations located eighteen hours apart ensured that apples travelling from Ontario or the Okanagan Valley arrived chilled at the docks in Montreal, Saint John, Halifax, and Vancouver. Heaters replaced ice in winter. By the 1930s, ships were also equipped with cold storage facilities, although this could increase shipping costs from 70 to 80 cents per box to well over 1 dollar.[63] Thus, Nova Scotia growers, close to their ports, still tended to ship without refrigeration.

Apples were sold in Britain primarily through public auction, where buyers could evaluate the quality of the fruit. Manchester and Liverpool featured salesrooms where fruit brokers gathered around a pit in which elevators raised sample barrels from the docks. Barrels were opened and the contents tumbled out into large baskets before the eyes of buyers.[64]

The IEC and then the EMB set out to reform this system. As had been recommended at the 1923 Imperial Conference, they tackled it by using science and from the perspective of the Empire as a whole, considering 'all the conditions from the orchard to the consumer.'[65] One of the first acts of the IEC was to commission a report on the Empire fruit industry. The report recommended that Empire fruit producers establish an organization and that producers have representatives in the United Kingdom overseeing what happened to their product. It also called for more scientific research. Finally, it recommended that the soon-to-be founded Empire Marketing Board establish a Fruit Intelligence Service in order to provide information for producers and for the publicity campaign that was to be one of the EMB's major tasks.[66] When the EMB was created, one of its first acts was to appoint a small committee to investigate problems of damage to fruit shipments in transit. The board also turned itself into a granting agency for scientific research. The first beneficiary was the Imperial College of Tropical Agriculture in Trinidad, which received between £20,000 and £30,000 to study the growing of cotton in the Empire. But the EMB sunk more funds into research on low temperature storage than into any other scientific activity. The existing Low Temperature Research Station at Cambridge University received a £38,500 capital grant, with an additional £8,000 per year for five years. The board also made a £55,000 capital grant, with £10,000 for one year and £6,000 for the next four years, for the building of a new research station at East Malling, Kent, for the study of cold storage methods with more directly commercial applications.[67]

These two efforts came together in a series of studies on factors leading to spoiling or 'wastage' in fruits shipped overseas. An initial set of comprehensive studies in 1926–27 examined fruit shipments from Canada, Australia, New Zealand, Palestine, the West Indies, Cyprus, and Zanzibar.[68] The report on Canada was carried out by a committee consisting of members of the EMB (including Canada's fruit commissioner in London, W.A. Wilson) and other people from industry and government bodies concerned with the fruit trade.[69] Problems needing laboratory analysis were referred to the Cambridge Low Temperature station. Conclusions demonstrated the difficulties in following apples from orchard to table. It proved very difficult, for example, to study conditions in ships in detail, as the temperature and ventilation could vary considerably depending on where in the hold the fruit sat. The condition of barrelled apples, which made up the majority of shipments from Canada, could not be investigated as barrels could not be opened and then resealed without spoiling the whole lot. Boxed apples from British Columbia were studied, instead, but the sample sizes were small, making conclusions suspect.

Consequently, the report concentrated on two factors that the investigators could hold constant: the variety of apple and the district in which they were grown. Results for districts were difficult to interpret, being plagued, again, by the complexity of the process. How to account for the fact that Jonathan apples from Salmon Arm, British Columbia, survived so much better than those of the same variety from Vernon? Was it something in the soil? The climate? (Salmon Arm is only about 60 km from Vernon but in a different valley.) The growing or storage conditions? The only really conclusive results related to variety. Yellow Newton, Winesap, and Stayman Winesap apples passed the tests with flying colours.

Perhaps this conclusion is unsurprising. We noted earlier how banana and lettuce production came to centre on one variety, selected because it grew and shipped well. That modern food systems reduce variety is a common criticism. Certainly, the Canadian apple industry has consolidated its offerings since the interwar period. In 1930, Nova Scotia growers sold more than eleven principle varieties on the British market, many of which were also grown in Ontario, while the business of British Columbia growers centred on nine varieties, all of them different from those grown in the east.[70] These were just the most important varieties. The actual number grown and shipped could be much larger. In 1924, South Australia shipped fifty-six varieties to Britain, and New Zealand sold fifty.[71] It is the rare supermarket today that stocks anywhere near these numbers.

Yet this process of consolidation was likely not a simple one of selecting the variety best suited for shipping. The causes of deterioration in apples were too complex for the EMB to conclude that variety was the key factor. They did conclude that something about the fruit itself was the key. A study of barrelled apples from Nova Scotia, for instance, stated that 'the method of packing adopted has less influence than might have been anticipated' and that the 'condition of apples themselves' was much more important.[72] Another study focused on Jonathan apples from British Columbia susceptible to a disease known only as 'internal breakdown,' in which older apples became mealy and brown. This study observed that larger apples were more susceptible to damage than smaller ones, that shipments from certain packing houses fared consistently worse than others, and that shipments early in the season did better than later ones. What to make of these findings was less obvious. The only solid advice that emerged was to pick and market the apples as early as possible since the disease was serious only after the apples reached a certain point of maturity, and took about a month to develop after picking. Yet, Canadian growers customarily stored some apples in Canada for shipping later in order to provide a continuous supply to Britain. More seriously, growers had to be careful not to pick the fruit before it was ripe. Experiments at the research station in Summerland, British Columbia, found that pressure tests, the colour of the seed, and the ease with which the fruit separated from the tree were not reliable ways to tell if this particular variety was ripe enough to pick. The taking on of a particular yellowish cast to the skin was a good indicator, and so the Summerland station produced a colour chart showing the proper shade and two other shades for comparison.[73]

These studies suggest the ways in which the application of science to a global food system could lead to the eventual narrowing of varieties produced and sold. Variety, for one thing, was a factor that could be effectively controlled by a government body that could not oversee every field, the technique of every packer, and the condition of every ship's hold. Further, when we think of the Jonathan apple colour chart, produced at the site of production for use specifically with one variety, we can see that narrowing production to a smaller number of varieties would have the virtue of lessening somewhat the enormous complexity of the task the EMB had set itself. Since science could not produce universal knowledge that could be applied to all local conditions, it must have made sense to simplify local conditions.[74] The market played a role as well. Only certain types of apples were popular in Britain, and marketing the enormous number of varieties that descended on the country was a challenge. The IEC recommended that countries focus on ten or fifteen staple varieties.[75]

Uniting the imperial food system from orchard to plate also meant overcoming the information gap posed by distance, through the establishment of the Fruit Intelligence Service recommended by the IEC. Information on Canadian fruit shipments came from telegrams sent regularly from the Canadian Ministry of Agriculture to the Empire Marketing Board's offices in London. Telegrams listed the name of the port, the ships destined for it, and the amounts of Canadian products each carried.[76] Fruit reports also included agro-ecological knowledge such as weather, types of crops planted, and size of the final harvest, which could be crucial in gauging likely prices. The reports, according to the Canadian Horticultural Council in 1932, meant that 'crop production programmes could be more intelligently arranged, plans for orderly marketing could be set up, gluts with consequent dumping of supplies at ruinous prices prevented while new markets could be searched for and their requirements studied.'[77] The initial report, issued in February, included a prediction as to the size of that year's exports, including the critical U.S. market. Lists of sailings were included as well.[78] Notes were received by governments across Canada, at least as of 1939, when a list of recipients was forwarded to the Department of Agriculture in Ottawa and, judging by the comments of the Horticultural Council, accessed by producers and marketers of fruits across the country.[79] In this way, the EMB created a global/imperial information field to replace what could be gained by local knowledge, agricultural papers, or national or provincial Departments of Agriculture.

Thus, we can see in the Empire Marketing Board's attempts to work out the contradictions between markets and apples the move towards integration and agro-ecological simplification, towards the stress on 'distance and durability,' that would characterize the global food system after the Second World War.[80] The imperial/global system that the EMB's supporters envisioned, however, would not come to pass. Criticisms of the costs of the board mounted as the world slipped into the Great Depression after 1929. The killing blow came in Ottawa, at the Imperial Economic Conference of 1932. The governments of the Empire set up a system of preferential tariffs as a desperate attempt to revive global trade. Since the EMB initially had been set up as a way for the British government to avoid implementing such measures, these tariffs made the board vulnerable. When the Dominions refused to contribute to its costs, another vulnerability of the board became clear. In the Depression, gestures towards imperial preference aside, internationalism and free trade were increasingly out of fashion. Countries took care of their own. The Empire was not quite the global family of EMB advertisements. Stuck with the whole costs of an increasingly anachronistic body, the British government decided to abolish the Empire Marketing Board.[81]

Conclusion

The Empire Marketing Board attempted to deal with the interwar problems of the global economy by reshaping trade around the Empire. Since it was banned from using the most direct and obvious tool for influencing trade – tariffs – it ended up conceiving of a market in its widest possible sense, as one encompassing not just economic, but also cultural exchange. A global market in food was to be built on imperial sentiment as much as on price; and on knowledge, information, and packing, storage and grading techniques as much as on supply and demand. In evaluating the board, we must focus on this wider work and this wider idea of what made up a global market. If we do this, we can see that the board attained a fair measure of success. Despite the disappearance of the propaganda campaign, most of what the EMB built survived. Many of the scientific projects it created continued under the Colonial Development fund, and its market research and intelligence activities were given to the Imperial Economic Committee. This, too, is critical: the IEC was *not* abolished, although its name was changed to the Commonwealth Economic Committee after the Second World War. This is a point that historians of the EMB have missed.

Ultimately, only the propaganda activities of the EMB were gone.[82] In attempting to assess their effectiveness, Stephen Constantine looks at changes in the buying habits of Britons and the increases in Empire imports. More broadly, though, we might argue that EMB propaganda played a role in legitimizing the market tools that survived the campaign's demise. Even as the EMB reminded everyone that the Empire was a single family and a single economy, it set up research exchanges and marketing schemes that worked to make these claims into reality. The IEC continued to investigate the trade in commodities between Empire countries, while broadening its scope by the late 1930s into 'World Surveys' of trade in cattle, beef, and other commodities. Annual reports were issued for a select group of commodities, including grains and fruit. The committee published five intelligence notes at both weekly and monthly intervals. In addition to those on fruit, dairy, and wheat established during the era of the EMB, newer notes covered canned and dried fruits, tomatoes, and wool.[83] In these intelligence notes 'certain classes of information are compiled and presented in a manner not to be secured elsewhere,' foreign information being made available in a more timely way than otherwise possible. The various branches of the Canadian Department of Agriculture all found the reports valuable.[84] The Department of Agriculture agreed again in 1951 that IEC publications provided information not available elsewhere. Other international agricultural bodies published reports, but where these summarized national legislation, the IEC concentrated on the movements of markets. Where these bodies operated on a national level, the IEC occupied a global space.

By 1951, the Empire was rapidly receding into history. Yet, the attempt of the EMB and the IEC to reshape Britain's food imports around the Empire had foreshadowed the deeper global integration of food chains that would characterize the postwar food system. These included its research schemes, marketing information programs, and the acceptance of the idea that there had been a revolution in food and that this revolution was a good thing. The global food system did not arise naturally. It was built, out of the culture of imperialism, and via the actions of the British and Dominion governments. The Empire Marketing Board and the Imperial Economic Committee, taken together, have to be seen as a part of the building of the interwar global/colonial food system that provided one of the bases for the global food system after the Second World War. John Bull and Sons lives.

ACKNOWLEDGMENT

I offer thanks for research assistance by Jennifer Evans, Dustin Wall, Nicole Cybulskie, and Emily Weiskopf-Ball. Anne Clendinning first put me on to the Empire Marketing Board. Funding was provided by Nipissing University and the Social Sciences and Humanities Research Council of Canada.

NOTES

1 Harold S. Williamson and Empire Marketing Board [EMB], *untitled [shoppers at John Bull and Sons (1928) Ltd]*, photomechanical print on wove paper, 1928, 1983-27-99, Library and Archives Canada (LAC) and Harold S. Williamson and Empire Marketing Board, *untitled [woman shopping at John Bull and Sons (1928) Ltd]*, colour lithograph on wove paper, 1928, 1983-27-101, LAC.

2 The sources I cite above do not actually specify that JB&S existed in London (nor do they employ the abbreviation JB&S) – I have invented these details.

3 By the 1920s, the British Empire had been divided, in common parlance and for administrative purposes, into two groups. The 'Dominions' were the largely self-governing former settler colonies, where descendants of Europeans were in the majority – Canada, Australia, New Zealand, South Africa, and Newfoundland. The rest of the Empire was referred to as the 'Colonial Empire.' The Irish Free State, India, and, occasionally, Southern Rhodesia, for different reasons, occupied somewhat ambiguous positions between the two categories.

4 Joan Thirsk, *Alternative Agriculture: A History from the Black Death to the Present Day* (Oxford: Oxford University Press, 1997), 2.

5 Quotes from Trevor J. Barnes, Roger Hayter, and Elizabeth Hay, 'Stormy Weather: Cyclones, Harold Innis, and Port Alberni, BC,' *Environment and Planning A* 33 (2001): 21–33; Karl Polanyi, *The Great Transformation* (Toronto: Farrar and Rinehart, 1944); Harold Innis, *The Fur Trade in Canada: An Introduction to Canadian Economic History* (Toronto: University of Toronto Press, 1999 [1930]).

6 John Soluri, *Banana Cultures: Agriculture, Consumption, and Environmental Change in Honduras and the United States* (Austin, TX: University of Texas Press, 2005), 217.

7 Gabriella M. Petrick, '"Like Ribbons of Green and Gold": Industrializing Lettuce and the Quest for Quality in the Salinas Valley, 1920–1965,' *Agricultural History* 80/3 (2006): 269–95.

8 Soluri, *Banana Cultures*, 57, 161–92.

9 Jeffrey A. Frieden, *Global Capitalism: Its Fall and Rise in the Twentieth Century* (New York: W.W. Norton, 2006), passim, but see xvi–xvii. The banana example is from Soluri, *Banana Cultures*, esp. 14 and 24.

10 Ted Steinberg, *Down to Earth: Nature's Role in American History* (New York: Oxford University Press, 2002), 178–9.

11 William Cronon, *Nature's Metropolis: Chicago and the Great West* (New York: W.W. Norton, 1991), chapters 3 and 5.

12 Harriet Friedmann, 'Circles of Growing and Eating: The Political Ecology of Food and Agriculture,' in Raymond Grew, ed., *Food in Global History* (Boulder, CO: Westview, 1999): 33–57. Also by Harriet Friedmann, see: 'Distance and Durabil-

ity: Shaky Foundations of the World Food Economy,' in Phillip McMichael, ed., *The Global Restructuring of Agro-food Systems* (Ithaca, NY: Cornell University Press, 1994): 258–76; 'The Political Economy of Food: The Rise and Fall of the Postwar International Food Order,' *American Journal of Sociology* 88 (Supplement: Marxist Inquiries: Studies of Labor, Class, and States) (1982): S248–S286; 'Remaking Traditions,' in Deborah Barndt, ed., *Women Working the NAFTA Food Chain: Women, Food and Globalization* (Toronto: Sumach Press, 1999), 36–60.

13 But see Harriet Friedmann, 'World Market, State, and Family Farm: Social Bases of Household Production in the Era of Wage Labour,' *Comparative Studies in Society and History* 20/4 (1978): 545–86.

14 This is true as well of Steven Stoll, *The Fruits of Natural Advantage: Making the Industrial Countryside in California* (Berkeley, CA: University of California Press, 1998), 273; Steinberg, *Down to Earth*, chapter 11; Kathryn Morse, *The Nature of Gold: An Environmental History of the Klondike Gold Rush* (Seattle, WA: University of Washington Press, 2003).

15 Although Friedmann's newer work moves in this direction. See her 'Remaking Traditions.'

16 On the EMB, see Stephen Constantine, *Buy and Build: The Advertising Posters of the Empire Marketing Board* (London: Her Majesty's Stationery Office (HMSO), 1986); Stephen Constantine, '"Bringing the Empire Alive": The Empire Marketing Board and Imperial Propaganda, 1926–33,' in John M. MacKenzie, ed., *Imperialism and Popular Culture* (London: Manchester University Press, 1985), 192–231; Mike Cronin, 'Selling Irish Bacon: The Empire Marketing Board and Artists of the Free State,' *Eire-Ireland* 39/3&4 (2004): 132–43; David Meredith, 'Imperial Images: The Empire Marketing Board, 1926–32,' *History Today* (1987): 30–6; Anandi Ramamurthy, *Imperial Persuaders: Images of Africa and Asia in British Advertising* (Manchester: Manchester University Press, 2003).

17 The quote is from Ian Macpherson, '"Creating Stability amid Degrees of Marginality": Divisions in the Struggle for Orderly Marketing in British Columbia, 1900–1940,' *Canadian Papers in Rural History* 7 (1990): 310.

18 Ibid., 311; Constantine, *Buy and Build*, 2. On wheat and the global food system, see Friedmann, 'World Market'; David B. Grigg, *Agricultural Systems of the World: An Evolutionary Approach* (New York: Cambridge University Press, 1974); R.C. Michie, 'The International Trade in Food and the City of London since 1850,' *Journal of European Economic History* 25/2 (1996): 369–404.

19 Constantine, '"Bringing the Empire Alive,' 192–3.

20 The EMB received requests from 23,000 British schools in 1928–29 for reproductions of their posters. The pro-Empire magazine *United Empire* reported that posters were being used across the Empire and particularly in Montreal, the result of the work of the Montreal Branch of the Royal Empire Society. EMB, *Empire*

Marketing Board, May 1928 to May 1929 (London: HMSO, 1929), 24; and Sir Stephen Tallents, 'Empire Marketing Board, 1926–33,' *United Empire* 24/8 (1933): 485.

21 Constantine, *Buy and Build*, 2–3; Meredith, 'Imperial Images,' 30–1.

22 Imperial Economic Committee (IEC), 'Report on the Functions and Work of the Imperial Economic Committee,' n.d., 7, LAC, RG 17, vol. 3310, file 4.

23 IEC, 'Note for the Imperial Economic Committee by Sir Thomas Allen on Marketing Organization,' 22 June 1925, LAC, RG 17, vol. 3309, file 848-1(1).

24 See the memo containing this speech from J. Reid Hyde, resident secretary, Imperial Conference 1923, to Dr Grisdale, 3 Oct. 1923, LAC, RG 17, vol. 3308, file 848-1(1). Quote at D1-D2.

25 W.L. Mackenzie King to L.C. McOuatt, 5 Feb. 1925, LAC, RG 17, vol. 3309, file 848-1(1).

26 O.D.S. [Skelton] to Mr King, 20 Mar. 1925, and J.H. Grisdale to Skelton, 10 Mar. 1925, LAC, RG 17, vol. 3309, file 848-1(1).

27 L.C. McOuatt, High Commissioner for Canada, to O.D. Skelton, 25 June 1925, LAC, RG 17, vol. 3309, file 848-1(1).

28 External [likely Skelton] to McOuatt, 20 July 1925 (telegram), LAC, RG 17, vol. 3309, file 848-1(1).

29 McOuatt to External (telegram), 29 July 1925; Secretary of State for Dominion Affairs to Governor General, 29 July 1925; Skelton to Grisdale, 30 July 1925; all in LAC, RG 17, vol. 3309, file 848-1(1).

30 Constantine, *Buy and Build*, 3.

31 Dominion to [obscured], 3 Mar. 1926, LAC, RG 17, vol. 3310.

32 The following is based on Constantine, *Buy and Build*, 5, and other sources as noted.

33 Constantine, *Buy and Build*, 5–6, 11.

34 W.A. Wilson, Agricultural Products Representative for Canada, to Grisdale, 16 June 1927, LAC, RG 17, vol. 3310, file 3.

35 EMB, *Empire Marketing Board, May 1932 to May 1933* (London: HMSO, 1933), 119.

36 See EMB, Publicity Committee, 'Daily Mail Ideal Home Exhibition 1927: Report from the Department of Overseas Trade on Participation by the Empire Marketing Board,' LAC, RG 17, vol. 3310; 'Canadian National Exhibition [CNE] Association, Toronto: Annual Report, 1928,' 'Official Souvenir Catalog & Program, Canadian National Exhibition, Toronto, 1928,' and selections from photograph collection – all at CNE Archives.

37 John Grierson, 'The E.M.B. Film Unit,' *Cinema Quarterly* 1/4 (1933): 205.

38 Meredith, 'Imperial,' 31–2; Constantine, *Buy and Build*, 16–17.

39 Charles Pears and EMB, *Every Time You Buy Empire Produce You Help the*

Empire to Buy the Goods You Make at Home, photomechanical print on wove paper, 1926–34, 1983-027 PIC 00237, LAC; 'Our Empire Garden' and 'Buy Canadian Apples' [newspaper ads], LAC, RG 17, vol. 3310, file 3.

40 EMB, 'The Empire Marketing Board,' 1927, LAC, RG 17, vol. 3310, file 3.

41 EMB, 'Winter Visitors' [ad], LAC, RG 17, vol. 3310, file 3. Wilson to Grisdale, 13 Jan. 1928, LAC, RG 17, vol. 3310, file 3, notes that this ad appeared in the *Times* and 'ten other papers of that class.'

42 Constantine, *Buy and Build*, 3.

43 Ramamurthy, *Imperial Persuaders*, 136.

44 See EMB, 'The Men Talk and Talk, But –' [ad], and G. Huxley, 'Empire Marketing Board. Press Advertisements' [memo], n.d., LAC, RG 17, vol. 3310, file 3.

45 EMB, 'From the Home Farms' [ad], ibid.

46 EMB, 'Buy Canadian Apples' [ad], ibid., and EMB, 'A Calendar of Empire Apples' [ad], ibid., file 848-1(5).

47 Although Canadian apple producers did have an advantage over other Empire producers in being relatively closer to the United Kingdom. Apples took only 8–10 days to make the trip from eastern Canadian ports, as opposed to a month from Australia, and cold storage was less important because many of the journeys took place in winter. See EMB, *Canadian Fruit Shipments: Report of an Investigation by the Economic Section of the Empire Marketing Board into the Deterioration in Transit of Imported Canadian Fruit, 1927–29* (London: HMSO, 1930), 10.

48 Friedmann, 'Circles of Growing and Eating.'

49 EMB, 'The Empire Marketing Board,' 1927, 3.

50 IEC, *Apples and Pears* (London: HMSO, 1938), 36; 'Imperial Economic Conference. Canadian Horticultural Council Memorandum Re Preference on Fresh Apples,' n.d. [1932 from context], 1–2, LAC, RG 17, vol. 3308, file 846-6-2 (hereafter 'Horticultural Council Memo'); George Elmore Reaman, *History of Agriculture in Ontario* (Toronto: Saunders, 1970), 147.

51 'Horticultural Council Memo,' 3; Secretary of State for Dominion Affairs to the Governor General, 3 April 1926, LAC, RG 17, vol. 3310, file 848-1.

52 'Appendix III. Imperial Co-operation in Food Preservation Research: The Application of Science and Research to the Problems of Overseas Transport of Fruit and Vegetables,' in *Imperial Economic Conference. Co-ordination of Research in the Empire. Memorandum by the Department of Scientific and Industrial Research*, IEC (23)-16, 1923, p. 14, LAC, RG 17, vol. 3308, file 848(1).

53 IEC, 'Marketing and Preparing for Market of Foodstuffs,' [draft copy (4th)], 24 July 1925, 352, LAC, RG 17, vol. 3309, file 848(1)-1.

54 'Imperial Economic Conference, 1923. Summary of Conclusions,' n.d. [forwarded to Canadian Delegation on 13 Nov. 1923], LAC, RG 17, vol. 3308, file 848(1), and

L.F. Burrow, Secretary-Treasurer, Canadian Horticultural Council, to Grisdale, 12 April 1926, LAC, RG 17, vol. 3310.

55 Soluri, *Banana*, 230–2.

56 Canada, Department of Agriculture, Branch of the Commissioner of Agricure and Dairying, Fruit Division, and W.A. MacKinnon, *Export Apple Trade* (Ottawa: Department of Agriculture, 1903), ·12.

57 'The Fruit Marks Act, 1901 (1 Edward VII, Chap. 27), as amended in 1902 (2 Edward VII, Chap. 10),' reproduced in whole in the appendix of Canada, *Export Apple Trade*, 17–19; citation at 17.

58 EMB, *Canadian Fruit Shipments*, 8–9; 'Horticultural Council Memo.'

59 Canada, *Export Apple Trade*, 7–8.

60 Ibid., 13.

61 1 imperial bushel = 8 imperial gallons or roughly 36 L.

62 Canada, *Export Apple Trade*, 15–16.

63 'Horticultural Council Memo.'

64 Canada, Department of Agriculture, Branch of the Commissioner of Agriculture and Dairying, Extension of Markets Branch, *Notes on the Export Apple Trade* (Ottawa: Government Printing Bureau, 1904).

65 'Appendix III. Imperial Co-operation,' 15.

66 Secretary of State for Dominion Affairs to the Governor General, 3 April 1926, summarizes the conclusions of the report.

67 EMB, 'The Work of the Empire Marketing Board, Report No. 1,' July 1926, 4–6, LAC, RG 17, vol. 3310, and EMB, *Note on the Work and Finance of the Board … from July, 1926, to March 31st, 1929* (London: HMSO, 1929), 17.

68 EMB, *Note on the Work and Finance*, 11.

69 EMB, 'Report on the Fruit Investigation during the Canadian Season, 1926–27. Special Report No. 1,' Sept. 1927, LAC, RG 17, vol. 3310, file 4. The following discussion is from this source.

70 EMB, *Canadian Fruit Shipments*, 7.

71 IEC, *Report on Methods of Marketing and Preparing for Market within the United Kingdom of Food Products of the Overseas Parts of the Empire* (London: HMSO, 1926), 92.

72 EMB, *Report on Experimental Shipments of Nova Scotian Barrelled Apples* (London: HMSO, 1928), 20.

73 EMB, *Canadian Fruit Shipments*, 22–36.

74 James Scott argues that modern states tend to produce a simplified reality in order to make management easier – see *Seeing Like a State: How Certain Schemes to Improve the Human Condition Have Failed* (New Haven, CT: Yale University Press, 1998).

75 IEC, *Methods of Marketing*, 92.

76 A large collection of telegrams is contained in LAC, RG 17, vol. 3315, file 848-1-1(1), and other files in this volume.

77 'Horticultural Council Memo,' 18–19, quote at 19.

78 See examples of Weekly Fruit Intelligence Notes from 1927 included in LAC, RG 17, vol. 3310, file 848-1.

79 The list is attached to High Commissioner to Secretary of State for External Affairs, 12 Jan. 1939, LAC, RG 17, vol. 3314, file 848-1(15).

80 Friedmann, 'Distance and Durability.'

81 Constantine, 'Bringing the Empire Alive,' 219–20.

82 Given that EMB posters were used in schools, it may be that the propaganda campaign continued in this form. No one to my knowledge has considered how long such materials continued to be used to educate children in Britain and the Dominions.

83 'Publications of the Imperial Economic Committee,' 1937, LAC, RG 17, vol. 3313, file 848-1(14).

84 See correspondence in LAC, RG 17, vol. 3313, file 848-1(14).

14 Spreading Controversy: The Story of Margarine in Quebec

NATHALIE COOKE

If spices were pivotal to the earliest centuries of Western civilization, then another food substance has proved to be the focus of culinary (or perhaps, more accurately, chemical) creativity, contrivance, and competition during the past two centuries. Despite a charged history that involves inflated rhetoric reminiscent of liquor prohibition debates, some version of this product is likely to be found in many of our home refrigerators at this very moment, whether those fridges are in Canada, the United States, Europe, or Australia.

Margarine, invented in 1869 in response to a challenge issued at the Paris World Exhibition of 1866, addressed the problem of rising costs of animal fats during rapid urbanization. By 1886, however, there were laws prohibiting its production and sale in seven U.S. states, followed soon after by taxation (in Russia and the United States) and various regulations concerning its identification (in Sweden, Holland, England, and Norway), coloration (Russia, Denmark, France, New Zealand, Australia, and South Africa, and thirty U.S. states), and storage (Russia, Denmark, Germany, and Holland).[1] In Canada, restrictions were tougher still. With the exception of a temporary reprieve (1917–1922), margarine was banned entirely between 1886 and 1949.[2] Quebec banned coloured additives through June 2008;[3] and Ontario has allowed coloration only since 1995.[4] In Quebec, debates continue to rage about the future of margarine and its appropriate classification.

In ways similar to other studies of specific food items, such as sugar,[5] my chapter explores the broader social, cultural, and political ramifications emerging from the production, marketing, and distribution of a single food item in Canada: margarine. By looking to a product history that extends from the late nineteenth century (when margarine entered European markets) to the 1960s, and by drawing on a variety of sources, from professional periodicals and scholarly tracts to corporate advertising campaigns and popular newspapers and radio broadcasts, this essay places the post-1945 debates in Quebec and Canada more generally within the wider context of international debates provoked by the invention of this edible product. It further highlights the significant degree to which the debates were generated, even fuelled, by narrative scenarios that cast the principal characters in dramatically different ways, and it points to the role played by gender performance in corporate branding efforts to improve the image of margarine.

A source of heated controversy, margarine here serves as a lens through which to address the theme of mindful eating – a theme also addressed in this volume by Catherine Carstairs and Valerie Korinek in their respective chapters on the postwar health movement and vegetarianism and sexual politics – as well as more specific issues such as the fine balance between the interests of food producers and consumers, the shaping of consumer taste, and the impact of distinctive national and provincial food policies on agricultural, corporate, and consumer behaviour. A consideration of the remarkable flexibility of a processed food product also affords a glimpse into changing notions of nutrition and health over the long twentieth century, a theme that receives close attention in Ian Mosby's chapter on nutritional knowledge and its impact on social policy and in Caroline Durand's on the ideological content of Quebec domestic science manuals.

Background

Different versions of the story of margarine exist, distinguished largely by the disciplinary approach of the storytellers themselves. While there seems to be general consensus around the central facts,[6] conclusions differ dramatically. Despite variations between national margarine policies, there are some broad trends that cut across national and continental divides. First, the emergence of the new product was followed quickly by the adoption of legislative measures, around 1885, to restrict its production or distribution. Second, a depression struck the dairy industry despite restrictive measures and subsequent lobbying from that sector. Third, resulting protective policy measures were introduced ostensibly to protect consumers 'by ensuring purity and good quality' of margarine. Fourth, it was acknowledged that policy measures, however strict, cannot be reliably enforced. Finally, there was an eventual relaxation of restrictions, as early as 1925 in Denmark and most commonly in the mid-twentieth century elsewhere.[7]

There are also some notable exceptions. New Zealand is one, since the strong dairy industry largely banned the production and importation of margarine altogether.[8] Norway is another, since margarine production has been consistently promoted since the Second World War, presumably because of the abundant supply of marine oil for its production.[9] Canada is another exception; and, since the 1990s, scholars have begun to trace lines of difference between Canada and its neighbour to the south, as well as distinctions between provincial policies.[10] Notably, when margarine's centennial in 1969 was marked by the publication by University of Toronto Press of a major study of the product's history, featuring economic, social, and scientific perspectives, there was virtually no examination of the Canadian scene. In a book of 342 pages published by a Canadian press, only four references are made to the Canadian case. Recent years, however, have seen interesting analyses by W.H. Heick (1991), Ruth Dupré (1999), and Charlene Elliott (2009).[11] The present study aims to complement and extend these discussions of the Canadian case.

Rather than participate in the margarine debate, this chapter further aims to identify the ways in which the debate is generated, even fuelled, by narrative scenarios that cast principal characters in dramatically different ways. While Dupré and Heick comment on the debate and the narrative scenarios emerging from it, they also participate in the construction of narrative scenarios. They do, however, carefully and quite rightly resist becoming directly involved with the characterization of either butter or margarine as 'good' or 'bad,' as narrative protagonist or antagonist. Stakeholders do not share such hesitation; and the relative characterization of butter and margarine is cause for fierce, heated, and creative debate. Dairyman Erle Kitchen, in an interview aired on CBC radio on 14 December 1948, the day on which the ban on margarine production was lifted in Canada, spoke of dramatic and far-reaching consequences. If Canadian consumers were to buy and eat less butter, he argued, farmers would raise fewer cows, which would lead to the production of less manure and natural fertilizer, the depletion of the soil, and the farmers' inability to produce feed for other livestock including pigs and poultry.[12] In addition to the protectionist argument, butter advocates cast aspersions on margarine itself, an argument that was particularly strong in the early days when it was known as 'oleomargarine' because of its primary ingredient, beef fat.

On the other side of the debate, margarine advocates felt threatened by the positive expressive connotations of butter. They were right in thinking that restrictions on coloration did affect margarine sales[13] and that butter's readily comprehensible composition was more appealing than a processed food product that elicited much confusion.[14] Until mid-century, margarine suffered from its connotation as a poor man's substitute for butter. A friend of mine recently noted that her husband, who grew up in Winnipeg, 'remembers some pretty terrible margarine being all that his poor family could afford.'[15] Advertising campaigns for butter and margarine took direct aim at such connotative assumptions. From my own childhood, I can quite clearly remember television advertisements for Imperial margarine, where the slogan 'fit for a king' was accompanied by the almost miraculous appearance of a crown on the head of the one astute enough to spread the right spread. In other words, the debate hinged on conflicting narratives that diverged according to the way in which the primary characters – butter and margarine – were depicted.[16]

Story Elements

Scholars and commentators seem to agree that the story of margarine in Canada involves four plot elements that correspond to chronological markers related to the economic and political landscape. The story opens in 1869 with the invention of margarine and its appearance on the Canadian scene. Legislated regulations begin soon after, in 1886, and only ease during the First World War in response to butter shortages. Between the two wars, legislative restrictions resume, only to be repealed at the federal level on 14 December 1948, when the production of margarine is permitted in Canada. However, restrictions fall under provincial jurisdiction and, more specifically, restrictions on coloration continue after this point – until 1995 in Ontario and through 2008 in Quebec. In narrative terms, the story reaches its climax just after the Second World War, and the denouement involves the gradual easing of restrictions subsequent to 1948.

Not only is there consensus surrounding the plot, but commentators also seem to agree on the cast of principal characters: in addition to the farmer, the consumer, the policy maker, and the marketer, butter and margarine feature as characters in their own right. As a result, the corporate producer is curiously absent from centre stage, receiving relatively infrequent mention and often reduced to the role of puppeteer and makeup artist who controls the movements and appearance of the principal player on stage: margarine.[17]

By contrast, the farmer consistently plays a leading role in the narrative action, his fate inextricably linked to both the production of butter *and* of margarine. (Margarine was first produced from beef fat, and can be produced from a variety of oil products, including soy and marine.) Further, the farmer is the most rounded of the central characters. As one whose livelihood is vulnerable to social, political, economic, and environmental forces, he frequently plays the role of the sympathetic protagonist, challenged by the antagonist margarine. For economist Patrick Allen in 1955, for example, the Quebec farmer is the most important character, and one particularly vulnerable to a province whose geography makes the transport of dairy produce expensive and inefficient, battling against a product that is manufactured from largely imported raw materials. 'Ce ne sont ni les consommateurs, ni les distributeurs, ni les fabricants de margarine qui sont les premiers et les plus fortement touchés par la présence ou l'absence de la margarine sur un marché comme celui de Québec, mais bien l'agriculteur. Pour le moment il semble bien que ce soit là les elements du problème qui l'emportent sur tous les autres.'[18]

Forty years later, economist Ruth Dupré emphasizes the farmer's sympathetic appeal. In her account, the public perceived the Canadian farmer as beset not only by big business, but also by *foreign-owned* big business.[19] In this way, both Allen and Dupré depict a protectionist sentiment, one noted explicitly by Heick's title – *Propensity to Protect*. Dupré's protectionist arguments are admirably nuanced, and based on economic evidence rather than sentimentality. In her 1990 article, she points to the industry's recognition of the need for self-regulation. Such a move to self-regulation during the early twentieth century was prompted by a number of factors: to regulate quality in the 1900s, price by the 1930s, and quantity by the 1950s.[20] At first glance, this would suggest Dupré's recasting of the farmer into the role of a proactive protagonist, characterized by vehemence rather than vulnerability. But, a key insight involves the composition of the SIL, or Societé d'Industrie Laitière. As she points out, the association's name, which translates to the 'Quebec Dairymen's Association,' is misleading since its members came from different sectors, and included 'dairy farmers and butter and cheese makers' as well as 'agronomists, officials from the Department of Agriculture, politicians such as the Minister of Agriculture, and members of the federal and provincial parliaments from rural ridings, Montreal butter and cheese dealers, members of the clergy and of the liberal professions – doctors, lawyers, and notaries.'[21] Not surprisingly, such an organization endorsed the move to 'compulsory inspection, licensing, and grading in order to get rid of the poor-quality producers' in the early years of the twentieth century in Quebec.[22] The result was the industry's ability to dispel negative perceptions of Quebec cheese, dubbed derogatively as 'Joseph' (the first name given to Catholic males at christening) by its detractors on the other side of the Atlantic.[23]

Not all commentators cast the farmer in a sympathetic light, however. Indeed, the farmer frequently appears as a savvy and effective lobbyist, victorious in the epic battle against the foreign invader margarine, to the detriment of a vulnerable consumer. This recasting of characters, which places the farmer in the role of antagonist and the consumer in the role of protagonist, is the predominant storyline of social historical analysis, which focuses on the expressive and connotative implications of butter and margarine. Speaking of margarine, in phrases evoking a story character rather than an edible oil product, Ball and Lilly lament: 'It was the misfortune of margarine to become entangled in the structural transition from one social order to another, and in the expressive redefinitions accompanying this shift, and to find itself confronted with an opponent with special clout.'[24] That opponent, of course, was butter.

A social and cultural historian, Heick places a similar emphasis on the misfortune of margarine and, by extension, on the consumer in Canada who is denied access to an inexpensive and inoffensive food product. For him, 'the history of margarine is a prime example of applied technology meeting the changing needs and desires of the consumer. Margarine was invented as a cheap substitute for butter so that the poorer elements of society could have some spread on their bread.'[25] Heick's analysis hones in on the protectionist impulse, but he privileges and advocates for the protection of the consumer over the protection of the dairy farmer. And he clearly celebrates Canadian consumers who 'use the state to achieve their goals.'[26] It is a victory shared by margarine itself, which, through Heick's use of the active voice, seems to be an agent of its own transformation: 'The standards of excellence have been those of butter in flavour, consistency, appearance and utility. Margarine has met and even, in the area of cholesterol, surpassed these standards.'[27]

The accounts of Dupré and Heick differ in significant ways, as Dupré herself notes before providing a succinct and firm rebuttal. 'Heick wants to show that the evolution toward a more liberal margarine policy corresponded to the shift from a rural to an urban culture. Unfortunately, the two largest and most urbanized provinces, Quebec and Ontario, do not fit this thesis.'[28] Dupré's rebuttal is based on the long delays in easing regulations on coloration in Ontario and Quebec, as well as Quebec's hesitation to lift the ban on production.[29] Heick, presumably, would counter by describing Quebec and Ontario as two provinces with significant dairy production and a strong dairy lobby.

What, then, can the story of margarine tell us? For scientists, it is a story of triumph, the success of inventor Hippolyte Mege-Mouriez to respond to a challenge issued to the scientific community in a timely and remarkably effective manner. For consumer analysts, it is an invaluable example of the efficacy of nutritional labelling and efficient transmission of health information.[30] For social historians, it is evidence of the remarkable flexibility of a processed food product and the adaptability of the consumer who welcomes it, and a lens through which key moments of social change can be identified.[31] For economists, margarine's threat to butter offers an opportunity for comparative case study analysis.[32]

If, however, we step back to examine the secondary literature surrounding the margarine controversy rather than the controversy itself, what emerges? Together, these stories provide a wealth of evidence to illustrate the expressive potential of food items (such as butter and margarine) and the shifting definitions of 'health' over time (as advocates endorsed one, then the other, and most recently, neither).[33] Similarly, Catherine Gidney's discussion (in this volume) of how university students protested the lack of milk in their residence meals in 1948 by bringing a cow into the dining hall, and Julie Guard's discussion (in this volume) of how assumptions about the essential goodness of milk helped to mobilize Depression-era housewives to protest against price hikes, underscore the expressive connotations of milk. Most obviously, margarine stories speak to the circumscribed and scripted nature of consumer selections, exposing along the way some forces involved in the shaping of consumer taste and Quebec's determination to forge a path of distinction.

The story of margarine in Canada, as told in the voices of various stakeholders in the raging debates, reveals a striking ambivalence to novelty – a simultaneous attraction and resistance to the novel and the new – on the part of Canadians and their policy makers. This ambivalence is noticed by Charlene Elliott who, in her article on 'Canada's Great Butter Caper,' suggests that Canada's reaction to margarine can be understood within a larger discussion of society's discomfort with impurity – a concern most famously signalled by anthropologist Mary Douglas in 1996. Elliott tells the story of margarine as a biography, invoking Arjun Appadurai's assertion that material objects can have a 'life' of their own to justify her personification of margarine in a way that is entirely appropriate in that it parallels the anthropomorphic transformations of butter and its substitutes by their promoters and commentators.[34] How, she asks, can we ignore margarine's biographical potential, its challenge to be recognized as something 'different,' something that presented not only a textbook example for the economics classroom, but 'a new sociocultural and legal challenge'?[35] Her answer, quite simply, is that we can't. Margarine clearly posed a threat to societies that, to differing degrees, resisted its advances. Elliott looks to Douglas' model of societal resistance to explain both what prompted that resistance ('the concern for purity') and the form of that resistance (Douglas' three stages of 'dealing with pollution or anomaly': naming, regulating, renaming or reclassifying).[36] The result is a remarkably neat parallel between Douglas' three stages and what Elliott identifies as the three plot developments in the story of margarine in Canada: identification of margarine as unhealthy, legislated prohibition, and the subsequent legislated colour prohibitions.

The False Dichotomy of Farm and Industry

A number of false dichotomies emerge from the margarine controversy. The first is related to an assumption that the farmer's world is far removed from that of science or industry.[37] Dupré and others do point out that the farmer is directly implicated in the production of both butter and margarine, rather than simply the former – but at the supply rather than management end of things. However, we do farmers a disservice to assume that their world was far removed from the technical advances of the twentieth century – a pastoral and timeless world distant from timely innovations. It was quite the opposite. Indeed, while margarine was being developed during the last decade of the nineteenth century, so too, were farmers being urged to bring sophisticated knowledge to the care of the soil. In an 1898 report, the Minister of Education illustrates the paradoxical assumptions at play as he distinguishes between the moral virtues of the farmer who is both 'industrious' and 'frugal' and the unstated but clearly less positive characteristics of those who have abandoned the land and let it go to waste in their flight to urban centres. 'Could we add [to] the rural population of the country but a tithe of the population now seeking employment in our towns and cities,' he asserted, 'we would add greatly to the wealth of the country, and at no time did agriculture need more scientific attention, in view of the competition and the low price of farm produce than it does at the present day.'[38] Ironically, the minister urges farmers not only to tend the land, but also to take advantage of scientific advances and train themselves in order to tend the land in efficient ways; but training was to be had at institutions located in towns and cities and involved transforming farm boys into skilled and highly educated agricultural scientists.[39]

'When does Guelph start its short "butter" course – that is, take the smart kid off the farm and train him?' asks Gwendolyn Owens, granddaughter of dairyman Ross J. Quirie.[40] Evidence suggests this process begins at the turn of the twentieth century. A postcard from 1913 reads: 'The Ontario Minister of Education aims to have agriculture taught in our schools.'[41] Such an initiative leads directly to the institutionalizing of agricultural education. The career path of dairyman Quirie sheds light on such educational initiatives and some of their implications. Born outside London, Ontario, Quirie earned a certificate in 'butter' and an undergraduate degree from the University of Guelph, after which he worked in Creemore, Ontario. He earned his Master of Science degree from Iowa State University (Ames, Iowa) in 1924, and subsequently worked in Flint (Michigan), Kitchener and London (Ontario), Boston, and New York City.

In addition to illustrating the transformation of farm boy into university graduate and highly trained agricultural specialist, Quirie's story illustrates two further points. First, his career trajectory suggests that despite differing dairy regulations between countries and provinces, the border between Canada and the United States was a relatively permeable one during the early decades of the twentieth century for dairymen themselves.[42] The same seems to have been true for liquid milk. Consider the Heward family cow: she lived in the backyard of 3467 Peel Street in Montreal in the 1880s while her milk supplied Delmonico's restaurant in New York City, it being shipped by Efa Heward via Ogdenberg, New York.[43] The distinctions between rural and urban life were not always so rigid, nor were the protective barriers between Canada and the United States.

Second, Quirie's role as president of the Ontario Dairyman's Association, in 1921–22, and his Master's thesis on dairy pricing strategies, underscores the close relationship of the dairy farmer with business. 'The farmer versus the businessman is a false dichotomy,' mused Owens in a discussion with me. 'Dairymen's associations were on the agri-business side. They were promoting pasteurized milk [in the late 1920s]. So they were big business.'[44]

The effectiveness of the dairy lobby provides further evidence of the need to examine the farmer's role more closely. Very recently, the dairy association of Quebec successfully defended its protectionist position despite a court challenge from Unilever Canada that lasted nine years and went to the Supreme Court of Canada. The challenge begins in 1997 when 'Unilever, which has about 60 per cent of the Canadian margarine market, deliberately provoked the province into a court fight in 1997 by shipping 480 containers of pale yellow margarine from the U.S. into Quebec.'[45] The Quebec Federation of Milk Producers was quick to react because stakes were very high. The cost, according to a spokesperson for the association, Jean Vigneault, would be in the order of '3,000 jobs in Quebec and maybe 100 million dollars of sales per year.'[46] Canadian grocers favoured abolishing the coloration laws. 'Well I don't know about the citizens of Quebec, but I would venture to guess,' writes George Condon in the *Canadian Grocer* of 1999, 'that they are every bit as smart as the citizens of every other province. And they *can* tell the difference between butter and margarine. Migawd, even if you can't read "butter" or "margarine" on the package, surely you can tell the difference between a brick of butter and a tub of margarine!'[47] While initial court rulings in favour of regulation seemed to quell the industry challenge, the fight resumed in 2002.[48] By 2004, Unilever's case was before the Supreme Court and summarized by the media as forcing a ruling on whether 'Quebec laws that prohibit margarine from being the same colour as butter violate freedom of expression.'[49] By 2005, though, the challenge was quashed. The Supreme Court upheld the ruling of the Quebec Superior Court in 1999 and the Quebec Court of Appeal in 2003 'that validated the Quebec regulation which prevents the sale of margarine in the same colour as butter.'[50]

Industry leader Unilever, in other words, continued to be outmanoeuvred by the Quebec dairy lobby until very recently, the latter having managed to wage a very effective media campaign and lobby program.[51] One cannot help but sense the influence of the dairy lobby behind the inflated rhetoric of Parti Québécois agriculture critic Maxime Arseneau who, in 2005, 'tabled a Becel margarine tub in the Quebec national assembly, charging that Unilever Canada Inc. and Wal-Mart Stores Inc. Canada were conspiring to bring yellow margarine into Quebec.'[52] Behind such a claim is the implication of a related binary motivated by a protectionist impulse: *local* farmers and *foreign* business interests.[53]

By the summer of 2008, the story's outcome seemed to favour margarine interests: the Quebec cabinet adopted a decree to repeal the provincial law banning coloured margarine on 25 June 2008,[54] and coloured margarine went on sale in the province on 20 August 2008.[55] However, characterizing the distinction between butter and margarine as one of victor and vanquished is another false dichotomy. Both sides of the battle had their supporters, and both were formidable competitors. Margarine, of course, had economics on its side. It was cheap to produce and endlessly versatile in its sourcing so could be adapted to take advantage of pricing fluctuations and availability of raw material. With the regulation of colouring, however, producers were forced to convince consumers either to eat a bland-looking substance or to take on the task of blending the yellow colouring for themselves. For years, in the mid-twentieth century, margarine was sold with a small colour packet included at point of sale. An advertising campaign that showed smart-looking and very tidy young women illustrating the techniques of mixing and using margarine served to convince consumers that the process would be easy, and, judging from the women's expressions, painless. The success of such media campaigns is underscored by my friend's recent memory. 'As a child I got to mix the yellow in. I recall that clearly and with affection, although I can't abide margarine now and cannot remember when I last ate it.'[56]

Brenda York of Canada Packers, played by Kathleen 'Kay' Hodgins, promoted the potential of that company's margarine product, 'Margene' – the first to be sold in Canada.

As explained by the woman who personified her, 'Brenda York was created as an advertising personality' in 1947 by Canada Packers, upon the urging of Grant Advertising Agency. 'The goal was to increase brand awareness and product identification, although I never actually saw this in any document.'[57] Certainly, there was a close affiliation between the product and the spokespersonality.[58] A portrait of Brenda York appeared on the Margene packaging such that a consumer would quickly associate one with the other.

Grant Advertising led a strategic campaign to introduce Brenda York to the Canadian public. Kay Hodgins remembers that 'they ran a series of teaser billboards' with 'Brenda's coming' and then 'Brenda Who?' and finally 'Who is Brenda York?'[59] Once on the scene, Brenda and her assistants led cooking

14.1 Kay Hodgins portraying Brenda York for Canada Packers Margene, 1948. Photograph courtesy of Kay Hodgins.

14.2 Cover of the iconic Margene Recipe Book bearing image and signature of pseudonymous corporate personality Brenda York, produced by Canada Packers, 1949. Scanned image courtesy of Mary F. Williamson.

classes for women's groups, these classes serving both as fundraisers for the groups themselves and as a wonderful advertising venue for the company.

Also involved in a media campaign were Canadian dairy producers, who engaged their own home economists as spokespersonalities during the mid-century. In the years when Kathleen Hodgins was modelling the marvels of margarine under the corporate pseudonym Brenda York, Jean Fewster was extolling the virtues of dairy products in general under the bilingual pseudonym of Marie Fraser.

Fewster believes she was the first home economist with a trade name to be hired by a farm organization when, in December 1951, she was hired by Dairy Farmers of Canada to serve as Food Editor for the Dairy Foods Service Bureau.[60] Fewster notes that the word margarine was seldom spoken aloud since 'the focus of the DFSB was on all dairy foods, including the great flavor of butter. And since margarine was not a dairy food, it was of course never mentioned.'[61]

14.3 Jean Fewster (who portrayed Marie Fraser) with assistant Jocelyne Leduc (on the left) in Dairy Foods Service Bureau test kitchen on Davenport Road in Toronto, late 1950s. Image courtesy of Jean Fewster.

If imitation is the highest form of flattery, then Fraser was clearly good at her job and the initiative was successful. Fewster believes that the American Dairy Association soon posted a similar position, and a number of other producer-distributor groups hired home economists. She remembers Dorothy Batcheler McKinnon from the poultry and egg producers (who came up with the affectionate nickname 'Moo' for Marie Fraser, for which she was dubbed 'Cackle McKinnon') and Corinne Trerice with Bakery Foods Foundation. At DFSB, a test kitchen was built and an assistant hired to oversee its work so that the bureau no longer contracted out the testing of recipes and food photography to *Chatelaine*.[62] These associations suggest a sense of camaraderie between the home economists of the time, perhaps belied by the intimations of competition inherent in retrospective discussions of the media 'wars.'

Marie Fraser was very busy during her years with DFSB, producing releases for press, radio, and television, authoring many recipe booklets, making regular guest appearances on television and radio, delivering speeches to 'producer, consumer and professional groups on invitation,' travelling extensively from coast to coast, providing consultation on ad campaigns, and appearing at the annual Winter fair.[63] Her scrapbook photos also show her making appearances at the National Cheese Festival Dinner sponsored by the National Dairy Council, which included media representatives, 'home economists in business and government' and 'government people.'[64] Trained as a home economist (B. Sc., 1946),[65] not as a media personality, Marie Fraser nevertheless appeared regularly on *Down Dairy Lane*, a professionally produced radio program that included a cast of singers and announcers. 'Media people,' remembers Fewster, 'were constantly looking for and welcoming authentic information for Canadian readers, listeners and viewers. So operations such as DFSB (and our commercial colleagues) helped respond to these needs.' At the DFSB, 'we mailed out to these media, monthly releases with copy, tested recipes and photos with cutlines.' According to Fewster, 'DFSB credibility was high, perhaps because we were not branded and hence not pushing particular branded products.' Fewster also notes that DFSB 'employed two ad agencies not split by products, as was the usual way, hence providing the DFSB with the combined thinking of two agencies.'[66]

A different reason for DFSB's credibility was that its work was consistent with a deeply held nostalgia for Canada's rural heritage. Dairy promotion, even after margarine's decisive victory in 1948 alerted dairy producers to the need for a sophisticated and strategic marketing campaign, was consistent in its emphasis on the timeless appeal of the pastoral vision.[67] One other possible ally in the dairy marketing campaign was a humble food item that developed iconic status in English Canada during the twentieth century: the butter tart. Despite the name, the tart's main ingredients are sweeteners, yet most recipes call for at least three tablespoons of butter per batch. Calling for margarine in a butter tart recipe would surely be both a contradiction in terms and an admission of compromise. Could the promotion of the butter tart and its rise to iconic status be linked in any way to the dairy lobby's promotion of butter?

Irrespective of the differing impulses prompting promotional initiatives for butter, taken together they clearly articulate to consumers a sense of the timeless appeal of dairy products. Cows and butter tarts appeal to Canadians' sense of a shared rural past, as does the title of the radio program to which Marie Fraser was such a frequent visitor. By contrast, margarine's supporters had no equivalent argument to make. Although margarine has a remarkably long history, as a versatile processed food product it embodies change rather than continuity, timely innovation rather than timelessness. Scrutinizing consumer behaviour, Chang and Kinnucan find that the Canadian Dairy Bureau's 1978 promotion of dairy's timeless value as source of energy continues to have a positive effect on consumers despite 'the growing presence of unfavorable information' and despite the fact that 'health information is relevant for understanding food consumption behavior.'[68] Literally and figuratively, then, and as margarine advertisers have realized, there is no equivalent of the timeless appeal of the pastoral. It is the dairyman's trump card.

All of the media personalities used the annual Canadian National Exhibition in Toronto as a key promotional venue. Kay Hodgins remembers that Canada Packers had four demonstration kitchens in the Food Building and hired eight home economists for the event. Hodgins provides a wonderful description of the kinds of activities staged by Canada Packers at the CNE in the late 1940s. 'The girls (behind glass) had to follow the voice as they made cherry pies, pigs in blankets, garnished hams (in my innocence I gave this demo to a Jewish friend who has never let me forget!), cheese tea biscuits, chocolate brownies, party sandwiches and how to colour and use the new Margene margarine (the first margarine on the market in Canada).'[69]

Despite the scale of the Brenda York campaign, the involvement of an advertising agency, and the corporate sponsor, there is a distinctly homemade feel to the whole thing as Hodgins described it. Since there was 'no such thing as a prop girl in those days,' she used her own dishes and accessories or borrowed what she needed from friends for the promotional photographs.[70] The art director for the first Margene cookbook was A.J. Casson of the Group of Seven,[71] which might suggest a high level of professionalism and a large corporate budget. However, the Group of Seven did not have the iconic status it holds today, in an era prior to the founding of the Art Gallery of Ontario and the establishment of the McMichael Gallery in Kleinberg. The president of Canada Packers, J.S. McLean, was an art collector, and presumably was on close terms with Casson. McLean had a tremendous art collection and used the blue walls of the Food Clinic to mount about thirty paintings by the Group of Seven and their contemporaries. As Hodgins herself later recalled, 'needless to say, these pictures would be more appreciated today. It seems incredible now that such art should have been hung above the hog killing floor!'[72]

Conclusion

Taken together, accounts of the media war between butter and margarine from

Hodgins and Fewster reinforce the similarities rather than the differences between them, and underscore the fallacy of establishing a clear dichotomy between them. Hodgins remarks that 'in retrospect, despite real success and lasting interest, it was a marketing program that was very simple in concept,'[73] revealing her insider's perspective on the marketing campaign undertaken by the corporate giant, Canada Packers. Inversely, Fewster's description of the high credibility of the DFSB and its multifaceted media campaign illustrates the effectiveness of the Canadian Dairy Foods Service Bureau in anticipating, meeting, and rising to the challenge of corporate innovations.

ACKNOWLEDGMENT

I gratefully acknowledge the Social Sciences and Humanities Research Council of Canada and the Max Bell Foundation, for supporting research that led to this chapter.

NOTES

1 Ruth Dupré, 'Margarine Regulation in Quebec: A Long Story,' unpublished ms., July 2005. Table 1, 'An International Comparison of the Severity of Margarine Regulation.' See also Ruth Dupré, 'Regulating the Dairy Industry, 1905–1921: Peeling Off the Joseph Label,' *Journal of Economic History* 50/2 (1990): 339–48.

2 Ruth Dupré, '"If It's Yellow, It Must Be Butter ": Margarine Regulation in North America since 1886,' *Journal of Economic History* 59/2 (1999): 353.

3 The Quebec cabinet adopted a decree to repeal the provincial law banning coloured margarine on 25 June 2008. See Kevin Dougherty, 'Don't Reach for Your Glasses, That Margarine Is Yellow,' [Montreal] *Gazette*, 9 July 2008, A2. Coloured margarine went on sale in the province on 20 August 2008. Mark Cardwell, 'Quebec Warns Unilever about Margarine: "New Product Introduces New Notion to Mislead Consumers,'" Minister Says,' *Gazette*, 22 Oct. 2008, B2.

4 Dupré, 'If It's Yellow, It Must Be Butter,' 353.

5 See Sidney W. Mintz, *Sweetness and Power: The Place of Sugar in Modern History* (New York: Penguin, 1985).

6 Disagreements emerging might be dismissed as typos or minor variations. Heick, for example, notes that Katharine Snodgrass cites 1914 as the date of 'the first Canadian legislation prohibiting manufacture, sale or importation.' W.H. Heick, *A Propensity to Protect: Butter, Margarine and the Rise of Urban Culture in Canada* (Waterloo, ON: Wilfrid Laurier University Press, 1991), 176n2. The correct date was 1886.

7 Johannes Hermanus van Stuyvenberg, *Margarine: An Economic, Social and Scientific History, 1869–1969* (Toronto: University of Toronto Press, 1969), 319–21.

8 Ibid., 313. Ironically, given the protectionist rhetoric of policy makers who decried

the threat of butter substitutes, margarine could be obtained by New Zealanders through prescription. Janet Mitchell, personal communication, 2008.

9 Stuyvenberg, *Margarine*, 317. Margarine can be manufactured from a variety of different oils, both vegetable and marine.

10 One exception: Patrick Allen, a professor at HEC in Montreal, did publish a study examining the viability of margarine as a replacement for butter, with a chapter scrutinizing the Canadian case, as early as 1955. See Patrick Allen, *La margarine, peut-elle remplacer le beurre?* (Montreal: École des hautes études commerciales, 1955).

11 Heick, *Propensity to Protect*; Dupré, 'If It's Yellow,' 353–71, and 'Regulating the Quebec Dairy Industry,' 339–48; Charlene Elliott, 'Canada's Great Butter Caper: On Law, Fakes and the Biography of Margarine,' *Food, Culture and Society* 12/3 (2009): 379–96.

12 Bill Reid, '"On This Day": Housewives Save with Margarine,' *CBC News Roundup*, CBC Archives, 1948; CBC Canada, '"On This Day": Housewives Save with Margarine,' *CBC News Roundup*, Radio Broadcast, 20 Feb. 2008.

13 Hui-Shung Chang and Henry W. Kinnucan actually suggest that blend bans are even more effective in influencing consumer choice; see their 'Blend Bans and Butter Demand,' *Review of Agricultural Economics* 15/2 (1993): 269–78.

14 Julie A. Caswell and Daniel I. Padberg, 'Toward a More Comprehensive Theory of Food Labels,' *American Journal of Agricultural Economics* 74/2 (1992): 461. See also Julie A. Caswell and Eliza M. Modjuszka, 'Using Informational Labeling to Influence the Market for Quality in Food Products,' *American Journal of Agricultural Economics* 78/5 (1996): 1251.

15 Fiona Lucas, personal communication, 2008.

16 Caswell and Mojduszka, 'Using Informational Labeling'; Chang and Kinnucan, 'Blend Bans and Butter Demand'; Reid, 'On This Day'; CBC Canada, 'On this Day.'

17 Ball and Lilly do note, within the body of their article, that 'Kraft Foods entered the margarine industry in 1938 and Standard Brands entered in 1946.' However, the thrust of their discussion is the companies' marketing 'spin' as they insisted 'that their product was better than butter' by 'stressing new values such as nutrition, standardization, versatility, and ease of storage.' Richard A. Ball and J. Robert Lilly, 'The Menace of Margarine: The Rise and Fall of a Social Problem,' *Social Problems* 29/5 (1982): 495. See also n14 for Dupré's mention of Unilever's dominance until 1949, when American subsidiaries Proctor and Gamble and Swift Canadian enter the scene. Dupré, 'If It's Yellow,' 359.

18 'It is neither the consumers, nor the distributors, nor the manufacturers of margarine who are the first and most significantly impacted by the presence or absence of margarine in a market like that of Quebec, but rather the farmer or agricultural producer. Herein lies the crux of the problem that, for the moment, overrides all others.' Allen, *La margarine*, 87; translation by N. Cooke and Ariel Buckley.

19 Dupré, 'If It's Yellow,' 359.

20 Dupré, 'Regulating the Quebec Dairy Industry,' 339.

21 Ibid., 342–3.

22 Ibid., 343.

23 Ibid.

24 Ball and Lilly, 'Menace of Margarine,' 488.

25 Heick, *Propensity to Protect*, 2.

26 Ibid., 4.

27 Ibid., 163.

28 Dupré, 'If It's Yellow,' 370n31.

29 In 1948, margarine legislation came under control of the provinces. Quebec continued to ban margarine production until 1961, and Prince Edward Island until 1965. Ontario lifted its ban on coloration in 1995; Quebec resisted doing so until June 2008 despite legal challenges from Unilever (see n3 above), while other provinces let it lapse in the 1970s.

30 Julie A. Caswell, 'Current Information Levels on Food Labels,' *American Journal of Agricultural Economics* 74/5 (1992): 1196–1201; J. Edward Russo, Richard Staelin, Catherine A. Nolan, Gary J. Russell, and Barbara L. Metcalf, 'Nutrition Information in the Supermarket,' *Journal of Consumer Research* 13/1 (1986): 48–70.

31 Ball and Lilly, 'Menace of Margarine'; Heick, *Propensity to Protect*.

32 Dupré, 'If It's Yellow,' 370.

33 'Today, nutritionists say to go easy on both butter (high in saturated fat) and margarine (high in trans fatty acids). The American Heart Association still recommends margarine over butter but also advises consumers to choose the soft liquid or tub varieties.' Louisa Dalton, 'Margarine,' *Science and Technology* 82/33 (2004): 24.

34 Arjun Appadurai, *The Social Life of Things: Commodities in Cultural Perspective* (Cambridge : Cambridge University Press, 1986).

35 Elliott, 'Canada's Great Butter Caper,' 389.

36 Ibid.

37 I am grateful to Gwendolyn Owens not only for pointing this out, but also for providing details of her own grandfather's training as a dairyman that reveal the fallacy of the dichotomy between the world of the farm and that of the science lab.

38 *Report of the Minister of Education*, 1898, xxxviii, cited in Government of Ontario, 'Agricultural Training. Government of Ontario' (2005), http://www.archives.gov.on.ca/english/on-line-exhibits/education/agriculture.aspx.

39 Government of Ontario, 'Agricultural Training.'

40 Gwendolyn Owens, personal communication, 2008.

41 Government of Ontario, 'Agricultural Training.'

42 Owens, personal communication, 2008.

43 John Heward, personal communication, 2008. Grandmother Efa Jones Heward

kept a cow in the backyard of her home at 3467 Peel Street in Montreal for tax reasons, since one would be taxed at the farm, rather than the higher residential, rate. A terrific image of cows being herded down Côte des Neiges in Montreal, held at the McCord Museum, suggests cattle were a common sight on the streets of nineteenth-century Montreal. Bettina Bradbury confirms that many Montreal families raised animals to supplement small incomes prior to the introduction of stricter livestock regulations in the late nineteenth century. Bettina Bradbury, 'Pigs, Cows and Boarders: Non-Wage Forms of Survival among Montreal Families, 1861–1891,' *Labour / Le travail* 14 (Fall 1984): 9–46.

44 Owens, personal communication, 2008.

45 Cristin Schmitz, 'Yellow Margarine Won't Spread in Quebec,' *CanWest News*, 18 March 2005, 1.

46 Ibid., 2.

47 George Condon, 'Oh that Darn Quebec Margarine Regulation: When Will Reason Prevail?' *Canadian Grocer* 113/7 (1999): 94.

48 CTV, 'Margarine Fight Resumes in Quebec,' *CTV News*, CTV Television, Scarborough, ON, 2002.

49 Elizabeth Thompson, 'From Hitler to Margarine: Supreme Court Looks at Free-Speech Cases,' *CanWest News*, 6 May 2004, 1. Characterizing restrictive margarine legislation in terms of a challenge to the freedom of individual rights echoes rhetoric emerging around the margarine issue more than a century earlier. Henry Bannard, writing in 1887 after the Oleomargarine Law was passed, argues: 'Legislation runs wild at our state capitals. Grant the doctrine that state laws may prescribe or prohibit certain drinks, and it is an easy step to interfere with or prohibit certain foods, as has been done in the case of oleomargarine. If this tendency continues, we of this generation may live to see laws passed to regulate our clothing or our religion, that will be as arbitrary as anything against which our forefathers rebelled.' Henry C. Bannard, 'The Oleomargarine Law: A Study of Congressional Politics,' *Political Science Quarterly* 2/4 (1887): 545.

50 Anonymous, 'Supreme Court Uphold [*sic*] Quebec Regulation Preventing Yellow Margarine,' *Canadian Press Newswire*, 17 March 2005, 1.

51 As Mark Cardwell recently reported, the battle between the Quebec Dairy Farmers Federation and Unilever Canada continues: 'Now two words might re-ignite the butter vs. margarine war in Quebec. Acting on a complaint by the Quebec Dairy Farmers Federation, officials from Quebec's Agriculture Department have warned consumer products giant Unilever that its new Becel Gold Buttery Taste margarine contravenes the province's food laws.' Cardwell, 'Quebec Warns Unilever.'

52 CanWest, 'Quebec Margarine Police See Yellow,' *CanWest News*, 5 Nov. 2005, 1.

53 Such an implication lends further credence to Elliott's invocation of the 'concern

for purity' as key motivator for the challenge to margarine. See Elliott, 'Canada's Great Butter Caper,' 381, 389–92, 394.

54 See Kevin Dougherty, 'Don't Reach for Your Glasses.'

55 Cardwell, 'Quebec Warns Unilever.'

56 Fiona Lucas, personal communication, 2008.

57 Kathleen Hodgins, personal communication, 2002.

58 My thanks to Shelley Boyd for this observation.

59 Hodgins, personal communication, 2002.

60 Jean Fewster, personal communication, 21 July 2002.

61 Ibid.

62 Jean Fewster, personal communication, 24 March 2008.

63 Fewster, personal communication, 2002.

64 Fewster, personal communication, 2008.

65 Fewster later went to the University of Wisconsin for a graduate degree in Home Economics Journalism, was quickly hired as part-time faculty in the Department of Agricultural Journalism, and pursued doctoral study at the university.

66 Fewster, personal communication, 15 April 2012.

67 Dairy farmers also had one other well-known and much beloved trade character: Elsie. Elsie the Borden cow, whose fame quickly surpassed that of other 'spokes-cows,' was 'born' in the 1930s during the 'well-publicized milk wars between farmers and dairy processors.' Borden Organic, 'The Story of Elsie,' http://bordenorganic.com/elsiesplace/storyofelsie.htm. Although American by birth and nationality, so to speak, Elsie also appeared regularly in Canadian venues, including the Canadian National Exhibition. She spent her time in costume, ensconced in a carefully decorated room, 'with curtains, framed pictures, four-poster bed, and a telephone,' and a portrait of her husband, Elmer the bull, in uniform complete with military medals, greeting eager viewers. Government of Ontario, 'Strength in the Community,' *The Archives of Ontario Celebrates Our Agricultural Past* (2005), http://www.archives.gov.on.ca/english/on-line-exhibits/agriculture/strength.aspx.

68 Hui-Shung Chang and Henry W. Kinnucan, 'Advertising, Information, and Product Quality: The Case of Butter,' *American Journal of Agricultural Economics* 73/4 (1991): 1202.

69 Hodgins, personal communication, 2002.

70 Ibid.

71 Ibid.

72 Ibid.

73 Ibid.

PART SIX

Protests, Mindful Eating, and the Politics of Food

15 The Politics of Milk: Canadian Housewives Organize in the 1930s

JULIE GUARD

The chapter begins with a question: how did radical women fighting rising prices during the Great Depression overcome the significant obstacles to political involvement and mobilize a large, broad-based grassroots movement? The short answer is: by tapping into the material and symbolic meanings of milk. Communist and other socially progressive women activists had campaigned through the 1930s on a wide range of issues, including high food prices, low relief benefits, and inadequate housing, but failed to attract the public support necessary to have an impact. When some of the same women, along with many others, focused their efforts on rising milk prices, however, they were transformed from an obscure group at the fringe of local politics into an integral part of a highly respectable consumer organization, the Toronto Housewives Association. Speaking as citizen-consumers and concerned mothers, and led by a then political neophyte, twenty-three-year-old Bertha Lamb, the Housewives called for the same reforms as the Canadian left, but with far better results. Their legal challenges threatened the ability of the Ontario Milk Control Board to set milk prices. The Housewives' citywide milk boycott forced the dairy companies to alter their pricing strategies. Housewife-activists became local celebrities who held meetings with powerful political authorities. A few ran successfully for public office, including at least one, Elizabeth Morton, who was likely a communist.

Dairy companies eventually capitulated to the Housewives to the extent that they gave up their plans to implement additional price increases (although they refused to reduce prices) while stepping up advertising to increase milk consumption.[1] But the Housewives' most important achievement was not lower prices but rather the stimulation of an informed public debate about the politics of food prices and the possibilities for popular participation in developing social and economic policy. Women with no previous experience of activism who participated in Housewives' campaigns became self-confident political actors. As the Ward Four captain of the Housewives, Mrs Durno explained, 'Belonging to the Housewives Association has been a wonderful education for most of us,' adding that 'we can appreciate now that while we have had a vote for a long time we have not used it intelligently.'[2] Rae Luckock, a founding member of the Ontario Co-operative Commonwealth Federation (CCF) who, in 1943, was one of the first two women elected to the Ontario legislature, explained her decision to work within the Housewives with the declaration that 'there is not another way out of our present predicaments but through organization.' 'We should never miss a chance,' she asserted, 'to ask our political representatives in government to help us better our lives.'[3] In similar fashion, Housewife Mrs E. Dunn assured those attending a meeting of the Local Council of Women, a mainstream women's group with a history of supporting liberal reforms, that 'we are here to look at the whole question from the broadest possible point of view to see what can be done about it.'[4]

And so they did. My case study demonstrates that, by keeping the issue in the news and by provoking debate about milk pricing from all of the interested parties, the Housewives' milk price campaign fostered popular education about the political economy of milk. The Housewives' leaders did not start with a radical analysis, and some of them, including founding president Bertha Lamb and executive member Mrs Ena Albon, who was also Lamb's mother, were actually anti-communist in political outlook. However, as information about milk pricing, the local market, and the state activities that supported the dairy industry became better known, it became clear to the Housewives and their supporters that corporations, with the active support of the provincial government, were reaping benefits at the expense of consumers and farmers. Detailed information in the daily newspapers about the differences in the price of wholesale, discounted, and retail milk, the extraordinary price-setting power of the highly profitable dairies, the low incomes of struggling farmers, and the difficult working conditions of delivery truck drivers educated urban consumers about the market activities behind the production, distribution, and purchase of milk. Increased public knowledge about milk's political economy also laid bare the conflicting class interests of the farmers, drivers, and consumers who produced, delivered, and bought milk and the dairy companies that processed, distributed, and sold it.

Building a Mass Movement

The Toronto Housewives Association was inaugurated, in November 1937, by women who were outraged when the Ontario Milk Control Board approved an increase in the price of milk while wages remained low and many had no work at all. The Milk Board, created by the Ontario Milk Control Act of 1934 to stabilize and support the economically important dairy industry, established milk prices for the province.[5] Consumers rightly suspected the Milk Board of deliberately keeping prices high to protect the industry at their expense. Three years previously, overproduction had prompted a milk 'price war' in which prices dropped from 11 cents to as low as 6 cents per quart.[6] But in fall 1937, despite a surplus of milk on the market, the Milk Board approved a 1 cent per quart increase to 13 cents. The Milk Producers' Association joined with the Milk Board in assuring consumers that the price increase would benefit only the underpaid farmers, but small producers denied these claims, observing that the association that ostensibly represented all dairy farmers was actually dominated by a few large producers who also had ties to the dairies.

Milk was universally regarded as an essential food that was critical to children's health. It therefore followed, the Housewives argued, that the state was obliged to ensure it was available in sufficient quantities to even the poorest of families. Its failure to do so enraged them. 'Government officials ask us to send our children to war for what they claim is the protection of the country,' Lamb charged, pointing out a cruel irony, 'but they allow children of the country to go unprotected in peace time by protecting the profits of such trusts as control milk and allow them to boost the price beyond the reach of average wage earners.' Already, 'oranges and cod liver oil are beyond the reach of the average family,' she added, 'and now they are putting milk beyond reach as well.'[7]

Lamb's claims rang true for many women and their families. After almost a decade of low wages and high unemployment, even an apparently small increase in the price of milk, a nutritious food that could replace more expensive items such as meat and eggs, could play havoc with family budgets. A 1938 study by Toronto's Visiting Homemakers' Association pegged basic weekly food costs for a family of five at 8 dollars.[8] Such a cost would have strained the budgets of those – and there were many – who lived on average weekly earnings of 17 dollars, or the very low-paid, who earned less than 13 dollars.[9]

Hoping to win the support of local government, Lamb led several delegations of women to Toronto's Municipal Council and Board of Control, where they urged city officials to pressure the province to lower prices and investigate the high profits earned by the dairies. Bolstered by city officials' unanimous endorsement, Lamb called on all concerned housewives to attend a mass meeting in Toronto's Labour Temple, a trade union meeting hall, to organize against the milk price rise. Refusing to be silenced by an anonymous threat to the life of her infant son, a stance the press lauded as courageous and one that enhanced her popular appeal, she declared a housewives-led 'war on prices.' Eight hundred women filled the hall to capacity, pledging to reduce their household milk consumption to a bare minimum until the price dropped from 13 cents to

10 cents a quart. Banner newspaper headlines announced a 'price war' as the Housewives vowed to establish a 'city-wide union' of consumers that would strike against every dairy in the city unless their demands were met.[10]

The newly formed Housewives Association took swift action, starting immediately with a door-to-door campaign to encourage others to support their citywide milk boycott. They built membership over the next few months by holding frequent public meetings, where they educated consumers about the political economy of the dairy industry and promoted the boycott.[11] They lobbied officials at all levels, sending hundreds of letters to the Milk Board and dispatching countless delegations to the provincial and federal legislatures and municipal councils across the province.[12] In February 1938, four thousand Housewives and supporters filled Toronto's Mutual Street arena and vowed to buy no milk until the price came down.[13] Soon afterwards, the Housewives expanded the boycott to include butter, at one point parading for two days up and down the city's busy streets bearing placards charging that 'dairy combines are unfair to housewives' and urging women to 'not buy any more butter until it is 30 cents a pound or less.'[14] In the spring, they bombarded the members of the provincial legislature with letters urging them to support a change in provincial legislation to permit producer-consumer co-operatives, so that they could establish and run not-for-profit co-operative dairies.[15] By the summer, they were also demanding reductions in the price of bread and had also established a number of neighbourhood-based food co-operatives that sold farm produce directly to consumers.[16] Moreover, they made food prices a central issue in the 1938 and 1939 civic elections, running several candidates on a Housewives' ticket and reporting publicly on the positions that other candidates were taking on prices.[17]

The Housewives' campaign was enormously popular. Within weeks of the association's founding, ten thousand middle- and working-class women in the Toronto area and across the province were paid-up members. Although the Housewives Consumers Association that emerged from these beginnings has been dismissed by some scholars as a communist-led movement,[18] in fact, it was a diverse organization representing a wide spectrum of political views. Its members included several communists and CCF members as well as Liberals and many political neophytes. In addition to their all-female membership, the Housewives attracted strong support within the wider community. Advocates of the Housewives' campaign included religious organizations and women's groups, clergy, social workers, and nutrition experts, as well as organized labour, milk truck delivery drivers, small dairies, retailers, and farmers. Their trenchant critique of the powerful dairy industry and its friends in the provincial government raised hackles among those in the milk producers' associations, the major dairies, and in the federal and provincial governments; Ontario Premier Mitchell Hepburn was a particularly powerful opponent. But a number of politicians of every stripe and at every level of government – including several Cabinet ministers – endorsed the Housewives. Whether despite, or (partly) because of, such formidable opposition, the Housewives were treated as serious political actors by community and political authorities as well as by the news media. They demanded, and eventually secured, meetings with the provincial premier and the chair of the Milk Board and they used these opportunities to argue publicly with powerful men and to advance their views in the press. As we shall see, the extensive coverage of their activities provided by the mainstream media assured that their campaign remained visible and inspired wide public debate.

The Meanings of Milk

The Housewives' popularity rested on milk's extraordinary material and symbolic significance, and was bolstered by the hyperbole that exaggerated milk's importance to health. A so-called protective food that was widely viewed as essential to the well-being of children and a critical necessity for mothers desperate to feed their families on inadequate breadwinner wages, milk allowed even apolitical women to take to the street in noisy protest and demand state ownership of the dairy industry in the name of responsible motherhood. The apparently natural connections assumed to exist between milk, motherhood, and children's health hints at another aspect of this struggle: the Housewives' and the media's apparently unreflective and unself-conscious acceptance of milk's popular and official meanings. Scholars have only begun to plumb the complicated and often contradictory social meanings attached to milk. A focus in the literature on milk regulation, pasteurization, production, and marketing has more recently shifted to questions about the way that milk has been bound up historically with meanings of class and gender, safety and danger, authority and power, cleanliness and filth, nature and science, trust and deception.[19] The space limitations of a case study preclude an in-depth examination of these broad themes, but suffice it to say that recognizing that such meanings adhere to milk, even when they were not recognized or acknowledged by the historical actors involved, alerts us to the ways in which the Housewives simultaneously embraced and deployed unconscious and official notions about milk to reinforce the legitimacy and apparent naturalness of their demands.

The enormous popularity of their demand for affordable milk, expressed in the organization's broad-based, heterogeneous support, along with the maternalist framing of their campaign, enabled ordinary women to overcome the gendered assumptions that normally deterred them from engaging in direct political action. It also deflected, for a time, the red-baiting that typically undermined the legitimacy even of groups that, like the Housewives themselves, were not communist organizations but did include a handful of active communists.

Along with the communist left, which advocated nationalization, state management of the economy, and direct democracy, the Housewives called for lower milk prices and proposed that government 'municipalize' the dairy industry, control basic commodity prices, and create a position for consumers on the Milk Board. In developing their critique, they may well have been influenced by the *Daily Clarion*, a Communist party paper that ran a series of encouraging articles about the Housewives and also published detailed information about the rising profits of the dairy companies and the generous salaries paid to their high-ranking executives, even in the midst of the Depression.[20] This could have been politically dangerous given the pervasive anti-communism of the period, which led many to vilify anyone, no matter how respectable, who endorsed ideas known to be supported by the Communist party. It was, therefore, truly remarkable that, in the context of the Housewives' campaign, these calls for price fixing and state takeover of private industry shed their leftist stigma and entered mainstream discourse. Free, at least temporarily, from the demonizing that generally dogged those who supported socialist ideas, tens of thousands of ordinary people, few of whom would have identified as socialists, lobbied government to adopt what were effectively socialist policies.

The Housewives' campaign was fuelled, in part, by the stark evidence of government disregard for the needs of ordinary people when it came to milk. The fact that milk prices were rising, despite clear evidence of continued profits in the dairy industry, and that they did so with the complicity of the government-appointed Milk Board, provided an unusually clear case of the state's role in perpetuating social and economic inequality. While the state protected profits, middle- and working-class families struggled to get by, and the poor starved. The milk price campaign thus became a vehicle by which ordinary people, most of them women who had never been involved in radical political movements, as well as a few radicals, were mobilized to challenge the state.

Grassroots politics based on maternalist claims like those of the Housewives have, as Temma Kaplan has compellingly demonstrated in her histories of politicized Latin American, Spanish, South African, and U.S. women, enabled protesting women to draw on conventions of motherhood and female fragility, thus legitimizing their participation in political protest and suspending or delaying state repression of their movements.[21] Nor were the Canadian-based Housewives the only ones to frame their movement around their rights as citizen-consumers. European, British, Australia, and U.S. historians, such as Belinda Davis, Karen Hunt, Judith Smart, Annelise Orleck, and Dana Frank, have examined the gendered histories of politicized consumer movements in different places and time periods.[22] Also providing useful context are the chapters in this volume by Sonia Cancian, Catherine Carstairs, and Marlene Epp, which illustrate just how readily women's socially constructed relationship to food has been politicized, both by themselves and by others, while Franca Iacovetta's chapter reminds us that, in the hands of the 'experts' (self-claimed or otherwise), and the state, such constructions have sometimes been used to contain and control women.[23] More specifically, Catherine Gidney's chapter on university students' food protests, and Krista Walters' on Canadian nutritional surveys of Aboriginal women, examine in different contexts some of the many meanings with which milk resonates. In Depression-era Canada, the combination of maternalism, politicized consumption, and women's special relationship to food, particularly milk, helped to create a social space that legitimated the Housewives' political engagement.

Promoting Milk's Essential Goodness and Protesting Social Injustice

The Housewives' remarkable appeal hinged on milk's symbolic and material importance, both of which became more pronounced during the Depression. In her excellent social history of milk in the United States, E. Melanie Dupuis observes that the exaggerated claims about milk's unparalleled health benefits that fuelled the dramatic increase in milk consumption in the twentieth century can be traced to the dairy industry's successful marketing strategy together with state programs designed to promote milk consumption.[24] In Canada, as elsewhere, virtually no one (including the Housewives) challenged the belief that milk was essential. Its status as an especially nutritious food – vital for babies and children – was well entrenched by the 1930s. That decade's concern with public health, as noted by Ian Mosby in this volume, spurred calls to drink more milk.

Health and nutrition experts uniformly urged increased milk consumption – at least one quart per child per day and one pint per adult – to combat rising levels of malnutrition and illness. The Health League of Canada, revived after a decade of decline in response to public concerns about the rise in contagious diseases such as tuberculosis and poliomyelitis, identified milk as one of the 'four pillars' of public heath. The league advised everyone to drink at least 30 per cent more milk to 'ward off disease.'[25] A variety of other medical experts prescribed milk as an antidote to contagious diseases. The most eminent of

these was the Scottish medical researcher Dr John Boyd Orr, a social progressive whose 1936 report, *Food, Health and Income*, revealed widespread malnutrition in Britain. Speaking to a Toronto audience in April 1939, Orr affirmed
the prevailing medical opinion that consuming enough of the right foods, one
of the most important of which was milk, would help prevent diseases such as
rickets and tuberculosis.[26]

An emerging awareness of malnutrition gave rise to public health scares
about inadequate diets in the 1930s. Official measures of malnutrition provided
quantitative evidence of the social consequences of poverty. As Mosby notes,
Leonard Marsh's important 1938 study, *Health and Unemployment*, which
identified that up to 35 per cent of the unemployed suffered from malnutrition,
added substance to popular worries about the impact of the Depression on public health. Given the central importance accorded milk in maintaining health,
both popular and official discourses inevitably associated inadequate nutrition
with insufficient milk. Although federal policy makers rejected Marsh's recommendations, and those of other critics on the political left who advocated
state intervention in the economy, the public education programs designed to
shift responsibility from the state to the individual (as in the housewife) provided advice about adequate diets that, among other things, advised people to
consume more milk (see Ian Mosby's chapter in this volume).

The government may have hoped to silence its critics by offering nutritional advice in place of income support, but the Housewives' campaign drew
impetus precisely from popular outrage at state-approved price increases on
such a vitally important food. From the outset, the Housewives had stressed
the social consequences of higher priced milk. Framing their campaign as a
compassionate response to the desperate need of those living on low incomes,
Housewives' spokeswomen stressed that while some 'may be able to afford the
increased price of milk,' there were 'thousands of children not getting the food
they need.'[27] Newspaper coverage about the inability of low-income families
to provide their children with sufficient milk pricked the consciences of their
better-off neighbours. An examination of the scores of letters sent to the liberal
and populist-oriented *Toronto Daily Star* strongly indicates that many people,
including many ordinary Torontonians, blamed the dairies and the government
for pricing milk beyond the reach of low-income families and also saw the
Housewives as offering a solution. Signing her letter 'an Under-Consumer,'
one such writer observed that 'at the present price it is almost impossible for
adults of many a family to consider themselves where milk is concerned.' She
thus urged that people 'make an extra effort to support the Housewives' association for a reduced price' because 'only then will we be able to increase
the consumption.'[28] Another 'Consumer' who wrote in support of the boycott

explained that she intended to halve her own family's normal milk supply of '728 to 800 quarts annually' and urged others to do the same. 'If all housewives cooperate in such a movement,' she declared, 'a new milk price will surely result.'[29] Others expressed similar views, including the writer who asserted that 'the advance in price of both bread and milk ... threatens the life of the poor,' especially those 'fighting for existence on some of the disgracefully low salaries still offered in Toronto,' adding, 'the government had better take over the milk supply in municipal depots, as they have the water supply.'[30]

The spectre of malnourished, unhealthy children, depicted almost daily in the populist mainstream press and invoked by a variety of authorities, animated the campaign for affordable milk. Speaking to the Ward Three branch of the Housewives, Margaret Stern of the Toronto Children's Welfare Council linked insufficient milk to malnutrition and disease among the poor, arguing, 'There is no use denying we have thousands of little white mice – little guinea pigs – in Toronto involved in a cruel experiment to determine how little a child can be fed without dying.' Physical defects, she explained, were the product of 'an inadequate diet; for one thing, not enough milk.' She also warned that 'the exorbitant price of milk is robbing children, especially those of relief recipients, of a vitally important food ... [and] making it all the more difficult for the housewife to stretch an already burdened food voucher.'[31] Other women involved in social welfare organizations agreed. In statements to the press, Miss J.V. Moberly, secretary of the Toronto Infants' Home, Mrs J.E. Shaw, secretary of the Downtown Church Workers, and Mrs Newton Magwood of the Local Council of Women bluntly asserted that '13-cent milk means many poor families will have to drop milk from their list.'[32] Medical authorities weighed in as well. Dr Gordon Bates of the Health League of Canada argued that 'milk should [not] be withheld from any citizen, especially a child, because of poverty.' Similarly, Dr W.C. Hopper told the Canadian Council on Nutrition that, while ethnic background influenced the milk consumption of some Canadian households, the single most important factor 'was the family income.' In short, 'families on relief were the smallest consumers.' Even Dr E.W. McHenry, perhaps Canada's most prominent authority on nutrition, and a male 'expert' who generally blamed ignorant mothers, not poverty, for malnutrition, noted publicly that 33 per cent of children in low-income families got no milk. 'What is the use of telling the mother of a family of five that every adult in the family should have a pint of milk a day and every child a pint and a half,' he asked rhetorically, 'when the cost of this would be $2.99 a week?' Clearly, this was an amount out of reach for low-income families.[33] (On McHenry's views, see Ian Mosby's chapter in this volume.)

Although the worst of the Depression was over, the economy took a downward turn in 1937, and the misery of many continued. Approximately 10 per cent of Torontonians were still dependent on municipal assistance, while as many as half of all of the city's wage earners earned less than the legal female minimum wage of $12.50 a week, and hundreds more scraped by on wages as low as, or lower than, the relief rates.[34] A self-help guide to menu planning compiled by the Emergency Unemployment Relief Committee of Montreal in 1932 reveals that even the most careful homemaker struggled to feed her family on relief rates or low earnings. With careful planning, a family of five or six could eat on the relief allocation of $3.25 a week, but menus relied heavily on starch, and some suppers consisted of nothing but boiled rice, milk, sugar, bread and butter.[35]

The milk price campaign focused attention on the gap between basic food costs and the income of many families, and the harmful effects it produced. As an editorial in the *Toronto Daily Star* explained, few understood that 'people can actually starve for some time without actually dying from starvation,' adding that 'children who grow up without adequate nourishment are damaged in health, often beyond repair.'[36] Significantly, medical authorities and civic politicians affirmed the accuracy of the charges issued by the communist-led Ontario Federation of Unemployed Association that people on relief were 'slowly starving to death.'[37] In the context of the Housewives' campaign, the communist-led protests that earlier had been largely ignored, became newsworthy. One such instance of this shift that was recorded in the press involved a group of twenty-five women relief recipients who appealed for help to the Toronto Board of Control in February 1938 because their children were 'being methodically starved.' The group's leader, Mrs Jean Finlayson, explained that 'we as mothers face week in week out the impossible task of feeding our families. We know the limit of human endurance is fast being reached. Speaking plainly, our children to say nothing of ourselves are hungry for food.'[38]

Just as the Housewives' campaign shone light on the injustices that communists had been protesting for years, so the Housewives themselves, including the organization's avowedly anti-communist leaders, employed rhetoric normally associated with the left to denounce the dairy companies. Fiercely anti-communist president Lamb, for example, denounced the dairies as 'profiteering organizations that would make us pay through the nose for the things we need' and dismissed the Milk Control Board as 'a dictatorship.' Resisting the pressure to blame milk delivery drivers and farmers for higher-priced milk, the Housewives also made common cause with the drivers' union and the small-scale milk producers. They rejected the claims of the dairy companies that price increases were warranted by rising wages and that the farmers, rather than themselves, would benefit most from the 1 cent increase. Instead, they insisted that a price decrease could 'very easily be absorbed in the spread there is between the price the farmer gets and the price we are charged by the dairies' and should not be borne by milk producers.[39] This alliance of consumers, workers, and farmers, although only partially successful was, of course, a version of the strategy advocated by the Communist Party of Canada which, as part of its Popular Front program sought to forge such collaborations itself but without success.[40]

Conclusion

By fostering broad public debate about the political economy of milk, educating consumers about the relations of milk production, distribution, and sale, and organizing events in which self-respecting women could participate without conflict or embarrassment, the Toronto Housewives Association created a vehicle for direct democratic participation in governance. Participation in the Housewives Association transformed ordinary women from apolitical homemakers into citizen-consumers who demanded government accountability and called for reforms that were, in their essence, socialist. In this regard, the Housewives' history provides an especially clear instance of how, in the absence of vilifying attacks and red-baiting, a good many socialist ideas – universal medicare, public pensions, state provision of essential services, to name a few – have been embraced by ordinary Canadians and, indeed, even become integral to definitions of a Canadian national identity. As the milk campaign so compellingly demonstrates, communist insistence that government account to the governed, that it protect the interests of ordinary people and not just those of capital, and that it adopt measures to ameliorate the worst effects of the Depression rather than leaving the poor and their families to starve and suffer, were ideas that ordinary people would support, so long as they were not stigmatized as 'radical.'

ACKNOWLEDGMENT

My thanks to the Social Sciences and Humanities Research Council for supporting this research, and to Carl Klassen and Zac Saltis for research assistance.

NOTES

1 'Trying to Weld Milk Producers in One Big Unit,' *Toronto Daily Star*, 17 Feb. 1938, 1.
2 'Ask Control Board Aid on Prices: Housewives Present Resolution Demanding Probe into High Costs,' *Daily Clarion*, 24 March 1938, 1.

3 'London Women Elect Officers,' *Daily Clarion*, 25 Feb. 1939, 1.

4 'Support Plan for Municipal Milk Supply,' *Evening Telegram*, 30 Nov. 1937, 4.

5 E.H. Clarke, *A History of the Toronto Milk Producers' Association, 1900 to 1966* (Toronto: Toronto Milk Producers' Association, 1966), 57–65.

6 Veronica McCormick, *A Hundred Years in the Dairy Industry: A History of the Dairy Industry in Canada and the Events that Influenced It, 1867–1967* (Ottawa: Dairy Farmers of Canada, 1968), 21–2, 55–6.

7 'Housewives Plan Boycott of Milk,' *Daily Clarion*, 4 Nov. 1937, 1.

8 Toronto Welfare Council, *The Cost of Living: Study of the Cost of a Standard of Living in Toronto which Should Maintain Health and Self-Respect* (Toronto, 1939).

9 'Food Costs Said up 20 PC Average Wage Held at $17,' *Toronto Daily Star*, 15 July 1938, 21.

10 'Housewives Plan "High Prices" Boycott: Plan City-Wide Union to Fight Food Costs Control Board Told,' *Toronto Daily Star*, 3 Nov. 1937, 1; 'Women Uniting against Prices, Mrs Lamb Says,' *Daily Clarion*, 8 Nov. 1937, 1. For a more detailed account of this event and of the Housewives' milk price campaign, see Julie Guard, 'A Mighty Power against the Cost of Living: Canadian Housewives Organize in the 1930s,' *International Labor and Working-Class History* 77/1 (2010): 27–47.

11 'Lakeshore Women Unite to Fight Milk Increase,' *Toronto Daily Star*, 13 Nov. 1937, 6; 'Price Boycott Cuts Milk Consumption: Toronto Housewives to Hold Meetings throughout City,' *Daily Clarion*, 13 Nov. 1937, 1; 'Women Milk Boycotters Now Claim 5,000 Members,' *Toronto Daily Star*, 16 Nov. 1937, 7; '5,000 Housewives Cut Milk, Some Drinking Only Water,' *Toronto Daily Star*, 18 Nov. 1937, 25; 'Milk Price Scored as Robbing Infants,' *Toronto Daily Star*, 9 Feb. 1938, 6; 'Relief System in Toronto Said Costly to Taxpayers,' *Evening Telegram*, 10 March 1938, 28; 'Laborite Tells Housewives Boycotts and Probes Useless,' *Evening Telegram*, 28 March 1938, 16; 'London Women to Fight Prices,' *Daily Clarion*, 18 April 1938, 1; 'Housewives Send Speakers,' *Daily Clarion*, 10 Nov. 1938; 'Housewives Plan Parleys to Terminate "Monopolies,"' *Evening Telegram*, 30 Nov. 1938, 1.

12 'Ten-Cent Milk Sale Planned by Housewives,' *Toronto Daily Star*, 7 Jan. 1938, 1; Phyllis Poland, 'International Women's Day: The Cost of Living and March the Eighth,' *Daily Clarion*, 28 Feb. 1938; 'Ask Control Board Aid on Prices: Housewives Present Resolution Demanding Probe into High Costs' *Daily Clarion*, 24 March 1938; 'Urge Officials Query Spread in Food Prices,' *Evening Telegram*, 22 March 1938, 34; 'Housewives in London Urge Federal Probe into High Food Prices,' *Daily Clarion*, 12 May 1938, 1.

13 'A Call to All Women,' *Globe and Mail*, 21 Feb. 1938, 11; 'Women Urge Federal Probe of Food Prices,' *Daily Clarion*, 19 Feb. 1938, 1; *Daily Clarion*, 21 Feb.

1938, 1; 'Council to Support Housewives' Fight,' *Toronto Daily Star*, 22 Feb. 1938, 6.

14 'Toronto Women Picket High Food Cost; Women Boycott Costly Butter, Groups Grow,' *Daily Clarion*, 26 Feb. 1938, 1.

15 Ontario's Milk Control Act forbade the existence of co-operative dairies unless the purchaser held shares in the company. The Housewives sought and won a change in the law so they could establish consumer-producer dairy co-operatives. 'Housewives Seek Law Allowing "Co-op" Dairies,' *Evening Telegram*, 17 March 1938, 20.

16 'Housewives Sign Contract with Farmers,' *Evening Telegram*, 23 June 1938, 30; 'Farmers Join Housewives' Co-operative,' *Globe and Mail*, 23 June 1938, 5; 'First Vegetables Friday for Housewives' Union,' *Toronto Daily Star*, 7 July 1938, 6; 'Housewives' Co-operative Finds Business Going Up,' *Toronto Daily Star*, 30 July 1938, 6.

17 'York Reeve Gives Promise to Seek Lower Milk Price,' *Toronto Daily Star*, 29 Dec. 1937, 6; 'Aspirant to Council Wants Public Dairy,' *Toronto Daily Star*, 30 Dec. 1937, 6; 'Housewives Ask Gas Rate Cut and Urge Milk Probe,' *Evening Telegram*, 1 Dec. 1938, 43; 'Women Show Interest in Election of Ald. Smith,' *Daily Clarion*, 29 Dec. 1938, 1.

18 Studies of the Canadian left that identify the Housewives Consumers Association as a branch of the Communist party or as communist-led include Dan Azoulay, '"Ruthless in a Ladylike Way": CCF Women Confront the Postwar "Communist Menace,"' *Ontario History* 89/1 (1997): 23–52; Joan Sangster, *Dreams of Equality: Women on the Canadian Left, 1920–1950* (Toronto: McClelland and Stewart, 1989). The characterization is not consistent with my more extensive research, which reveals a much more diverse organization that, while it included a number of communists, existed separately from the party.

19 For example, see Denyse Baillargeon, 'Gouttes de lait et soif de pouvoir: Les dessous de la lutte contre la mortalité infantile à Montréal, 1910–1953,' *Canadian Bulletin of Medical History* 15/1 (1998): 27–57; Daniel E. Bender, 'Perils of Degeneration: Reform, the Savage Immigrant, and the Survival of the Unfit,' *Journal of Social History* 42/1 (2008): 5–29; Daniel Block, 'Saving Milk through Masculinity: Public Health Officers and Pure Milk, 1880–1930,' *Food and Foodways* 13 (2005): 115–34; Alan Czaplicki, '"Pure Milk Is Better than Purified Milk": Pasteurization and Milk Purity in Chicago, 1908–1916,' *Social Science History* 31/3 (2007): 411–33; Michael Egan, 'Organizing Protest in the Changing City: Swill Milk and Social Activism in New York City, 1842–1864,' *New York History* 86/3: 205–25; Jane E. Jenkins, 'Politics, Pasteurization, and the Naturalizing Myth of Pure Milk in 1920s Saint John, New Brunswick,' *Acadiensis* 37/2 (2008): 86–105; Thomas J. Kriger, 'Syndicalism and Spilled Milk: The Origins of Dairy Farmer Activism in New York State, 1936–1941,' *Labor History* 38/2–3 (1997): 266–86.

20 For example, 'How the Milk Trust Milks the Citizens,' *Daily Clarion*, 5 Nov. 1936, 2; 'New Milk Price Costs Citizens $270,000 Yearly,' *Daily Clarion*, 26 Feb. 1937, 1; 'Milk Dominated by 5 Huge Units,' *Daily Clarion*, 4 May 1937, 1.

21 Temma Kaplan, *Crazy for Democracy: Women in Grassroots Movements* (New York: Routledge, 1997), and *Taking Back the Streets: Women, Youth and Direct Democracy* (Berkeley, CA: University of California Press, 2004).

22 Belinda Davis, *Home Fires Burning: Food, Politics, and Everyday Life in World War I Berlin* (Chapel Hill, NC: University of North Carolina Press, 2000), and 'Food, Politics and Women's Everyday Life during World War I,' in K. Hagemann and S. Schüler-Springorum, eds., *Home Front –Battle Front: Military and Gender Relations in the Two World Wars* (New York: Berg, 2002), 115–38, and 'Food Scarcity and the Empowerment of the Female Consumer in World War I Germany,' in Victoria de Grazia, ed., *The Sex of Things: Gender and Consumption in Historical Perspective* (Berkeley, CA: University of California Press, 1996), 287–310; Dana Frank, 'Housewives, Socialists, and the Politics of Food: The 1917 New York Cost-of-Living Protests,' *Feminist Studies* 11/2 (1985): 255–86; Karen Hunt, 'The Politics of Food and Women's Neighborhood Activism in First World War Britain,' *International Labor and Working-Class History* 77/1 (2010): 8–26, and 'Negotiating the Boundaries of the Domestic: British Socialist Women and the Politics of Consumption,' *Women's History Review* 9/2 (2000): 389–410; Annelise Orleck, '"We that Mythical Thing Called the Public": Militant Housewives during the Great Depression,' *Feminist Studies* 19/1 (1993): 147–73; Judith Smart, 'The Politics of the Small Purse: The Mobilization of Housewives in Interwar Australia,' *International Labor and Working-Class History* 77/1 (2010): 48–68, and 'The Politics of Consumption: The Housewives' Associations in South-eastern Australia before 1950,' *Journal of Women's History* 18/3 (2006): 13–39.

23 See also Marlene Epp, *Mennonite Women in Canada: A History* (Winnipeg: University of Manitoba Press, 2008), esp. chapter 5; Franca Iacovetta, *Gatekeepers: Reshaping Immigrant Lives in Cold War Canada* (Toronto: Between the Lines, 2006), esp. chapter 6.

24 E. Melanie Dupuis, *Nature's Perfect Food: How Milk Became America's Drink* (New York: New York University Press, 2002).

25 Gordon Bates, 'Health League of Canada,' *Canadian Journal of Public Health* 61 (Jan./Feb. 1970): 60–2.

26 Robert Reeds, 'Half Low-Income Families in Toronto Said "Under-fed,"' *Toronto Daily Star*, 18 April 1939, 1; Amy L.S. Staples, '"To Win the Peace": The Food and Agriculture Organization, Sir John Boyd Orr, and the World Food Board Proposals,' *Peace and Change* 28/4 (2003): 495–523.

27 'Drive for Cheaper Milk Not Dead, Declare Women,' *Evening Telegram*, 10 Dec. 1937, 30.

28 An Under-Consumer, 'Milk Consumption,' letter to the editor, *Toronto Daily Star*, 20 Jan. 1938, 4.

29 Consumer, 'Cost of Milk,' letter to the editor, *Toronto Daily Star*, 2 Nov. 1937, 4.

30 'Important to Health,' letter to the editor, *Toronto Daily Star*, 3 Nov. 1937, 4.

31 'Ten-Cent Milk Sale Planned by Housewives,' *Toronto Daily Star*, 7 Jan. 1938, 1; 'Milk Price Scored as Robbing Infants.'

32 'Fears Rise to Make Poor Use Less Milk,' *Toronto Daily Star*, 9 Nov. 1937, 21.

33 'Urges Canadian Law to Pasteurize Milk,' *Toronto Daily Star*, 2 March 1938, 5; 'Value of Milk as Diet Not Appreciated, He Says,' *Toronto Daily Star*, 21 April 1938, 11; 'Ignorance, Lack of Money Seen Causing Malnutrition,' *Toronto Daily Star*, 18 Dec. 1937, 3.

34 'Toronto's Relief Figures,' *Toronto Daily Star*, 15 March 1939, 4. For a detailed discussion of poverty and earnings, see Marcus Aurelius Klee, 'Between the Scylla and Charybdis of Anarchy and Despotism: The State, Capital, and the Working Class in the Great Depression, Toronto, 1929–1940,' doctoral dissertation, Queen's University, 1999, 192–201.

35 My thanks to Elizabeth Driver for this source. *How We Do It: A Report of Thrifty and Imaginative Food Planning and Preparation by Montreal's Homemakers in the Troubled Times of the Thirties*. Emergency Unemployment Relief Committee of Montreal: first issued in 1932; reprint, n.d.; private collection of Elizabeth Driver.

36 'Relief Diets and Mother Nature,' *Toronto Daily Star*, 6 April 1938, 4.

37 'Cites Low TB Death Rate to Deny Relief Starvation,' *Toronto Daily Star*, 10 Jan. 1938, 2; 'Relief or Taxpayers' Rebellion Is Coming, Trenton Mayor Warns,' *Toronto Daily Star*, 22 Feb. 1938, 1.

38 'Sign-Carrying Women Charge Children Starve,' *Toronto Daily Star*, 23 Feb. 1938, 1.

39 'Dairies Here Propose Cut of Cent a Quart on Milk,' *Toronto Daily Star*, 11 Feb. 1938, 21.

40 The Communist International encouraged Communists everywhere to forge alliances with all progressive groups, including liberals, to combat the rise of fascism. On the Communist party's Popular Front program, see Norman Penner, *Canadian Communism: The Stalin Years and Beyond* (Toronto: Methuen, 1988), 128–34.

16 'Less Inefficiency, More Milk': The Politics of Food and the Culture of the English-Canadian University, 1900–1950

CATHERINE GIDNEY

Today, most residence students find their food at university food courts or cafeteria-style eateries. The dining culture they encounter is self-serve, pick-your-own, with cash registers and meal vouchers. Students eat at odd hours, sometimes with a regular gang of friends but just as likely with strangers. Yet, less than fifty years ago, students sat down to dinner together, were served by waitresses, and learned table etiquette and methods of polite conversation. On a regular basis, female students 'retired' for coffee and after-dinner talks in their well-cared-for common rooms. In the modern university, food is conceived of as fuel to sustain the body through classes or extracurricular activities; however, in the past the dining hall was part of an elaborate and refined residence culture considered central by university authorities to the creation of cultured and productive middle-class citizens.

Unfortunately, we know little about the role of food in university culture. Historians of higher education have begun to examine a variety of facets of student experience such as residence life and extracurricular activities.[1] Scattered evidence suggests that food played an important role in all aspects of student culture, from daily life to special events. Nevertheless, historians have generally made reference to the activity or event rather than to the food, emphasizing, for example, the socializing function rather than the ritual of food at a YMCA tea or the gathering of athletes rather than their act of collective consumption at an athletics banquet.[2]

This inattention to food in institutions of higher education is perhaps not surprising given the limited work in the social history of that field. Moreover, students' relationship to food is not easily researched. Despite the fact that university students spent a significant amount of time eating, records about their reaction to food are difficult to find, neither systematically reported on in student newspapers nor recorded in residence minutes. There are, however, clear moments when the politics of food has been at the centre of university life. In 1766, for example, students at Harvard protested the use of rancid butter in the dining hall, sparking off 'a decade of confrontations and rioting that spread' to universities 'throughout the colonies.'[3] Over a century later, Virginia Woolf, in one of the most powerful feminist tracts on women's education in Britain, illuminated the educational disadvantages faced by women through a comparison of the dining-hall food in women's and men's Oxbridge colleges.[4]

This chapter focuses on students' relationship to food primarily through the residence dining hall. I start by briefly examining the role of food within the intellectual, social, and moral culture of the university. I then turn to two incidents of student protest at Victoria College, University of Toronto, one in 1913 in Annesley Hall, the women's residence, and the other in 1948 in the men's residence, Burwash Hall.[5] Although specific in time and place, taken together these two events provide insight into the role of the dining hall in students' moral and social education, the relationship between student governments and university administrations, and the growth of expertise in food management. By drawing our attention to disruptions in the functioning of the dining hall, these protests help reveal the extensive rituals associated with the dining hall and the concomitant class and gender relations embedded within these rituals.[6] In the process, these incidents provide insight into a culture that now seems distant but which permeated the university well into the 1960s. This culture – reflective of particular societal values and beliefs – became reinforced in, and transmitted to, future generations through the everyday customs of university life.

The Culture of Food on Campus

In 1941, the University of Toronto student newspaper, the *Varsity*, printed an article on what it considered to be the most common student pastime: eating. The article noted, 'For the average undergraduate any time is time to eat – food is the logical conclusion of a Big Evening, the obvious diversion at club meetings, after skating or the movies, the natural welcome intermission in an evening's study, and almost a "must" before bedtime.'[7] The consumption of food was central to students' evening activities, but equally it formed part of the rhythm of students' annual events. Senior students regularly integrated food into initiations, for example, forcing new students to ingest strange substances. Through the year, students attended and hosted numerous teas. Often put on to facilitate social introductions, teas appeared as part of any number of events, from formal receptions to an opening club meeting to welcome new students. In the first decades of the twentieth century, the tea-dance was a central feature of heterosocial activity. Food was integrated into students' charity work – through the preparation of food baskets for needy families or monetary donations for Christmas baskets. During wartime, food became a symbol of women's patriotic duty, with students abstaining from luxuries such as candy, or, as at Victoria College, organizing a Patriotic Tea Room, the profits of which went to the Red Cross. At the end of the year, students sat down for a final meal together at end-of-year banquets and graduation dinners.[8]

Food was also a significant feature of residence culture. Students often turned residence meetings into social events, with food and refreshments appearing before or after residence business.[9] Food played a particularly significant role in women's residence culture. Historians in Britain, the United States, and Canada have noted the importance to female students of 'spreads,' as they were called in the United States, and 'feeds' by some students in Canada – feasts of cocoa, cakes, breads, or even cooked chicken sent from home and enjoyed late in the evening with friends. These meals became sites for the formation of close friendships, and moments during which students could temporarily shed school anxieties, as well as gatherings facilitating political and social discussion.[10]

Residence students encountered food most frequently, however, in the dining hall. Anecdotal evidence suggests that some students enjoyed residence food while others regularly complained.[11] Only occasionally, however, did individual complaints become expressed in a collective manner. Two such cases occurred at Victoria College. As we will see, complaints that appear specific to consumption, quickly reveal themselves to be grounded in broader concerns about the efficiency of the dining hall and the running of the residence more generally. The culture of the dining hall was embedded within the larger purposes and aims of residence life for which the dean of women or dean of men was responsible. The successful implementation of those aims and purposes relied, at least in part, on the efficiency of the household for which the housekeeper or dietician was responsible.

Food Protests of 1913 and 1948

The first student protest about the quality of food served and level of cleanliness occurred in the women's residence, Annesley Hall, in the fall of 1913. In spring of that year, the long-term housekeeper retired. The Committee of Management, which oversaw the running of the residence, consulted Annie Laird, head of the Faculty of Household Science at the University of Toronto, and then hired Helen G. Reid, a dietician at Toronto General Hospital.[12] Just one month into the school year, the students had already become dissatisfied with the quality of the meals served, the manner in which they were served, and the 'tardiness of serving them.'[13] Residents organized a deputation of senior women to present their complaints to the Committee of Management. These were numerous. For example, on 13 October, students were served crackers instead of bread. On 24 October, they received applesauce for dessert. On 27 October, 'soup, salads and bananas ran out before all were served,' students were given stale salty biscuits instead of fresh soda biscuits, and staff refused requests for second helpings of bananas. Students also complained about the quality of Sunday tea.[14] They requested improvement in the attractiveness of the tea table and that there be 'sufficient food and palatable food,' complaining that they were served 'stale brown bread half buttered' as well as boiled and bitter tea and coffee. They suggested that the maids should be on duty, that tea should be served promptly, and that there be sandwiches, 'iced cakes or something dainty,' and 'no mussy fruit like grapes.'[15]

Students complained not only about the food but also about the running of the residence more generally and the attitude of the dietician. They noted that their rooms were never thoroughly cleaned, especially under the beds and desks, that the corridors were always dusty, that only one face towel was provided a week, and that on one occasion the dietician refused to provide some of the girls with fresh linen. In addition, Margaret Addison, the head of residence, reported to the Committee of Management that the laundry room was 'never ready or in fit condition' for student use and that Reid refused 'to lend things that girls have been in custom of having.'[16] After hearing a litany of complaints – from both students and the head of residence – the Committee of Management met with Reid who, in turn, tendered her resignation.[17]

The protest held in the men's residence over thirty years later was less easily resolved. On 9 February 1948, students sitting down for breakfast at Burwash Hall found not 'the customary jugs of milk and the pots of jam' but instead 'only milk for cereal and a small dab of jam.'[18] By the 13th of that month, a number of students had organized a demonstration to bring attention to the mismanagement of the dining hall. Students led two calves into the dining hall and attempted to extract milk from them for breakfast. An article in the *Varsity* reported, 'maintaining that their breakfast beverage could be restored and no increase would be necessary if the hall were run on a more efficient basis, the protestors had adorned the calves with sandwich boards saying "Less Inefficiency – More Milk."'[19] In drawing attention to the reduction of milk, students drew on a long-established rhetoric that, as Julie Guard's chapter in this collection illustrates, linked the nutrients in milk to the creation and maintenance of strong, vigorous bodies.[20] In doing so, students cast university officials as a threat to the development of the future leaders of the nation.

As at Annesley Hall in 1913, student grievances addressed more than just the efficiency of food services. In 1948, they extended to complaints about the violation of fire protection by-laws and residence maintenance, including lack of cleanliness and insufficient linen.[21] Problems within the residence stemmed at least in part from postwar conditions faced by all Canadian households and residential institutions. Postwar inflation had adversely affected the financial position of the dining hall, which ran deficits in 1946 and 1947.[22] Yet, that was not the only problem. Paul Chester, a third-year student, told a reporter from the *Varsity* that the bursar, W.J. Little, and the Board of Regents refused to pay attention to student proposals and petitions. He complained that 'various petitions and suggestions, such as re-organization of the over-crowded staff, the establishment of a cafeteria system, and the investigation of the management by experts, have been ignored. The higher cost of living by no means justifies the abnormal conditions that exist, and the recent curtailment of milk at breakfast is a feeble attempt to cover up the inefficiency of the management.'[23]

On 16 February, the Residence Council, composed of students, dons, and the senior tutor, accepted a student report demanding the removal of residence management.[24] On 26 February, members of the council presented this request, along with their other complaints, to a residence subcommittee of the Board of Regents.[25] In the meantime, the Burwash Hall dietician, Miss D. Falconbridge, and the assistant dietician, Elizabeth Hewson, while angry at the very public charges made against them, wrote the senior tutor in support of students' request 'that an authority on institutional cafeterias be consulted to promote a more efficient food service.'[26] The subcommittee responded by agreeing to bring the residence up to fire code and to improve the efficiency of cleaning services by the following session. It decided that the Residence Council, which normally took complaints to the senior tutor, could have direct access to the president of Victoria College in regard to the dining hall. It also hired a qualified expert, Miss Park, a lecturer in institutional management at the university, to undertake a survey and analysis of the dining hall. The subcommittee did not, however, accept the recommendation of Residence Council that the management of the hall be taken out of the hands of the current dietician and bursar.[27]

The response of the subcommittee seemed to prevent further protest by students, although as the senior tutor noted, the absence of continued agitation may also have been due to the approach of exams.[28] In the end, however, students would find themselves the victors. While Miss Park laid the blame for the inefficiency of the dining hall on university administrators rather than the director of household services, she also noted that 'milk is one of the important protein foods and a popular beverage and since the amount saved per student was almost negligible, I believe there was really no justification for eliminating it from the breakfast menu.'[29]

Moral Regulation and Etiquette in the Dining Hall

The 1948 and 1913 protests differ both in their nature and context. In combination with fragmented evidence from other universities, however, these incidents offer key insights into university culture in the first half of the twentieth century. Historians have documented the important role of residence life in the process of character formation. Particularly strong in women's residences, but extending also to male residents, deans of men and women attempted to instil and reinforce values, attitudes, and behaviour expected of middle-class Christian men and women. This included such things as the supervision of residence curfews, chaperonage of co-ed activities, and oversight of student government.[30]

The dining hall was central to this type of regulation. Indeed, administrators perceived the dining hall as a place that could help recreate what they assumed to be the elevating and refining influence of the family home and to inculcate such refinement in students who might be a little rough around the edges. This sentiment can be clearly seen in a 1927 complaint made by Florence Dodd, adviser to women students at the University of Alberta, to the president of that university, about the limited size of the women's dining hall. Dodd noted that 'among the most important things that form social habits and cultivate social ease must be placed the training in courtesy and demeanour that a well-conducted dining-room affords.'[31]

The etiquette of the dining hall was elaborate, especially at dinner time. Well into the 1960s, it involved proper dress – a requirement true of attendance at university more generally. At Victoria College, and elsewhere, women students wore skirts and blouses and men wore jackets and ties.[32] In many places, dinner was at a set time and students entered the dining hall together, as a group. Often this was a means of inspecting students. At Regina College in the 1920s, for example, 'the girls lined up in pairs for inspection before entering the dining-room. Girls with uncombed hair, untidy stockings, or crooked hemlines were sent back to their rooms to make themselves presentable.'[33] It also allowed the dean daily personal contact with each student. In 1927, at the University of Alberta, Dodd noted, 'for the evening meal, the students enter and leave the dining-room as a body, and it is while they are assembling for dinner, that the Adviser to Women Students has the opportunity of a word or at least a nod of greeting to every student in the Building.'[34]

Once assembled, students at Victoria College said Grace before dinner.[35] As in most residences, students sat in groups at a table in a preapproved arrangement. Administrators usually implemented some form of dining rotation so that students would have the opportunity to become better acquainted with each other as well as with the dean.[36] Students were then served by waiters or waitresses or food was placed on the table and students learned the etiquette of serving. For example, at Regina College in the 1920s a faculty member sat at a table of eight, admonishing students for improper use of bread and butter plates, eating before the whole table was served, and improper use of forks and spoons.[37] Similarly, as late as the mid-1960s, one student at Victoria College remembers residents being chastised for passing platters of food the wrong way.[38] Students remained at their tables until everyone was done. Well into the 1950s, female students at Victoria College, as at many other women's residences, gathered after dinner in the common room for tea and coffee.[39]

Mary Douglas has argued that 'the ordered system which is a meal represents all the ordered systems associated with it.'[40] A similar argument could be made of the campus dining hall which encoded the class and gendered social relations that existed within broader society and into which administrators expected students would take their place upon graduation. Dining-hall activities demarcated students from servers and, where in some instances financially strapped students acted as servers, differentiated between students.[41] Rules of etiquette stringently reinforced to students the fact that some of their colleagues still needed to learn 'how to manage a knife and fork, how to approach soup.'[42] Equally, while coffee hours contributed to the intellectual life of the women's residence, they also became occasions to train female students in the art of pouring and serving, reinforcing the idea of their future role as hostesses.[43] The dining hall, then, became one means by which administrators could help students acquire the cultural capital, or reinforce in them the need to maintain that capital, for success in later life. While there is certainly scattered evidence to suggest that some students resisted or rebelled against elements of this process, in the main, the requisite daily participation in the rituals of the dining hall familiarized students with, and reinforced their adherence to, the dominant social relations of the day.[44]

If administrators used residence life as a central site of social and moral education, students, in turn, expected a particular type of service commensurate with their own upbringing and social standing, and assumed the right to critique standards not meeting their expectations. As the 1913 case indicates, they expected a certain level of cleanliness and order, from thorough cleaning of individual rooms and common areas to sufficient provision of towels and linens.[45] They also had specific food standards they expected to be met. Applesauce, for example, was not considered a dessert but a condiment. Bread should be fresh daily. Food should not be scrimped on, and seconds should be available. There was a proper way in which to serve food – with both the food and table presented attractively and sufficient staff to ensure prompt and orderly service.

Changing social and economic conditions, however, also presented challenges to administrators' abilities to maintain the cultural aims and purposes of university life. This was particularly true in the 1940s. Taking advantage of federal funding opportunities to further their post-secondary education, veterans swelled university enrolments at war's end. Cafeteria-style eating became one means of feeding students in halls that could no longer accommodate all students in one sitting.[46] The efficiency of the dining hall was also affected by limited availability of staff. During the war, this was likely caused by the opening up of more attractive job opportunities for women. Yet, the shortage continued after the war. Park's survey of the Burwash dining hall found only one trained cook and no head waitress.[47] To help alleviate the problem, administrators decided in February 1948 to rent a nearby home as a furnished residence for female waitresses.[48]

The shortage of staff affected not only the quality but also the type of service students received. Examining McGill's women's residence, Paula LaPierre notes that from its origins in the late-nineteenth century, 'the maids woke the students in the morning, first closing their windows, answered the telephones, and served afternoon tea and milk and biscuits each evening. A student could have her meals in her room for a charge of 25 cents. These lavish services were only abolished in 1941 when World War II created a shortage of domestic workers.'[49] Such services were not widely available at other university residences. Yet, the belief in the importance of the formal meal – and the service it depended on – existed elsewhere. At the University of Manitoba, the dean of women noted in 1947–8: 'In these days of general unrest there is more need for some emphasis on gracious living. A reasonable compromise might be reached if at least one evening per week throughout the session table service, table linens, saucers for cups etc. were provided, and a more attractive menu offered.'[50] Similarly, while in 1946 administrators at St Francis Xavier University in Nova Scotia instituted cafeteria-style eating in order to deal with postwar overcrowding, they soon began planning the expansion of the dining hall so that the entire student body could once again sit together at meals, a plan 'designed to restore the cherished pattern of college life.'[51] Administrators clearly believed in the importance of table service both as a process of socialization and a means of cultivating manners. However, wartime and postwar conditions challenged their ability to provide a refined residence culture.

Students versus Administrators

While administrators attempted to produce students with cultivated manners, their aim was not simply refinement, but also to instil qualities of leadership. Indeed, they integrated elements of leadership training into the rituals of the dining hall: students sat in groups in which seniors provided advice and guidance. Following the lead of deans and dons, they set the tone and standards – which they themselves would have learned as juniors. This type of leadership formed part of a broader system of student government, itself designed to train students for their future role as community leaders.

Students' methods of protest in 1913 and 1948, and administrators' reactions, provide important insights into the historical role and nature of student government. In 1913, students sent a delegation to the residence Committee of Management. Female students at Victoria College had been given some modicum of responsibility for setting and enforcing residence rules as early as 1906. This was done, in part, in the belief that students would be more likely to follow rules created by their peers but also because Margaret Addison, the head of residence, believed self-government to be an important part of the learning environment of the university. The creation of a petition thus fit within Addison's and the committee's vision of the workings of democracy in the residence. Addison's own views also likely aided in the Committee of Management's immediate receptiveness of student complaints and demands. She lived in the residence, ate with the students, and would have been well aware of the situation.[52] Thus, during the 1913 protest against the dietician, the students had the backing of the head of residence.

The 1948 incident witnessed much more strained relations between student leaders and administrators. For one thing, administrators perceived students' turn to the press as bringing negative publicity to Victoria College and thus as a violation of the rights of student government. In concluding his letter to the president of the college, in which he detailed the events leading up to the February protest, the bursar, W.J. Little, argued that 'in view of the fact that Mr Bailey, a member of the sub-committee of the Residence and Burwash Hall Committee has made statements and charges in the public press, I would submit that he has consequently forfeited the right to be the representative of the Residence Council on the Sub-Committee.'[53] Taking up Little's position, the president threatened to withdraw recognition of the Residence Council if it continued to show itself incapable 'of representing the students,' or in other words, of putting a cap on the protests.[54]

Unlike in 1913, in 1948 tensions between students and administrators resulted in the escalation of the situation. Students felt that administrators had ignored their petitions for almost two years. They were also angered by the bursar's reference to them in a local newspaper as 'boys.'[55] Indeed, in a letter to the editor of the *Varsity*, two Victoria students noted that 60 per cent of one residence 'House' were ex-servicemen with an average age of twenty-three. Little, they argued, was not 'dealing entirely with teen-age Joe Colleges of the pre-war era.' They continued on, 'It might be well for some of the authorities themselves to take a more "grown-up" view of the existing conditions and stop beating around the bush in trying to squelch publicity.'[56] On their side, administrators at Victoria – like those at other institutions – constantly worried about negative attention – be it the result of students or faculty – for fear it would lead to a decline in enrolment and lost revenue.[57] In addition, the incident illustrates administrators' perception of student government not as a right but a privilege.[58]

The 1948 case reveals that when administrators seemed unwilling to respond, and student government ineffective, students found alternative means to express their discontent. The turn to publicity in 1948 may well have resulted not only from a breakdown in communication but to the presence of war veterans who were less amenable to a heavy-handed administration. Moreover, this protest fits within broader consumer discontent at the time. Historians have documented the reaction against price gouging and the elimination of controls by groups such as the Housewives Consumers Association, the Canadian Association of Consumers, and the National Council of Women.[59] Whether students drew inspiration from these groups is unknown. Certainly, this protest represents a youthful, male contribution to a consumer movement historians have generally portrayed as dominated by women. The immediate postwar period thus provided conditions ripe for the 1948 protest. The protest, in turn, illustrates the consequences for administrators perceived as unwilling to respond to student demands.

The Scientifically Managed Dining Hall

The protests against food services by students in 1913 and 1948 provide insight into the nature of student government and the role of the dining hall in the moral education of students. The incidents also reveal the growing role of expertise in the area of food management. The early decades of the twentieth century witnessed the growth of academic programs in household science as well as the application of nutritional science in hospitals, schools, and public dining rooms. This process occurred gradually. As a profession, dietetics was largely unknown in the 1920s, with a Canadian professional association created only in 1935. At the University of Toronto's Faculty of Household Science, for example, Annie Laird worked hard to develop household science on a scientific basis and to train women for a career in dietetics. Women trained in this fashion themselves contributed to the emphasis on scientific management of cafeteria and hospital work. Violet Ryley, a student of Laird's, became superintendent at the University of Toronto dining hall in 1910 and then in 1917 the dietician for the Military Hospitals Commission. During the First World War, she pressed her supervisors for the development of food services along the principles of labour and management efficiency. In doing so, she aimed to elevate the profession by the creation of the position of executive dietician who would train student dieticians and nurses as well as supervise and administer a whole kitchen and its ancillary functions.[60] Residence administrators recognized the growing drive towards the scientific management of food services. They also encountered difficulties applying that expertise to a system modelled on the domestic home.

In hiring Helen Reid, in 1913, the members of the Committee of Management clearly recognized the desirability of employing the skills of a dietician. The new dietician replaced Mina Richardson, a capable, well-organized, efficient woman, who had no formal training but rather had learned the skills of organizing a dining room on the job. As director of household, she was responsible for overseeing the general running of the residence and dining facilities. She ordered food, did the accounts, planned menus, and oversaw food preparation and service, as well as the general running and cleanliness of the household.[61] When she retired in 1913, the Committee of Management decided to hire a trained dietician 'to reconstruct the administration of the household along modern scientific lines.'[62]

The shift in approach was reflected in Reid's title as both dietician and director of household. The Committee of Management hired Reid to set up a model kitchen that would also employ and train pupil-dieticians from the School of Household Science. Some of Victoria's female students were enrolled in household science, and so this was also an effort to integrate Victoria with the school and further the role of the residence as a place of education. The expectations of trained dieticians were not easily met, however, within the household structure of the residence. Unfortunately, Reid's perspective on her employment at Victoria is unknown. There is some evidence that she felt she was being asked to perform tasks not properly hers, such as overseeing the transfer of graduation gowns from one building to another.[63] Certainly, the director of household who replaced Reid had duties well beyond those of dietician, overseeing, for example, the repair of eavestroughs, the interior painting of the residence, the repair of the furnace, and the building of new cupboards.[64]

The problems of running a large institution along the lines of a small household re-emerged in 1948. University administrators clearly recognized that the management of their food services had remained informal. In awaiting the report of Miss Park's survey of food services, for example, the university decided that during the summer months it would send two of its dieticians to the Food Institute at Northwestern University in Illinois.[65] Much of Park's survey of the working of the dining hall and kitchen focused on bureaucratic inefficiency – a criticism directed towards the university's administration. Park argued that the dietician and her assistant were overworked, responsible for 'routine ordering, bookkeeping, checking invoices and answering the telephone' leading to 'insufficient time for constructive planning,' and having to 'perform tasks which are properly not theirs,' resulting in the neglect of 'the important work' of 'staff training and supervision to promote efficiency.'[66]

One example of that inefficiency was the continued reliance on home canning. In 1913, the housekeeper at Annesley did a significant amount of preserving and canning for the year. The practice remained in place in Burwash Hall in 1948. Indeed, one of the criticisms of the dietician's survey was the amount of time required to complete this task and the fact that 'all such condiments may be purchased quite reasonably and are just as acceptable to the students.' This continued reliance on home canning, she argued, was part of a larger problem of outdated equipment and the organization of the kitchen. Ultimately, Park saw the need for the creation of a proper bureaucratic structure, the division of tasks, and sufficient and trained staff. She noted, for example, that the dietician's responsibilities included both food services and housekeeping but that she did not hold any executive authority. Park recommended that the title of dietitian become an executive position responsible directly to the president of Victoria College. She also advised that a second assistant dietician and a secretary be appointed, so that the dietician could focus her attention on supervisory duties. And she recommended the appointment of a head waitress responsible for training and supervising waitressing staff.[67]

Park's survey of the dining hall illustrates the way in which its operation had remained modelled on the household. In 1948, as in 1913, a single dietician/housekeeper oversaw the entire management of the kitchen and domestic staff. While university administrators increasingly turned to trained dieticians to help them improve the efficiency of the kitchen and household, the shift to a scientifically managed dining room was slow. The inefficiency of the kitchen was complicated in 1948 by problems rooted in the lingering effects of the war – lack of available staff, increasing food prices, and outdated equipment. In the long run, however, the household model would give way to trained professionals in food management. While postwar conditions affected the traditional dining-room service, over the course of the twentieth century the drive for greater efficiency and the need to cut costs would result in the transformation of many dining halls into cafeterias. In the process, the idea of the dining hall as a centre of moral training and refinement would disappear. This was certainly not due solely to the rise of food management. The cultural and social transformation of the 1960s reshaped residence life and student culture.[68] Nevertheless, the search for efficiency also played a part.

Conclusion

The transformation of the ideals and culture of the dining hall occurred only gradually. In Victoria's women's residences, administrators attempted to maintain the traditions and rituals of the dining hall at least into the mid-1960s.[69] Historians have drawn attention to the classroom, extracurricular activities, or even the residence hall, as sites of moral education and middle-class formation. The dining hall was clearly an extension of these other educational venues. There, administrators reinforced and taught students the niceties of table manners, the ability to engage in polite conversation, and general comportment for public life. It became a site in which students could gain the refinement and cultivation deemed necessary for their future endeavours so that they might take their place as the leaders of the nation.

If administrators had particular ideals they wanted to instil in students, students, in turn, expected particular standards. Students often accepted – even assumed – the paternalism of the university. After all, many institutions recreated elements of the middle-class home with which most students were familiar. That they accepted the paternalism of the university, however, did not entail being passive subjects. When, as in 1913, they perceived those standards to be failing, they petitioned administrators to rectify the situation. If administrators were unresponsive, as in 1948, students resorted to public protest. In doing so, students played a role in shaping the nature of university life.

Students' protests about dining-hall management, as well as their broader experience of food on campus, provide an important window onto the social and cultural history of higher education. From the time of their arrival on campus for their first orientation or initiation tea to their last event – the graduation dinner – students' encountered the university through a culture of food. Through the daily act of communal consumption, as well as at special events, administrators used food as a means of socialization and to cultivate in their students at least an air of refinement. The rituals of the dining hall, in particular, helped administrators maintain, teach, and reinforce existing boundaries of respectability. Students, in turn, incorporated food into their own expressions of residence and campus culture, from late-night residence feeds to patriotic teas, and, of course, protests. Indeed, students used food to solidify intimate friendships, create class and college bonds, and ensure moments conducive to homosocial and heterosexual socialization. Many of these encounters would result in lifelong bonds. Both administrators' vision of the aims and purpose of the university and students' university experience can thus be more fully gleaned through analysis of the social meanings of dining-hall culture. In turn, that culture not only tells us a great deal about the nature of the university in the first half of the twentieth century, but also provides insight into the broader society of which it was a product.

ACKNOWLEDGMENT

The research for this project was funded by Associated Medical Services and the Social Sciences and Humanities Research Council of Canada.

NOTES

1 For the twentieth century see, e.g., Paul Axelrod and John G. Reid, eds., *Youth, University and Canadian Society* (Kingston and Montreal: McGill-Queen's University Press, 1989); Paul Axelrod, *Making a Middle Class: Student Life in English Canada during the Thirties* (Montreal and Kingston: McGill-Queen's University Press, 1990); Catherine Gidney, *A Long Eclipse: The Liberal Protestant Establishment and the Canadian University, 1920–70* (Montreal and Kingston: McGill-Queen's University Press, 2004), and 'Dating and Gating: The Moral Regulation of Men and Women at Victoria and University Colleges, University of Toronto, 1920–60,' *Journal of Canadian Studies* 41/2 (2007): 138–60; A.B. McKillop, *Matters of Mind: The University in Ontario, 1791–1951* (Toronto: University of Toronto Press, 1994); Alyson E. King, 'The Experience of the Second Generation of Women Students at Ontario Universities, 1900–1930,' doctoral dissertation, University of Toronto, 1999, and 'Centres of "Home-Like Influence": Residences for Women at the University of Toronto,' *Material History Review* 49 (1999): 39–59.

2 In general, historians in North America and Britain have paid scant attention to the role of food in the culture of the university. An exception is Margaret A. Lowe, *Looking Good: College Women and Body Image, 1875–1930* (Baltimore, MD: Johns Hopkins University Press, 2003).

3 J. Angus Johnston, 'Student Activism in the United States before 1960: An Over-

view,' in Gerard J. DeGroot, ed., *Student Protest: The Sixties and After* (London: Longman, 1998), 13.

4 Virginia Woolf, *A Room of One's Own*, chapter 1, in *A Room of One's Own/Three Guineas*, edited, with an introduction and notes, by Michèle Barrett (London: Penguin, 1993), 9–10, 15–16.

5 Victoria College was founded as a Methodist institution in Cobourg, Ontario, in 1841. In 1887, it federated with the University of Toronto, relocating to the city in 1892. A female residence, Annesley Hall, was built in 1903, and a men's residence, Burwash Hall, in 1913. See C.B. Sissons, *A History of Victoria University* (Toronto: University of Toronto Press, 1952).

6 On the cultural significance of food, see Mary Douglas, 'Deciphering a Meal,' *Daedalus* 101 (1972): 61–8; Margaret Visser, *The Rituals of Dinner: The Origins, Evolution, Eccentricities, and Meaning of Table Manners* (New York: Grove Weidenfeld, 1991), ix; Jeffrey M. Pilcher, *Food in World History* (New York: Routledge, 2006), 2. On the role of rituals in student culture, see Keith Walden, 'Hazes, Hustles, Scraps, and Stunts: Initiations at the University of Toronto, 1880–1925,' in Axelrod and Reid, *Youth, University and Canadian Society*, 94–121.

7 'Eating and Sleeping Are Old Student Habits,' *Varsity*, 14 March 1941.

8 Walden, 'Hazes, Hustles, Scraps, and Stunts,' 105, 110; Gidney, 'Dating and Gating,' 144; Diana Pedersen, '"The Call to Service": The YWCA and the Canadian College Woman, 1886–1920,' in Axelrod and Reid, *Youth*, 201–2.

9 Gidney, 'Dating and Gating,' 143; King, 'The Experience of the Second Generation,' 248.

10 Paula J.S. LaPierre, 'The First Generation: The Experience of Women University Students in Central Canada,' doctoral dissertation, University of Toronto, 1993, 239–40; Jean O'Grady, *Margaret Addison: A Biography* (Montreal and Kingston: McGill-Queen's University Press, 2001), 119; James M. Pitsula, 'Student Life at Regina College in the 1920s,' in Axelrod and Reid, *Youth*, 136. For Britain and the United States see, e.g., Elizabeth Edwards, 'Educational Institutions or Extended Families? The Reconstruction of Gender in Women's Colleges in the Late Nineteenth and Early Twentieth Centuries,' *Gender and Education* 2/1 (1990), 17–35; Dulcie Groves, 'Dear Mum and Dad: Letters Home from a Women's Hall of Residence at the University of Nottingham, 1952–55,' *History of Education* 22/3 (1993): 293; Helen Lefkowitz Horowitz, *Alma Mater: Design and Experience in the Women's Colleges from their Nineteenth-Century Beginnings to the 1930s*, 2nd ed. (Amherst, MA: University of Massachusetts Press, 1993), 63, 169; Lowe, *Looking Good*, 33–4.

11 See, e.g., Mary Dulhanty, cited in Janne Cleveland and Margaret Conrad, 'Mary Dulhanty,' in Kathryn Carter, ed., *The Small Details of Life: 20 Diaries by Women*

in Canada, 1830–1996 (Toronto: University of Toronto Press, 2002), 345, and King, 'The Second Generation,' 187.

12 'Helen Reid' is likely 'Helen Reed,' who had been one of Annie Laird's students in household science and was appointed dietician at Toronto General Hospital in 1910. See Ruby Heap, 'From the Science of Housekeeping to the Science of Nutrition: Pioneers in Canadian Nutrition and Dietetics at the University of Toronto's Faculty of Household Science, 1900–1950,' in Elizabeth Smyth, Sandra Acker, Paula Bourne, and Alison Prentice, eds., *Challenging Professions: Historical and Contemporary Perspectives on Women's Professional Work* (Toronto: University of Toronto Press, 1999), 150–1.

13 United Church of Canada/Victoria University Archives (hereafter UCC/VUA), Fonds 2069, 90.064v, box 3-24, Committee of Management (hereafter CoM), Report, n.d.

14 Students did not have a sit-down dinner on Sunday evening. Instead, they had their large formal meal at noon, after church, and then in the late afternoon consumed a lighter meal consisting of tea, sandwiches, fruit, and squares.

15 UCC/VUA, Fonds 2069, 90.064v, box 1-2, CoM, Minutes of Special Meeting, 3 Nov. 1913.

16 Ibid.

17 Ibid., box 3-24, CoM, Report, n.d.

18 'Charge Burwash Inefficient,' *Varsity*, 10 Feb. 1948.

19 'Victoria Males Demand Milk; Bring Calves to Burwash Hall,' *Varsity*, 16 Feb. 1948.

20 For the symbolic connections between milk, youth, and national identity in New Zealand, see Philippa Mein Smith, *A Concise History of New Zealand* (Cambridge: Cambridge University Press, 2005), 143.

21 'Victoria Males Demand Milk' and 'Residence Council Requests Changes in Burwash Staff,' *Varsity*, 17 Feb. 1948.

22 UCC/VUA, Fonds 2000, 87.195v, box 1-4, Burwash Hall and Men's Residence Minutes, 16 Feb. 1948.

23 Ibid., E. Paul Chester, letter to the editor, 'Burwash Hall,' *Varsity*, 13 Feb. 1948.

24 'Residence Council Requests Changes.'

25 Burwash Hall and Men's Residence Minutes, 26 Feb. 1948.

26 UCC/VUA, Fonds 2000, 87-195v, box 1-4, letter from D. Falconbridge and E. Hewson to W.J. Little, 18 Feb. 1948.

27 UCC/VUA, Fonds 2000, 87.195v, Burwash Hall and Men's Residence Minutes, 26 Feb. 1948. Listed only as 'Miss Park,' she is likely Edna Wilhelmine Park, a graduate of the Faculty of Household Science at the University of Toronto. A member of the faculty from 1919 until 1962, she conducted research on the relationship between nutrition and children's academic performance. See Heap, 'From

the Science of Housekeeping to the Science of Nutrition,' 149.

28 UCC/VUA, Fonds 2000, 87.195v, box 1-4, Burwash Hall and Men's Residence Minutes, 17 June 1948.

29 Ibid., 'Survey and Analysis of the Situation at Burwash Hall.'

30 See, e.g., Axelrod, *Making a Middle Class*, chapter 5; King, 'Centres of "Home-Like Influence,"' 39–59; Gidney, 'Dating and Gating,' 138–60.

31 University of Alberta Archives (hereafter UAA), Office of the President, RG 3, Tory, 68-9-308, Report, Florence Dodd, Adviser to Women Students, May 1927.

32 Gidney, 'Dating and Gating,' 145.

33 Pitsula, 'Regina College in the 1920s,' 132. Although in 1925 Regina became affiliated with the University of Saskatchewan, offering the first two years of an arts program, it was also a Methodist residential high school (123). Thus, rules and regulations may have been stricter at Regina than at universities that had a slightly older student population.

34 Report, Florence Dodd.

35 O'Grady, *Margaret Addison*, 97.

36 In the 1920s, at the University of Alberta, the seating plan changed every three weeks. See Report, Florence Dodd.

37 Pitsula, 'Regina College in the 1920s,' 132.

38 Jane Pitblado, personal correspondence, 12 Aug. 2008.

39 Gidney, 'Dating and Gating,' 145–6; Margaret Gillette, *We Walked Very Warily: A History of Women at McGill* (Montreal: Eden Press, 1981), 249–50.

40 Douglas, 'Deciphering a Meal,' 80.

41 For example, students acted as servers at St Francis Xavier University. See St Francis Xavier University Archives (hereafter StFXA), Students' Representative Union, Minutes, 4 Nov. 1945.

42 Cited in Patricia Clark Smith, 'Grandma Went to Smith, All Right, but She Went from Nine to Five: A Memoir,' in Michelle M. Tokarczyk and Elizabeth A. Fay, eds., *Working-Class Women in the Academy: Laborers in the Knowledge Factory* (Amherst, MA: University of Massachusetts Press, 1993), 135.

43 Pitsula, 'Regina College in the 1920s,' 132; Gidney, 'Dating and Gating,' 145–6; Gillette, *We Walked Very Warily*, 249–50.

44 In terms of resistance, there is certainly evidence to suggest that a fair number of students regularly broke their curfews or engaged in undesirable behaviour such as smoking. See Gidney, 'Dating and Gating,' 148–9, 153.

45 Such demands were not unique to Victoria. Alison King has found that, in 1915, students in the Queen's University women's residence demanded that the house-keeper improve the cleanliness of the residence by cleaning stairs weekly, dusting lamps, and removing cobwebs. See King, 'The Experience of the Second Genera-

tion,' 188.

46 In 1946, officials at St Francis Xavier University introduced cafeteria-style dining for that reason. See 'St F.X. Students Now Eat Cafeteria Style,' *Xaverian*, 19 Oct. 1946, 1.

47 'Survey and Analysis of the Situation at Burwash Hall.'

48 UCC/VUA, Fonds 2000, 87-195v, box 1-4, letter from the Bursar to President Brown, 12 Feb. 1948.

49 LaPierre, 'The First Generation,' 233.

50 'Report of the Dean of Women,' in University of Manitoba, *President's Report*, 1947–48.

51 StFXA, RG 5/11/25, Rev. Dr D.J. MacDonald, Address Delivered at Commencement Exercises, 1947, 1.

52 O'Grady, *Margaret Addison*, 103, 140–1.

53 Letter from the Bursar to President Brown, 12 Feb. 1948.

54 UCC/VUA, Fonds 2000, 87.195v, box 1-4, letter from Walter T. Brown, president, to Mr F.T. Hoare, Residence Council, 16 Feb. 1948.

55 'Victoria Males Demand Milk.'

56 Harry H. Green and Stan Kurisko, 'Burwash Boys,' *Varsity*, 20 Feb. 1948. In 1948–49, veterans comprised 42 per cent of the student body at the University of Toronto. See Peter Neary, 'Canadian Universities and Canadian Veterans of World War II,' in Peter Neary and J.L. Granatstein, eds., *The Veterans Charter and Post-World War II Canada* (Montreal and Kingston: McGill-Queen's University Press, 1998), 122.

57 Axelrod, *Making a Middle Class*, 114.

58 Gidney, 'Dating and Gating,' 152–3.

59 Joy Parr, *Domestic Goods: The Material, the Moral, and the Economic in the Postwar Years* (Toronto: University of Toronto Press, 1999), chapter 4; Magda Fahrni, *Household Politics: Montreal Families and Postwar Reconstruction* (Toronto: University of Toronto Press, 2005); Julie Guard, 'Women Worth Watching: Radical Housewives in Cold War Canada,' in Gary Kinsman, Dieter K. Buse, and Mercedes Steedman, eds., *Whose National Security? Canadian State Surveillance and the Creation of Enemies* (Toronto: Between the Lines, 2000), 73–88.

60 Heap, 'From the Science of Housekeeping,' 143–52, 158–9, 161.

61 Richardson likely took a 'Housekeeper's course in Domestic Science' at Toronto Technical School once she received the position. See UCC/VUA, 90.064v, box 4-3, letter from Mina Richardson to Addison, 23 Jan. 1904.

62 UCC/VUA, Fonds 2069, 90.064v, box 2-10, Dean's Report in the Annual Report for the Senate of Victoria College, 1914.

63 Ibid., box 1-2, CoM, Special Meeting, 3 Nov. 1913.

64 Ibid., box 1-4, CoM, Minutes, 14 Sept. 1916.

65 UCC/VUA, Fonds 2000, 87.195v, box 1-4, Burwash Hall and Men's Residence Committee Minutes, 17 June 1948.

66 'Survey and Analysis of the Situation at Burwash Hall.'

67 Ibid.

68 Gidney, *A Long Eclipse*, chapter 7.

69 M. Van Die, personal correspondence, 21 July 2008; Jane Pitblado, personal correspondence, 12 Aug. 2008.

17 The Granola High: Eating Differently in the Late 1960s and 1970s

CATHERINE CARSTAIRS

In the late 1960s and early 1970s, as concern about food additives, water pollution, pesticide use and the nutritional value of processed foods mounted, an increasing number of Canadians began growing their own sprouts, baking whole grain breads, and shopping at health food stores. The health food movement is often associated with baby boomers and the counterculture.[1] Although the counterculture did play an influential role, health food in Canada as elsewhere had much longer roots, and drew customers from across the generations. Arguably, the modern health food movement began with nineteenth-century health reform movements in both Europe and the United States; it was infused by the optimism of early nutritional investigators who hoped that science would reveal the exact combination of food required for perfect health, and it was influenced by interwar eugenicists who hoped that better nutrition and healthy living could improve racial quality. Not surprisingly, given its diverse roots in progressive science, eugenics, and anti-modernism, health food appealed to a broad constituency of people, but especially women, on both the right and the left including spiritual seekers, environmentalists, and hypochondriacs of all ages and classes. Athletes, the elderly, women concerned about their children's health, and last but not least, young hippies, all shopped at health food stores. What they had in common was a desire to find a sense of control in their lives through carefully monitoring what and how they ate. Health food was an individualistic movement, which more often than not, promoted conservative gender norms and glorified certain types of healthy bodies. Health food promoters also believed that most illness was the result of a poor diet and, as a result, they ignored the social inequities that often result in sickness and disease.

Health food exploded in popularity in the 1960s and 1970s because it spoke to widespread concern about the safety of our food, growing distrust of experts including doctors, scientists, and governmental regulators, and a desire for a more holistic approach to health. In the early 1960s, there was growing concern about nuclear fallout in milk, water, and food crops. In 1962, Rachel Carson's *Silent Spring* raised awareness about the health dangers of pesticides, especially DDT. Then in 1969, the Canadian government banned the widely used sugar substitute cyclamate out of fear that it caused cancer. In the early 1970s, newspaper articles drew attention to the dangers of mercury and PCB contamination of our food. Books like *The Chemical Feast* and *Eating May be Hazardous to Your Health*, warned people about the dangers of food additives, growth hormones, and pesticide residues and condemned regulatory authorities for failing to protect the public.[2] People were despairing about food quality: as one journalist put it in 1972: 'Mr Grocer, please supply me with half a pound of chemicals, a quarter pound of deadly pesticides, a pint of hormone growth stimulant and some apples, chicken and beef to give them flavour.'[3]

At the same time, journalists, health activists, and others were attacking regular medicine for treating the disease and not the patient.[4] In the early 1960s, thousands of European and Canadian mothers who had taken the drug thalidomide gave birth to children with severe deformities. People began to wonder if other medicines were safe, and if they were being appropriately tested. The women's health movement questioned the safety of the birth control pill, critiqued the overmedicalization of the birthing process, and condemned the medical profession for treating women callously.[5] Many Canadians wanted a more spiritual approach to healing; they longed for explanations of illness that drew connections between the mind and the body.[6] A growing number of Canadians were critical of the idea that Western science had all the answers and were interested in exploring Eastern medicine (interest in acupuncture exploded in the early 1970s), herbalism, and alternative medicine such as homeopathy and chiropractics. Part of the appeal of these alternative medical practices was that they combined the spiritual and the medical and seemed to treat the whole patient, instead of treating the body as a machine in need of repair.

While Canadians were becoming more sceptical about the promises of medicine, science, and technology, there was still considerable hope that new discoveries would reveal the path to total health. Much like the mainstream food advertisers discussed by Cheryl Warsh in her chapter in this volume, health food promoters promised that their foods and supplements would provide strength and vitality. (Vitalist ideas, with their emphasis on unseen forces affecting health, resurged in the 1970s, thanks to the growing strength of alternative medicine.) Consumers held out great hope that vitamins, most of which were discovered by nutritional scientists in the interwar years, would lead to great improvements in health, especially if they were taken in the right combination and in the correct amounts.[7] The same principle extended to herbal remedies and supplements. The 'naturalness' of these products gave them a credibility that was increasingly denied to pharmaceuticals. And yet, it was important that they be supported by science. Health food stores and activists often drew on the authority of nutritionists, Ph.D.'s, and naturopathic doctors, and cited scientific research to make their case for their remedies and diets. So, while people worried about the safety of pharmaceuticals and were sometimes distrustful of doctors, they still wanted expert advice on how to eat and improve their health.

Part of the appeal of health food stores was that they empowered people, especially women, to manage their own health. Health food stores sold books on health and nutrition, and health food stores owners and workers were pleased to share their knowledge about supplements, vitamins, and diets. Many health food consumers read voraciously. They took pride in their knowledge of health and nutrition and in their ability to improve their own health through their diets. Unlike medical journals or textbooks, health food books required no scientific background and were written at the same reading level as newspapers or popular fiction. And yet, they promised advanced medical knowledge, and let everyone become an expert. As such, health food had considerable appeal to people of all knowledge levels and across economic classes. The health food ideology also helped to explain to people why they felt sick when mainstream doctors insisted there was nothing wrong with them. Allopathic medicine works best when doctors can diagnose a disease and provide a treatment. When people were tired and stressed, coming down with never-ending colds or yeast infections, or suffering from arthritis, mainstream medicine had little to offer. By contrast, health food writers and educators promised that there was a product or a diet that could restore you to health.

Health food had a fascinating gender politics. The assumed audience of most health food texts was women. This was not surprising because, despite the growing influence of second-wave feminism in the early 1970s, it was still primarily women who cooked the family meals and shopped for food. Women often authored health food texts, but it was mostly men who owned health food stores and businesses and played an important role in the Canadian Health Food Association. Many of the women who wrote about health food, such as Adelle Davis (in the American context) and Rebecca Clarkes and Kareen Zebroff (in the Canadian context) never explicitly embraced feminism and they assumed that a woman's primary responsibility was to look after her family. Even so, by their very presence, they showed that it was possible for women to have successful careers. Moreover, health food had an understandable appeal for young countercultural women, who, disillusioned by male-dominated medicine, were eager to take health into their own hands. Health food books and magazines provided instructions on how to spot and cure potential nutritional deficiencies, how to ensure that children ate a complete diet, and how to heal minor health problems. Health food's attention to environmental issues and animal rights spoke to many women, who had a long history of activism on those issues.[8] At the same time, a surprising number of men shopped at health food stores, wrote letters to health food magazines, and read the health food literature.

As the chapters by Julie Guard, Valerie Korinek, Franca Iacovetta, and Ian Mosby in this collection demonstrate, our beliefs about food have important political consequences. The Toronto Housewives Association focused on milk because they believed that it was the 'perfect' food for their children. k.d. lang's vegetarianism prompted her PETA ads, which led to a homophobic backlash in cattle-dependent Alberta. Government nutritionists promoted the idea that malnutrition was not the result of poverty, but of poor eating habits, while International Institute workers believed that immigrants would be healthier if they ate at least a little more like Anglo-Canadians. Health food, with its critique of the industrial food system and the medical monopoly and its atten-tion to environmental issues, has often been associated with the counterculture and the left. But instead of advocating political solutions to the problem of food safety and contamination, the health food movement told people that by consuming differently, they, as individuals, could overcome these industrially created risks and achieve optimum health. Because they believed that everyone could improve their own health through diet, they were frequently intolerant of sickness and disability and had little sympathy for the argument that pov-erty was an impediment to good health. Indeed, the counterculture often led to unexpected political alliances. Lynn Weiner shows, for example, that young hippies embraced the La Leche League, a group started by Conservative, Cath-olic women with a maternalist agenda; while Thomas Frank demonstrates that big business embraced the counterculture as a money-making opportunity.[9]

The History of Health Food

The first health food activist in the United States was the evangelical lecturer Sylvester Graham (inventor of the Graham cracker) in the 1830s. A Jacksonian individualist, who feared stimulation of all kinds, especially sexual stimula-tion, Graham told people that temperance, 'unbolted' bread, and vegetarianism would help them achieve a long life and Christian serenity.[10] One of his adepts was Ellen White, the founder of the Seventh Day Adventists. Her followers were told to avoid meat, drugs, and alcohol. White also established the Battle Creek Sanatorium, which under the leadership of John Harvey Kellogg became a prestigious health resort where wealthy patients ate individually tailored vegetarian diets (with a strong emphasis on chewing repeatedly), took hydrotherapy and other medical treatments, and listened to lectures on the dangers of masturbation.[11] North American health food writers also drew on the teachings of German and American hydrotherapists, naturopaths, and herbalists. These included the German hydrotherapist Sebastein Kneipp who counselled his followers to take plant-based medicines and follow nature's laws with regards to dress, sleeping, and time in the sun, and the Swiss doctor Maximilian Bircher-Benner (1867–1939) who recommended a diet of raw fruits, vegetables, and nuts.[12] In fact, many of the key health food players in Canada were postwar German immigrants who had been influenced by German life reform movements. Thus, from the beginning, health food had strong ties to new religious movements and alternative medicine and promoted an ascetic approach to eating and sometimes to sex. It also had significant appeal to eugenicists and fascists throughout Europe and North America.[13]

In Canada, the first health food stores opened up in the 1930s, and possibly earlier.[14] Despite their names, early health food stores carried relatively little in the way of food, which spoiled quickly, and instead focused on herbs, vitamins, tea and coffee substitutes, as well as a few health food staples like wheat germ and brewer's yeast. George Macmillan, who opened his first store in Toronto in 1939, also sold fresh fruit juices and whole wheat bread sandwiches.[15] They were usually small, family-run businesses, operated by people with little formal education. Often health food store owners had been ill themselves and had been healed by diet and naturopathy. For example, a health food store owner in Medicine Hat, Alberta, Elsie Czember, had been bedridden for six years before being cured by two naturopaths. Wanting to share her knowledge of food and health, she opened her first store in 1962. She eventually ran six stores and a substantial mail order business.[16]

Health food store owners prided themselves on their extensive knowledge about health and nutrition, much of which was garnered from books by Gayelord Hauser, the German-born author of *Look Younger, Live Longer* (1950) and *Be Happier, Be Healthier* (1952); Lelord Kordel, the Polish-born author of *Eat and Grow Younger* (1952); Carlton Fredericks, author of *Eat, Live and Be Merry* (1951); and Cathryn Ellwood, author of *Feel Like a Million!* (1952).[17] As the titles make clear, many of these books focused on how to achieve a long and healthy life. Written for a largely female audience, they often suggested that one's appearance and waistline could be improved through healthy eating. The books provided long descriptions of what vitamins, minerals, and protein could do for the body and a short section of recipes. Another source for health food fans in Canada was the *Healthful Living Digest*, a small magazine operated by J.B. Gladstone of Winnipeg. From 1940 onwards, Gladstone recommended and sold easy natural cures for indigestion, menopause, skin rashes, and other problems and advised that we could all be healthier by following the natural laws of health, bestowed upon us 'by the Creator.'

One of the most prominent health food writers was the American Adelle Davis, the author of *Let's Eat Right to Keep Fit* (1954) and other books on cooking, child care, and illness. Her books sold more than ten million copies before she died in 1974.[18] Unlike the authors mentioned above, Davis had a Master's degree in biochemistry from the University of Southern California, giving her greater scientific credibility. Davis did her first degree in domestic science at Berkeley, and her books reflected her training in scientific cookery and scientific motherhood. They also assumed that women would be responsible for child rearing and cooking. Davis argued that American soil was poor, fruits and vegetables were grown with dangerous pesticides, and packaged food had all the vitamins and minerals processed out of them. American women cooked badly, destroying the remaining nutritional content of their foods. Moreover, Americans did not get enough exercise. Sedentary lifestyles meant that people needed fewer calories than they did in the past, but this made it even more difficult to get the required nutrients. As a result, Americans were suffering from subclinical deficiencies of vitamins and minerals, making them tired, sick, irritable, and old before their time. Davis was an enormous fan of protein, and recommended that people consume liver daily and 'pep-up drinks' throughout the day. A pep-up drink was a mixture of blended milk (preferably raw certified milk), eggs, brewer's yeast, skim milk or soy flour, fruit juice, and lecithin.

A wide range of Canadians were influenced by these health food writers in the 1950s and early 1960s. Health food appealed to many elderly people looking to extend their life spans and improve their quality of life. In 1964, 69-year-old Charlie Gibson wrote to the Nutrition Division of Health Canada from a seniors' housing complex in working-class East York (Toronto) to inquire about the Vitamin C content of Canadian apples. Enclosing a picture of himself standing topless in the middle of winter, he announced: 'I eat only natural foods, no civilized processed junk and I feel like a million and raring to go.' He elaborated: 'I realize the detrimental effect that synthetic fertilizers and poison sprays have on the human body over a period of years,' and signed the letter, 'Yours in Healthful Living.'[19] Women were another receptive audience. A middle-class 'housewife' from Mississauga interviewed by the *Toronto Star* in 1970 claimed that she had learned about the health food philosophy in 1962. She fed her family whole grain bread which she made from scratch, wheat germ and brewer's yeast, 'pep-up' drinks, and served up a high-protein breakfast with eggs and often liver.[20] Another route into health food was through sports and body building. Bruce Reid, the owner of Vitamin Shop in Victo-

Figure 17.1   Health Food Stores in Selected Cities

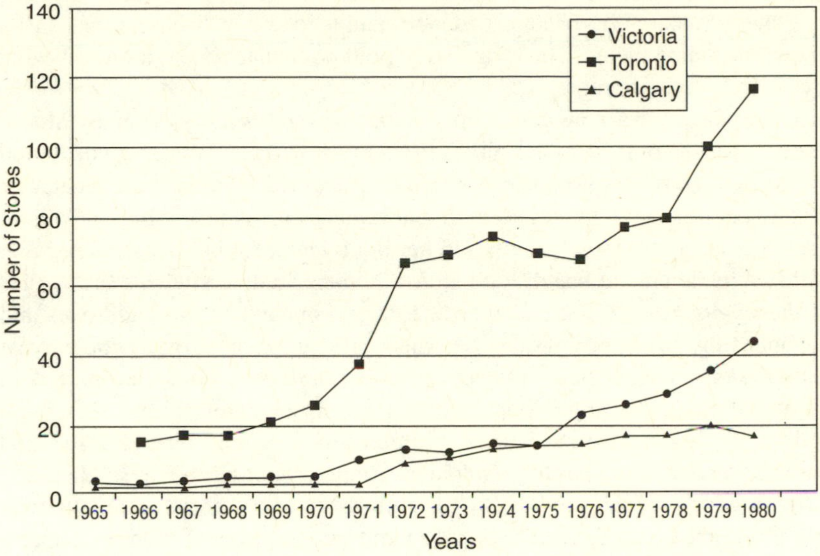

ria, British Columbia, inherited his interest in health food from his father, a competitive swimmer, who had attempted to improve his performance through vegetarianism and vitamins in the 1930s.[21]

In the late 1960s and early 1970s, the food additive bans, growing concern about pesticide residues, and alarm about the mercury contamination of fish helped lead to an explosion in the number of health food stores, as Figure 17.1 shows. Adelle Davis was at the centre of the 1970s health food revival. The press frequently referred to her as the 'high priestess' of 'natural foods' or 'Earth Mother to the Foodists.'[22] By this time, her critique of food additives and depleted soil had considerable support from environmentalists and academics. Despite an obsession with meat, Davis had a certain amount of countercultural credibility. She was open about her long psychotherapy, gleefully told reporters about her daily swims in the nude, and had published a book, *Exploring Inner Space* (1961) on her early LSD experiments.[23] Other popular authors included Jethro Kloss, the author of *Back to Eden: The Classic Guide to Herbal Medicine, Natural Foods and Home Remedies,* a book that was originally published in 1939 but was reprinted frequently in the early 1970s and seems to have been particularly popular among back-to-the-landers. Kloss had trained at John Harvey Kellogg's sanatorium and went on to a career as a health food manufacturer and lecturer. Kloss claimed that true health would come from following the 'laws of nature.' God had provided remedies for every disease; it was just a matter of finding them.[24] His ideas likely held particular appeal to the growing 'Jesus freak' movement.[25]

There was also a new generation of health food writers. Frances Moore Lappé's best-selling *Diet for a Small Planet* (1971) argued that the world food crisis could be solved if people in the Western world switched to a vegetarian diet. Lappé was more interested in global hunger than in promoting individual health. Even so, the simple recipes in her book included many ingredients that were available only at health food stores.[26] Many student kitchens had copies of the *Whole Earth Cookbook* whose authors condemned food additives and the unhealthy conditions of dairy and meat production and urged people to eat natural and organic foods.[27] Others came to health food out of an interest in Eastern religion and yoga. Macrobiotic diets, which carefully balanced 'yin' and 'yang' foods, were particularly popular among young hippies fascinated with the 'exotic' East. As Julie Stephens argues, adopting the dress, diet, and religion of the 'other' provided a particularly dramatic form of rebellion in that it critiqued both Western rationality and imperialism.[28] While the popular media often represented macrobiotics as an extreme diet that at its highest level consisted of nothing but brown rice, most macrobiotic diets included grains, vegetables, and even some fish.[29] Nevertheless, macrobiotics was an austere discipline. Georges Ohsawa's popular *Zen Macrobiotics* told people that if they were still sick after ten days of following his diets, it was because they did not fully desire to be cured.[30] Truly healthy people never felt fatigue or caught colds, had perfect memories, and were 'free from anger, fear or suffering' and 'cheerful and pleasant under all circumstances.'[31] He promised that leukemia could be cured on a diet of nothing but brown rice and other cereals while the flu could be overcome with whole rice cream, kuzu cream, and ume-syo-kuzu.

While the older type of health food store continued to expand in the early 1970s, many of the newer stores looked different from their predecessors; they sold more food and often cultivated an anti-modern appeal. Goldberrys in Toronto looked like 'an old-fashioned general store' with barrels of organically grown apples and handmade signs for exotic products like tahini and tamari.[33] In Vancouver, the turban-wearing Arran Stephens, a young hippie who had found spiritual enlightenment with his guru Sant Kirpal Singh in India, opened the natural foods supermarket, Lifestream. Lifestream had a mill that ground whole wheat flour daily. It sold organic fruits and vegetables from California as well as Asian foods such as tofu and soymilk.[34] At the same time, supermarkets and drug stores created 'natural food' sections.[35]

In Canada, one of the key sources of information for people interested in health food was *Alive Magazine*, which was given out free at health food stores across the country. The force behind *Alive* was Siegfried Gursche, who had immigrated to Canada in 1951 after doing an apprenticeship in a German health food store. In the late 1950s, he began selling imported herbal remedies at his bookstore in Vancouver. Through his involvement in the Canadian Health Food Association, he began a small magazine to promote the industry.[36] Much of the content was advertiser generated. Willie Pelzer, the founder of Sunny Crunch (and another postwar German immigrant), wrote an article praising the benefits of Sunny Crunch granola over other breakfast cereals without ever mentioning his personal interest in the company; while Sloan Alma Smith, the proprietor of the vitamin company Trophic, published articles on the merits of vitamins, again without any mention of his day job.[37] The magazine frequently highlighted the benefits of products that could be purchased in health food stores such as lecithin, vitamin E, soya beans, and golden seal. Not surprisingly, *Alive* also told people that shopping in health food stores could save them money.[38] Indeed, health food writers had little patience for the argument that health foods were expensive. As Adelle Davis argued, supplements were cheap compared with medical bills.[39]

In addition, there was a regular column on natural skin care by the German-trained esthetician and hydrotherapist Giselle Roeder and a column on herbs by Ella Birzneck, the owner of the Dominion Herbal College in Vancouver. Croft Woodruff, a health food store owner in Vancouver and a radio host, wrote a regular column on environmental issues called 'Five Minutes to Midnight' in which he warned about nitrites in meat products, water fluoridation, lead and arsenic poisoning, and the dangers of the nuclear industry. There were also recipes, gardening tips, and interviews with leading health food writers including Frances Moore Lappé, Beatrice Trum Hunter (the author of *Consumer Beware!*), and McMaster University biochemist Ross Hume Hall (a leading Canadian commentator on health, the environment, and food.) The magazine encouraged a strict and unforgiving approach to diet. An article on Halloween questioned whether parents who allowed their children candy truly cared about their kids, while another article threatened that by drinking water straight from the tap: 'you are exposing yourself and your family to a higher risk of cancer and arteriosclerosis, not to mention the viruses and bacteria which can cause illnesses such as hepatitis and gastroenteritis.'[40]

Alive offered people with long-standing health problems the promise that they could be cured through natural methods and encouraged them to take an active (and empowering) approach towards their own health. One woman wrote to tell fellow readers that her migraine headaches had been solved with Vitamin B6.[41] Another writer credited her 'youthful appearance and healthy complexion' to brewer's yeast, kelp powder, desiccated liver, lecithin, bee pollen, cod liver oil, wheat germ, and extensive vitamin supplementation.[42] A third claimed that a diet free of sugar and refined foods had improved their children's grades and behaviour.[43] But health food was not just about getting well. Much like teenage anorectics, who exert their independence through controlling their food intake, health food advocates prided themselves on their strict diets, and felt superior to those who lacked their will power and self-control.

The star of *Alive* was the Finnish-born health food writer, Paavo Airola. Like several other important players in the Canadian health food movement, Airola was a member of the Church of Jesus Christ of Latter Day Saints. The Mormon Church, which has strict edicts against smoking, drinking alcohol, and caffeine consumption, also has an interest in spiritual healing techniques.[44] Like J.B. Gladstone and Jethro Kloss, Airola believed that good health was simply a matter of following God's laws. Airola claimed to be an N.D. and Ph.D., but his N.D. was from a naturopathic diploma mill, and his Ph.D. was supposedly from Leningrad University, although he had not spent much time in Russia.[45] Airola recommended a regimen of fruits and vegetables, whole grains, seeds, and nuts. He described 'white sugar' and 'white flour' as 'nutritional mon-strosities.' Airola stressed that there were many dangers in our food, even at health food stores. He was particularly wary of rancid oils, but he also warned that 'leafy vegetables lose 50 per cent of their vitamin C *in just one day* after they have been harvested! Whole wheat flour turns rancid *in just a few days.*'[46] He thus left health food enthusiasts in a difficult position – it was important to eat as naturally as possible, but healthy natural foods would be almost impos-sible to obtain.

Fortunately, Airola did have a solution: fasting. Fasting is what animals do when they are sick. It was what Hippocrates, Galen, and Paracelsus recom-mended, as did Eastern philosophers and yogis. Rather than dieting to lose weight, it was better to fast. Europeans were already adopting it, and the famous Karolinska Institute in Stockholm had carried out studies proving its benefits.[47] The body could heal itself. 'During a prolonged fast,' he wrote, your body will wisely 'decompose and burn those cells and tissues which are diseased, dam-aged, aging or dead' while accelerating the 'building up of new health cells.'[48] In addition to curing arthritis, psoriasis, high blood pressure, headaches, and asthma, fasting would also increase the sex drive.[49] Airola made fasting sound appealing, but when *Globe and Mail* restaurant critic Joanne Kates wrote an amusing piece about following Airola's fast, she focused more on her hunger pains and ensuing domestic squabbles, although she was pleased by her weight loss.[50]

Canadians (especially stay-at-home mothers) also learned about health food through daytime television. *Yoga with Kareen* (Zebroff), was nationally syndicated on CTV for six years from 1971 to1977. The German-born Zebroff became interested in yoga in the late 1960s while living in the interior of British Columbia with her husband and three children.[51] Like many people in the industry, she inherited her interest in alternative medicine and diet from her parents, who had been interested in alternative medicine in Germany. Zebroff promised that yoga would provide renewed energy, enhance one's sex life, and take off unnecessary pounds. She recommended a yoga diet, consisting of organically grown 'natural foods' including whole wheat and other grains, fruits, and vegetables. She suggested the following 'rule of thumb': 'if it is white and refined, if it is instant, if it has chemical additives in it, if it has been chemically changed (hydrogenation of fats) – it's a no-no.'[52] She advised that food should be eaten slowly, and one should only eat when hungry. She warned that 'sugar is addictive' and that if one stopped eating sugar and refined flour one would lose weight quickly.[53] Indeed, Zebroff's obsession with weight loss probably won her many converts among women eager to reduce their waistlines at a time when a thinner female form was becoming increasingly fashionable.[54]

In Winnipeg, another German immigrant, Giselle Roeder, had her own show focusing on beauty and fitness. Trained in hydrotherapy by the Kneipp Institute in Germany, she taught Winnipegers how to alternate cold and warm baths for better health, and how to make their own fruit and vegetable juices.[55] In Vancouver, Michael Kingscott (also known as Sat Sewak Sing), a yoga and meditation teacher, had a weekly television show called 'Natural Foods Conscious Cooking.' Kingscott suggested: 'It is possible to give your friends, husbands and wives, ulcers without ever seeing them. Simply cook them a meal while you are upset and slide the food through a door to them – they'll absorb that vibration without a doubt.'[56] While Kingscott referenced the wise ways of the East for this insight, an earlier generation of health food writers had also argued that food prepared with love would be healthier for you.[57]

Others encountered natural food through the health food restaurants that were springing up across the country. Harry Stinson, who would later establish a reputation as Toronto's 'condo-king' and is a good example of how business and the counterculture could go hand-in-hand, opened up his first Groaning Board restaurant in Yorkville in 1972 when he was just eighteen years old. Two others followed. In addition to serving his special 'hot salad,' the restaurants often featured local folk musicians. At one, staff offered free cookies to anyone who could play a recognizable tune on the piano.[58] At the Beggars' Banquet restaurant in Toronto, the room was lit with oil lamps and decorated with tie-dyed fabrics. The menu changed daily and offered a wide variety of world cuisine.[59] Those searching for a more spiritual experience could go to the Hare Krishna restaurant in Toronto which opened in 1976. The vegetarian Hare

Krishnas avoided drugs and alcohol, and believed that sex should only be for procreation. Joanne Kates described it as 'austere in the extreme' but said that the food was good and cheap.[60]

In Vancouver, one of the most popular new restaurants was the Golden Lotus, which Arran Stephens opened in Kitsilano, Vancouver's 'hippie haven,' after he returned from India in 1967. Over the next few years, a small spiritual community formed around the restaurant. According to Stephens, many of the people came from the 'hippie/drug culture,' but 'at the Golden Lotus, drugs, alcohol and promiscuity' were not allowed.[61] Another local restaurant was the Naam, which was started by a former cook at the Lotus. (The space had originally been the Love Café. According to one of the current owners of the Naam, 'Their idea of pancakes was to take red dye number 2 and swirl it into a pancake and that was a psychedelic pancake. They were completely stoned all of the time, real acid heads.'[62]) The Naam was both a vegan restaurant and health food store. The food was served at a long communal table, and most of the staff were turban-wearing followers of Sant Kirpal Singh. In Winnipeg, one could eat at the natural foods co-operative, The Banyan Tree, while Calgary offered Pimpernels, The Sun Rising, and The Soup Kitchen.[63]

Canada's health food movement was best organized in Quebec, where the charismatic Jean-Marc Brunet tried to reform the way Quebecers thought about food and their health. Brunet was a former boxer who became interested in Quebec nationalism after joining the English-dominated Royal Canadian Air Force. He got involved in the Alliance laurentienne headed by the right-wing nationalist and naturopath, Raymond Barbeau. After Brunet became ill from overwork in the early 1960s, he too, began taking courses in naturopathy. In 1966, at 26 years of age, he completed his doctorate in naturopathy in the United States. That same year, he began Le Mouvement Naturiste Social (MNS) with the goal of regenerating Quebec society through the principles of 'le naturisme.' His first book outlined the philosophy and goals of the movement. *La Réforme Naturiste* began with a long cry about 'biological degeneration.' Brunet argued that this was occurring all over the Western world, but that it was of particular concern to Quebec, where there was a small francophone population in a sea of anglophone North Americans. The problem was that the laws of nature were not being respected – there were chemicals in the food, pollution in the air, and chlorine and fluoride in the water. Quebecers were poisoning themselves through medicines and vaccines and their lifestyles were too sedentary.[64] Brunet saw many signs of this 'degeneration' including a declining life expectancy, a high rate of tooth decay, and baldness. Following in a long tradition of looking to nature for lessons on how to live, Brunet argued that trees only lost their leaves when the soil was poisoned – hair loss was a clear sign that Quebecers, too, were being poisoned.[65] In his typically florid prose, he condemned the physical weakness of 'modern men,' saying: 'The most minor physical shock breaks him. A minor change in temperature weakens him. The least effort makes him sick. Slave to his voluptuous spirit, and his physical and mental laziness, he is only interested in huge stuffed arm-chairs, gargantuan dinners, super-comfortable automobiles and mansion-pal-aces where he can stretch out in front of the television in the coming evening – tired, depressed, out of breath from so much cowardliness and stupidity.'[66] Even more worrying, this sedentary lifestyle was feminizing men, especially young men. He was particularly alarmed about the 'scrawny' hippies with a 'greenish tint and pimples.'[67]

Brunet believed in eugenics and argued that people should not marry into families where there was a history of cancer, diabetes, tuberculosis, mental ill-ness, or addiction.[68] He recommended that the state should provide everyone with a biological identity card, which would classify people according to their health. Only individuals in 'perfect biological condition' should be allowed to assume important government posts.[69] He thought the state should exert careful control over advertising to ensure that none of it contributed to the physical and moral corruption of man and that the press be controlled so that it taught the lessons of 'le naturisme.' Brunet believed that modern medicine only treated the symptoms of disease and failed to cure the underlying causes. Moreover, modern medicine was at the mercy of the pharmaceutical industry whose only goal was profit. In his view, chemical medicines were 'a worse danger than the atomic bomb' and were responsible for the 'biological weakness of the human race.' He condemned vaccination as 'dangerous and ineffective.'[70]

In the early 1970s, thousands of people (mostly older women) attended annual weekend conferences sponsored by the MNS, and Brunet claimed that the organization had 100,000 members.[71] Certainly, the Mouvement attracted enormous publicity, especially in Quebec's lively tabloid market. This was partly due to the star power of Marie-Josée Longchamps, an actress on *Rue des Pignons*, a popular Quebec television show, who was also the vice-president of the MNS. (She and Brunet would later marry.) The Mouvement petered out in the mid-1970s, probably because its strident Catholicism and opposition to abortion were unpalatable to many people who were interested in what Brunet had to say about food and medicine.[72] On the advice of media baron Pierre Peladeau, the owner of Québecor, Brunet turned away from politics and began devoting more attention to expanding his network of health food stores. He began writing a daily column on naturopathy in the *Journal de Montréal* in 1978 and in the *Journal de Québec* in 1980. He continues to publish widely on health and nutrition, although his later books do not deal with eugenics.[73]

Brunet was not the only voice of health food in Quebec. There was also a net-work of co-operatively run health food stores with strong links to the growing environmental movement.[74] Nor were his views all that unusual. Adelle Davis was also concerned with biological degeneration. In *Let's Cook It Right*, for example, Davis claimed: 'Most recipe books appear to have only one designed purpose: to bring about the physical degeneration of the race at all possible speed.'[75] Her *Let's Have Healthy Children,* started with the claim that 'too many American parents are settling for mediocre children when they could have the joy and satisfaction of superior ones.'[76] Davis argued that women who did not eat well during pregnancy were likely to suffer from toxaemia and give birth prematurely and that 'these infants carry emotional scars through life.' She claimed that their children would have a high incidence of hearing defects, eye abnormalities, cerebral palsy, rickets, and anemia, and that they would do badly at school.[77] Like Brunet, this occasionally took on a nationalist tone. Her *Let's Eat Right to Keep Fit* (1970) concluded: 'If our nation is to survive as a world leader' it needs to solve its nutritional problems.[78] *Alive* also talked about the need to produce 'blue ribbon children' through good nutrition, which included laboriously prepared homemade baby food.[79]

The blossoming of the health food movement took place at the same time that second wave feminism was gathering strength. And yet, there was little evidence of this in health food writings, which often promoted quite traditional gender roles and stereotypes. Adelle Davis worried that poor nutrition was leading to boys with 'round-cheeked hips' or 'girls with narrow masculine hips.'[80] Davis warned women not to change their spouse's diets too suddenly, as it would be resented by any man who was 'not a hopeless Milquetoast.'[81] Paavo Airola described motherhood as the reason why women were created and as 'the ultimate self-realization.' He warned that in the pre-liberation era 'a woman felt secure in her home surrounded by her loving family, with children and later grandchildren ... Now, divorced or unmarried, she is thrown into the competitive dog-eat-dog man's world, forced to work and support herself, lonely, insecure, unloved and unprotected.'[82] On the other hand, writers like Frances Moore Lappé and even Adelle Davis showed that women could combine successful careers with child rearing, and that women were capable of translating complex scientific and economic ideas to a mass audience.

The movement gave people the ability to take their health into their own hands, gave them natural solutions to ongoing health problems, and encouraged them to eat a healthier diet, probably improving many people's health in the process. But it also created impossible expectations of health and an intolerance of disease and disability. In *Better Eyes without Glasses*, Gayelord Hauser declared that good nutrition and eye exercises would allow anyone to discard their prescription lenses. In *Let's Get Well*, Davis asserted that psychotherapy and diet would cure most ulcers, while diabetics could reverse their condition with vitamin B6 and other supplements.[83] The idea that nutrition could cure most ills bled easily into the idea that the sick were responsible for their fate through their own poor habits.

Despite its often-expressed social conservatism, the health food movement did much to increase environmental awareness. Health food activists drew attention to the health risks of pesticide use and promoted organic food and gardening. Their stores and books increased knowledge about the use of synthetic estrogen (DES) to promote the growth of cattle, mercury contamination of fish, and the impact of pollution on health. The health food movement also helped to make Canadians aware of the degree to which regulatory authorities were influenced by big business, especially the pharmaceutical industry, and drew attention to the use of dangerous food additives by the food processors.

The issue that most galvanized health food store owners and consumers, however, was restrictions on their ability to sell and buy vitamins and supplements. In 1967, the Food and Drug Directorate wanted a warning label on high-potency vitamins and planned to schedule vitamins and minerals as drugs. The Canadian Health Food Association defeated the proposed changes by meeting with federal officials and organizing a letter campaign. In 1971, the Ontario College of Pharmacy sent a letter to health food stores telling them that it was illegal for them to sell high-potency vitamins. The Canadian Health Food Association hired a legal team to fight back. In the mid-1970s, the Canadian Health Food Association also fought proposed restrictions in Saskatchewan and British Columbia. Although the campaigns were framed in the language of protecting people's health, they were also self-interested – vitamin sales were the biggest money maker for most health food stores.[84]

Conclusion

Young hippies were not the only Canadians interested in eating differently in the late 1960s and early 1970s. Although a few baby boomers took an active role in health food in Canada – Arran Stephens and Harry Stinson are two examples – the most prominent voices in the health food industry were somewhat older, often had roots in Europe, and were frequently quite conservative. Siegfried Gursche, Paavo Airola, Giselle Roeder, and Kareen Zebroff were all immigrants to Canada and helped to bring European, particularly Germanic and Nordic, ideas about healthy eating and body culture to a Canadian audience. Many people involved in the industry were deeply religious. The food teachings of Jean-Marc Brunet and Paavo Airola were tied to their desire to live according to what they saw as God's laws. Health food writers were frequently intolerant of illness or disability and often promoted traditional roles for women (including long hours in the kitchen.) The industry helped to raise awareness about pollution and environmental destruction but their political activities most frequently revolved around protecting their right to sell vitamins and supplements. Ultimately, health food was an individualistic enterprise. The followers of health food hoped to protect their own health in a dangerous age by taking a wide array of vitamins and supplements, eating organically, and consuming less processed food. Consumers embraced health food because it allowed them to take control of their health into their own hands. This was important in an era when faith in experts, especially physicians, was in decline, and science and technology had apparently created many new hazards in food additives, pesticides, and nuclear fallout. Although health food store owners and wholesalers were usually sincere in their desire to improve people's health, they also wanted to increase their business and protect their profits. The story of health food is part of a much broader political and cultural re-analysis of the 'long 1960s' which shows how new conservative movements were springing up alongside the new left, demonstrates how and why big business often embraced the counterculture, and explains how the radical 1960s turned into the more individualistically oriented 1970s.

ACKNOWLEDGMENTS

Thanks to the Canadian Health Food Association, especially Donna Herringer and Inga Shelton, who arranged for me to do interviews, and thanks also to all of the people who consented to be interviewed. I am grateful to Bob McMillan, Sharon Weaver, Brianna Greaves, Michelle Dubois, and Rachel Elder for research and editorial assistance.

NOTES

1 Warren Belasco, *Appetite for Change: How the Counterculture Took on the Food Industry* (Ithaca, NY: Cornell University Press, 2007 [1993]).
2 These included the following: James S. Turner, *The Chemical Feast: The Ralph Nader Study Group Report on Food Protection and the Food and Drug Administration* (New York: Grossman, 1970); Beatrice Trum Hunter, *Consumer Beware! Your Food and What Has Been Done to It* (New York: Simon and Schuster, 1971); Gene Marine and Judith Van Allen, *Food Pollution: The Violation of Our Inner Ecology* (New York: Holt, Rinehart and Winston, 1972); Jacqueline Verrett and Jean Carper, *Eating May Be Hazardous to Your Health* (New York: Simon and Schuster, 1974); Linda Pim, *Additive Alert: A Guide to Food Additives for the Canadian Consumer* (Toronto: Doubleday, 1979). For a summary, see Catherine

Carstairs, 'Food, Fear and the Environment in the Long 1960s,' in Lara Campbell, Dominique Clement, and Greg Kealey, eds., *Debating Dissent: Canada and the 1960s* (Toronto: University of Toronto Press, in press).

3　Anne Wanstall, 'Consumer Worried about Those Food Additives,' *Toronto Star*, 11 Aug. 1972, 53.

4　Paul Starr, *The Social Transformation of American Medicine* (New York: Basic Books, 1982); James Whorton, *Nature Cures: The History of Alternative Medicine in America* (Oxford: Oxford University Press, 2002).

5　Sandra Morgan, *Into Our Own Hands: The Women's Health Movement in the United States, 1969–1990* (New Brunswick, NJ: Rutgers University Press, 2002); Ruth Rosen, *The World Split Open: How the Modern Women's Movement Changed America* (New York: Viking, 2000).

6　Anne Harrington, *The Cure Within: A History of Mind-Body Medicine* (New York: W.W. Norton, 2008), 175–205.

7　Rima D. Apple, *Vitamania: Vitamins in American Culture* (New Brunswick, NJ: Rutgers University Press, 1996).

8　Women have had a long history of involvement in anti-vivisection movements and in the environmental movement. See, e.g., Lynda Birke, 'Supporting the Underdog: Animal Rights and Citizenship in the Work of Alice Morgan Wright and Edith Goode,' *Women's History Review* 9/4 (2000): 693–719; Adam Rome, '"Give Earth a Chance": The Environmental Movement and the Sixties,' *Journal of American History* 90/2 (2003): 525–54.

9　Lynn Y. Weiner, 'Reconstructing Motherhood: The La Leche League in Postwar America,' *Journal of American History* 80/4 (1994): 1357–81; Thomas Frank, *The Conquest of Cool* (Chicago, IL: University of Chicago Press, 1997).

10　Stephen Nissenbaum, *Sex, Diet and Debility in Jacksonian America* (Westport, CN: Greenwood, 1980).

11　Ronald Numbers, *Prophetess of Health: A Study of Ellen G. White* (New York: Harper and Row, 1976); Harvey Levenstein, *Revolution at the Table: The Transformation of the American Diet* (Berkeley, CA: University of California Press, 2003).

12　For a list of natural health pioneers, see the following: Siegfried Gursche and Rona Zoltan, *Encyclopedia of Natural Healing: The Authoritative Reference to Alternative Health and Healing, A Practical Self-Help Guide* (Burnaby, BC: Alive Books, 1998); Michael Hau, *The Cult of Health and Beauty in Germany: A Social History, 1890–1930* (Chicago, IL: University of Chicago Press, 2003); Corinna Treitel, 'Nature and the Nazi Diet,' *Food and Foodways* 17 (2009): 139–58.

13　Robert C. Fuller, *Alternative Medicine and American Religious Life* (New York: Oxford University Press, 1989); Robert Proctor, *The Nazi War on Cancer* (Princeton, NJ: Princeton University Press, 1999); Treitel, 'Nature and the Nazi Diet';

Arnaud Baubérot, 'Un projet de réforme hygiénique des modes de vie: Naturists et vegetarians à la belle époque,' *French Politics, Culture and Society* 26/3 (2008): 1–22; Corinna Treitel, 'Max Rubner and the Biopolitics of Rational Nutrition,' *Central European History* 41 (2008): 1–25; Richard Moore-Colyer, 'Towards "Mother Earth": Jorian Jenks, Organicism, the Right and the British Union of Fascists,' *Journal of Contemporary History* 39/3 (2004): 353–71.

14 The first health food book that I know of in Canada is Robert Jackson, *How to Always Be Well* (Toronto: Print-Craft, 1927).

15 Mary Jukes, 'Once over Lightly,' *Globe and Mail*, 11 Sept. 1961, 16.

16 Canadian Health Food Association, *A Historic Look at the Life and Times of the Canadian Health Food Association and the People Who Made Them Happen* (Vancouver: Author, 2004).

17 Gaylord Hauser, *Look Younger, Live Longer* (New York: Farrar and Straus, 1950), and *Be Happier, Be Healthier* (New York: Farrar, Straus and Young, 1952); Lelord Kordel, *Eat and Grow Younger* (Cleveland, OH: World Publishing, 1952), and *Cook Right – Live Longer* (New York: Putnam, 1966); Carlton Fredericks, *Eat, Live and Be Merry* (New York: Paxton-Slade, 1951), and *Psycho-Nutrition* (New York: Grosset and Dunlap, 1976); Cathryn Elwood, *Feel Like a Million!* (New York: Devin-Adair, 1956 [1952]).

18 Daniel Yergin, 'Let's Get Adelle Davis Right: Supernutritionist,' *New York Times*, 20 May 1973, 286; James Harvey Young, 'Adelle Davis,' in Barbara Sicherman and Carol Hurd Green, eds., *Notable American Women: The Modern Period* (Cambridge, MA: Harvard University Press, 1980), 179–80; Adelle Davis, *Let's Have Healthy Children* (New York: New American Library, 1972); Adelle Davis, *Let's Cook It Right* (New York : Harcourt, Brace and World, 1962), *Let's Eat Right to Keep Fit* (New York: Harcourt, Brace and World, 1954), and *Let's Get Well* (Scarborough: Signet, 1972 [1965]).

19 Letter from Charlie Gibson to Dorothy Sinclair, Nutrition Division, 15 Oct. 1964, in Library and Archives of Canada (LAC), RG 29, vol. 931, part 2, file 386-4-5.

20 Anne Wanstall, 'Health Food Fans Say Man Pollutes Himself,' *Toronto Star*, 17 April 1970, 61.

21 Interview with Bruce Reid, 15 July 2004. Physical culture advocates such as Bernarr Macfadden and Charles Atlas were important promoters of 'natural' ways of health. Janet Golden and Elizabeth Toon, '"Live Clean, Think Clean and Don't Go to Burelsque Shows": Charles Atlas as Health Advisor,' *Journal of the History of Medicine* 57/1 (2002): 39–60.

22 'Outspoken Adelle Davis Ate Her Way to Fame,' *Toronto Star*, 24 May 1972; Jane Howard, 'Earth Mother to the Foodists,' *Life*, 22 Oct. 1971, 67–70.

23 Jane Dunlop, *Exploring Inner Space* (New York: Harcourt, Brace and World,

1961). This book was initially published under a pseudonym but she was quite open about it in discussions with reporters in the 1970s.

24 Jethro Kloss, *Back to Eden: The Classic Guide to Herbal Medicine, Natural Foods and Home Remedies* (Santa Barbara, CA: Woodbridge Press, 1975), v–viii.

25 Robert S. Ellwood, *The Sixties Spiritual Awakening: American Religion Moving from Modern to Postmodern* (New Brunswick, NJ: Rutgers University Press, 1994); Timothy Miller, *The 60s Communes: Hippies and Beyond* (Syracuse, NY: Syracuse University Press, 1999), 92–127.

26 Frances Moore Lappé, *Diet for a Small Planet: Twentieth Anniversary Edition* (New York: Ballantine, 1991).

27 Sharon Cadwallader and Judi Ohr, *Whole Earth Cookbook: Access to Natural Cooking* (Boston, MA: Houghton Mifflin, 1972).

28 Julie Stephens, *Anti-Disciplinary Protest: Sixties Radicalism and Postmodernism* (Cambridge: Cambridge University Press, 1998), 51.

29 George Alexander, 'Brown Rice as a Way of Life,' *New York Times*, 12 March 1972, SM87; 'Zen Diet Assailed by AMA Council as Peril to Health,' *New York Times*, 19 Oct. 1971, 29.

30 Georges Ohsawa, *Zen Macrobiotics* (Los Angeles: Ohsawa Foundation, 1965), 8–9.

31 Ibid., 7–20, quote at 15.

32 Ibid., 67–8.

33 Gale Garnett, 'More on Mother Muesil's Health Foods,' *Toronto Star*, 25 Jan. 1972, 9; 'The Flowering of the Health Food Industry,' *Saturday Night*, May 1980, 3.

34 Interview with Arran Stephens, 30 June 2003. For more, see Stephens' spiritual biography: *Journey to the Luminous: Encounters with Mystic Adepts of Our Century* (Seattle, WA: Elton-Wolf, 1999), 204–5.

35 'New Health Food Centre,' advertisement in *Toronto Star*, 23 Nov. 1971, 18; Sidney Katz, 'Pollution Makes Health Foods Boom in the Suburbs and Supermarkets,' *Toronto Star*, 1 May 1971, 18.

36 Interview with Siegfried Gursche, 23 July 2003. The magazine was initially under the auspices of the Canadian Health Food Association, but not everyone liked the magazine, so Gursche began operating it independently.

37 Willie Pelzer, 'Granola versus Brand X,' *Alive* 3 (1975): 12; Al Smith, 'Vitamins Are Not Toxic,' *Alive* 3 (1975): 19; Sloan Alma Smith, 'Natural or Synthetic,' *Alive* 5 (1976): 6.

38 'Are Health Foods Expensive: It Depends on What You Get for What You Pay,' *Alive* 5 (1976): 21.

39 Davis, *Let's Get Well*, 408.

40 Lucy Mekler, 'Halloween: Is It Good for Your Children?' *Alive* 21 (Sept. 1979): 27; Rebecca Clarkes, 'Your Tap Water: Does It Smell Like a Swimming Pool?'

Alive 24 (April 1979): 17.

41 Mrs Phyllis Reeves, 'Aid for Angela,' *Alive* 4 (Nov. 1975): 4.

42 Reva Spence, 'Youthful Appearance,' *Alive* 32 (Sept. 1980): 5.

43 Isobel Wilson, 'Hyperactive No More,' *Alive* 20 (May 1978): 5.

44 Steven Simmerman, 'The Mormon Health Traditions: An Evolving View of Modern Medicine,' *Journal of Religion and Health* 32/3 (1993): 189–96.

45 Rebecca Clarkes, 'Paavo Airola: The Scientist and the Man,' *Alive* 28 (Dec. 1979): 22.

46 Paavo Airola, *Are You Confused?* (Tucson, AZ: Health Plus Publishers, 1971), 93.

47 Ibid., 104–5.

48 Ibid., 112–13.

49 Ibid., 119.

50 Joanne Kates, 'Slimming Down for Spring,' *Globe and Mail*, 25 April 1981, F7.

51 Eve Rockett, 'How to Get Started in Yoga before You Really Get Started,' *Chatelaine* (Feb. 1973): 64.

52 Kareen Zebroff, *The ABC of Yoga* (Vancouver: Forbez, 1971), 8.

53 Ibid., 9.

54 Peter Stearns, *Fat History: Bodies and Beauty in the Modern West* (New York: New York University Press, 2002).

55 Canadian Health Food Association, *A History*, 24; Interview with Giselle Roeder, 19 Feb. 2004.

56 Michael Kingscott, 'Conscious Cookery,' *Alive* 3 (Sept. 1975): 7.

57 See, e.g., Hauser, *Be Happier, Be Healthier*, 184.

58 Joanne Kates, 'Fine New Groaning Board Hedges on Health Food Redo,' *Globe and Mail*, 6 Oct., 1975, 14.

59 Joanne Kates, 'A Vegetarian Dinner for $4,' *Globe and Mail*, 16 Dec. 1974, 14.

60 Joanne Kates, 'Krishna for Those of Purer Bent,' *Globe and Mail*, 6 Dec. 1976, 16.

61 Interview with Arran Stephens, 30 June 2003.

62 Interview with Bob Woodsworth, 5 Aug. 2003.

63 Siegfried Gursche, 'Hungry in Canada,' *Alive* 5 (Jan. 1976): 8.

64 Brunet, *La réforme naturiste* (Montreal : Éditions du Jour, 1969), 11–14.

65 Ibid., 43–4.

66 Ibid., 44–5. Original: 'La moindre choc physique le brise. Le moindre écart de température l'affaiblit. Le moindre effort lui fait mal. Esclave de son esprit de volupté et de sa paresse physique et mentale, il n'a d'intérêt que pour les gros fauteils rembourrés, les dîners gargantuesques, les automobiles super-confortables et les maisons-palaces où il peut aller s'étendre devant son téléviseur, de soir venu, fatigué, déprimé, essoufflé par tant de lâcheté et de stupidité' (my translation, CC).

67 Ibid., 45–6.

68 Ibid., 95.

69 Ibid., 110.

70 Ibid., 48, 49, 51.

71 Clipping from *Le Journal de Montréal*, 17 March 1973, Bibliotheque and Archives nationales de Québec, Montreal (hereafter BANQ), Fonds Jean Marc Brunet, box 1, file 26A; Daniel Pinard, 'Le Combat Naturix.' *Le Magazine Maclean*, Oct. 1974, 22, 50–1, 57–8.

72 See, e.g., 'Les naturistes se politisent,' *La Patrie*, 14 June 1972, in BANQ, Fonds Jean Marc Brunet, box 1, file 26A.

73 Interview with Jean-Marc Brunet, 8 July 2003.

74 Jean-Gay Vaillancourt, 'Évolution, diversité et spécificité des associations écologiques québecoises: De la contre-culture et du conservationnisme à l'environnemntalisme et à l'écosocialisme,' *Sociologie et sociétés* 13/1 (1981): 85.

75 Davis, *Let's Cook it Right*, 3–4.

76 Davis, *Let's Have Healthy Children*, 3.

77 Ibid., 92.

78 Davis, *Let's Eat Right to Keep Fit* (New York: Signet, 1970), 272.

79 Natalie Rogers, 'Feeding Your Baby Naturally,' *Alive* 6 (March 1976): 19.

80 Davis, *Let's Eat Right to Keep Fit*, 166–7.

81 Ibid., 6.

82 Airola, *Everywoman's Book*, 408.

83 Gayelord Hauser, *Better Eyes without Glasses* (London: Farber and Farber, 1974); Davis, *Let's Get Well*, 82–105.

84 Rebecca Clarkes, 'Are Vitamins Drugs?' *Alive* 3 (Sept. 1975): 17–18; 'Lawyer for Health Food Dealers Says Sale of Vitamins Legal,' *Toronto Star*, 3 Aug. 1971, 17.

18 'Meat Stinks/Eat Beef Dyke!' Coming Out as a Vegetarian in the Prairies

VALERIE J. KORINEK

In June 2008, singer k.d. lang was awarded an honorary doctorate from the University of Alberta. Timed to coincide with lang's concert tour stop in Edmonton, this privilege was intended to celebrate a native Albertan's accomplishments in arts and activism. The organizers also sought to claim, in some fashion, lang's endeavours for the University of Alberta. What went unstated were the past controversies, or any suggestion that one of Alberta's famous exports might have an uneasy history with the people of her home province. The brief summary of her activism noted that she was 'a champion of sexual minority rights who is committed to the celebration of diversity across all areas of human difference' and a member of 'artists against racism.'[1] In her brief comments to the assembly, lang urged everyone to realize that 'we have a moral obligation – not just to Alberta, not just to this University, not just to this country, not just to human beings – but to every living being on the globe.'[2] lang's spare address was moving and eloquent but one wonders how many in the convocation audience were completely attuned to the nuances of her speech?

Drawing on her Buddhism, the message lang chose to share with the graduates was one of outreach in the form of global connections, spirituality, and open-mindedness. While unstated, her ambivalence about the province and her experiences of growing up in a conventional Alberta small town echo throughout her speech, which repeatedly encouraged the graduates to embrace growth and personal development. One may speculate that lang's comments were partly motivated by the events of eighteen years prior, when her ranching community had denounced her as traitor for her vegetarian political views. A public service announcement advocating vegetarianism found lang pilloried rather than praised by her fellow Albertans. This chapter analyses this controversial episode, which spanned the spring and summer of 1990, highlighting in particular, the local, provincial, and national reactions to lang's vegetarian politics.

This illuminating case reveals critical but little explored linkages between food history and the histories of sexuality and activism. In this regard, the essay can be usefully read alongside several contributions in this volume, including Catherine Carstairs' chapter on the postwar health movement and Julie Guard's chapter on milk and political mobilizing. Furthermore, the lang case study also sheds light on the role that gender, sexuality, region, and food symbolism have played in the shaping of contemporary viewpoints on matters of social diversity. Like Maura Hanrahan's chapter on Newfoundland foodways, S. Holyck Hunchuck's chapter on Ukrainian food monuments in western Canada, and Megan Davies' chapter on foods of the Peace River, a regional analysis is central. However, my focus is not on foodways as a signifier or marker of ethnic Canadian identity but on food choices as signifiers of contested notions of 'radical' and 'traditional' sexualities with the region.

'Absolute Torch and Twang':[3] Queering the Prairies

In their important histories of sexuality and community formation, scholars such as George Chauncey, Marc Stein, Elizabeth Lapovsky Kennedy, Nan Alamilla Boyd, and others have highlighted the importance of an intricate network of bars (working class, tourist and, later, gay and lesbian places) and, less commonly, restaurants, diners, and coffee shops that served as the site for gay, lesbian, bisexual, and transgendered (glbt) socializing, identity formation, and political activism.[4] But, while it is a given that such sites are focal points for glbt histories, the heavily urban-focused scholarship has yet to explore the full range of the venues involved, including those based in small towns or heavily rural regions. In my larger project, which seeks to historicize the creation of gay and lesbian communities in the Canadian prairies, social spaces figure prominently because of the importance of local sites to forging identity. Moreover, it seeks to show that while much prairie-based gay and lesbian community socialization and identification paralleled developments elsewhere, there were also some significantly unique regional experiences. One particularly noteworthy pattern specific to western Canada, for example, was the existence of membership-only gay and lesbian clubs and bars. Working-class cafés were also popular regional locations for gay and lesbian socializing in the prairies and also offered a potential opportunity for forging alliances and interrelationships between members of racially and sexually marginalized groups. Moreover, food, and in particular, prairie food traditions, allowed gays and lesbians to build queer communities, and to establish bridges to mainstream communities, in ways that were authentically western Canadian. That is, familiar modes of prairie-based socializing could be used to new queer ends. Naturally, there were also moments of conflict and contestation, and those episodes illustrate much about the region's supposedly strong 'community' values and the often fragile respect that mainstream communities held for diversity and unconventionality.

The lang episode of 1990 provides one such contested moment. Her decision to publicly 'come out' as a vegetarian was interpreted as a politically charged attack on the economy, culture, and lifestyle of rural Albertans. The episode reveals the extent to which small town people can stretch their community values to accommodate a range of political, gendered, and sexual differences, and, conversely, what factors precipitate the collapse of that tenuous type of tolerance. A close reading of the episode reveals a particularly fascinating and multilayered story about food, sexuality, rural dwellers, and popular culture. The case study also touches on some of the important contemporary issues concerning food politics, raising questions about the production and marketing of food commodities and the ways that our seemingly simple 'food choices' are actually linked to much larger economic, political, and international dynamics. By exploring the gendered, class, and regional biases evident in so-called food choices and by demonstrating that food and sexual politics were sometimes closely linked, this chapter also aims to offer some thought-provoking insights into the construction and expression of western Canadian cultural values.

'Ingenué':[5] Decoding the PETA Ad

In spring 1990, lang donated her time to film a public service announcement for People for the Ethical Treatment of Animals (PETA),[6] who, clearly, had hoped to harness her celebrity for the promotion of vegetarianism in the United States. A vegetarian since her teenage years and a PETA member for one year, lang filmed the ad in Los Angeles. The ad was part of a larger series of celebrity vegetarian endorsements. According to *Alberta Report*, PETA had also recruited musicians such as Paul McCartney, the B-52s, and Belinda Carlisle as well as actor Bea Arthur to pitch vegetarianism.[7] In contrast to more recent PETA television or YouTube videos or print ads, which employ shock tactics or heterosexualized displays of attractive models and celebrities to garner attention for their campaigns against animal cruelty and exploitation, the 1990 'Meat Stinks' commercial featuring lang used a relatively low-key approach.[8] As country music plays in the background, the youthful and androgynous lang (who is dressed in jean jacket and overalls) comments on the offensiveness of eating beef in a seemingly innocent manner, asking: 'We all love animals but why do we call some pets and some dinner?' Moving on to the harsher truths, she delivers the key statement of the ad and one that would be replayed, critiqued, and ultimately condemned: 'If you knew how meat was grown you'd lose your lunch. I know, I'm from cattle country and that's why I became a vegetarian. Meat stinks!'[9] Following that declaration, the ad returns to a more playful tone with lang reassuring viewers that they need not worry about conversion to vegetarianism marginalizing them because 'there's millions of us.'

In retrospect, this ad initially strikes one as being quite tame, its moderate tone underscored by the visual, which features a friendly celebrity playfully hugging her bovine friend 'Lulu.' Yet, it was also emblematic of lang's forthright determination to speak out about political matters. According to her manager, they had talked about the potentially negative impact of the advertisement on her hometown folk, but either she was naïve about being able to win over Albertans or she actively sought out the debate. Recently, in a retrospective interview with the *Globe and Mail* which profiled lang's twenty-five-year career, her long-time songwriting partner Ben Mink offered the observation that she had, in the past, been 'a little free with her thoughts and didn't understand the repercussions that some of her words might have.'[10] The ad proved to be a lightning rod for controversy, and protest came from a variety of corners – cattle ranchers, Albertans, rural dwellers, and country music fans. Support would also be forthcoming, but that support, from vegetarians, champions of free speech, and people who called themselves 'liberal-minded' was most prevalent in areas outside of Alberta, and more guarded when it emerged from within cattle country. For PETA, all of the media exposure provided significant free publicity.

'Angel with a Lariat':[11] lang's Biography

Given her international success, many people are now familiar with lang's biography but a brief sketch is in order. Born and raised in a professional middle-class Alberta family, lang spent her formative years in Consort, Alberta, a small wheat and ranching community southeast of Edmonton. After high school graduation, lang attended Red Deer College (212 kilometres west of Consort), where she began her professional recording career. In 1985, she achieved national recognition within the Canadian music recording scene and was awarded the Juno Award for most promising female vocalist. A series of three progressively more successful country music albums – *Angel with a Lariat* (1987), *Shadowland* (1988), and *Absolute Torch and Twang* (1989) – solidified her national reputation, and resulted in five more Juno Awards, including the 1989 award for best female vocalist. Internationally, she became increasingly known in American country music circles, winning two Grammy awards (a 1988 award with Roy Orbison for best Country Vocal Collaboration, followed by a 1989 award for Best Female Country Vocalist). Up to this point, she had made no public disclosure about her sexual orientation but those who listened to her music and observed her idiosyncratic fashion and personal style recognized that she was a unique presence within the country music world. Fans chose to appreciate her talent and either accepted or wilfully ignored the more complicated questions raised by her androgynous appearance. According to *Alberta Report*, 'she's seen as a weird-but-good local kid who hit the big time.'[12]

In a 2002 article published in the gay newsmagazine, the *Advocate*, Dan Mathews recollected that 'kd lang's journey to coming out as a lesbian actually began in June 1990, when she came out as a vegetarian.'[13] Indeed, until lang openly denigrated the beef industry, most people were content to turn a blind eye to her unconventionality, preferring to describe her as talented if 'quirky' (one of the most common adjectives applied to the singer). The town of Consort formally proclaimed their pride in her achievements in 1986 with the installation of two large highway signs that declared 'Consort, Home of k.d. lang.' The signs were also part of an official civic thank you to lang, who had performed at a benefit concert that raised over $10,000 for the town's recreation facilities.[14] But when lang criticized the cattle industry – a sector so integral to historical and mythic representations of Alberta society and economy – the relationship was deeply tarnished.

Alberta's Ranching and Cattle Industry

Ranching and cattle production are significant economic drivers in Alberta. According to 2007 Statistics Canada figures, 40 per cent of Canada's beef cow herd were resident in Alberta.[15] As the academic Gwendolyn Blue has insightfully observed, for Albertans, 'beef' is no simple commodity but rather a potent symbol of provincial identity.[16] This is not surprising given the agricultural and commercial realities: a significant proportion of Canada's production and processing of beef cattle is situated in Alberta. But Blue also acknowledges the role played by sophisticated marketers at Alberta Beef Producers in transforming this food commodity into an iconic representation of the province's geographical splendour, independent spirit, agricultural industries, and ultimately, social values. Her work analyses how the marketing board employs classically Albertan scenes of cattle, wide-open skies, ranch lands, mountains, male and female cowboys, and ranching iconography to effectively brand beef as Albertan. This association was aided and abetted by the long-standing adoration of Albertans with the cowboy iconography so publicly displayed and bolstered by the annual Calgary Stampede. Thus, it follows that those opposed to beef would be portrayed as anti-Albertan. Enter lang and her PETA ad and the tensions between provincial food symbolism, gender, and sexuality proved combustible.

'Invincible Summer'[17]

The story of lang's vegetarianism first broke on the U.S. entertainment television newscast *Entertainment Tonight*, but the news rapidly spread across North America as both Canadian and U.S. media producers and consumers entered the fray. An examination of the coverage the story received in four major Canadian regional and national papers – the *Edmonton Journal*, *Calgary Herald*, *Toronto Star*, and *Globe and Mail* – and in the right-wing provincial newsmagazine, *Alberta Report*, indicates a noticeable difference in evaluations of the controversy. In the non-western media reports, journalists adopted a jocular tone, often using puns, wordplay, and humour to describe the 'beef' that Canadian cattlemen had with lang. There was no jocular tone to the articles published in the *Calgary Herald*, the *Edmonton Journal*, and *Alberta Report*, where journalists were far more critical of lang's outspokenness and of the way in which she had quite literally raised a 'stink' in country circles.[18] Very quickly, a backlash began to mobilize. A *Calgary Herald* article reported that small town country music stations in Stettler and High River were prepared to pull lang's music out of rotation if the controversy continued. It was reported that '60% of callers in a country radio station poll said k.d. lang's anti-meat advertisements stink.'[19] A few days after the reports of the poll, Larry Steckline, a Wichita broadcaster who owned country music stations in several small Kansas communities, declared that he would not air lang's music. 'I have no problem with her being a vegetarian,' he stated, adding, 'she can eat what she wants.' But he did have a 'problem' with 'somebody with a name in this industry coming down hard on the number one industry in our state. That's not what I call ladylike.'[20] Other stations in western U.S. states, including in Nebraska, Montana, Missouri, and Wyoming, quickly followed suit. It would be her hometown, however, that offered lang the sharpest rebuke for her actions, and their response made Steckline's criticism seem quaint by comparison.

Given the direct or indirect economic importance of agriculture and ranching in Consort (then a population of 700 people), it was not surprising that the mood of the townsfolk was testy. Residents who agreed to be interviewed by the press were clearly experiencing a range of emotions – shock, hurt, anger, and incredulity that lang could have spoken so critically of the local economy and, by their reasoning, openly criticized her hometown. They personalized her message and regarded her comments as a clear critique of their lives and livelihood. A local rancher, Roger Buxton, was quoted in the *Edmonton Journal*, saying, 'We feel betrayed ... we were pretty proud of her up until she did this. That pride is kind of half dead right now.'[21] Throughout this event, daily reactions from Consort appeared as the front page news in the *Edmonton Jour-*

nal. Both of its local radio stations, CFCW and CFOK, pulled her music from rotation because, according to music director Byron Trekoffy, their economic interests (that is, their advertising) were highly dependent on the agricultural business and rural listeners.

The news coverage was dominated by the many negative responses of people who criticized lang for issuing intemperate comments and worried about their possible economic ramifications, but a minority viewpoint did also emerge, and it, too, got some media play. For instance, a front page story on the *Edmonton Journal* reported that thirty-six-year-old Marjorie Hannah, a lifelong Consort resident, intended to organize a weekend rally where she hoped her sign 'We still love you k.d! And we still love beef!' might reduce tensions and bring the two sides together. People who commented publicly rationalized their authority to speak by virtue of their tenure in the community or their occupations (cattle ranchers). Hannah indicated she felt compelled to offer support to the Lang family, particularly Audrey Lang (k.d.'s mother) who at that time still resided in Consort. Reportedly, Mrs Lang found herself being harassed by abusive phone calls. There had been an escalation in local ire once the initial shock receded, and soon there were local threats about burning down the k.d. signs.[22] Few of those quoted in the article gave Hannah's attempts to make peace, and bridge the two sides, much credence. The mayor claimed that ranchers would picket any pro–k.d. lang rally in town, but Roger Buxton quashed that notion with evident machismo, stating, 'We don't do things like that here. If cattlemen don't like it, they just leave it. It's a big country. There's lots of room for ding-a-lings to do whatever they want.'[23] The president of the National Farmers Union, Wayne Easter, also entered the fray by endorsing the radio ban. 'I like her music,' he said, 'but if she's on some kind of a witch hunt or endangering the livelihood of cattlemen I would be in favour of not having anything to do with her music.' In all seriousness, he also told the *Journal* reporter that lang should be careful lest she become the 'Brigitte Bardot of the cattle industry.'[24] Easter was clearly keen to protect the 'cattlemen' (and they were always men) from the economic peril caused by female, animal-hugging celebrities. Such women were either dangerously idiotic or misguided about the appropriate purpose of animals raised or harvested for food, fur, and by-products – and not as pets.

The rally itself became the site for the most contested moment of the controversy. The k.d. supporters tried to amplify her right to freedom of speech, and to not be branded by her hometown as a traitor, but they were handed a less than ideal set of circumstances. First, the event drew slightly more than a dozen participants, primarily young people. Second, the town signs were defaced. Initially, they had been covered in 'I Love Alberta Beef' stickers, but on the night before Sunday's rally, someone had covered one of the signs with graffiti that bore the hateful message 'Eat Beef Dyke.'[25] The rally organizer expressed shock, stating, 'I'm ashamed of whoever did it ... it was a spineless coward. They have to sneak away in the dead of night to do it.' Whoever defaced the sign was well versed in the classic derogatory epithets for lesbians but also clearly intended the homophobic message to publicly 'out' the singer, and by implication, damage her both socially and economically. The lang supporters valiantly tried to remove the degrading graffiti, and when that proved only partially successful, they marched along the main street to the Consort Sportex for their rally. Significantly, few of the townspeople wished to be associated with the sign's message, suggesting that they viewed this slur as having stepped over the line of acceptable behaviour. But the *Edmonton Journal* did manage to capture the views of oil rig worker Cliff Carpenter who offered this blunt observation: 'this is where she comes from. This is a beef-eating community. You don't screw where you come from. She should use her brains before she opens her mouth.'[26]

The Consort signs, which had been permanently defaced by the graffiti, were removed for repainting. Even this bureaucratic matter became fodder for the press, as the *Edmonton Journal* published a self-congratulatory article about the community-mindedness of most Albertans. It reported that Consort resident Jack Sumner had graciously offered to repaint the signs free of charge. Since Sumner was 'branding and inoculating his herd' and, hence, preoccupied, his wife Frances spoke to the press on her husband's behalf, stating, 'I know she made a horrible mistake, but it doesn't do any good to deface her sign. That's just meat heads that did it.'[27] Two town officials, the mayor and the recreation director, both denounced the action of the vandals while professing they had no idea who the perpetrators might be. The RCMP was reportedly investigating the incident, but when asked about potential suspects, Corporal Terry McMahon's public statement revealed the Mounties' scepticism. Claiming that 'everybody who has ever barbecued, raised, trucked, or otherwise benefited from the production of beef is a suspect,' he added, 'We're always hopeful, but when you have 10,000 suspects, it's hard to limit it down.'[28] When Audrey Lang returned to Consort from Vancouver, where she had been staying with her daughter, she indicated she was encouraged by the considerable support shown to them. She particularly commended Marjorie Hannah for being 'the most courageous person in town.' Interestingly, Mrs Lang reported that 'there was a count of [k.d. lang's] mail' which was received in Vancouver at her management office, 'and well over 50 per cent of it was from ranchers, farmers and beef eaters – they made a point of saying that. But they were broad minded enough to know she should be able to speak her mind.'[29] While we cannot know whether the 'ranchers and beef consumers' were Albertans, what is evident is that privately a significant proportion of those who wrote to k.d.'s management offices were prepared to give her their support even if publicly the debate had become quite polarized between urbanities and rural people, vegetarians and beef consumers.

Alberta Report's Perspective and Reader Responses

Given the polarization in Alberta, it was not surprising that *Alberta Report*, the very popular, albeit right wing, homophobic 'newsmagazine' entered the fray with a series of articles. Elsewhere, researcher Gloria Filax has comprehensively enumerated how the instalments of this weekly newsmagazine 'produced' homophobia within Alberta in the 1990s.[30] Driven by their publisher Link Byfield's ambitious circulation goals, *AR* routinely published sensationalistic articles that, as Filax claims, 'cultivated a moral panic about homosexuality.' Most disturbing of all, Byfield's comprehensive regional news coverage, and the policy of providing free copies throughout the province, meant that the paper's 'sensationalized representations of "homosexuals" and "homosexuality" were everywhere – on school and library shelves and bank counters, in doctors' and dentists' offices, and on the coffee tables in Albertan households. The paper thus informed and influenced thinking about homosexuality, discussions over gay issues, and government actions and policy in relation to queer Albertans.'[31] Such a magazine would hardly ignore the lang episode. In total, *AR* published two articles and one editorial on the subject as well as a series of readers' letters. In the most substantive article, writer Peter Shawn Taylor described the singer as a 'wrecker' of Alberta's rural economy who, in concert with 'veggie activists,' sought to inflict the same economic sanctions on the cattle industry that had befallen the Newfoundland seal hunt. Taylor noted that the executive director of the Canadian Sealers Association, Art Pearce, reported that PETA was responsible for gutting their industry (he claimed a drop 'from $12 million in 1982 to $100,000').[32] Pearce's economic warnings and the article's overall tone were intended to stress the severity of PETA's threat to the cattle industry, and perhaps more insidiously, to rural values and small town life.[33]

As for Byfield's editorial, it began with some half-hearted praise for lang's singing abilities, and her courage 'to look and act as weird as she does,' adding: 'It isn't only of the approved kind of weirdness, like those of pop artists and the more flamboyant homosexuals. It is a weirdness very much her own.'[34] Like the homophobic graffiti on the Consort sign, the homophobic message in Byfield's editorial was evident. According to Byfield's disturbingly apocalyptic message, vegetarian politics derived from 'the morality of the jungle' and the 'vegetable militants [sic]' are in alignment with those who agitate for 'the right to divorce, the right to sex, a right to any form of medicine, a right to a comfortable income, a right to kill unwanted children … the list is getting very long.'[35] Given its core audience of politically and economically right-wing provincial readers, *Alberta Report* was seldom subtle in its campaigns against socialism, feminism, or activism related to 'special rights' for homosexuals, although when it came to publishing letters, it did allow for some variety of opinion because the publishers knew it stimulated interest in the periodical. Similar to those in the *Calgary Herald* or the *Edmonton Journal*, correspondents to *AR* were not shy about criticizing the magazine, but especially curious in this case is that the majority of the published letters were critical of *AR* coverage. (The opposite was usually the case.) Criticizing the collapsing of vegetarianism and radical politics, Peter Lyle of Toronto, for example, rhetorically asked 'why this reference to homosexuals. What has this got to do with her beliefs?' He then added: 'Remember Jane Fonda? Everybody said she was "weird" as well, but she turned out to be right in her disgust for the Vietnam War.'[36] Significantly, Lyle also indicated that he was a vegetarian. So, too, did David Stowe from Calgary, Alberta, another letter writer who was critical of the paper's coverage. He wrote: 'I find your recent attack on KD Lang … pathetic and ill-informed. If anyone represents the true Alberta heritage of originality, independence of spirit, and lack of pretentiousness it is k.d. lang. The attempts made by said writers to belittle her many accomplishments are due solely to envy and jealousy.'[37]

'Even Cowgirls Get the Blues':[38] Marketing Alberta Beef

However, few defenders, let alone western critics, would have agreed with Stowe's claim that lang epitomized the 'true Alberta heritage.' For the critics, lang represented the antithesis of 'Alberta values' attached as they were to working, living, and believing in cattle. Blue's analysis of the award-winning advertising campaigns of the Alberta Beef Producers, entitled RancHERS, is especially helpful here. The ads conveyed an explicitly heterosexual message by depicting images of multigenerational groups of grandmothers, mothers, and daughters from the ranching industry. Their current campaign, 'Raised Right,' which simultaneously trumpets their environmentally respectful farming protocols and their multigenerational ranching families, similarly shows how beef marketers brand their product as a potent symbol of provincial family values.[39] It thus follows that anyone critical of the industry was not merely criticizing the health or environmental impacts of beef consumption or produc-

tion but also implicitly criticizing Alberta families. As Blue observes, 'unfor-·
tunately, alongside creating a sense of continuity and cohesion, collective
identification also conceals a certain foundational violence because it excludes
the differences, contradictions or problems that make this unity possible.' 'This
is perhaps why,' she adds, that apart from 'a few dissenting voices in student
newspapers or vegetarian and environmental publications, the promotion of
Alberta beef is rarely challenged in the province.'[40] Thus, lang's PETA ad was a
rare, albeit very well publicized, moment of dissent that, as Blue characterized
it, represented a 'severe transgression of orthodoxy.'[41]

While Blue's research does not offer any sustained analysis of the gendered dynamics of beef marketing, other scholars have productively utilized
gender analysis to explore both histories of vegetarianism and meat consumption. Notably, backlash from pro-cattle, pro-meat forces is exceedingly common according to vegetarian scholars. Carol J. Adams and Julia Twigg have
observed how challenges from vegetarians (usually female) are frequently constructed as anti-patriarchal and anti-male.[42] In her book *Vegetarianism: Movement or Moment?* Donna Maurer assessed the reactions of the beef and cattle
industry in the United States and Canada to both vegetarian activists and to animal rights activists such as PETA. Maurer notes that the beef industry expends
considerable money on lawyers, litigation, government lobbying, and advertising to counteract any and all negative statements issued about beef consumption
or cattle ranching.[43] For the industry, then, these are not matters of 'freedom
of expression' but, instead, clear threats to their economic viability, and so
they utilize every means at their disposal to confront, silence, and denigrate
vegetarian political activists and those who advocate for the health benefits
of vegetarian diets. Famously, a number of well-known celebrities who have
endorsed beef consumption in print and television ads, including James Garner and Cybill Shepherd, have found their contracts terminated abruptly when
either their health (Garner's heart by-pass surgery) or their wavering commitment (Shepherd's statements about consuming other protein sources) diverged
from the pro-beef message. In lang's case, however, the counter-attack focused
not on countering her claims about the human and environmental benefits of
a vegetarian diet but, instead, struck at her Achilles heel, her 'closeted' lesbianism. They did this in several ways. First, her opponents challenged lang's
motivations for critiquing meat consumers and producers and publicly speculated as to the real reasons she betrayed her former neighbours and friends.
Was she opposed to the 'lifestyle' of rural North Americans, they asked, and
their reliance on agricultural pursuits? Using a familiar country metaphor, they
also rhetorically asked whether she was now too big for her britches or too
'quirky' an entertainer to realize the economic ramification of her offensive

statements. Certainly, many Albertans believed that the latter was true. In an interview on *Entertainment Tonight*, Alberta Agriculture Minister Ernie Isley shared his thoughts on the reaction in Alberta. 'I think any repercussions she suffers, she fully brought on herself,' he stated, adding, 'I have no problem with her promoting her belief to be a vegetarian but what she did was a frontal attack on non-vegetarians and cattle producers in particular. They've got every right to respond in any way they see fit.'[44] Similarly, George Schoepp, chairman of the Alberta Cattle Commission, wrote to lang to convey his dismay over her behaviour, stating, 'We are extremely disappointed to say the least to have you stab us in the back by condemning us for our way of life. Perhaps you should have another look at your "roots" before you sever them completely'[45]

The situation grew more ominous as lang remained mute in the face of the controversy and the various threats and questions, neither apologizing nor qualifying her statements in the press. As a result, many people became all the more convinced that she had intentionally criticized the Albertan way of life. Moreover, a few citizens of Consort obviously felt fully justified in offering more vituperative attacks against lang's personal life. Explicit vegetarian politics visibly altered public perceptions of lang and, one could speculate, enabled people to publicly voice a critique of her politics and sexuality that for years may have been circulating privately. Locally, it was well known that lang had been a vegetarian since her teenage years, but her impressive singing abilities had resulted in a certain degree of acceptance and support of her life choice. Yet, at the heart, this was a fragile tolerance that was predicated both on her continued artistic success and political silence and on the willingness of the more conservative townsfolk to ignore certain inconvenient truths about the performer. An editorial in the *Edmonton Journal* reprimanded the town for its hypocrisy. It began by noting that 'before lang cut her anti-beef commercials she was the pride of the southeastern Alberta community' and that 'Consort and environs were front and centre in a national TV special featuring the singer earlier this year – which they wouldn't have been without her.'[46] After briefly recapping the events of the past weekend, the editorial then offered the community and the ranchers this stinging rebuke: 'Whether Consort and cattle growers like it or not, lang will be the most famous export from the community for a long time to come – probably long after her anti-beef commercials have been forgotten. Rather than shun and attempt to quiet her for her beliefs she has held for a long time, the town and cattle growers everywhere should show a degree of tolerance.'[47]

The lang episode corroborates Blue's assertions about the mythic nature of beef production in Alberta. It was very clear within the province, and certainly in Consort and its environs, that few could depersonalize lang's comments;

they could not differentiate between someone being critical of beef production and consumption from a critique of rural producers. While the handful of her supporters expressed shock and regret at the turn of events, Corporal McMahon probably represented the views of a great many people when he articulated the opinion that nearly everyone who ate, grew, hauled, or profited from the beef industry could have been motivated to put that hateful graffiti on the town sign. The violence implicit in the homophobic message was apparently lost on the police who viewed the incident rather benignly, but it was not lost on some of those who wrote letters to the media. Paula Eve Peterson from Camrose Alberta told the *Alberta Review* that 'I am shocked and appalled ... at the audacity of your publication to have printed them, thereby implying credibility.' 'Your ignorance,' she added emphatically, 'astounds me, and the underlying violence insinuated in these articles is enough to shock anyone.'[48] Nor was 'the underlying violence' lost on lang and her family. In subsequent interviews with family members, this episode is routinely cited as the watershed moment that forced lang to make two critical career decisions. First, she concluded that country music was anathema to her political and social realities. Second, having outed herself as a vegetarian, it was time to consider formally coming out of the by now rather transparent closet as a lesbian.

Interestingly, however, the lang episode differed considerably from a more recent political brouhaha that broke out within the world of country music. In 2003, the Texas country music group, the Dixie Chicks, infamously bemoaned the fact that they shared the same birth state as President George W. Bush. This flippant comment, made before an audience in London, England, resulted in a nearly complete ban on their music in the United States, plummeting record sales, and public destruction of the group's recordings and cultural ephemera.[49] By contrast, while lang's music was pulled from some prairie and Midwestern country music stations, in general, the publicity had a positive impact on the sales of her then current album *Absolute Torch and Twang*. According to Australia's the *West Magazine*, sales of the disc soared from '250 a day to 1200 a day' after the PETA controversy erupted. In addition, PETA got millions of dollars worth of free advertising from the constant news spin on this item.[50] All of this proved that lang's fan base was far broader than traditional country music radio audiences. Indeed, her next recording, *Ingénue*, 'became her breakout album ... and ushered in the yearning, torchy pop that made her a star (the single *Constant Craving* hit No. 2 on the U.S. charts). That was the first real watershed in her career and marked a permanent shift in her singing style.'[51]

'Reintarnation':[52] Assessing the Regional and National Reactions

While the reactions from Consort and the cattle industry were predictable enough, what about those of other western Canadians? What did they think of lang's 'tofu-tongued utterances'?[53] In this regard, the newspapers, and the letters they generated, offer an intriguing mélange of perspectives. In one editorial, the *Calgary Herald* declared that the lang episode was a 'wing-ding-daddy-o of an uproar' and 'hoped that cooler heads would soon prevail.' Still, even this editorial couldn't help but take a shot at lang, by rhetorically asking whether or not 'lang really is a vegetarian' and then answering it with 'You'd never know it – not by the way she sinks her teeth into the hand that feeds her.'[54] Business writer Vern Simaluk offered up a song lyric which proclaimed his misogynistic opinions on the matter. To the tune of 'Ruby, Don't Take Your Love to Town,' Simaluk wrote, 'I know that it was cruel of me to lock you in the can, every time you cut yer hair like some truck drivin' man … Oh kaaaaay-deeeeeee, don't take yer beef to town.'[55]

Despite the mixed messages involved, even in Calgary, urban Albertans could be critical of the paper's views. Calgary reader Michael Alverez spoke up in defence of lang, noting that 'the attitude of the cattle industry … is truly pathetic … thousands of dollars, and countless numbers of hours of commercials and printed ads are given to the glorification of, and continued eating of dead animals; and yet, when one person stands up and offers her feelings – that are contrary – slurs, vandalism, threats and censorship toward her are the result.'[56] For the record, Alverez noted that he was not a vegetarian. Readers Tanja and Inge Timmermanns, also from Calgary, reported on how amazed and disappointed they were by the 'substandard journalism' to which the usually 'professional *Calgary Herald*' had stooped in covering the lang controversy. Moreover, they were 'frightened by the rising public intolerance to any opinion that differs from the norm.'[57]

Other letter writers pondered the issue of free speech, including Art Thormann from Edmonton, who wrote 'must everything we say please everybody before it becomes acceptable?'[58] Meanwhile, Chris Macleod of Sidar, British Columbia, offered this stinging rebuke of the whole debacle: 'What a pathetic if not ludicrous spectacle small-town Albertans, reactionary as ever, are making of themselves in condemning k.d. lang for uttering the truth about beef,' adding, 'Albertans previously had no more cause to feel proud of and take credit for lang's success than they now have to spurn it. Kudos to her and shame on the hidebound and disloyal of her fans.'[59]

Given that lang offered no new commentary on the subject, it might seem curious that the media coverage of the controversy continued, but it was the timing that was critically important. The story originally broke in June, but merely a month later, Calgary was again hosting its annual Stampede. The Calgary Stampede is nationally famous for its two week-long celebration of all things western and specifically cowboy clothes, food, music, and recreation.

Urban Calgary is transformed as commerce comes to a virtual standstill while lawyers, oil industry executives and employees, politicians, and regular folks alike don their western gear – Stetsons, fancy shirts, tight jeans, and expensive leather cowboy boots – and celebrate. Food is central to these celebrations and the images of politicians at pancake breakfasts and, later in the day, at barbecues of all variations of beef – ribs, burgers, and particularly steak – take culinary centre stage. The confluence of all of the pro-cowboy cuisine, rodeo events, and western celebration created another opportune context for engendering anti-lang commentary. Conversely, Edmonton, the provincial capital, which doesn't share in this western bacchanalia, differentiated itself by occasionally offering more cautiously liberal assessments of the ongoing coverage of the Consort media drama.

The country music stations also played an important role in fuelling the controversy. The ongoing ban of lang's music, first in the United States, and then in some Canadian prairie stations, had the affect of keeping the story current. These actions were criticized by the *Edmonton Journal*, which encouraged the radio stations to 'be leaders instead of witless followers' and admonished them to 'begin playing her unique music again – before her large number of fans start getting on the phone or looking elsewhere on the dial.'[60] Reactions to the *Edmonton Journal* editorial were negative. Barry Felstad, from Dapp, Alberta, wondered 'how fast *The Edmonton Journal* would knuckle under if suddenly confronted with a 45 percent drop in ad sales?' He explained that cattlemen like him were upset for two reasons. First, the message that healthier beef was available to people was just slowly getting out to Canadian consumers and the lang incident didn't acknowledge this fact. Second, he expressed disdain for lang's views because it was 'a campaign based on emotion rather than on scientific fact.'[61] Felstad did not comment on the appropriateness of the emotional counter-campaign that had been waged against lang nor of the ways that the beef industry relied on equally emotional images of multigenerational ranching families and extended family celebrations, or used images of rugged western individualism, to encourage beef consumption.

But because beef production was and remains big business in Alberta, the *Edmonton Journal*, although willing to show sympathy towards lang, could not appear to be too overwhelmingly supportive of her. To negotiate this tricky terrain, the paper followed in the tradition of newspaper lifestyle sections, which routinely publish features that provide a supportive environment for important advertisers. Thus, the newspaper ran articles supportive of the beef industry, such as the one entitled 'Meat Consumption Down,' which offered an analysis of the changing pattern of beef consumption in Canada. The *Journal* linked this downward trend to the interest of Canadians in better health and, perhaps, too, to the appeals such as lang's about animal rights. The article employed some of the gendered analysis that was used in other articles, particularly those criticizing the healthiness of a vegetarian diet, and it cited a series of male experts – academics, farmers, and ranchers – who noted the importance of beef protein in people's diets.[62] One expert, a University of Alberta professor emeritus of animal science, Roy Berg, offered his analysis of the centrality of beef in people's diets, stating, 'We evolved with meat and as a result, our diet is best balanced when meat is included.' Another expert quoted remarked, 'You can't have a working man go home and eat lettuce at night. He has got to have something substantial.'[63] Of course, the association of beef consumption with male virility and masculine strength, and even with nationalistic and ethical notions of male citizenship, is not at all original. As studies of vegetarianism document, there have long been class-based and gendered notions of food consumption.[64] Curiously, however, at least one reader of *Alberta Review*, Allen Attrill, offered a contrasting perspective on the gendered stereotypes of vegetarians, and a trenchant analysis of some of the reasons why those arguments were often advanced. A resident of Grand Central, Alberta, Atrill wrote, 'Something tells me that the meat industry is running scared. It must have an inferiority complex. I'm a vegetarian and have been one for fifteen years. I'm 5' 7" and weigh 230 lbs. I'm no weakling. I can lift 225 lbs and I don't work out. I have endurance and time after time I've lasted longer on the job than my fellow workers.'[65]

Outside of the prairies, the responses to lang's campaign met with less complicated support. This reflected several factors, including the greater numbers of vegetarians living in cities outside the west who voiced their opinion. It was also in these cities that one was more likely to find a higher concentration of people whose political perspective involved support for animal rights as well as artistic freedom and licence. And, in fairness to Albertans, these people lived long distances away from beef country and thus lacked an awareness of the daily realities and challenges of farming and ranching. Indeed, outside of western Canada, the lang incident was seldom front page news, but instead, reserved for the entertainment section or, less frequently, editorial and political essays. Nor were the events in Consort covered as a daily breaking news feature as they were in Alberta.

In political terms, it was more common to find press coverage of the lang episode that also offered a more comprehensive analysis of the larger picture involved in either the national or eastern newspapers, such as the *Globe and Mail* and *Toronto Star*. Robert Sheppard, a *Globe* political columnist, used the episode as the focal point for writing a perceptive article about Canadian regionalism. Thus, he asked, 'Is this just a Canadian phenomenon, to do with our failed constitutional maneuverings and the inability to define ourselves as a country? Or is it broader? Does it have anything to do with the end of liberalism, as a widely held look-after-your neighbour philosophy? Or the growing economic imbalances among countries, regions and even individuals – what has been referred to as emerging middle-class warfare – stemming from the uneven eighties?'[66] More specifically, and pointedly, Sheppard questioned, 'Why can't the people of Consort, and the U.S. Midwest for that matter, accept without retribution that one of their number, albeit a celebrated one, does not like meat?' In answering such a question, the editor of the *Consort Enterprise*, Mary Readman characterized the whole incident as simply a family spat, stating, 'We're possessive about Kathy; this is her hometown. But it's like a member of our family that has gone wrong.'[67] By contrast, Sheppard's more nuanced answer suggested that the breakdown of larger national alliances had strained regional relations and placed greater pressures on smaller, regional communities to offer a 'united front to the outside world, to protect their hard-won economic gains.'[68]

Jay Scott, entertainment reporter at the *Globe and Mail*, offered a more blunt and gendered assessment of the episode and lang's apparently career-threatening decision to publicly espouse her vegetarianism. 'It doesn't take a degree in psychology,' Scott wrote, 'to presume that lang, represented on her albums as a cowgirl when she is, in fact, the daughter of a pharmacist and a schoolteacher, is in some ways getting even, as so many of us privately do but so few of us have the opportunity to do publicly, with her roots,' adding, 'She's economically biting the hand that may have refused spiritually to feed her.'[69] Scott speculated about the challenges lang probably faced growing up 'as a headstrong tomboy in a culture that prizes frilliness in fillies.' He offered an analysis of some of her lyrics, including 'Nowhere to Stand,' which openly talks about gendered violence and life in small towns. While correctly noting that one should not infer 'autobiographical exactness' from her lyrics, he nevertheless observed that 'there is a hip constituency, away from country, that would not consider vegetarianism radical nor lang's look "weird."' If she did make the switch, Scott felt certain that she could 'truly leave childhood behind, find somewhere to stand, and tell the folks who scrawled "Eat Beef Dyke" to eat … whatever they want.'[70]

Mitch Potter, writing for the *Toronto Star*, offered a similar appraisal of the incident. He began it with this memorable observation: 'If you haven't had the pleasure of living in Alberta, take heed of these fundamental taboos. Never threaten a cowboy's sexuality. Never threaten a cowboy's cows. At 28, in all her big-boned, Southern Albertan resplendence, k.d. lang has fully trampled both no-no's.'[71] Potter reminisced about watching the reaction that lang's music and appearance had on the real cowboys during her 1984 debut at a Calgary cowboy bar. The boys, he said, 'liked what they heard, but the very sight of lang ... made them crazy. Bad crazy. And her performance seemed to feed upon that very tension.' Potter predicted lang would return to the music scene with 'a style much further removed from the country music to which she has so far hitched her wagon.'

Conclusion

What does k.d lang's vegetarian public service announcement and its aftermath tell us about the history of the prairie region, diversity, and social cohesion? As many commentators pointed out at the time, lang was not the first celebrity or popular musician to support vegetarianism. Some of those celebrities rallied to support her, including Paul McCartney, who reminisced that 'when they banned the Beatles in the '60's it only helped to make us more popular.' He also accurately predicted that 'the same will happen with k.d. We support her 100 per cent.'[72] Subsequently, in countless print interviews, lang would point to this controversy as a key professional and personal crossroads where she reconsidered her commitment to the country music industry. As Dan Mathews put it, 'That surreal summer inspired k.d. to "move on" from country music, recording *Ingénue* and scoring her biggest hit "Constant Craving."'[73] Ultimately, the tussle over vegetarianism looked tame against lang's decision only two years later to officially come out as a lesbian in print interviews in *Rolling Stone* and the *Advocate*. More adventurously, she would famously appear in drag in a celebrated *Vanity Fair* cover photo with American model Cindy Crawford. Since 1990, k.d lang has been inducted into the Order of Canada (1996), won numerous achievement awards, and received an impressive array of North American music awards. All of this success culminated recently with the honorary doctorate from the University of Alberta. Far from ruining lang's career, the 1990 PETA controversy proved to be an important catalyst for personal change and career success. Those honours and accomplishments have no doubt blunted the impact of the 'Meat Stinks' controversy, but the wounds in Consort may not have entirely healed. While the town's website acknowledges their famous expat, there are no images of the singer on the website, only a link redirecting people to lang's official website.

From a historical perspective, this rich episode, which sits at the intersection of prairie histories of sexuality and food, offers a window on the politics of people's food choices. The discourses generated by the incident reveal both majority and minority views on such central themes as social organization and rural economies and culture and allow us to explore a distinctly prairie perspective on difference – culinary, sexual, and gendered. This study also enables us to think critically about local, provincial, and national reactions to 'quirky' queer westerners. While contemporary research indicates a growing tolerance and gradual acceptance of sexual minority individuals and communities in the prairies, there are still important limits to that tolerance. First, rural areas lag considerably behind their urban counterparts in their tolerance or acceptance of lesbians and gays. Additionally, gays and lesbians have and continue to negotiate certain tacit and unwritten but highly significant rules regarding behaviour, appearance, and expression. Should people 'transgress orthodoxy,' pace Blue, such as when lang criticized Alberta's local industry and the hallowed myths of the independent Alberta rancher, it gave industry supporters open permission to retaliate. Instead of challenging lang's vegetarian assertions about the health and environmental benefits of vegetarian diets, her critics personalized their criticism, focusing on her sexuality, her mental acuity, her celebrity status, and her feminism. While the media attention eventually dissipated over the course of the summer of 1990, the fallout from it remained. As Filax details, in January 1993 the controversy erupted anew when Premier Ralph Klein's Conservatives refused to congratulate lang for winning a Juno award (standard practice for award-winning Albertans). Klein defended his actions by recalling lang's snub of beef producers three years earlier, while his cabinet minister, Ernie Isley, did so on the grounds that lang was now a declared lesbian.[74] Only in March 1993, when lang won a Grammy award, and national attention was focused on his Conservative government, did Klein issue a commendation to lang. His actions appear to be motivated by a desire to avoid more negative press, rather than sincere recognition of lang's accomplishment.

An analysis of the regional politics of food provides an intriguing vantage point on the subject of queer politics and social inclusion in rural western Canada and the role played by gender in its local hierarchies and political elites. While social and political commentators from outside might mock the regional unrest created by lang's PETA ad, or paint lang's adherence to the country music scene as some ill-considered choice, the reality was far different. Lang was used to negotiating her difference within the region, and she had a strong base of fans who were prepared to support and encourage her as long as she abided by certain unspoken rules about supporting one's community and not openly flaunting differences (sexual, political, gendered, or classist). However, the explicit declaration of her political views – first, her vegetarianism, then her lesbianism – made for an untenable situation in a region noted for valorizing farm families, virile cowboys, appropriately feminized heterosexual women and small 'c' conservative political values. Thus, ultimately, the politics of food choices offers a glimpse into the dichotomies of prairie life – the tensions between rural and urban dwellers, the reception of difference in small town communities, and the challenges facing small town and rural gays and lesbians who are forced everyday to negotiate a tightrope of expectations about how not to 'flaunt' their difference.

NOTES

1 Express News Staff, 'k.d. lang accepts honourary degree.'
2 Author transcript of the k.d. lang University of Alberta commencement speech, provided on the website www.expressnews.ualberta.ca/media/9410_1.mp3.
3 k.d. lang, 'Absolute Torch and Twang,' released May 1989; http://www.kdlang.com/home.php.
4 A sample of North American literature includes the following: N.A. Boyd, *Wide Open Town: A History of Queer San Francisco to 1965* (Berkeley, CA: University of California Press, 2003); George Chauncey, *Gay New York: Gender, Urban Culture and the Making of the Gay Male World, 1890–1940* (New York: Basic Books, 1994); Elizabeth Lapovsky Kennedy and Madeline D. Davis, *Boots of Leather, Slippers of Gold: The History of a Lesbian Community* (New York: Routledge, 1993); Marc Stein, *City of Sisterly and Brotherly Loves: Lesbian and Gay Philadelphia, 1945–1972* (Chicago, IL: University of Chicago Press, 2000); Gary Kinsman, *The Regulation of Desire: Homo and Hetero Sexualities* (Montreal: Black Rose Books, 1996); Tom Warner, *Never Going Back: A History of Queer Activism in Canada* (Toronto: University of Toronto Press, 2002); Elise Chenier, 'Rethinking Class in Lesbian Bar Culture: Living "The Gay Life" in Toronto, 1955–1965,' *left history* 9/2 (2004): 85–117; David Churchill, 'Mother Goose's Map: Tabloid Geographies and Gay Male Experience in 1950s Toronto,' *Journal of Urban History* 30/6 (2004): 826–52; and the extensive work of Steven Maynard on Toronto, including: 'Through a Hole in the Lavatory Wall: Homosexual Subcultures, Police Surveillance, and the Dialectics of Discovery, Toronto, 1890–1930,' in Joy Parr and Mark Rosenfeld, eds., *Gender and History in Canada* (Toronto: Copp Clark, 1996), 165–84.
5 k.d. lang, *Ingenué*, released March 1992; http://www.kdlang.com/home.php.
6 Those interested may download the video from the PETA website. The url is www.petatv.com/tvpopup/viceo.asp.video.kd.lang.
7 While the ad attracted much attention and commentary, I have not been able to verify that it did actually air on network television. Where it did originally air was on the entertainment program, *Entertainment Tonight*, and then the contents of the ad was repeated in countless newspaper and magazine venues as the controversy built.

8　PETA maintains a website where one can view their past print ads and their com-mercials. Most recently, for example, another famous Canadian woman, Pamela Anderson, has offered her stinging critique of the KFC food chain, and chicken processors in general, for their inhumane treatment of animals.

9　k.d. lang, 'Meat Stinks,' PETA ad, 1990. Accessed on the PETA website, July 2008.

10　Robert Everett-Green, 'i om k.d.,' *Globe and Mail*, 2 Feb. 2008, R7.

11　k.d. lang, *Angel with a Lariat*, released March 1987; http://www.kdlang.com/home.php.

12　Peter Shawn Taylor, 'K.D. Lang Sings a Sour Note,' *Alberta Report* 17/32 (1990): 32.

13　Dan Mathews, 'Bold Beginnings,' *Advocate*, 12 Nov. 2002, 52.

14　David Staples, 'Defaced k.d. lang Signs to Be Fixed; Ranchers Offer to Do the Work,' *Edmonton Journal*, 10 July 1990, A7.

15　'Canada's Beef Industry Fast Facts,' www.beefinfo.org.

16　Gwendolyn Blue, 'If It Ain't Alberta, It Ain't Beef: Local Food, Regional Identity, (Inter)National Politics,' *Food, Culture and Society* 11/1 (2008): 69–85.

17　k.d. lang, *Invincible Summer*, released June 2000; http://www.kdlang.com/home.php.

18　Julia Nunes, 'Cattlemen Have a Beef with k.d.,' *Globe and Mail*, 23 June 1990, C13. Alison Mayes, 'Ads Raise Stink in Country Circles,' *Calgary Herald*, 23 June 1990, C15.

19　Mayes, 'Ads Raise Stink.'

20　Bob Curtwright, Knight-Ridder, 'Radio Jumps on k.d's Ban Wagon,' *Calgary Herald*, 30 June 1990, E9.

21　David Staples, 'DJs Have a Beef with "Meat Stinks" k.d. lang,' *Edmonton Journal*, 6 July 1990, A1.

22　David Staples, 'Hometown Has No Beef with k.d., Rally Organizer Says,' *Edmonton Journal*, 7 July 1990, A1.

23　Staples, 'DJs Have a Beef with 'Meat Stinks' k.d. lang.'

24　'National Farmers Union Backs Radio Ban of k.d. lang's Music,' *Edmonton Journal*, 8 July 1990, B2.

25　'Anti-lang Feelings Harden,' *Calgary Herald*, 10 July 1990, B3.

26　Quoted in David Staples, 'k.d.'s Teen Friends Erase the Hate Graffiti,' *Edmonton Journal*, 9 July 1990, A1.

27　Staples, 'Defaced k.d. lang Signs.'

28　Ibid.

29　David Staples, 'k.d. Enjoys Support for Free Speech; No Need to Bring k.d. Signs Back, Singer's Mother Says,' *Edmonton Journal*, 21 July 1990, A7.

30　Gloria Filax, 'Producing Homophobia in Alberta, Canada in the 1990s,' *Journal of*

   Historical Sociology 17/1 (2004): 87–120. Also, see Gloria Filax, *Queer Youth in the Province of the 'Severely Normal'* (Vancouver: UBC Press, 2006).
31 Filax, 'Producing Homophobia,' 88.
32 Taylor, 'K.D. Lang Sings a Sour Note,' 33.
33 Ibid.
34 Link Byfield, 'Behind "Animal Rights" Lies the Morality of the Jungle,' *Alberta Report* 17/32 (1990): 4.
35 Ibid.
36 Peter Lyle, Toronto, Ontario, letter to the editor, *Alberta Report* 17/35 (1990): 3.
37 David Stowe, Calgary, Alberta, letter to the editor, *Alberta Report* 17/37 (1990): 4.
38 k.d. lang, *Even Cowgirls Get the Blues,* released October 1993; http://www.kdlang.com/home.php.
39 To watch the videos from the 'Raised Right' campaign, see www.raisedright.ca. For Alberta Beef Producers, see: http://albertabeef.org/.
40 Blue, 'If It Ain't Alberta, It Ain't Beef,' 79–80.
41 Ibid.
42 Carol J. Adams, *The Sexual Politics of Meat: A Feminist-Vegetarian Critical Theory* (New York: Continuum, 2000); Julia Twigg, 'Vegetarianism and the Meaning of Meat,' in Anne Murcott, ed., *The Sociology of Food and Eating* (Aldershot, UK: Gower, 1984).
43 Donna Maurer, *Vegetarianism: Movement or Moment?* (Philadelphia, PA: Temple University Press, 2002), 62–5, 135–6.
44 Staff reporter, 'Lang Caused Her Own Problem – Isley,' *Edmonton Journal*, 12 July 1990, A7.
45 Duncan Thorne, 'k.d. Invited to Visit Cows in Feedlot,' *Edmonton Journal*, 25 July 1990, D8.
46 Editorial, 'Ballad of a Country Star,' *Edmonton Journal*, 10 July 1990, A8.
47 Ibid.
48 Paula Eve Peterson, Camrose, Alberta, letter to the editor, *Alberta Report* 17/37 (1990): 4–5.
49 Natalie Maines' 2003 critique of President Bush has been the focus for much discussion and debate about the politics of the country music industry, its fan base, and of differences between Canadian and American audiences. The 2006 documentary film *Shut Up and Sing* chronicles the aftermath of the controversy that nearly destroyed the Dixie Chicks American recording career, and interestingly, illustrates the supportive nature of the Canadian music audience.
50 Ray Purvis, 'k.d. lang and the Art of Finding a Life Off the Beaten Track,' *West Magazine* (Western Australia), 23 Aug. 1997, 7.
51 Everett-Green, 'i om k.d.'
52 k.d. lang, *Reintarnation*, released April 2006; http://www.kdlang.com/home.php.

53 William Gold, 'Too Many People Want Other People to Change,' *Calgary Herald*, 11 July 1990, A5.
54 Editorial, 'Radio K.O. on k.d.,' *Calgary Herald*, 11 July 1990, A4.
55 Vern Simaluk, 'Now Just Take that, k.d.,' *Calgary Herald*, 11 July 1990, A10.
56 Michael Alvarez, letter to editor, *Calgary Herald*, 22 July 1990, C5.
57 Tanja and Inge Timmermanns, letter to the editor, *Calgary Herald*, 5 Aug. 1990, C5.
58 Art Thormann, Edmonton, letter to the editor, *Calgary Herald*, 29 July 1990, C5.
59 Chris Macleod, Sidar, B.C., letter to the editor, *Calgary Herald*, 12 Aug. 1990, A6.
60 Ibid.
61 Barry Felstad, Dapp, Alberta, letter to the editor, *Edmonton Journal*, 19 July 1990, A11.
62 See Maurer, *Vegetarianism: Movement or Moment?* for an informative overview of the gendered nature of vegetarian adherents and organizations, their political strategies, and the beef industry's persistent critique that vegetarianism is an unhealthy and dangerous form of dieting.
63 Journal staff writer, 'Meat Consumption Down – and k.d. Ad Certainly No Help to Alberta Cattlemen,' *Edmonton Journal*, 15 July 1990, E1.
64 Carol J. Adams, *The Sexual Politics of Meat: A Feminist-Vegetarian Critical Theory*, 10th anniversary ed. (New York: Continuum, 2000); Nick Feddes, *Meat: A Natural Symbol* (London: Routledge, 1991); Tristram Stuart, *The Bloodless Revolution: A Cultural History of Vegetarianism from 1600 to Modern Times* (New York: Harper Collins, 2007).
65 Allen Atrill, Grand Central, Alberta, letter to the editor, *Alberta Report* 17/35 (1990): 5.
66 Robert Sheppard, 'The Provinces: It's a Small World, and It's Getting Smaller,' *Globe and Mail*, 12 July 1990, A17.
67 Andrew Duffy, 'Alberta Ranchers Fit to Be Tied over Singer's Pitch against Meat,' *Toronto Star*, 5 July 1990, A15.
68 Sheppard, 'The Provinces.'
69 Jay Scott, 'Cross Current: It's Puzzling that k.d. lang Continues to Court Steak-Loving Country Market,' *Globe and Mail*, 16 July 1990, C1.
70 Ibid.
71 Mitch Potter, 'k.d. lang Doesn't Step Lightly into Cow Flap,' *Toronto Star*, 7 July 1990, F1.
72 Mitch Potter, 'Vega Delicate as ever Despite All the Gear,' *Toronto Star*, 9 July 1990, B1.
73 Dan Mathews, 'Bold Beginnings: Dan Mathews Notes that k.d. lang Came Out as a Lesbian Only after First Coming Out as a Vegetarian,' *Advocate*, 12 Nov. 2002, 52.
74 Filax, 'Producing Homophobia in Alberta,' 97–8.

PART SEVEN

National Identities and Cultural Spectacles

19 Nationalism on the Menu: Three Banquets on the 1939 Royal Tour

MOLLY PULVER UNGAR

The study of food is defined by a central irony: the fact that human beings cannot survive without food,[1] and yet their reasons for eating are not always connected to survival. Sometimes we eat to assuage hunger; if we have some choice and have available more food than we need for subsistance, we eat for taste, or to satisfy our senses. Beyond these reasons, we eat to create a fantasy in which food becomes a symbol, and meals or menus become cultural products – representations or images of the society that produced, arranged, prepared, and consumed them.[2]

On the 1939 Royal Tour, food and the venues for its presentation and consumption – the subject of this chapter – were key elements in a fantasy of national identity and social democracy. In this respect, my case study bears a resemblance to Julia Roberts' reading of colonial public house dinners as occasions for the enactment and solidification of social roles and identities. Almost one hundred years after the famous snipe dinner at the British North American tavern, the foods offered at the royal meals in 1939 similarly represented 'powerful messages of social inclusion, exclusion, and negotiation ... encoded in public space' (Julia Roberts in this volume).

The 1939 Royal Tour

Royal visits to Canada were not a new phenomenon. Ian Radforth's book *Royal Spectacle* describes the intense excitement and unprecedented celebrations provoked by the Prince of Wales' visit of 1860.[3] From Confederation to 1939, there had been three royal visits to Canada (1901, 1919, 1927), each one accompanied by pomp and enthusiasm. Nevertheless, claims for the singularity of the 1939 visit were justified. Never before had a reigning monarch come to Canada; never before had a Royal Tour taken place in the shadow of impending war and amid international alarm and foreboding. As well, King George VI and Queen Elizabeth arrived on the heels of the 1936 abdication crisis, and thus their favourable reception in Canada was not guaranteed. It is, therefore, almost impossible to exaggerate the contemporary importance accorded to the 1939 Royal Tour.[4]

From 17 May to 17 June the tour dominated the feelings, activities, and imaginations of millions of Canadians. Cheering crowds greeted the King and Queen everywhere they went, and newspapers described their appearances in superlatives. For all that was unique, however, the commemorative and celebratory aspects of 1939 shared with other such events the qualities of theatricality in the service of social cohesion and national pride.[5] Conceived as an elaborate promotion of the British Empire and its future on the world stage, the flood of positive images, commentary, and publicity generated by the Royal Tour all but eclipsed the few voices raised in criticism or opposition.

Co-operative Commonwealth Federation leader J.S. Woodsworth dared to advocate publicly for restraint in expenditures for receptions and displays.[6] The Communist party's *Daily Clarion* chided the mainstream press for stooping to political manipulation by inflating the size of the crowds in Toronto, but nevertheless concentrated on how labour would benefit from the King's visit.[7] In general, the majority of Canadians seemed delighted to contribute to the royal festivities, to buy thousands of royal souvenirs, and read endless descriptions of the Royals' activities, whether great or small.

On the surface, therefore, the tour might appear to be another in a long series of royal impositions on the hospitality and budgets of Canadians. Indeed, occurring ten weeks before the outbreak of the Second World War, the tour is rarely mentioned amid the avalanche of attention given to the war years that followed. Nevertheless, the menus for the 1939 Royal Visit embodied much about Canadians' image of themselves, and about their collective sense of self.

The Royal Tour featured thirteen ceremonial meals and six smaller occasions such as a tea or a garden party, each precipitating minute examination in the print media. In their elaborate descriptions of sumptuous dishes and glittering banquets, newspapers encouraged a form of culinary tourism and escapism in the midst of the privations and anxieties of the Depression. Unconnected to the more ordinary fare eaten by the King and Queen in their private dining car on board the Royal Train, the three specific banquets examined in this chapter were all extraordinary – public meals that fit easily into the category of symbol and fantasy.

These grandiose luncheons and dinners were edible expressions of national pride, representing Canadians' collective ability to produce foodstuffs of the highest quality, to prepare sophisticated, one-of-a-kind dishes, all the while preserving their more casual, democratic Canadian identity. At the same time, the banquets were statements of imperialist enthusiasm, showing that Canadians could celebrate their British heritage and measure up to the exclusive standards of the royal palate. The specific food served, the manner of its preparation, and the way in which it was presented metaphorically offered up Canada and its bounty to be consumed by the King and Queen.

Inclusiveness: Local and Provincial Identities

The chief chefs of the Empress, Frontenac, and Windsor hotels chose dishes that acknowledged Canada's British past, but they also reached for inclusiveness with menu items recalling the varied European pasts of certain provinces or localities. For the luncheon banquet at Victoria's Empress Hotel, one of the symbolic ingredients of the meal was British Columbia's heritage. Early connections to Spain were conjured up by the 'Essence of Tomato, Madrilene,' a tomato soup served cold, in the Spanish style. The more recent provincial identity was represented in the fact that Vancouver Island crabs had created the crab cocktail with Thousand Island sauce, and that local sources had supplied the trout, fried and served with chopped burned almonds, for the 'Mountain Trout Sauté Amandine,' as well as the peas cooked in and served with mint leaves for the 'New Peas à la Menthe,' the potatoes for the hazelnut-sized 'New Potatoes Noisette,' and the asparagus for the 'Asparagus Mousseline.'[8]

British Columbians who read about these dishes might be encouraged to think that they themselves were represented in the ingredients. Through the produce of their home province, they too, could attend the royal meal, and even their familiarity with these local foodstuffs included them in the occasion. To underscore British Columbia's emphatically British character, Chef Anderegg had chosen a traditional British game bird, the pheasant. On this occasion, a bird to remind the guests of manor homes and lordly hunting grounds, was also served 'in the English way,' the bread sauce made with bread crumbs that had been buttered.[9]

The people of Quebec could claim a symbolic seat at the Château Frontenac banquet table, with dishes that bore names redolent of Quebec localities and their history. The chicken soup was named 'Consommé de Volaille Montmorency'; the trout cooked in white wine for 'Truites des Laurentides au Vin Blanc' came from the St Lawrence River; and the lamb to be served in a crown with fresh seasonal vegetables as 'Couronne d'Agneau de Québec aux Primeurs,' was local lamb. Local wild birds from the Quebec City area were served in aspic as 'Petits Oiseaux Blancs de l'Île d'Orléans en Belle Vue.' 'Salade Gauloise' (Gallic salad) emphasized the contributions of France.[10]

At Montreal's Windsor Hotel, the theme of national unity superseded the need to promote local ingredients. Here, the menu emphasized dishes that joined together English and French traditions. The origins of 'La Tortue Claire Printanière' (turtle soup with spring vegetables) were French and British, while the roasted Cornish game hens ('Le Poussin Poêlé') combined a British-named bird with a French recipe. Port wine, long associated with British food culture, laced the truffled goose liver pâté ('Foie Gras Truffé au Porto'), a French dish. The Norman contribution made its appearance in the sauce blanketing the halibut medallions for 'Médaillon de Flétan à la Normande.'[11] Thus, the harmonious fantasy of Canada's 'two founding (European) nations' was offered up to Canada's monarch.

Exclusivity: Ingredients and Preparation

These banquet menus established Canada's national identity as a product of its provincial history and local characteristics. The inclusion and representation of Canadians indicated a desire to depart from the colonial past and establish a more modern, democratic, and specifically Canadian identity. However, the banquets were inclusive only at the symbolic level, and the reality was somewhat different. When it came to the actual edibles, the hallmarks of exclusivity came to the fore, as shown by the often-described rarity of ingredients, complexity of preparation, artistry of presentation, and excruciating, time-consuming perfectionism.[12] Participants at these rarified occasions ingested painstakingly prepared, one-of-a-kind dishes that acknowledged the privileged, elite status of the guests. Not least of all, regardless of origin, which was not always local, almost all the dishes bore French names, capitalizing on the cachet of foreign travel and sophistication available only to the wealthy. At the Empress Hotel, the tomatoes for the soup needed to be passed through two fine sieves between boilings, after which the purée was again passed through muslin. For dessert, in an exceptional moment of culinary theatre, waiters entered bearing an ice sculpture bathed in coloured lights, revealing a glacial forest in which two beavers attended to their time-honoured work. Nestled in an icy tree stump, the 'Charlotte Printanière' (spring Charlotte) made with frozen, cognac-flavoured cream and seasonal fruit inside a moulded cake, provided a suitably luxurious ending.[13]

For the Château Frontenac meal, poached tapioca thickened the chicken soup, after which it was strained and garnished with asparagus tips, quenelles, rice, and chervil. Rarity could be claimed for the Laurentian trout, which had been caught in a provincial wildlife reserve by specially issued government order, and holes had to be cut in the ice-covered lake to get at them. With bones and skin removed, the trout was poached in white wine 'whipped up in sweet butter.' A small army of men had been commandeered to capture the 2,500 black-eyed juncos, better known as finches, at their winter home on Île d'Orléans to create a bite-sized delicacy for which only the breasts of the snowbirds were used. About an inch in length and less than half an inch thick, each breast was mounted on a platform of pâté de fois gras, a truffle placed on top, and the entire creation enveloped in gleaming, transparent aspic.[14]

The food in Montreal shared the characteristics of complex, time-consuming preparations to produce tiny edibles. The clear, slightly peppered turtle soup was garnished with a special sauce, and contained thin strips of vegetables and beans cut into lozenges. Fish stock, mushroom liquor, cream, butter, and egg yolks made up the sauce normande for the medallions of halibut. Stuffed with liver and rice, the Cornish game hens were served with miniscule green peas and marble-sized sautéed potatoes.[15] Finally, Canadians were invited to consume the Royals' own home in a hotel named for them, because the Windsor Hotel's head pastry chef had prepared a spectacular cake in the shape of Windsor Castle.[16]

Dining with Royalty

At these highly choreographed meals, the intimate act of 'breaking bread' was transformed by the presence of royalty into a transcendent occasion that bound the participants to something greater than themselves: the solemnity of ritual, tradition, and history. The ordinarily unreachable, untouchable world of monarchy and privilege momentarily opened its gates as the food was consumed, and the guests as well as the Royals acted out a collective fantasy about the benevolent relationship between ruler and subject. The royal banquets conferred elite status on those who attended them, but simultaneously included all who were connected to the production of the ingredients, or what the ingredients and the final dishes represented.

As Canadians served up the best that their country had to offer, their King and Queen ate sparingly. This was noticed time and again by the press and indicated both the primary reason for the tour, as well as the fantasy that concealed it.[17] Britain's imminent appetite for Canadian soldiers and Canadian resources provided the subtext for every occasion of public dining. At each meal, in reality an acknowledgment of the ancient custom of offering sacrifices to a divinity, Canadians were reminded that the foodstuffs and the cuisine were personifications of Canadians themselves, and how much these had impressed the King and Queen. It is, therefore, significant that at these ceremonial meals the rulers recognized the need for restraint and ate very little, as if not wanting to exhibit an unseemly gusto for Canada's human and material resources, or a disregard for the people who had so generously created the repast.

Nationalism in the Making

In their repeated culinary expressions of home-grown nationalism, and gastronomic assertions of provincial accomplishment, Canadians indicated self-awareness as a nation, and announced that their colonial past was behind them. Yet, in their eagerness to participate in the protocol, formalities, and exclusiveness of royal dining, Canadians clung to their enthusiasm for all things British, and symbolically embraced the trappings of their colonial past. As much as Canadians may have promoted a wholly Canadian nation on the world stage, an analysis of the symbolic function of the foods served at three royal banquets on the 1939 Royal Tour reveals the fault lines of competing notions of national identity.

NOTES

1 Raymond Grew, 'Food and Global History,' in Raymond Grew, ed., *Food in Global History* (Boulder, CO: Westview Press, 1999), 1.
2 Margaret Visser, *Much Depends on Dinner* (Toronto: McClelland and Stewart, 1987), 12, 14; Grew, 'Food and Global History,' 2–5, 36, 41; Bonnie Huskins, 'From *Haute Cuisine* to Ox Roasts: Public Feasting and the Negotiation of Class in Mid-19th Century Saint John and Halifax,' *Labour / Le travail* 37 (Spring 1996): 9–32; Sidney Mintz and Christine du Bois, 'The Anthropology of Food and Eating,' *Annual Review of Anthropology* 31 (2002): 99–100, 107–9; Nancy Rosenberger, 'Patriotic Appetites and Gnawing Hungers: Food and the Paradox of Nation-Building in Uzbekistan,' *Ethnos* 72/3 (2007): 340, 341, 356; Jayanta Sengupta, 'Nation on a Platter: The Culture and Politics of Food and Cuisine in Colonial Bengal,' *Modern Asian Studies* 44/1 (2010): 81, 82, 97, 98; Peter N. Stearns, 'Food and History,' *Journal of Social History* 36/1 (2002): 165, 168, 169, 171, 172, 174.
3 Ian Radforth, *Royal Spectacle: The 1860 Visit of the Prince of Wales to Canada and the United States* (Toronto: University of Toronto Press, 2004). The 1860 Royal Tour also revealed the processes of identity formation in the colonies, and the importance of 'provincial identities.'
4 Peter Bell, 'The Foreign Office and the 1939 Royal Visit to America: Courting the USA in an Era of Isolationism,' *Journal of Contemporary History* 34/4 (2002): 599–616; R.B. Fleming, *The Royal Tour of Canada: The Royal Visit of King*

George VI and Queen Elizabeth (Toronto: Lynx Images, 2002); Tom MacDonnell, *Daylight upon Magic: The Royal Tour of Canada, 1939* (Toronto: Macmillan, 1989); David Reynolds, 'FDR's Foreign Policy and the British Royal Visit to the United States,' *Historian: A Journal of History* 45/4 (1983): 461–72; Benjamin D. Rhodes, 'The British Royal Visit of 1939 and the Psychological Approach to the White House,' *Diplomatic History* 2/2 (1978): 197–211. Considering the fact that the Royal Tour was seen by contemporaries as one of the key opportunities to save the world from the aggression of Hitler's Germany, the lack of scholarly attention given to this event is remarkable.

5 H.V. Nelles, *The Art of Nation-Building, Pageantry and Spectacle at Quebec's Tercentenary* (Toronto: University of Toronto Press, 1999); Ronald Rudin, *Founding Fathers: The Celebration of Champlain and Laval in the Streets of Quebec, 1878–1908* (Toronto: University of Toronto Press, 2003). Both Nelles and Rudin examine public celebrations as cultural products and their ability to transmit messages about national identity.

6 *Globe and Mail*, 18 Jan. 1939, 1.

7 *Daily Clarion*, Monday, 27 May 1939, 3; Saturday, 20 May 1939, 1; Monday, 22 May 1939, 1, 4. The *Clarion* praised the King for signing into law 'The Labor Charter.' This was an amendment to the Criminal Code making it a criminal offence for employers to prevent employees from joining a trade union. Labour saw this as a great victory, and credited the King with bringing this about. A few other incidents of negative commentary with regard to the Royal Tour included B.K. Sandwell's appeal, quoted in the *Winnipeg Free Press*, Friday, 24 Feb. 1939, 15. Sandwell, editor of *Saturday Night*, drew attention to Canada's urban slums, asking that the Royals should be shown these parts of the Dominion as well. Sandwell said that Canadians' money could be put to better use in building subsidized housing instead of erecting statues of Queen Victoria and King Edward VII. See also *Globe and Mail*, Monday, 27 Feb. 2.

8 *Vancouver Sun*, 30 May 1939, 8.

9 Ibid.

10 *Le Devoir*, 10 May 1939, 4; Molly Ungar, 'Royal Banquets in La Belle Province,' *Culinary Chronicles* 45 (Summer 2005): 8; *Vancouver Sun*, 18 May 1939, 3. http://www.culinaryhistorians.ca/newsletters/CC_45.pdf. Joan Elson Morgan, *Castle of Quebec* (Toronto: J.M Dent, 1949), 175.

11 McCord Museum of Canadian History, Fonds Mr C.B. Brown, P452/c, Royal Visits to Montreal, Menu and Programme.

12 *Vancouver Sun*, 25 May 1939, 10, 11; 27 May 1939, Supplement 6; *Le Devoir*, 10 May 1939, 4; *Vancouver Sun*, 29 May 1939, 17.

13 Ibid., 30 May 1939, 8. The Charlotte has a lengthy and complex history. The theory that it was named after Queen Charlotte, wife of King George III has not

been proved. The Apple Charlotte was a traditional English dessert, and the Old English word 'charlyt' pre-dates the eighteenth century. The celebrated French chef Antonin Carême is said to have invented the Charlotte Russe in 1802. It is also claimed that he originally named the dessert Charlotte à la Parisienne, but changed it out of respect for Czar Alexander of Russia, at whose court Carême was employed. To date, the origins of the Charlotte dessert are obscure. Darra Goldstein, 'Russia, Carême, and the Culinary Arts,' *Slavonic and East European Review* 73/4 (1995): 715; David Shulman, 'Culinary Americanisms,' *American Speech* 34/1 (1959): 26, 27; *The Big Apple* (Weblog), http://www.barrypopik.com/index.php/new_york_city/entry/charlotte_russe/.

14 *Montreal Gazette*, 16 May 1939, 18.

15 I am grateful to Mary Williamson for her culinary annotations and comments on the menu for the Montreal banquet.

16 MacDonnell, *Daylight upon Magic*, 72, 73; *La Presse*, 17 May 1939, 25.

17 *Time*, 29 May 1939, http://www.time.com/time/magazine/article/0,9171,931236,00.html; *Vancouver Sun*, 18 May 1939, 3; *Globe and Mail*, 17 May 1939, 11; *Montreal Gazette*, 19 May 1939, 22.

20 Food Acts and Cultural Politics: Women and the Gendered Dialectics of Culinary Pluralism at the International Institute of Toronto, 1950s–1960s

FRANCA IACOVETTA

As the first director of the International Institute of Metropolitan Toronto, Nell West initiated a series of Ethnic Weeks in 1957 to showcase immigrant customs and other cultural gifts and encourage mutual respect between new and old Canadians. In recruiting Anglo-Torontonians to the events, she promised such delightful treats as colourful handmade crafts, exciting folk dance performances, and delicious festive food. Of the dinner scheduled for Latvian Week in March, she predicted 'a gala occasion' with 'the Latvian women' wearing their 'varied and colourful' ethnic costumes and the banquet table set 'with the Easter motif used by Latvians in their homeland, fresh birch branches, green stalks of corn and multi-coloured Easter eggs.' They would serve popular Latvian meat dishes and 'the national bread in which the centre is filled with the whole kernel of wheat.'[1]

A decade later, in 1968, another woman director, Tina Stewart, announced plans to publish an 'International Cookbook' that would celebrate the culinary gifts that immigrants had brought to Canada and reflect the transformation in 'Toronto's eating habits' since the 1940s. The 'great influx of newcomers from Europe,' she noted, had encouraged a greater variety of restaurants and more experimentation with ethnic foods. She also acknowledged the role of postwar tourism, saying 'the enormous increase of travel' had also 'acquaint[ed] the native-born Canadians with the pleasing variety of European and Eastern dishes at home.' As an agency promoting interethnic relations, Stewart declared, the Toronto International Institute was well poised to produce a multi-ethnic cookbook that would 'enable a hostess to entertain with a variety of foreign dishes' or with 'a whole meal from one country.' She appealed to the institute women 'to send us your favourite recipes,' adding 'don't worry if they are in your own language, we will get them translated and the measurements converted to English measurements.'[2]

As the directors of the Canadian member of a U.S.-based network of immigrant agencies that promoted pluralism as part of its integration campaigns, West's and Stewart's emphasis on the immigrants' cultural contributions, or gifts, to Canada met with the goals of the wider International Institute movement.[3] It also fit with a history of Canadian experiments in pluralism that both celebrated and appropriated ethnic customs through a mosaic discourse in which Canada emerged as benevolent brewer of enriching cultures.[4] This chapter considers the role that food-related acts played in promoting a cultural politics of pluralism at the Toronto International Institute, highlighting the mix of Anglo and ethnic Canadian[5] and immigrant women involved. I examine the various programs, from charity baskets for poor mothers to multi-ethnic banquets and cook booklets (Stewart's grand cookbook never materialized) implemented as part of the institute's mandate to incorporate immigrants into the mainstream and build an international community, or local United Nations, in Toronto that might also serve as a model for postwar Canada.[6] My analysis draws on the scholarship that explores the multifaceted character of food as material resource, political tool, social practice, cultural marker, and site of contest between dominant and less powerful groups,[7] and that highlights women as food providers, cookbook writers, and community builders (including the essays by Andrea Eidinger and Marlene Epp in this volume).[8]

Furthermore, in assessing the wider significance of this food activism, my essay probes the possibilities as well as limits of the pluralism that women, both professional and volunteer staff, enacted in the intercultural space of the International Institute.[9] Rather than adopting a glass half-full or half-empty approach, it adopts a gendered dialectical approach sensitive to the tensions revealed by the women's well-intentioned activities that, in concert with the efforts of others, did help to bring about a modest discursive shift from a hegemonic politics of Anglo conformity to one more respectful of cultural difference, even if it hardly erased class and racial-ethnic hierarchies.[10] My examination of how the International Institute women negotiated class and cultural boundaries, and experimented with a 'multicultural re-imagining'[11] of the city and nation after the Second World War, is mindful of a central paradox of the early post-1945 era, where a liberal pluralist ethos that encouraged Canada's 'ethnics' to celebrate their cultural distinctiveness while adapting to middle-class 'Canadian ways' bumped up against more intrusive measures and a repressive Cold War state that censured those with divergent politics or values.[12] Although hardly uncontested, food emerged in this era as a comparatively safe site on which to negotiate Canada's growing ethnic diversity.

Origins and Backdrop

Following the merger of its precursors, the Toronto institute joined the American Federation of International Institutes in 1956. Despite America's dominant melting pot ideology, these multilingual agencies consciously pursued intercultural approaches to immigrant integration and to education and social work. In contrast to the '100 per cent Americanizers,' or assimilationists, the institutes' pluralist approach combined settlement-house type programs promoting Americanization, such as English language, civics, and mother's classes, with those aimed at exhibiting immigrant cultural gifts, such as folk music concerts and multi-ethnic cookbook projects. Originating out of the Progressive-era Young Women's Christian Association movement and its work with immigrant women, the first International Institute was founded in New York City in 1910; in subsequent decades, institutes cropped up in cities across the United States. Following the Second World War, a few new institutes emerged in the United States, and one in Toronto.[13]

As Canada's most popular immigrant destination, Toronto made great sense as a site for a Canadian International Institute. The huge influx of newcomers arriving in the decades after 1945 reinforced and enlarged Toronto's older ethnic neighbourhoods, with their ma and pa bakeries, butchers, eateries, and grocery stores. Moreover, it truly challenged for the first time the city's reputation as a primarily 'wasp' city. Approximately half of the 2.5 million newcomers who entered Canada by 1965 were continental Europeans, many of whom settled in Toronto. By 1971, with more than 43 per cent of its population (713, 315) composed of foreign-born persons, Toronto had become a more decidedly multi-ethnic if still largely white city.[14] Since the Toronto Institute collapsed in 1974, its efforts to attract immigrants who arrived from South Asia, the Caribbean, and other 'new' sources after 1967 were short-lived. Its experiment in community-based pluralism, like Ottawa's adoption in 1971 of official multiculturalism, occurred in a primarily white, Anglo, and Euro-Canadian context.

The Toronto International Institute began life in a small downtown church building on Jarvis Street, fairly distant from any immigrant neighbourhood. In 1959, it moved west to larger quarters in a two-building address on College Street amid a major immigrant reception area. Here, a mix of Anglos, ethnic Canadians, and immigrants resided. The area included Toronto's oldest Little Italy, which was attracting new Italians and other Europeans, and Kensington Market, the open air ethnic market. The 'ethnic' mix of these neighbourhoods was reproduced inside the institute.[15]

The institute personnel included both male and female professionals, students, and volunteers, but women composed an overall majority of the staff (including volunteers) and were most active in the food programs. Far from being a homogeneous group of middle-class Anglo Canadians, the female staff represented a mix of Anglo and ethnic Canadian and immigrant women of different social backgrounds. They included professionally trained Canadian social workers such as West and group workers from the University of Toronto Social Work School. There were ethnic Canadian women on the multilingual counselling staff (some of whom earned social work degrees) as well as educated refugees with linguistic skills. A few immigrants trained in social work back home were also hired.[16]

The volunteers were mostly Anglo-Canadian middle-class women recruited through the institute's co-sponsors, the Toronto Junior League and the Imperial Order Daughters of the Empire, which also hosted the annual children's Christmas party where needy kids feasted on cookies and ice cream. (Even in these 'wasp' circles, a few ethnic Canadians emerge.) There were also ethnic Canadian middle-class women like the ladies auxiliary members of the Italian Canadian Professional and Businessmen's Association who acted as home visitors for Italian clients, and immigrant volunteers of working-class background who also helped out. The composition of the institute's female personnel was thus more diverse than would have been found in a mainstream English Canadian social agency. [17] And while middle-class women dominated, they shared with the others a pluralist agenda, one that stressed the beneficial effects of their efforts to preserve and celebrate immigrant food and folk cultures. By cultivating a sense of belonging among immigrants, they agreed, the programs facilitated the newcomers' integration into Canadian society.[18] By encouraging among Canadians a greater knowledge of and respect for cultural diversity, it was also argued, they helped Anglo-Torontonians become enlightened citizens of Canada and the wider world.[19] In addition, women's labours helped get the food programs off the ground, and many of the participants appreciated the events and attached positive meaning to them.

Charitable Food Acts and Limits of Pluralism

Immigrant women have heroically sacrificed their own health and endured multiple indignities to feed their families in challenging old and new world contexts, and their success or failure has profoundly informed their personal identities as well as their status within their family and community (see, e.g., Stacey Zembrzycki's chapter in this volume).[20] Food has been a major charitable or welfare item and middle-class women, whether religious or secular, professional or volunteer, have played key roles in distributing food to struggling women and their families.[21] We also know that charity among the poor, especially women, has its own long and enduring history.[22] As a social agency serving non–English-speaking immigrants, the Toronto International Institute saw feeding hungry newcomers as necessary to avoiding individual anomie or crisis and equated a healthy nation with social stability. Notwithstanding the heterogeneity of the institute's female staff (including volunteers), their organized charitable food acts certainly reinforced class and ethnic hierarchies, although the evidence, most of it produced by the institute and thus requiring careful scrutiny,[23] shows few instances of class resentment or conflict.

In carrying out their welfare activities, the staff of the Toronto International Institute prescribed to the professional and bourgeois codes of a mainstream social service agency surveying resources and selecting suitable recipients. They routinely solicited food vouchers from ethnic stores (like Johnny Lombardi's nearby deli) and supermarkets (such as Dominion Stores) and thanked the donors for contributing to the newcomers' integration into Canadian life. During the busy Christmas season, the institute distributed close to one hundred baskets to poor immigrant families in the neighbourhood. It obtained many of its donors through the Christmas Bureau of the Toronto Social Planning Council, another institute co-sponsor, but generated its own list of recipients through its counsellors and home visitors. The home reports on eligible families suggest how illness, injury, debt, or divorce could push struggling mothers and their families onto the brink of disaster.[24] As individual donors, Brownies and Boy Scout troops, teachers, and grocery store truck drivers dropped items off, the institute women filled the baskets with a Christmas turkey or chicken dinner, food voucher, and toys, and then delivered them or had the families pick them up. The work was sufficiently labour intensive that it interrupted normal duties for several weeks. Ever vigilant, the staff tried to protect their clients from intrusive donors, usually Anglo-Canadian women, wanting to see what an appreciative immigrant family looked like – although a few of them got their way. The staff also encouraged donors and recipients to join the institute.[25]

In selecting deserving families, the institute staff expected the mothers to make effective use of a modest food donation. As in the past, those who made what staff considered an impulse or unnecessary purchase came under criticism: an Italian mother of seven young children, for instance, was dubbed irresponsible for using part of her institute Christmas food voucher for 'buying chestnuts' and other unnecessary 'merchandise.' Ironically, the criticism ignored the cultural and emotional significance of this holiday treat for Italians. The woman's effort to rekindle nostalgic memories of roasted chestnuts at Christmastime also hurt her chances of getting similar help the following year.[26]

The reports reveal plenty of sympathy for struggling newcomer women albeit sympathy that bordered on class pity. An Anglo-Canadian home visitor was so moved by the plight of a mother of six young children burdened with hospital and mortgage costs that she asked whether, in addition to a large Christmas basket, the mother could receive money. As her report suggests, the parents' work and family ethic influenced the request: 'The parents are making a real sacrifice to keep the children in school, and have put everything toward buying a home … Food and Clothing needed, especially for the older ones.'[27] An Italian Canadian visitor used similar language in her report on a sick and 'very depressed' Italian mother whose family was facing crippling medical costs on account of her spine operation ('proud people,' 'good manners'). She showed sympathy for non-Italians, too, including a Portuguese mother of five whose husband had recently died in a car accident.[28] On occasion, the home visitors recommended women they considered immoral because the children were truly hungry: this happened to a Jamaican woman, one of the few racial minorities to appear in these records, with four children reportedly fathered by different men.[29]

True to their pluralist mandate, International Institute workers were sensitive to the food preferences of their mostly European recipients. When donors asked what to give, they said 'southern European' foods, easily obtained in Toronto's ethnic shops, would appeal to the largest number of families. A suggested list included 'Ham – smoked and cooked; sardines; macaroni; rice; tomato – peeled and paste; beans, peas but not in tins – dry; fruit, vegetable oil, cotton seed oil, olive oil mostly; Jam, coffee, tea, sugar, butter unsalted; cod fish; turkey; chicken.'[30]

The institute also pressured the Visiting Homemaker's Association, whose nutritionists drew up model baskets, to adopt a multicultural approach. The VHA's recommendations for a festive and nutritious Christmas family meal did reflect Anglo-Canadian or North American models. (Nutritional science itself is socially constructed, and the experts are themselves products of their class and culture; see the chapters by Ian Mosby, Krista Walters, and Caroline Durand in this volume.) For example, the seven-dollar VHA Christmas basket for a family of five included a '5–6 lb chicken or turkey, 1 lb onions, 3 lbs each of turnips and potatoes, 1 tin peas (20 oz), 1 dozen each of oranges and apples, 1 lb each of sugar, cranberries, dates, mixed nuts or candy, 1 loaf bread, and 1 lb margarine.' Instead, institute staff created a list of 'Suggested Food Gifts' for 'Italians, Greeks, Slavic, and Others' that had both individual items and brand names of Italian foods. It included: 'oil for cooking; canned goods – Unico or Brava products; canned tomatoes (peeled); dried beans (red, kidney, lima) and lentils; peas; fruit; nuts; raisons; prunes; Jams; tea and cocoa – Canadian brands or others; Italian Coffee; Macaroni – Lancia; Rice, Olives; Sugar; Flour; Sardines; Milk in tins; Barley; and Canned fruit.' A 'Portuguese and Spanish' column had most of the same items plus corn flour for making bread.[31] Still, the gap between the sort of 'Canadian' foods recommended in Canada's Food Guide and 'southern European' foods was fairly easy to close, especially in Toronto (see Ian Mosby's chapter in this volume). As Krista Walters notes in this volume, Canada's nutritionists largely dismissed the value of Aboriginal 'country foods' like big game meat, whales, and wild rice.

As their correspondence suggests, the International Institute women drew great satisfaction from their charity work and they exhibited a mutual respect for each other. Even allowing for an expected degree of politeness or effusiveness, we can detect in the friendly letters between staffers and volunteers evidence of women forging bonds of friendship and articulating a sense of themselves as a community of women involved in worthy projects (see below).[32] By contrast, their interactions with the overburdened mothers they met were overlaid with a paternalism that reinforced the class and cultural (if not ethnic) divide between them.[33] Still, the records suggest that if accepting charity proved embarrassing for some mothers, no one rejected the Christmas baskets, a finding that likely reflects the institute's selection process and record-keeping as well as the depth of need.

As scholars of 'the gift' observe, the recipient of charity often becomes in some way beholden to the giver while the giver, feeling virtuous, might yet expect something in return.[34] Institute staff encouraged the mothers to become members and enrol in their mothers' clubs and other Canadianization programs, but they did not limit their donations to institute members. However complicated their response to charity, the recipients of institute food (or vouchers), many of whom already had been forced by war and displacement to rely on aid, expressed their appreciation in thank-you letters written on cheap cards or scraps of paper, in their own language or in rudimentary English. A typical batch arrived during Christmas 1961 penned by Polish, Slavic, and Italian mothers (and some daughters) who struggled to say thanks in English. They included Yugoslav-born Magdalena T., who wrote, 'I can't find the proper words to express my gratitude, therefore I am just saying "THANK YOU EVER SO MUCH,"' and an Italian mother deeply moved by the large basket she received. 'O[n] this date which I never forget,' Maria D. wrote, 'it was a big surprise for me but more great to my children ... [a] memorable day ... unforgeble [unforgettable] ... great avent [event].' 'I together with my family' she added, 'adresse [with] poor words but grea[t] spirit of my fede [faith] to thank you and all children of this great organization.'[35]

Ethnic Eating and Cultural Mingling

If charitable food acts hold few possibilities for building a democratically based international community, the receptions and banquets organized by the International Institute for its immigrant, ethnic, and Canadian members created comparatively more egalitarian contexts for cultural mingling. For such events, the staff invited men and women from their roster of individual and ethnic group members, which helped ensure the desired ethnic mix. While the catering varied depending on the size and purpose of the gathering, the staff often aimed for a mixed-ethnic menu. For its annual garden party in 1957, for example, female staff shopped and prepared the simple party food on their own, at the downtown home of one of the volunteers. Their shopping list reveals a mix of 'Canadian' (North American) and 'European' food items: '150 hot dogs and buns,' '2 jars peanut butter,' '15 loaves of white bread,' '1 jar canned corned beef,' '½ half lb. fish – English style sandwiches,' '1 jar mustard' and '½ lb. Danish salami [for] Danish sandwiches,' '1 package liver paste,' and '4 loaves of German bread.'[36] Cost also influenced the choices; indeed, staff often shopped for deals at Kensington Market and asked for donations from bakeries and stores.

The catered receptions held at the International Institute by the Canadian Citizenship Branch of the federal government, IODE, and other groups created a forum for cultural mingling and sociability that encouraged a modest degree of cultural pluralism. On such occasions, young Greek, Estonian, Hungarian, and other immigrant women dressed in colourful 'traditional' costumes might act as the 'pretty attendants' greeting people and serving nationality pastries, thereby literally embodying an attractive and feminine ethnicity.[37] But they were also considered 'nationality workers,' an institute term meaning intermediaries, expected to facilitate friendly conversation across cultures.[38] On occasion, men, too, filled this role: a Christmas Tea flyer for 1958 advertised 'Hosts and Hostesses in National Costume.'[39]

The institute staff particularly approved of members who planned their own intercultural events, including dinners, as it encouraged participatory democracy and sociability within a multi-ethnic, community-based organization. There was never complete autonomy, however, because a staff member always acted as adviser – a situation that annoyed certain members.[40] Still, an early success was the gender-mixed Supper Club, whose adult members met on two Sundays of each month to share a meal and enjoy a movie, music, or speaker, and a final evening 'social.'[41] Indeed, rather than simply following institute designs, the mostly European participants were drawing on their own food customs with meals punctuated by story telling, debate, and entertainment. They clearly understood that sociability could facilitate and reinforce social bonds, and that, to cite food theorists Carol Counihan and Penny Van Esterik, eating is 'an evolving enactment of gender, family, and community relationships.'[42] Given the intense anti-communism of both staff and members, the group's politics no doubt overlapped with the institute's anti-communist position. Both women and men helped organize these events and the ethnic dinners were varied.

Another successful group, the Outdoor Club, served a mix of Canadian (North American) camp fare, such as hamburgers, and easy-to-cook food bought from ethnic butchers, such as Hungarian pork sausages. The most adventurous of the institute groups – and criticized for being too independent-minded – the Outdoor Club organized day and weekend trips outside of Toronto. Composed mostly of Balts and other Eastern Europeans, the group went on summer camping trips or rented housekeeping cottages and took bus tours to see the autumn colours. Eventually, a few of them bought a modest cottage and invited institute friends for the weekend. As the logbook shows, the group sometimes ate hot dogs and 'mac and cheese,' at other times, tongue. They cooked European dishes that, like spaghetti and meatballs (already mainstreamed in the United States), could be made from scratch or with manufactured products like tinned sauce.[43]

The most elaborate ethnic dinners held at the International Institute were the banquets connected with the Ethnic Weeks, described as 'a community project' that showcased the 'cultural attributes' of Toronto's 'local ethnic communities' and 'promoted closer understanding between "New" and "Old" Canadians.'[44] Each week featured a different group but followed a general pattern: Sunday tea with music and dances; a cultural lecture or film and perhaps a musical performance on Wednesday; a nationality dinner on Thursday; and Friday night folk dancing sometimes followed by ballroom dancing or a party. Throughout the week, the group's art and crafts were on display as well as ethnic snacks and food.[45]

To help ensure a collaborative effort, institute staff tried to pair one major organization (or umbrella group) representing the ethnic group being featured with a few 'general community groups,' meaning Canadian groups such as a Local Council of Women or Kiwanis Club branch. West even proposed a mixed menu for the opening tea and ceremonies with the community group bringing 'fruitbread or sandwiches' and the ethnic group 'the nationality cakes and pastries.' Still, the ethnic sponsors took on greater responsibility for securing the performers, lecturers, displays, and the dinner. The institute helped with the advertising and preparations. All of the co-sponsoring groups tried to get some of their members out to the modestly priced banquet (usually about two dollars) but it was hoped that members of the public would also be enticed into coming to dinner.[46]

The public spectacles connected with these Ethnic Weeks reflected a cultural gifts or treasure chest approach to integrating immigrants, with its paradoxical mix of simultaneously celebrating and containing ethnic customs – and mining them for larger national objectives.[47] In one respect, the celebration of immigrant customs was all about colour, as suggested by West's description of the Latvian hostesses and Easter buffet table cited at the outset of the chapter. The publicity delivered the message that people would be treated to an exciting but orchestrated presentation of colourfully costumed musicians and folk dancers, decorated rooms, beautiful handicrafts, and festive ethnic food. In performing this packaged ethnicity, the performers were filling an assigned role as pleasing symbols of Canadian pluralism. This pluralism also had voyeuristic elements: Torontonians could become domestic tourists exploring an exotic cultural landscape and consuming foreign cultures in the safety of their own city.[48]

But these were not simply top-down events. The institute could not have mounted them without the active participation of ethnic organizations based in Toronto (both local ones and the Toronto branches of national federations such as the Canadian Polish Congress) and the immigrant or ethnic Canadian performers, hostesses, cooks, and attendees. Many of the immigrant and ethnic Canadians involved saw these events as an opportunity to shape the public commemoration and consumption of their culture in a Canadian milieu. Deeply invested in their own ethnic organizing and lobbying for more public recognition, ethnic leaders regularly invited institute directors and board members to their banquets and commemorative events. An institute gathering, then, might include, in addition to individual immigrant members like the Eastern European–dominated chess club, representatives of the Estonian Association of Toronto, the German Canadian Club Harmonie, and the Co-ordinating Committee of the Czechoslovak Democratic Organization in Toronto, an umbrella organization representing nationalist Czech groups such as St Wenceslaus Catholic Church in Toronto, Council of Free Czechoslovakia, Czech Boy Scouts, gymnastics, and veterans, Protestant church groups, and the Masaryk Memorial Institute.[49] While they might not wholly agree with the institute's ideals, these ethnic representatives also wanted to influence the making of a multi-ethnic Toronto and Canada.[50]

Like the artists, craftspeople, dancers, and musicians who welcomed the chance to attract an audience or sell their wares, the bakers, restaurant owners, and caterers hoped to build up a clientele. The dinner menu for Latvian Week in spring 1957, for example, offered a valuable plug for Little Riga Restaurant, which had prepared the buffet according to a Mrs Kronis-Balduma's arrangements. It included a starter of head cheese with horseradish and rye bread ('spudins ar marrutkiem un rudzu maizi') and three entrees: roast ham baked in dough ('mikla cepts zavets skinkis'), roast veal ('tela cepetis'), and roast chicken ('cepti cali'). The side dishes included leaf lettuce salad ('lapu salati') and radishes ('redisi'), country style peas and buttermilk ('zirni ar paninam'), and cottage cheese ('biezpiens'). The desserts reflected a Latvian preference for yeast doughs with crushed nuts, poppy seeds, and pot cheese: country style buns with honey and honey loaf cottage cheese. The much-loved caraway seeds were in the buns.[51]

The institute staff saw the participation of both Canadian and ethnic organizations as essential to the success of the Ethnic Weeks and dinners, yet also recognized that without the latter the events were doomed. In getting German Week off the ground in February 1957 (in the original Jarvis Street building), for example, West worked hard to secure the support of several different German immigrant and ethnic organizations in Toronto. The Citizenship Committee of the Toronto Local Council of Women and the Parkdale Travel Club, a local travel group, were the Canadian sponsors. The menu for the dinner featured common German fare: 'Kraftbruhe mit Leberkloessen' (consomme with liver dumplings) followed by main dishes: 'Kasseler Rippenspeer' (smoked pork chops) and 'Schwaebisches Kalbschnitzel mit Spaetzle' (Swabian veal steak with noodles). There were side dishes of red cabbage ('Rotkohl'), probably steamed and buttered in the German manner, and cucumber salad ('Gurkensalat'). The dessert was 'Apfelstrudel' (apple strudel). During the week, pastries were served with tea courtesy of German bakeries in the city: Freimann's Pastry, Hilda's Fancy Cake Bar, and Rudolph's Pastry. It was probably money well spent for the exposure and good will created.[52]

The participation of the ethnic organizations also had an important gender dimension. Men dominated the leadership of the major ethnic associations (whether composed mostly of immigrants or a mix of immigrant and ethnic Canadians) and their approval was necessary, but it was the women and their auxiliary or affiliated societies who usually were more actively involved in preparations. It was these immigrant and ethnic Canadian women who worked closely with the women of the International Institute and its co-sponsoring Canadian groups.

Take, for example, the Polish banquet held during the (inaugural) Polish Week in February 1957 and catered by Mr W. Szymczak of the Parkside Grill, a west-end restaurant. The ethnic co-sponsor was the Canadian Polish Congress, an umbrella organization representing a variety of social, cultural, men's, women's, and youth groups. The status of its male executive was evident in their placement at the head table; the president and vice-president, along with the wives, sat with speaker Father Mulvihil, a priest active in Catholic migration work and chair of the institute's board. As official host to this largely Catholic gathering, Mulvihil noted the historic and multicultural nature of the evening, reportedly saying that 'in this gathering, history was in the making' and the organizers 'were dreaming dreams for the future.'[53] But there were also women there who had been more directly involved in planning the event. They included the president of the Catholic Women's League (Mrs Ward Markle), the president of the Canadian Polish Women's Federation, and several institute board members, including Irene Ungar, singled out for special praise for her handling of the liaison work between the different sponsoring groups.[54] Other board members included seasoned Anglo volunteers like Mrs Fred Porter (Toronto Junior League), Mrs R.D. Jennings (IODE), and social worker Charity Grant of the Social Planning Council. Director Nell West (along with Richard Kolm, director of group services) represented the institute professional staff.[55] Similar gender dynamics characterized the organizing of the Croatian,[56] Ukrainian,[57] and other Ethnic Weeks.

There was also cross-gender collaboration. Just as the institute staff and volunteers dealt with both male and female artists and artisans, they worked with both male and female caterers, bakers, and restaurant owners. If institute women did not always put the food on the table, they frequently served it and, afterwards, helped with clean-up. Women also took care of other logistical details, devising a seating plan for the head table, making place cards for the dinner guests (so as to ensure mixing), and ordering tablecloths and napkins. If they used a commercial laundry, they saved themselves hours of washing up.[58] Feminist scholars have argued that the portrayal of housewifery as artistry in popular women's self-help and cookery books effectively disguised the reality of women's domestic labour. The institute's pluralist mandate could also serve to disguise women's labours as contributions to this greater goal, but the women's correspondence also suggests that they expected some recognition for all of the legwork, too.[59]

The Ethnic Weeks attracted a mix of immigrant, ethnic, and Canadian participants and institute immigrant and ethnic members praised them. For the staff, there were never enough Anglo-Torontonians at the events, especially men, but they, too, reported on the positive interethnic mingling. Some of the participating 'Anglos' were teachers, nurses, and other women with links to the institute; a few of them developed friendships with their ethnic counterparts. Some of the participating members developed romantic relationships, and a few interethnic European couples got married.[60] Within a year of launching the Ethnic Weeks at the institute's Jarvis Street home, West had to suspend the program because of increased workload and lack of space (also signs of success), but relaunched it after the move to College Street. The increased capacity (an auditorium with a 1,000 person capacity and a banquet or cabaret space for 350 to 400 people) allowed for larger week-long crowds. The total numbers appear to have grown from a few hundred to about a thousand.[61] Mounting the events was also time-consuming and costly, however, and so the institute also shifted to Ethnic Nights and Sundays, which drew respectable audiences of a few hundred people.[62] By the early 1960s, the program featured 'Eastern' events such as an Indonesian exhibit and dinner.[63]

Multi-ethnic Cookbooks and Immigrant Gifts

The Toronto International Institute adopted another food-related strategy long popular with the U.S. institutes, the multi-ethnic cookbook. One such project was a 1963 Christmas booklet and, it, too, was heavily European in focus. Promoting ethnic foods in Christian contexts provided another way of stripping the immigrants of their more threatening features and of creating a safe context in which to endorse cultural diversity (by contrast, Michel Desjardins and Ellen Desjardins' chapter in this volume on today's multiethnic food banks describe a more activist Christian pluralism). Done badly, it could reduce ethnicity to novelty. The institute's project, however, aimed not simply to entertain but to promote a pluralist message, and its creation involved a significant degree of intercultural collaboration. In both regards, it mirrored the cookbook projects of its U.S. counterparts, and the central International Institute body, whose 1956 cookbook, compiled by New York City staff with recipes from 'new and old Americans,' declared, 'When we prepare and eat the food of a foreign country we are not only exploring unique gustatory delights but bridging a gap in international understanding.'[64] Like the U.S. books, the Toronto institute's 1963 Christmas cookbook was also a fundraiser that helped pay the costs of Christmas baskets and parties. A few men contributed a recipe,[65] or sold copies,[66] but the women were most directly involved in creating and selling the inexpensive (one dollar) booklet.[67]

The scholarship on women and cookbooks, including the chapters in this volume by Marlene Epp and Andrea Eidinger, show that recipes are the products of personal and community relationships. Certainly, the Toronto International Institute women responded with enthusiasm to West's call for recipes; a Mrs R. Jensen sent in her favourite recipes for Danish Christmas 'Goodies' and was delighted that West included them.[68] They worked hard at choosing easy recipes or, when passing on 'a family tradition,' writing out easy-to-follow steps so other women would try them out. Mrs Lazic's Hungarian recipes were very basic: her 'Bachelor Gulash' involved frying onions, green peppers, tomatoes, and an egg with salt and pepper to taste; her smoked spare ribs had a few more ingredients (cooked spare ribs, potatoes, flour, paprika) and took just a little bit longer to prepare.[69]

A self-deprecating tone often associated with women characterized several letters, including that penned by a contributor of Ukrainian recipes for kutya (wheat pudding) and holubtsi (cabbage rolls). In neat and precise handwriting, she wrote, 'Both are so long – so much to explain so hope it helps you in your booklet idea.'[70] When Marie Dymes, in large loopy handwriting, sent in her detailed Czech recipes for fish soup (carp), red carp in bread crumbs, blue carp in aspic, and Yule loaf (Czech, vanocka), she told West, 'I only hope you will be able to decipher them.' Although asked to provide her favourites, Dymes, probably Czech Canadian, took the project so seriously that she 'copied them out of an old cookery book to make them more reliable,' but added, 'they certainly evoked some old memories.' She also included personal comments, asking after West's health and saying she hoped to see her soon.[71]

West is equally friendly in her replies to the contributors, which included Hungarian Canadian staffers Elizabeth Szalowski, a home visitor, and Irene Szebeny, a bookkeeper who also handled many Hungarian clients. Significantly, Szalowksi was emphatic about including her borscht and beef à la Stroganoff as 'everyday recipes' representing 'a mixture of old country and Canadian foods, adapted to the needs of a busy Canadian housekeeper, who still loves to cook and serve interesting meals.' In both cases, ketchup and a package of dried onion soup mix appeared as the convenient 'Canadian' (North American) processed ingredients. The borscht recipe also added wieners to the hamburger, consomme (a can), diced beets (also tinned), and celery and potatoes. In addition to the familiar emphasis on quick and inexpensive meals is their flexibility: that the recipes could be prepared in advance and reheated, and refrigerated leftovers used for another meal 'is of great help to the Hostesses' disposition and appearance.' Referring to her borscht recipe ('I find it very nice to serve this stew-type soup on cold winter nights'), Szalowksi offered a familiar encouragement to women to be playful with meal making and vary the recipe to keep family members from becoming bored eaters. One could use a ham base for borscht, for instance, or add lima beans, cabbage, or tomatoes. Even more fun, she exclaimed, 'for the ones who do not count calories!' were her 'quick tasty potato pancakes': 'this is excellent for a kitchen party – everybody ready with a plate waiting for the pancakes to be served right off the skillet (or skillets – you can have a couple of them going).'[72]

Szebeny's recipe for a chicken with rice dish, which included convenience items of cream of mushroom soup and condensed milk, also suggests that by this point the mainstreaming of European dishes already had occurred in Canadian cities like Toronto and that busy ethnic Canadian women had adopted quicker versions of old world dishes. She, too, stressed ease and flexibility. The dish was 'excellent to prepare in advance for a nice relaxed Sunday – dinner ready – just heat it and serve it.' One could then vary the leftover soup produced by adding some dumplings or fresh vegetables.[73] By contrast, a self-described Anglo-Canadian lawyer who contributed one of the few 'Anglo' or 'British' Christmas recipes, for light fruit cake, wished to establish authenticity, even a royal pedigree, for her recipe. In reference to the Royal family, Margaret P. Hyndman, QC, wrote: 'I sent one of these cakes to Queen Mary for Christmas 1949, having been first invited to visit her in the summer of that year, after which we corresponded – thereafter I sent one to her each Christmas, the last one in 1953.'[74]

The cookbook is a multilayered cultural, political, and gendered text requiring interpretation. An understanding of the makers' aim and intended audience can help unpack the encoded messages, even paradoxes, of a given book. The Toronto International Institute women never explicitly defined their audience but it is clear that *Season's Greetings in Food – Christmas 1963* was targeted mainly at Canadian women and ethnic Canadian women operating in both an English and ethnically Euro-Canadian milieu. No doubt, they hoped to sell copies to immigrant women, too, especially those enrolled in institute classes or programs.[75] As an English-language booklet promoting culinary pluralism among Toronto women, it used the familiar techniques of food writers and nutritionists who touted cheap, flexible, and healthy meals and tried to make cooking sound like fun.[76] It adopted the cheery style of food writers like Margaret Carr, whose *Cooking Chat* column appeared in the *Toronto Star.* Institute staff even clipped her ethnic holiday recipes for their files.[77]

The booklet begins by declaring that 'each nationality within the Canadian "mosaic" celebrates the Christmas season in the tradition of its forefathers,' a statement that ignores non-Christians, and that 'the melding of these distinctive customs brings a richness to the festive season.'[78] It then offers brief descriptions of the Christmas customs of different European groups. Although written in an obviously festive manner, the booklet's emphasis on the most colourful or fantastical of customs has the overall effect of transforming particularly rural Europeans into simple folk figures bearing quaint traditions. The Italians, for example, have their 'Befana, the benefactress,' who appears as 'a charitable witch coming down the chimney filling the children's shoes with gifts' and the Czechs their St Nicholas, who 'comes down from the heavens accompanied by an angel carrying a bag of gifts for good children and leading the devil who has switches for the bad ones.' There is also a focus on the more intimate, familial, and less commercial nature of Christmas in Europe (as compared with North America), where people enjoy a quiet family meal on Christmas Eve, attend mass, and hand out gifts. Christmas is presented as a magical time, especially in the villages, where children are delighted by magical pigs or talking animals and people tell each other's fortunes. The playful take on pagan rituals is continued in the section on New Year's Superstitions; it includes the book's only two British examples: the Irish, who must have 'their lucky Irish bread' and the English, who believe that 'for every mince pie you eat you will have a wish come true.' The only acknowledgment of non-Europeans is an entry on the Japanese who 'drink the first pail of water drawn from a well on New Year's morning' in the belief that it 'drives evil spirits from their body.'[79] Thus, while West and colleagues included a few quaint 'Anglo' customs (but no mention of Santa Claus, North America's Saint Nick),[80] the main portrait is of colourful European villagers.

The major part of the booklet is devoted to the ethnic recipes collected, all but eight of the total thirty-six presented as popular foods eaten at Christmastime. Most are assigned a nationality label although some may have easily crossed European borders. The breakdown was as follows: two Lithuanian; six British (Christmas cake, pudding, and sauce recipes); two each for Danish, Yugoslav, and Ukrainian; and four each for Czech, Italian, Portuguese, and Italian. Only two of the eight 'Year Around Recipes' were ethnically marked, 'Finger Frets' (Austrian pastry) and 'German Cake.' The remaining 'Canadian' recipes would have been familiar to Anglo-Torontonians: pumpkin pie, tuna casserole, and chicken and rice combinations. As Szalowski hoped, the borscht and beef à la Stroganoff, although European in origin, were also presented as Canadian recipes perfect for the busy mother. (Her cute asides for the borsht and pancake recipes were also included.) Again, the recipes reflected and reinforced the mainstreaming of economical and nutritious European-origin foods, with commercially prepared ketchup and tinned or packaged soups acting as the items of homogenization.

Still, most of the recipes are presented as immigrant cultural gifts, that is, as old world dishes transplanted to Toronto by the latest waves of Europeans. There was Lithuanian red beet salad with herring and poppy seed rolls as well as Italian lasagna and the dessert zabaglione and Christmas fruit bread, Panettone alla Milanese. There was Hungarian porkolt (goulash) and hazelnut cake and Danish cookies, klejner (deep-fried cookies) and vanille kranse (vanilla and almond cookies). The booklet also featured 'typical' Christmas meals of recent immigrants, including the Portuguese, who, it claimed, ate cod fish for Christmas Eve but turkey dinner for Christmas Day with turkey soup, stuffed turkey, fish fillets, pumpkin croquettes, flan pudding, salad, jams, oranges, and dried fruits. It noted, through a silly sexist joke, that many Toronto Portuguese bought live turkeys: 'Before killing the turkey,' the recipe advises the wife, 'give him [husband] a drink of brandy so he gets drunk, then let him rest without food for 24 hours.'[81]

The Toronto International Institute's 1963 Christmas cook booklet fit with other multi-ethnic Canadian and U.S. cookbooks that helped to create a safe cultural terrain on which particularly the dominant 'hosts' could be encouraged to accept 'difference.' It was a hybrid culinary text, the product, really, of the food acts of a group of mostly Anglo and ethnic Canadian middle-class women enacting liberal pluralism at the Toronto institute during a time of heavy European immigration (on culinary hybridity see the chapters by Julia Roberts, Marlene Epp, and Julie Mehta in this volume).[82] Such cultural politics inevitably involved a process of mainstreaming the foreign food until it was no longer considered dangerously foreign yet still retained enough of the exotic to make experimentation worthwhile. By having fun with ethnic foods that, as a bonus, were generally cheap, women across class and cultures could engage in mutual cultural exchange and share a healthy respect for culinary diversity. In short, these foods were cultural gifts that could be used to enrich the treasure trove, or smorgasbord, of Canadian national unity. A few immigrant and working-class women participated in the project but West held the cultural reigns of power and she and her middle-class friends decided what got into the booklet. Nor did their pluralism preclude promotion of 'Canadian' cookbooks with recipes for flapjacks, biscuit cheese squares, pies, and French Canadian pea soup.[83]

Still, the institute's 1963 multi-ethnic cook booklet, like its ethnic dinners and Europeanized Christmas baskets, represented a collective effort to help shift, if only modestly, a hegemonic notion of a once staunchly 'wasp' Toronto, and Canada (notwithstanding the French fact), to a more tolerant pluralist society. In that regard, these booklets, though slim, cheap, and even amateurish, were not only vehicles for the exchange of ideas among liberal-minded women. To borrow from food theorist John C. Super, they constituted sites of a gender-influenced production of nationalist ideology that linked culinary experimentation and celebrations of multi-ethnic diets to participation in a new national culture,[84] one that officially espoused tolerance and respect for cultural difference as common Canadian values. The 1947 Canadian Citizenship Act did just that: it promoted Canadian citizenship as a set of common values – democracy, freedom, liberalism – with which a diverse people could be made to identify and support.[85] Institute staff similarly believed that a modest multicultural reimagining of the nation could foster unity among an increasingly heterogeneous population, although none of this was supposed to challenge Canada's ruling elites or major institutions.[86]

Conclusion

According to U.S. historian Kirstin Hoganson, liberal pluralist 'Americanizers' like the International Institute's interwar nationality workers 'celebrated immigrant gifts even as they promoted national homogeneity.'[87] In postwar Toronto, too, the institute staff and volunteers who taught English, civics, and nutrition celebrated immigrant customs as they worked to make newcomers into Canadians. For them, Canadianization (which invariably involved some homogenizing of ethnic cultures into a Canadian mould) and pluralism existed in symbiotic relationship to each other: eating ethnic involved a positive, indeed enriching, process of absorbing the other and rendering it Canadian while still a touch exotic. Their food-related cultural projects (as opposed to charitable ones) encouraged some cross-ethnic and cross-class bonds among the women involved, even opening up some possibilities for building a multicultural community within the institute's intercultural space.[88] Toronto's expanding immigrant and mixed-ethnic neighbourhoods and ethnic eateries also encouraged a degree of 'bottom-up' culinary experimentation and the rise of hybrid diets across class and cultural boundaries (see Zembrzycki on Ukrainians, in this volume).[89] The International Institute's pluralism also had serious limits: it was largely confined to white, Anglo, and Euro-Canadians, middle-class women dominated its programs, and non-European customs were promoted only sporadically.

NOTES

1 The quotations are from two letters: Archives of Ontario (AO), International Institute of Metropolitan Toronto Collection (IIMT), Fonds 884, MU6413, File: Ethnic Occasions, 1957, Mrs W.E. West, executive director, to Controller Jean Newman, City Hall, Toronto, 28 March 1957; and MU6415, File: Latvian Federation, 1957, W.E. West to Mr Ian McIntosh, Television news editor, CBC, Toronto, Memoranda on Latvian Week – March 31st to April 6th, 26 March 1957.
2 AO, IIMT, F884, MU6446 (B28383), File: International Club, *Intercom*, April 1968. Column headed 'Institute Cookbook,' 1.
3 Ibid., MU6413, File: Ethnic Occasions, 1957, 'The Ethnic Weeks at the International Institute of Metropolitan Toronto,' and 'Suggested Schedule for Ethnic Weeks at IIMT'; Kristin L. Hoganson, *Consumers' Imperium: The Global Production of American Domesticity, 1865–1920* (Chapel Hill, NC: University of North Carolina Press, 2007), chapter 4.
4 See, e.g., Robert Cupido, 'Appropriating the Past: Pageants, Politics and the Diamond Jubilee of Confederation,' *Journal of the Canadian Historical Association* 9/1 (1998): 155–86; Stuart Henderson, '"While There Is Still Time …": J. Murray Gibbon and the Spectacle of Difference in Three CPR Folk Festivals, 1928–31,' *Journal of Canadian Studies* 39 (2005): 139–74; Ivana Caccia, 'Managing the

Canadian Mosaic: Dealing with Cultural Diversity during the World War Two Years,' doctoral dissertation, University of Ottawa, 2006, chapter 2. See also, John Murray Gibbon, *Canadian Mosaic: The Making of a Northern Nation* (Toronto: McClelland and Stewart, 1938).

5 By ethnic Canadian I mean foreign-born or Canadian-born women who had grown up or spent much of their adulthood in Canada and were thus significantly Canadianized. Some of them had also experienced upward mobility into the middle classes and were active in older or new ethnic organizations.

6 For example, AO, IIMT, F884, MU6413, File: Ethnic Occasions, 1957, 'The Ethnic Weeks at the International Institute of Metropolitan Toronto'; Mrs W.E. West to His Worship, Mayor Phillips, City Hall, Toronto, 1 April 1957, and other correspondence and flyers in the file; Franca Iacovetta, *Gatekeepers: Reshaping Immigrant Lives in Cold War Canada* (Toronto: Between the Lines, 2006), chapter 4.

7 For example, Mary Douglas, ed., *Food in the Social Order: Studies of Food and Festivals in Three American Communities* (New York: Basic Books, 1984); Stephen Mennell, Anne Murcott, and Anneke H. van Otterloo, *The Sociology of Food: Eating, Diet and Culture* (London: Sage, 1992); Harvey Levenstein, *Paradox of Plenty: A Social History of Eating in Modern America* (New York: Oxford University Press, 1993); James Miller, *Skyscrapers Hide the Heavens: A History of Indian-White Relations in Canada* (Toronto: University of Toronto Press, 1989); and on women, Joan Jensen, *New Mexico Women: Intercultural Perspectives* (Albuquerque, NM: University of New Mexico Press, 1986); Marlene Epp, *Women without Men: Mennonite Refugees of the Second World War* (Toronto: University of Toronto Press, 2000); Mary Ellen Kelm, *Colonizing Bodies: Aboriginal Health and Healing in British Columbia* (Vancouver: UBC Press, 2001).

8 For example, Carol Counihan and Penny Van Esterik, eds., *Food and Culture: A Reader* (New York: Routledge, 1997); Arlene Voski Avakian and Barbara Haber, eds., *From Betty Crocker to Feminist Food Studies: Critical Perspectives on Women and Food* (Amherst, MA: University of Massachusetts Press, 2005); Sherrie A. Inness, *Dinner Roles: American Women and Culinary Culture* (Iowa City, IA: University of Iowa Press, 2001); Valerie Korinek, *Roughing It In Suburbia: Reading Chatelaine in the Fifties and Sixties* (Toronto: University of Toronto Press, 2000).

9 My concept of intercultural space has some parallels with a contact zone approach that treats the subjects in terms of 'interlocking understandings and practises, often within radically asymmetrical relations of power.' Mary Pratt, *Imperial Eyes: Travel Writing and Transculturation* (New York: Routledge, 1992), 2.

10 On paradox, see also, the theoretically sophisticated Viranjini Munasinghe, *Callaloo or Tossed Salad? East Indians and the Cultural Politics of Identity in Trinidad* (Ithaca, NY: Cornell University Press, 2001).

11 This is a play on Benedict Anderson's influential *Imagined Communities: Reflections on the Origin and Spread of Nationalism* (London: Verso, 1991). For a positive position on Canadian multiculturalism, see, e.g., Will Kymlicka, *Multicultural Citizenship: A Liberal Theory of Minority Rights* (Toronto: Oxford University Press, 2001).

12 On these themes see, e.g., my *Gatekeepers*.

13 The Toronto International Institute's precursors were the New Canadians Service Agency and St Andrew's Memorial House. The AFII was later renamed the American Council for Nationalities Service. Raymond A. Mohl, 'Cultural Pluralism in Immigrant Education: The International Institutes of Boston, Philadelphia, and San Francisco, 1920–1940,' *Journal of American Ethnic History* 1/2 (1982): 35–5 8; Hoganson, *Consumer's Imperium*, 222–3; Iacovetta, *Gatekeepers*, chapters 3 and 4.

14 Statistics from Ninette Kelley and Michael Trebilcock, *The Making of the Mosaic*: *A History of Canadian Immigration Policy* (Toronto: University of Toronto Press, 1998), 315; and Dominion Bureau of Statistics, unpublished census, Toronto, 1971.

15 James Lemon, *Toronto since 1918: An Illustrated History* (Toronto: Lorimer, 1985).

16 For example, the female social workers included one from Italy and Greece and, in the Portuguese case, Algiers.

17 This profile is drawn from personnel files, committee minutes, board minutes, and newspaper clippings in the IIMT collection. The male profile was also diverse and included a Caribbean and a South Asian counsellor.

18 AO, IIMT, F884, MU6413, File: Ethnic Occasions, 1957. Mrs W.E. West, director, to Mr Z. Jaworski, president, Toronto Branch, Canadian Polish Congress, 6 March 1957; Mrs W.E. West, executive director, to Mr Hans Kames, 27 March 1957.

19 This explains the institute's celebration of international events such as United Nations Week. Ibid., MU6382, File: Board of Directors Minutes June 12, 1956 – Dec. 5, 1957, Minutes of Programme Committee, 5 June 1957.

20 A small sample also includes: Marlene Epp, 'The Semiotics of Zwieback: Feast and Famine in the Narratives of Mennonite Refugee Women' (314–40), Franca Iacovetta and Valerie Korinek, 'Jello-O Salads, One-Stop Shopping, and Maria the Homemaker: The Gender Politics of Food' (190–230), and Paula Draper, 'Surviving Their Survival: Women, Memory and the Holocaust' (399–414), all in Marlene Epp, Franca Iacovetta, and Frances Swyripa, eds., *Sisters or Strangers? Immigrant, Ethnic, and Racialized Women in Canadian History* (Toronto: University of Toronto Press, 2004); Frances Swyripa, *Wedded to the Cause: Ukrainian-Canadian Women and Ethnic Identity, 1891–1991* (Toronto: University of Toronto Press, 1993); Ellen Cole, Oliva M. Espin, and Esther D. Rothblum, eds., *Refugee Women and Their Mental Health: Shattered Societies, Shattered Lives* (Binghamton, NY: Haworth Press, 1992); Marlene Epp, *Women without Men: Mennonite Refugees of*

the Second World War (Toronto: University of Toronto Press, 2000); Hasia Diner, *Hungering for America: Italian, Irish and Jewish Foodways in the Age of Migration* (Cambridge, MA: Harvard University Press, 2001); and references above.

21 For just a few North American modern era histories, see Cathy James, 'Gender, Class and Ethnicity in the Organization of Neighbourhood and Nation: The Role of Toronto's Settlement Houses in the Formation of the Canadian State, 1902 to 1914,' doctoral dissertation, University of Toronto, 1996; Rivka Shpak Lissak, *Pluralism and Progressives: Hull House and the New Immigrants, 1890–1919* (Chicago, IL: University of Chicago Press, 1989); Linda Gordon, *Pitied but Not Entitled: Single Mothers and the History of Welfare, 1890–1935* (Cambridge, MA: Harvard University Press, 1994); Margaret Little, *No Car, No Radio, No Liquor Permit: The Moral Regulation of Single Mothers in Ontario, 1920–1977* (Toronto: Oxford University Press, 1998).

22 See, e.g., Ellen Ross, *Love and Toil: Motherhood in Outcast London, 1870–1918* (London: Oxford University Press, 1993).

23 My reading of these slippery sources acknowledges the professional paradigms and class biases imbedded in such discursively constructed texts while rejecting the extreme postmodern position that they are merely the record-makers' fictive products. My approach is articulated in 'Post-Modern Ethnography, Historical Materialism, and De-centring the (Male) Authorial Voice: A Feminist Conversation,' *Histoire sociale / Social History* 32/64 (1999): 275–93.

24 For just one example, see 1963 list of home visitor reports on 73 families composed of Italian (49), Hungarian (11), Portuguese (9), Polish (1), Jugoslav (1), Croatian (1), and German (1) families in AO, IIMT, F884, MU6471, File: Christmas 1961, Nov. 14th and Nov. 13th, 1963, 'Xmas List for Needy Families (72)'. By this time, landed immigrants in several provinces could apply for certain health and welfare supports, but these varied across region, and many newcomers feared that accepting welfare might make them vulnerable to deportation.

25 Ibid., Margurite Streeruwitz, supervisor, Reception Centre, IIMT RC – Xmas 1963, 'Receiving and Giving Out of Xmas Gifts to Needy Families.'

26 'Xmas List for Needy Families (73).' The home visitor, Mrs A. (perhaps an IODE volunteer), put down 'maybe' for a basket for the following year. I found no record of what happened.

27 She was probably an IODE volunteer. 'Xmas List for Needy Families (73).'

28 Ibid. The visitor likely belonged to the Women's Auxiliary of the Italian Businessmen and Professional Men's Association or its Italian Immigrant Aid Society.

29 AO, IIMT, F884, MU6471, File: Christmas 1961, 'List, Xmas Needy Families Help, 1964/65.'

30 Ibid., 'List Starting Dec. 16th,' 1964 MS.

31 AO, IIMT, F884, MU6471, File: Xmas Lists 1962, Memo Diana Wilson to Mrs M.

Streeruwitz, 29 Nov. 1962; Reception Centre – Xmas 1965, Food Gifts Suggested for Italians; Spanish; Portuguese; 17 Nov. 1965, Margurite Streeruwitz, supervisor.

32 See, e.g., ibid., MU 6474, File: IODE Thank-you Letters, Margurite Streeruwitz (a newcomer who ran the Institute Reception Centre) to Mrs E.H. Hugenholtz, 12 May 1965; Streeruwitz to Mrs A. Stermac, Glen Alton Chapter, IODE, 11 May 1965 (describes Hugenholtz as 'a charming person'). For related activities, Mrs Streeruwitz to Mrs H.J. Heslop, 10 Jan. 1964; Mrs W.L. Smart, 17 Dec. 1962; Mrs Streeruwitz to S. Perri, 19 July 1962.

33 Here, I refer to encounters between acculturated and established ethnic Canadian women and struggling newcomers who came from the same country or belonged to the same nationality group.

34 For example, Gareth Stedman Jones, *Outcast London: A Study in the Relationship between Classes in Victorian Society* (Harmondsworth: Penguin, 1984), 251–71.

35 AO, IIMT, F884, MU6476, File: Thank you Letters, 1961, Letters (originals and translations).

36 Ibid., MU6413, File: Programme Committee Minutes, 1957.

37 This is a growing literature but the best Canadian work on the subject is Patrizia Gentile, 'Queen of the Maple Leaf: A History of Beauty Contests in Twentieth-Century Canada,' doctoral dissertation, Queen's University, 2006.

38 For examples, see AO, IIMT, F884, MU6427, File: Publicity Scrapbook Clippings from *Globe and Mail*, *Toronto Star*, *Toronto Telegram*; MU 6389, File: Immigration (General) 1957–66; MU6413, File: Ethnic Groups – Clippings, 1971–74; MU 6398, File: Croatian Organizations, File: Bulgarian 1961–64; MU6411, File: Mrs Stewart's Log; MU 6413, File: Ethnic Organization Lists, Godfrey Barrass to Nell West, 27 June 1960.

39 Ibid., MU5405, File: Xmas 1957–58, Flyer Christmas 1958, 'Tree Trimming Party, Wed. Dec. 17, 1958' and 'Christmas Tea, Sun. Dec. 21st.' The tea program included a Christmas play, Hungarian carols, and Chinese carols.

40 Ibid., MU6406, File: Programme Committee Reports, 1959–61, Programme Committee – Group Work Section, Minutes of Meeting, 31 March 1960.

41 In spring 1947, it had about 30 adult members, male and female, who came from a number of Toronto's ethnic groups. Ibid., MU6382, File: Board Minutes, June 12, 1956 – Dec. 5, 1957, Minutes of Programme Committee, 13 March 1957.

42 Counihan and Van Esterik, Introduction, *Food and Culture*.

43 AO, IIMT, F884, MU6381, File: Outdoor Group Logbook, 1954–59; on institute criticism of group, see, e.g., MU6382, File: Board of Directors: 1959, Minutes, Committee Statistics, Reports, Programme Committee – Group Work Services Minutes, 25 Feb. 1960. Levenstein, *Paradox of Plenty*.

44 AO, IIMT, F884, MU6413, File: Ethnic Occasions, 1957, 'The Ethnic Weeks at the International Institute of Metropolitan Toronto.'

45 Ibid., MU6411, File: Cultural Festival (Member Organizations), Institute Direc-
    tor, Harry Forbell, 'Notes from an Organizing Meeting.' See also MU 6415, File:
    Latvian Federation, 1957.
46 See, e.g., ibid., MU6413, File: Ethnic Occasions, 1957, Mrs W.E West to Mr T.W.
    Lovet, Don Mills, Kiwanis Club (Ukrainian week), 28 March 1957.
47 Hogarson, *Consumer's Imperium*, chapter 4. A more sympathetic treatment of
    grassroots U.S. pluralism is Russell A. Kazal, 'The Lost World of Pennsylvania
    Pluralism: Immigrants, Regions, and the Early Origins of Pluralist Ideologies,'
    Journal of American Ethnic History 27/3 (2008): 7–42. On spectacles with ethnic
    themes, see also Cupido, 'Appropriating the Past'; Henderson, 'While There Is
    Still Time'; Ian Radforth, *Royal Spectacle: The 1860 Visit of the Prince of Wales to
    Canada and the United States* (Toronto: University of Toronto Press, 2004); John
    Bodnar, *Remaking America: Public Memory, Commemoration and Patriotism in
    Twentieth-Century America* (Princeton, NJ: Princeton University Press, 1994).
48 For just two examples, see garden party flyer in AO, IIMT, F884, MU6429,
    B2800566, File: 1-St Andrews, Flyer 'A Garden Party,' 19 June 1954, and bazaar
    flyer in MU6472, File: Letters of Appreciation 1959–62, International Institute of
    MT Newsletter, 415 Jarvis, n.d. but 1957, Front Page, 'Old World Bazaar.'
49 For other examples, see ibid., MU6413, File: Ethnic Occasions, 1957, Invitations.
50 For example, see Cupido, 'Appropriating the Past.' A more detailed treatment is
    my 'Immigrant Gifts, Canadian Treasures and Spectacles of Pluralism: The Inter-
    national Institute of Toronto in North American Context, 1950s–1970s,' *Journal of
    American Ethnic History* 31/1 (Fall 2011): 34–7.
51 AO, IIMT, F884, MU6413, File: Ethnic Occasions, 1957, Flyer, 'Latvian Week,
    International Institute of Metropolitan Toronto, 414 Jarvis St, WA 5-1121, March
    31 to April 6, 1957'; Thelma Barer-Stein, *You Eat What You Are: A Study of Ethnic
    Food Traditions* (Toronto: McClelland and Stewart, 1979), 54–60.
52 AO, IIMT, F884, MU6413, File: Ethnic Occasions, 1957, Flyer 'German Week
    at the International Institute of Metropolitan Toronto, February 17 – February 23
    1957, 415 Jarvis St'; Barer-Stein, *You Eat What You Are*, 218–32.
53 AO, IIMT, F884, MU6413, File: Ethnic Occasions, 1957, 'The Polish Dinner,
    February 15th, 1957.'
54 Ibid., Mrs W.E. West, director, to Mr Z. Jaworski, president, Toronto Branch,
    Canadian Polish Congress, 6 March 1957. Ungar honed her multicultural organ-
    izing skills in these years and later became a citizenship judge.
55 Ibid., 'The Polish Dinner, February 15th, 1957.'
56 The main organizers were the Croatian Women's Organization and Toronto Local
    Council of Women (International Committee). West particularly thanked the
    Croatian president, saying her 'exhibit of [Croation] folk art and the dinner were
    quite outstanding.' Ibid., W.E. West to Mrs M. Ashby, Croatian Women's Organi-

zation, 'Kat. Zrinskh,' Toronto, 27 March 1957; W.E West to Mrs Ridell [LCW], 27 March 1957.

57 The week was sponsored by the established Ukrainian Canadian Committee, whose leadership was male, and a Kiwanis club, but it was the Ukrainian Women's Organization, an affiliated society, which was more actively involved than UCC male executives in the on-site organizing. Ibid., W.E. West, executive director, to Mr E.D. Kyle, Kiwanis Club of West Toronto, Toronto, 27 March 1957.

58 Ibid., Ethnic Weeks 'Points to Be Arranged 24 Hours before the Dinner.'

59 An excellent discussion of these nineteenth-century books is Julia Rady-Shaw, 'The Culinary Imagination: Canadian Cookbooks and the Construction of Identity,' Graduate History, University of Toronto, 2008, ms. in author's possession.

60 The Institute newsletter, *Intercom*, contains many positive reviews and letters written by members as well as the occasional wedding announcement and other reports on members' social activities and relationships.

61 AO, IIMT, F884, MU6413, File: Ethnic Occasions, 1957, Mrs W.E. West, executive director, to Dear…, 29 Oct. 1959.

62 These preliminary calculations are based on fragmentary evidence in the files dealing with ethnic weeks. The capacity for Jarvis St dinners was 50 people.

63 AO, IIMT, F884, MU6400, File: Administration 1958–66, 'Fact Sheet 1964.' There is also a reference to a Japanese Week and Dinner but I found no information about it in the records. Some of the Canadian Weeks also featured 'Eastern' food.

64 Immigration History Research Center, University of Minnesota, RG 3, Immigration and Refugee Services of America, Box 265, Folder: 8, Cookbook – Claim to Copyright, Manuscript, 1955–56, not paginated.

65 For example, AO, IIMT, F884, MU6415, File: Ethnic Recipes 1956–63, Joe Vatileroti (?), handwritten signature, to Mrs Nell West, 26 Nov. 1962, and attached typed recipe for 'Turkey Stuffing Greek Recipe,' which included minced meat, wine, turkey livers and heart, as well as onions, bread crumbs, tomato paste, and sweet butter.

66 For example, ibid., Don B[ellamy] to Mrs W.E. West, 21 Dec. 1962; ibid., West to Mr Don Bellamy, School of Social Work, University of Toronto, 27 Dec. 1962.

67 Ibid., see lists of women selling copies of booklet, which include staffers, volunteers, and two nuns; see also correspondence with Mrs Casey, SPC Christmas Bureau, and other lists and letters.

68 Ibid., Mrs W.E. West, director of services, to Mrs R. Jensen, Scarborough, 14 Nov. 1962.

69 Ibid., Mrs Lazi's recipes, Jugo-Slav, 'Bachelor Gulash,' 'Spare Ribs.'

70 Ibid., 'Olia' to Mrs West, 3 Nov. 1962. She wrote, I 'wish that your leg is not giving you any trouble' and that 'we' would like to see her soon, probably meaning she and her husband.

71 Ibid., Mrs Marie Dymes to Mrs West, 5 Nov. 1962. It ends with 'kindest regards from both of us,' presumably referring to herself and husband.

72 Ibid., I determined that the messily written signature referring to a Mrs 'Schalasky' or 'Schalosky' is Szalowski. See 'Everyday Recipes,' n.d., probably 1962. (The potato pancakes recipe involved basic items of potatoes, flour, and egg, but notes that the more traditional sour cream could be substituted with cranberry sauce, presumably tinned.) See also final entries in *Season's Greetings in Food – Christmas 1962*.

73 Ibid., Szebeny recipe for chicken and rice; final entry in *Season's Greetings in Food – Christmas 1962*, 19.

74 AO, IIMT, F884, MU6415, File: Ethnic Recipes 1956–63, 'Light Fruit Cake,' Margaret P. Hyndman, Q.C., 151 Sandringham Dr, Downsview, Ont. (n.d. but clearly 1962).

75 *Intercom* occasionally ran a column called 'Let's Exchange Recipes,' where members shared recipes in English.

76 AO, IIMT, F884, MU6415, File: Ethnic Recipes 1956–63, Flagged for *Intercom*, n.d.

77 Ibid., Clippings Margaret Carr, *Cooking Chat*, 'Chicken with Cherry Scandinavian Dish,' 'Chowder Is Good Winter Meal,' and 'Let's Have Fun with Food' with photo of challah bread with caption 'Twisted Challah Loaf Deserves a Place on Every Table.' She coaxes Canadian mothers to experiment with 'Chicken Scandinavia' by saying it was similar to the Canadian practice of serving 'Chicken with cherry sauce,' adding, 'the tart cherry has the same refreshing quality as the cranberry, and a peppy cherry sauce suits chicken as well as cranberry sauce suits turkey.' After explaining that cherries traditionally accompany meat dishes in Scandinavia, she notes two other attractive qualities: it is easy to prepare and the cherries make it a 'cheerful' dish.

78 Ibid., *Season's Greetings in Food – Christmas 1962*, International Institute of Metropolitan Toronto, 709 College St, Christmas Recipe Book. On International Institutes and similar cookbook projects see, e.g., Donna Gabaccia, *We Are What We Eat: Ethnic Food and the Making of Americans* (Cambridge, MA: Harvard University Press, 1998).

79 *Season's Greetings in Food – Christmas 1963*, 4.

80 On the spectacle and commercialism of Christmas in Toronto, see Steve Penfold, '"A Whole Cavalcade of Dear, Queer People": The Toronto Santa Claus Parade as Urban and Virtual Spectacle, 1905–1982,' *Histoire sociale / Social History* 44 (May 2011): 1–28. I thank him for sharing the unpublished paper with me.

81 *Season's Greetings in Food – Christmas 1963*, 10–11.

82 See also, Munasinghe, *Callaloo or Tossed Salad?*; Gabaccia, *We Are What We Eat*, 31.

83 For example, it promoted a Canadian Centennial cookbook called *Discovering*

Canadian Cuisine (1967), see AO, IIMT, F884, MU6415, File: Ethnic Recipes
1956–63; also, the dinner menu for Irish Week (March 1957) featured fare familiar
to anglophone Torontonians: fruit cup, roast beef, green beans and carrots, potato
croquettes, rolls and butter, celery, pickles, olives, and lemon sponge for dessert,
and coffee, tea, and mints. This, too, was commercially prepared, by Anne Smith
Catering. See ibid., MU6413, File: Ethnic Occasions, 1957, Flyer 'Irish Week,
March 10–15, 1957, International Institute of Metropolitan Toronto, 415 Jarvis
Street, WA 5-1121.'

84 John C. Super, 'Food and History,' *Journal of Social History* 36/1 (2002): 165–78.

85 The Canadian state endorsed multiethnic cookbooks as nation-building tools.
On the broader themes, see Paul Martin, 'Citizenship and the People's World,' in
William Kaplan, ed., *Belonging: The Meaning and Future of Canadian Citizen-
ship* (Montreal and Kingston: McGill-Queen's University Press, 1993), 64–78;
Heidi Bohaker and Franca Iacovetta, 'Making Aboriginals "Immigrants Too": A
Comparison of Federal Citizenship Campaigns towards Immigrants and Indig-
enous Peoples in Post-War Canada, 1940s–60s,' *Canadian Historical Review* 90/3
(2009): 427–62; Iacovetta, *Gatekeepers*, chapter 4.

86 Library and Archives Canada (LAC), Canadian Citizenship Branch, MG31, D69
Col 12, File: 1950, Liaison Officer (Kaye), Report of Trip to Toronto and Hamilton, 27 Sept. – 2 Oct. 1950.

87 Hoganson, *Consumers' Imperium*, 210.

88 They did so in ways that resemble how *Chatelaine*'s engaged readers and writers
forged a 'community of women,' in Korinek, *Roughing It in Suburbia*.

89 Iacovetta, *Gatekeepers*, chapter 4, on hybrid diets.

PART EIGHT

Marketing and Imposing Nutritional Standards

21 Vim, Vigour, and Vitality: 'Power' Foods for Kids in Canadian Popular Magazines, 1914–1954

CHERYL KRASNICK WARSH

Childhood nutrition has been a concern for Canadian parents, especially mothers in charge of the family diet, throughout the twentieth century. Having to seek out safe alternatives to breastfeeding, cope with gastrointestinal problems caused by rancid or adulterated food products, and deal with fussy young eaters, mothers turned to physicians, health manuals, and popular magazines for advice. The nutritional information provided in these sources has shifted over the years,[1] but one constant has been the targeting of parental fears, anxieties, and desires by commercial producers and their advertisers.[2]

While parental anxieties and aspirations may have been the focus of advertising campaigns, these emotional responses were based on the health realities of a particular time and place. Before the 1940s, high rates of infant and child mortality and morbidity were reflected in advertisements for infant formulas and nutritional supplements, while improvements in child health by the Second World War were demonstrated in texts relating to optimal health, in keeping with Ian Mosby's analysis of Canada's Food Rules in this volume. Allusions to food purity reflected public health campaigns and the enactment of food adulteration legislation before the Great War,[3] as well as the relative quality of food for the rich and the poor, as noted in Nathalie Cooke's examination in this volume of the reception of margarine by Quebec dairy farmers. The nineteenth-century characterization of optimal health as related to Vitalism and blood health persisted for much of the twentieth century. Indeed, as Caroline Durand notes in her chapter, a Quebec school health manual of the 1940s was entitled *Vitalité*. Furthermore, as Catherine Carstairs observes in her chapter on health food, the Vitality paradigm survived even longer in the health food movement. By mid-century, the Vitalist focus, at least in the advertisements, shifted to bone strength.

This chapter is a photo-essay that examines advertisements concerning children's health that appeared in two leading Canadian journals, the *Family Herald and Weekly Star*, and *MacLean's* magazine, during selected years (1914, 1924, 1934, 1944, and 1954). By 1908, the *Montreal Star*, and its weekend edition, the *Family Herald*, had by far the highest circulation (over 100,000 for each) of any Canadian periodical, and subsequently were the leading national advertisers.[4] *MacLean's* magazine, inaugurated in 1905 for the urban, white-collar 'busy man and his family,' sought advertisers who would appeal to consumers in a higher economic bracket.[5] These ads were directed at parents, especially mothers, and other primary caregivers, and the audience was likely, although not totally, urban, middle-class, and anglophone Canadians. The advertising also assumed a racialized whiteness; there were no images of people of colour, and few references to ethnicity beyond products like spaghetti, which had entered the mainstream Canadian diet by mid-century.

To date, the U.S. historiography on the rise of advertising and its sociocultural influences in North America is more developed than in Canada. In the United States, Jackson Lears has analysed the iconic significance of American advertising within the context of urban-industrialization, while Richard Ohmann focuses on marketing, class formation, and mass culture. James Norris traces the origins of national advertising, and Roland Marchand picks up the story for the crucial interwar period when the advertising agency was professionalized. In their respective histories, Susan Strasser and Richard Tedlow analyse the growth of mass markets and national branding. Michael Schudson has investigated the relative importance of advertising campaigns in shaping consumer culture. An important Canadian contribution is Russell Johnston's *Selling Themselves*, which traces the origins of the Canadian advertising industry; a central argument is that in advertising strategies, Canadian marketers and copywriters were heavily influenced by American models.[6]

Building on this North American literature, and with a view to contributing, in particular, to the smaller body of Canadian work in advertising, I highlight a number of themes that emerged in my sample of advertisements for children's food which, in turn, suggest patterns of continuity and change. A key pattern of continuity uncovered by this research is that vestiges of nineteenth-century advertising strategies and consumer concerns continued into the years leading up to the Great War as evidenced, for example, by the concern over infant mortality, the nutritional needs of older children, and the persistence of the Vitalist paradigm in the twentieth century. The analysis also reveals some changes that occurred in the twentieth century: in 1914, advertisements for foods directed towards child consumption were limited to sweets, including chewing gum, yeast, cocoa, baby foods, breakfast cereals, and cereal-based drinks, for example,[7] and by 1924, were joined by canned meals and nutritional supplements.[8]

Prepared meals, including soups, would dominate the advertising from 1934 onwards.[9] The 1940s saw the addition of soft drinks, bread, and prepared meat products,[10] while the 1950s included fruit juice.[11]

Vestiges of Victorianism

There were several features in pre-1914 advertising which can be seen as vestiges of late Victorian and Edwardian life. In nineteenth-century British advertising, products ranging from U.K. Tea to Beecham's Pills were marketed to both rich and poor.[12] In the Canadian journals, class divisions (which escaped the radar of food advertisers in the postwar years, if not reality) were alluded to in 1914 with the assurance that Savory & Moore's [Infant] Food was 'used by parents in every station of life from the highest to the lowest.'[13] Quaker Oats were served by mothers of all walks of life, 'All the world over – in cottage and mansion.'[14]

Food adulteration and unsanitary packaging were common in the nineteenth-century marketplace, and consumers were suspicious of prepared and processed foods.[15] That this suspicion lingered well into the twentieth century was evident in the Canadian journals with the use of the popular descriptors: 'pure' and 'wholesome.' Wholesome foods included Cowan's Maple Buds chocolate and Baker's Cocoa.[16] Henry Heinz built his food empire, initiated in 1869, largely on scrupulously sanitary practices, which were highlighted in company advertising for a century.[17] By 1934, Heinz spaghettis and soups were 'packed in a modern plant where cleanliness is positively a fetish' (advertisers read lots of Freud).[18] A decade later, Heinz changed its claim to producing foods that were 'scientifically prepared, always uniformly good,' which was just as well, since fetishes might, after all, be cured.[19]

In 1914, convenience foods had not yet had an impact, although an ad for Symington's soups, which displayed a picture of a maid relaxing in the kitchen, portended the end of maids, or more accurately, the possibility for homemakers to put their feet up in the kitchen.[20] By 1924, mothers were encouraged to make mealtime easier with Clark's beans and soups, which 'enable you to serve excellent meals at moderate expense and little labor.'[21]

In 1914, men were making food purchases, whether it was the grandfather treating his grandson to Maple Buds or to cocoa,[22] or the father whose pocket always had a supply of Wrigley's Spearmint Gum for his little girl: 'It's very good for her teeth, appetite and digestion ... Chew it after every meal.'[23] Expense was alluded to in 1914, even though it was avoided in the Great Depression. The addition of Crown Brand Corn Syrup encouraged 'little Miss Muffet' to eat plain foods, such as bread.[24] Homemade bread consumption also

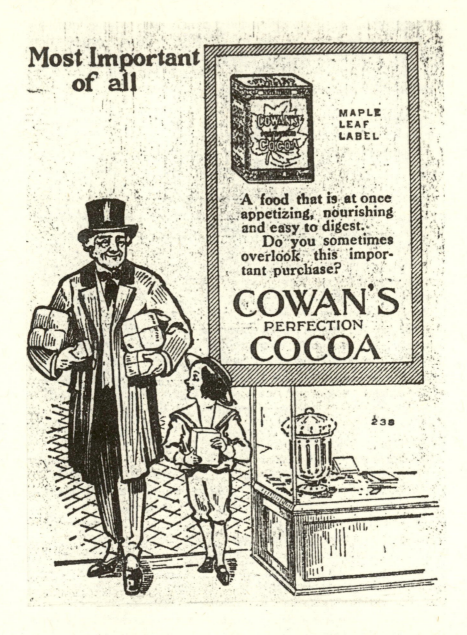

21.1 Cowan's Cocoa, *Family Herald & Weekly Star* [*Herald*], 4 February 1914, p. 6.

was encouraged by Royal Yeast Cake, not for its superiority to store-bought bread, but because it reduced the high cost of living to substitute homemade bread for meat at the dinner table.[25] The bread industry weighed in again during the Second World War, encouraging families to 'eat one more slice of bread each [wartime] meal.'[26]

Babies Died

From our twenty-first-century vantage point, and concern for childhood obesity, it is easy to forget a time only three generations ago when skinny babies died.[27] The spectre of baby death and serious childhood illnesses was omnipresent in the 1914 ads and in those of decades to come.[28] In 1926, the Canadian infant mortality rate was 101 per 1,000 live births, and that dropped to 73 per 1,000 by 1932. The decline slowed to 1 per cent per year until 1936, rose to 76 per 1,000 in 1937, and then dropped to 61 per 1,000 in 1939. The rate continued its decline in the 1940s.[29] The dry statistics and antiseptic label of infant mortality were magnified into the heart-wrenching reality that many babies died despite their parents' best, desperate efforts. The stage was set with ads for the Montreal Children's Hospital, with a row of happy, round faces of the saved – or at least cared for – the crippled victims of rickets, polio, and birth defects.[30] Richard Middleton's poem, 'On a Dead Child,' reminded all of the fate of too many – a fate which, perhaps, could be prevented with the purchase of the proper nutritional products.[31]

Mothers had to be assured that infant feeding products adequately replaced breast milk both in terms of nutritional value and safety.[32] The fact that so many babies died after weaning was not lost on the public. Savory & Moore's foods, for instance, which could be used in conjunction with nursing, provided the 'essential elements of nutrition, relieve[d] constipation [and promoted] healthy bones and good teeth.' 'Baby thrives on it amazingly. Each week there is steady progress. Particularly marked in the case of weakly or delicate infants.'[33] The delicate child is a term that is lost in our time, but resonated throughout the years. Little Eva of *Uncle Tom's Cabin* was a delicate child. So, too, was Beth March of *Little Women*. Both of them died young. In the first half of the twentieth century, childhood delicacy was a reminder of the fragility of childhood.

The year 1924 saw no let-up in concern over infant fragility. Knox Gelatine 'helps the underweight baby' by helping a mother create a supposedly safer formula: 'Cow's milk was intended for the calf – add gelatine to use as formula.'[34]

Virol dramatically asserted that 'more boy babies die than girls. Arrest wasting, protect his little life by giving Virol … to tide over the dangerous moments

More boy babies die than girls

BABY PIRKS.

At birth he was so small and weak that his life was despaired of. On Virol he soon improved, and is now a plump, strong, happy child.

Be specially careful of your baby boy. Arrest wasting, protect his little life by giving Virol.

Virol is the food which gives strength to tide over the dangerous moments in Baby's life.

Because it contains just those valuable foods that Baby needs and car assimilate.

VIROL

Sole Importers: BOVRIL., LTD., 2725, Park Avenue, Montreal.

21.2 Virol, *MacLean's*, 15 February 1924, p. 62.

in Baby's life.' Even more dramatic was Virol's picture of a burning candle, with the text, 'A Baby's Life is like a Candle ... so easily extinguished.'[35]

The gut-wrench award, however, goes to Nestle's Milk Food, an infant formula. In a full-page ad entitled, 'The Valley of the Shadow: The diary of a brave little pioneer,' the narrator is the infant who, from birth, describes his or her deadly eating problems and the reactions of the adults around. 'I wonder why they are all so unhappy? Dearest cries and cries and Father dear walks, and the big persons with fur [those are the doctors – all doctors in the ads are at least sixty and most resemble Sigmund Freud] are here all the time ... it is getting darker ... darker ... It is no use. I must go back.'[36] Luckily, after many tries with other formulas, the doctor recommends Nestle's food and the baby recovers. This ad would have been beyond the pale if it were not based on a reality that spoke to its audience.

By 1944, Heinz baby foods portrayed infants who were 'so sturdy, contented, so well-fed, that their mothers and doctors [were free] to make greater contributions to the war effort.'[37] While there was still notice made of babies who didn't gain, the solution (apart from feeding them Heinz baby food) was to keep a permanent record of their growth.[38] This, of course, presumes a positive outcome. For the most part, fussy babies were now characterized as a nuisance 'to busy mothers.'[39] By 1954, the Canadian baby was portrayed as a safe and happy baby. The Heinz Baby won baby contests and was hearty rather than fragile.[40]

Eating Habits of the Older Child

Malnutrition among toddlers and young children provoked anxiety in 1914. Wrigley's Spearmint Gum, for instance, was promoted as an appetite stimulant.[41] A nurse serves an older boy in a hospital bed St Vincent Arrowroot: 'The Most Nourishing Food for the Convalescent.'[42] By 1924, there was still concern over older children's appetites, although the emphasis was more on flavour than on fear of malnutrition. A toddler with a bowl of Quaker Puffed Wheat and Rice, 'a joyous temptation no child can resist,' also would be tempted by puffed wheat macaroni, 'Here's lightness and brightness to tempt the childish appetite!'[43] Sugar-Crisp Corn Flakes would entice appetites 'a little jaded these warm days.'[44] Certainly, this emphasis on the taste of foods, which presumed variety and children's choice, spoke to a more prosperous audience than in 1914.

By 1924, the picture was brightening as well on another front regarding childhood nutrition. Concerns over wasting and malnutrition, exacerbated by dysenteries and other diarrheas, were now accompanied by concern over con-

MacLean's Magazine 35

Every Woman should read this true story!

The Valley of the Shadow

The Diary of a brave little Pioneer

June 1

WELL, here I am at last, and it's certainly a queer world I must say. This world has a white top and pink sides, and is inhabited by a lot of funny people.

There is a large creature all in white, with fur on his face, and everybody jumps when he says anything. Then there is another white person, rather nice I think, with a cap on her head.

There is another queer large person who walks up and down and says "Oh Lord, I'm glad it's over."

And finally there is The Person, who lies on a big white thing they call the bed. She seems very tired, somehow, but when they put me alongside of her she almost broke me with a terrible squeeze.

Nevertheless, I am going to like this person . . . She said, over and over again, "Oh, my baby, my little baby."

Baby. That must be me, I'm going to call her "Dearest." That's what the Walking Person called her. He bent over us and hugged us both . . . I guess I'm going to like them, too.

Just now they tried to take me away from Dearest, and of course I howled.

Then the White Person in the cap gave me what she called a bath. It was awful. But I have lots of toes and things, and I got interested in them. They are very pink.

. . . . I am going to like the Walking Person almost as much as Dearest. I am going to call him Fatherdear. He says I can . . .

June 2

Goodness! They have changed the world while I was asleep. It isn't pink and white now. It's brown, and the air is mostly gold. It was all black before. They call the gold "sunlight." Huh! A lot they know about sunlight. They ought to see it where I came from.

Just had a wonderful adventure. Dearest gave me my lunch. Now I know what was the matter with the things inside of me before it happened. They wanted lunch. . . .

Oh dear!

I just lost that lunch.

I lost some more lunch.

It isn't such a nice world after all. Guess I'll sleep some more.

June 3

The Big Person with fur on his face is back again. His name is Doctor. They told him about the lunch and he said "Ilum" and scratched his head, and Dearest looked very unhappy, and Fatherdear began to walk again. There must be something wrong.

June 5

"Try him again," said Doctor, so they put me in Dearest's arms, and it was just as great as ever. If they would only leave me with Her all the time! I would try so hard not to lose my lunch.

I lost it. Somehow, I don't feel quite so good as I did. When I came, I could kick quite well. I can't kick much any more. . . .

Had a lot of adventures. Every so often they come to me with a hard thing you can see inside of, only you can't get at the inside; and they put the soft end in my mouth, and I think it's Dearest, only it never is. It's awful. I lose my lunches right along.

All the people are acting very queer. Dearest cries a lot, and Fatherdear walks around and says things to himself. I wonder what's the matter.

June 7

Doctor brings in other people with fur on their faces, and they stand around and look at me, and talk long words nobody can understand.

Then they all go into the kitchen and bother the big black thing in the corner that has sunlight in its middle and makes warm feelings, and then they come at me with the Thing. Its name is Bottle. It is never Dearest any more, no matter how we both cry.

Today they put me on a thing that bounced up and down, and Fatherdear said "Oh Lord, he's lost eight ounces." Then he told Dearest I had gained nearly a pound.

Each time they come at me with the bottle, it tastes different. It never stays long. I wish they could find something . . . the things inside of me are very unhappy . . . I cried almost all day, and Fatherdear started to walk with me, only they stopped him.

June 9

The world is better today. They let me stay with Dearest all the time . . . She got all excited and cried, and I cried, and she said they were going to take me away from her, and began to laugh out very loud mixed with crying, and started to get up out of the big white thing she lies on, so they left me with her. High time, too. It would be a very nice world . . . if the things inside would stop.

June 10

Today I slept most all day. I do not care much for the world. Dearest held me all day, and Fatherdear sat alongside. Dearest said "Shouldn't you go to the office, dear?" and Fatherdear choked.

I wonder why they are all so unhappy? Dearest cries and cries, and Fatherdear walks, and the big persons with fur are here all the time, and the white person with the cap cries too. . . . It is getting darker . . . darker.

It is no use. I must go back. I am sorry to leave Dearest, who is so soft and pink and white, and I love my toes and things. Yes, I will, go to sleep, in the lovely dark. There . . . Darker . . . It was Fatherdear who woke me up that time. He tried to give me that awful bottle, but I wouldn't take it although I heard them say it was something new. What is the use? It never stays; and then they get unhappy.

But I looked at Dearest and her hair was all around her face, and she was sitting up in bed and crying with her shoulders shaking something awful, and Fatherdear looked as if something was going to happen to him right away . . . so I took it just to please them.

. . . . Well, it was *certainly* very good. Fatherdear didn't give me nearly enough of it. And then he took me ever so carefully and laid me in Dearest's arms . . . and they both bent over me . . . and waited . . . and I waited—for it to come up—and Dearest's hair was all soft around me, and I loved it . . . and it forgot to come up, that time, and Dearest and I went to sleep . . . but it was not so dark, and the things inside felt better . . . and just as I was drifting off, very comfy, I heard the Doctor say "Cheer up, old man, Nestlé's Food has saved many a baby's life." I wonder what he meant?

June 11

I woke up early in the gold air, and howled, much louder than I could before . . . and right away they came running, and brought me more of the good stuff, whatever it's name is . . . and it *stayed*, and I kicked all the blankets off.

And Dearest held me in her arms all day long, and over and over she said "Oh, my baby, my little baby, you're *not* going away after all!"

And I guess I won't. But I think it's time for another lunch!

Epilogue

This is a true story written by the father of the little adventurer who went down into The Valley of the Shadow and came safely back again. It has been true of hundreds of thousands of babies all over the world for the past fifty years. The experience of the Brave Little Pioneer in his journey into The Valley of the Shadow, his brave fight for life, is one which is going on every day in hundreds of homes.

If you have a little pioneer who is undergoing similar difficulties, Nestlé's Food may play its part in bringing your little one back to health and strength.

If this little story accomplishes anything in the way of helping other small adventurers to avoid the hazardous experiments that took the Brave Little Pioneer into the Valley of the Shadow, it has not been written in vain.

If you will write to Nestlé's Food Company of Canada, Limited, 323 St. James Street, Montreal, they will send you a sample package of Nestlé's Milk Food sufficient for twelve feedings—also their Mother's Book which gives full directions on the care and feeding of babies.

21.3 Nestle's Milk Food, *MacLean's*, 15 October 1924, p. 35.

21.4 Wrigley's Spearmint Gum, *Herald*, 4 February 1914, p. 3.

stipation. Nujol, a fibre agent, was 'more important than soap and water' for a boy's internal cleanliness.[45] Constipation should not be taken lightly, however. Nujol also warned that a healthy and happy home required that a mother 'Guard your children ... Headache, fretfulness, loss of appetite, coated tongue ... all indicate that clogging is present and that poisons are saturating the body. Vital resistance is lowered and the child is prey to contagious diseases.'[46]

By 1934, all that overfeeding of milk products to sustain infants had taken its toll, as constipation advanced front and centre. Over the next twenty years, there is nothing quite like the domestic dramas of petty and griping adults surrounding constipated children as in the Fletcher's Castoria ads.

Configured in the highly popular comic strip format, the tag lines varied from 'I have a war job ... and a little mother-in-law trouble,' or 'next thing you'll be tying pink ribbons in Bobby's hair!'[47] (speaking to both absentee parenting and threatened masculinity) to the ominous (with a toddler girl standing in the corner with her blankee, and her father looming over and scolding): 'Sometimes the world turns against a baby.'[48] Fletcher's Castoria did more to de-idealize the family image than anything else in the magazines.[49] The issue here, however, was not saving the child's life, but promoting proper parenting skills and domestic harmony through regular bowel movements.

The malnourished child of 1934 was transformed into the 'fussy eater,' as characterized by Ovaltine, which promised to add 'a pound a week in weight' to young children.[50] The 1930s ads saw 'ravenous youngsters' dashing home from school for Heinz tomato juice and soups. With a brief nod to the value of domesticity – 'No mother would rebel at spending whole mornings in the kitchen cooking for children' – convenience is quickly embraced: 'but it is totally unnecessary, in fact, it's old fashioned.'[51]

Vim, Vigour, and Vitality for Boys and Girls

The *MacLean's* ads in 1914, which centred on cereals, generally were more positive, and promoted vigour and vitality rather than delicacy. Vigour and vitality (vim was a companion which has lost its currency) hearken back to the Vitalist school of physiology of the late nineteenth century.[52] The Vitalists argued that modern civilization, with its streetcars, telegraphs, and overcrowded hustle and bustle, was enervating to urban dwellers, especially among the middle classes. The popular interpretation of Vitalism, which resonates throughout the early twentieth century and even today, was that the nervous system was overloaded causing neurasthenia or the general complaint of 'nerves,' a predominantly female-gendered disorder.[53] A parallel aspect of Vitalism was concern over anaemic blood, since iron-fortified blood promotes

21.5 Fletcher's Castoria, *MacLean's*, 15 June 1944, p. 24.

energy.[54] As noted in the Nujol ad cited above, Vitalism is represented not just by input but by outflow.[55]

From 1914 onwards, there was a great deal of interest in the vim, vigour, and vitality of children, and the descriptors were gendered. In a Quaker Oats ad, a picture of a girl tobogganing accompanied the text, 'Any oat food is a great vim-producer. Any supplies an abundance of what brains and nerves are made.'[56] Vitalism and strong blood – as well as feminine beauty – were reflected in ads for Postum, a cereal-based hot beverage. A round-cheeked girl was described, 'Eyes, cheeks and lips reflect one's health as a mirror ... The precious blood current – when pure and laden with vitality – is Nature's greatest beautifier.'[57] Note that in a decade prior to the extensive use of diagnostic tools and chemical blood testing, it is the outward appearance which represents the clinical expression of health.

Along with vitality, brainpower – a code for academic achievement – was conferred by oatmeal, particularly for boys. A series of ads in 1914 displayed adolescent boys in classrooms, 'it abounds in the elements which active brains require.'[58]

Boys, as young men in training, needed preparation for future material success, as parents were warned in a Quaker Oats ad, with one boy raising his hand while the other was sprawled across his desk, asleep: 'Some Do / Some Don't: Get Vim-Food in the Morning.'[59] Male success also was cited in the Grape-Nuts ad with a boy playing sports: 'To do it effectively – in sports, business or any other game of life – one needs a vigorous body controlled by a clear brain.'[60]

The concern with male achievement was even more pronounced in 1924. Famed American illustrator Norman Rockwell was commissioned for a series of Quaker Puffed Wheat ads, including a portrait of a teenaged boy in a necktie: 'That million dollar Boy of yours – do this to give him strength to meet life's later problems. Much of your boy's future depends on how well you build his body now. For without health and strength, early manhood will find him handicapped.'[61] Fourteen was 'The Anxious Age' for a boy, with a picture of a sad young man, too skinny to be a good athlete, holding a tennis racquet: 'A time of special strain for boys and girls.'[62] The antidote to the angst and physiological stresses of puberty was Virol: 'The Food for Growth.' This beef-based supplement (produced by the Bovril Company) employed many of the gendered and health attributes routinely claimed by beef producers. Similar to the analysis offered in Valerie Korinek's chapter in this volume, where vegetarians and beef consumers/producers contested different gendered notions of healthy eating, Virol identified itself with the red-blooded health boost supposedly conferred by beef.

Vitality

Any oat food is a great vim-producer. Any supplies an abundance of what brains and nerves are made.

The difference lies in flavor. Puny oats lack richness and aroma. The taste which makes oatmeal delicious comes from big, plump oats.

That's why millions of mothers, all the world over, serve Quaker Oats to children. They do this to foster the love of oatmeal. Then the food children need, beyond all else, becomes the wanted dish.

Quaker Oats

The Big, Luscious Flakes Alone

For Quaker Oats we pick out only the big, richly-flavored grains. A bushel of the choicest oats yields only ten pounds of Quaker.

Thus you get in Quaker just the big, luscious flakes. And you get a flavor which has won the world. Because of that flavor, a billion dishes of Quaker Oats are consumed each year.

Yet Quaker Oats costs no more than others. Simply say "Quaker," then, at no extra trouble, no extra price, you get the utmost in oatmeal.

Regular Size package, 10c

Family Size package, for smaller cities and country trade, 25c.

Except in the extreme West.

Look for the Quaker trademark on every package

The Quaker Oats Company
Sole Makers

(519)

21.6 Quaker Oats, *MacLean's*, March 1914, p. 61.

Some Do————————Some Don't

Get Vim-Food
In the Morning

Some children go to school on Quaker Oats—perhaps five millions of them. They get all the vitality, all the energy that the greatest vim-food can supply them. Children and grown-ups all need an abundance of this spirit-giving Quaker.

You know that—all folks know it

They get in addition a delicious dish. You serve nothing so luscious, so tempting to children as well-cooked Quaker Oats.

Quaker Oats

Matchless in Taste and Aroma

Quaker Oats comes in big flakes, made only from the plump and luscious grains. All the puny, starved grains are discarded. So careful are we that we get but ten pounds of Quaker Oats from a bushel.

The Quaker process includes hours of dry heat and steam heat, which enhance the flavor. Thus we bring to the tables of a hundred nations the most delicious oat dish that's known.

You get this when you ask for Quaker Oats, and you pay no extra price. Don't you consider that worth while?

**10c and 25c per Package
Except in Far West.**

(702)

21.7 Quaker Oats, *MacLean's*, November 1914, p. 73.

"Play Ball"

To do it effectively—in sport, business or any other game of life—one needs a vigorous body controlled by a clear brain.

Food Plays a Big Part

Many play a losing game because their food doesn't contain the elements necessary to build up strong bodies and healthy brains.

Most white flour foods are lacking in these elements—the vital mineral salts—necessary for mental and physical balance.

Grape-Nuts
FOOD

admirably supplies this lack.

Made of choice whole wheat and malted barley, Grape-Nuts retains the mineral salts and other nutritive values in just the right proportion, as grown in the grain. It is an ideal food for winners in any game.

Grape-Nuts comes in tightly sealed packages—perfectly baked and ready to eat with cream or good milk. Fresh, crisp, and delicious!

"There's a Reason" for Grape-Nuts

—sold by Grocers everywhere.

21.8 Grape-Nuts, *MacLean's*, May 1914, p. 41.

Virol's advertisements were particularly hard-hitting warnings of the dangers of an enervated, disease-prone population. Virol was 'Building up food' for the seven ages of man: 'It rescues babies from wasting; protects at the critical school age of growth; makes the weak man strong; fortifies expectant mothers; prolongs youth and vitality into later years ... in a form that the most delicate can assimilate.'[63] The school years had special dangers and challenges for both boys and girls. 'The active boy or girl who works hard to get to the top of the form ... Virol *feeds* the blood.'[64] Virol displayed a giant hand holding an adolescent girl: 'you hold that child's future in your hand. The body that must last your child for life is built during the age of growth. Once that body is built the mistakes made cannot be rectified.'[65] 'Your children are bound to take risks when they go to school,' but Virol, mothers were urged, helped their children resist infection.[66] Certainly, the early 1920s was a period of concern over childhood epidemics, for a population still reeling from the influenza pandemic, and the annual threats of polio, diphtheria, and meningitis.

By the 1930s, the Vitalist paradigm was receding, as child strength was measured not so much through the vascular, but through the muscular-skeletal system. Shredded Wheat made children (especially boys) 'sturdy' and provided the 'bone and tissue building elements' which gave the body 'vitality, energy and endurance.'[67] Pep Bran Flakes were also 'body building' for girls, keeping 'young minds [now including female ones] alert for school.'[68] For boys, school success was measured by more than academic achievement. Edwardsburg Crown Brand Corn Syrup pictured a young boy playing football: 'The leader among boys and girls – is the one who has the superabundant energy that makes for joy of living ... the one whose boundless vitality attracts both classmates and teachers.'[69] What is striking here is these are not the characteristics of the ideal student. Indeed, in the twenty-first century, a boy with superabundant energy and boundless vitality would be a candidate for Ritalin.

That energy made sense in 1944, as Heinz promised 'the proper feeding of the generation that will inherit tomorrow's peacetime world.'[70] While the exigencies of absentee military fathers and working mothers interfered with the rigidity of gender roles, they were reformulated, albeit awkwardly. Kellogg's Corn Flakes portrayed both a daughter and a son doing housework, but while the girl dusted to teach 'my dolls to keep house too,' the boy beat a rug to help his 'batting arm.'[71]

The gender roles were firmly realigned by 1954, with toddler boys called 'single-minded'[72] and 'two-fisted little fire engines'[73] (as well as voters),[74] while much older girls' 'vitality' and 'energy' were channelled into cheerleading[75] and frolicking.[76] In the world of advertisements, at least, their mothers had retired from their wartime jobs to be farmers' wives ('worthy wife ... devoted mother ... partner in progress')[77] or perhaps Angels of Mercy by a

21.9 Canadair, *MacLean's*, 15 October 1954, p. 7.

child's bedside. More appropriate to the Cold War universe of the Canadian popular magazine, mother's healthy sons were sustained by a hearty Thanksgiving dinner. As Canadair Aircraft avowed, 'Freedom from Want' separated Canadians from dominated peoples, and was 'Worth Defending.'[78]

Conclusion

From the waif facing imminent death in the nursery to the robust lad tumbling down the football field, the Canadian baby, child, and adolescent, as portrayed in food advertisements, was becoming healthier over the course of the first half of the twentieth century. Advances in maternal and children's health were claimed by shrewd marketers and manufacturers, as they exhorted mothers to purchase an array of new products (baby formulas, supplements, and baby food) or touted the 'health benefits' of sugary confections and candy (cocoa, corn syrup, and chewing gum). Interestingly, marketers were quick to change their messages, from sustaining fragile infants to promoting 'optimal' health and the increasing affluence that allowed for the purchase of more products. What continued to sell products, though, were messages laden with guilt for mothers – worries about fussy eaters; whole families stalked by the spectre of irregularity; and fears about supplying sufficient brain food for future male leaders. Thus, the challenges for mothers remained: to provide appealing meals and supplements for the optimal health (whether defined by ruddy cheeks, sturdy bones, pleasant dispositions, or open bowels) of boys and girls, regardless of financial or time constraints. The stark prospect of infant mortality was receding as the century progressed; nevertheless, the desire to rear strong and healthy Canadian children remained, and was addressed by food advertisers.

As the examples analysed here have indicated, most of the messages were exceedingly gendered. Gender historians have observed that recurrent 'threats' to masculinity (real and imagined) were regularly invoked in the late nineteenth and twentieth centuries and those notions appear in these advertisements. Whether couched in the findings of science (more boy babies died) or employing sporting notions of male activity, or highlighting the necessity of supplying sufficient 'brain food,' entreaties to feed male infants, children, and adolescents appropriately were a constant refrain. Food ads featuring female children were noticeably different, often playing on images of beauty, innocence, charm, and the health attributes of such. 'Dads' seldom made appearances in food advertisements (probably because the audience for these ads were mothers, the primary grocery purchasers). When fathers did appear, it was often with female children, thus heightening the emotional or dramatically gendered messages. While the gendering of such food advertisements in the first half of the twentieth century is not surprising (it parallels the gendered social histories of this era), it is worth noting how many of these advertising tropes are still utilized in contemporary advertisements for processed foods and health supplements. Powering food sales by utilizing medicalized, gendered messages of vitality and vigour proved an enduring strategy because it fed into wives' and mothers' anxieties about providing for their families.

ACKNOWLEDGMENT

I acknowledge a grant from Vancouver Island University and thank research assistant Deb Stackhouse. I dedicate this essay to Clarence Karr's memory,

NOTES

1 For more on childhood nutrition in Canada and other Western nations, see the essays by Aleck Ostry (on Canada), Judith Sealander (U.S.), and Lisa Featherstone (Australia), in Cheryl Krasnick Warsh and Veronica Strong-Boag, eds., *Children's Health Issues in Historical Perspective* (Waterloo, ON: Wilfrid Laurier University Press, 2005).

2 Katherine Arnup, *Education for Motherhood: Advice for Mothers in Twentieth-Century Canada* (Toronto: University of Toronto Press, 1994); Cynthia R. Comacchio, *Nations Are Built of Babies: Saving Ontario's Mothers and Children, 1900–1940* (Montreal and Kingston: McGill-Queen's University Press, 1993); Julia Grant, *Raising Babies by the Book: The Education of American Mothers* (New Haven, CN: Yale University Press, 1998).

3 Gary Gnirss, 'A History of Food Law in Canada,' www.foodincanada.com. May 2008, 38.

4 Russell Johnston, *Selling Themselves: The Emergence of Canadian Advertising* (Toronto: University of Toronto Press, 2001), 228.

5 Ibid., 243.

6 Jackson Lears, *Fables of Abundance: A Cultural History of Advertising in America* (New York: Basic Books, 1994); Richard Ohmann, *Selling Culture: Magazines, Markets and Class at the Turn of the Century* (London: Verso, 1996); Roland Marchand, *Advertising the American Dream: Making Way for Modernity, 1920–1940* (Berkeley, CA: University of California Press, 1985); James D. Norris, *Advertising and the Transformation of American Society, 1865–1920* (Westport, CT: Greenwood, 1990); Susan Strasser, *Satisfaction Guaranteed: The Making of the American Mass Market* (New York: Pantheon, 1989); Richard S. Tedlow, *New and Improved: The Story of Mass Marketing in America* (New York: Basic Books,

1990); Michael Schudson, *Advertising, the Uneasy Persuasion: Its Dubious Impact on American Society* (New York: Basic Books, 1984); Johnston, *Selling Themselves*.

7 The companies and their products were the following: Wrigley's Spearmint Gum, Dominion Molasses, Cowan's Maple Buds, Baker's Cocoa, Savory & Moore's Food, Royal Yeast Cakes, Crown Brand Corn Syrup, Bovril, Quaker Oats, St Vincent Arrowroot Growers, Postum, and Grape-Nuts Foods.

8 Clark Soups and Beans, Virol, Sugar-Crisp Corn Flakes, Horlick's Malted Milk, Fletcher's Castoria, Royal Baking Powder, Nestle's Milk Food, Dominion Chocolate Bars, Nujol, Ovaltine, Knox Gelatine, Oxo Cubes, and Purity Salt.

9 Canada, Department of Trade and Commerce [maple syrup], Heinz Foods, Canadian Shredded Wheat, Windsor Salt, Kellogg's Cereals, Beech-Nut Fruit Drops, Cox's Gelatine, Klim Milk (Borden), and VIP Chocolate Drink.

10 Ogilvie Flour Mills, Fleischmann's Yeast, George Weston, Canada Dry, Coca-Cola, Life Savers, and Swift Meats.

11 Willards Regency Sweets, Toastmaster (McGraw Electric), Florida Orange Juice.

12 Lori Anne Loeb, *Consuming Angels: Advertising and Victorian Women* (New York: Oxford University Press, 1994), 175–7.

13 Savory & Moore's Food, *Family Herald and Weekly Star* [*Herald*], 7 Jan. 1914, 6.

14 Quaker Oats, *MacLean's*, Feb. 1914, 54. Quaker Oats was one of the first U.S. companies to use industrial methods in the food industries and develop national (then international) branding through mass marketing. See Tedlow, *New and Improved*, 14; Ohmann, *Selling Culture*, 86, 106; and Schudson, *Advertising, the Uneasy Persuasion*, 165.

15 Nancy F. Koehn, 'Henry Heinz and Brand Creation in the Late 19th Century: Making Markets for Processed Food,' *Business History Review* 73/3 (1999): 350.

16 Cowan's Maple Buds and Baker's Cocoa, *Herald*, 7 Jan. 1914, 4 and 5. Chocolate had been notorious for being adulterated in the nineteenth century. See Koehn, 'Henry Heinz,' 356.

17 Koehn, 'Henry Heinz,' 356.

18 Heinz, *MacLean's*, 15 Feb. 1934, 33. Edward Bernays, top public relations man for the J. Walter Thompson advertising company in the 1930s, was a nephew of Sigmund Freud. See Cheryl Krasnick Warsh, 'Smoke and Mirrors: Gender Representation in North American Tobacco and Alcohol Advertisements before 1950,' *Histoire sociale / Social History* 31/62 (1998): 187.

19 Heinz Baby Foods, *MacLean's*, 15 May 1944, 41.

20 Symington's Soups, *Herald*, 7 Jan. 1914, 3.

21 W. Clark Ltd., *MacLean's*, 15 June 1924, 75.

22 Cowan's Maple Buds, *Herald*, 7 Jan. 1914, 4, and Cowan's Cocoa, *Herald*, 4 Feb. 1914, 6.

23 Wrigley's Gum, *Herald*, 28 Jan. 1914, 4. For more on Wrigley marketing, see
    Daniel Robinson, 'Marketing Gum, Making Meanings: Wrigley in North America,
    1890–1930,' *Enterprise and Society* 5/1 (2004): 4–44.
24 Crown Brand Corn Syrup, *Herald*, 18 March 1914, 6.
25 Royal Yeast Cakes, *Herald*, 7 Jan. 1914, 8.
26 Fleischmann's Yeast, *MacLean's*, 15 Sept. and 15 Nov. 1944.
27 Comacchio, *Nations Are Built of Babies*, passim; Denyse Baillargeon, 'Entre la
    revanche et la veillée des berceaux: Les médecins québécois francophones, la mor-
    talité infantile, et la question nationale, 1910–1940,' in Warsh and Strong-Boag,
    Children's Health Issues, 101–30.
28 Loeb, *Consuming Angels*, 114–15.
29 Comacchio, *Nations Are Built of Babies*, 218.
30 Children's Hospital, *Herald*, 7 Jan. 1914, 3.
31 Richard Middleton, 'On a Dead Child,' *Herald*, 15 April 1914, 3.
32 Rima Apple, *Mothers and Medicine: A Social History of Infant Feeding* (Madison,
    WI: University of Wisconsin Press, 1987), passim.
33 Savory & Moore's Foods, *Herald*, 7 Jan. 1914, 6, and 15 April 1914, 9.
34 Knox Gelatine, *MacLean's*, 1 Feb. 1924, 56. Gelatine, of course, is made from
    by-products of the cattle and pork industries.
35 Virol, *MacLean's*, 15 Feb. 1924, 62, and 15 March 1924, 62.
36 Nestle's, *MacLean's*, 15 Oct. 1924, 35.
37 Heinz, *MacLean's*, 15 Feb. 1944, 37.
38 Heinz, *MacLean's*, 15 Dec. 1944, 53.
39 Heinz, *MacLean's*, 15 Sept. 1944, 64.
40 Heinz, *MacLean's*, 15 Dec. 1954, 37, and 15 Aug. 1954, 51.
41 Wrigley's, *Herald*, 4 Feb. 1914, 3.
42 St Vincent Arrowroot, *MacLean's*, April 1914, 50.
43 Quaker Puffed Wheat, *MacLean's*, 15 July 1924, 44. Lightness and brightness sold
    products ranging from automobiles to corsets in the 1920s, as part of the Art Deco
    aesthetic. See Penny Tinkler and Cheryl Krasnick Warsh, 'Feminine Modernity
    in Interwar Britain and North America: Corsets, Cars and Cigarettes,' *Journal of
    Women's History* 20/3 (2008): 113–43.
44 Sugar Crisp Corn Flakes, *MacLean's*, Aug. 1924, 37.
45 Nujol, *MacLean's*, 15 Jan. 1924, 47.
46 Nujol, *MacLean's*, 15 Feb. 1924, 33.
47 Fletcher's Castoria, *MacLean's*, 15 March 1944, 34.
48 Fletcher's Castoria, *MacLean's*, 1 July 1934, 47.
49 See also, Fletcher's Castoria, *MacLean's*, 1 March 1934, 39.
50 Ovaltine, *MacLean's*, 15 March 1934, 69, and 15 April 1934, 61.
51 Heinz, *MacLean's*, 15 Feb. 1934, 33.

52 For more on the Vitalist school of physiology, see Elizabeth A. Williams, *The Physical and the Moral: Anthropology, Physiology and Philosophical Medicine in France, 1750–1850* (Cambridge: Cambridge University Press, 1994); John S. Haller Jr, *Kindly Medicine: Physio-Medicalism in America, 1836–1911* (Kent, OH: Kent State University Press, 1997).

53 Lears discusses vitalism in advertising in *Fables of Abundance*, 179–80.

54 That these beliefs pervaded popular culture is evident in Dona Davis' study of folk health concepts in outport Newfoundland, *Blood and Nerves: An Ethnographic Focus on Menopause* (St John's, NL: ISER Press, 1983).

55 Nujol, *MacLean's*, 15 Feb. 1924, 33.

56 Quaker Oats, *MacLean's*, March 1914, 61. See also, Feb. 1914, 54.

57 Postum, *MacLean's*, April 1914, 51.

58 Quaker Oats, *MacLean's*, Sept. 1914, 61.

59 Quaker Oats, *MacLean's*, Nov. 1914, 73.

60 Grape-Nuts, *MacLean's*, May 1914, 41.

61 Quaker Puffed Wheat, *MacLean's*, 15 June 1924, 81.

62 Virol, *MacLean's*, 15 July 1924, 66.

63 Virol, *MacLean's*, 1 Sept. 1924, 68.

64 Virol, *MacLean's*, 15 Sept. 1924, 43.

65 Virol, *MacLean's*, 1 Nov. 1924, 56.

66 Virol, *MacLean's*, 1 Oct. 1924, 72.

67 Shredded Wheat, *MacLean's*, 1 June 1934, 48.

68 Pep Bran Flakes, *MacLean's*, 15 Sept. 1934, 62. See also, 15 April 1934, 68, and 1 May 1934, 58.

69 Edwardsburg Crown Brand Corn Syrup, *MacLean's*, 1 Dec. 1934, 28.

70 Heinz, *MacLean's*, 15 May 1944, 41.

71 Kellogg's Corn Flakes, *MacLean's*, 15 July 1944, 34.

72 Kellogg's Corn Flakes, *MacLean's*, 1 April 1954, 7.

73 Kellogg's Corn Flakes, *MacLean's*, 1 Oct. 1954, 33.

74 Kellogg's Corn Flakes, *MacLean's*, 15 June 1954, 65, and 15 Aug. 1954, 51.

75 Florida Orange Juice, *MacLean's*, 15 Nov. 1954, 58.

76 Florida Orange Juice, *MacLean's*, 15 June 1954, 35.

77 George Weston, *MacLean's*, 15 Nov. 1954, 59.

78 Canadair, *MacLean's*, 15 Oct. 1954, 7.

22 Making and Breaking Canada's Food Rules: Science, the State, and the Government of Nutrition, 1942–1949

IAN MOSBY

During the 1940s and 1950s, Canada's Food Rules were perhaps the single most recognizable symbol of good nutrition in the country. First introduced in 1942 as Canada's Official Food Rules, this simple list of daily food requirements formed the central message of Canada's first large-scale national nutrition campaign. With minor revisions made in 1944 and 1949, they could be seen anywhere: in newspaper advertisements, on posters in factory lunchrooms, in cookbooks, and on flyers included along with family allowance cheques. The recommendations ranged from the very specific (milk, butter, tomatoes, potatoes, bread, liver, eggs, and cheese) to the more general (citrus fruits, leafy green or yellow vegetables, whole grain cereal, and meat) and were designed to meet a scientifically determined set of nutritional requirements. The overall message was a straightforward one and would form the basis of Canadian nutrition advice until the introduction of Canada's Food Guide in 1961: 'These foods are good to eat. Eat them every day for health. Have at least three meals a day.'[1]

This chapter attempts to problematize the seemingly simple message of this iconic nutrition campaign by critically examining the concept of 'health' that formed the basis of the recommendations contained within the three revisions of the Food Rules. While a number of Canadian historians have examined the ways in which various official and unofficial 'gatekeepers' have used dietary advice as a means of normalizing the ideal of a white, middle-class, male-breadwinner–centred nuclear family, decidedly less attention has been paid to the role played by scientists, doctors, and other nutrition experts in reproducing many of the same kinds of gender, class, and racial ideologies at the level of basic nutritional science.[2] This essay therefore focuses specifically on the central role played by scientific experts in the production of popular nutrition advice as well as the ways in which changing definitions of key concepts such as 'health,' 'illness,' and 'malnutrition' reflected larger transformations in the relationship between the state and its citizens during the Second World War and early postwar periods. Building on a growing international literature on the history of nutrition, I argue that the Food Rules were part of larger efforts by leading Canadian nutrition experts to advance their own particular political and professional interests by defining healthy eating in a way that prioritized a certain vision of the wartime labour, military, and agricultural needs of the nation.[3] Through an examination of how changing ideas about the concept of 'malnutrition,' in particular, were constructed and deployed by nutrition experts and governments throughout this period, this chapter situates the Food Rules as the central message of a public health campaign that was ultimately less concerned with preventing serious illness than it was with normalizing a largely unrealized physical and cultural ideal of good citizenship.

A Canadian Malnutrition Crisis

When Canada's Official Food Rules were first unveiled to the public by the Department of Pensions and National Health in 1942, they were a key component of what would prove to be an unprecedented expansion of Canadian state-sponsored nutrition programs. Prior to the 1940s, nutrition had played an important, albeit secondary role in a range of scattered municipal, provincial, and federal public health campaigns. Nutrition was rarely the sole focus of these campaigns and, even when it was, educational materials and programs were unevenly distributed throughout the country and frequently offered conflicting advice.[4] Starting with the creation of the Nutrition Services Division within Pensions and National Health in 1941, however, nutrition began to emerge as a priority at all levels of government and, by 1950, nearly every province and dozens of municipal health departments had created their own nutrition programs. Central to these developments was the creation of the Canadian Nutrition Program in 1942. With Canada's Official Food Rules as its first public announcement, the Canadian Nutrition Program was the country's first large-scale, truly national public health effort aimed exclusively at improving Canadians' dietary habits.[5]

Like most public health campaigns, the Canadian Nutrition Program was created in response to a perceived health crisis. In this case, the crisis was the discovery of widespread malnutrition among Canadians based on the results of five dietary studies conducted by the newly created Canadian Council on Nutrition (CCN) in the cities of Edmonton, Toronto, Quebec City, and Halifax.[6] The studies, published between 1939 and 1941, found that a majority of the mainly low-income families examined were failing to consume sufficient quantities of a range of nutrients. In the first Toronto survey, for instance, widespread nutritional deficiencies were found in almost every category examined. Only 3 per cent of families were securing sufficient caloric intake, and only 7 per cent of families were consuming sufficient protein. Vitamin and mineral consumption was even lower, with mothers and children showing the highest rates of malnutrition.[7] The results of the other four surveys were perhaps somewhat less bleak but they still showed serious deficiencies in vitamin and mineral consumption. In the Halifax survey, for instance, the same kinds of gender inequalities were apparent and, overall, average family intakes of calcium, vitamin B1, and vitamin C were are all seriously deficient.[8] Even a second Toronto study, this one of higher-income families, found less malnutrition overall but evidence of widespread nutritional deficiencies among women. Ultimately, it was the authors of the Edmonton survey who provided an estimate that became a kind of shorthand for Canada's nutrition crisis as a whole when they suggested that at least 40 per cent of those surveyed 'get about three-quarters of what they need' while nearly 20 per cent 'get little more than half of what they need.'[9]

Warnings of a nationwide malnutrition crisis were not new during this period. Throughout the Depression years of the 1930s, a range of vocal social critics accused the government of ignoring what they saw as widespread malnutrition among Canada's unemployed. As James Struthers has shown, social reformers, political activists, and labour leaders frequently used malnutrition statistics to bolster their arguments against unfair wages and relief rates.[10] In particular, many pointed to studies by Leonard Marsh and other social critics that showed nutritionally adequate meals to be out of reach for poor families.[11] As Julie Guard's contribution to this volume shows, the issue of affordable, nutritious food also formed an important rallying point for popular protest throughout this period. Perhaps more than any other single issue, the inability of so many to meet basic nutritional requirements formed both a compelling and scientifically backed critique of Canada's inadequate institutional response to poverty and unemployment.

What differentiated the Canadian Council on Nutrition's warnings of a nationwide malnutrition crisis from these earlier warnings, however, was the willingness of various levels of government to take the problem seriously. In part, this was because the council – which was composed of the country's leading nutrition experts and had expressly been created by Pensions and National Health to advise them on nutrition policy – carried a kind of official legitimacy that critics and social reformers of the 1930s did not. Even more important, however, was the way that the council managed to frame the problem of malnutrition. For one thing, the scale of the problem had changed. No longer simply a problem of the unemployed, the council's studies suggested that upwards of 60 per cent of the population of Canada was suffering from inadequate nutrition. Particularly in the context of Canada's mobilization for total war, the council's representatives rarely neglected to mention the serious impacts that malnutrition could have on the war effort. Furthermore, the way in which the scientists responsible for the studies framed both the causes and solutions to the problem of malnutrition also facilitated a change in government nutrition policy. E.W. McHenry, a professor of nutritional science at the University of Toronto and the primary author of the two Toronto studies, outright rejected the idea that insufficient income was the primary cause of malnutrition. Despite the fact that, in general, the five surveys by the Canadian Council on Nutrition showed a direct correlation between income and malnutrition among the families examined, McHenry argued that the data did not provide 'a clear-cut conclusion regarding the effect of income,'[12] and he went so far as to suggest that this was because higher-income families 'obtained better food value for their money than the families in the low income group.'[13] The same sentiment was conveyed in the reports on the other surveys. While the authors of the Edmonton study acknowledged that their findings indicated that 'diet tends to improve automatically with increase in income,' they suggested that it was 'a slow process' and that 'the only means left to try to maintain the health of the population ... is to teach people to make the most of their available money.'[14]

Because the CCN studies represented the largest and most comprehensive statements on the dietary status of Canadians ever conducted, their authors wielded significant power in framing the nature of this crisis. When Nutrition Services was created in 1941, government officials stated explicitly that 'the results of the dietary surveys should form the basis for a national campaign of education to improve the nutrition of Canadians,' and they even hired one of the co-authors of the Edmonton survey, Leonard B. Pett, as the division's first director.[15] Not only did these developments have a profound effect on the authority and legitimacy granted to Canada's fledgling nutrition professions, they also proved to have a significant influence on the Canadian Nutrition Program and its first public announcement, Canada's Official Food Rules.

Measuring for Hidden Hunger and Perfect Health

What is perhaps most surprising about the wartime malnutrition crisis uncovered by the five CCN studies is the fact that it has largely been erased from Canadians' collective memory and merits almost no attention from historians of the period.[16] In part, this is because official statistics tend to provide little indication that such a crisis existed, with overall mortality rates from infectious diseases and other illnesses steadily declining throughout both the 1930s and 1940s. According to nutrition historian Aleck Samuel Ostry, deaths from deficiency diseases were actually lower during the height of the Depression than they were in the 1920s, and he suggests that there is little evidence that Depression-era changes in Canadians' dietary practices did anything to arrest the general population level improvements in health that occurred during this period.[17] Despite the seeming disconnect between the dramatic claims that upwards of 60 per cent of Canadians were malnourished and these kinds of vital statistics, the CCN's findings were not atypical for the period and, in many ways, mirrored similar studies conducted by the world's leading nutrition experts. Studies conducted by Hazel Stiebeling, the head of the section on food economics of the U.S. Department of Agriculture, found that more than 30 per cent of Americans were not consuming nutritionally adequate diets.[18] In Britain, the prominent scientist Sir John Boyd Orr found that over half of the population was living on diets deficient in a wide array of nutrients.[19] Moreover, the formation of the Canadian Council on Nutrition itself was initially spurred by a call from the League of Nations Health Organization for its member countries to begin dealing with what it warned could be a worldwide malnutrition crisis.[20]

To a large degree, the malnutrition crises in Canada and other industrialized nations during this period are perhaps best understood as artefacts of a number of important transformations that the science of nutrition was undergoing during the 1930s and 1940s. The catalyst for these changes was the discovery of the importance of vitamins and minerals during the interwar period.[21] Prior to the 1920s, good nutrition had been premised primarily on an individual's ability to maintain a thermodynamic equilibrium of energy inputs and outputs based on the consumption of the right proportions of what were understood to be the constituent components of food – namely, carbohydrates, proteins, and fats. The discovery in the 1910s and 1920s of the connection between what we now know as vitamins and minerals and a number of deficiency diseases including scurvy, pellagra, beriberi, and rickets forced a major rethinking of dominant ideas about nutrition. Not only could an individual be consuming enough calories to avoid hunger and still be malnourished but, by the 1930s, it had become widely recognized that this 'hidden hunger' had an impact far beyond deficiency diseases alone. Nutrition experts drew explicit connections between these newly discovered nutrients and the proper functioning of a number of bodily processes including growth, the immune system, eyesight, and motor functions. However, while there was at least some consensus as to the minimum human requirements necessary to avoid starvation and deficiency diseases, it proved to be much more difficult to measure for the impacts of less overt malnutrition. This was a particular problem when it came to the establishment of basic human requirements for vitamins and minerals in the form of dietary standards.

In 1933, Hazel Stiebeling posed a novel solution to this problem by creating a dietary standard that adopted a model of health based on 'optimum' as opposed to 'minimum' dietary requirements. During this period, dietary standards – which set out the daily requirements for a range of nutrients based on factors such as age, gender, and occupation – represented one of the few ways of measuring the nutritional adequacy of an individual's or group's diet without resorting to a clinical examination. Prior to the 1930s, dietary standards had primarily been designed to show the minimum calories and protein necessary to prevent hunger or to enable individuals to do certain kinds of work. For the most part, these early standards were directed almost exclusively at the destitute and at institutions like schools, prisons, and hospitals.[22] The novelty of Steibeling's 'optimal' standard was that it recognized the importance of maintaining a level of consumption above that necessary to prevent starvation or deficiency diseases. In order to do this, Stiebeling included a 'margin of safety' in her calculation of dietary requirements. Requirements for vitamins, for instance, were calculated at twice that required to prevent the occurrence of deficiency diseases. For minerals, requirements were based on accepted calculations of basic maintenance requirements plus an additional 50 per cent allowance.[23]

Steibeling's optimal dietary standard proved to be very influential in Canada and internationally. In 1936, the League of Nations Health Organization had called on all member nations to begin studying their own malnutrition problems, and to this end, the LNHO produced one of the first internationally recognized dietary standards based on a set of unambiguously optimal requirements. [24] Although there were other competing standards for vitamin and mineral consumption produced during the 1930s, Steibeling's optimal standard was popular among many nutrition experts particularly because it inserted nutrition into the heart of a number of key social and economic debates.[25] It was these social meanings of nutrition that initially attracted British scientist John Boyd Orr to Stiebeling's standard. As one of the earliest adopters and most vocal proponents of optimal nutrition, Orr drew a direct connection between the measurement of proper nutrition and Depression-era debates over what constitutes an adequate standard of living. As a progressive reformer seeking greater state intervention into the redistribution of wealth, Orr felt that the goal of proper nutrition was not simply to keep the poor alive but, rather, to raise their standard of living and make actual improvements in their health. He argued that dietary standards, therefore, needed to encourage positive social change by promoting the goal of 'perfect health' or, more specifically, 'a state of well-being such that no improvement could be effected by a change in the diet.'[26] While some proponents of optimum nutrition may not have shared Orr's political aims, they were in agreement that the dividends of promoting optimal health would not only be greater growth, increased productivity, reduced rates of illness, and lower mortality rates but also a major economic transformation. According to Orr and Stiebeling, efforts to improve nutrition would help bring the world out of the Depression by stimulating the economy through encouraging the consumption of the agricultural surpluses faced by many Western nations in the 1930s.[27]

When the Canadian Council on Nutrition adopted its own dietary standard in 1939, it used the League of Nations Health Organization and Steibeling optimal standards as a guide but made some adaptations. McHenry, in particular, worried that the LHNO standard described an adequate diet that greatly exceeded the cost relief diets provided in Canadian cities. In part, he attributed this to LNHO's nutritional requirements for women, which he felt were too high because they were based on European women who 'must work, of necessity, in the fields and must expend as much energy as men.'[28] The Canadian standard, therefore, adopted lower energy requirements for women as a way to account for both issues. Overall, however, the requirements adopted for vitamins and minerals approximated those outlined in other optimal standards and included 'margins of safety' well above those required to prevent deficiency diseases.[29] When put to use in surveys, the result was that the new standard, like its international counterparts, had the effect of greatly increasing estimates of the number of Canadians at risk of the 'hidden hunger' of malnutrition. This was because it was ultimately measuring whether or not an individual was living up to what nutrition experts determined to be an ideal of 'optimal health' rather than any specific clinical manifestations of malnutrition.

Although the dramatic estimates of malnutrition in the wake of the CCN surveys brought unprecedented attention to Canada's growing malnutrition crisis by both the public and all levels of government, the nature of the survey methods used also meant that Canadian nutrition experts had to be particularly cautious in their predictions of the possible health outcomes of their findings. The published findings of the second Toronto survey, for instance, made no specific predictions as to the clinical effects of the levels of malnutrition identified. Instead, they used the language of the eugenics movement and quoted the president of the American Medical Association who stated that the future 'promises those races who will take advantage of the newer knowledge of nutrition, a larger stature, greater vigor, increased longevity and a higher level of cultural attainment.'[30] The Edmonton survey report attempted to be more specific, predicting that in a more comprehensive survey, 'it is almost certain that clinical evidence of faulty bone, anaemia, and vitamin deficiency would be found.'[31] Even as such, the report acknowledged that the CCN studies were 'physiological only by inference.'[32]

While the CCN survey results could do little to connect the rates of malnutrition shown to the actual incidence of nutrition-related diseases, Canadian nutrition experts were quite successful in their ability to connect the high rates of 'sub-optimal' nutrition shown in the surveys to two of Canada's most serious wartime crises. Perhaps the most pressing of these was the perceived crisis among military recruits. Figures released publicly by the military in 1942 showed that upwards of 43 per cent of Canada's first 50,000 recruits had been rejected for medical reasons. Although the reasons for these rejections ranged anywhere from foot trouble to bronchitis, the results of the CCN surveys offered a ready explanation for their alarming scale. The perceived impact of sub-optimal nutrition was wide ranging: it could be a predisposing cause to infectious diseases like tuberculosis, it affected growth and structural development, and it could have serious effects on one's capacity for physical activity. Moreover, many of the specific reasons for rejection appeared to be directly related to diet. Not only were problems such as 'stomach or intestinal trouble' responsible for 8.49 per cent of the rejections but other problems associated with poor nutrition were also leading reasons for rejections on medical grounds, including faulty bones, eyes, feet, and teeth, as well as respiratory problems and heart disease.[33] These claims were further supported by studies in Britain showing that recruits who had initially been rejected on medical grounds were able to pass their second medical examination after only a few weeks on a nutritionally supervised diet.[34]

Sub-optimal nutrition was also frequently connected to one of the most pressing threats facing Canada's war effort on the home front. Although Canada's 'manpower crisis' was primarily understood to be the product of the labour shortages caused by military recruitment of able-bodied men, it was also perceived to be a problem of efficiency and productivity.[35] Surveys in war industries suggested that rates of absenteeism due to preventable minor illnesses had led to the loss of as many as 9,000,000 man-days in 1942 alone.[36] Canadian nutrition experts were quick to draw connections between these figures and malnutrition statistics. According to a 1942 article by the director of nutrition services, the impact of malnutrition was far reaching: '[Malnutrition] means increased sickness and fatigue. It means backaches and sore eyes, and sore muscles, and tired eyes, and apathy, and accidents, and stomach troubles, and worry, and more colds, and many other common causes of absenteeism or decreased production.'[37] According to nutrition experts, other common results of malnutrition included reduced 'health,' 'mental alertness,' 'pep,' 'vitality,' and 'working efficiency.'[38] This common connection between malnutrition and working efficiency is made explicit in the Halifax survey report, which suggested that the average lower-than-optimum calorie consumption of those surveyed might 'raise the question whether the Maritimer works as hard as the standard allows for muscular effort.'[39]

In this sense, malnutrition was constructed primarily as a threat to the nation's virility and strength. Both the language used to describe the results of the CCN surveys as well as the philosophy underlying the dietary standard the surveys were based on suggested that the rates of malnutrition found in the surveys probably said more about 'productivity,' 'efficiency,' and 'optimal performance' than they did about physical manifestations of illness or disease. Throughout the war, it became more common for the public pronouncements of nutrition experts to discuss malnutrition in Canada specifically in terms of lost man-hours or even the number of bombers not produced than it was for them to discuss it in terms of effects on mortality or incidence of specific nutritional diseases.[40] Moreover, if the commitment of Canada's leading nutrition experts to the somewhat utopian goals of optimum nutrition was ever in doubt during this period, it was reaffirmed in 1942 when the Canadian Council on Nutrition adopted a new dietary standard that was even more unambiguously grounded in the notion of 'perfect health.'

In 1941, the U.S. National Research Council created the most comprehensive dietary standard produced up to that point in the form of a set of 'recommended dietary allowances' (or RDAs). While it was widely acknowledged by nutrition experts that the RDAs contained a number of recommendations that had 'no experimental basis,' they were quickly adopted as the new Canadian Dietary Standard by the Canadian Council on Nutrition in 1942, partially to ensure uniformity in international standards but also because many CCN members had already begun using the more comprehensive American standard.[41] What is perhaps most interesting about the RDAs, however, was the rationale used to justify the theoretical optimum employed in order to calculate the various dietary allowances. For instance, the National Research Council stated outright that the RDAs were intended specifically for the purpose of 'building up [the American] people to a level of health and vigor never before attained or dreamed of.' In order to achieve this goal, the RDAs were designed to be 'sufficient for maximum health and vigor of any individual under any normal circumstances.'[42] This meant that the 'margin of safety' used to define what constituted 'optimal' nutrition requirements was intentionally set at the theoretical needs of the largest and most active individuals, even though most people in a population would actually require far less, often only half as much as the recommended allowances. When Canada adopted the ambitious and utopian RDAs as the Canadian Dietary Standard, it therefore meant that they also adopted a notion of malnutrition that had become unambiguously tied to notions of productivity, efficiency, and perfect health in a way that no previous standard had done.

Making Canada's Official Food Rules

The official response to the malnutrition crisis uncovered by the CCN dietary surveys reflected both the priorities of optimum nutrition and the privileging of faulty education over lack of income as the cause of malnutrition. When Nutrition Services was created in 1941, priority was placed on two areas of intervention: a large-scale popular education program and the inspection of food service facilities in key war industries. However, even the latter function of Nutrition Services was primarily aimed at education rather than the structural causes of malnutrition. This was because, although Nutrition Services staff inspected and rated the food facilities for 723 war production plants during the course of the war, they had limited power to make any meaningful changes. Legal sanctions such as fines were never used, and Nutrition Services, instead, relied on persuasion through education and promises of increased production in order to convince factory owners to improve food facilities.[43]

The Canadian Nutrition Program was the public face of the work being done by Nutrition Services and its purpose was to serve a similar function to these war industry inspections. Both approaches defined malnutrition primarily as a problem of poor food choices and both placed significant priority on the threat malnutrition posed to production and the war effort. It was a priority that was stressed by the slogan of the Canadian Nutrition Program: 'Eat Right, Feel Right – Canada Needs You Strong.' It was also a priority that formed the basis for the message contained within Canada's Official Food Rules, whose July 1942 release marked the Canadian Nutrition Program's first public announcement.

From the very outset, the Food Rules were designed to act as the central message of a much larger educational campaign that would, by the end of the war, see the Nutrition Services produce dozens of different educational pamphlets, brochures, monographs, filmstrips, displays, and posters in both English and French. While nutrition education and public health programs were largely a provincial and municipal responsibility, the federal government managed to make significant strides towards guiding and coordinating the efforts of all three levels of government, as well as voluntary organizations interested in nutrition, by promoting the unified, consistent message of the Food Rules.

As dietary advice, Canada's Official Food Rules and its 1944 and 1949 revisions were a reflection of the malnutrition crisis that the Canadian Nutrition Program had been created to solve. To this end, the primary goal of the Food

EAT RIGHT
— FEEL RIGHT
CANADA NEEDS YOU STRONG

CANADA'S OFFICIAL FOOD RULES

These are the Health-protective foods. Be sure you eat them every day in at least these amounts.

(Use More if You Can)

Milk — Adults, ½ pint. Children, more than 1 pint. And some cheese, as available.

Cereals and Bread — One serving of a whole-grain cereal and 4 to 6 slices of Canada Approved Bread, brown or white.

Fruits—One serving of to-matoes daily, or of a citrus fruit, or of tomato or citrus fruit juices, and one serving of other fruits, fresh, canned or dried.

Meat, Fish, etc.—One serving a day of meat, fish, or poultry. Liver, kidney and heart once a week.

Vegetables—(In addition to potatoes of which you need one serving daily)— Two servings daily of vegetables, preferably leafy, green or yellow, and frequently raw.

Eggs—At least 3 or 4 eggs weekly. Cooked any way you choose or in "made" dishes.

Eat these foods first, then add these and other foods you wish

DO YOUR PART IN THE CANADIAN NUTRITION PROGRAM

22.1 An early image of Canada's Official Food Rules, from the widely distributed Swift Canadian Co. pamphlet *Eat Right to Work and Win* (Toronto: Swift Canadian Co., 1942). Used with permission from Maple Leaf Foods Inc., Toronto, Ontario, Canada.

Rules was the promotion of optimal intakes of vitamins, minerals, and protein as set out in the 1942 Canadian Dietary Standard.[44] They were designed to act as a simple, meal-based guide to nutritional planning based on the concept of 'health protective' foods – foods like milk, tomatoes, potatoes, bread, and eggs which 'supply minerals, vitamins and good quality protein, or any one of these, in suitable amounts according to reasonable daily intakes.'[45] The Food Rules were, therefore, organized into six groups of protective foods, and when put into practice, they represented a model for how a person should be eating every day. However, rather than representing a total diet, the Food Rules did not actually reflect an individual's total energy needs. Instead, based on the assumption that individuals would easily make up the remainder of their energy needs with non-protective foods, the Food Rules suggested that a person 'eat these foods first, then add these and other foods you wish.'[46]

While the 1942 Food Rules made some minor concessions to wartime supply concerns – recommending only minimal rather than optimal requirements for the nutrient riboflavin in order to reflect the possibility of milk shortages – they largely defined the ambitious ideals of optimum nutrition as the norm by which individuals should judge their diets. Moreover, even the minor concession to the Department of Agriculture that the sub-optimal milk recommendations represented were ultimately rejected by the Canadian Council on Nutrition who, with support of the dairy industry, passed a motion in 1943 stating that they could not 'take any part in food lists based on "existing supply" nor "expediency"' and that the food rules needed to be 'based on optimal nutrition requirements.'[47] Thus, in the face of formal protests from the Department of Agriculture and the Wartime Prices and Trade Board, the 1944 revision of the Food Rules was altered so as to fully reflect optimal dietary requirements through the addition of cheese to the 'Meat and Fish' rule, butter to the 'Cereals and Bread' rule, and by changing the 'Milk' rule to read 'Adults, 1/2 to 1 pint' and 'Children, 1 1/2 pints to 1 quart.' While other, more cosmetic changes were also made – including the removal of the word 'official' from its title and the reduction of the number of rules from six to five by adding the recommendation to consume at least three eggs per week to the 'Meat and Fish' rule – the nutritional message remained consistent: good nutrition is optimal nutrition.[48] By basing the Food Rules and the other educational materials of the Canadian Nutrition Program on the ideal of optimum nutrition, the Canadian Council on Nutrition and Nutrition Services were setting an ambitious goal for Canadians. The utopian vision of optimum nutrition is reflected in the hyperbole of the editors of *Saturday Night* who, in a January 1943 editorial, suggest that the Canadian Nutrition Program 'is going to effect what is probably the most radical change in the living habits of a nation that has ever been brought about by the conscious effort of its rulers and its scientific and intellectual leaders' – a goal which they suggest is ultimately the creation of 'a race of super-Canadians.'[49]

While this physical ideal reflected in the recommendations for the Food Rules is essential to understanding their larger meaning, the Food Rules also represented a similarly ambitious set of culinary assumptions and goals. As the chapters by Caroline Durand and Krista Walters in this volume both show, nutrition can be adapted to a range of ideological and cultural projects, whether that be to buttress the traditionalist goals of Catholic educators or to reinforce the colonial power structure of government relations with Aboriginal peoples. The same was true of the Food Rules. Although the staff of Nutrition Services claimed to have designed the Food Rules to 'conform to the average food pattern of Canadians as nearly as known,' it would probably be more accurate to say that they reflected a specific Anglo-European cultural ideal rather than the reality of many Canadians' diets.[50] In part, this was because the Food Rules closely mirrored the interests of Canada's main domestic agricultural producers. The promotion of agriculture had always been one of the central goals of optimal nutrition. While the recommendations for the consumption of citrus fruits are the exception to this rule, the core recommendations of the Food Rules had a clear agricultural purpose in mind. Not only did they recommend the daily consumption of a number of specific staples of Canadian agriculture, but they also recommended quantities 'definitely in excess of those actually consumed in order to provide a clear goal for improvement.' The staff at Nutrition Services estimated that, if all Canadians were to eat based on the Food Rules, consumption of products such as milk and tomatoes would increase by between 25 and 35 per cent, with similar increases in domestic consumption of fruits, vegetables, and whole grains.[51] This support for the goals of Canadian agriculture was similarly reflected in the long-term opposition by both the Canadian Council on Nutrition and Nutrition Services to the use of vitamin supplements and the fortification of foods. While both the United States and Britain encouraged the fortification of certain foods like bread or margarine as a low-cost response to specific deficiencies shown in dietary surveys, these practices were actively discouraged by Nutrition Services and the Canadian Council on Nutrition. Thus, the 1942 and 1944 revisions of the Food Rules even went so far as to contain recommendations for 'Canada Approved Bread' – a product that, instead of being fortified with B vitamins, used an alternative milling technique to boost its vitamin content.

Regardless of the motivation for the specific foods chosen, however, the end result was that the Food Rules did not simply 'conform to average food patterns.' Instead, they promoted an idealized culinary template that actively pathologized eating habits that did not fit its specific Anglo-European cultural parameters. Not only did the combination of foods laid out in the Food Rules have little application to a number of Canadian regions, particularly for the inhabitants of the country's north, but they also stigmatized culinary traditions of ethnic groups whose cuisines were less centred around dairy products like milk, cheese, and butter – particularly for Aboriginal and Asian cuisines. But, it was not only certain ethnic groups or certain regions that were not living up to the Food Rules. According to a January 1943 national Gallup Poll, the vast majority of Canadians were deficient in at least one of the six food groups laid out in the Food Rules. Upwards of 25 per cent were not eating enough milk and cheese, 40 per cent were failing to consume enough breads and cereals, and upward to 83 per cent of those polled were not eating enough fruit. While the food groups for vegetables, meat, and eggs seemed to fare better, the overall picture was one of a population that, as a whole, was not eating enough of the right foods.[52] In large part, these results reflected the fact that most Canadians – but low-income individuals, in particular – were unable to meet the requirements set out in the Food Rules because they were based on a set of optimal dietary requirements that were 'sufficient for maximum health and vigor of any individual under any normal circumstances.' Calculations of the cost of a diet based on optimal nutrition requirements done by the Toronto Welfare Council and other groups consistently showed that income remained one of the major barriers families faced in living up to the kind of diet represented by the Food Rules.[53]

While both the United States and Britain introduced major redistributive as well as educational programs to deal with wartime malnutrition problems, the Canadian Nutrition Program remained focused almost exclusively on education, an approach that was applauded by the magazine *Canadian Business* for being 'designedly set against a conservative background.'[54] Thus, while Britain introduced efforts to redistribute protective foods to the poorest through a system of milk depots, communal restaurants, and nutrition-based rationing, and the United States offered food stamps to over four million low-income Americans and set plans in motion for a national school lunch program, Canada's national nutrition program included little in the way of wealth redistribution.[55] While rationing, price controls, and increased employment probably had the largest effect on the quantity and types of foods available to low-income Canadians through the course of the war, Canadian food policies were based overwhelmingly on supply rather than nutritional considerations. Most rationed food items were non-protective foods of little nutritional value like sugar, coffee, tea, jam, and certain cuts of meat. Moreover, as studies done during the 1940s showed, even with certain agricultural products like milk and citrus fruits heavily subsidized during the course of the war, they still remained out of reach of the poorest Canadians.[56]

In the end, Canada's wartime nutrition program was premised on the notion that good nutrition was a personal rather than collective responsibility. In this sense, the program was a fundamentally moral one, framed in terms of the needs of the nation and the family. This was further reinforced by the images in popular materials either produced or approved by Nutrition Services during the war, which consistently portrayed a normative white, middle-class model of domestic stability. Aside from early efforts to include educational materials in the pay envelopes of both male and female industrial workers, popular educational materials which carried the message of the Food Rules like the booklets *Healthful Eating*, *Eat Right to Work and Win*, or *The Lunch Box Is on the March* were overwhelmingly aimed at mothers, and they consistently framed the proper feeding of the family as an essential duty of wartime citizenship. Just as the Food Rules gave a scientific justification for the promotion of a specific Anglo-European culinary tradition and a utopian physical ideal, the Canadian Nutrition Program as a whole reinforced the gender norms of a dominant male-breadwinner–centred domestic order and, ultimately, did little to address the serious gender-based nutritional inequalities within families that were shown so clearly in the CCN surveys.

The Crisis of Optimal Nutrition

By the time the third and final revision of the Food Rules was published in 1949, Canada's malnutrition crisis had undergone a profound transformation. In fact, by 1945, most Canadian nutrition experts were no longer willing to stand by their earlier claims regarding malnutrition rates, and they had effectively abandoned the optimal dietary standards that had been adopted only a few years earlier. In large part, this had to do with the changing social and political uses of malnutrition following the publication of the five CCN surveys.

Despite their prominence, the Food Rules were simply one among many different ways that a diet based on the ideal of optimum nutrition could be presented. As advocacy groups like the Toronto Welfare Council argued throughout the 1940s, the Canadian Dietary Standard could also be used to calculate the minimum cost of a nutritionally adequate diet in a way that showed the actual cost of good nutrition to be 'far above prevailing wages.'[57] Although these kinds of conclusions were contradicted by the official findings of the CCN surveys, they gained traction during the 1940s. Leonard Marsh's 1943 *Report on Social Security for Canada* – one of the foundational documents in Canada's postwar welfare state – placed nutrition at the centre of attempts to produce scientifically grounded minimum standards of living.[58] And, in 1943, welfare advocates and prominent CCN members Frederick Tisdall, Alice Willard, and Marjorie Bell were even able to convince the City of Toronto to adopt a new relief schedule based, in large part, on the requirements set out in the Canadian Dietary Standard. Because this meant increases in relief payments of anywhere between 20 to 70 per cent depending on the size of the family, Ontario's provincial government responded by refusing to match the costs associated with the new schedule.[59]

For some in the Canadian Council on Nutrition, these kinds of uses of the Canadian Dietary Standard were a cause for alarm. In 1944, E.W. McHenry expressed concern that people had been making 'unnecessarily exaggerated statements about the prevalence of malnutrition' and had been using such statistics as, among other things, 'evidence of iniquities in the present social order.' After conceding his own 'considerable responsibility' for claims of widespread malnutrition, he argued that 'because of the lack of scientific evidence it is not possible, at present, to assemble a precise standard of adequacy' and suggested that the use of dietary standards be reconsidered.[60] In part, this was based on McHenry's more recent research which, perhaps unsurprisingly, found little correlation between sub-optimal dietary intake and actual physical manifestations of malnutrition.[61] However, his emergence as the leading critic of the 1942 standard also had much to do with the fact that he had been asked in 1943 by the government of Ontario to produce his own report on the adequacy of provincial relief levels in relation to proper nutrition. Unlike his colleagues Tisdall, Willard, and Bell, McHenry chose not to use optimal dietary requirements in his calculation of minimum dietary needs of families on relief and, as a result, he presented a significantly lower estimate of the cost of an adequate diet. In the process, however, McHenry was forced to publicly repudiate both the work of Tisdall, Willard, and Bell, as well as a dietary standard that the Canadian Council on Nutrition had unanimously voted to adopt only two years earlier.[62]

Ultimately, McHenry was able to recruit other allies within the Canadian Council on Nutrition to his perspective. From early on, it was widely recognized that the margins of safety adopted within all optimal dietary standards were essentially arbitrary, which was reflected in the tendency for many Canadian scientists to draw the equally arbitrary distinction between diets that were 70 per cent below the standard as being 'markedly deficient' from those that were only 'borderline' deficient.[63] Within a few years, however, even this distinction was put into question as the predicted rates of clinical malnutrition failed to materialize. It was in this context that the Canadian Council on Nutrition issued a June 1945 statement warning of the 'lack of correlation between the results of dietary surveys and the physical condition of the subjects' and therefore recommending that researchers discontinue the use of the 1942 Canadian Dietary Standard.[64]

Although the official rationale was that the lack of correspondence between claims of the incidence of malnutrition and its clinical manifestations forced a rethinking of the Canadian Dietary Standard, a 1945 article on the construction of dietary standards co-authored by Pett and two colleagues at the Department of National Health and Welfare, C.A. Morrel and F.W. Hanley, suggested that this rather abrupt change in attitudes among Canadian nutrition experts was spurred as much by Canada's altered post-1945 social conditions as by any specific advances in the science of nutrition. In what might be one of the most revealing statements from any scientist of the period about the socially constructed nature of 'malnutrition' as a medical category, the article proposed that all dietary standards up to that point had 'arisen as a direct result of certain national or international situations of a critical nature in which food played a decisive or important role.' They argued that Stiebeling's 1933 standard had been produced in light of the 'existence of huge undistributed surpluses of food in a world where inadequate nutrition of all degrees abounded.' The requirements used as the basis for Canada's 1942 standard, on the other hand, had originally been developed in response to 'the need for a program of action to mobilize all the nation's resources for large-scale and protracted warfare.' What Canada needed, therefore, was a new dietary standard that, they argued, could be 'adapted to the provision of freedom from hunger in the immediate post-war world.'[65]

For Pett, Morrel, and Hanley, the problem was not so much that dietary standards grounded in the concept of optimal nutrition had been proven wrong. When the Canadian Council on Nutrition adopted its 1939 and 1942 dietary standards, it did so with the full knowledge that the figures used included significant 'margins of safety' and that many of the figures used had 'little experimental evidence.'[66] While the Canadian Council on Nutrition could have adopted a more conservative standard, it chose to use optimum requirements because they reflected a biological response to the needs of a nation at war. In the postwar period, however, the relevance of such an ambitious standard was put into question when nutrition began to be invoked regularly by leftist social critics and the claims of a Canadian malnutrition crisis were considered alongside the reality of mass starvation in war-ravaged Europe and Asia.

These concerns about the political uses of malnutrition and its relevance to Canada's postwar international role were ultimately reflected in the requirements set out in the new Dietary Standard for Canada that was adopted by the Canadian Council on Nutrition in 1948.[67] The most important difference from earlier standards was the adoption of two separate categories of malnutrition, with one set of requirements provided to measure the minimum nutritional needs of an individual alongside another set of optimal requirements.

The former set of requirements were given the name 'nutritional floor,' and they essentially described a nutrient intake beneath which 'the maintenance of health in people cannot be assumed.'[68] Optimal requirements, on the other hand, were provided specifically for categories including work, pregnancy, and lactation. The intention was that these optimal figures be added to the 'maintenance' requirements to calculate the nutritional needs of a 'normal' or 'active' person. Although the optimal requirements were somewhat lower than those in the 1942 standard, they continued to be based on an arbitrary ideal and its authors readily admitted that 'there are no quantitative experimental data bearing on the question of how much more than enough is better.'[69]

In effect, the introduction of the 'nutritional floor' to the 1948 standard managed to simultaneously reflect the priorities of both optimum and minimum standards of health. The 'nutritional floor' responded to McHenry's criticism of the earlier standards by providing one set of measurements for the purposes of planning minimum nutritional requirements for use in the calculation of relief or institutional diets while, at the same time, promoting a model of 'optimal' health that reflected a set of aspirational goals for both health and agricultural production.[70] While undercutting the kinds of malnutrition claims that had been used by social critics in their efforts to reform the Canadian state, the new dietary standard allowed nutrition experts to straddle the line between social and medical uses of nutrition in a way that consciously reflected the new socio-political circumstances of a postwar international order. This was made even more explicit when, for the first time, the Canadian Dietary Standard also contained warnings that 'excess ingestion of nutrients should not be confused with an adequately nourished state' and that the 'ingestion of more of a nutrient than serves a clear physiological purpose is undesirable in the face of the world scarcity of food and may even be harmful to the individual under certain circumstances.'[71]

Conclusion

When the final revision of Canada's Food Rules was introduced, in 1949, it continued to reflect the priorities of the malnutrition crisis that had sparked the creation of the Canadian Nutrition Program in the first place. As Catherine Carstairs' contribution to this volume shows, the basic assumptions behind optimal nutrition continued to find an eager following in the postwar years as the emerging 'health food' movement placed much of its faith in the promise of nutritional science and the goal of perfect health. But optimum nutrition remained at the heart of popular nutrition advice as well. Although the ambitious dietary standard that the first two versions of the Food Rules had been based on was replaced in 1948, the general message remained consistent. Some small alterations were made to reflect changes in the postwar food supply and to encourage greater consumption of some protective foods. Overall, however, the five rules looked remarkably similar to their 1944 counterparts and, according to calculations done by the Canadian Council on Nutrition, the utopian goal of optimum nutrition that had formed the basis of the Food Rules since 1942 continued to be their primary message, well after the scientific justification for such recommendations had been brought into question and warnings against 'over-nutrition' as a form of malnutrition became more common.[72]

As with its predecessors, the deceptively simple message of the 1949 version of Canada's Food Rules masked the controversy and uncertainty that underwrote its basic assumptions about health and nutrition. And, like these earlier incarnations, the advice represented as much a political as it did a scientific consensus about healthy eating. This continuity between the 1949 Food Rules and its predecessors suggests the ways in which wartime notions of citizenship and health continued to resonate among Canada's leading nutrition experts and policy makers long after the Second World War had ended. In part, this was related to the fact that such educational materials supported their professional and political aspirations. Not only did the sizeable and very specific recommendations of the Food Rules suggest to most Canadians that they were in need of at least some expert guidance in order to meet the nutritional requirements of their families, but they also continued to represent both a nutritional and cultural model of social stability that stressed the role of individuals in the maintenance of their own well-being. As the central message of a campaign that had originally been designed to promote the maximum industrial, agricultural, and military capacity of a nation at war, the Food Rules would continue to represent a model of 'health' that had only ever been conceived of as an unmet ideal well into the postwar period.

ACKNOWLEDGMENTS

This chapter is dedicated to the memory of Gina Feldberg. Financial support for this research was provided by the Social Sciences and Humanities Research Council of Canada.

NOTES

1 This quote is from the 1949 revision of the Food Rules. See Health Canada, *Canada's Food Guides, 1942–1992* (Ottawa, 1992).

2 See Franca Iacovetta and Valerie J. Korinek, 'Jell-O Salads, One-Stop Shopping, and Maria the Homemaker: The Gender Politics of Food,' in Marlene Epp, Franca Iacovetta, and Valerie Korinek, eds., *Sisters or Strangers? Immigrant, Ethnic, and Racialized Women in Canadian History* (Toronto: University of Toronto Press, 2004), 190–230; Franca Iacovetta, *Gatekeepers: Reshaping Immigrant Lives in Cold War Canada* (Toronto: Between the Lines, 2006); Mary-Ellen Kelm, *Colonizing Bodies: Aboriginal Health and Healing in British Columbia, 1900–50* (Vancouver: UBC Press, 1998); Cynthia R. Comacchio, *Nations Are Built of Babies: Saving Ontario's Mothers and Children, 1900–1940* (Montreal and Kingston: McGill-Queen's University Press, 1993). For a history of the nutrition policy, see Aleck Ostry, *Nutrition Policy in Canada, 1870–1939* (Vancouver: UBC Press, 2006).

3 See, for example, James Vernon, *Hunger: A Modern History* (Cambridge: Belknap Press, 2007); Nick Callather, 'The Foreign Policy of the Calorie,' *American Historical Review* 112/2 (2007): 1–60; John Coveney, *Food Morals and Meaning: The Pleasure and Anxiety of Eating*, 2nd ed. (London: Routledge, 2007); David F. Smith and Jim Philips, eds., *Food, Science, Policy and Regulation in the Twentieth Century: International and Comparative Perspectives* (London: Routledge, 2000); David F. Smith, ed., *Nutrition in Britain: Science, Scientists and Politics in the Twentieth Century* (London: Routledge, 1997); Rima Apple, *Vitamania: Vitamins in American Culture* (New Brunswick, NJ: Rutgers University Press, 1996); Harmke Kamminga and Andrew Cunningham, eds., *Science and Culture of Nutrition* (Amsterdam: Rodophi, 1995).

4 See Ostry, *Nutrition Policy in Canada*.

5 For discussions of the early years of the Canadian Nutrition Program, see Tara D. Corless, 'Lunch Boxes on the March: Women, Family-Feeding, and the Nova Scotia Nutrition Programme, 1935–1959,' M.A. thesis, Dalhousie, Saint Mary's, and Mount Saint Vincent Universities, 1998, and Alana J. Hermiston, '"If It's Good for You, It's Good for the Nation!" The Moral Regulation of Nutrition in Canada, 1930–1945,' doctoral dissertation, Carleton University, 2005.

6 L.B. Pett, 'Nutrition as a National Problem,' *Canadian Welfare* 18/1 (1942): 21–9; E.W. McHenry, 'Nutrition in Toronto,' *Canadian Public Health Journal* (hereafter *CPHJ*) 30/1 (1939): 4–13; E. Gordon Young, 'A Dietary Survey in Halifax,' *CPHJ* 32/5 (1941): 236–40; George Hunter and L. Bradley Pett, 'A Dietary Survey in Edmonton,' *CPHJ* 32/5 (1941): 259–65; J. Ernest Sylvestre and Honore Nadeau, 'Enquête sur l'Alimentation Habituelle des Familles de Petits-Salaries dans la Ville de Québec,' *CPHJ* 32/5 (1941): 241–50; Jean M. Patterson and E.W. McHenry, 'A Dietary Investigation in Toronto Families Having Annual Incomes between $1,500–$2,400,' *CPHJ* 32/5 (1941): 251–8.

7 McHenry, 'Nutrition in Toronto,' 5.

8 Young, 'A Dietary Survey in Halifax,' 236–40.

9 Hunter and Pett, 'A Dietary Survey in Edmonton,' 265.

10 James Struthers, 'How Much Is Enough? Creating a Social Minimum in Ontario, 1930–44,' *Canadian Historical Review* 72/1 (1991): 39–83.

11 Leonard Marsh et al., *Health and Unemployment: Some Studies of Their Relationship* (New York: Oxford University Press, 1938).

12 McHenry, 'Nutrition in Toronto,' 9.

13 Patterson and McHenry, 'A Dietary Investigation in Toronto,' 257.

14 Hunter and Pett, 'A Dietary Survey in Edmonton,' 265.

15 Department of Pensions and National Health, *Annual Report for the Year Ending March 31, 1941* (Ottawa: Author, 1941).

16 See Jeffrey A. Keshen, *Saints, Sinners and Soldiers: Canada's Second World War* (Vancouver: UBC Press, 2004); J.L. Granatstein and Peter Neary, *The Good Fight: Canadians and World War II* (Toronto: Copp Clark, 1995).

17 Ostry, *Nutrition Policy in Canada*, 90–7.

18 Harvey Levenstein, *Paradox of Plenty: A Social History of Eating in Modern America* (Berkeley, CA: University of California Press, 1993), 58.

19 John Boyd Orr, *Food Health and Income: Report on a Survey of Adequacy of Diet in Relation to Income,* 2nd ed. (London: Macmillan, 1937).

20 League of Nations, *Nutrition: Final Report of the Mixed Committee of the League of Nations on the Relation of Nutrition to Health, Agriculture and Economic Policy* (Geneva: Author, 1937).

21 For an overview, see Harvey Levenstein, *Revolution at the Table: The Transformation of the American Diet* (Berkeley, CA: University of California Press, 1988); Apple, *Vitamania*.

22 I. Leitch, 'The Evolution of Dietary Standards,' *Nutrition Abstracts and Reviews* 11/4 (1942): 509–21; L.B. Pett, C.A. Morrell, and F.W. Hanley, 'The Development of Dietary Standards,' *Canadian Journal of Public Health* (hereafter *CJPH*) 36 (June 1945): 232–9.

23 Orr, *Food Health and Income*, 39.

24 Technical Commission of the Health Committee of the League of Nations, *The Problem of Nutrition*, vol. 2, *Report on the Physiological Bases of Nutrition* (Geneva: League of Nations, 1936).

25 See, Vernon, *Hunger*, 137.

26 Orr, *Food Health and Income*, 11.

27 David F. Smith, 'Nutrition Science and the Two World Wars,' in Smith, *Nutrition in Britain*, 142–65.

28 E.W. McHenry, 'Dietary Standards for Use in Canada,' 15 March 1938, LAC, RG 29, vol. 958, file 387-9-1.

29 The requirements adopted for use in the final four CCN surveys for vitamins A,

B1, and C, for instance, were optimal requirements with margins of safety ranging anywhere from 50 to 100 per cent above accepted minimal requirements. See Frederick F. Tisdall to C.A. Morrell, 1 Oct. 1940, LAC, RG 29, vol. 959, file 387-9-1.

30 Patterson and McHenry, 'A Dietary Investigation in Toronto,' 251.

31 Hunter and Pett, 'A Dietary Survey in Edmonton,' 265.

32 Ibid., 259.

33 Rica McLean Farquharson, 'Startling Army Revelations – So What Now!' *Canadian Home Journal* (Feb. 1942): 8–9, 23–4. Also see, Pett, 'Nutrition as a National Problem,' 21–9.

34 'The Need for Action in Nutrition,' *CPHJ* 32/6 (1941): 317–18.

35 See Jennifer A. Stephen, *Pick One Intelligent Girl: Employability, Domesticity, and the Gendering of Canada's Welfare State, 1939–1947* (Toronto: University of Toronto Press, 2007).

36 Hiram McCann, 'Scientific Feeding to Build a Healthier Race,' *Saturday Night* 58/19 (1943): 6; Leonard L. Knott, 'Hidden Hunger,' *Canadian Business* (Jan. 1943): 24–9, 92–6.

37 L.B. Pett, 'Food Makes a Difference,' *CPHJ* 33/12 (1942): 567.

38 L.B. Pett, 'Applied Nutrition,' *CJPH* 34/1 (1943): 1–5; Pett, 'Food Makes a Difference,' 565–70; W.A. Crandall, 'Vitamins: A Review of Present Knowledge,' *National Health Review* (hereafter *NHR*) 9/35 (1941): 222–8; E.W. McHenry, 'Some Observations on Canadian Nutrition,' *CPHJ* 31/12 (1940): 584–8; and C.A. Morell, 'Nutrition in Canada,' *NHR* 8/32 (April 1940): 84–6.

39 Young, 'A Dietary Survey in Halifax,' 238.

40 Pett, 'Food Makes a Difference,' 565.

41 'Canadian Dietary Standards, April 1942,' LAC, RG 29, vol. 960, part 15, file 387-9-1.

42 L.B. Pett, 'Vitamin Requirements of Human Beings,' *Vitamins and Hormones* 13 (1955): 217.

43 L.B. Pett et al., *Nutrition in Industry* (Montreal: International Labour Office, 1946).

44 See 'Canada's Food Rules,' *Canadian Nutrition Notes* 2/7 (1946): 1–2.

45 L.B. Pett, 'Outline of the Canadian Nutrition Program,' 1942, LAC, RG 17, vol. 3670, file N-9-12.

46 'Canada's Official Food Rules,' LAC, RG 17, vol. 3670, file N-9-12.

47 Agenda Item 5, Canadian Council on Nutrition (CCN), 9th Meeting, 8 May 1944, LAC, RG 17, vol. 3670, file N-9-12A.

48 Other changes included the addition of recommendations regarding water and iodized salt and the omission of kidney and heart 'because of the very limited supplies available and the uncertainty of their necessity in addition to meat.'

49 'Nutrition Campaign,' *Saturday Night* 58/17 (1943): 1.

50 'Canada's Food Rules,' 1–2.

51 Ibid., 1.

52 'Gallup Poll Checks Canada's Diet,' *Toronto Daily Star*, 6 Jan. 1943, 5.

53 See F.F. Tisdall et al., 'Relief Diets,' *Bulletin of the Ontario Medical Association* (Dec. 1933): 15–16; Marsh et al., *Health and Unemployment*; and Toronto Welfare Council, *The Cost of Living* (Toronto, 1939).

54 Knott, 'Hidden Hunger,' 26.

55 Levenstein, *Paradox of Plenty*, 62–3; David F. Smith, 'The Rise and Fall of the Scientific Food Committee during the Second World War,' in Smith and Philips, eds., *Food, Science, Policy and Regulation*, 101–16.

56 Frederick F. Tisdall, Alice C. Willard, and Marjorie Bell, *Report on Study of Relief Food Allowances and Costs* (Toronto: City of Toronto, 1941); Toronto Welfare Council, *The Cost of Living*, rev. ed. (Toronto: Author, 1944).

57 Toronto Welfare Council, *The Cost of Living*, (Toronto: Author, 1939), 43.

58 Leonard Marsh, *Report on Social Security for Canada* (Toronto: University of Toronto Press, 1975).

59 Struthers, 'How Much Is Enough?' 76–9.

60 McHenry, 'Recent Trends in Nutrition,' 154–6.

61 E.W. McHenry et al., 'A Nutrition Survey in East York Township,' *CJPH* 34/5 (1943): 193–204.

62 E.W. McHenry et al., *A Report on Food Allowances for Relief Recipients in the Province of Ontario* (Toronto: Ontario Department of Public Welfare, 1945).

63 L.B. Pett, 'What's Wrong with Canada's Diet?' *NHR* 10/36 (1942): 1–7.

64 CCN, 'The Construction and Use of Dietary Standards,' *CJPH* 36 (July 1945): 272.

65 Pett, Morrell, and Hanley, 'The Development of Dietary Standards,' 23–35.

66 'Minutes of the Meeting of the Scientific Advisory Committee of the Canadian Council on Nutrition, June 4th, 1942,' LAC, RG 17, vol. 3670, file N-9-12.

67 CCN, 'A Dietary Standard for Canada,' *Canadian Bulletin on Nutrition*, vol. 2 (Ottawa: Author, 1950).

68 Ibid., 6.

69 E.W. Crampton, 'Canadian Nutritional Problems, with Reference to the Canadian Dietary Standards,' *CJPH* 41/9 (1950): 361.

70 'Minutes – 12th CCN Meeting – 5 May 1947,' LAC, RG 29, vol. 961, part 22, file 387-9-1.

71 'A New Dietary Standard for Canada, 1949,' *Canadian Nutrition Notes* 5/9 (1949): 65–72.

72 While most of the rules remained largely the same, recommendations for (1) 'Canada Approved Vitamin B Bread' were officially removed from the rules following its failure to make any headway into the market and ongoing opposition

from industry and synthetic vitamin supplements and (2) fortified margarine were included for the first time. Changes in milk recommendations were made, in part, to recognize the different nutritional needs of children and adolescents, but also because of concern that the maximum recommendations provided in the previous version were discouraging milk consumption. The ranges in milk consumption that characterized the 1944 revision were, therefore, replaced with recommendations for 'at least' 1/2 pint for adults, 1 pint for children, and 1 1/2 pints for adolescents. Overall, however, the Food Rules remained consistent and continued to reflect an optimal consumption of vitamins and minerals. L.B. Pett, 'A New Dietary Standard for Canada, 1949,' *CMAJ* 61 (Nov. 1949): 452.

23 'A National Priority': Nutrition Canada's *Survey* and the Disciplining of Aboriginal Bodies, 1964–1975

KRISTA WALTERS

In 1973, the Department of National Health and Welfare released the results of Canada's first national nutrition survey, referred to as Nutrition Canada.[1] Published as a series of reports under a primary summary, *Nutrition: A National Priority*, this decade-long project (1964 to 1975) studied 'scientific' evidence of physical health based on medical examinations. The data examined included questionnaires, blood samples, food tracking, and body measurements. In undertaking the *Survey*, the nutrition analysts grouped those belonging to white settler society together with immigrants into the category of Canada's 'national population,' which was understood as being separate from two other distinct groups: *Indians* and *Eskimos*.[2] The construction of these groupings underscores the special otherness of Aboriginal bodies, and the form of data collection and conclusions drawn well illustrate that this government-funded project aimed not simply to raise the standard of health in Canada but was part of the state's ongoing agenda to assimilate Aboriginal peoples. It served to reinforce the disciplinary colonial power structure of Aboriginal-government relations in Canada.[3]

By the late 1960s, the Canadian government, under the Department of National Health and Welfare and the Department of Indian Affairs, had launched various initiatives in an attempt to discipline culturally deviant bodies, particularly those of Indians and Eskimos.[4] In addition to the better-known efforts at increasing the regulation of First Nations peoples, such as the Trudeau government's infamous 1969 White Paper on Indian Policy,[5] there were more subtle national projects being carried out through data collection that reflected efforts to produce a more homogeneous society. The Nutrition Canada *Survey* was one such project; indeed, it embodied the liberal ideology that provided justification for what was touted as benevolent state intervention into Aboriginal peoples' lives. Accordingly, this chapter seeks to explain why, in late twentieth-century Canada, food and nutrition were declared a 'national priority.' The essay also explores how the Canadian government and its cadres of experts analysed the diets of Aboriginal peoples in Canada and, moreover, how the state sought to regulate those family diets as a means of assimilation.

Colonizing Aboriginal Health and Nutrition

Food and nutrition policy in Canada from the late 1960s to the 1970s, a period significantly shaped by incoming immigrants from more 'exotic' regions around the globe, should be considered in the context of resistance to assimilation by both recent immigrants and Aboriginal people. The Canadian government responded to the growing ethnic diversity of its post-1945 population, and the increasing pressures created by groups maintaining their distinct cultural identities, by hyperanalysing the mothers of families, in part, through studying dietary habits. That is, they singled out the mother for special scrutiny on the ground that she was the person most responsible for the habits or behavioural patterns of all the other family members. Thus far, the historiography has looked at the ways in which immigrant women have negotiated the complex dynamics created by the health and nutritional campaigns that sought to change immigrant families by 'reforming' mothers,[6] but little careful attention has yet been paid to the Canadian government's interest in the food customs and nutritional profiles of Aboriginal mothers and their families in the period after the Second World War.

In addressing the subject, I am mainly concerned not with analysing the statistical data but, rather, with how Nutrition Canada's research on bodies fits within a colonial discourse on Aboriginal health. Family and food authorities expect mothers to take care of their families, a theme highlighted by other chapters in this volume, including Ian Mosby's on Canada's Food Rules and those dealing with cookbooks. The modern experts behind the Nutrition Canada *Survey* similarly placed heavy responsibility for the nutritional status of Aboriginal people on mothers. Equally important, however, Aboriginal women were also vulnerable to a more deeply pathologizing medical discourse than were Euro-Canadian or immigrant women.

As scholars of encounter have documented, food has been central to constructing both racial identity and colonial projects.[7] In the Nutrition Canada *Survey*, a colonial framework that pathologized non-Western foodways was central to defining acceptable levels of national nutrition and to determining who fit within the category of the 'national' (population) and who required separate categories of analysis. The *Survey* was presented as an expression of governmental concern for a healthy national body, which it was hoped would be strengthened by a shared understanding of appropriate dietary choices through increased national nutrition education. When the Canadian Council on Nutrition conceived of the project in 1964, it proposed three objectives: to examine 'the mean consumption of selected food groups and their contribution to nutrient intake of Canadians,' as well as 'patterns of food consumption and nutrient intake at various times of the day' and, third, to 'provide information on the changes in eating habits during pregnancy.'[8] The data collected were to 'serve as a basis for the development of nutrition programs, construction of food guides, evaluation of changes of food patterns in Canada over a period of time' and 'as a basis for food legislation.'[9]

As food and its consumption became increasingly monitored and regulated, and nutrition legislation standardized and professionalized, the emerging science of Aboriginal nutrition fast became a site of colonization. Moreover, gendered colonial power relations informed the approach to nutrition data collection: that is, predominantly male urban 'experts' oversaw the collection of data that was carried out primarily by women studying Aboriginal bodies in what were understood to be 'isolated' areas of Canada.[10] The *Survey* was supported by government health officials from both provincial and federal levels under the supervision of the Department of National Health and Welfare, and it was conceived of and structured with 'related' scientific communities in conjunction with the Department of Indian and Northern Affairs. The content of the program and *Survey* funding were approved in August 1969.[11]

Creating a National Survey

The national *Survey* fieldwork was carried out between 1970 and 1972, when data were collected according to categories based on divisions between age groupings and gender as well as pregnancy. Bodies were studied beginning with infancy; then nutrition patterns (and diversions from them) were measured in participants representing the different life stages from early childhood to adolescence and then adulthood with the latter capped at a category defined as '65+.' The *Survey* was 'designed to assess nutritional status according to region, population type, income and season' and included population samples from five distinct regions: Atlantic, Quebec, Ontario, Prairies, and British Columbia. The *Survey* further stratified the Enumeration Areas within each region by population types, defined as metropolitan, urban, or rural, and by income levels.[12] The most striking stratification among these population groupings was the separation of Indian and Eskimo peoples into distinct categories while all of the other cultural, religious, class, or ethnic groups appeared as a nondescript Canadian citizenry, distinguished in the published reports only by region, age, and gender.[13]

Separate sample designs were created for the Indian and Eskimo surveys to assess the nutritional status of non-urban Aboriginal people in Canada.[14] The *Indian Survey* was carried out from September 1971 to September 1972 and the *Eskimo Survey* between April and June 1972.[15] Most of the participants in the Eskimo study who were over the age of 20 required translators as did some of the *Indian Survey* participants living in 'remote areas.' The translators were drawn from the local population.[16] Divisions by age and gender mirror those in the national model with one exception: the oldest age category in both the Indian and Eskimo samples was cut off at 55 years out of recognition of the low numbers of Aboriginal people over 65 years of age living in the areas surveyed.[17] The participants included members of Indian bands from six culture areas defined by Indian and Northern Affairs for the *Survey* as Algonkian, Iroquoian, Plains, Plateau, Pacific, and Mackenzie River, and Eskimos from the four settlements of Frobisher Bay, Coppermine, Pelly Bay, and Eskimo Point.[18]

In its published form, the *Survey* (which was accessible to the public) consists of a set of bound books, printed in twelve volumes, and accompanied by a separate preliminary summary of the project entitled, *Nutrition: A National Priority*. Ten of these volumes cover each of the regional-based findings while the final two publications were the separate *Indian Survey* and *Eskimo Survey* reports released in 1975. The publication of the series was followed by a report on food consumption patterns based on the findings of the study as well as the *Health and Protection Branch Report on the Relationship between Income and Nutrition Based on Analysis of Nutrition Canada Data*.[19]

The chapters in the regional, Indian, and Eskimo reports are organized along a model that begins with a synopsis of the study, where technical and methodological issues such as sample designs, procedures, and data interpretation are discussed. This is followed by the presentation of regional results, showing a breakdown of various vitamins and minerals consumed for the specific population studied, which are then measured against the national findings. The findings for each group of participants, a total of 19,000 individuals overall, are then medically presented, detailing nutritional intake and status as well as areas of deficiency or 'risk.'[20] No photographs are included in any of the publications, nor are there any specific details that would identify individual *Survey* participants. The questions asked concern not only location details and the number of individuals in a home but specific aspects of everyday living conditions. A 'List of Household Members Form,' for example, is laid out in columns that ask for the interviewee's 'Sex and Pregnancy Status,' 'Highest School Grades Obtained,' and 'Employment Status.'[21] The surveyors also tabulated household details including where food was purchased, who prepared it, whether there was storage space for perishables, and how much was spent on weekly purchases.

The form's individual subject boxes contain nutritionally incriminating evidence of the 'problem' of national health. For instance, Box H, 'Type of Cook Stove,' allows for the following options listed in order from top to bottom: 'electric range or rangette,' 'natural gas range,' 'hot plates,' 'wood/coal/oil,' 'primitive,' and 'other.' The various options, which are presented as a kind of hierarchy of modernity which then spirals downwards to below 'primitive' means of cooking, seem to have little to do with nutrition. Instead, they position subjects who check the lower boxes outside of modernity and thus outside of the professional middle-class knowledge of household science. As historians have documented, the discourses surrounding the type of stove that women did or did not use often said more about the educational and ideological objectives of the schools, physicians, dieticians, nurses, and government publications dispensing advice than about nutrition per se (see, e.g., Caroline Durand in this volume).[22]

In the *Survey*, the participants employing methods of food preparation that are deemed 'primitive,' which arguably include the methods used by primarily Aboriginal communities living in subsistence conditions or on combinations of 'country' and imported foods, are pathologized as practising poor nutrition. Similar treatment is given to food storage, with options listed from top ('refrigerator') to bottom ('other'), along with a second section that indicates a range of choices from 'refrigerator & freezer' down to 'other.' The message seems clear: for the mothers storing their food in the less than ideal conditions of a refrigerator and freezer, poor nutrition, and the accompanying stigma of unhealthy children and high infant morbidity, appear to be the inevitable results.

The categories are organized hierarchically based according to a middle-class model in which the ideal household is composed of a single, nuclear family dwelling. In addition, the tasks of purchasing and preparing family meals are gendered. Boxes Q and R, inquiring consecutively into 'who usually decides what food to purchase' and 'who usually prepares food,' have the option of 'wife' squarely positioned at the top of the list. Below in box Q, the options of 'husband,' 'husband & wife,' 'other adult,' and 'other' are listed in descending order, while box R offers the same options with the exception that 'other' is replaced with 'child (12–18 YRS).' Again, the message seems clear: not only are women the appropriate option to check in both boxes, but these women are to be wives and mothers. This underlying assumption that mothers are the family's food provider is not unique to this *Survey*, of course, but fits with a larger gendered discourse regarding food preparation in Canadian families.[23]

Pathologizing Aboriginal Mothers

Most nutrition education campaigns in Canada, and the United States,[24] were directed at mothers as a fairly inclusive and broadly defined category. It is not surprising, given that Canadian officialdom had created separate educational campaigns for Aboriginal mothers on the ground that they and their children constitute a separate class and culture in need of special education, that Nutrition Canada chose to separate Indian and Eskimo families from the national population for the purposes of its nutrition *Survey*. Indeed, it is consistent with a history of othering First Nations women. In Canada's colonial projects, health education has reinforced the notion of Aboriginal mothers and their domestic arrangements as a threat to the 'physical, social, and spiritual survival' of their children.[25]

In the survey, the organization of families in some Aboriginal communities was also framed as deviant, particularly in the northwest, where the central organizing unit was an extended rather than nuclear family structure. Such findings challenge the main tenets of a postwar nutrition ideology that presupposes, and therefore normalizes, the nuclear family. For instance, in the period after the Second World War, observers noted that the emergence of organized caribou hunts 'represents the institutionalization of the share ethic of the extended family.'[26] In these extended families, men were charged with procuring food, thus denying women the supposedly natural role of shopping and securing meals for the family. This impacted the ability of nutrition experts to place blame on mothers, who did not so easily fit the normalized role of a mother as nurturer and feeder.

Similarly, the presence of Aboriginal children as family cooks is understood as posing yet another problem in family organization because, according to the dominant ideology, children in 'normal' Canadian families are fed, not feeders.[27] The *Survey* reflected this strain of thought. For example, the lowest acceptable age listed for youths who acted as family cook (on Form 1) is 12 years, indicating that there is no room for younger children to take on this role. There is no 'other' box to allow for such a perversion. The methodology involved in creating this form, and the cultural assumptions informing such methods, place all of the responsibility for living up to middle-class standards of family 'normalcy' on the mothers. Conversely, it creates 'bad mothers' out of those who do not fulfil expected roles.[28]

The Cold War witnessed the resurgence of a conservative domestic ideology that idealized a homemaker mother in her nuclear family, and in the post-1945 decades, both immigrant and Aboriginal women were isolated for special attention as 'part of a wider campaign to reform Canadian women and elevate postwar family life.'[29] Viewing the immigrant woman as key to the education and uplift of her family, the experts sought to expose her to Canadian customs through such outlets as adult English language and 'home management' classes.[30] It reflected their view that immigrant women potentially could become better mothers and elevate their families. By contrast, contemporary nutritionists considered the antithesis of this homemaker and family ideal to be the Aboriginal mother. This pathologizing of Aboriginal women was not unique to the *Survey* but part of a larger project of assimilation through educational programs aimed at Aboriginal mothers. As part of various ongoing efforts to transform the bad mother into the 'Clever Mother,' for example, Indian and Northern Health Services published in 1958 a text entitled *The Pre-Schooler*, which recommended lifestyle changes for northern Aboriginal mothers who were presented as being in need of re-education.[31] Nutrition Canada similarly drew on the colonial discourse that Aboriginal parents and their homes were inherently diseased.[32] These and other publications and educational pamphlets from the period send an implicit message that 'A Clever Mother' who follows 'expert' guidelines will have a healthy child, whereas Aboriginal mothers relying on knowledge provided by those without professional credentials will raise sick children.[33]

The increasing presence of health officials and services in northern communities on account of these poverty-related diseases also directly impacted who was chosen to participate in the nutrition *Survey*. The authors of the published reports explain how 'Indians in Bands on Reserves and Crown Lands' were studied on the basis of a sample 'according to region, distance from urban centres, and cultural area.' The six 'Indian Culture Areas' in Canada chosen for the *Survey* sample (as listed above) were based on stratifications defined by Indian and Northern Affairs.[34] According to the published *Survey*, 'in recognition of cultural differences,' Nutrition Canada 'selected bands representative of each culture area.'[35] In effect, Indian and Northern Affairs provided Nutrition Canada with a list of bands, along with a selective list of members from these bands, thereby shaping the scope of participants in the *Survey* and, therefore, its results.

The participants, states the *Indian Report*, 'were not informed beforehand of the nature of the dietary interview so that they would not deviate from their usual eating habits.'[36] The interview required the completion of both the '24 Hour Dietary Recall Form' and 'Food Frequency Questionnaire.' The three variations of the Recall Form, appended to the *National Priority* report, were each created with specific questions for distinct age groups of participants and organized by age: thirty-six months and over, up to thirty-six months, and expectant mothers.[37] The '36 Months and Over Form' asked interviewees to recall when and what they had consumed for the past twenty-four hours, with tracking recorded for time of day, place, type (food or drink), description, and amount consumed. The recall forms for expectant mothers and infants under thirty-six months reflect the heightened concern for pregnant bodies and the nation's future citizens. Here, questions dealt with whether children were bottle or breast fed, and whether table food – home or commercially prepared – was fed to the child.

The greatest degree of scrutiny was reserved for expectant mothers. Devising the interview required an additional page of fact gathering by nutritionists. The list of special concerns includes whether moms-to-be have made any dietary changes, and there is a detailed box on what food groups have either decreased or increased because of pregnancy. The form asks, 'How did you know how to make these changes?' and the optional responses listed begin with the expert 'Doctor or Clinic' and end with 'Other,' right below 'Self Imposed.'[38] These categories reflected the pervasive view of pregnancy as 'an illness of nine months' duration,' when unborn babies are 'desperately vulnerable to harm or neglect.'[39] The postwar notion that a mother's diet has consequences for her unborn baby's health was central to the Nutrition Canada *Survey*; the pregnancy as pathology thesis was an established medical discourse that contributed to both the *Survey*'s methodology and its approach to data collection.

In the collection of data, the recall form was used in combination with a dietary interview. This included inquiry into foods consumed by the interviewee over the previous month based on a 'Food Frequency Questionnaire' that listed only seventy-eight food items. The authors of the *Survey* assert that interviewers were 'thoroughly trained in the use of the questionnaire forms and food models before going into the field' and instructed on 'the importance of nonverbal, as well as verbal communication.'[40] In data collection interviews, interviewers assisted interviewees by 'encouraging a review of the previous day's activities' and using portion-sized models designed for the study to 'define objectively the quantities of foods consumed.'[41] Information on demographics, food purchase, and meal preparation was recorded in preliminary sessions by an advance team visiting chosen participants in their homes. For the Indian and Eskimo surveys, district public health nurses were charged with these visits.[42]

Surveying Eating Habits

Central to this project was the disciplining of bodies through monitoring food consumption. In considering the links between reclaiming indigenous foodways and Aboriginal health, Monica Bodirsky and Jon Johnson argue that, although colonialism ultimately failed to sever indigenous peoples from the lifeways and traditional teachings of their ancestors, 'the intergenerational impacts of colonial institutions including the reserve system, Indian Act, and residential schooling point to the specific and largely deleterious effects on traditional Indigenous diets and food knowledge.'[43] The *Survey*, however, ignored this history and, instead, treated all study participants as representing a comparable cross-section of the nation despite crucial differences in class, income, and access to resources between urban and non-urban populations.[44] It effectively denied the material realities of those First Nations and other non-urban communities whose food costs, particularly those deemed healthy by nutritionists, continue to be far higher than in urban centres.[45]

The data collected on food intake for the *Survey* were based on the Department of National Health and Welfare model of four food groups, which were rigidly outlined in the Department of National Health and Welfare educational pamphlet described by Mosby, namely, *Good Eating with Canada's Food Guide*.[46] However, to mediate the concern that if 'too many foods were grouped together the usefulness of the data would be impaired,' the department decided to use the nine groups developed by the U.S. Department of Agriculture (USDA).[47] These nine groups, which represent a breakdown of foods at the time condensed into the five-category Canadian model, included dairy products; meat, poultry, fish and eggs; cereal products; fruit and fruit products; vegetables; fats; nuts and dried legumes; foods primarily sugar and beverages and soft drinks; and lastly, miscellaneous.[48] Like Canada's food groups, these USDA-based categories privilege Western dietary choices, such as milk and milk products, which are the primary category, while the example foods for each category reinforce these norms. For cereal products, for instance, while the Indian and Eskimo reports include bannock, the standardized sample considers breads, rolls, or pastas as normative choices.[49]

Aside from a brief mention of the slight modification to food groups to include wild game,[50] reflections of culture were removed from the Indian and Eskimo surveys. National and international Western nutritional standards during the period were closely adhered to in Nutrition Canada's *Survey*. As these standards present examples of foods for each group reflective of Western food choices, most are accessible only to those with adequate storage facilities[51] and in close proximity to urban centres with such facilities. Moreover, they emphasize fresh over packaged or frozen food for cost effectiveness and better health.[52] Alongside rules for what should be consumed, the guide outlined when it should be eaten and in what combination. A 'pattern for a day's meals' was proposed based on three sittings a day, starting 'with a good breakfast for all!' at seven a.m. (see Ian Mosby in this volume).[53]

There is little room in postwar nutrition programs for negotiating class or cultural variations such as 'country' or indigenous foods consumed primarily by non-urban Aboriginal communities. (As Iacovetta's chapter suggests, nutritionists were more willing to find food substitutes for immigrant families from southern Europe.) The term 'country foods' refers to an Aboriginal diet of natural resources that are harvested regionally and seasonally, including 'big game' meat, birds, fish and whales (and their eggs or grease), and smaller fur-bearing animals, as well as the cultivation or collection of fruits, greens, tubers, berries, wild rice, and other foods available from the land. 'Country foods' are both high in nutritional value, and equally important in their contribution to maintaining cultural tradition through the acts of hunting and sharing the wealth.[54]

While these features were increasingly acknowledged in the mid-1980s by the Department of Indian and Northern Affairs and its nutritionists,[55] in the period of the *Survey* the interests and lifestyles of the many unique Aboriginal communities in Canada were yet to be considered by nutrition professionals. When they were recognized, as in the *Survey*, indigenous foods were treated as limited and supplementary, rather than as normative, legitimate dietary choices with adequate nutritional composition and consumed on a regular basis. Inuit diets, which ranged from game to marine mammals, were supplemented by a variety of land and sea vegetables, such as berries, willow buds, herbs, and some roots.[56] The traditional Inuit diet focused on consumption of meat and fat, and the limited technology available for cooking foods encouraged consumption of what communities believed to be nutritionally complete raw, frozen, or aged foods. While these diets were increasingly supplemented with heavily processed and sugary foods by the 1960s, consumption of traditional or 'country foods' continued to be both nutritious and affordable for many Aboriginal households.[57]

Despite this continued incorporation of indigenous foods into non-urban Aboriginal diets, in particular, both small gardens and larger-scale agriculture supplemented intakes. Some British Columbian Aboriginal women grew vegetables, including beets, corn, lettuce, and potatoes. Others practised agriculture, including occasional dairying to provide both food and income.[58] This was combined with an overall increased access to Western foods through community stores, including Hudson's Bay Company outlets located in many communities, and small community markets run by non-Aboriginal residents, which were often either co-operatives or locally owned.[59] In the postwar decades, the bulk of west coast Aboriginal diets included grains, sugars, oils, and canned goods purchased at markets in smaller centres, such as Tofino on Vancouver Island.[60]

Further inland across the Northwest Territories, northern health officials expressed concern that Aboriginal buyers consumed too many sweets and too little fresh produce, a trend also present in parts of British Columbia.[61] By the 1980s, the Bay addressed these concerns, launching a Nutrition Upgrading Program that provided educational information to Aboriginal communities that instructed people on how to 'choose economical and nutritious foods.'[62] Local retailers like the Bay thus participated in nutritional uplift programs, following the lead of Indian and Northern Affairs, whose medical and nutrition 'experts' had already recognized dramatic dietary shifts in the postwar decades.[63] Such programs attempted to manage starvation and malnutrition in the northwest based on a colonial model, which sought to reform and discipline diet.[64]

Efforts at improving health tended towards increasing Western foodways and reducing the reliance on game meats and other 'country foods.' However, communities in northern Manitoba, who consume large quantities of Western packaged foods brought in from the South, as well as those on the northwest coast, who have engaged in vegetable gardening for generations, at present face epidemic rates of Type 2 diabetes.[65] Negating the significance of indigenous dietary staples and supplements to Aboriginal communities and imposing the normalcy of Food Guide choices not only created the postwar conditions of Aboriginal nutritional health, but also perpetuated a narrow view of the diverse diets of equally diverse Aboriginal cultures in Canada. Moreover, this approach reinforced colonial relations between Aboriginal people and the Canadian state.

Based on such relations, the samplings of Indian and Eskimo peoples used in the *Survey* provide an essentialist approach to studying Aboriginal peoples in Canada, patterned, in part, after mass government data collections such as the census. Like the census, the Nutrition *Survey* should be read not as a harmless head count but as an inherently disciplinary practice.[66] As Bruce Curtis argues, 'census making involves identifying political subjects and centralizing knowledge. It serves to increase the possibilities for intensive administration.' The *Survey* demonstrates what Curtis refers to as the creation of 'social equivalencies,' in which hegemonic groupings do not reflect actual diversities but minimize or deny them in favour of uncomplicated statistical samples.[67]

Overdetermined Survey Results

The published Indian and Eskimo surveys reflect the persistence of nineteenth-century colonial relations, employing notions of scientific approaches to studying bodies used by Victorian experts. The anthropometric body measurements[68] used in the *Survey* indicate that a small proportion of underweight children were at risk with 'severe growth retardation and wasting': 'generally, the prevalence of moderate weight deficits were higher among Indians and Eskimos than the General Population.'[69] For example, the category of 'Protein-Calorie Malnutrition, Moderate Risk,' based on evaluations of five-year-old children produced results of 4.7 per cent of the General Population, 7.7

per cent of Indians, and 6.1 per cent of Eskimos 'at risk.'[70] In addition to the overall problems of the results from such surveys, this 'scientific' approach to studying humans based on racially distinguished dietary difference and measures of anthropometry mirror past problematic and insidious studies of anatomy.[71]

Not surprisingly, the bodies Nutrition Canada identified as most often lacking adequate nutrients were those of pregnant mothers and young children. Iron, caloric intake, and protein were found deficient in expectant women, thus, shortages were also present in babies and young children. Thiamin deficits were found in pregnant women, particularly among Indian populations while calcium and vitamin D shortages were seen in infants, children, and adolescents. And there were vitamin A shortages among pregnant Indians and Eskimos, but 'no indication of deficiency among adolescents and adults.'[72] Ironically, the pregnant women in this study were expected to demonstrate 'a superior picture of health to that which actually exists in the pregnant population.'[73]

This seems a fairly insignificant distinction, since the women studied among the General Population generally presented with minimal 'risks' and deficiencies, with some shortages – such as iron and serum folate – indicating a need for closer dietary monitoring. However, severe shortages of iron and serum folate, as well as moderate to severe protein deficiencies, were identified in both the Indian and Eskimo populations, and Eskimo populations showed a higher 'risk' (for example, aneamia indicators placed 65 per cent of Eskimos at risk, with deficiencies in only 25 per cent of the General and Indian populations).[74] Most notable, though, are the vitamin C deficiencies among Eskimo and Indian women, and especially the observation that 'foods high in vitamin C may not be currently available in remote areas of the north nor do they form part of the customary Indian and Eskimo diet.'[75] Indeed, this statement directly contradicts the assertion made only three pages earlier that 'the food distribution system in Canada seems to be effective.'[76]

Soon after the *Survey* was published, the 1975 *Health and Protection Branch Report on the Relationship between Income and Nutrition Based on Analysis of Nutrition Canada Data* was released, which studied the overlooked significance of income on the *Survey*'s conclusions.[77] This follow-up study emphasized the problems pertaining to the *Survey* by addressing its published assertion that income levels have little to no relation to nutrition.[78] Yet the 'problem' of nutrition in Aboriginal bodies is ultimately a problem of access to affordable fresh food, which hinges on the high cost of food in many northern communities. This income analysis, in contrast to the original *Survey*, provides evidence that nutritional deficits should be directly linked to income: as the report clearly states, 'for most physiological groups a relationship does exist

between income and nutritional status.'[79] Unlike more recent government publications and studies concerning the health of Aboriginal people in Canada,[80]
the Nutrition Canada *Survey* denies the role that Canada's colonial history of
government-initiated relocation, settlement, and disciplinary 'continuous monitoring' of Aboriginal peoples played in creating the conditions of poverty as
well as the decreased access to both traditional and Western foods.

Conclusion

The government attempts in the 1960s and 1970s to regulate indigenous foodways, from production to consumption, stemmed from a colonial relationship
between the Canadian government and Aboriginal peoples. This was driven
both by a state desire to fully realize the colonial project through the disciplining of Aboriginal bodies and by the continual resistance by those targeted for
assimilation. As Myra Rutherdale writes, 'those involved in colonizing Aboriginal bodies, from Euro-Canadian doctors to field matrons, missionaries, and
Indian agents,' historical figures who all played a role in the *Survey*, 'generally
believed that in order to "capture" the minds of Aboriginal peoples, they had to
"capture" their bodies first.'[81]

On its own, the Nutrition Canada *Survey* may appear as simply one piece
of the Canadian colonial project, but it is best understood as a significant 'top-
down' study that contributed to a large body of research and publications on
Aboriginal health compiled by non-Aboriginal professionals. This and similar
smaller-scale studies from the period were met with an intensified backlash by
many Aboriginal communities who, by the mid-1970s, asserted their right to
study and monitor nutrition and health on their own terms.[82] In sum, the *Survey* was a highly racialized, classed, and gendered project, one informed by a
discourse, present since colonial encounters, that has constructed Aboriginal
women as bad mothers and the bodies of their family members as inherently
weak and diseased. As part of an ongoing effort to assimilate these mothers
and their families into an urban Canadian citizenry through various studies
and educational programs, Nutrition Canada declared food and nutrition 'a
national priority.'

ACKNOWLEDGMENTS

I acknowledge research support from the Social Sciences and Humanities Research
Council of Canada and the University of Manitoba Institute for the Humanities, and
thank Adele Perry and Franca Iacovetta for their guidance.

NOTES

1 Nutrition Canada is the name of the *Survey* project, and refers both to the *Survey* and the committee of experts who carried out the *Survey* for the Department of National Health and Welfare (DNHW).

2 The terms *Indian* and *Eskimo* should be understood as the legal terminology used by Ottawa and Nutrition Canada. They are used here *only* in reference to usage by Nutrition Canada. The groups that I identify collectively as Aboriginal likely included people who identify as Metis, but they were not recognized as such until the surveys conducted after 1990 on both national and regional levels. See James B. Waldram, D. Ann Herring, and T. Kue Young, *Aboriginal Health in Canada: Historical, Cultural, and Epidemiological Perspectives*, 2nd ed. (Toronto: University of Toronto Press, 2006). More recently, Metis people have been identified as participants in health and nutrition research, reflecting in part the Metis Nation's consolidation. See Metis Nation, *Metis National Council*, http://www.metisnation.ca/index.html. While recognizing that the Metis were overlooked as a unique people in this study, attempting to reconcile this and decipher where Metis people 'fit' in Nutrition Canada's *Surveys* is beyond the scope of this chapter.

3 The concept of discipline is informed by Michel Foucault's work. Of particular utility in analysing the nutrition *Survey* is his writing on surveillance, ritual, and registers in medical examinations related to disciplinary power. Michel Foucault, 'The Means of Correct Training,' in *Discipline and Punish: The Birth of the Prison*, 2nd ed. (New York: Vintage, 1995), 170–94.

4 See Mary Jane McCallum, 'This Last Frontier: Isolation and Aboriginal Health,' *Canadian Bulletin of Medical History / Bulletin canadien d'histoire de la médecine* (hereafter *CBMH/BCHM*) 22/1 (2005): 103–20.

5 See Canada, Department of Indian Affairs and Northern Development (DIAND), *Statement of the Government of Canada on Indian Policy* (Ottawa: Hon. Jean Chrétien, PC, MP Minister of Indian Affairs and Northern Development Ottawa, 1969); Indian Chiefs of Alberta, *Citizens Plus: A Presentation of Indian Chiefs of Alberta to Right Hon. P.E. Trudeau, Prime Minister and Government of Canada* (Edmonton: Indian Association of Alberta, 1970); Alan Cairns, *Citizens Plus: Aboriginal Peoples and the Canadian State* (Vancouver: UBC Press, 2001); Dale Turner, *This Is Not a Peace Pipe: Towards a Critical Indigenous Philosophy* (Toronto: University of Toronto Press, 2006).

6 See Marlene Epp, Franca Iacovetta, and Frances Swyripa, eds., *Sisters or Strangers? Immigrant, Ethnic, and Racialized Women in Canadian History* (Toronto: University of Toronto Press, 2004); Franca Iacovetta, *Gatekeepers: Reshaping Immigrant Lives in Cold War Canada* (Toronto: Between the Lines, 2006).

7 See Mary-Ellen Kelm, *Colonizing Bodies: Aboriginal Health and Healing in*

British Columbia, 1900–1950 (Vancouver: UBC Press, 1998); John S. Milloy, *A National Crime: The Canadian Government and the Residential School System, 1879–1986* (Winnipeg: University of Manitoba Press, 1999); Cole Harris, *Making Native Space: Colonialism, Resistance and Reserves in British Columbia* (Vancouver: UBC Press, 2002). While these and other authors identify the centrality of diet, it is not the focus of their studies.

8 Canada, Nutrition Canada, and the Bureau of Nutritional Sciences, *Food Consumption Patterns Report* (Ottawa: DNHW, 1975), 6.

9 Ibid.

10 Canada, Nutrition Canada for the DNHW, *Nutrition: A National Priority* (Ottawa: DNHW, 1973), 125–36. These divisions are documented in the list of *Survey* committees, directors, and staff. On isolation as a framework used by Indian Health Services, see McCallum, 'This Last Frontier,' 104.

11 *Nutrition: A National Priority*, 2.

12 Ibid., 5–7. Population types were *metropolitan* (100,000 and greater), *urban* (5,000 to 100,000), or *rural* (5,000 and less), and income was based on the 1961 census data.

13 While there is a box in the 'Household and Family Profile Form 1' asking for 'Residence of Family Head (in years),' asking participants to state their regional background or, if not from Canada, their country of origin, all non-Aboriginal cultural or ethnic statistics are fully integrated in the published report and appear only as crunched data for the regional and national populations. *Nutrition: A National Priority*, Appendix C, I.

14 Canada, Nutrition Canada for the DNHW, *Eskimo Survey Report* (Ottawa: DNHW, 1975), 5; Canada, Nutrition Canada for the DNHW, *Indian Survey Report* (Ottawa: DNHW, 1975), 5–6.

15 *Indian Survey Report*, 6; *Eskimo Survey Report*, 6.

16 *Eskimo Survey Report*, 9; *Indian Survey Report*, 11.

17 *Eskimo Survey Report*, 5; *Indian Survey Report*, 6.

18 *Indian Survey Report*, 7; *Eskimo Survey Report*, 7. Spellings as used in the *Survey*.

19 *Food Consumption Patterns Report*.

20 *Nutrition*, 3.

21 Ibid., Appendix C, II.

22 See Joy Parr, 'Shopping for a Good Stove: A Parable about Gender, Design, and the Market,' in Joy Parr, ed., *A Diversity of Women: Ontario, 1945–1980* (Toronto: University of Toronto Press, 1995), 75–97.

23 Franca Iacovetta and Valerie Korinek, 'Jell-O Salads, One-Stop Shopping, and Maria the Homemaker: The Gender Politics of Food,' in Epp et al., *Sisters or Strangers?* 190–230; Iacovetta, *Gatekeepers*, chapter 6, 'Culinary Containment? Cooking for the Family, Democracy, and Nation.'

24 Rima D. Apple, *Perfect Motherhood: Science and Childrearing in America* (New Brunswick, NJ: Rutgers University Press, 2006).

25 Kelm, *Colonizing Bodies*, 57.

26 Robert M. Bone, *Changes in Country Food Consumption: Report 3-85* (Ottawa: DIAND, 1985), 7.

27 On Canadian postwar 'normalcy,' see Mary Louise Adams, *The Trouble with Normal: Postwar Youth and the Making of Canadian Heterosexuality* (Toronto: University of Toronto Press, 1997); Mona Gleason, *Normalizing the Ideal: Psychology, Schooling, and the Family in Postwar Canada* (Toronto: University of Toronto Press, 1999). The *Survey* was conducted in what Catherine Carstairs and Rachel Elder have called the 'child-centred culture of the postwar years,' when, for example, debates over water fluoridation included claims that denying the advice of experts was tantamount to child abuse. See their 'Expertise, Health, and Popular Opinion: Debating Water Fluoridation, 1945–80,' *Canadian Historical Review* 89/3 (2008): 360, 352.

28 See Molly Ladd-Taylor and Lauri Umansky, eds., Introduction, in *'Bad' Mothers: The Politics of Blame in Twentieth-Century America* (New York: New York University Press, 1998), 3. The authors argue that 'bad mothers' tend to fall into three groups: those living outside of a 'traditional' nuclear family; those who 'would or could not protect their children from harm'; and 'those whose children went wrong.' On Canada, Julie Guard, 'Women Worth Watching: Radical Housewives in Cold War Canada,' in Gary Kinsman, Dieter Buse, and Mercedes Steedman, eds., *Whose National Security? Canadian State Surveillance and the Creation of Enemies* (Toronto: Between the Lines, 2000), 72–88; Iacovetta and Korinek, 'Jell-O Salads,' 193–4.

29 Iacovetta and Korinek, 'Jell-O Salads,' 194.

30 Ibid.; Canada, Department of Citizenship and Immigration, Indian Affairs Branch, *Indian News* 12/1 (1969): 5.

31 Canada, Indian and Northern Health Services, *The Pre-Schooler: From the Age of One to Six Years* (Ottawa: DNHW, 1958).

32 Kelm, *Colonizing Bodies*, 57. See also her 'Diagnosing the Discursive Indian: Medicine, Gender, and the "Dying Race,"' *Ethnohistory* 52/2 (2005): 371–406.

33 For a discussion of child health in Canadian history, see CBMH/BCHM 19 (2002).

34 *Nutrition*, 16, and *Indian Survey Report*, 7.

35 *Nutrition*, 17.

36 *Eskimo Survey Report*, 9.

37 *Nutrition*, Appendix C, III-IV and VIII.

38 Ibid., V.

39 Barbara Clow, '"An Illness of Nine Months' Duration": Pregnancy and Thalidomide Use in Canada and the United States,' in Georgina Feldberg, Molly Ladd-

Taylor, Allison Li, and Kathryn McPherson, eds., *Women, Health, and Nation: Canada and the United States since 1945* (Montreal and Kingston: McGill-Queen's University Press, 2003), 50.

40 *Food Consumption Patterns Report*, 8.

41 *Eskimo Survey Report*, 9.

42 Ibid. See also Kathryn McPherson, 'Nursing and Colonization: The Work of Indian Health Service Nurses in Manitoba, 1945–1970,' in Feldberg et al., *Women, Health, and Nation*, 223–46.

43 Monica Bodirsky and Jon Johnson, 'Decolonizing Diet: Healing by Reclaiming Traditional Indigenous Foodways,' *Cuizine* 1/1 (2008): par. 3. Journal online. Available at Indigenous Foodways,' *Cuizine* 1/1 (2008): par. 3. Journal online. Available at http://id.erudit.org/iderudit/019373ar. On the disciplining of Aboriginal bodies, see Milloy, *National Crime*, and Harris, *Making Native Space*. This was not particular to Aboriginal peoples: see Franca Iacovetta, Roberto Perin, and Angelo Principe, eds., *Enemies Within: Italian and Other Internees in Canada and Abroad* (Toronto: University of Toronto Press, 2000); Mona Oikawa, 'Cartographies of Violence: Women, Memory, and the Subject(s) of the "Internment,"' in Sherene Razack, ed., *Race, Space, and the Law: Unmapping a White, Settler Society* (Toronto: Between the Lines, 2002), 71–98.

44 See Hugh Shewell, *'Enough to Keep Them Alive': Indian Welfare in Canada, 1873–1965* (Toronto: University of Toronto Press, 2004).

45 The persistence of the myriad reasons for food insecurity in northern Manitoba continues to be reflected in unaffordable staple food prices; in some communities, for example, a four-litre jug of milk can cost over twelve dollars. Debora Lyell, *Northern Food Prices Project Report* (Winnipeg: Healthy Child Committee of Cabinet, Government of Manitoba, 2003). Shirley Thompson, Natural Resources Institute, University of Manitoba, has collaborated with First Nations and Northern Manitoba communities to address the lack of affordable foods and food insecurity in northern Manitoba stemming from the impact of colonialism. See Thompson's participatory video, *Growing Hope in Northern Manitoba*. Available at http://home.cc.umanitoba.ca/~thomso4/Movie.html.

46 Canada, *Good Eating with Canada's Food Guide* (Ottawa: DNHW, 1967); *Canada's Food Guide Handbook* (Ottawa: DNHW, 1977), 40. See also Aleck Ostry, *Nutrition Policy in Canada, 1870–1939* (Vancouver: UBC Press, 2006).

47 *Food Consumption Patterns Report*, 10.

48 Ibid., 14–15.

49 Ibid., 14.

50 Ibid., 10; on intake data, which reflects these modifications, 202, 221.

51 See Joy Parr, *Domestic Goods: The Material, the Moral, and the Economic in the Postwar Years* (Toronto: University of Toronto Press, 1999).

52 See Valerie Korinek, *Roughing It in the Suburbs: Reading Chatelaine Magazine in the Fifties and Sixties* (Toronto: University of Toronto Press, 2000).

53 *Good Eating with Canada's Food Guide*, inside panel.

54 Bone, *Changes in Country Food*; Kelm, *Colonizing Bodies*.

55 See Canada, *Nutrient Bar Graphs: A Teaching Aid to Learn the Value of Native Foods* (Ottawa: Health and Welfare Canada, 1984).

56 Otto Schaefer and Jean Steckle, *Dietary Habits and Nutritional Base of Native Populations of the Northwest Territories* (Yellowknife, NWT: Science Advisory Board of the Northwest Territories, 1980), 2.

57 Pauktuutit, *The Inuit Way: A Guide to Inuit Culture* (Ottawa: Pauktuutit/Inuit Women's Association of Canada, 1991), 20.

58 Kelm, *Colonizing Bodies*, 36.

59 *Indian News* 8/ (1966): 2; Bone, *Changes*, 28.

60 Kelm, *Colonizing Bodies*, 36.

61 Bone, *Changes*, 28; Kelm, *Colonizing Bodies*, 36.

62 Bone, *Changes*, 28.

63 See *Indian News* 2/2 (1956): 1.

64 Consistent with this approach, men and boys were encouraged to labour as agriculturalists, while women and girls were taught domestic duties such as how to feed a family. See Sarah Carter, *Aboriginal People and Colonizers of Western Canada to 1900* (Toronto: University of Toronto Press, 1999); Milloy, *National Crime*; Carter, *Lost Harvests: Prairie Indian Reserve Farmers and Government Policy* (Montreal and Kingston: McGill-Queen's University Press, 1990).

65 Waldram et al., *Aboriginal Health in Canada*, 97–101.

66 Bruce Curtis, *The Politics of Population: State Formation, Statistics, and the Census of Canada, 1840–1875* (Toronto: University of Toronto Press, 2002), 26.

67 Ibid., 3–4.

68 Anthropometry refers to the study of human body measurement for use in anthropological classification and comparison.

69 *Nutrition*, 58.

70 Ibid., 67.

71 See Matthew Frye Jacobson, *Barbarian Virtues: The United States Encounters Foreign Peoples at Home and Abroad, 1876–1917* (New York: Hill and Wang, 2000), particularly chapter, 'Theories of Development: Scholarly Disciplines and the Hierarchy of Peoples,' 139–172; Jennifer Morgan, *Laboring Women: Reproduction and Gender in New World Slavery* (Philadelphia, PA: University of Pennsylvania Press, 2004).

72 *Nutrition*, 112–14.

73 Ibid., 103.

74 Ibid.

75 Ibid., 114.

76 Ibid., 111.

77 Canada, DNHW, *Health Protection Branch Report on the Relationship between Income and Nutrition Based on Analysis of Nutrition Canada Data* (Ottawa: Minister of National Health and Welfare, 1975).

78 *Nutrition*, 111.

79 *Health Protection Branch Report*, 'Summary of Report,' 1.

80 Robert Allec for Inter-governmental Committee on First Nations Health, *First Nations Health and Wellness in Manitoba: Overview of Gaps in Service and Issues Associated with Jurisdictions: Final Report* (2005): 11–13. Available at http:// www.gov.mb.ca/ana/publications/1st_nations_health_final 2005.pdf.

81 Myra Rutherdale, '"She Was a Ragged Little Thing": Missionaries, Embodiment, and Refashioning Aboriginal Womanhood in Northern Canada,' in Katie Pickles and Myra Rutherdale, eds., *Contact Zones: Aboriginal and Settler Women in Canada's Colonial Past* (Vancouver: UBC Press, 2005), 228–45.

82 Canada, DNHW, Medical Services Branch, *Indian Health Discussion Paper (draft)* (Ottawa: DNHW, 1979). In 1977, the National Indian Brotherhood launched the Commission of Inquiry on Indian Health, after the group 'called on the federal government to put aside its unilateral approach to the development of Indian Health policy and to support Indian efforts to contribute meaningfully to such efforts' (1–2). Since 1994, the First Nations Regional Longitudinal Health Survey has worked to challenge projects like the *Survey* by collecting longitudinal data from regions and peoples often overlooked, generating reports on the health and well-being of First Nations and Inuit peoples in Canada, and incorporating both traditional and Western knowledge into survey models. See Assembly of First Nations, *First Nations Regional Longitudinal Health Survey*, http://www.rhs-ers. ca/english/.

Contributors

Sonia Cancian is a postdoctoral fellow affiliated with the Immigration History Research Center, University of Minnesota, and Concordia University's Simone de Beauvoir Institute. A scholar of immigrant letters, international migration, gender, and family, she is the author of *Families, Lovers, and Their Letters: Italian Postwar Migration to Canada* (2010).

Catherine Carstairs is an associate professor of history at the University of Guelph. A historian of health and the body, she is the author of *Jailed for Possession: Illegal Drug Use, Regulation and Power in Canada, 1920–1961* (2006).

Nathalie Cooke is associate provost and professor of English at McGill University. Her publications focus on moments of pivotal change and continuity in Canadian literature, culture, and foodways. Most recently, she is editor of *What's to Eat? Entrées in Canadian Food History* (2009), and founding editor of *CuiZine: The Journal of Canadian Food Cultures*.

Megan J. Davies is an associate professor in the Health and Society Program at York University. Her research interests and publications focus on ageing, rural health, marginal medical practices, and madness. For recent work see historyofmadness.ca.

Michel Desjardins is a professor of religion and culture at Wilfrid Laurier University. A 3M Teaching Fellow, he teaches and writes about the role that food plays in people's religious lives.

Ellen Desjardins has had a long career as a public health nutritionist. Now, with a Ph.D. in human geography, she is conducting research on the politics and culture of the food environment.

Caroline Durand is an assistant professor at Trent University, teaching the history of Quebec and food and conducting research on nutrition in Quebec, 1942–75. Her thesis, 'Le laboratoire domestique de la machine humaine: La nutrition, la modernité et l'État québécois, 1860–1945,' is the object of a forthcoming article in *Revue de Bibliothèque et Archives nationales du Québec.*

Andrea Eidinger teaches Canadian and women's history at the University of Victoria. Her dissertation, 'What My Mother Taught Me: The Construction of Canadian Jewish Womanhood in Montreal, 1945–1980,' is currently being revised for publication.

Marlene Epp is an associate professor of history and peace and conflict studies at Conrad Grebel University College at the University of Waterloo, where her teaching includes a course on food, culture, and history. She publishes mainly in the fields of Mennonites and gender, including *Mennonite Women in Canada: A History* (2008).

Catherine Gidney is an adjunct professor in the Department of History at St Thomas University. She is the author of *A Long Eclipse: The Liberal Protestant Establishment and the Canadian University, 1920–1970* (2004) and winner of the Canadian History of Education Association Founders' Prize, 2004–6.

Julie Guard is an associate professor and program coordinator of the labour studies program at the University of Manitoba. Co-editor with Wayne Antony of *Bankruptcies and Bailouts* (2009), she studies women, gender, and ethnicity in left, labour, working-class, and social justice movements.

Maura Hanrahan is the award-winning author of eleven books, the latest being *Sheilagh's Brush: A Novel* (2010). She has an interdisciplinary Ph.D. from the London School of Economics and is Special Adviser to the President for Aboriginal Affairs at Memorial University.

S. Holyck Hunchuck is a feminist artist and art historian in Ottawa. Her recent work can be found in the *Material Culture Review* and in *Re-Imagining Ukrainian Canadians: History, Politics, and Identity* (2011).

Franca Iacovetta is a professor of history at the University of Toronto and president of the Berkshire Conference of Women Historians. Her most recent monograph, *Gatekeepers: Reshaping Immigrant Lives in Cold War Canada* (2006), won the John A. Macdonald Prize for the best book in Canadian history.

Valerie J. Korinek is a professor of history at the University of Saskatchewan. A cultural and gender historian, she is the author of *Roughing It in the Suburbs: Reading Chatelaine Magazine in the Fifties and Sixties* (2000) and co-editor of *Finding a Way to the Heart* (2012).

Julie Mehta, author of *Dance of Life: The Mythology, History and Politics of Cambodian Culture* (2001), is a specialist in post-colonial literatures and diasporic studies and teaches in the Canadian Studies Program at the University of Toronto.

Ian Mosby is a SSHRC postdoctoral fellow at the University of Guelph. His current research examines the history of postwar food technologies and the industrial transformation of the Canadian diet. This project builds on his doctoral research on the politics, culture, and science of food in Canada during the Second World War.

James Murton is an associate professor of History at Nipissing University. An environmental historian of agriculture and food, he is currently working on a larger study of the creation of global/imperial markets for food in the early twentieth century.

Alison Norman holds a SSHRC postdoctoral fellowship at Trent University for a project on the history of Aboriginal teachers in southern Ontario, 1800–1970. Her doctoral dissertation (University of Toronto, 2010) looks at public life among the Six Nations of Grand River, Ontario, in the early twentieth century.

Julia Roberts is an associate professor in the Department of History at the University of Waterloo. She studies colonial societies and public identities within them and is author of *In Mixed Company: Taverns and Public Life in Upper Canada* (2009).

Molly Pulver Ungar is a historian of culture in Canada and Quebec. She is a faculty member in the Department of History at University of the Fraser Valley in Abbotsford, British Columbia.

Krista Walters is a doctoral student in history at the University of Manitoba. Her dissertation focuses on the history of nutrition education programs in mid-twentieth-century Canada, particularly those aimed at Aboriginal mothers and children in northern communities.

Cheryl Krasnick Warsh is a professor of history at Vancouver Island University and a former editor-in-chief of the *Canadian Bulletin of Medical History*. Her books include *Prescribed Norms: Women and Health in Canada and the United States since 1800* (2010).

Stacey Zembrzycki's first book, entitled *Sharing Authority with Baba: Wrestling with Memories of Community*, is forthcoming with University of British Columbia Press. To learn more about this project go to: www.sudburyukrainians.ca.